INTERNATIONAL CALVINISM
1541–1715

INTERNATIONAL CALVINISM

1541–1715

Edited by
MENNA PRESTWICH

CLARENDON PRESS · OXFORD

1985

Oxford University Press, Walton Street, Oxford OX2 6DP
Oxford New York Toronto
Delhi Bombay Calcutta Madras Karachi
Kuala Lumpur Singapore Hong Kong Tokyo
Nairobi Dar es Salaam Cape Town
Melbourne Auckland
and associated companies in
Beirut Berlin Ibadan Nicosia

Oxford is a trade mark of Oxford University Press

Published in the United States
by Oxford University Press, New York

British Library Cataloguing in Publication Data
International Calvinism 1541–1715.
1. Calvinism—History
I. Prestwich, Menna
230´.42´09 BX9415
ISBN 0-19-821933-4

Library of Congress Cataloging in Publication Data
Main entry under title:
International Calvinism 1541–1715.
Includes bibliographies and index.
1. Calvinism—History—Addresses, essays, lectures.
I. Prestwich, Menna.
BX9422.2.I57 1985 284´.2´09 85-10667
ISBN 0-19-821933-4

Photoset by Cotswold Typesetting Ltd, Gloucester
Printed in Great Britain
at the University Press, Oxford
by David Stanford
Printer to the University

Editorial Note

In planning and editing this book I have contracted many debts of gratitude. A major debt is owed to Élisabeth Labrousse, who came to St Hilda's College as a Sacher Visiting Fellow in Trinity Term 1979. She encouraged the project from its outset; her inexhaustible stock of knowledge and ideas and her infectious sense of enjoyment conveyed in many talks in Mauvezin, Paris, and Oxford have been a constant stimulus; the annual loan of her flat in Paris, a library in itself, has been invaluable; and she has served as a key to unlock many doors.

One of the pleasures of editing this book has been the making of new friends, and I am especially grateful to Myriam Yardeni, Philippe Joutard, and Herbert Lüthy for their ready co-operation with an English editor and for meals and talks enjoyed together in Paris, Basle, Marseille, and the Cévennes. I wish that I could also speak of Richard Stauffer in the present tense. I first met him when he gave a paper in Oxford, and I have vivid and grateful memories of the hospitality which he and his wife, Irène, gave me in their chalet high above the Lake of Lucerne. Any notion that those interested in Calvinism might have something of the austerity attributed to its founder was finally dispelled by Richard Stauffer. But his sudden illness and tragic death last year have meant that he was unable to annotate his contribution as he would have wished.

I am grateful to all the contributors for the patience and tolerance they have shown in listening to my suggestions. Some explanation of the plan of the book should be given. The occasion for it was the tercentenary of the Revocation of the Edict of Nantes in October 1985. But in a work intended primarily for English readers it seemed appropriate to take a wider view of Calvinism, taking account of the great volume of recent work, and especially that by continental scholars. There are many legitimate approaches to Calvinism. Here it has been treated as an international religion which sought to cast society in a new mould, and the main purpose has been to consider how it affected, and was affected by, the very different societies in which it took root. Readers will appreciate that it would not have been sensible or tactful to issue detailed directives to established scholars who have elsewhere contributed so much in their own fields. Hence no attempt has been made to require contributors to cover between them the whole span of time and all aspects of the general subject. No attempt has been made to secure uniformity of interpretation, and where there is agreement it results only from a common concern to understand the evidence, not from any other shared allegiances. It was originally intended that there should be a sparing use of footnotes, but here too it proved undesirable or impracticable to attempt uniformity. Each essay is designed to be read as a self-contained piece. There are therefore some repetitions, but they are inevitable: the Calvinists of the first generation intended that there should be the same creed and the one Discipline in all regions.

Keith Thomas's advice and encouragement were immensely helpful when I was first considering the project. And in the later stages members of the Press have surpassed themselves. Ivon Asquith combined shrewd guidance with warnings about the difficulties of translation and of getting so many horses under starter's orders. Robert Faber handled a harassed editor, herself the last to come under starter's orders with her own contribution, with just the right mixture of firmness, tolerance, interest, and practical help. In Leofranc Holford-Strevens I found not merely a copy-editor but an exacting and helpful critic whose scholarship and sense of language enabled him to make many improvements, especially to the translations. But he had little time, and for that and the faults that remain the responsibility is mine. I am grateful to the staff of the Bodleian Library, and especially to Georgina Warrilow, who showed unfailing interest and solved many practical problems.

My thanks go to Michelle Magdelaine for permission to include the map showing the geographical origins of the refugees after the Revocation. This is based on her important work on the registers preserved at Frankfurt; and I also thank Armand Colin, publishers of Le Refuge Huguenot, 1685–1985 (Paris, 1985), and Éditions Verlag C. H. Beck, publishers of Die Hugenotten, 1685–1985 (Munich, 1985), for kindly allowing it to be reproduced. Again, I am grateful to the Librairie Protestante, 140 boulevard Saint-Germain, Paris, for permission to use the map of Calvinist churches in France taken from Samuel Mours, Le Protestantisme en France au XVIᵉ siècle (Paris, 1959).

Finally, and as always, I owe the greatest of my debts to my husband, whose historical concerns are far removed in time from my own, but whose lively interest in the enterprise, once it had begun, has sustained it throughout. A happy by-product has been our travels in France, taking advantage of the fortunate overlap between the territories controlled by the Angevin kings in the twelfth century and the regions of Huguenot strength in the sixteenth and seventeenth centuries. We were both attracted by a painting by Sébastien Bourdon in a Paris exhibition. He turned out, surprisingly, to have been a Calvinist from Montpellier, and this led to a rewarding search for his paintings in the Midi. It would be inappropriate to dedicate what has been the work of many hands; but I should like to dedicate my part in it to my husband and to Élisabeth Labrousse, who between them have made this book possible.

Contents

Maps

Contributors

RICHARD STAUFFER (d. 1984) was President of the Section des sciences religieuses, École des Hautes Études, Sorbonne, and Professor in the Faculté de théologie protestante de Paris.

GILLIAN LEWIS is a Fellow of St Anne's College, Oxford, and a University Lecturer.

MENNA PRESTWICH is a Fellow of St Hilda's College, Oxford.

ALASTAIR DUKE is a Lecturer in History, The University of Southampton.

HENRY J. COHN is Senior Lecturer in History, The University of Warwick.

R. J. W. EVANS is a Senior Research Fellow of Brasenose College, Oxford, and a University Lecturer.

PATRICK COLLINSON is Professor of Modern History, The University of Sheffield.

MICHAEL LYNCH is Lecturer in Scottish History, The University of Edinburgh.

W. A. SPECK is Professor of Modern History, The University of Leeds.

L. BILLINGTON is Senior Lecturer in American Studies, The University of Hull.

ÉLISABETH LABROUSSE is a Maître de recherche honoraire, CNRS, Paris, and an Honorary Fellow of St Hilda's College, Oxford.

MYRIAM YARDENI is Professor in the Department of General History, The University of Haifa.

PHILLIPPE JOUTARD is Professor of History, The University of Aix-Marseille.

HERBERT LÜTHY is an Emeritus Professor, The University of Basle.

Abbreviated References

AHR	*American Historical Review*
Annales ESC	*Annales. Économies, Sociétés, Civilisations*
BHR	*Bibliothèque d'Humanisme et Renaissance*
BIHR	*Bulletin of the Institute of Historical Research*
BSHPF	*Bulletin de la Société de l'Histoire du Protestantisme Français*
EHR	*English Historical Review*
P&P	*Past & Present*
PHSL	*Proceedings of the Huguenot Society of London*
RH	*Revue historique*
SCH	*Studies in Church History*
SHR	*Scottish Historical Review*

INTRODUCTION

The Changing Face of Calvinism

MENNA PRESTWICH

THE year 1685 is memorable for the Revocation of the Edict of Nantes, by which Louis XIV withdrew from the Calvinist Reformed Church the status and privileges accorded to it in 1598 after almost four decades of intermittent civil war. The Revocation set in motion the Huguenot diaspora with the flight of refugees to Holland (described by Bayle as the Noah's ark of the exiles), to Switzerland, Brandenburg, and other welcoming German states, to England, Ireland, and North America. Indeed Calvinism had rapidly become an international religion from 1541 when Calvin, a Frenchman, settled permanently in Geneva, whence his copious writings, ranging from the *Institutes* to his catechisms for children, were widely disseminated. John Locke, who travelled widely in France between 1675 and 1679 and stayed in Languedoc, the heartland of French Calvinism, had noted the discriminatory moves against the Huguenot minority. Increase Mather preached a sermon at Boston, printed in 1682, describing it as 'Occasioned by the Tidings of a great Persecution Raised against The Protestants in France'.[1] A consequence of the Glorious Revolution in 1688 was war against France, welcomed by Locke, who expressed the hope that 'God Almighty preserve the freedom of the Reformed churches and of all Europe' from 'that design which France seems to have of extirpating heresy'. The Revocation was thus not merely a French affair but an event of international concern.

John Knox wrote of Geneva in the time of Calvin that it was 'the most perfect school of Christ that ever was on the earth since the days of the Apostles', while Lambert Daneau, one of the Genevan Company of Pastors, compared Dutch towns, whose governments had been set up by popular votes, unfavourably with Geneva and its government established according to God's word and the rules of the ancient church.[2] The apocalyptic mood was shared by others of Calvin's disciples who looked to establish Geneva in their own countries and cities. *An Admonition to the Parliament*, printed in

---

[1] G. Spini, 'Remarques sur la Réforme française dans l'historiographie puritaine de la Nouvelle Angleterre', in P. Joutard (ed.), *Historiographie de la Réforme* (Paris, 1977), 103.

[2] P. Chaunu, *Église, Culture et Société: Essais sur Réforme et Contre-Réforme (1517–1620)*, (Paris, 1981), 278.

1572 and in effect a Calvinist manifesto, asked: 'Is a Reformation good for France? And can it be evil for England? Is discipline meet for Scotland? And is it unprofitable for this Realm? Surely God hath set these examples before your eyes to encourage you to go forward to a thorough and a speedy reformation.' The sense of a Calvinist International was expressed by a Scottish Presbyterian at this time, for on receiving a letter from La Rochelle, the fortress and headquarters of Calvinism in western France, he wrote enthusiastically to a correspondent in London that 'it is no small comfort brother . . . to brethren of one nation to understand the state of the brethren in other nations.'[3]

These expressions of Calvinist solidarity raise the questions of how Calvinism became a European religion and what it stood for. Calvinism is an indispensable term, but it was one which Calvin himself rejected and considered odious. He was never an isolated figure, for the Reformation scholars constituted a kind of *République des Lettres*. Calvin's stay in Strasburg between 1538 and 1541 brought him into close contact with Martin Bucer, from whom he borrowed much. He knew and got on with Philip Melanchthon and he made an ally of Heinrich Bullinger, Zwingli's successor in Zürich. Calvin did not put predestination in the forefront of the *Institutes* and he held that Christ died for all men, while he considered the Eucharist more than a commemorative service, though less than the Lutheran mass. His ecclesiology resting on pastors, elders, and deacons and on the pyramidal structure of consistory, colloquy and synod, although deriving its authority from the New Testament, did not mean that in practice Calvin was not prepared to allow bishops or patriarchs, as he made clear in his correspondence with the governors of England in Edward VI's reign and with the king of Poland. His fundamental doctrines were salvation through Christ and the absolute authority of the Bible, *sola scriptura*, giving equal weight to the Old and New Testaments.

After 1541 three Protestant capitals, Wittenberg, Zürich and Geneva, represented the Lutheran, Zwinglian, and Calvinist strands in the Reformation. This was a house divided against itself and Calvin saw the danger. In 1549 he and Bullinger made the Accord of Zürich or *Consensus Tigurinus*, by which the Zwinglian tenet that the Eucharist was only symbolic was upheld, while Calvin reserved his own position by having an affirmation of the spiritual presence of Christ included. The Lutheran doctrine of the ubiquity of Christ was not recognized and the breach with the Lutherans was never healed. The Zürich agreement was basic to the united front of Zwinglo-Calvinism and opened up a new zone of influence in western Germany, notably in the Palatinate. This was an age of definition, of decrees and confessions. The Catholic Church promulgated

---

[3] P. Collinson, *Godly People: Essays on English Protestantism and Puritanism* (London, 1983), 248–9.

the decrees of the Council of Trent in 1563, and in that year the Catechism of Heidelberg was issued, followed by the Second Helvetic Confession in 1566. Both owed much to Bullinger; both drew upon Calvin; and both were widely disseminated in Protestant Europe from the Low Countries and Scotland to Poland and Hungary, while the Catechism found its way to New England.

The first synod of the French Reformed church which met in Paris in 1559 issued the Discipline and a Confession of Faith, independent of but close to the Genevan versions, and in 1571 the Confessions of La Rochelle and Emden demonstrated Calvinist solidarity. In all these Confessions, the Calvinist tenet of parity between individual churches was upheld, while rules of conduct, following the Genevan pattern, were spelt out. Moreover, the Reformed churches were engaged in a campaign for a Christian and biblical ordering of daily life. Like other churches, the Reformed churches were fortified by their belief that they held a monopoly of truth. Beza, Calvin's adjutant and successor, firmly declared that the Calvinist church order was faithfully modelled on that of the primitive church as contained in the Acts of the Apostles. In 1617 at the academic festivities held in Heidelberg to celebrate the centenary of the Reformation, the theologian Pareus upheld 239 theses denouncing the doctrinal errors, pagan idolatry, and Antichristian tyranny of the Roman church.[4]

Through Calvin's insistence upon the Bible as the primary source of knowledge and authority, Calvinism had a common cultural foundation. Beza's Genevan Bible was a work of some forty years' scholarship carried out in collaboration with the Genevan Academy. In 1588 it was published in French, with helpful aids to readers: a line at the head of each chapter summarizing the contents and marginal cross references. In 1596 the Assembly of Saumur decided to compete with Geneva; in consequence the Haultin press at La Rochelle brought out an annotated edition of the Bible in French, with an index and at a cheaper price. This was followed in 1616 by a pocket Bible with a special index devised to give Calvinists the edge when engaged in argument or controversy. The Geneva version of the English Bible published in 1560 also had marginal cross references and Calvinist glosses, while quarto editions after 1579 had predestinarian catechisms bound up with them. Ninety-six editions of Calvin's works had been printed in England by 1640; they were surpassed in popularity only by those of William Perkins.[5] The martyrology of Jean Crespin, published in 1554, and John Foxe's *Book of Martyrs*, published in 1563 and started

[4] B. Vogler, *Le Monde germanique et helvétique à l'epoque des Réformés, 1517–1618* (Paris, 1981), ii 516–17).

[5] E. Trocmé, 'La Rochelle de 1560 à 1628. Tableau d'une société réformée au temps des guerres de religion' (unpubl. thesis, Strasburg, 1950), 305; N. R. N. Tyacke, Arminianism in England in Religion and Politics, 1604–40, (unpubl. thesis, Oxford, 1968), 2–3.

during his exile in 'the far parts of Germany', created a Calvinist consciousness by a cult of martyrdom which linked sixteenth-century persecution to the sufferings of the early Christians.

The Reformed Church was a learned church owing much to humanism, and the unity of Calvinism was strengthened by the Calvinist academies and by the welcome given to Calvinism in the universities, not least in Cambridge, the home of so many Calvinists and new Calvinist foundations. The academy of Geneva was founded in 1559, playing an important role in the training of ministers for the French Church and having amongst its alumni Olevianus, a key figure in Heidelberg, Philippe Marnix de Sainte-Aldegonde, nobleman and close friend of William of Orange, François du Jon or Franciscus Junius, professor at Leiden, and Thomas Bodley, the founder of the great library at Oxford. The university of St Andrews played its part in promoting Calvinism in Scotland, just as the university of Leiden, founded in 1574 after the heroic siege, did in Holland. An academy was founded in Ghent in 1578 simultaneously with the Calvinist urban revolution there, but failed to survive the Catholic reconquest of Flanders. French academies were founded in the wake of the Edict of Nantes: Montauban, Die in Dauphiné, Saumur, and Sedan, the capital of the independent duchy of the duc de Bouillon. The academy of Herborn in Hanau, close to Frankfurt, where there also operated the great humanist Wechel press, attracted scholars from Bohemia, Hungary and Poland, while at Heidelberg, which with Leiden was the most renowned of Calvinist universities, 35 per cent of the foreign students in the early seventeenth century were drawn from Central and Eastern Europe.[6] In 1636, six years after the *Arbella* sailed for New England, Harvard was founded to avoid having 'an illiterate Ministry in the Church, when our present Ministers shall lie in the dust.'

The strength of these academies and universities lay in their cosmopolitan character, though some were more regional and less well endowed than others. Lambert Daneau was professor at Ghent before returning to Geneva. John Cameron was pastor at Bordeaux and then became professor at Saumur in 1618. William Ames aroused irritation in Cambridge by disapproving of card-games and the wearing of surplices. He failed to become Master of Christ's College, but became rector of the new university of Franeker in Holland. When he died in 1633 his widow is said to have taken his writings with her to America, and Ames posthumously became one of the Calvinist voices of New England. Heidelberg had outstanding professors in the French Hebraist Franciscus Junius and his Italian father-in-law Tremellius who had lectured in Cambridge in Edward VI's reign. The Rhinelander Olevianus and the Silesian Ursinus drew up the

[6] R. J. W. Evans, *The Wechel Presses: Humanism and Calvinism in Central Europe, 1572–1627* (P. & P., Supplement, 1975), pp. 41, 46.

Heidelberg catechism. The logic taught by Peter Ramus, a victim of the massacre of St Bartholomew, was welcomed in Herborn and his works were printed by the Wechel press. New England looked to the Continent as well as to Cambridge, for the works of Junius and Tremellius were in the libraries of ministers there, while Ramist logic was the stern fare served up at Harvard. Both Ames and Ramus had a following in Hungary, and Lewis Bayly's *Practice of Piety* (1612), a best-seller in England, was translated into Hungarian.

Calvinism was marked by a sense of international solidarity. When La Rochelle was besieged in 1572 the magistrates requested and obtained a loan from the city of London. When Geneva was threatened by the duke of Savoy in 1589, 1590, and again in 1602, the Swiss Protestant cantons, the Count Palatine, the states of Holland and Frisia, all responded with loans, while collections were made in churches all over western Europe as well as in Bohemia, Hungary, Transylvania, and Poland. The Habsburg conquest of the Palatinate in 1621 stimulated fund-raising in England and Holland for the refugees. The synod of Flushing in 1626 asked the Walloon churches to send what they could for 300 refugee pastors from the Upper Palatinate stranded in Nuremberg. In 1636 a collection was made in Middelburg for the churches in Zweibrücken to relieve famine there, and in 1650 there were again appeals to the Walloon churches on behalf of the Palatinate ministers and their churches. When Cromwell made his appeal in 1655 on behalf of the Vaudois 'slaughtered saints', he was following a well-established tradition of fund-raising.

The flight of the Calvinist refugees at the time of the Revocation of the Edict of Nantes raised major problems and stimulated generous responses. The States-General of the United Provinces voted money for the refugees, and under the direction of the consistories of Rotterdam and Amsterdam collections were made for the galley-slaves and for the prisoners in the *Tour de Constance* at Aigues-Mortes. Refugee hostels were established under the patronage of Mary, princess of Orange, for widows and girls of good family, who were to support themselves by sewing, embroidering, and teaching French.[7] Sympathy for the refugees in England led Charles II in 1681 to ask Henry Compton, bishop of London, to 'represent the sad state of these poor people' to the clergy, who were to ask their parishioners to contribute freely to a fund for the Huguenots.

From the French Wars of Religion to the Thirty Years' War ideology coloured international politics, and the Protestant Interest was invoked against Catholic Spain, the Austrian Habsburgs, and the Papacy. The great Huguenot nobles were on terms of friendship with the leaders of the Netherlands nobility in revolt against Spain, and these links were

---

[7] P. Dibon, 'Le Refuge wallon précurseur du Refuge huguenot', *XVIIe Siècle*, 76–7 (1967), 63; H.-H. Bolhuis, 'La Hollande et les deux refuges', *BSHPF* 115 (1969), 421–2.

strengthened by the marriage of Coligny's daughter, Louise, to William of Orange. In both countries help was sought from Protestant England and the Calvinist Palatinate. Frederick III saw himself in the role of Joshua and his was the model Calvinist state, but in practice he exacted a heavy price for the troops he sent to his coreligionists in France and the Netherlands, and looked to territorial rewards. Elizabeth I could play the Protestant Queen, but she was sceptical and cautious, though there were those at her court committed to the Protestant cause. The earl of Leicester and Sir Francis Walsingham, English ambassador in Paris during the massacre of St Bartholomew, pressed for a Protestant foreign policy, while Sir Philip Sidney by his death at Zutphen became the Protestant paladin. The second cycle of the French Religious Wars between 1621 and 1629 saw the duc de Rohan in this role, but he failed to enlist international Protestantism. James I made only hollow responses, while Charles I and Buckingham had a responsibility for the disaster at La Rochelle in 1628.

It was at Heidelberg that the Calvinist cause came to be preached most fervently. At the centenary celebrations of the Reformation in 1617, the theologian Pareus claimed that Heidelberg was the mother of all Calvinist churches and preached the crusade against Rome, the seat of the Beast, a Babylon where the worship of idols was worse than it had been in Egypt.[8] In England Archbishop Abbot, a Calvinist in doctrine, on hearing that the Elector Palatine had accepted the crown of Bohemia echoed this apocalyptic message. He looked forward to a Protestant alliance extending from Scotland to Hungary, which would perform the work of God, so that 'by piece and piece, the Kings of the Earth that gave their power unto the Beast (all the work of God must be fulfilled) shall now tear the whore, and make her desolate, as St. John in his revelation hath foretold.'[9] Cromwell inherited the crusading tradition of the Protestant Interest. His was the voice of authentic Calvinism when he spoke of providences which 'so hang together'. He applied diplomatic pressure to Cardinal Mazarin on behalf of the Vaudois, and one of his aims in acquiring Dunkirk was to provide him with a 'backdoor' into France to safeguard the interest of the Huguenots. He had dreams of a European Protestant federation, and sent John Dury, a Scot who had taught in a Huguenot household, became minister at Elbing, and had spent long years pressing the cause of Protestant unity, as his agent to Holland and Switzerland. In one of his last speeches Cromwell spoke with emotion of Protestants driven out of Bohemia, Moravia, and Silesia by the sword and 'tossed out of Poland . . . ready to perish for want of food', while on the other side of Europe they were threatened by the persecuting power of Spain and of a 'Pope, fitted to accomplish this bloody work'.

[8] Vogler, 517.
[9] Quoted by S. L. Adams, 'Foreign Policy and the Parliaments of 1621 and 1624', in K. Sharpe (ed.), *Faction and Parliament: Essays on Early Stuart History* (Oxford, 1978), 147.

Calvinism was an international religion seeking not to adapt itself to society but to cast society into a new mould. John Winthrop could start from scratch in the 'wilderness' of America and on the deck of the *Arbella* he preached that the future settlement would be a new Jerusalem, a city set upon a hill. The doctrine of predestination, which came into the forefront when Beza succeeded Calvin, led Calvinists to identify themselves with the Elect and with the children of Israel. The Old Testament was for them both a mirror and a guide, in which they found inspiration for their victories over the forces of Babylon and consolation for their tribulations in the desert or the wilderness on their way to the Promised Land. Providence and the dispensations of God had immediacy and reality for them. When Coligny crossed a ford on the Loire in 1568 this was at once compared to the crossing of the Red Sea, and in the skirmishing before the Battle of Dunbar, Cromwell saw 'high acts of the Lord's Providence', especially when a cloud conveniently obscured the moon. The sense of being of the Elect gave high moral purpose to Calvinists, though this could draw them apart from society. Elizabeth Clinton, countess of Lincoln, who campaigned against the practice of wet-nursing, used as one of her arguments the consideration that the baby might be 'one of God's very elect . . . to whom to be a nursing-mother is a queen's honour'. Indeed her own son showed his Calvinist mettle by raising troops for the defence of the Palatinate. Again, the minister of the English church at Flushing, when dedicating a theological treatise to Sir Francis Barrington, his son, and his son-in-law, congratulated all three on being chosen by God 'with that glorious Advantage and Prerogative, to be called his Saints'.[10]

Calvin emphasized the importance of the family unit in which the father set the moral tone with Bible-readings and instruction through the catechism, adjuncts of the sermons given by the ministers. Despite Calvin's own accommodating attitude towards bishops, the startling change introduced by Calvinist ecclesiology was parity between the individual churches and the destruction of priestly hierarchy. In 1576 Beza wrote to Lord Glamis denouncing the institution of episcopacy as man-made, since there was nothing in the New Testament to justify putting one pastor above his brethren. This view had already been expressed at the Geneva Academy in lectures attended by two leading English Presbyterians, Thomas Cartwright and Walter Travers, and by the Scot, Andrew Melville, the proponent of the uncompromising Calvinism of the *Second Book of Discipline*.[11] Calvin's revolutionary innovation was to require his churches to be established on the basis of a consistory, composed of elders elected by

[10] N. Tyacke, 'Puritanism, Arminianism and Counter-Revolution', in C. Russell (ed.), *The Origins of the Civil War*, (London, 1975), 136–7; J. T. Cliffe, *The Puritan Gentry: The Great Puritan Families of Early Stuart England* (London, 1984), 11.

[11] P. Collinson, *The Elizabethan Puritan Movement* (London, 1967), 110.

the congregation and a minister, a new social unit disruptive of the old communities. The consistories enforced the moral and social discipline on the pattern of Geneva which Calvinists sought to impose upon society. If they failed to capture the whole of society, their separate identity, advertised by their dress, manners, and conduct, was a challenge which could lead to riot and disorder, civil war and persecution, or emigration.

The powers, duties, and functioning of the consistory were set out in the various Confessions, Catechisms, and Books of Discipline. But how did the consistory function in practice? Were Calvinists drawn from the whole spectrum of society or were the Calvinist Elect already an élite, drawn from the nobility, the professional classes, and the more skilled occupations? And how did the social recruitment of Calvinism affect its success or failure in different countries? The relation of Calvinism to its social background helps to explain why Calvinism was welcomed by some elements in society and not by others, why a religion supposedly of the élite could be associated with mob violence and iconoclasm, and why it took firmer root in some countries than in others.

An investigation of the actual working of consistories also helps in seeking answers to these questions. The apparent democracy of Calvinist consistories and congregations becomes questionable in view of the re-election and co-option of the elders, a common practice which transformed the consistory into an oligarchy and the Discipline into an exercise in social controls. Beza himself spoke of 'the aristocratic principle of the consistory'.[12] Nicolas Des Gallars, sent by Calvin to the Strangers' Church in London, turned to Bishop Grindal for help in upholding the elders against the congregation, while John Cotton in Massachusetts declared that God never ordained democracy 'as a fit government for either church or commonwealth'. But if internal controls made for disciplined flocks, externally Calvinism presented a challenge to authority in the political theories of resistance which emerged from the rebellions and civil wars of the second half of the sixteenth century. France produced the most telling propaganda, especially in the *Franco-Gallia* of Hotman in 1573 and in the *Vindiciae contra Tyrannos* of 1579, probably written by Duplessis-Mornay, with arguments which were both cogent and practical. In 1622 the *Vindiciae* was condemned and burned at Oxford; in 1648 it was translated into English and then invoked to justify the execution of Charles I. Milton in *The Tenure of Kings and Magistrates* cited Buchanan of Scotland and Pareus of the Palatinate, together with Hotman of France, as authorities for the deposition of kings. Dryden at the time of the Exclusion Crisis was quick to trace the lineage of Whig views back to Milton and the monarchomachs, writing in the prologue of his play, *The Duke of Guise*:

[12] R. M. Kingdon, *Geneva and the Consolidation of the French Protestant Movement, 1564–1572* (Geneva, 1967), 103.

What e'er our hot-brain'd sheriffs did advance,
Was, like our fashions, first produced in France.

The legacy of the *Vindiciae* was impossible to shake off, however much Huguenot writers deplored the action of the Long Parliament and subscribed to royalist theories of absolutism and obedience. There were no doubts in the mind of a government agent in Saintonge in 1680 who, reporting to Paris on the happy progress of the campaign for conversion and the destruction of temples, spoke of the need to humble 'le Consistoire, dangereux gouvernement qui fait les républicains'.[13]

When E. G. Léonard came to sum up Calvin's achievements he considered that the greatest of these was the creation in Geneva of 'a new type of man, the Calvinist', and that it was there that Calvin sketched out the lineaments of the modern world. Léonard identified the 'Calvinist man' by his moral rectitude, his sense of vocation, his capacity for social organization, and a faith which, nourished on the Old Testament rather than on the New, was more concerned with the grandeur of God than with Christian love. But Léonard did not subscribe to the view of 'the great German sociologists', Max Weber and Ernst Troeltsch, that the Reformation was 'the mother of capitalism', a view he considered hasty and fragile.[14]

The affinity between Protestantism and capitalism advanced by Weber has been the subject of keen debate. E. Le Roy Ladurie touched on this in his great study of Languedoc, where Calvinists ranged from the peasants of the Cévennes to the rich merchants of Nîmes. Although he held that Calvinism did not prefigure capitalism in the way Weber had argued, he concluded that it had nevertheless helped to change and to modernize the society of Languedoc. The silk industry, a dynamic element in the economy, was in Protestant hands, and in Olivier de Serres, celebrated for his best-selling *Le Théâtre d'Agriculture*, first published in 1600, Le Roy Ladurie saw Weber's Protestant ethic fully exemplified. Olivier de Serres had a keen sense of vocation, and his belief in predestination pervaded his book. He preached the virtues of the patriarch presiding over his family and household, enforcing strict moral standards, chasing vagabonds off his estates, and paying as little as possible to his workers, who were liable to cheat and steal, and whom he likened to oxen whose only value lay in their physical strength. Olivier de Serres had heard Calvin's teaching at Geneva.[15] Yet it can be argued that here the substance of his recommendations, as distinct from his Calvinist terminology, differed little from that

[13] P. Collinson, *Archbishop Grindal, 1519–1583* (London, 1979), 130–3; Perry Miller, *The New England Mind* (Harvard, 1939), 423; E. Guitard, *Colbert et Seignelay contre la religion réformée* (Paris, 1912).

[14] E. G. Léonard, *Histoire Générale du protestantisme* (Paris, 1961), i, 307–09.

[15] E. Le Roy Ladurie, *Les Paysans de Languedoc* (Paris, 1966), i, 353–5.

of the thirteenth-century English treatises on estate management, similarly concerned with efficiency and improvement and equally informed by a deep distrust of the idleness and chicanery of servants. The comparison of workers to beasts seems to derive, directly or indirectly, from Aristotle and not from Calvin.

While Calvinism has been regarded as the friend of capitalism, it has been commonly considered the enemy of art. It has often been associated with iconoclasm, but iconoclasm occurred only in particular places and at particular times and was deplored by Calvin. He condemned the veneration of images, citing the example of the temples of the primitive church which were not polluted and profaned by idols. But Calvin also denounced mob action, and insisted that nothing should be done except under the direction of the magistrates. Frederick III's iconoclastic campaign in the Palatinate in 1565 obeyed Calvin's directive, in this respect again making the Electorate a model Calvinist state. Marnix de Sainte-Aldegonde, the friend and adviser of William of Orange, was horrified by the destruction in Flanders in 1566. That summer saw spectacular outbreaks of iconoclasm in Antwerp, Ghent, Ypres, and Valenciennes where altars, fonts, organs, chalices, reliquaries and vestments were all attacked, mutilated or destroyed. In 1562 there was widespread iconoclasm in France and sporadic outbreaks in the following years, while in the second cycle of religious wars between 1621 and 1629 Languedoc experienced a wave of violence, when Nîmes cathedral, newly rebuilt after its destruction in the late sixteenth century, was again demolished. Iconoclastic attacks were directed against objects rather than people, since objects were held to be the carriers of superstition, and their timing coincides with periods of tension and of war, when there were hopes of revolution or victory following a period of persecution.

The whitewashed walls of Calvinist churches were denied to artists. In contrast, the reinvigorated and proselytizing Catholic Church which emerged from the Council of Trent saw the adoption of the baroque style and lavish commissions for visual aids to piety in ornate altars, paintings of the Virgin, saints, flagellations, and crucifixions. But how did Calvinist doctrine affect artistic talent? In the post-Tridentine period canons of taste in architecture and painting were imported from Rome, denounced from Calvinist pulpits as Babylon. The Heidelberg Catechism of 1563 banned visual aids, and in Dutch churches only the doors to the organ lofts were painted. Calvin himself forbade images of God, disapproved of idle fancies, and considered that paintings and sculpture should be concerned only with the visible world. But he also considered that it was permissible to paint commemorative historical pictures, or, even though they served for pleasure only, portraits, landscapes and townscapes.[16] He was therefore allowing

---

[16] Quoted by C. Tümpel in A. Blankert et al., *Gods, Saints and Heroes: Dutch Painting in the Age of Rembrandt* (Washington, DC, 1980), 53 n. 7.

plenty of scope, especially since history painting came to be largely concerned with biblical scenes which had a moral content.

But what patronage did Calvinist artists enjoy and did they suffer discrimination as a result of their faith? The United Provinces provided Calvinist painters with a court and affluent burghers who liked to buy pictures. The landscapes, the domestic scenes, and the still-life paintings met the Calvinist requirement of realism, but they were relatively cheap, and low in the scale of approved artistic values. Dutch and French art critics of the seventeenth century gave the highest rating to history painting, drawn from the Bible or from mythological themes. Dutch burghers commissioned history paintings on a large scale, and since Calvinists identified themselves with the children of Israel they responded to biblical scenes. Rembrandt was not alone in painting biblical scenes but followed the fashion, responding to the demand: the difference lay in the quality of his painting. Rembrandt never left Holland, but Italy exercised an important influence and there was the Caravaggio school at Utrecht. History paintings were expensive and were commissioned by the wealthier burghers, by the Orange court in The Hague, and by municipalities.[17]

France offered Protestant architects and artists a full range of patronage from the reign of Henri IV until the early years of Louis XIV's reign. The crown gave a lead on building, while there were lavish commissions to be earned from ministers enriched by office, nobles in receipt of pensions, and financiers in charge of tax collecting and royal borrowing. Calvinism was a minority religion, but there was no discrimination against Calvinists, whose work was in keeping with the artistic culture of the age. Salomon de Brosse built for Henri IV and for Marie de Médicis when she was Regent; he was commissioned by the great Protestant nobles, by the duc de Sully and also by Richelieu. There was no austerity in the bills de Brosse presented to his clients, while although he never went to Italy himself, he had the folios of drawings bequeathed by his Calvinist grandfather, Jacques du Cerceau. He played a key role in the development of French classicism, composing splendidly in mass and giving his patrons the sense of grandeur and status which they sought. De Brosse belonged to a dynasty of Protestant architects, who never wavered in their Calvinism and who took the road of exile to Hesse-Cassel in 1685.[18]

Protestant artists formed a tight group, congregating in the Faubourg Saint-Germain, going by river to the temple at Charenton on Sundays, drawn close by marriage and by membership of the Académie Royale de

[17] A. Blankert, 'General Introduction' and C. Tümpel, 'Religious History Painting', ibid. I am very grateful to Professor Michael Kitson for the loan of this catalogue and for helpful conversations on Dutch and French seventeenth century painting.

[18] R. Coupe, *Salomon de Brosse and the Development of the Classical Style in French Architecture from 1565 to 1630* (London, 1972).

Peinture, founded in 1643. Out of the twenty-three original members nearly a third were Calvinists. Simon Vouet had returned from Rome in 1627 and his studio, the most important art centre in Paris, was open to Protestants. Louis and Henri Testelin, the first two secretaries of the Academy, specialised in murals and grisailles, and Henri Testelin became a designer for the Gobelins. He survived his brother, refused to abjure and died in the Hague in 1692. The two miniaturists, Louis du Guernier and Samuel Bernard, both trained by Vouet, were among the first Academicians. The latter abjured when a very old man after 1685, but Jean Michelin, the painter of charming street scenes, which have been taken to be the work of the Le Nains, was excluded from the Academy in 1681 and emigrated to Hanover, where he opened a tapestry factory. Abraham Bosse, the celebrated engraver, was a strict Calvinist, whose work included moving hospital and prison scenes, fashionable ladies in church and rich Huguenot households in Paris.

The most famous of these Calvinist artists was Sébastien Bourdon, too versatile and perhaps too derivative to have been placed in the very top flight, but immensely talented. He came from Languedoc, where Calvinism was still militant, and in 1634 contrived to get to Rome where the French artistic colony was dominated by Poussin and Claude Lorrain. He practised history painting, was expert in copying Lorrain, and when Rome became too dangerous for an impetuous Calvinist he had the good fortune to be rescued by a rich French patron who rose to hold the agreeable post of *Intendant des plaisirs du roi*. Bourdon quickly prospered in Paris. He had many commissions from members of the court, churches in Paris, and the canons of Chartres. He was a founding member of the Academy, rising to become its rector; accepted an invitation to Stockholm as court painter to Queen Christina; and on her abdication returned to his native Montpellier in 1656. There the canons were rebuilding the cathedral and, in association with the governor of the town, invited Bourdon to paint a picture for the high altar. The result was one of his finest paintings, *The Fall of Simon Magus*. But his Calvinism was a liability in troubled Montpellier, and he returned to Paris with a splendid commission to paint the murals of the most sumptuous *hôtel* on the Île Saint-Louis. He died while painting a ceiling in the Tuileries. He was an extraordinarily rapid worker: indeed he is said to have made a wager that he could paint twelve heads life-size in a single day, and to have won his bet in what may be regarded as a triumph for the Calvinist work-ethic. Yet despite the range and volume of his output the quality of his best work was very high, earning the praise of Bernini in the seventeenth century, of Sir Joshua Reynolds in the eighteenth, and of Constable in the nineteenth.[19]

    [19] C. Ponsonailhe, *Sébastien Bourdon* (Paris, 1886); A Félibien, *Entretiens sur les vies et les ouvrages des plus excellents peintres anciens et modernes* (Paris 1705); P. Rosenberg *et al.*, *La Peinture française du*

It may be thought that Bourdon's Calvinism wore thin under the influence of success and of his Catholic patrons and clients. But all the evidence indicates that it remained firm. His wife, a talented miniaturist, was a Calvinist of the Du Guernier family. Bourdon died in 1671. But his only surviving daughter, accompanied by her aunt, gave the strongest proof of her upbringing when she succeeded in reaching England in 1686 after being captured in the first attempt at escape. Although neither de Brosse nor Bourdon wavered in his Calvinism, their styles were uninfluenced by their religion. Patrons chose their architects and artists for their work, not for their religion. Gédéon Tallemant, a member of the very rich Protestant banking family, his father-in-law the financier Pierre Montauron, and Barthélemy Hervart, the Protestant financier whose timely loan enabled Mazarin to acquire Alsace, all employed the Catholic artists La Hyre and Mignard. Coexistence in the upper reaches of French society in the middle decades of the seventeenth century was eased when St François de Sales was advocating urbanity of manner both in social life and in controversy, and when Moïse Amyraut of the Academy of Saumur was recommending passive obedience, enjoyment of life, good manners, and 'une affabilité qui nous rend facilement accessibles les uns aux autres'.

What then was Calvinism? Strict definitions make for clarity of exposition; and if we adopt the strict definitions given by the Synod of Dort in 1618 and the *Consensus Helveticus* of 1675, Calvinism can be, and has been, represented as a harsh, austere, and intolerant creed. Its theology centred on the forbidding and divisive dogma of double predestination, degenerating into arid scholastic disputes; its requirement of conformity to an unnaturally stiff code of conduct was productive of bigotry or hypocrisy; and its structure of consistories, colloquies, and synods formed an unyielding straitjacket. So defined, Calvinism appears as a reactionary movement which has been illegitimately linked with the quite separate intellectual developments which came to fruition in the Enlightenment and with the economic achievements of capitalism.[20]

But to adopt this strict definition has awkward consequences. It requires us to hold that Calvin was in many respects not a Calvinist, for it was Beza, not Calvin, who emphasized the doctrine of double predestination and made it the core of reformed orthodoxy. It ignores too Calvin's humanism and his flexibility or opportunism on the issue of church government. It requires us to exclude such men as Amyraut and Bayle, has no room for the painters and

XVIIᵉ siècle dans les collections américaines (Paris, 1982), introduction by M. Fumaroli; Menna Prestwich, 'Patronage and the Protestants in France, 1598–1661: Architects and Painters', in J. Mesnard and R. Mousnier (eds.), *L'Age d'or du mécénat, 1598–1661* (Paris, 1985). I am very grateful to Professor Francis Haskell for the help and advice he gave me when, investigating the career of Bourdon and the Protestant circle in Paris, I ventured into the world of art-history.

[20] See the stimulating essay by H. R. Trevor-Roper, 'The Religious Origins of the Enlightenment' in *Religion, the Reformation and Social Change* (London, 1967).

architects, and encourages us to deny that there was anything Calvinist in the work of the Huguenot political theorists of the sixteenth century on the grounds that they merely stole their arguments from their Catholic opponents.[21] It is at least plausible to think that in the seventeenth century Calvin's influence was greater outside the narrow confines of the orthodoxy of Dort than within it. Historians have found it necessary to speak of Calvinist episcopalianism in the Anglican Church and of the decentralized Calvinism of the Independents. Scholars concerned with continental Calvinism in the seventeenth century have been unable to force it into a single mould, and, while writing of Calvinist orthodoxy, have also identified a liberal and an ultra-Calvinist orthodoxy. It is revealing that the supposedly orthodox Calvinism of the *Consensus Helveticus* of 1675 proved distasteful to the Huguenot pastors who took refuge in Switzerland after the Revocation. Indeed the *Consensus* was to be discarded by the Company of Pastors of Geneva, the very body which had once done so much to make Calvinism an international religion.

[21] Q. Skinner, *The Foundations of Modern Political Thought* (Cambridge, 1978), ii, 320–1.

I

Calvin

RICHARD STAUFFER[1]

AFTER the death of the majority of the Reformation leaders of the first generation (Luther died in 1546, fifteen years after Zwingli and Oecolampadius and five years before Bucer), the work which they had begun was carried on by successors, who in general were not of the same intellectual calibre. Two men, however, emerged in the second generation, Henry Bullinger, the successor of Zwingli at Zürich, and John Calvin. Both had the stature of great men and the origins of the Reformed as distinct from the Lutheran tradition are linked to their names. Calvin, by his actions and by his thought, gave a new impulse to the Protestant cause, which after the death of Luther, had lost some of its dynamic.

Calvin's Life

Calvin was born on 10 July 1509 in the cathedral city of Noyon in Picardy about seventy miles north-east of Paris. His father, Gérard Cauvin (whose surname, latinized as 'Calvinus', became Calvin in French), was a man of modest origins. He was the son of a bargeman and became himself a municipal clerk. He rose to be a man of business to the bishop and to the local clergy, thus gaining admittance to the urban bourgeoisie. Jeanne Lefranc, Calvin's mother, was the daughter of a bourgeois sufficiently influential to be a member of the Noyon town council. Little is known about her, except that she was pious, attached to the devotional cults of the time, and died quite young. Calvin was not an only child. He had an older brother, Charles, and two younger brothers, Antoine and François, but the latter died in childhood.

As a result of the bishop of Noyon's patronage, the Cauvin boys, destined by their father for ecclesiastical careers, obtained chaplaincies which provided them with enough income to pursue their studies. Thus John Calvin probably received the tonsure at the age of twelve. He was highly

[1] This essay, translated into German, was published in vol. 6 of *Gestalten der Kirchengeschichte, Die Reformationszeit II* (Verlag W. Kohlhammer, Stuttgart, 1981), ed. Martin Greschat, Professor at the University of Münster, 211–41. The French text appeared in *Hokhma, Revue de réflexion théologique*, 23 (1983). This shortened English version appears with the kind permission of Verlag W. Kohlhammer. Owing to his sad death, Professor Stauffer was unable to see the translation or to add more footnotes. References to books and articles in the essay will be found under *Further Reading*.

talented and did not stay long at the Collège des Capettes of his native town, where he had been placed along with his brother, Charles. In 1523, as is generally agreed, he was sent to Paris to continue his studies there. He did not go alone. He accompanied three young men with whom he had ties of friendship and who belonged to the noble family of Hangest, which had given several bishops to Noyon. In Paris, Calvin entered the Collège de la Marche, where his master in grammar was Mathurin Cordier, who was to become one of the founders of Protestant education in French-speaking countries. He did not stay long at this establishment but soon matriculated at the Collège Montaigu, which had a reputation for asceticism and orthodoxy. The principal was the theologian Noël Bédier, a savage opponent of evangelical ideas.

During the four or five years he spent at Montaigu reading for the degree of Master of Arts, which seems to have been conferred on him in 1528, Calvin no doubt had occasion to hear talk of the Lutheran 'heresy'. In 1523, just when he arrived in Paris, the Augustinian monk Jean Vallière, suspected of heterodox beliefs, was burnt at the stake. In 1524 Francis I's sister, Marguerite of Angoulême, Duchess of Alençon and later Queen of Navarre, published her *Dialogue en forme de vision nocturne*, in which she proclaimed the doctrine of justification by faith alone. In 1525, following the battle of Pavia, the Paris *Parlement*, backed by the Sorbonne, took advantage of the captivity of Francis I to launch severe action against those who were termed *mal pensants de la foi*. In 1526 the execution in the Place de Grève of Jacques Pavannes (or Pauvant) struck a serious blow at the evangelical movement centred on Meaux. All those events were probably known to Calvin, but they did not lead him to take the side of the Reformation.

When his philosophical education was completed (for philosophy and dialectic constituted the essential disciplines of the Faculty of Arts), Calvin left the University of Paris for that of Orléans, then famous for its Law Faculty. This change of residence, which appears to have taken place in 1528, meant also a profound change of direction. Whereas Calvin's father had originally sent him to study theology, because he wished to make a churchman of him, the young man now found himself switched to the study of law. Why was this new career chosen for him? Partly because Gérard Cauvin had quarrelled with the Chapter at Noyon over money matters, but, even more certainly, because he had realized, as his son puts it in the preface to his *Commentary on the Psalms*, that 'the study of law commonly brings wealth to those who pursue it'.

Calvin, as a dutiful son, accordingly applied himself to the study of law. At Orléans he attended the lectures of Pierre de l'Estoile, described by Theodore Beza as 'the most acute-minded jurist among all the doctors of France'. However, Calvin did not let himself become wholly absorbed in juridical problems. To satisfy a taste for letters which he had acquired in Paris, he set himself to learn Greek, under Melchior Wolmar, a scholar from Württemberg who was interested in the ideas of Martin Luther, if not won over to them. Calvin, like all students, was susceptible to the fame that certain teachers can acquire. He was drawn to the University of Bourges, apparently in 1529, by the teaching which, at the request of Marguerite of Angoulême, the Italian Andrea Alciati had begun to give there as professor of Roman law. Moving from the lecture-room of Pierre de l'Estoile to that of Alciati meant moving from a medieval conception of law to one which, putting Roman law in its historical setting and studying the texts in the light of classical scholarship meant making a place for the methods of humanism. Calvin, perhaps surprisingly, was not captivated by Alciati. Even though it is to the latter that he owed his clarity of expression, he stayed loyal to Pierre de l'Estoile and defended him against Alciati in his first published work, a preface to Nicolas Duchemin's *Antapologia*.

In the spring of 1531, soon after gaining his degree as *licencié ès lois*, Calvin was recalled to Noyon by his father's illness. Gérard Cauvin died on 26 May, excommunicated by the Chapter. His death enabled his son to take up the career which corresponded to his real tastes. Calvin settled down to the study of letters in Paris, though without entirely neglecting law, since, in the course of 1533, we find him carrying out in the University of Orléans the duties of deputy proctor, representing the students on the academic council of the 'Picard nation'. In order to pursue his studies, he followed in Paris the courses given by the royal lecturers, the embryo of the Collège de France, recently created by Francis I on the model of the Collegium Trilingue of Louvain. Two of the Readers particularly caught his attention. Both had been influenced by Lefèvre d'Étaples, the humanist of Saint-Germain-des-Prés and moving spirit of the Meaux circle, which aimed to advance the reform of the Church. They were the Hellenist Pierre Danès and the Hebraist François Vatable. Under Danès Calvin improved the knowledge of Greek he had obtained from Wolmar, while Vatable appears (we have no formal proof of this) to have initiated him into the mysteries of Hebrew.

The fruit of Calvin's first researches in literature appeared in April 1532. It was a *Commentary on Seneca's 'De Clementia'*. This work, applying as it does the method used by Valla, Erasmus, and Budé, bears witness not only to Calvin's erudition and qualities of style but also to his individuality and originality. However, despite these virtues, it was coolly received by the humanists. Calvin was blamed for presumption because he had dared to criticize Erasmus. Whatever the merits or the shortcomings of this *Commentary*, it should be noted that in it religious questions are kept in the background. When he wrote this work Calvin was not yet involved with the problems that were soon to preoccupy him to the exclusion of all else.

These problems literally burst into his life in 1533. The new rector of the

University of Paris, the humanist Nicolas Cop, a friend of Calvin's from his youth, not only took action against those who had dared to attack Marguerite for the favour she showed to Reformers, but went even further. At the beginning of the academic year, on All Souls' Day, he dared to give a quasi-sermon on the Beatitudes instead of the usual rectorial address. Drawing inspiration from Erasmus and Luther, he touched on themes dear to the Reformers in particular on justification by faith. This was going too far! Taking advantage of the King's absence from Paris, the *Parlement* prosecuted Cop, who had to flee abroad. Calvin, who also felt threatened, took refuge in Angoulême, at the home of his friend Louis du Tillet, the *curé* of Claix. But why did the young author of the *Commentary on Seneca's 'De Clementia'* feel the need to seek safety? No doubt because he had taken a hand, in one way or another, in the drafting of Cop's address. Long accepted as an established fact, then doubted by several historians, the view that Calvin composed the address to the university on All Souls' Day, 1533, has now found new defenders thanks to the researches of the Strasburg historian, Jean Rott.

Calvin's flight to Angoulême gives rise to an important question, the date of his conversion, or, more precisely, of his adhesion to the cause of the Reformation. By seeking to escape from the proceedings launched as a result of Cop's address, Calvin showed that he possessed acquaintance with the evangelical ideal. In November 1533 he must have been at the least a supporter of the reformism that Lefèvre d'Étaples had tried to set in train. It is tempting to go further, but it is difficult to do so because Calvin never willingly spoke of himself in his writings. In the passage in his preface to the *Commentaries on the Book of Psalms* (1557) where he recalled the *subita conversio ad docilitatem* by virtue of which God, turning him away from 'the Popish superstitions', 'tamed his heart and reduced it to obedience', no date is given. However the most likely hypothesis is that it was at the end of 1533 that he passed from the mild reforming views of Lefèvre d'Étaples to an unambiguous Reformation platform. For it was in the spring of 1534 that he visited his native town in order to surrender all the church livings he had enjoyed up to then, and to terminate his position as a cleric.

On his return from Noyon, Calvin first stopped in Paris and then stayed in several places, Orléans in particular. There it was that he put the finishing touches to his first theological work, the *Psychopannychia* ('The Vigil of Souls'), in which he sought to prove, in opposition to the Anabaptists, that 'souls watch and live after they have left the body'. Hardly had he completed this treatise when a resounding event forced him to leave France. During the night of 17–18 October 1534 placards directed against the Mass, written by Antoine Marcourt, pastor at Neuchâtel, were posted up in Paris and at Amboise, even in the King's own apartments. Francis I could not let this insult pass. Encouraged by the Sorbonne, by the *Parlement*, and even by some humanists, he had a number of people executed. To escape from the danger to which his beliefs exposed him, Calvin decided to take refuge in Basle at the beginning of 1535.

In Basle the young Frenchman found safe asylum, but, as he wished to remain incognito, he assumed the name of Martinus Lucanius. Devoting himself wholly to theological studies, he completed within less than a year, by intensive effort, a work which he had certainly put on the stocks before he left France: the *Institutes of the Christian Religion*. Published in Latin in March 1536, this book, which begins with an *Epistula apologetica* addressed 'to the King of France', takes the form of a manual of theology consisting of six chapters dealing respectively—it should be noted that this format was inspired by Luther's *Short Catechism*—with the Law (the Ten Commandments), Faith (the Apostles' Creed), Prayer (the Lord's Prayer), the Sacraments (Baptism and the Lord's Supper), False Sacraments, and Christian Liberty. From the moment of publication, Calvin's *Institutes* made its author the herald of the French Reformation, a herald who was never to cease, throughout his career, from revising and expanding his work. The last edition of the *Institutes*, published in 1559 (and translated into French in 1560), bore no resemblance to the original manual, being composed of eighty chapters, divided into four books dealing, successively, with theology in the strict sense (concerning God as creator and 'sovereign ruler of the world'), with soteriology (concerning Christ as redeemer), with pneumatology (concerning the Holy Spirit, or, more precisely in this case, the action of the Holy Spirit in man and the fruits of the grace of Jesus Christ), and with ecclesiology (concerning the Church and the Sacraments).

When the *Institutes* had been written, Calvin set off for Italy together with his friend Du Tillet. After a short stay at the Court of Ferrara, where a small circle of supporters of the Reformation had gathered around the Duchess, Renée de France, he returned to Basle. From there he soon afterwards departed for France, with a view to winding up his affairs before finally taking the path of exile. Intending to settle in Strasburg, he arranged for the sale at Noyon of the lands he held with his brothers, and left his native country without hope of return. As the war between Francis I and Charles V, which had begun again in 1536, made it impossible for him to take the shortest way into Alsace, he was obliged, after leaving Paris, to go round by Geneva. He had just arrived in that city, in July 1536, when Guillaume Farel (1489–1565), who, assisted by Pierre Viret, had recently introduced the Reformation there, persuaded him by 'an awesome entreaty' to remain there and help him consolidate his work.

By keeping Calvin in Geneva Farel showed his discernment. He had the wit to perceive in the author of the *Institutes of the Christian Religion* the man who would be able to carry through the task of regeneration that had just been started in this city of some ten thousand inhabitants whose citizens, jealously guarding their liberties, had recently thrown off the tutelage of their Bishop, their theoretical sovereign, and also their dependence on the dukes of Savoy. Having been assigned the duties of 'lecturer in Holy Scripture', Calvin was not content with commenting on the Epistles of St Paul in the cathedral. Since there was as yet 'no Reformation' in Geneva and everything was 'in disorder' (as he was to say, on his deathbed, to his colleagues in the ministry), he set himself to organize the Church with all possible speed. Together with Farel he drew up four Articles which he submitted to the City Council. In the second of these articles he advocated the singing of the Psalms, in the third he proposed the introduction of a catechism for children, and in the fourth suggested a reform in the marriage-law. The first article dealt with the most important problem of all, the Lord' Supper. Though Calvin himself was in favour of weekly communion, he agreed to celebrate the Eucharist only once a month by reason of the 'infirmity of the people'. On the other hand, because he desired that the Lord's Supper should not be 'polluted and contaminated' by unworthy persons, he claimed for the Church the right to excommunicate impenitent sinners. Besides these Articles, Calvin, in order to provide his new parishioners with a catechism drew up the *Instruction and Confession of Faith in use in the Church of Geneva* (1537), in which he presented in popular form and in a cool, eirenic tone the teaching of the *Institutes of the Christian Religion*. He also composed (perhaps with Farel) a profession of faith in twenty-one articles which he intended to be signed by all the citizens of Geneva.

These efforts, aimed at equipping the Church of Geneva with a solid framework of discipline and doctrine, aroused vigorous resistance. The civil authorities fearing to lose some of their prerogatives if they were to allow the Church the right to exercise discipline, insisted on reserving for themselves the supervision of public morals. As for the citizens, they refused in many cases to put their names to the confession of faith, either because they were still faithful to the Church of Rome or because, in the name of a misunderstood evangelical freedom, they were opposed to all ecclesiastical discipline. Consequently, one year after Calvin's arrival in Geneva, he and his colleagues ran into an opposition which soon became threatening. To these internal problems were added other external difficulties which he had to face. Calvin had been obliged to stifle an Anabaptist offensive originating in the Netherlands. Above all, he had to defend himself against the accusations of Pierre Caroli, a former member of the Meaux circle who had become a pastor in Lausanne, and who by unjustly suspecting him of Arianism, made Calvin for ever afterwards highly sensitive on the subject of the dogma of the Trinity.

The latent conflict between the civil authorities and the Reformers became acute in 1538. Calvin and his colleagues having judged it their duty to exclude from the Lord's Supper all who opposed the confession of faith, the Council decided that communion should not be refused to anyone. This was an extremely grave decision, which presupposed that the political authorities were entitled to intervene with sovereign power in religious affairs. It made the civil power the master of the Church. Accordingly, when the Council, acting once more *ultra vires*, resolved, in order to please their ally, the canton of Berne, to adopt the liturgical usages practised there (use of fonts for baptism, and of the host for communion), the Reformers reacted vigorously. Refusing to submit to the orders of the civil authorities, the Reformers mounted the pulpit to preach on Easter Day, 1538, but abstained from celebrating the Lord's Supper. The riposte by the authorities was rapid and draconian. Calvin and Farel were dismissed and ordered to leave Geneva within three days.

While Farel installed himself in Neuchâtel, Calvin considered going to Basle to resume his studies there. But an urgent appeal from Martin Bucer, who requested him not to act like Jonah when he refused to fulfil his mission to the Ninevites, diverted Calvin from this plan and convinced him that it was his duty to continue 'with the task of teaching'. In September 1538 he assumed responsibility for the community of French refugees in Strasburg. His stay in the Alsatian capital, though short (only three years), was of decisive importance. He learnt much, especially in the spheres of liturgy and ecclesiology, through contact with the Strasburg Reformers. He took over from Bucer, in particular, the doctrine of the four ministries, which will be discussed later.

Enjoying as he did the confidence of both the religious and political authorities, Calvin was able to give of his best in Strasburg. Besides performing his duties as pastor of the French church, he took on those of professor of exegesis in the *Haute École* which had just opened under the directorship of Johann Sturm and also became assistant and later delegate to the colloquies of Hagenau, Worms, and Regensburg, where, at the instigation of the Emperor, Roman and Evangelical divines sought in vain to re-establish religious unity. Calvin displayed extraordinary productivity with the pen. He prepared the second Latin edition (1539) and drew up the first French edition (1541) of the *Institutes of the Christian Religion*. He inaugurated a long series of exegetical works by publishing a remarkable volume, *Commentaries on the Epistle to the Romans*. He wrote the incisive work known as the *Epistle to Sadoleto* in reply to a humanist prelate who, after Calvin's departure for Strasburg, had sent a letter to the Senate and people of Geneva calling on them to return to the bosom of the Roman Church. Finally, troubled by the divisions which the problem of the Eucharist caused among supporters of the Reformation, and which the Marburg Colloquy (1529) had failed to overcome, he composed the *Short Treatise on the Lord's Supper*. While opposing the Romanist doctrine, he distanced himself from both Luther's and Zwingli's views, and sought to show that 'when we receive the sacrament with faith . . . we are truly made partakers in the proper substance of the body and blood of Jesus Christ.'

During Calvin's stay in Strasburg the Genevan church was troubled by grave dissensions. The supporters of the banished Reformers—the Guillermins as they were called in memory of Guillaume Farel—opposed the new pastors appointed by the civil authorities. Calvin, vexed from afar by disputes which were dangerous for the future of the Reform,[2] exerted a moderating influence on the Genevans and succeeded in re-establishing peace in their church. However, it very soon became apparent that the preachers entrusted with the defence of the cause of the Gospel in Geneva lacked the stature to face the confused situation created by the citizens of Berne, who, having themselves been won over to the Reformation, sought to exercise ascendancy over Geneva. Therefore, following elections favourable to the Guillermins, the Small Council decided to recall Calvin, who alone could control the situation. The French Reformer, happy in Strasburg, though unable to understand the language spoken there, had no wish to become involved once more in the difficulties of his first parish. However, when the solicitations from Geneva became more and more pressing, he decided that he could not shirk a task which, he thought, God had imposed upon him. He agreed, 'with grief, tears, great anxiety, and distress' (as he says in the preface to his *Commentaries on the Book of Psalms*) to return to the city from which he had been expelled three years before.

In September 1541 Calvin returned to Geneva, intending to stay there only as long as should be necessary to re-establish a little order in the Church. He was to end his days there after a ministry lasting twenty-three years, which some of his modern detractors, such as Stefan Zweig, have represented as nothing short of a dictatorship. This judgement is not only unjust, but a calumny. Until the last years of his life, Calvin was a foreigner in Geneva who did not belong to the Councils of the city. He was granted citizenship only in 1559, eighteen years after his return from Strasburg and five years before his death. His authority, long subjected to attack by the civil power, was due to his being, as Jean-Daniel Benoît has shown, a genuine pastor, a pastor with an acute intelligence, an extraordinary capacity for work, a tenacity in face of all odds and, finally, a personal magnetism which is only too often now forgotten.

As soon as he arrived in Geneva, Calvin set about organizing the Church. For this purpose he drew up a form of discipline which, under the title of *Ecclesiastical Ordinances*, was presented to the political authorities. After undergoing various amendments by them, aimed at safeguarding their prerogatives (in particular, the right to take part in the nomination of

---

[2] It has become customary among historians to employ the term 'Reform' for the specifically Calvinist form of the Reformation.

pastors and also to some extent, in the procedure for excommunication), the *Ordinances* were adopted by the authorities in November 1541. The *Ordinances*, drawing upon the concepts of Martin Bucer, the Strasburg Reformer, distinguished four ministries in the Church. There was the ministry of the pastors, whose mission was to 'proclaim the Word of God' and to 'administer the sacraments'; that of the Doctors, whose role was to 'teach sound doctrine to the faithful'; that of the Elders, on whom fell the task of ensuring respect for discipline; and that of the Deacons, who were responsible for aiding the poor and caring for the sick.

Besides the doctrine of the four ministries, the *Ordinances* included precise provisions for the religious instruction of children. To implement these it was necessary to possess a 'formulary', a manual containing the true 'doctrine'. Accordingly, Calvin drew up in 1542 a catechism in the form of questions and answers, better adapted to the needs of the young than his *Instruction and Confession of Faith* of 1537. Following the plan of Bucer's *Kurtzer Katechismus*, the *Catéchisme de l'Église de Genève* (as the 1542 text was entitled) abandoned the Lutheran structure of the 1537 catechism, and treated of faith before proceeding to the Law and to prayer. Finally, besides the *Ordinances* and the *Catechism*, Calvin gave the Church of Geneva, in order to perfect its organization, a liturgy, *Forme des prières et chants écclésiastiques*, which borrowed heavily from the Strasburg ritual, the *Psalter mit aller Kirchenübung* of 1539. Having thus laid the foundations of Reform in the city, Calvin engaged in a difficult struggle to make Geneva what Georges Goyau has called 'une ville-Église'. He aimed, with the help of the Consistory, a church authority composed of twelve Elders and some Pastors, to bring the Genevans to 'live in accordance with the Gospel and the word of God,' as they had committed themselves to doing in May 1536.

While thus dedicating himself to the reform of the Church of Geneva, Calvin did not forget his native country. Already in 1537 he had denounced the dangers run there by those who, though won for the Gospel, continued to take part in the ceremonies of the Church of Rome, that is, those laymen who persisted in attending Mass and those priests who did not renounce their sacerdotal functions. He had then stigmatized in two important epistles these 'middle-of-the-road men' and condemned all compromise between the evangelical faith and participation in the official form of worship. The first epistle, addressed more particularly to the laity (*De fugiendis impiorum illicitis sacris*) explained how necessary it was 'to avoid and to flee from popish ceremonies and superstitions'. The second, addressed to the clergy (*De christiano hominis officio in sacerdotiis papalis ecclesiae*), demonstrated 'what is the duty of a Christian with regard to the administration or rejection of the benefices of the Popish Church'.

These writings did not in Calvin's eyes exorcize the danger arising from harbouring Evangelical sentiments while pretending attachment to the established form of worship, with the excuse that for those who did not inwardly accept them, Roman ceremonies were a matter of indifference. Calvin therefore returned to the charge in 1543 with his *Petit Traité montrant ce que doit faire un homme fidèle connaissant la vérité de l'Évangile quand il est entre les papistes*. His advice came down to this: a Christian must be consistent. If he cannot confess his faith openly, he must depart out of Babylon. If he cannot escape, then he must abstain from all 'idolatry'. These recommendations, pregnant with consequences, dismayed numerous followers of the Gospel in France. To those who felt neither called to martyrdom nor obliged to go into exile, and accused Calvin of lacking humanity, he replied in his *Excuse à Messieurs les Nicodémites* (1544), in which he refused to make a single concession. He scolded these timid and shamefaced 'evangelicals' who excused themselves by invoking the example of the Pharisee Nicodemus, who for fear of compromising himself came to question Jesus by night.

Nicodemism was condemned, but another danger threatened those French who were receptive to the teaching of the Gospel, namely Illuminism. Founded by a certain Coppin from Lille and protected by Marguerite of Navarre, the sect of 'Libertines' (or *Spirituels*, as its initiates preferred to call themselves) constituted in the 1540s a formidable deviation on the left wing of French Protestantism. The sect, which was both pantheist and antinomian, held that since everything came from God and was a manifestation of the Spirit, the distinction between good and evil had no foundation. Calvin, seeing the truth of God thus assailed', thought it his duty to intervene. He did so in two pamphlets, *Contre la secte fantastique et furieuse des Libertins qui se disent Spirituels* (1545) and *L'Épître contre un certain Cordelier, suppôt de la dite secte* (1547). By these interventions, and also because thanks to the *Institutes of the Christian Religion* and other works, Calvin's thought was propagated widely, he helped to give those of his compatriots who had been won for the Gospel the doctrinal cohesion which they lacked.

While waging these battles aimed at promoting the Reformed cause in France, Calvin was at the same time engaged in a hard struggle in Geneva, where what was at stake was church discipline. Because he was convinced of the necessity of reserving communion to Christians whose conduct was consistent with the principles of their faith, and anxious to keep away from the Lord's Supper those who did not respect God's Commandments, he stirred up a number of reactions. In the first place, the civil authorities considered that it was for them to pronounce or suspend excommunications. To this resistance on the part of the political authorities was added the discontentment of an entire section of the population that was restive under the moral control to which it was subjected. Exposed to a popular opposition which did not miss any opportunity to express itself in jokes or insults (more than one Genevan of this period named his dog 'Calvin'), he had, furthermore, to face from 1546 onwards the hostility of two notables. These were Ami Perrin and François Favre, who had done much to bring Calvin back to Geneva. Exasperated at having been several times reprimanded by the consistory, without respect shown to their social status, Perrin, the leader of the Guillermins, and Favre, his father-in-law, turned against Calvin and rallied round themselves those Genevans who, without wishing to renounce the Reformation, nevertheless rebelled against the rigour of the ecclesiastical regime that had been installed in their city. Perrin's supporters, called 'Libertines' by the 'Calvinists' (who were drawn mainly from among the French or Italian refugees), triumphed in the elections of 1548. For seven years—until 1555—they had a majority in the Councils of Geneva. Their accession to power, as may be imagined, did not make any easier the relations between the Church and the civil authorities.

While Calvin's very strict views on ecclesiastical discipline evoked much hostility, his determination to defend the truth of the Gospel (or, at least, what he considered the truth) created just as many enemies. In 1543 he attacked the Savoyard humanist Sébastien Castellio, the principal of the College, whose refusal to accept the canonicity of the Song of Songs seemed to him to bring into question the authority of the Bible. In 1551 he had to reply to attacks by the former Carmelite Jérôme Bolsec, who, rejecting the doctrine of double predestination, accused Calvin of regarding God as the cause of sin. In 1553 he lodged a complaint against the Spanish physician Michael Servetus, who was condemned to death by the civil authorities for having denied the dogma of the Trinity in his *De Trinitatis erroribus*. (Capital punishment was the tragic fate reserved for heretics in the sixteenth century by the civil authorities, Protestant and Catholic alike.) After having thus extirpated in Geneva the 'false' doctrines which might otherwise have contaminated the Church, Calvin was in a position to take the offensive against his adversaries abroad. In 1553 he engaged in a polemic, as violent as it was fruitless, with Joachim Westphal, a Lutheran pastor in Hamburg who, alarmed by the advance of the 'Reformed' religion in northern lands, had found in the *Consensus Tigurinus* (the Agreement of Zürich), to which we shall return later, the occasion to merge Calvinists and Zwinglians and to denounce them together.

Calvin's efforts to transform Geneva into a city subject to the Gospel, and his polemics in defence of the true faith, have been judged severely by some historians, who regard them as expressions of a deplorable intolerance. In passing such a judgement on the battles fought by Calvin in the double sphere of discipline and doctrine there is a risk of forgetting that tolerance, as Joseph Lecler has shown, was in its infancy in the sixteenth century, and a risk also of failing to appreciate that, in this period, theologians threw themselves heart and soul into controversy. There should therefore be no misunderstanding: although Geneva seemed a hell to Papists and to some Lutherans, for thousands it was the new Jerusalem, where they wished to live and die. (The city was so welcoming to refugees that it received a thousand new citizens between 1540 and 1564.) If Calvin seemed to his adversaries a haughty doctrinaire or an unbearable tyrant, to his supporters he was the Doctor raised up by God to help them better to understand the Scriptures.

As well as being the Doctor of a Church, reformed according to the Word of God, Calvin was also an extraordinary worker for unity. He spared neither time nor trouble in trying to reconcile the churches which had issued from the Reformation. After many years of approaches to and discussions with Bullinger, Zwingli's successor, he succeeded in concluding in 1549 the *Consensus Tigurinus*. In this document, consisting of twenty-six articles, which rejected both Roman transubstantiation and Lutheran consubstantiation, Calvin maintained the reality of the spiritual presence of Christ, a concept which he cherished, even while making some necessary concessions to satisfy Zwingli's disciples. As a result, the destinies of the Calvinist Reform and the Zwinglian Reform gradually merged. The Zürich Church, however, was not alone in having discussions with Calvin, who also made contact with the Anglicans. He addressed between 1548 and 1553 a series of letters of advice to the young King Edward VI and to Protector Somerset. He proposed to them a full-scale plan for the reform of the Church, which—a fact worth recording—preserved episcopal government. Lastly, soon after his controversy with Westphal, in 1557 Calvin entered into discussion with Luther's successors. His intermediaries were Theodore Beza and Guillaume Farel, who went several times to Germany without, however, managing to reach agreement on the question of the Lord's Supper. These various approaches testify to Calvin's need to achieve concord. Given his concern to unite the families of Protestantism, he well deserves the title of *Calvinus oecumenicus* given him by Willem Nijenhuis.

Calvin not only sought to unite the Churches, but was also a remarkable organizer. The gifts that Farel had discerned in him and had considered necessary for the triumph of the Reform in Geneva were generously put at the disposal of those of his own countrymen who had been won for the Gospel. He had acquired considerable authority among them as a result of putting them on their guard against Nicodemism and Illuminism. Thus in 1549 when the Crown was sending French Protestants to their deaths, Haller, the Reformer of Berne, was able to write to Bullinger that the whole of France depended on Calvin. The Reformer of Geneva, enjoying such prestige, was well placed to organize his brethren. Did he go about this in the right way? We can ask this question since Professor Étienne Trocmé has shown that Calvin, in his anxiety not to alienate the king of France whom he hoped to persuade to undertake the reform of the Gallican Church, put a brake on the creation of Reformed churches in France: that is to say, he imposed over-rigorous conditions by insisting that every congregation should have a pastor and a consistory responsible for discipline. The question raised by Trocmé remains open. Whatever the answer, the fact is that from 1555 little groups for prayer and edification formed by the faithful touched by the Gospel began to be transformed into congregations given life by a consistory and each provided with a minister of the Word able to administer the sacraments. In endowing themselves with such a structure, the Reformed French felt that they now had churches that were set up (*dressées*), whereas before their churches had only been set down (*plantées*).

Calvin used various means to direct this organizing effort. His letters lavished encouragement and guidance on those who cried out for the Gospel. But it was above all through the medium of the preachers he sent from Geneva that he succeeded in organizing the French Reformed churches. The men he delegated to the communities which asked him for 'doctors' were, as Robert M. Kingdon has shown, mostly emigrés. They returned to their country at the risk of their lives and were wholly dedicated to Calvin's programme. Although they were not as numerous as has sometimes been claimed (from 1555 to 1562 their number did not exceed eighty-eight), they nevertheless exercised a decisive influence on the foundation of the French Reformed churches.

The *églises dressées*, led by pastors and provided with consistories, needed a structural link to ensure a modicum of cohesion. Such a link was found in government by synods. A meeting of pastors held at Poitiers in 1557 or 1558 to settle a question of discipline concluded that certain problems needed to be discussed by a body composed of representatives of all the churches. In May 1559 the first national synod of the Reformed churches of France was held in Paris, presided over by Pastor François de Morel. This assembly, summoned at the instigation of the Huguenot nobility in the hope of exercising pressure on King Henri II, failed to mobilize delegates from all the *églises dressées*, but nevertheless seventy-two churches were represented.

Calvin did not look favourably on the convening of the Synod of Paris. The moment, just after the signing of the Treaty of Cateau-Cambrésis in April 1559, which by making peace between Henri II and Philip II of Spain, enabled the king of France to devote all his energies to fighting heresy, did not seem propitious. But Calvin seemed to fear even more the difficulties which could arise from an assembly entrusted with the task of drawing up, under unfavourable conditions, a declaration that would be treated as a *credo*. When he realized that he could not oppose the intentions of his compatriots and co-religionists, he sent them the draft of a confession of faith. This text, consisting of thirty-five articles, was accepted after a Discipline had been agreed upon, though not without slight modifications by the representatives of the French Reformed churches. In particular, the first article, which affirmed very strongly that faith was based exclusively on biblical revelation, was replaced by five articles in which, before the Scriptures, the attributes of God and his revelation in the creation were set out. In its final form, the 1559 Confession of Faith, consisting of forty articles, was to be recognized, after some small changes had been made, by the seventh national Synod of the Reformed Churches of France in 1571 and called the *Confession of La Rochelle*, in memory of the town where this Synod had held its sessions.

Calvin's capacities as an organizer, which in France had contributed to the establishment of the Reformed churches, were strikingly displayed at Geneva, in June 1559, at the time of the Academy's inauguration. The city had been provided with an establishment for public education as soon as it adhered to the Reformation. A college had been founded by Farel in 1536. Two years later Calvin, aided by Mathurin Cordier, his old teacher at the Collège de la Marche, had drafted the statutes. Once he was freed from the opposition of the 'Libertines', Calvin began to think of associating it with an institute of more advanced learning. He was helped in his aim by a dispute which broke out between the authorities in Berne and the professors of the Lausanne Academy. When several of the latter, after their dismissal, fell back upon Geneva, Calvin was able to use them and to found in 1559 the Academy that he had projected. He entrusted it to Theodore Beza (1519–1605), who was to succeed him as the head of the Genevan Church, and together with him, Calvin gave theological teaching devoted essentially to the Scriptures. As a result of the wide range of its teachers, the Academy of Geneva, from which the present university is descended, enjoyed notable success. A few years after its creation it already had three hundred students, drawn from all over Europe. Among its pupils were Philippe Marnix de Sainte-Aldegonde, the future adviser of William the Silent, and Gaspard Olevianus, who in 1562 introduced Calvinism into the Palatinate and who, with Zacharias Ursinus, composed the Heidelberg Catechism.

After the foundation of the Academy, Calvin, profiting from the goodwill shown towards him by the civil authorities, was free in 1561 to settle down to the revision of the *Ecclesiastical Ordinances* which he had drawn up on his return to Geneva in 1541. Although he proved unable to impose all his ideas, he succeeded at least in emphasizing 'the power of supervision which the Church must have so as to marshal all Christians in obedience and true service to God, and to impede and correct scandals'. After twenty years of struggle, Calvin now saw his spiritual authority recognized. But the legitimate satisfaction this gave him soon gave way to serious worries, and, in the first place, concern for the future of the Reform in France. Some months after the failure of the Colloquy of Poissy, called by the Regent, Catherine de Médicis in September 1561 with the aim of reconciling Catholics and Protestants, there occurred on 1 March 1562 the massacre at

Vassy in Champagne, which triggered off the Wars of Religion. A second cause for concern was that Calvin, exhausted by his innumerable labours and by his hard battles, felt his health failing. From 1563 he took a turn for the worse, and from the beginning of 1564 he prepared himself for death, taking leave successively of his students, his parishioners, the representatives of the civil authorities, and finally of his colleagues in the pastorate.

When Calvin died on 27 May 1564 he was not yet fifty-five, but he left behind him a considerable achievement: a literary achievement whose wide scope is attested by the fifty-nine volumes of *Calvini opera quae supersunt omnia* and the manuscript sermons, of which five volumes have so far been published in the *Supplementa calviniana*; and that even more astonishing achievement, the transformation of Geneva. John Knox, the Scottish Reformer, who knew the city well having found refuge there, said that Geneva was 'the most perfect school of Christ that ever was on earth since the time of the Apostles'. Knox's praise was doubtless exaggerated. It would be closer to the truth to say with Émile G. Léonard that Calvin succeeded in fashioning in Geneva 'a new type of man, the Calvinist'.

Calvin's Thought

We cannot enter here into a detailed examination of everything that Calvin, a man of the second generation, derived from the Reformers and from the humanists who preceded him. It will be enough to mention that he owed much to Martin Luther, that he derived much of his ecclesiology from Martin Bucer, that he was on the best of terms with Philip Melanchthon, and that, even after his conversion, he did not break with the methods and objectives of a Budé or an Erasmus. He had been won over to the Reformation, but he remained a humanist.[3] Indebted as he was to the theologians and scholars who had blazed the trail for the Reformation, Calvin was equally familiar with certain medieval authors, such as St Anselm of Canterbury, St Bernard of Clairvaux (whom he was fond of citing), Peter Lombard, St Thomas Aquinas, and Duns Scotus, who, whatever has been said to the contrary, certainly influenced his conception of God. Beyond the doctors of the Middle Ages, moreover, he assiduously studied the Fathers of the Church. The two he preferred were St John Chrysostom, whom he appreciated as an interpreter of the Bible, and above all, St Augustine, with whom he felt a deep affinity. To sum up, while Calvin was nurtured on the Bible, his reading of it was enriched by his astonishing knowledge of the great authors of the Christian tradition.

The most convenient way to present Calvin's thought is to pick out the main themes of the *Institutes of the Christian Religion*. This method will be followed here. Although this means placing most emphasis on Calvin the dogmatist, it should not make us forget that this dogmatist was also an

[3] Wendel (1976), 96.

incomparable exegete and an extraordinary preacher. Calvin commented in his lectures and sermons on an impressive number of the books of the Old Testament and most of those of the New. His exegetic and homiletic writings occupy the greater part of his *Opera omnia*. It is therefore wrong to claim, as has sometimes been done, that Calvin was the man of a single book, or that 'Calvinism' can be reduced to the *Institutes* alone. Great as that theological *summa* is, it does not eclipse the products of the exegete and the preacher.

The first book of the last edition (1559–60) of the *Institutes of the Christian Religion* deals with our knowledge of God as the 'creator and sovereign ruler of the world'. Calvin begins by defining this knowledge, which does not consist in rational speculation about the nature of God, incomprehensible as it is to human creatures. The knowledge that interests Calvin is 'practical'. His aim, like Luther's, is to bring men to fear, revere, and praise God. But how is it possible to attain this knowledge? Calvin answers this question by first appealing to a revelation, often been styled 'natural', but which it would be wiser to call 'general', because it has been given to all men, heathens included. By virtue of this general revelation God manifests himself in man, in the universe, and in history. As far as man is concerned, the human being has not only received from God an awareness of divinity (*sensus divinitatis*) or a seed of religion (*semen religionis*), he also receives from him, according to the discourse of Saint Paul on the Areopagus (Acts 17:27–8), life, movement, and being. With regard to the universe and history, God manifests himself in the 'fabric of heaven and earth, so beautiful and exquisite', (v. 1) and in all that happens outside the ordinary course of nature (v. 7).

Although Calvin thus underlines the existence of a general revelation, he does not derive from it a 'natural theology'. The knowledge of God which men could have obtained through it has been stifled by their sinfulness. The general revelation does not therefore lead men to God, but it deprives them of all excuses before God. This being so, the question needs to be asked anew: how is it possible to attain knowledge of God? Calvin's answer is through biblical revelation, which in contrast to the general revelation has sometimes been styled the special revelation, because it is addressed only to Jews and Christians. Scripture alone provides the means of discerning the 'true God from all the troop of idols that the world has invented' (vi. 1). The Bible, divinely inspired in the books of the Old and the New Testament— which does not mean that Calvin subscribed to the doctrine of literal inspiration—does not derive its authority from the Church. It is the Holy Ghost that proves to the believer by an inner, secret testimony that God speaks in it or by it.

What does Scripture say in its teaching about God? That he is unique, of course, but also that in him there are three persons, the Father, the Son, and the Holy Ghost. In defending the dogma of the Trinity, which Caroli had unjustly accused him of questioning, Calvin is anxious to avoid any interpretation which might countenance the idea of some sort of tritheism. Though he maintains, as one must, the distinction between the persons, he underlines the unity of God. At the same time he affirms the divinity of the Son and of the Holy Ghost, a divinity that he had always insisted on after the Caroli affair, a divinity that explains the severity he showed towards Servetus, who died crying 'Jesus, son of the everlasting God, have pity on me', whereas to be orthodox he should have said, 'Jesus everlasting son of God . . .'.

After the dogma of the Trinity, the Bible teaches us that God is the creator of the world and of all things. In his doctrine of the creation, at least as explained in the *Institutes*, Calvin did not dwell for long on cosmogony. He affirms that the creation of the world, performed six thousand years earlier according to the Word and the spirit of God, had taken six days. After devoting to the angels, 'ministers of God', discussions (xiv. 3–12) whose length surprised François Wendel, and extensive treatment to the devils, who, with Satan, were fallen angels (xiv. 13–19), Calvin concerned himself entirely with man, 'the most noble and most excellent masterpiece, in whom the justice, wisdom, and goodness of God appears' (xv. 1). Man was created in the image of God, formed of a body and soul (even though certain passages in the *Institutes* speak of a body, soul, and spirit), endowed by the Creator with a free will which he lost as a result of the Fall. That is to say, man was clothed with a dignity which distinguished him from all species of animals and that he was endowed in 'his spirit and heart, or in his soul and faculties' with 'some shining spark' that although not destroyed and stamped out by the fault of Adam, has at least been greatly corrupted.

The doctrine of Providence, which was not accorded a chapter of its own in the *Institutes* of 1536, and in the edition of 1539–41 was linked to the doctrine of predestination, closes the first book of the 1559–60 edition, in which it is separated from the doctrine of election. But why should Providence be placed immediately after the creation? Because for Calvin Providence is nothing else but the continuance of the creation (*creatio continuata*). After having created the world, God did not abandon it to its own devices: he preserves it, he sustains it, he directs it, he governs it at every moment, and his will is manifested not only in very small events but also—which faith alone makes acceptable—in the cruellest calamities. In thus taking up again from Luther, Zwingli, and Bucer the notion of the Creator's continuous action in the heart of his creation, Calvin was not indifferent to the problem of evil: indeed, he concluded his thoughts on Providence by showing that if the actions of the wicked serve to execute divine judgements, God cannot, even in a single instance, be regarded as the author of evil.

The second book of the 1559–60 *Institutes* treats of the knowledge of God 'in as much as he has shown himself to be our redeemer in Jesus Christ'. Before examining Christology as such, Calvin tackled three great problems: the Fall and its consequences, the Law and its usages, and lastly the relations between the Old and the New Testament.

Calvin was in agreement with St Augustine on the fall of Adam. He considered that man, as he emerged from the hand of God, was good. If he nevertheless fell, this was because God had willed it. But this fall did not in any way exclude man's responsibility. Man was guilty and the root of his sin lay in infidelity joined to pride. Following this original disobedience, the children of Adam are contaminated; they inherit the corruption and the perversity of their father and their reason and will are weakened, but without being destroyed. On the other hand, free will, as has already been explained, is totally lost in Calvin's eyes. In answer to those who reproached him for nevertheless asserting human responsibility, Calvin again resorted to the distinction made by Luther in *De servo arbitrio* between necessity and constraint; 'Man, after being corrupted by his fall, sins willingly and not against his own volition, nor by constraint . . .; and nevertheless . . . his nature is so perverse that he cannot be roused, driven, or led except to evil'.

Although fallen man is incapable of anything good, God does not abandon him. He restores contact with him, or rather, with the posterity of Abraham, by revealing his Law to him. The gift of the Law to the Jewish people was an act of grace; in fact, the Law prefigured Christ and was intended to 'keep minds in suspense' until his coming (vii. 1). After this, the Law lapsed only in respect of its ceremonial and judicial regulations. Its moral regulations, such as those set out in the Decalogue, remain valid for Christians, beneficiaries of the New Covenant. The Law embraces three aspects for them (here Calvin followed Bucer and Melanchthon). In the first place, as Luther had often affirmed, the Law served an educational function. In 'demonstrating' the justice of God, it revealed to everyone his own injustice; as the 'mirror of sin' the Law is like 'our schoolmaster to bring us unto Christ' (*Gal.* 3:24). In the second place, the Law has a political function in the broadest sense of the term: it prevents the unregenerate, the wicked who yield only to constraint, from doing evil. In the third place, the Law has a normative function: it prompts the faithful, who already have God's commandments inscribed in their hearts, to submit even more completely to his will. For Calvin the most important of these three functions is the last, the normative; by insisting on it, he may lay himself open to the charge of encouraging legalism.

In attributing to the Law the role that we have seen, Calvin could be accused of putting the Old Testament on the same plane as the New. Therefore, after underlining their 'similarity' in that both celebrate the grace of God manifested in Christ and both have the same 'signs and sacraments' (x. 5), he insists on pointing out the differences between them. These differences, which concern not the substance but the method used by the Holy Ghost to address first the Jews and then the Christians, are five in number: the fact that the New Testament, in comparison with the Old, reveals invisible things more clearly, that it contains the truth instead of representing it through images; that it displays the Gospel instead of proclaiming the Law (though this third difference was immediately whittled down by Calvin); that it sets consciences free instead of enslaving them, and finally that it calls to all nations instead of addressing only a single people.

After showing that the two Testaments, whatever their differences, bear witness to Christ, Calvin was free to tackle Christology. Faithful to the teaching of the Council of Chalcedon in 451, he accepted the dogma of the two natures, since it was necessary that 'he who was to be our Mediator should be truly God and truly man' (I xii. 1). Truly man, with this difference that Jesus Christ was a stranger to sin. By his obedience on Calvary, he was able to substitute himself for Adam, pay our debt, and reconcile us to God in satisfying his justice. Truly God, he was able to discharge to the Father the debt of all mankind and allow it to triumph over death. In conceiving redemption in terms of atonement Calvin was certainly influenced by St Anselm.

In defending the dogma of the two natures, Calvin, though recognizing their union, insisted upon their distinction. He dreaded 'contaminating' the divinity of Christ with his humanity. He did not, however, reject the doctrine (*communicatio idiomatum*) that Christ's divinity causes his humanity, through their union in him, to participate in its properties, while his humanity participates in those of his divinity. But he makes sparing use of it. Thus, unlike Luther, he will not attribute to Christ's human nature the ubiquity belonging to his divine one. From the same concern to safeguard Christ's divinity, Calvin affirmed—in what the Lutheran theologians of the seventeenth century were to call the *extra calvinisticum*—that although the Son of God, by his incarnation, united his divine essence with our nature, he did not become a prisoner of our humanity.

In order to describe Christ's achievement Calvin employed the doctrine—going back beyond Bucer to certain Church Fathers—of the three offices or ministries (*triplex munus Christi*). Christ is a prophet: he was the herald and witness of God's grace and taught 'all the branches of perfect wisdom' (xv. 2). Christ is king: he has inaugurated a kingship which is neither terrestial nor carnal, but spiritual, which is exerted over believers by the action of the Holy Ghost, and over the wicked by force. Finally, Christ is a sacrificial priest: he has made us pleasing to God by his holiness, appeased the anger of the Father, and immolated himself for us.

The third book of the *Institutes* treats of 'the manner of participating in the grace of Jesus Christ, the benefits we derive from it, and the effects which ensue'. The order is a little surprising. Calvin, after defining faith, instead of discussing justification by faith, which comes first in the order of salvation in Protestant theology, proceeds to regeneration by faith, and then to penitence and the Christian life. It is only after this long digression that he tackles justification, before setting out the doctrine of predestination. Why did Calvin adopt this order in the *Institutes*? Not because he ascribed greater importance to regeneration than to justification, but probably because he intended to show the Roman theologians that the Reform, in rediscovering justification by faith, had not discarded regeneration and the Christian life.

To obtain salvation and to benefit from grace, Calvin considered that man must enter into communion with Christ, a spiritual communion established by faith alone. Faith is not due to man's initiative; the Holy Ghost, working within him, bestows it on him. Faith means trust in Christ, and this is its fiduciary aspect, but it also means 'a firm and assured knowledge of God's good will towards us' (ii. 7). When the believer is seized by faith, he becomes in some way inhabited by Christ, who takes possession of his whole being. This act of possession by his Lord forms the very nature of regeneration or sanctification. By his regeneration the believer is associated with the death of Christ (the old Adam is crucified) and, at the same time, with his resurrection (he participates in a new life). But man nevertheless continues still a sinner, although regenerated and progressively sanctified. For this reason, he must throughout his life remain penitent.

Calvin considered that justification by faith was 'the principal article of the Christian religion' (xi. 1). In what does it consist? It means that man, renouncing the righteousness of good works, seizes hold by faith of the righteousness of Jesus Christ, and being clothed with this, he appears before the face of God, not as a sinner, but as a righteous man' (xi. 2). This definition shows very well that for Calvin, as for Luther and Melanchthon, justification implies an idea of a righteousness which is foreign to us but attributed to us by imputation. Calvin was indebted to the Wittenberg Reformers for his teaching on justification, although he gave a new stress to it by his doctrine of double justification. He thus showed that as the believer is justified, reputed righteous by faith, so are his works similarly justified, reputed righteous by the faith which enwraps them in the purity of Christ.

Predestination does not, contrary to the claims of numerous theologians, constitute the central doctrine of Calvin's thought. Certainly it occupies no negligible place in the *Institutes*, being examined over four chapters (xxi–iv). But it is not the kernel around which the different aspects of Calvinist theology are organized. Thus put into its proper place, predestination is defined by Calvin as 'the eternal decree of God, by which he determined what he wished to make of every man. For he does not create all in like condition, but ordains eternal life for some and eternal damnation for others' (xxi. 5). Predestination, independent of all foreknowledge and founded on the divine will only, is therefore double. It implies a decree of election, the fruit of God's goodness, and a decree of reprobation, the fruit of his justice, which 'should terrify us' (*decretum horribile*, xxiii. 7). Calvin's rigour draws him apart from St Augustine, for whom only the elect are the object of a special decision rescuing them from the 'mass of the damned' (*massa perditionis*) made up of humanity after the Fall. As for the reprobate, they are, in the eyes of St Augustine, abandoned by God to the ruin that their sin has brought upon them.

The fourth book of the 1559–60 *Institutes* which treats of 'the outward means or aids whereby God calls us into the fellowship of Christ, his Son, and keeps us in it', centres in fact entirely upon ecclesiology. The Church, as a divine institution, appears in two aspects. In its invisible aspect, which was dear to the young Luther, it is the communion of saints, the assembly of the elect who are known to God alone. In its visible aspect, it is the community of professed Christians. The Church has two aspects but it is a single entity and has Jesus Christ as its head. Calvin, anxious to establish the criteria which would permit the discovery of this church here below, drew inspiration from Article VII of the Augsburg Confession in recognizing two 'marks', the plain preaching of the Word of God and the administration of the sacraments as instituted by Christ. To these two marks it is tempting to add a third, ecclesiastical discipline. But, contrary to Bucer, he did not consider that he ought to treat this as part of the essential notion of the Church.

The Church, organized according to the principles fixed in the *Ecclesiastical Ordinances* of 1541 with four offices, those of the minister, doctor, elder, and deacon, is endowed with 'spiritual power' (viii. 1). In other words, the Church has doctrinal power, whose nature is submission to the authority of the Scriptures, and a legislative power, whose function is to enact ecclesiastical laws, without however 'binding consciences' as canon law had done. The exercise of this 'spiritual power' should not bring the Church into competition with the magistrate. This has its proper domain and is not subject to the Church. The two powers, civil and religious, are complementary. Calvin, contrary to what has often been stated, was not the apostle of a theocratic regime: he never proclaimed the necessity of putting the magistrate under the tutelage of the Church.

As has already been pointed out, the Church, if it is to fulfil its mission faithfully, must preach the Word of God and administer the sacraments. What are the sacraments? Calvin devotes to them six of the twenty chapters of the fourth book of the *Institutes* (chs. xiv–xix). He considers them as being, side by side with the preaching of the Gospel, 'an aid . . . to support and confirm our faith'. He defines them—following St Augustine, for whom they were visible signs of invisible grace—as 'the outward signs whereby God seals in our consciences the promises of his good will towards us', or as 'testimonies of the grace of God towards us, confirmed by outward signs' (xiv. 1). He limits them to two: baptism and the Lord's Supper, because there is a warrant for them in the Bible, because they were instituted by our Lord, and because they 'present . . . Jesus Christ clearly' (xiv. 22). He thus excluded as false sacraments, confirmation, penitence, extreme unction, ordination, and marriage, since these are only 'ceremonies . . . invented in the minds of men' (xix. 1).

Calvin's doctrine of baptism, following Bucer, combined the Zwinglian and Lutheran conceptions. He borrowed from Zwingli the idea that baptism, like other sacraments, should 'serve as our confession before men' (xv. 1), which is to say that it should be a token for the Church of our commitment to the service of God. Calvin owes to Luther his interest in the strictly religious content of baptism. In what, as far as he is concerned, does this consist? It is a sign of the remission of our sins 'it shows us our mortification in Jesus Christ and . . . our new life in him' (xv. 5); and finally it certifies to us that 'we are so united' to the Lord as to be 'partakers in all his good things' (xv. 6). In opposition to the Anabaptists he had encountered in Strasburg, Calvin defends the legitimacy of infant baptism. He strives to prove that infant baptism is not an invention of men nor an innovation of the post-Apostolic period, but had been instituted by God. Although Calvin was obliged to concede to his adversaries that the rite has no foundation in the New Testament, inspired by Bucer he made it the equivalent for Christians of circumcision for the Jews. It was a sign of God's covenant with his people.

The Calvinist doctrine of the Lord's Supper is much more original than that of baptism. Calvin distinguishes three aspects in the spiritual truth figured, indeed 'exhibited' (that is, presented and offered to communicants) through the visible tokens of bread and wine. These three aspects concern the significance, the matter or substance, and the virtue or effect of the Eucharist. The significance lies in the promises that accompany the outward rite and are identified with the words of the ceremony. The matter or substance consists in the fact that through communion the believer receives the body of Christ. The virtue or effect resides in the blessings brought by Christ, redemption, righteousness, sanctification, and life eternal.

The Lord's Supper was not for Calvin 'a vain and empty symbol' (xvii. 10). Through it the believer is 'fed with the substance' of Christ (xvii. 1). By employing the term 'substance' Calvin created an ambiguity which helped to sustain his conflict with Westphal. It must therefore be observed that the term does not bear here the material sense which it does in scholastic philosophy, where substance is opposed to accidents. It simply expresses the reality of the blessings offered by Christ in the Eucharist. Unlike the Lutherans, for whom, by virtue of consubstantiation, the body and the blood of Christ are substantially (materially) present in, with, and under the elements of bread and wine, Calvin considered that the body of Christ had no local or spatial relationship with these material elements in the communion service. He therefore rejected the Lutheran doctrine of ubiquity according to which the resurrected Christ is corporeally present in the eucharistic elements. But he stated positively that Christ is present in the Eucharist, truly present through the intermediary of the Holy Ghost.

Such is, in its main lines, Calvin's thought as set out in the *Institutes*. It strove in every possible way to make a system of the biblical data and to organize them in a coherent whole. In this attempt Calvin does not give priority to any particular doctrine: he means to do justice to all aspects of Scripture. As a biblical theologian he drew heavily on the dogmatic tradition, and was often inspired by St Augustine, Luther, Melanchthon, and Bucer. But however numerous his borrowings from his predecessors may be, they in no way detract from his genius. In composing the *Institutes* Calvin undoubtedly surpassed Melanchthon in his *Loci theologici communes* and Zwingli in his *De vera et falsa religione*. It was Calvin who gave the Reformation its most monumental theological *summa*.

Further Reading

The literature on Calvin is immense. Apart from the indispensable bibliographies, the books and articles cited here are those referred to in the essay, together with some of the main works on Calvin's life and thought.

Sources

Ioannis Calvini opera quae supersunt omnia, ed. Wilhelm Baum, Eduard Cunitz, and Eduard Reuss (59 vols., Brunswick and Berlin, 1863–1900).
Ioannis Calvini opera selecta, ed. Peter Barth and Wilhelm Niesel (5 vols., Munich, 1926–52).
Supplementa Calviniana (Sermons inédits), ed. Erwin Mülhaupt (5 vols. to date, Neukirchen, 1936–81).

Bibliographies

Erichson, A., *Bibliographia Calviniana* (1st edn. 1900, 3rd edn. Nieuwkoop, 1965).
Niesel, W., *Calvin-Bibliographie (1901–1959)* (Munich, 1961).

Studies

Benoît, J.-D., *Calvin directeur d'âmes: Contribution à l'histoire de la piété réformée* (Strasburg, 1947).

Fatio, O., 'Présence de Calvin à l'époque de l'orthodoxie réformée', in *Calvinus Ecclesiae doctor* (Kampen, Netherlands, 1980), 171–207.

Fraenkel, P., *De l'Écriture à la dispute: Le cas de l'Académie de Genève sous Théodore de Bèze* (Lausanne, 1977).

Goyau, G., *Une ville-Église: Genève (1535–1907)* (2 vols., Paris, 1919).

Hall, B., 'Calvin against the Calvinists', in G. E. Duffield (ed.), *John Calvin* (Abingdon, 1966), 19–37.

Kingdon, R. M., *Geneva and the Coming of the Wars of Religion in France, 1555–1563* (Geneva, 1956).

Lecler, J., *Histoire de la tolérance au siècle de la Réforme* (2 vols., Paris, 1955).

Léonard, E. G., *Histoire générale du protestantisme* (2 vols. Paris, 1961); English tr., ed. H. H. Rowley, *A History of Protestantism* (2 vols., London, 1967).

Nijenhuis, W., *Calvinus oecumenicus. Calvijn en de eenheid der kerk in het licht van zijn briefwisseling* (The Hague, 1958).

Parker, T. H. L., *John Calvin: A Biography* (London, 1975).

Rott, J., 'Documents strasbourgeois concernant Calvin. Un manuscrit autographe: la harangue du recteur Nicolas Cop', in *Regards contemporains sur Jean Calvin* (Paris, 1965), 28–43.

Stauffer, R., *L'Humanité de Calvin* (Neuchâtel and Paris, 1964).

—— *Dieu, la création et la Providence dans la prédication de Calvin* (Berne, 1978).

Trocmé, E., 'Une révolution mal conduite', *Revue d'histoire et de philosophie religieuses* (1959), 160–8.

Wendel, F., *Calvin: Sources et évolution de sa pensée religieuse* (Paris, 1950); tr. P. Mairet, *Calvin: The Origins and Development of his Religious Thought* (London, 1969).

—— *Calvin et l'humanisme* (Paris, 1976).

Zweig, S., *Castellion contre Calvin ou conscience contre violence* (Paris, 1946).

II

Calvinism in Geneva in the time of Calvin and of Beza (1541–1605)

GILLIAN LEWIS

THE city of Geneva possessed a significance which was symbolic and mythical. Her friends saw her as the mirror and model of true piety,[1] a haven of refuge,[2] a roosting-place for fledglings,[3] a stronghold[4] to train and despatch abroad soldiers of the Gospel and ministers of the Word.[5] Counter-myths developed by disillusioned Protestants and by Catholics presented Geneva as a hell of hypocrisy, Satan's sanctuary, a source of heresy, atheism, and libertinage and a centre for the active dissemination of sedition.[6]

These various legends were cultivated (and in part believed and acted upon) by outsiders. But native Genevans too began to show new perceptions of their city. They could hardly fail to notice that since Geneva had gained independence of her bishop and of the Dukes of Savoy, and had adopted the Protestant faith, she had been swamped by foreign religious refugees who had not only taken over the running of the local church but were using Geneva as a base from which to evangelize their homelands. The local response was ambivalent; there was some active hostility to this intrusion. But a significant (and ultimately dominant) minority among the leading families decided to swim with this current rather than to fight against it.[7] Their voice is heard in those new chronicles which begin to depict the city

---

[1] William Wittingham, *The New Testament of our Lord Jesus Christ* (Geneva, 1557). Letter to the Reader, sig. iiv; Alain Dufour, 'Le mythe de Genève au temps de Calvin', *Revue suisse d'histoire*, 9 (1959), 489–518.

[2] Antoine Froment, *Actes et gestes merveilleux de la cité de Genève*, ed. G. Revillioud (Geneva, 1854), p. xviii; Dufour, *Mythe*, 501 n. 21.

[3] Theodore Beza, letter to Durnhoffer, May 1581; Charles Borgeaud, *Histoire de l'Université de Genève, vol. I. L'Académie de Calvin* (Geneva, 1900), 169.

[4] The Pastors of Zürich to Calvin, 4 April 1541 Calvin, *Opera*, xi, cols. 186–8; Dufour, *Mythe*, 500 n. 19.

[5] Theodore Beza, inaugural address as Rector of the Geneva Academy, 1559 Borgeaud, *Académie*, 169.

[6] Dufour, *Mythe*, 511 n. 43, 512–13 n. 47; *Registres de la Compagnie des Pasteurs de Genève* (hereafter *RCP*). iii. 101 n. 1.

[7] Amédée Roget, *Histoire du peuple de Genève depuis la Réforme jusqu'à l'Escalade* (7 vols., Geneva, 1870–87), E. W. Monter, *Histoire de Genève*, ed. Paul Guichonnet (Toulouse, 1974). Monter, *Calvin's Geneva* (New York, 1967) is still the best introduction to the subject.

as chosen by God to provide a refuge for the faithful and to act as a shield and bulwark against the enemies of truth.[8] Warlike metaphors may have come easily to those who saw the whole of human life as a cosmic battle between good and evil. They also came easily to more mundane observers of the military dangers which beset Geneva in cold fact. Literally, as well as figuratively, she was a city under threat.[9]

This propensity to see things in dramatic terms was exploited not by Calvin (who abhorred the idolatrous personification of the city and who refused in any way to regard Geneva or his own role there as special)[10] but by other pastors and professors who used such imagery to create a legend which should keep up the morale of the beleaguered saints all over Christendom, and by canny magistrates who used it as a means of raising money for the city's defence.[11] Paradoxically their greatest success in this enterprise came between 1583 and 1603, when the danger to the city was acute, but when the legend was ceasing to correspond with the facts. Large sums were donated not only by rulers making shrewd political calculations (like the Elector Palatine) but by individual well-wishers and scattered congregations.[12] To those sympathizers from all over Protestant Europe from Scotland to Transylvania, who subscribed to the cause Geneva was still an evocative symbol, a citadel of the faith which must not be allowed to fall.

In practice, however, her significance was by 1600 little more than symbolic. Her church settlement was still intact, it is true, the Word was preached and the sacraments administered according to scriptural precept; godliness and zeal were still recognized and respected and the tone of her public life was still sober and austere.[13] But her celebrated role as a leading centre for the propagation of the Gospel was virtually at an end. Her Academy was no longer, as once it had been, the principal nursery of the ministers of France.[14] Her pastors and professors were by 1600 making only a mediocre contribution to the teaching and writing of theology and to the dissemination of the latest learned commentaries upon the Scriptures. They were no longer making as much running as once they had in crucial

[8] Froment, *Actes;* Michel Roset, *Les Chroniques de Genève*, ed. H. Fazy (Geneva, 1894).

[9] Especially after 1567; the situation was at its worst during the war with Savoy in 1589–93 and during the blockade which preceded it. Lucien Cramer, *La Seigneurie de Genève et la Maison de Savoie de 1559 à 1593* (vols. i–iii, Geneva, 1912–50; vol. iv, Alain Dufour, *La Guerre de 1589–93*, (Geneva, 1958).

[10] Dufour, *Mythe*, 498–9, 508–9.

[11] Eugène Choisy, *L'État chrétien calviniste à Genève au temps de Théodore de Bèze* (Geneva, 1902), 426–9.

[12] Martin H. Körner, *Solidarités financières suisses au seizième siècle*, (Lausanne, 1980), 259–61; Bernard Vogler, *Monde germanique* (see Further Reading), 478–9.

[13] Roger Stauffenegger, 'La piété genevoise en 1677', *Bulletin de la Société d'Histoire et d'Archéologie de Genève* (hereafter *BHG*), 12 (1962) 161–9.

[14] French churches did continue to appeal to Geneva for pastors, but after the earliest years the Company was almost always unable to help, since it was desperately short of men to serve even in its own parishes.

confessional debates. At the Synod of Dort their representatives carried little weight.[15] The Genevan book-trade had diminished in scale and changed in character. In place of religious books, it had gone over to cheap reprints of basic classical texts for the educational market.[16] Geneva's effectiveness in the international religious politics of the early seventeenth century was negligible. What resonance her voice had carried in Calvin's day, when money and men had come out of Geneva in support of the reformed religion, had long since died away.[17]

In retrospect it is possible to see that the heyday of Calvinist Geneva had been brief, no more than about thirty years, from around 1557 to around 1587. Why was this so? Was there a collapse in the zeal and the corporate energies of the Genevan church? Was it simply that times had changed, leaving Geneva less scope for an international role? Or was there a worm at the heart of Calvinism itself? All three explanations contain an element of truth.

There is no doubt that Geneva between 1557 and 1564 did create an extraordinary impression upon foreign visitors.[18] It may be that they saw only what they wanted to see, or that they were moving in untypically pious circles. But their testimony is corroborated by other sources, not only the register of the Company of Pastors, which shows a certain cautious optimism in these years,[19] but also by the Registers of the Small Council and of the Council of Two Hundred, which take on a tone of biblical solemnity.[20]

Between 1545 and 1555 there had been bitter animosity against Calvin and the ministers. Dogs had been set upon them in the streets. There was dislike of the high-minded way in which traditional practices had been dubbed 'superstitious'; there was resentment against the Consistory, which was said to be motivated by private malice and political animus; there was hostility towards the immigrant French. All these sentiments were shared (and exploited) by a group of families, the Favre–Berthelier–Perrin clan,

[15] William McComish, 'The Epigoni, The Contribution of Genevan Academic Theologians to the Synod of Dort', (unpubl. thesis for the degree of Doctor of Theology, Protestant Faculty of Geneva, 1980).

[16] Paul Chaix, *Recherches sur l'imprimerie à Genève, 1550–1564. Étude bibliographique, économique et littéraire* (Geneva, 1954); Chaix–Dufour–Moeckli, *Livres* (see Further Reading).

[17] Throughout the years 1557–87 the city of Geneva had, through private financiers and public loans, contributed money for military and diplomatic support for the Reformed religion, especially in France. But the money and arms it provided 'for the cause of the King of Navarre and of the churches in France' in 1587 was the last it was able to make. Increasing difficulties, culminating in the war of 1589–93, made it impossible for Geneva to contribute again. See *Bibliothèque publique et universitaire de Genève*, MSS Tronchin 3, No. 41; Körner, *Solidarités*, 142.

[18] John Bale, *Acta romanorum pontificorum* (Basle, 1558), dedicatory letter. Théophile Dufour, 'Bâle, Zurich et Genève en 1558', *Mémoires et documents publiés par la Société d'Histoire et d'Archéologie de Genève* (hereafter *MDG*), 22 (1884), 378–80.

[19] *RCP* I–II.

[20] Archives de l'État du Genève, *Registres de Conseil de Genève, 1557–1564* (hereafter *AEG, RC*).

who declared themselves to be the true 'Enfants de Genève'. More far-sighted diplomats and politicians on the Small Council disagreed. In 1555 Perrin was exiled and his followers scattered or executed. His hopes of making a come-back were disappointed by the loss in 1557 of the support he had once enjoyed in Berne. After that the spearhead of any political opposition to Calvin dropped away, and there is little further sign of organized animosity against the French.[21]

The importance of the French contribution to the transformation of religious institutions and of public life in Geneva was considerable. It was Calvin's own presence in the city which had attracted there many of the more educated and committed incomers, such as the jurist Germain Colladon, the printers and booksellers Laurent de Normandie, Jean Crespin, and Robert Estienne, and the humanists Michel Cop, Jean Budé, and Theodore Beza. Perhaps not every French incomer was a genuine religious refugee. The irreverent view was expressed at the time (and not only by Catholic propagandists) that some exiles were crooks and villains fleeing from their wives, their creditors, or the law. Certainly some of the gentlemen in this talented, pushy émigré society fretted to return to France, and engaged in intrigues and plots embarrassing to their Genevan hosts.[22] But others were indubitably godly, establishing their businesses and their reputations in Geneva, making a living out of their religious scruples and competing for Calvin's approval. This, at any rate, is the malicious description of them given by the ex-Carmelite ex-reformed Protestant Bolsec, who had lived in Geneva but who had fallen out with Calvin over the doctrine of predestination.[23] Even if allowance is made for his disillusionment, it still seems to have been the case that there was a distinct *beau monde* among the exiles, of which Calvin, in his austere way, formed a part. There was also a crowd of poorer refugees, some of them with tradesmen's skills which gave them a chance of employment, but many of them virtually destitute and dependent upon the charity of their richer compatriots.[24] A high proportion of these refugees moved on into the countryside beyond Geneva, or drifted gradually back home.[25] The eager idealists who had

[21] Monter, *Calvin's Geneva*, 64–92.
[22] Robert M. Kingdon, *Coming* (see Further Reading).
[23] Jerome Bolsec, *Histoire de la Vie, Mœurs, Actes, Doctrine, Constance et Mort de Jean Calvin ... publié à Lyon en 1577*, ed. Louis-François Chastel (Lyon, 1975), 63–6.
[24] *AEG*, Arch. Hosp. Kg. 1, 2, bourse française, *Grand Livre des Assistés, 1560–1579, 1580–1591*, and Arch. Hosp. Kg. 12–24, *Comptes des Caissiers 1550–1599* reveal a very large number of poor persons helped.
[25] Albert Perrenoud, 'La Population de Genève du seizième au dix-neuvième siècle. Étude démographique, *MDG* 47 (1979), 41–4; Walter Bodmer, *Der Einfluß der Refugianteneinwanderung von 1550–1700 auf die schweizerische Wirtschaft*, (Zürich, 1957, Robert Mandrou, 'Français hors de France aux XVIᵉ et XVIIᵉ siècles, I. A Genève: le premier refuge protestant 1549–1560', *Annales ESC* 14 (1959) 662–6; id., 'Les protestants français réfugiés à Genève aprés la Saint-Barthélemy', *Revue suisse d'histoire* 16 (1966), 243–9; Paul F. Geisendorf, 'Métiers et conditions sociales du premier refuge à Genève (1549–1587)', *Mélanges d'histoire économique et sociale en hommage au professeur Antony Babel* (2 vols., Geneva, 1963), ii. 239–50.

taken up posts as pastors in the French-speaking districts around the city, and further afield in areas under the jurisdiction of Berne, also returned to France in large numbers, especially after 1559, when a spectacular quarrel broke out in the Pays de Vaud and Lausanne between the church and the civil authorities. They were among the eighty-eight or more men who went back to France as ministers, placed through the good offices of the Geneva Company of Pastors with some Huguenot congregation which had appealed for pastoral help.[26] Some French exiles, on the other hand, took up permanent residence in Geneva, their sons and daughters marrying other French exiles, or into local families. By 1600 such households were well assimilated—indeed they had taken over and developed the worlds of law, medicine, theology, and letters in the town.[27]

Important though this contribution was, it could not have existed without the support which the civil power in Geneva afforded to the religious settlement. In order to understand why it did invite Calvin in to the city, and thereafter give its full backing to the Ecclesiastical Ordinances he had helped to draft, it is necessary to remember that Geneva had in 1536 undergone what amounted to a revolution in her political, jurisdictional, ecclesiastical, and even cultural life.

Geneva was not a great cosmopolitan city like Strasburg or Basle. She had once been a prosperous international *entrepôt*, frequented by Italian and German merchants and bankers, but between 1470 and 1530 her long-distance trade had declined.[28] This decline produced complicated cross-currents of hostility and mistrust. Intrigues and faction-fights defaced Genevan public life for a generation until in 1536, amid scenes of clamour and violence, the commune declared itself independent of all episcopal and ducal jurisdiction, abolished the Mass, and expelled the canons, the monks, the friars and the nuns.

The enemies of Bishop and Duke found that they had done more than topple from power a clannish establishment from which they had been excluded. They had smashed a working edifice of jurisdictions which now had to be repaired or replaced. The ecclesiastical changes of the 1530s had been nearly all destructive. No-one was sure any more just what the few remaining 'reformed' clergy could and could not do. Who was to baptize, to marry, to bury and according to what rite? What courts were to judge in matrimonial cases and all the other old canon-law concerns? In cases of disagreement on doctrine or church discipline who was to arbitrate?

The city's rulers decided that a comprehensive set of ecclesiastical ordinances was needed. A controversial decision was taken: Jean Calvin, the

---

[26] Kingdon, *Coming*, 5–42.

[27] Perrenoud, 'Population', 44, warns, however, against over estimating their cultural effect even upon the ruling families. He points out that the ruling class continued to use the Savoyard dialect to assert its independence of the ducal court, which spoke French.

[28] Antony Babel, *Histoire économique de Genève depuis les origines jusqu'au début du XVIᵉ siècle* (2 vols., Geneva, 1963); Jean-François Bergier, *Genève et l'économie européenne de la Renaissance* (Paris 1963).

young lieutenant of Farel, earlier expelled from the city, was invited back to help with this task. It was not immediately apparent that this had been a momentous choice. With hindsight it is obvious that in Calvin they had secured no mere functionary but a religious visionary and an extraordinary man. There is great disparity between an outlook which sees no further than the need for a secure and orderly city and one which hopes to see the transformation of an entire community by the Holy Spirit operating through the Word. The existence of this disparity may not at first have been obvious to those councillors who called in Calvin, and to the more mundane of the Genevans it may never have been clear at all. For there was between Calvin and the Genevan authorities a good deal of common ground, about the functions of a clergy, about the suppression of religious dissent, and about the policing of public morals. The broad measure of this consensus deserves more emphasis than it is usually afforded in accounts of the Geneva of Calvin: any amount of ingenuity and zeal on the Reformer's part would, without it, have been fruitless. It turned out that the Ordinances, in their assumptions and in the details of their provisions, secured from ruling councils and general public not only widespread acquiescence, but genuine support.

There was, for example, agreement about the duties allocated to each category of the new-fangled ministers of the Word, deacons, doctors, elders, and pastors.

Deacons proved uncontroversial. It is doubtful, in any case, whether they can reasonably be regarded as a 'Calvinist' innovation, in principle or in fact. *Procureurs* to oversee the finances and *hospitaliers* to take charge of the day-to-day care of the sick and impotent poor had been established in 1535, when the city had amalgamated a crowd of ecclesiastical charities and private funds into the centrally funded *Hôpital-Général*, established in a recently emptied convent. All that the 1541 article did was to confer upon these officials the Scriptural cognomen 'Deacon', and the dignity of being regarded as a part of the fourfold ministry. From the outset, however, they were in no real sense ministers, but lay office-holders elected by the civil power.[29] Nor was there anything novel or unconventional in their duties to support the view that we have here an example of a new and specifically 'Calvinist' attitude towards the poor.[30]

'The Doctors' office is to instruct the faithful in sound doctrine so that the purity of the Gospel be not corrupted either by ignorance or by false

[29] Robert M. Kingdon, 'The Deacons of the Reformed Church in Calvin's Geneva', *Mélanges d'Histoire du XVIᵉ siècle offerts à Henri Meylan*, Bibliothèque Historique Vaudois 43 (Lausanne, 1970), 81–90.

[30] André Biéler, *la Pensée économique* (see Further Reading), Robert M. Kingdon, 'Social Welfare in Calvin's Geneva', *AHR* 76 (1971), 50–69; Micheline Tripet, 'L'Hôpital-Général au temps de l'Escalade', *L'Escalade de Genève, 1602* (Geneva, 1980); Roger Stauffenegger, 'Réforme, richesse et pauvreté' *Revue d'histoire de l'Église de France*, 52 (1966), 47–58.

opinions', the Ordinances declare.[31] The municipality was content to hand over responsibility for the teaching of the young, for catechizing, and for secular as well as religious instruction to the ministers to share between them as they thought best. It was willing (although not in practice always able) to foot the bill, paying the salaries of schoolmasters and professors as it paid those of pastors, insisting only on having two representatives on the panels which chose the teachers.

The task of the elders was to keep an eye on the Christian life of the community. In effect, this meant dealing most of the time with people in trouble and with troublesome people, especially those who 'dogmatized against received religion', showed 'public contempt for the company of the faithful', refused to attend church, or were known or believed to be living an immoral life. Elders had to be 'decent and respectable men, beyond reproach and of unblemished reputation, above all God-fearing and carrying spiritual weight.'[32] They were chosen from members of the city's ruling councils. They usually found themselves carrying the burden of the office for years on end. This must surely have contributed to the development of a consistent style and tone in the Genevan church, and to some extent in Genevan public life. As the Ordinances had intended, their co-operation with the pastors did produce some genuine dovetailing of the activities of the spiritual and the civil power.[33]

If elders at first had been unfamiliar figures, pastors, in many ways, were not. There was much similarity between what had been expected of the old clergy and what was expected of the new. Ministers did not celebrate Mass, but only they could officiate at the Lord's Supper. They did not give absolution, but they did concern themselves with penitence. They did not administer Extreme Unction, but they did give solace to the dying. They were still needed to baptize infants and to conduct weddings and funerals. Only the earnest catechizing zeal, the relentless didacticism,[34] and the preoccupation with heresy and error struck, in Geneva, a novel chord.

Pastors were not exempt from surveillance; as guardians of 'purity and concord' in doctrine they were supposed to maintain fraternal vigilance and correction among themselves. Every Friday a congregation of doctors, elders, and pastors met to read the Scriptures and to discuss matters of doctrine and discipline. These congregations were usually followed by a

[31] Emile Rivoire and Victor van Berchem, *Les Sources du droit du Canton de Genève* (Aarau, 1927–35), (hereafter *SDG*), ii,.no. 794, p. 381.

[32] *SDG* 383.

[33] Harro Höpfl, *Christian Polity* (see Further Reading), 190–7, emphasizes that for Calvin the roles of civil and ecclesiastical (or spiritual) powers were not different in aim but were intended to complement one another, to dovetail perfectly in a common enterprise of edification, instruction, and discipline for the greater glory of God.

[34] Höpfl, *Christian Polity*, 203–4 is surely right to draw attention to the frequency with which Calvin and his successors used metaphors of teaching, admonishing, and chastizing. The whole Christian polity was, in a sense, an 'educational enterprise'.

smaller meeting of pastors (and occasionally doctors) only. Attendance was obligatory, and excuses were not well received; even country pastors were expected to turn up at least once every month. In addition there were special meetings four times a year before the Lord's Supper. These occasions produced, *de facto*, a 'Company of Pastors', which soon acquired a formal standing, an institutional existence, and its own record or Register.[35]

What gave both the Company and the congregations their particular complexion in Geneva was Calvin's personal ascendancy therein. Whether he actively sought this or not, he could not avoid it. At the beginning he had no rival, in intellectual energy, in seriousness of purpose, or in unremitting zeal; and later he could have brooked no rival had one had the temerity to appear. He lived in Geneva for more than twenty years. Only rarely in that time did he travel outside the town, and seldom far afield. Mostly he stayed within a small area, a network of steep and intersecting streets not much larger than the single parish of Saint-Pierre.

Here he preached his innumerable sermons, administered the sacraments, catechized, and taught. Here he attended the weekly congregations and the meetings of the Consistory. Here he met the syndics and town councillors, at their request or his own, to offer his reaction to some public issue or event. In the house the city had provided for him he dictated letters to his secretaries, went through his foreign mail, added to his long list of Scriptural commentaries, revised and elaborated the Institutions, spent long and wakeful nights, or passed quiet evenings with his friends.

Demands for pastoral guidance and for rulings in matters of faith and morals were made upon him all the time, by his fellow-ministers, by the city's rulers, by French, Italian, and English religious exiles, by students and parishioners. In Beza's (admittedly partisan) view 'he was like a father to us all'.[36]

There was a high turnover of pastors in the early years.[37] Some died in office, but disagreement on the Eucharist and on predestination accounts for the disciplining and deposition of several of them. Once such disagreement (or some other matter, such as negligence or quarrelsomeness)

---

[35] *RCP* (7 vols., Geneva, 1962–84).

[36] Theodore Beza, *Commentaire de M. Jean Calvin, sur le livre de Josué. Avec une preface de Theodore de Bèze, contenant en brief l'histoire de la vie et mort d'iceluy* (Geneva, 1564). The text is also to be found in Calvin, *Opera*, xxi, col. 19–71. The same phrase occurs in *RCP* ii, 103. 'Feu M. Calvin, qui avoit esté comme père au milieu de la compaignie . . .'

[37] Henri Heyer, *L'Église de Genève* (Geneva, 1909) 193–250, 379–414. Of the 10 pastors appointed before 1544 only 3 (Calvin, Jacques Bernard, and Abel Poupin) were still in office in 1554; 5 had been deposed and 2 had died. Eight more pastors were appointed in 1544 and a further 4 in 1545; out of these only 4 (Nicholas des Gallars, Michel Cop, Raymond Chauvet, and Francois Bourgoing) were still in office in 1554; 4 had been deposed and 4 had died. In the late fifties the depositions stopped but there was still a high turnover through death in office. It was not until the early 1560s that the position stabilized. The longevity in office of the pastors of Beza's own generation (which could not have been predicted), must have helped to ensure continuity in the Genevan church.

had come to light, earnest discussion and remonstration with the offender continued, in private, in the weekly pastors' meeting, or even in the Consistory until he toed the line, resigned in dudgeon, or was summarily deposed.

'Fraternal correction' may well have turned out in practice to have been more like an inexorable interrogation dominated by the interventions of Calvin. Calvin's command of the Scriptures from memory was formidable. He had an armoury of references from the Fathers at his instant disposal. He must have outgunned with little effort most of the disputants he met in Geneva. It was partly to challenge his easy (and in their eyes undeserved) supremacy in this that Bolsec (a trained scholastic theologian) had spoken out in a public congregation, and that Servetus (an old adversary) had, when apprehended in Geneva, put up so spirited a fight.

It was possible for Calvin to purge the pastorate with impunity only because of an artificially favourable situation when it came to replacing the deposed men. Recruitment of adequately educated and zealous ministers from among the local population was difficult, indeed impossible.[38] What made all the difference was the influx of the refugees. Not a single pastor in the sixteenth century was a native Genevan; all were in origin French.[39] To the earlier tasks of rooting out popery and administering to the local faithful was added the bother of finding and training ministers to send back to France. It is paradoxical that one aspect of the special character of the Genevan church was the duel identity of the Company of Pastors: at once the local ministry and a missionary enterprise for France.

Heresy and false doctrine, evidence to Calvin of the activity of Satan, not to be tolerated because it was an outrage to God, carried for the magistrates connotations of sedition, not to be tolerated for the trouble it might cause. Both agreed that one doctrine only should be upheld within the area of a secular jurisdiction; neither would listen to the argument that religious diversity might be harmless, even desirable, within a single state. Calvin had opposed Castellio on the question of pastors (or others) refusing to submit to the discipline of their church. He had answered Bolsec on the theological issue of predestination and the allegation that it made God the

[38] The difficulty was not unique to Geneva. Vogler, *Monde germanique*, p. 468; Henri Meylan, 'Le recrutement et la formation des pasteurs dans les Églises réformées du xvie siècle', *Miscellanea Historiae Ecclesiasticae* iii (Louvain, 1970), 127–50.

[39] All that is, except Jean-Baptiste Rotan, who was Italian. The Italian church in Geneva remained separate, with its own ministers. Although the Italian community in the city included many religious refugees and men of bookish education, it stood a little aside from the mainstream of political and ecclesiastical life. Its principal contributions lay in its wealth and in trade and manufacture, especially in silk-weaving. Later in the century Italian merchants and industrialists provided much of the skilled employment in the city. By 1600 the Diodati and Turretini families were allowing some of their sons to forsake commerce for scholarship and the church. There is no recent comprehensive study of the Italian community in Geneva. But see Monter, *Calvin's Geneva*, 165–90.

author of evil.[40] He had fought against the teaching of Gentile and
Biandrata on the Trinity,[41] against the illuminism and multiple heresies of
Servetus,[42] and he had quarrelled with Bauduin over just what might be
sacrificed for the sake of concord among Christians.[43] The Genevan
magistrates, in general, may not entirely have appreciated the theological
niceties involved in these disputes but like the magistrates of other states at
the time, Protestant and Catholic alike, they believed that dangerous
teachings should not go unchallenged and above all that authority should
not be defied.

Public acquiescence in what proved to be, in Geneva, an austere and
inquisitive regime has puzzled observers in later centuries more than it
need. Like that of other cities, the commune of Geneva—long before the
Reformation—had regularly passed edicts against fraud in commerce,
against usury, against excessive luxury in dress, against sexual offences and
prostitution, and against drunkenness and disorderly behaviour in the
street. There was a spate of such legislation between 1536 and 1541, when
the newly sovereign republic was asserting its authority in every sphere.
The edicts passed in Calvin's day, indeed in the whole period from 1541 to
the early 1570s, were a continuation of this process, and formed part of a
wide programme of clarifying and tidying up some of the anomalies, gaps,
and obscurities in the city's rudimentary legal code.[44] The ordinances
concerning public morals reveal the lineaments of what was, in the eyes of
the magistrates, acceptable social behaviour. They were designed not so
much to transform the community so that it became more godly as to protect
traditional decencies and preserve the *status quo*.

The Consistory contributed to this end. Its meetings were solemn and
formal occasions designed to overawe offenders (who were, by definition,
those whom earnest private admonition and counsel had failed to move) and

[40] *RCP* i. 76–131.

[41] Delio Cantimori, 'Profilo di Giorgio Biandrata Saluzzese', *Bollettino storico-bibliografico subalpino*, 38 (1936), 352–402, id., *Eretici italiani del Cinquecento* (Florence, 1949), 202–16; B. Nicolini, 'Bernardino Ochino esule a Ginevra (1542–45) in Cantimori (ed.), *Ginevra e l'Italia*, ed. Cantimori, 135–47; T. R. Castiglione 'La Impietas Valentini Gentilis e il corruccio di Calvino', ibid. 149–75; V. Subilia, 'Libertà e dogma secondo Calvino e secondo i riformatori italiani', ibid. 191–213.

[42] *RCP* ii. 3–47.

[43] Mario Turchetti, 'Concordia o tolleranza? Storia politica e religione nel pensiero di François Bauduin (1520–1573) e i "Moyenneurs"' (Unpubl. doctoral thesis, Geneva, 1982).

[44] Ernst Pfisterer, *Calvin's Wirken in Genf. Neu geprüft und in Einzelbildern dargestellt* (Essen, 1940; 2nd edn., Neukirchen 1957), assumes from the outset that Calvin sought to 'master' Geneva and that most of the initiative in sumptuary legislation, the controlling of luxury, the regulation of sociability was his. The institutions and the edicts are all seen by Pfisterer in this light. However, the chronology of the legislation, as well as its content, seems to suggest that the initiative lay with the Genevan city councils. Marie-Lucile de Gallatin, 'Les ordonnances somptuaires à Genève au xviᵉ siècle', *MDG* 36 (1938), 191–277; Erich-Hans Kaden, *Le Jurisconsulte Germain Colladon, ami de Jean Calvin et de Théodore de Bèze*, Mémoires publiés par la Faculté de Droit de Genève, 41 (Geneva, 1974); Robert M. Kingdon, 'Control of Morals in Calvin's Geneva', in Lawrence R. Buck, and Jonathan W. Zophy (eds.), *The Social History of the Reformation* (Columbus, Ohio, 1972), 3–16.

to secure a public admission of guilt and a declaration of penitence. The Consistory dealt primarily with religious offenders who persisted in 'superstitious' devotional practices, or who entertained Anabaptist errors, or who were simply negligent in church attendance or contumacious towards the ministers. It dealt too with notorious drunkards, adulterers, and bullies, with guardians who had misappropriated the inheritance of their wards, with forced betrothals between grown men and girls under age, and with ill-treated and deserted wives. Not for nothing was it known (with approval or derision?) as 'le paradis des femmes'.[45] Much of its business was in reconciliation, in infra-judicial settlement of pastoral matters which had got out of hand.[46] It acted (in effect) as a tribunal of first resort, sifting out those cases which should properly be passed on to the civil courts. The Consistory itself was not a lawcourt, as the Ecclesiastical Ordinances were at pains to point out. It was expressly forbidden to impose any civil penalty such as a fine, imprisonment, banishment, or death.

The code of morals adopted in its decisions was, explicitly, a Scriptural one. That is not to say that Genevans were to be subjected to Judaic taboos; what had been appropriate for the Children of Israel under the old dispensation was only in part still relevant for Christians under the new. Much ingenuity went into finding for every moral and social problem solutions suggested by the Scriptures, or, at least, compatible with the Word. Calvinists in later times sometimes laid themselves open to the charge that their morality was narrow, obsessively legalistic, and based upon a literal reading of the Scriptures which made for decisions which were ludicrous and harsh. If they did so, they had moved a long way from the spirit, and from the actual working in the Genevan Consistory, of this 'Scriptural' moral code. For Calvin consistently in his biblical commentaries, in his sermons, and in the Consistorial rulings in which he participated, was concerned not with a narrow search for Mosaic formulae, but with trying to find charitable resolutions for difficult human troubles by following the tenor of the guidance offered by the Holy Spirit operating through the Word.

Ready acceptance of most of the Consistory's rulings by the community in general suggests that there was a high degree of overlap between the morality the pastors extracted from the Scriptures, and the everyday assumptions about decency and the proprieties and justice which prevailed. Even so, the preachers were engaged incessantly in teaching, explaining,

---

[45] Roger Stauffenegger, 'Le mariage à Genève vers 1600', *Mémoires de la Société de l'Histoire de Droit et des Institutions des anciens pays bourguignons, comtois et romands*, 27 (1966), 317-29; E. W. Monter, 'Crime and Punishment in Calvin's Geneva', *Archiv für Reformationsgeschichte* 69 (1973), 281-7; Bernard Lescaze, 'Crimes et criminels à Genève en 1572', *Pour une histoire qualitative. Études offertes à Sven Stelling-Michaud* (Geneva, 1975).

[46] Compare Alfred Soman, 'Le registre consistorial de Coutras, 1582-4', *BSHPF* 126 (1980), 193-239.

expounding, weaning away from ignorance and error, admonishing and correcting.[47] Geneva in the 1550s and 1560s, would, if practice could have matched precept, have been one of the most inexorably didactic environments that an entire people has ever known.

The Consistory was a part of this continuum of edification. It was a solemn public extension of the counselling (sought or not), the urging and the admonition, the 'bonnes remonstrances' to which it was intended that Genevans should be subjected, at school, within the household, at their place of work. Significantly it was less concerned with punishment than with example, and as much with bringing errant minds to reason, as peccant souls to God.[48]

Disputes arose, however, over denying impenitent offenders access to Communion, which the Consistory regarded as a religious penalty within its right to impose, but which the civil authorities claimed as a civil penalty, improperly wielded by a body with no more than admonitory power. Calvin would not yield on what was for him a point of principle. There was nothing, he argued, to warrant the intrusion of the civil power into an area entirely the province of the Ministers of the Word. The Lord's Supper must not be profaned by the participation of a known uprepentant sinner; the Consistory must not be party to such blasphemy; it could not allow itself to be overruled. After a succession of such cases in the 1540s councillors began to give tacit recognition to the Consistory's sensitivity on the matter, while the Consistory for its part resorted to actual excommunication less frequently than before. But the dispute lay unresolved in principle; both sides backed a little away.[49]

By 1560 membership of the pastorate had stabilized. Indeed the first batch of pastors who had stood by Calvin in the darkest days was already passing away. His stalwart lieutenant Abel Poupin died in 1556, the talented Nicolas Des Gallars left in 1561, Francois Bourgoing died in 1561, and Raymond Chauvet in 1564. The veteran reformer Pierre Viret served briefly in the Genevan church before moving on to Lyon, as did the humanist schoolmaster Claude Baduel, soon to establish a Reformed academy in Nîmes. Younger men, all to serve in Geneva for many years, were already in place. They included Theodore Beza, Jean Merlin, Jean Pinault, Louis Enoch, and Nicolas Colladon.

By 1560 there was not only a well-entrenched godly minority of French

---

[47] Not always with success. In 1579 the Ministers lamented that 'Most men are so misguided as to show more respect for the rod of the civil power than for the sceptre of God's Word.' *AEG Pièces historiques*, No. 2022: Choisy, *État*, 165. Respect for the pastors was not always shown. In 1565 a woman called Beza a 'dumb-bell', the ministers 'riff-raff', and sang a song about the Consistory parodying the popular ditty 'Ce sont de beaux mignons' Choisy, *État*, 440.

[48] Calvin invoked reason, commonsense and the examples of Roman history as well as Scriptural guidance. Höpfl, *Christian Polity*, 200.

[49] Eugène Choisy, *La théocratie à Genève au temps de Calvin* (Geneva, 1897), 165–9, 243.

origin in the city, there was already a generation of native Genevans who did not remember the days of the old religion, and upon whom some at least of the assiduous instruction in godliness may have rubbed off. The registers of the Councils and of the Consistory suggest that among the general public as well as in the higher reaches of society this was so. Quite ordinary citizens, surprisingly, show 'une sorte d'érudition dogmatique'[50] while magistrates quote the Scriptures back at the ministers, swapping text for text.[51] One may perhaps wonder how universal was this change in tone, and whether or not the piety was for many Genevans more than skin-deep. Even preternaturally zealous pastors and schoolmasters numbering no more than thirty or forty can hardly have succeeded in reaching (let alone in transforming) many individuals in a fluctuating population of some fifteen thousand souls.

The rural parishes presented difficulties of their own. A memorandum written for his successor by Charles Perrot when he was a country minister reveals graphically the sense of frustration felt by an earnest young pastor in trying to deal with a canny, evasive, and unregenerate peasant flock.[52] It was hard work in the urban parishes, too. The registers of the Company of Pastors are full of references to the 'heavy burden' borne by the ministers of the Word.[53] Nevertheless there is a sense of exhilaration rather than discouragement discernible in these registers in the years 1559-64. The work of the Lord is proceeding. House-to-house visiting by elders had been instituted in 1557,[54] the year which saw also the Small Council adopting the *grabeau*, a monthly occasion at which the councillors were 'to remonstrate with each other . . . with zeal and fraternal charity, without animosity or rancour, to render account of their faults and negligence, in order that the grace of God may prevail'. As early as 1568 an edict reduced its frequency from monthly to quarterly, so that instead of being a constant fraternal surveillance it became little more than a formality, part of the ceremony of moral cleansing which preceded each of the four great celebrations of the Lord's Supper which punctuated the Genevan church year.[55]

Regular attendance at weekday sermons and at Sunday services was expected, formally at least, of the entire population. Heads of households were expected to bring their apprentices and maidservants with them to

[50] A. Cramer, 'Notes extraites des Registres du Consistoire', *Institut d'Histoire de la Réformation*, Geneva, Cramer MS, p. 3.

[51] Choisy, *État*, 456.

[52] *AEG, État Civil, Genthod 1*; Louis Dufour, 'Les notes d'un pasteur de campagne', *Étrennes réligieuses*, 41 (1890), 144-65.

[53] *RCP*, i. 21, ii. 66; ii. 193: Co-operation is needed to sustain 'the great weight of the responsibility, in order that the burden of it may be easier for each to bear'.

[54] A party composed of one syndic, one minister, one representative of the Consistory and one *dizainier* or local constable was to make 'visitations all over the city to learn of the faith, life, and manners of each man and record the names to encourage and favour the virtuous and know and cast out the wicked'; *RCP* ii. 172.   [55] *SDG* iii, no. 1082, p. 233.

church, as well as their wives and children. It was easier for the Consistory to rebuke a defaulting paterfamilias than to catch every seasonal immigrant, beggar-child, or soldier of fortune who had crowded within the walls.

In the 1570s the Geneva pastors agreed that the golden days had passed. Complaints were frequent from the pulpit and in the meetings of the Company that luxury and debauchery were increasing, that the young were ceasing to show deference to the ministers and when chided claimed that the magistrates were on their side.[56] To the pastors it seemed as if the co-operation they had been receiving from the civil power in disciplining the faithful was ceasing to obtain. In the Small Council, too, it was noted that the times were out of joint.[57] Epidemics of plague had provoked a hysterical witch-hunt of alleged 'plague-spreaders', immigration had re-awakened xenophobia and caused rents and bread-prices to rise. It became clear that the equilibrium of the decade 1557–67 had been a fragile one.

Calvin himself had been aware of this. On his deathbed he confided to the pastors that he had often been tempted to seek some amendments to the hurriedly drafted Ecclesiastical Ordinances of 1541, but that he had drawn back. All innovation, he believed, was fraught with danger; the Genevans were unreliable. All that could be said for them was that the magistrates, so far, had upheld the Gospel and the Discipline with their authority. It would be safest to leave things well alone. He counselled them, therefore, to 'Change nothing!', an admonition which they were, under Beza's guidance, to obey.[58]

Beza's succession was not a foregone conclusion. Although he had been close to Calvin and had been deputizing for him in public for several years, he was by no means the most senior of the pastors. On the other hand he was an able committee-man and arbitrator, he had been rector of the Academy, and his name was well-known and inspired confidence all over the world of the Reform. He was aware that he fell short of Calvin in presence, magnetism, learning, and above all in moral authority, but he had other qualities—sanity, level-headedness, a willingness to take up cudgels when he had to, but an instinct also to avoid unnecessary hostility, and to calm down—or outmanoeuvre—angry contestants. Above all he had stamina, a resolute (if increasingly weary) devotedness to duty, and a historical vision of the progress of the Gospel which looked far afield and to the long term as well as paying close attention to what was happening at home. In conscious imitation of Calvin, whose posthumous reputation he cultivated, Beza

[56] AEG, RC 13–17 May 1575; Beza declared in 1575 that 'the Spirit of God is already departing from among us . . . the good families of the city are gradually falling into decay': Choisy, État, 118–27.

[57] In 1576 an anonymous pamphlet denounced 'les pratiques de Bernard, l'ambition de Roset, le silence de Bèze' and claimed that a small coterie was monopolizing power and office, and creating 'un principaulté opposée à l'estat publique': Choisy, État, 149.

[58] In 1576 the Ecclesiastical Ordinances were thoroughly investigated and revised, but the revisions were not substantial.

occupied the same house, and followed for many years a very similar daily routine. It was a deliberate and sustained strategy to perpetuate the tradition. Beza pursued this strategy without wavering throughout the rest of his long life. But he was not the man Calvin had been, and in any case times changed.

His relations with his fellow pastors over forty years were not invariably amicable. His consistent supporters were the more flexible and pragmatic—as well as the ambitious climbers—in their ranks. The strong personalities, the awkward customers, and the saintly introverts among them liked and respected him less. But some of these were difficult people for anyone to get on with. They tangled with their colleagues in the Company, and with the city councillors, as much as they did with Beza.[59] By and large the solidarity of the Company of Pastors survived a succession of squabbles, and it was partly thanks to Beza that it did. He found the parish-pump mutterings in the Company uncongenial, and tried on several occasions to relinquish the moderator's role to which he was re-elected annually despite his genuine reluctance; he succeeded in retiring from it in 1580. The pastors then instituted a system which went to the other extreme: instead of an annual (but long-standing) moderator, they appointed chairmen for the absurdly short tenure of one week.[60] These *sepmainiers* rotated with such rapidity, that, paradoxically, the city council did not mind at all. It simply went on consulting Beza, unofficially, and he remained their real liaison with the pastors for a few more years.

There was from the mid 1570s a hardening in the attitude of the *Seigneurie* towards the ministers. The Syndics and the Small Council saw to it that ministers were kept in their place. But Beza did not, as has sometimes been argued, sell out to the magistrates.[61] Rather he served usefully to facilitate co-operation. He was impatient of the tender consciences of pastors who would not heed the fraternal admonitions of their colleagues, but if the tender conscience was the collective one of the Company, then on this Beza was sound. Such behaviour laid him open to the charge that he was not sensitive, as Calvin was said to have been, to the promptings of religious scruple. The awkward ones were claimed as Calvin's true heirs. But to say

---

[59] *RCP*, passim. Jacques Courvoisier, 'Théodore de Bèze et l'Etat chrétien', *Histoire de Genève des origines à 1798, publiée par la Société d'Histoire et d'Archéologie de Genève* (Geneva, 1951), 257–81, summarizes the still standard arguments of Eugène Choisy on this and other matters. Choisy had made extensive use of the Registers of the Council, the Company of Pastors, and the Consistory. More recent work on these, and on the correspondence of individual pastors, notably Beza, has done little to weaken Choisy's conclusions.

[60] The Geneva pastors, including Beza, seem genuinely to have feared the insidious reappearance of a 'popish' ecclesiastical hierarchy, which they called 'tyranny'.

[61] 'They are mistaken who have argued and written even in our own day that if the civil power is Christian, then all Church matters should be remitted to it; reason goes against such a view': *RCP* iii. 46; Choisy, *État*, 63–7.

this conveniently ignored the fact that Calvin had overruled the consciences of others in creating fraternal unanimity in the Genevan Church.

In Calvin's last years and later the Company of Pastors was a sort of Sanhedrin in the city, a force to be reckoned with. The ministers spoke of themselves as watchdogs of the Lord. However, Geneva was not a theocracy. Even at the height of their prestige and self-confidence the ministers had by no means taken charge. They operated only in their own sphere. Admittedly, by claiming that their sphere comprehended not only matters of doctrine and church-discipline but all moral questions too, they had given themselves *carte blanche* to speak their mind on every public issue where morality could be said to be involved.[62] Of course, speaking one's mind was one thing: it was quite another to possess the political muscle to affect the outcome, let alone the constitutional authority to legislate and to see the law enforced. The ministers never had such authority; occasionally, however, they successfully brought their moral influence to bear.

Their nose was keen for crookery in high places. They were always on the watch for such things as selling off at a profit grain bought cheaply or donated for the use of the poor, malversation of public funds, and especially the withholding of prosecution, or bending of justice, to preserve the indemnity of offenders who happened to have powerful friends. Many of the cases which caused friction between the pastors and the council may seem to be about adultery, or gambling, or larceny: so they are, in one sense, but they are above all cases where the ministers are determined that there shall not be in Geneva one law for the rich and well-connected, and another for the poor.[63]

It was the same thing over usury. Neither Calvin nor his successors took the thoroughgoing and simplistic view that all loans at interest were immoral, or that there was some mystic line which could be drawn between a percentage interest which was respectable and one which was not. Instead the Company, and Beza, like the careful reflective students of Calvin's teaching that they were, drew very different distinctions, and took all kinds of particular circumstances into account. They distinguished, for example, between the kind of loans which were indispensable to small vine-growers or small traders to tide them over until the grape-harvest or the next fair, and the kind at the other end of the spectrum where large-scale investment in manufacturing or in commerce was facilitated by credit on a vaster scale. Sensibly, they had no objection to credit which facilitated enterprise, or helped an intermittent cash-flow. What bothered them far more were loans

---

[62] On the other hand, Beza maintained that it was 'tyrannical and entirely contrary to the Word of God' for ministers 'not only to meddle in everything but also to be superior to the civil power in all matters and in all respects': *RCP* iii. 148–9; Choisy, *État*, 104–6.

[63] Choisy, *État*, 10–11. *AEG, RC*, lix, fol. 108[r-v].

at compound interest, or entanglements where the borrower could, by definition, never extricate himself from the toils.[64]

It used once to be argued that the Company of Pastors was hostile towards banking and that it successfully killed a project for the establishment in the city of a public bank.[65] However, it has more recently been demonstrated that this belief was quite mistaken and rested upon an oversimplified view of Genevan public finance and of the attitude of the ministers towards the moral implications of its technicalities.[66] In 1565 the *Seigneurie*, hesitating about whether or not to raise the interest rate it charged to borrowers, consulted the Company and met with a response which was far from prudish: the ministers robustly recommended that interest-rates should be raised, because otherwise 'many people who live here and make their money out of money-lending would move away, which would be our loss'. The Council Register records in detail a long discussion which followed.[67] In the end it was the Council itself, not the ministers, who drew back. In 1568 the debate was reopened, and again the ministers showed economic grasp and flexibility as well as a concern for the protection of the weak. They did not oppose the establishment by the *Seigneurie* of a public bank. In the event the scheme was wound up with many debts outstanding.[68] But its failure was in no sense the result of disapprobation from the ministers. They understood clearly that the financial situation in which the city found itself in the 1570s and later was quite different from what had obtained in Calvin's day: there was far more money about, and far more ingenuity was going into lending, borrowing, and investing. Although Beza might regret the worldliness which went with all this, and lament that foreigners might suppose that 'in Geneva everyone is a banker' he knew that there was little he could do about it.[69]

Perhaps the best single source of information about the activities, the preoccupations, and the collective morale of the Company of Pastors is its Register. The character of this document changes quite markedly over the years. Much depended on the pastor whose duty it was to keep a record of the Company's deliberations. Some secretaries made almost daily entries

[64] Biéler, *Pensée economique*, 453-76. Paul E. Martin, 'Calvin et le prêt à l'intérêt à Genève', in *Mélanges Babel*, I. 251-63; Jean-François Bergier, 'Taux de l'intérêt et crédit à court terme à Genève dans la seconde moitié du xvie siècle' in *Studi in onore di Amintore Fanfani*, iv (Milan, 1962), 89-119.

[65] André E. Sayous, 'La banque à Genève pendant les xvie, xviie et xviiie siècles', *Revue économique internationale*, 26 (1934), 437-74.

[66] Bergier, 'Taux de l'intérêt', op. cit.

[67] *AEG, RC*, vol. 60, fols. 129-31; Bergier, Taux de l'intérêt', 107 n. 58.

[68] E. William Monter, 'Le change public à Genève, 1568-81', *Mélanges Babel*, I. 265-90, Körner, *Solidarités*, 136-7.

[69] It was easy enough to denounce extortionate usurers in general, more difficult to secure the prosecution of an individual. Beza in 1582 complained that 'il y est deux ans qu'il a esté parlé tousjours des usures pour tout cela on n'en a chastié que trois on quatre. Cela est notoire par tout que la ville est pleine de reneviers': Monter, *Histoire de Genève*, ed. Guichonnet, 156.

and wrote fully; others were altogether more negligent or careless. There was even a point of view (expressed by Nicolas Colladon, secretary from 1565 to 1571) that since the Company was not a committee of the civil power it was improper to expect it to keep the kind of record appropriate to a department of state.[70] Where the Register is deficient it is possible, up to a point, to reconstruct what the Company was doing by using the Registers of the Council and the massive dossiers of surviving letters sent and received by members of the Company. The picture which emerges suggests that there is indeed some truth in the view that the Company after Calvin's death was plagued by bitter internal quarrels, and that it did after the mid 1580s suffer some kind of failure in its collective morale.

The trouble seems to have started almost as soon as Calvin was dead. There was perhaps some jealousy of Beza, and certainly some mistrust of his friendly working relationship with members of the Small Council. Nicolas Colladon kept the Register of the Company in such a way that Beza is scarcely mentioned by name; his activities for six years or more are thus (in this source at least) completely effaced. His successor Jean Pinault, on the other hand, wrote an altogether more detailed record in which Beza appears as a central figure. There is no undertone of mutiny here. The internal affairs of the Company were less fraught between 1571 and 1578, if we are to believe Pinault, but a succession of acrimonious disputes occurred over the refusal of the ministers to undertake not to criticize civic policy decisions from the pulpit, and over the diplomatic embarrassment caused to the city by the publication there of the *Franco-Gallia* of François Hotman and the *Du Droit de Magistrats* of Beza himself. In 1575 the distinguished theologian and moralist Lambert Daneau remarked that he and the other ministers from France who had (in the aftermath of the St Bartholomew massacre) returned to Geneva after an absence of several years all agreed that they found the place sadly changed for the worse and that there was a 'grande difformité' between the days of Calvin and the present.[71]

No register of the Company survives for the years 1579–84, when the Italian pastor Jean-Baptiste Rotan was secretary. This may be because he, like Colladon, did not hold with the idea that an official municipal-style register should be kept; or it may be simply that the record he did keep is lost. A gap in the record for these particular years is regrettable, because the evidence of the town council registers suggests that these were precisely the years in which a turning-point was reached in the history of the Company in its relations with the civil power. Up to 1579 the pastors had made vigorous and frequent interventions in public affairs. After 1584 they did so less often and less effectively. It becomes clearer than ever that the weight they had

---

[70] Hippolyte Aubert, 'Nicholas Colladon et les Registres de la Compagnie des Pasteurs et Professeurs de Genève', *BHG* 2 (1898–1904), 138–63.

[71] Olivier Fatio, *Méthode et Théologie* (see Further Reading), 6 and n. 53.

once carried in public counsels had been a moral weight unsupported by any constitutional authority, and that in exercising this moral weight they needed a spokesman of the calibre of Beza if not of Calvin himself. It is no coincidence that the decline in the Company's influence in public affairs followed very quickly after Beza relinquished the moderatorship in 1580.

In the 1590s things went from bad to worse. The pastors were ageing; many of them had been subjected to a demanding and unremitting weekly round of preaching and pastoral work now for over thirty years without a break, some of them with the additional responsibilities of teaching philosophy or theology in the Academy, supervising the theses of theological students, preparing works of religious instruction or of church history for the press, or collaborating on the Geneva Bible. On Charles Perrot, in Geneva since 1564, on Simon Goulart, a pastor since 1566, on Theodore Beza himself, the strain was beginning to tell. In Perrot's case it led to neurotic symptoms like the perpetual wringing of his hands and a habit of referring to himself in the third person as 'The Sinner';[72] in the case of the more robust Goulart it led to irritability and gloom.[73] In letters to old friends he declared: 'Our Company is no longer a company' and 'The School has gone cold; manners have become strangely corrupted. Many human hopes which once we held are dead and buried. We can no longer teach our pupils to say, "I believe in God." '[74] Beza was by this time old and ill; in 1597 Catholic rumours were spread about his death.[75] He was alleged to have apostasized. He roused himself and angrily refuted the allegation.[76]

Part of the trouble with the Company of Pastors was the difficulty it had experienced in finding suitable and willing young recruits for the ministry. In 1592 Beza had lamented that the ministry was 'nowadays the vocation held in most contempt'.[77] No local Genevan family of any standing had let a son of theirs become a minister and the supply of keen and educated Frenchmen had dried up.[78] It is symptomatic, perhaps, that Isaac Casaubon, himself the son of a pastor and a prize pupil of the Geneva

[72] J. E. Cellerier, 'Charles Perrot, pasteur genevois au seizième siècle. Notice biographique', *MDG* 11 (1859), 25–6.

[73] Leonard Chester Jones, *Simon Goulart 1543–1628, Étude biographique et bibliographique* (Geneva, 1917), 75–173.

[74] *RCP*, 16 November 1599: Borgeaud, *Académie*, I. 262; letter to Scaliger, 1602: ibid. n. 2.

[75] Choisy, *État*, 316.

[76] Theodore Beza, *Beza redivivus: Hoc est Theodori Bezae ad Ioan. Gvil-Stuckium. Epistola, et Pastorum et Professorum Genevensium Responsio. Ad putidissimum impudentissimum commentum Monachorum. de Theodori Bezae obitu et eiusdem ac totius Ecclesiae Genevensis ad Papismum defectione* (Geneva, 1597).

[77] Jean-François Bergier, 'Salaires des pasteurs de Genève au XVIᵉ siècle', *Mélanges d'Histoire du XVIᵉ siècle offerts à Henri Meylan*, Bibliothèque historique vaudois, 43 (Lausanne, 1970), 174, n. 52: Vogler, *Monde germanique*, 468.

[78] Ex-pastors of Geneva who had moved away remained deaf to the Company's appeal to them to return. *RCP* vii. p. viii.

Academy, chose to teach there not as a pastor but as a secular professor of Greek.

The title-page and the preface of the Geneva Bible of 1588 speak of the 'pastors and professors of Geneva', a fraternal company working together to establish and present a reliable text of Holy Scripture. Their friends and enemies alike often referred to them under this collective head and this was something they themselves approved of. They took a pride in the Geneva label, but at the same time they were sensitive to charges that they wanted to dominate other churches and to dictate to them in matters of doctrine or discipline.[79]

The close working relationship between the leaders of the French churches and the Church of Geneva was co-operative without being in any way deferential. The national synod at Lyon in 1563 entreated 'our brethren of the church in Geneva to write instructing us of their view touching certain principal points in church-discipline, such as the election of officers of the Church and the sentence of excommunication, and to send copies of their reply to the church in Lyon, which has orders to distribute them throughout the provinces of this Kingdom, so that the Deputies can come to the next National Synod well briefed in these matters'.[80] On the other hand there was no suggestion that the view of Geneva would necessarily be adopted as binding by the churches of France. Nor did the pastors and professors of Geneva think that it should.

The high-handed and managing style of Genevan church-discipline suited the peculiar political conditions of Geneva reasonably well. But it had its sharp critics among the French. Notable among these were the distinguished jurist and self-taught theologian Charles Du Moulin, the devout and earnest layman Jean Morély, and the celebrated university philosopher Pierre de la Ramée (Ramus).[81] Du Moulin in his writings took away the only leg the Reformed church-discipline had to stand on in France by denying it (with detailed textual reference) the Scriptural validity it claimed. He was reluctant to see the Gallican Church jettison the traditional mode of ordination and cast aside institutions long established in practice and in canon law.[82]

The writings and activities of Jean Morély were even more troublesome to the handful of French pastors (not all of them Geneva-trained) who were working between 1559 and 1572 to construct a network of local colloquies and provincial synods crowned by a 'national' synod for the entire kingdom,

---

[79] Choisy, État, 426–7. 'Aucune Eglise ne pourra pretendre primauté, ni domination sur l'autre'. Aymon, Synodes, i. 307. This principle remained fundamental. On the other hand individual churches continued to write to the Company for advice and rulings especially in matters of discipline and morals; this was still the case in the late 1590s: RCP vi, p. ix; vii, p. viii and annexes 4, 5, 28, 44, 46, 62, 89, 105.

[80] Aymon i. 48.

[81] Robert H. Kingdon, Consolidation Movement, 1564–1572 (see Further Reading).

[82] Ibid. 143–5.

and who regarded it as an indispensable part of this system that the authority of the ministers in congregation, colloquy, and synod should be supreme. Morély voiced the resentment of godly laymen who did not like to be dictated to by ministers in whose election they had had little voice.[83] Such church-discipline was 'tyrannical', he said. He would like to see it replaced by a 'democratic' arrangement in which all the adult male members of a local church participated as a matter of course in its direction and particularly in the choice of ministers.[84]

Beza in Geneva and Chandieu in France believed that it was necessary to discredit congregationalist notions like Morély's, for if they were once accepted as practice in Reformed churches all hope of universal acquiescence in synodical discipline would be at an end. If the principle of pastors' having the dominant voice in the selection of other pastors were to be weakened, congregations might elect as ministers all sorts of unsuitable people, synods would become jangling scenes of discord, true religion would splinter into a thousand fragments, and error would spread like wildfire. It would be a triumph for Satan.

This school of thought did prevail, although narrowly, at the national synods of Paris (1565), La Rochelle (1571), and Nîmes (1572). It took all the persuasion and procedural manipulation of which Chandieu, Beza, Des Gallars, and Colladon were capable to bring this about. Beza, in particular, was held by contemporaries to have been responsible for this victory for the authoritarian line.

Fresh trouble broke out in 1572. Ramus rallied support for a modified version of Morély's congregationalist scheme. Predictably, this seemed alarming to Beza. He attended the national Synod at Nîmes and 'stopped the mouths of the trouble-makers' through his intervention in the debates.[85] It seems unlikely that this would have put paid to the matter. What did so was the massacre of St Bartholomew, in which Ramus was killed. In retrospect the synods of La Rochelle and of Nîmes turned out to have been the high point of Genevan influence upon the Huguenot movement. At every level, military, diplomatic, financial, even doctrinal, the Huguenots found themselves caught up in an international maelstrom and they sought help and advice wherever they could, in Heidelberg and London and Leiden and Amsterdam as much as in Geneva.

Some churches still wrote in seeking the advice of the pastors and professors, as the Register of the Company reveals as late as 1599.[86] The Dutch and the Scots especially seem to have kept some regard for what the Genevan pastors had to say. Individual Reformers who had been educated

[83] Ibid. 45–62, 146–8.
[84] Ibid. 50–5.
[85] Ibid. 105–11.
[86] See n. 79 above.

in Geneva sometimes kept in touch by letter with their old preceptors.[87] But increasingly they too were preoccupied by developments in their own locality. Geneva was not so much cold-shouldered as swept into irrelevance by the force of international politics and war. Times had changed.

In addition, there was the problem of reconciling the denunciation of error with the principle of Christian charity. There might be agreement about the central truths of religion as revealed in the Scriptures, but what happened when disagreement occurred? How could preachers and theologians pursue harmony and concord among Christians without being too accommodating and conceding points of principle? Genevan ministers made conscientious efforts to resolve such problems, in their correspond-ence and in their publications as well as in their sermons, their teaching and their pastoral work at home.

Calvin himself had set the pattern, responding indefatigably to all these claims of conscience. Beza in his turn tried to play simultaneously the role of parish priest, university professor, preacher, moderator of the Company, international stateman, biblical scholar, controversialist, promotor of historical awareness among the Reformed, and architect of inter-confessional reconciliation. Calvin had understood the need for a clear head in the defence of true religion against all illuminist errors, Papist, Arian, or Anabaptist, and against all the temptations of the flesh, the compromises of Nicodemites and *politiques*. Also to be eschewed was the self-indulgence of the 'Libertines', who refused to acknowledge the right of church authorities to demand complete doctrinal assent, and who could be seen as intellectual poseurs, or as sceptics, or as persons guilty of 'vain curiosity'. Without Calvin's intellectual and moral forcefulness, the doctrinal unanimity of the Geneva pastors and professors would not have been so secure. But a price was paid for this. Geneva then (and later, under Beza) suffered from a slow haemorrhage of talent. Some of the ablest and most independent minds attracted there were, after a time, repelled. Some men moved away.[88] Others (like Charles Perrot) stayed but suffered torments of inward conflict. Perrot adopted for himself the motto *Gemere et silere*, to lament but hold one's peace.[89]

Beza, on the other hand, fully understood how strait was the gate for Calvin and agreed with him that in the face of error one must not hold one's peace. His development into a hard-liner (at first sight surprising in the light of his dilettante literary youth, and the suave affability of manner which he displayed in conversation) had already taken place by 1559, before

---

[87] Herman de Vries, *Genève pépinière du calvinisme hollandais, II Correspondance des élèves de Théodore de Bèze après leur départ de Genève* (The Hague, 1924).

[88] Monter, *Calvin's Geneva*, 169 n. 18.

[89] Bibliothèque nationale, MS Dupuy 700, f. 166, letter from Perrot to Nicholas Pithou, sieur de Chamgobert, 18 March 1592; Société historique et archéologique de Genève, MS 42 (Cellerier), p. 9.

he began to deputize for the ailing Calvin. At this time he still lived and worked as a schoolmaster in Lausanne, where he taught Greek and humane letters, took in student lodgers, and composed a popular and successful play, *Abraham sacrifiant*, which was to have a long future before it in the limited dramatic repertoire permitted in Calvinist schools. At Calvin's suggestion he had taken over the task started by Clément Marot of translating the Psalms into metrical French. The *Psalter* which resulted was to be one of the best-sellers of the Genevan book-trade and to become familiar to generations of Calvinists.[90] As early as 1554 he produced a pamphlet attacking Castellio, for whose arguments in favour of toleration he was to display a fierce hostility all his life, a hostility which, it must be said, was almost universally shared in that day. In 1555 he brought out what was perhaps a rather ill-advised leaflet[91] in which the difficult doctrine of predestination was compressed into the sort of diagrammatic dichotomies then fashionable in textbooks of philosophy, medicine, and law. This was a rash course to take with a doctrine acknowledged by seasoned theologians and pastors (neither of which Beza was) to be a mystery best not popularized too readily, since a misunderstanding (or even an understanding) of it had been found to trouble many souls. The presentation of the doctrine in this tabular form had the effect of drawing to the reader's notice the fact that Beza was in any case advancing a particularly stark version of predestination in which election and damnation were seen as symmetrical processes. This was an idea he was later to develop further.[92] It proved unacceptable to many of those who in other respects were fair and square in the centre of the Reformed tradition. Bitter divisions were to develop among Calvinists over this issue.

Beza' readiness to take on new tasks was also apparent in an ambitious project which he undertook in 1555 at the request of the printer Robert Estienne. This was nothing less than a fresh rendering of the New Testament, based on the best available Greek and Latin texts and furnished with annotations. There were places in the text where his reading of the Greek (in the light of the general doctrinal sense he imputed to certain key passages) differed from that of Erasmus, and where his version came to supplant the Erasmian one, as he intended that it should. The annotations came to occupy a more and more important part of the work in the later

[90] Eugénie Droz, 'Antoine Vincent et la propagande protestante par le psautier', in each (ed.), *Aspects de la propagande religieuse* (Geneva, 1957), 276–93.

[91] *Summa totius Christianismi, sive descriptio et distributio causarum salutis electorum et exitii reprobatorum ex sacris literis collecta* (Geneva, 1555). A translation into French appeared in 1560, into English in 1556, 1575, 1576, 1581, and 1613, into Dutch in 1571 and 1611. The tables were reprinted in Beza's widely known *Tractationes Theologicae* in repeated editions between 1570 and 1582: Frédéric Gardy, *Bibliographie* (see Further Reading), 47–53, 144–7.

[92] John S. Bray, *Theodore Beza's Doctrine of Predestination* (Nieuwkoop, 1975), 69–85, which dissents from some of the conclusions of Johannes Dantine, 'Les Tabelles sur la doctriné de la prédestination par Théodore de Bèze', *Revue de Théologie et de philosophie*, 16 (1966), 365.

editions, after 1565, in particular serving as a vehicle for his views on predestination. It was because of his well-deserved reputation as a Hellenist that Beza (who like Calvin had no formal theological training in the old style of the traditional schools) became saddled with these heavy responsibilities, and found himself well known as a specialist in biblical exegesis, his annotations widely read. The irony of this situation was not lost on his Catholic critics during the next century and a half.[93] Indeed they made more of it than was perhaps fair. Richard Simon was to be especially caustic. Beza 'made the Evangelists sound like pastors of Geneva' he said, and to read him one would suppose that 'the pure Word of God was to be dredged up nowhere but from the bottom of that lake . . .'.[94]

By 1559 Beza had committed himself, in print, to the defence of Calvin against the Catholic Cochlaeus on relics,[95] and to Calvin's views on the Eucharist against those of the Lutheran Westphal.[96] He had written against the ex-Calvinist François Bauduin, whose views on the price worth paying for concord among Christians he (like Calvin) could not share.[97] It has even been argued that he had already committed himself in print to what was later to develop into a fully-fledged theory of the right to resist (in the name of the Gospel) a tyrannical and persecuting civil power.[98] In these years Beza plunged for the first time into the deep waters of technical theology.

The same stresses which are evident in Beza's career are evident in the collective deliberations of the Company of Pastors and in the letters the Company and individual pastors sent and received. These documents, like Beza's own correspondence, are full of references to war and to politics, to missionary efforts by Capuchins and Jesuits, and to endless disputes (especially over the Eucharist) between representatives of the Lutheran and the Reformed traditions. After the failure of the Colloquy at Montbéliard in 1586, where the efforts of Beza and others to secure some kind of fraternal accord with the Lutherans came to nothing, and after the outbreak of war between Geneva and Savoy in 1589, more and more of the material is taken up with external affairs and more and more of the news is bad news. The

[93] Jean-Blaise Fellay, 'Théodore de Bèze, Exégète. Texte, traduction et commentaire de l'Épître aux Romains dans les "Annotations in Novum Testamentum"' (unpublished thesis, Protestant Faculty of Theology, Geneva, 1978), p. 6.

[94] Richard Simon, *Histoire critique des commentateurs sur la Sainte Bible* (Rotterdam, 1693), 751, and *Histoire critique des Versions du Nouveau Testament* (Rotterdam, 1690), 293.

[95] *Brevis et Vtilis Zographia Ioannis Cochleae, Theodoro Beza Veselio authore* (Basle, 1549), written in the form of a letter to the Zürich naturalist Conrad Gesner; Gardy, *Bibliographie* 17–18.

[96] *De Coena Domini, plana et perspicua tractatio. In qua Ioachimi Westphali calumniae postremum editae refelluntur. Theodoro Beza Auctore* (Geneva, 1559): Gardy, *Bibliographie*, 59–60.

[97] *Ad Francisci Baldvini apostatae Ecobolii convicia. Theodori Bezae Vezelii responsio* (Geneva, 1563): Gardy, *Bibliographie*, 102.

[98] Robert M. Kingdon, 'The First Expression of Theodore Beza's Political Ideas', *Archiv für Reformationsgeschichte* 46 (1955), 88–99; id. 'Les idées politique de Bèze d'après son *Traitté de l'authorité du magistrat en la punition des hérétiques*' *BHR* 22 (1960), 566–9.

Edict of Nantes itself aroused mixed feelings. And all the time the church in Geneva was more than a passive recipient of all this information. Jointly and singly its members were contributing to the international struggle, through the two instruments of the Academy and of the printed word.

As early as 1541 the Ecclesiastical Ordinances had declared that it was desirable that schools should be established to provide an education in Christian piety and eloquence and to produce a supply of godly men for the ministry and for leading positions in public life.[99] It was not until 1559 that Calvin's detailed plans became a reality.[100] In the preparatory school pupils were to read morally acceptable classical texts, gaining thereby a general literary education and an introduction to rhetoric. This in turn was to lead to logic and dialectic. In the more advanced *schola publica*, students were to be given long hours of daily tuition in Latin, Green, and Hebrew for the purpose of the close textual study of the Old and New Testaments. The teaching of dogmatics was not a separate item. It was incorporated into the teaching of exegesis.[101]

It proved difficult to attract professors to Geneva and to persuade them to stay. Life there was difficult and dangerous, there were more attractive posts available elsewhere. Geneva was not alone among academies and universities at that time in appointing local men of unproved worth to its posts rather than outsiders. The proliferation of institutions of higher education, Catholic and Protestant alike, in the second half of the century had made this (and the more restricted local recruitment of students) an almost universal phenomenon. Only a handful of universities stood out above the rest as places which could attract an international clientele and which could compete successfully for the most prestigious and choosy professors. Among institutions of the Reformed faith Heidelberg was the leader in competitiveness with Leiden not far behind. Herborn became fashionable, Geneva much less so. Even so, it was possible for Beza to remark as late as 1585 that he had never seen the schools in Geneva so well frequented; he may have been whistling in the dark. The blockade set up by Charles Emmanuel, duke of Savoy, was affecting Geneva very seriously. Very few foreign students were getting through. Audiences for lectures dwindled, as the Register of the Company of Pastors records in April 1586. Even Casaubon had 'hardly any audience', and this in November 1585. The magistrates concluded that the schools must be closed down and the professors paid off. Beza argued eloquently but in vain against this extreme

[99] *SDG*, 382. Pattison, *Casaubon*, 10, warns against romanticism: 'An elementary school, and a seminary for ministers—this was what was wanted, and this is what Calvin supplied. A grand Academy of letters or science, such as historians find in his scheme, was as little in Calvin's thoughts as the steamboats which now ply on the lake Leman.'

[100] *L'Ordre du Collège de Geneve. Leges Academicae* (1559), *Corpus Reformatorum* xxxviiia, 65–90.

[101] Irena Backus, 'L'enseignement de la logique à l'Académie de Genève entre 1559 et 1565', *Revue de théologie et de philosophie* Cahier III (Lausanne, 1979), 153–63, Pierre Fraenkel (see Further Reading).

course.[102] However, the schools opened again in 1588 and the *Livre du recteur* shows that the numbers (in most years) kept up well even after 1600; certainly there were still Scots, and Poles, and Bohemians, and Dutchmen among them often paid for by scholarships provided by their local churches or even by the Estates of their province: many Frenchmen still came, and some of these went back to be pastors as in the great days.[103] But Geneva's drawing power for Swiss and Germans and Slavs and Hungarians (despite her old links) was now much less than that of Heidelberg. More surprising still, many French students went to Heidelberg rather than to Geneva.[104] In addition she had to compete with French reformed academies, notably Saumur and Sedan.[105]

As the years went by talent was more thinly spread: never again did Geneva have such a distinguished batch of student as she enjoyed in the Academy's early years: between 1559 and 1564 there studied in Geneva Jean and Philippe Marnix de Saint-Aldegonde (later tutor to Henri of Navarre), Olévian (later professor at Heidelberg and co-author of the Heidelberg Confession), Jacob Ulrich (later professor in Zurich), Jean de Serres (later reorganizer of the Nîmes academy and an advocate of concord among conflicting faiths), Jean-François Salvard (later prominent in the efforts to establish a 'harmony' of Reformed confessions), Lambert Daneau (author of a wide range of works of Reformed theology and morals), François Du Jon (later a leading international theologian and professor at Leiden) and Thomas Bodley (later founder of the Bodleian library in Oxford).[106] Many more could be named.[107] Personal acquaintanceships formed in Geneva in those years were to have a far-reaching effect in the international Reformed network in the second half of the sixteenth century. There was a second concentration of talented students between 1573 and 1581 when the massacre of St Bartholomew brought a new flood of refugees, among them the celebrated jurist François Hotman, whose public and private tuition in law attracted to Geneva a whole succession of ambitious youths from

[102] Pattison, *Casaubon* , 23 and n. 25; *RCP* v. 131; *AEG, RC* 5 August 1956; Bourgeaud, *Académie*, 192–3.
[103] See n. 102 above.
[104] Vogler, *Monde germanique*.
[105] Richard Stauffer, 'Le Calvinisme et les universités', *BSHPF* 126 (1980), 27–51; Henry Meylan, 'Collèges et Académies Protestants en France au XVIᵉ siècle', *Actes du 95ᵉ Congrès nationale des Sociétés Savantes, Reims 1970* (Paris, 1975), i. 301–8, Daniel Bourchenin, *Etude sur les Académies protestantes en France au XVIᵉ et au XVIIᵉ siècle* (Paris, 1882).
[106] Borgeaud, *Académie*, 145 remarks with justice that a review of all the students of the Geneva Academy in the sixteenth-century would be well worth doing since it would reveal much of the lineaments of a 'Calvinist' culture stretching into every country in Europe.
[107] *Livre du recteur de l'Académie de Genève* (1559–1578), ed. Sven Stelling-Michaud (6 vols, Geneva 1959–81). Lambert Daneau, in a letter written to the magistrates in Geneva in 1576, recalled that in 1560 he had attended the Academy 'avec joie de l'âme. non parce qu'elle était voisine de la France (il y en avait des autres en effet) mais parce que c'était la source la plus pure de cette doctrine céleste', Fatio, *Méthode*, 5 and n. 44.

Germany as well as from France and the Low Countries.[108] Even in the 1590s Geneva retained some attraction for students if not for professors: numbers revived and two young princes of the House of Anhalt, one zu Sayn-Wittgenstein, a Zastrisell, and Robert Devereux (later the Parliamentary general Essex) all came there to study.[109] There had grown up in Geneva a thriving printing industry, a tradition of publishing and a well-established trade in books.[110]

The printers had come to Geneva in the first place only on the heels of ideologically committed refugees like Laurent de Normandie and Jean Crespin who had capital and contacts in Paris, Lyon, Strasburg, Basle, and Frankfurt. These businessmen had to find in the 1550s an area where a market existed, or could be stimulated, but where they did not have to compete with centres already established in the game. They succeeded by specializing. Between 1551 and 1564, 160 separate titles of works by Calvin were printed in Geneva, forty by Pierre Viret, and a score of others by miscellaneous pastors like Jean Garnier (Reformed minister in Marburg, Cassel, and Metz), Nicolas Des Gallars, and Michel Cop. French translations or Latin reprints were made of works by Luther, Melanchthon, Bucer, Hyperius, Ochino, Vermigli, Oecolampadius, Bullinger, and Gwalther. Of the 35,000 volumes which Laurent de Normandie had in stock at his death no less than 10,000 were copies of works by Calvin, and a further 3,500 were copies of works by Viret. Of the 312 items in his stock, 258 were religious books, sixty of these in turn being editions of the Bible, the New Testament, or the Psalms, which had been produced in exceptionally large print-runs.[111]

After 1564 the character of the Geneva book-trade began to change, in response to changing markets. Dictionaries, lexicons, classical texts, and schoolbooks of all kinds became fashionable, especially with small printers who could not afford the risk of a speculative venture. But even Jean Crespin went over to educational publishing, his grandest project in this line being the Justinian completed between 1568 and 1571, his more profitable stand-by being pocket Homers and pocket Ciceros. His *Livre des Martyrs* continued to reappear, each new edition larger than the last.[112]

[108] Borgeaud, *Académie*, 140–4.
[109] Stelling-Michaud, *Livre du Recteur;* Borgeaud, *Academie*, 146–7.
[110] Hans Joachim Bremme, *Buchdrucker und Buchhändler zur Zeit der Glaubenskämpfe, Studien zur Genfer Druckgeschichte, 1565–1580*, Travaux d'Humanisme et Renaissance (THR), 104 (Geneva, 1969), 76–96; Chaix, *Recherches*; Chaix–Dufour–Moeckli, *Livres;* Jean-Daniel Candaux and Bernard Lescaze (eds.), *Cinq Siècles d'imprimerie genevoise. Actes du colloque international sur l'histoire de l'imprimerie et du livre à Genève, . . . 1978*, (2 vols., Geneva, 1980).
[111] Chaix, *Recherches*, 91–109; Heidi-Lucie Schlaepfer, 'Laurent de Normandie', in Droz (ed.), *Aspects*, 176–230.
[112] Jean-Paul Gilmont, *Jean Crespin, une éditeur réformé du XVIe siècle*, Travaux d'Humanisme et Renaissance, 186 (Geneva, 1981); Gabrielle Berthoud, *Notes sur 'Le Livre des Martyrs' de Jean Crespin* (Neuchâtel, 1930); Ferdinand Vander Haegen, Th.-J. I. Arnold, and R. Vanden Berghe, *Bibliographie des Martyrologies protestantes néerlandaises*, Bibliotheca Belgica (2 vols., The Hague, 1890).

French churches continued to appeal to Geneva for a supply of printed Bibles. Jean-Baptiste Rotan had organized a system of ordering, supply, and payment through agents. There were complaints in the 1590s that some of these agents were unreliable, and that Geneva Bibles were hard to get, and too expensive. The Company, taxed with this, replied that the price reflected the expense of publishing, and that churches would be well advised to emulate the example of Dieppe, and order (and pay for) their Bibles in advance.[113]

Beza produced steadily for the press for half a century. His most productive years were 1554–64 when (as we have seen) he cut his teeth as a controversialist, and 1568–89.[114] He wrote ceaselessly, on polygamy and divorce, on predestination, on excommunication and the presbytery, and the Song of Songs.[115] Many of his works touch directly or indirectly upon the eucharistic controversy which preoccupied Protestant theologians throughout this period. Again and again Beza was prompted to reply to some new Lutheran attack.[116] He returned to the matter repeatedly in his correspondence, and this issue above all lay behind his decision to publish some of his letters, and to seek wide circulation for his controversial pamphlets. He continued to elaborate his *Annotations to the New Testament*, he produced a set of *Questions and Responses* on doctrinal matters which went into many editions,[117] he published his version of what had transpired at the Colloquies of Poissy and of Montbéliard,[118] he added new items to his youthful collections of poems and epitaphs of famous reformers,[119] he brought out an illustrated set of pocket biographies,[120] and he committed himself to a provocative defence of resistance to governments in *Du Droit des Magistrats*.[121] Beza was the voice of Geneva as Calvin had been before him, and if 'Geneva' did become a legend and an idea it was largely as a result of the energies and the talents and the sense of mission and of duty of these two men.

It has often been maintained that Beza was responsible for making Calvinist theology more rigid and more dialectical than it had been in Calvin's own day, and that his penchant for Aristotelian terminology was one of the root causes of a 'new scholasticism' which is said to have overcome Reformed theological teaching in the late sixteenth and early seventeenth centuries. This has been argued with force by some modern

---

[113] *RCP* v. 142 and n. 11; vii. 24 and annex 23, 236–7.
[114] Gardy, *Bibliographie*, 44–126, 136–204.
[115] Ibid. 137, 47, 55, 185, 148, 191.
[116] Ibid. 59, 80, 126, 157, 165, 180, 185, 190, 211.
[117] Ibid. 148–57.
[118] Ibid. 85, 197.
[119] Ibid. 1–17, 157, 188.
[120] Ibid. 180.
[121] Ibid. 162–5.

theologians temperamentally hostile to the intellectualization of religious discourse, and who see Reformed theology at that time moving away from what they take to be the existential insights of the early Reformers towards a deadening rationalism, that 'poison of profane natural theology' which led in the end, they believe, to deism and a secular outlook which has nothing in it of religion at all.[122]

Whether or not that has been the outcome of the undoubted dialectical expression of Reformed theology does not concern us here. But that dialectical expression was not a late development. It goes right back to Melanchthon, Bucer, and Peter Martyr Vermigli, and there are signs of it in Calvin himself. 'Since scripture alone had settled few arguments', a recent scholar has pointed out 'it became necessary to show that the opposite doctrine contained logical flaws or philosophical absurdities or that it logically implied an ancient heretical teaching repudiated by the early church . . . This inevitably involved . . . scholastic discussion of scholastic questions.'[123]

In his *Life* of Calvin, Beza makes the recognition and repudiation of error a central theme of the Reformer's concerns, and fairly so.[126] In his own lifetime the demands made by polemic pushed this process further. Beza had an acute sense of the political implications of what he was doing.[122] His correspondence (as it survives) is not a collection of private or personal letters at all.[124] It is a vehicle for conveying to carefully chosen correspondents precisely where he stands on the controversial religious issues of the day, and for imparting political information to his fellow Reformers, especially to Bullinger, who sat like a spider at the heart of the whole web, and who relied upon Beza for news out of France. This political awareness is discernible also in the way in which Beza timed the publication or the republication of his works, and in the choice he made of individuals and bodies of people to whom to dedicate them. There are dedications, for example, to the Elector Palatine, to the Duke of Württemberg, to the French

[122] This perspective goes back to the work of Otto Ritschl, *Dogmengeschichte des Protestantismus*, iii (Göttingen, 1927), 293–9, Ernst Bizer, *Frühorthodoxie und Rationalismus*, Theologische Studien 71 (Zürich, 1963), and Walter Kickel, *Vernunft und Offenbarung bei Theodor Beza. Zum Problem des Verhältnisses von Theologie, Philosophie und Staat* (Neukirchen, 1967). It is reflected to some extent by John S. Bray, *Theodore Beza's Doctrine of Predestination* (Nieuwkoop, 1975), and in Brian G. Armstrong, *Calvinism and the Amyraut Heresy: Protestant Scholasticism and Humanism in Seventeenth-century France* (Madison, 1969). A rather different view is taken by Olivier Fatio, 'Theodore Beza', in M. Greschat (ed.), *Gestalten der Kirchengeschichte* (Stuttgart, 1981), 255–76, and by Jill Raitt, 'Theodore de Bèze', in ead. (ed.), *Shapers of Religious Traditions in Germany, Switzerland and Poland* (New Haven, 1981), 89–104.

[123] John Patrick Donnelly, *Calvinism and Scholasticism in Vermigli's Doctrine of Man and Grace*, Studies in Medieval and Renaissance Thought, (Leiden, 1976), 196.

[124] Beza, *vie et Mort de Calvin*. The status and intentions of this work are discussed by Daniel Ménager, 'Théodore de Bèze, biographe de Calvin', *BHR* 45 (1983) 231–55. Its numerous editions and translations are listed in Gardy, *Bibliographie*, 104–28.

church in Basle, to the faithful in Poland, Bohemia, Lithuania, and Russia, to the Elector of Saxony, to the Landgrave of Hesse, to the Estates of various provinces in the Low Countries, to the Queen of England, to the King of Scotland, and to the pastors, deacons, and elders of the churches of France.

It has sometimes been argued that on matters of church-government Beza was less flexible than Calvin. Certainly he did write with more reservation about episcopacy, and certainly he was forced in the course of controversy to make decisions and statements about ecclesiology upon which Calvin had (whether deliberately or not) remained silent.[125] But the final impression left by Beza's writings is one of generosity as well as severity. From his correspondence, his acquiescence in the Second Helvetic Confession, and his co-operation with Salvard over the *Harmony of Confessions* it is clear that he very much wanted to see the different Reformed traditions flourishing side by side, each maintaining its own credal formulation within the larger scope of commonly shared Reformed principles.[126] At the Colloquy of Montbéliard he tried in vain to explain to a belligerent Andreae, who represented the Lutherans there, that he himself was not a spokesman for all the different confessions of the Reform, and that it was not realistic to expect him to be able (even if he were willing) to promise on their behalf some kind of collective submission to the Lutheran Formula of Concord.[127]

It cannot be said that there had been, by the early seventeenth century, a collapse in the zeal and the effectiveness of the pastors and professors of Geneva. But Beza's formidable energies had flagged; he was now an old man. There was no one in Geneva who could take his place. Simon Goulart was a veteran of the fight, a seasoned pastor, widely respected in the French-speaking world, and well known as the author of works of religious edification and of history. Jacques Lect, native Genevan, jurist and diplomat, was known as a good friend of the international cause of Reformed religion. Antoine de La Faye, Beza's successor as professor of theology in the Academy, did his best to keep up the tradition, but compared with the leaders of Reformed theology, Zanchius, Pareus, Junius, Arminius, Gomarus, Daniel Chamier, he carried little weight.

The war against Savoy had brought hard times; but Geneva was still an independent state. The failure of the Escalade (an attempt by the ducal forces to seize the city by surprise) soon became a patriotic legend. Henri IV and his successor Louis XIII extended their protection over Geneva,

[125] Tadataka Maruyama (see Further Reading).

[126] Olivier Labarthe, 'Jean-François Salvard, ministre de l'évangile (1530–1585). Vie, œuvre et correspondance' *MDG* 48 (1979) 343–480.

[127] Jill Raitt, 'The French Reformed Theological Response', in L. W. Spitz and W. Lohff (eds.), *Discord, Dialogue and Concord. Studies in the Lutheran Reformation's Formula of Concord*, (Philadelphia, 1977).

but showed no sign of wanting to gobble her up. Some foreign students still came to the Academy. But times had changed. All over Europe the Reformed cause had ceased to make new gains; in many places it was on the retreat. At the same time some of the old doubts which had plagued reflective Protestants were still alive, and some of the old certainties had become more difficult to hold. Political conflict and intellectual questioning had volatilized them; if they were any longer held, it had to be as pure articles of faith.

In all this perplexity and danger the heirs of Calvin and of Beza may not have had much room for optimism, but they firmly believed that they had grounds for hope. They know where their duty lay. It lay, as Calvin and Beza believed, in the struggle against Satan, in uncompromising denunciation of error, in refusal to be tempted into prudent or charitable compromise with falsity, and in resolute preaching of the Word. In 1637 the pastors and professors of Geneva declared; 'It is not good that our students should be vain disputants, or that they should be learned in a theory without savour or strength. The true aim which we should set before ourselves . . . is to provide a holy nursery-garden of devout pastors, pure in their faith, strong in their zeal to teach, well conducted and sober, keeping guard with a clear conscience over the grand mystery of piety, and administering with justice the Word of Truth.'[129]

Such had been the aim of Theodore Beza in watching over the Academy and the Company for so many years. Such had been the aim of the constant and indefatigable Jean Calvin. There is nothing in all this which is uniquely 'Calvinist'. But in it can be heard the authentic voice of that wider tradition of Reformed Christianity in which the Calvinism of Geneva formed a central part.

[129] Aymon, *Synodes* ii. 611; Stauffer, *Universités*, 47–8.

Further Reading

Beza, T., *Correspondance de Théodore de Bèze*, ed. H. and F. Aubert, H. Meylan, A. Dufour, *et al.*, THR (11 vols. so far, Geneva, 1960–   ).

Biéler, A., *La Pensee économique et sociale de Calvin* (Geneva, 1961).

Bray, J. S., *Theodore Beza's Doctrine of Predestination* (Nieuwkoop, 1975).

Chaix, P., Dufour, A., and Moeckli, G., *Les Livres imprimés à Genève de 1550 à 1600*, THR, 86 (Geneva, 1966).

Fatio, O., *Méthode et Théologie, Lambert Daneau et les débuts de la Scholastique réformée*, THR, 147 (Geneva, 1976).

Fraenkel, P., 'De l'Écriture à la Dispute. Le Cas de l'Académie de Genève sous Théodore de Bèze', *Revue de Théologie et de philosophie*, cahier I (Lausanne, 1977), 1–42).

Gardy, F., *Bibliographie des œuvres théologiques, littéraires, historiques et juridiques de Théodore de Bèze*, THR 41 (Geneva, 1960).

Geisendorf, P-F., *Théodore de Bèze* (Geneva, 1949, repr. 1971).

Höpfl, H., *The Christian Polity of John Calvin* (Cambridge, 1982).

Kingdon, R. M., *Geneva and the Coming of the Wars of Religion in France, 1553–63* (Geneva, 1956).

—— *Geneva and the Consolidation of the French Protestant Movement, 1564–1572. A Contribution to the History of Congregationalism, Presbyterianism and Calvinist Resistance Theory*, THR 92 (Geneva, 1967).

Maruyama, T., *The Ecclesiology of Theodore Beza. The Reform of the True Church*, THR 166 (Geneva, 1978).

Ménager, D., 'Théodore de Bèze, biographe de Calvin', *BHR* 45 (183) 231–53.

Monter, E. W., *Calvin's Geneva* (New York, 1967).

Potter, G. R., and Greengrass, M., *John Calvin*, Documents of Modern History (London, 1983).

Raitt, J., *The Eucharistic Theology of Theodore Beza: Development of the Reformed Doctrine* (Chambersburg, Pa., 1972).

—— 'Théodore de Bèze', in ead. (ed.), *Shapers of Religious Traditions, Poland, Switzerland and Germany* (New Haven, Conn., 1981).

Registres de la Compagnie des Pasteurs de Genève ed. J.-F. Bergier, A. Dufour, *et al.* (7 vols. so far, covering 1546–99, Geneva, 1962–   ); English tr. of vols. i and ii (1546–64) by P. E. Hughes (Grand Rapids, 1966).

Stauffenegger, R., *Piété et société à Genève*, Mémoires et Documents publiés par la Société d'Histoire et d'Archéologie de Genève (forthcoming).

Stauffer, R., 'Le Calvinisme et les universités', *BSHPF* 126 (1980), 27–51.

Vivanti, C., *Lotta politica e pace religiosa in Francia fra Cinque e Seicento* (Turin, 1963).

Vogler, B., *Le Monde germanique et hélvetique à l'epoque des Réformes, 1517–1618* (2 vols., Paris, 1981).

III

Calvinism in France, 1555–1629

MENNA PRESTWICH

THE history of French Calvinism possesses all the attractions often attributed to minority movements and lost causes. The years between 1555 and 1629 have an epic quality with their record of massacres and battles and their heroes ranging from Gaspard de Coligny and François de la Noue to Henri IV and Henri de Rohan. In 1555 the Calvinist church in Paris was founded, giving an internal focal point distinct from the international Calvinist capital at Geneva. In 1598, after nearly a half-century of civil war, the Huguenots gained by the Edict of Nantes the privileged political status of 'a state within a state'. In 1629, after the collapse of the citadel of La Rochelle and the crumbling of the duc de Rohan's resistance in the Midi, the Peace of Alès deprived the Huguenots of their political privileges and made them a vulnerable religious minority. Yet to bring the Peace of Alès into immediate perspective raises the question of the character, strength, and aims of the Calvinist movement in the sixteenth century. Professor P. Chaunu has offered the challenging opinion that 'it should be recalled that until the fall of La Rochelle (29 October 1628) the Catholic future of France was neither solidly nor irreversibly assured'.[1] In contrast, Professor Léonard, the outstanding authority on French Protestantism, considered that when Rohan raised the standard of revolt in the South in 1621 he saved the honour of French Calvinism, but fought 'the last battle of a lost cause'.[2]

An examination of the 'lost cause' shows French Calvinist ambitions in the mid-sixteenth century extending both to the conversion of society and to political power in the state. The years from around 1555 to 1562 saw an explosion of Calvinist conversions. The foundation of the Paris church set the tone for a mood of defiance, almost of triumph, and the will to resist replaced the cult of martyrdom.[3] In May 1558 Jean Macar, a minister of the Paris church, wrote to Calvin that 'the fire is lit in all parts of the kingdom and all the water in the sea will not suffice to extinguish it,'[4] shortly afterwards, Calvinist demonstrators occupied the Pré-aux-Clercs on the left

---

[1] P. Chaunu (see Further Reading), 291.
[2] E. G. Léonard, 'Le protestantisme français' (see Further Reading), 166.
[3] D. Richet (see Further Reading), 768–9.
[4] L. Romier, *Les Origines politiques des guerres de Religion* (Paris, 1914), ii. 250.

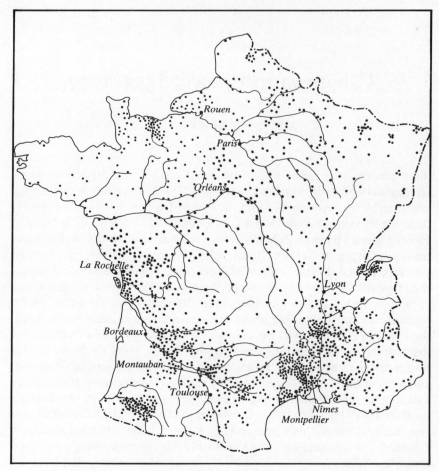

Map 1. Calvinist Churches in Sixteenth-Century France
After S. Mours, *Le Protestantisme en France au XVIe siècle* (Paris, 1959)

bank of the Seine, much frequented by Parisians for evening strolling, and for six nights three to four thousand of the faithful paraded and sang psalms.

This Calvinist activity coincided with a royal policy of harsh repression, culminating, after the peace with Spain at Cateau-Cambrésis in April 1559, in the Edict of Écouen of 2 June which outlawed Protestantism. The edict linked the making of peace with the renewed drive against heresy and was a response to the challenge of the first Calvinist national synod held in late May. This was the crucial moment for French Calvinism, which ceased to be a congeries of separate churches and became the Reformed Church of France. The Confession of Faith defined doctrine and the Discipline laid down the pyramidal structure of consistories, colloquies, and synods.

Three years later Coligny, of the house of Montmorenci and Admiral of France, who shared with Louis, prince of Condé, the political leadership of the Huguenot party, gave the figure of 2,150 Calvinist churches in France. This was an exaggeration and 1,750 would be more accurate, while modern estimates put the number of Calvinists in 1560 at around two million, 10 per cent of the population of France.[5] But it would be wrong to assess the strength of Calvinism by numbers; its social and regional composition is more important. The marked defection of court nobles to Calvinism in the late 1550s was of decisive importance, for they carried their clients in the provinces with them, so that 50 per cent of the nobility is said to have been Calvinist in 1559.[6] Further, Calvinism from the start had a regional base in the Midi, where a strong concentration of Calvinist churches reinforced existent provincial loyalties. The Wars of Religion, as a result of defeats in the north and tenacious resistance in Gascony and Languedoc, led to the organization of what has been called the United Provinces of the Midi.[7] When the Huguenots acknowledged defeat at Alès in 1629, the Cévennes continued to be a bastion of Calvinism and saw the last stand of resistance with the Camisard revolt of 1703.

To understand these events the nature and impact of Calvinism needs to be examined, and various questions arise. Why was Calvinism welcomed in some sections of society and not in others? How is its geographical dispersion to be explained? Why was Calvinism a religion of artisans rather than of peasants? How were Calvinist ideas disseminated, and what is the relative importance of anti-clericalism, economic factors, and intellectual appeal in accounting for their impact? Could Calvinism have been assimilated into French society or was it an alien growth, rejected because it challenged traditional values and ways? Did the behavioural patterns of Calvinism arouse antipathies which counted for more than did disputes over dogma? The consistory was the most original of Calvinist institutions and the reproductive cell essential to the spreading of the Reformed faith. But how did it function? Was the consistory democratic in its structure or was it an oligarchy in which the Calvinist discipline of manners and morals acted as a social control? If the latter, why did Calvinism acquire the reputation of being socially and politically subversive? And what part did iconoclasm play?

The questions can be the more easily answered if they are put into a historical context. The Calvinist ferment of 1555 to 1562 needs to be linked to the Erasmian and Lutheran influences of the earlier period. Up to the

[5] J. Garrisson-Estèbe, *Midi* (see Further Reading), 62–6; J. Estèbe, *Protestants en France* (see Further Reading), 55.

[6] Chaunu, 291 (where the date 1589 is a misprint for 1559, information from author); *Protestants en France*, 59–60.

[7] J. Delumeau, (see Further Reading), 181.

1550s French Protestantism was a religion of small groups devoted to prayer and mutual edification. Lutheran ideas seeped through the porous plaster of traditional Catholic beliefs, and Beza wrote complacently to Bullinger in 1554 that there was hardly any part of France which was not showing some fruits of the Gospel, while the flames from the burnings of Protestants were rising daily in a number of famous towns. The *Pays d'Aude*, the *Pays basque*, and Brittany were unaffected, but Picardy, Dauphiné, Provence, Languedoc, and Normandy, christened 'little Germany', were receptive to Reformation ideas.[8]

The importance of printing for the diffusion of Protestantism was emphasized by Henri Hauser, who wrote that 'La Réformation du XVIᵉ siècle est une hérésie du Livre—du Livre sacré et des livres qui le répètent et le commentent.'[9] Paris and Lyon were the main printing centres, and, despite censorship, the texts of Luther, Bucer, and Calvin rolled off the presses. Robert Estienne, later to emigrate to Geneva, gave lustre to Lyon as a publishing centre, while the Protestant towns of Strasburg, Basle, Neuchâtel, and Geneva helped to meet the French demand. Alençon was another printing-centre, which saw the publication in 1523 of the French translation of the New Testament by Lefèvre d'Étaples, with a preface stressing justification by faith.[10] It was at this time that the inhabitants of Châteaudun in the Beauce had the Bible read to them in French in church instead of Books of Hours.[11] The Alençon presses tapped a popular market early with cheap tracts, such as *Quatre Instructions pour les Simples et les Rudes*, but Lyon became the main centre for propaganda with its large output of tracts, anthologies, and pamphlets, printed in octavo, the equivalent of paper-backs. There were besides the almanacs and alphabet-books, which combined teaching how to read with instruction in the new doctrines.[12]

The tempestuous radical, Guillaume Farel, made Neuchâtel a propaganda centre from which were launched the violent anti-clerical pamphlets of his friend, Antoine Marcourt, whose *Placards* of 1534, denouncing the mass, were pasted up in Paris and Amboise to the fury of the king. In Calvin's time Geneva came to possess thirty-four printing houses. Calvin was an erudite humanist, but he knew the importance of popular appeal. Commentaries, homilies, and sermons poured out, and his two catechisms of 1542, one for adults and the other for children, which were written in dialogue form, had great success.

---

[8] P. Imbart de La Tour, *Origines* (see Further Reading), iv. 446; iii. 382.

[9] H. Hauser, *Naissance* (see Further Reading), 59.

[10] *Origines*, iii. 380–1.

[11] J.-M. Constant, *Nobles et paysans en Beauce au xviᵉ et xviiᵉ siècles* (Service de Reproduction de thèses, Lille, 1981), 327.

[12] Imbart de La Tour, iii. 336–7, 380–1.

Music played an important part in Calvin's liturgy and gave a special stamp to the French Reformèd church. As pastor to the French community at Strasburg he had composed hymns himself, and he published in 1539 *Aulcuns Psaumes et Cantiques mis en Chant*. This was an immensely important collection, since it included a number of psalms, sensitively translated into metrical form by Clement Marot and hitherto circulated only in manuscript. A translation of fifty psalms by Marot appeared in 1543, by which time he was a refugee in Geneva, and an enlarged edition was made by Beza in 1562. Calvin enjoyed music, and Bourgeois and Goudimel composed for him tunes for congregational singing, a form of audience-participation which became one of the hallmarks of the Calvinist churches. Bernard Palissy, the ceramic artist and manufacturer, a founder-member of the Calvinist church in Saintes, gave a lyrical description of the countryside in Saintonge, where peasants and artisans recited the psalms, while 'young girls and virgins sitting in groups in the gardens took delight in singing about holy things.' In the harsh world of confrontation the psalms of Marot were sung by martyrs on their way to the stake, by journeymen in the streets of Lyon, by demonstrators at the Pré-aux-Clercs, and by the Huguenot troops of Condé and Coligny, while Ps. 68, 'Let God arise, let his enemies be scattered' was to be a Marseillaise for the Camisard guerrillas descending from their mountain fastnesses.[13]

An index of prohibited books issued by the Sorbonne in 1544 testified to the success of the contraband trade. In 1551 the Edict of Châteaubriant was still wrestling with the problem, seeking to apply stricter censorship and also to stop emigration. But closing the frontiers was beyond the government's resources, and the traffic in books smuggled in by merchants and pedlars continued. Hauser long ago paid tribute to the role of the packman with tracts hidden among his combs and pins. When Anne du Bourg, a councillor of the *Parlement* of Paris, was tried in 1559 for heresy he explained that he had bought 'the works of Calvin and others from these packmen who come and go between countries'. Calvin's bookseller and publisher friend from his home town of Noyon, Laurent de Normandie, emigrated to Geneva, where he published the Beza psalter and devoted his fortune to the contraband trade in books, sending packmen to France. One of these hawking his wares in Troyes unwisely tried to sell a scurrilous anti-clerical pamphlet to a fervent Catholic, was duly arrested, and went to the stake singing psalms.[14]

The activities of the packmen bring into focus the routes by which the Reformed doctrines were disseminated and the importance of geographical contacts. With the exchange of wares went the exchange of ideas in towns

[13] Hauser, *Naissance*, 60–1; L. Wencelius, *L'Esthétique de Calvin* (Paris, 1937), 280–6.
[14] Hauser, *Naissance*, 57–8; L. Romier, *Royaume* (see Further Reading), ii. 185–6; A. N. Galpern, *The Religions of the People of Champagne* (Harvard, 1976), 115–16.

and fairs along rivers and maritime commercial routes. The influence of the printed word is incontestable, but this still begs the question of the degree of literacy. The sermon was as important as the tract, even for the literate, since oratory makes a direct emotional appeal, and the *rues des pasteurs* were the same roads as the packmen used. The diffusion of the Reform owed much to the itinerant preachers. The most striking of these was Guillaume Farel, outstanding for his forcefulness and stamina. He came from a notary family in Gap, joined the early reformist circle of Meaux, where his radicalism made him suspect, and he returned to Dauphiné. His missionary journeys took him to Basle, Strasburg, and Metz, from which he had to flee disguised as a leper in a cart full of genuine lepers. After evangelizing work in Montbéliard he set up his propaganda centre in Neuchâtel, then went on to Lausanne, and finally to Geneva. There he encountered Calvin, passing through on his way to Strasburg, and in the most decisive act of his life persuaded Calvin to join him in striving to make Geneva the perfect city of Christ. Similarly Pierre Viret evangelized in the Midi, organizing churches at Lyon, Montpellier, and Nîmes, while Jean le Masson pursued a trail from the Pyrenees to Carcassonne and then to Montauban on the Tarn.

News of anti-fiscal revolts in the time of Richelieu went upstream from Bordeaux along the Garonne, penetrating Périgord by the Lot and Dordogne. The Garonne had earlier played a role in the diffusion of Calvinism, and the trade in woad which linked Toulouse to Bordeaux and then Flanders was one of the agencies which transmitted Protestant ideas.[15] Beza, himself a gentleman from Burgundy, was astonished that the uncouth inhabitants of the Cévennes should have embraced the Gospel with such enthusiasm, but the valleys there were busy silk-weaving and textile areas within the magnetic field of Nîmes and Montpellier, whose merchants traded at the international fair of Beaucaire and had connections with Lyon.[16] The Durance and the Rhône connected Dauphiné and Languedoc with the Vaudois area of Provence. Farel established connections with the Vaudois, who in 1532 abandoned their separate identity just when Reform groups were appearing in Languedoc. The Rhône was the trade artery from Lyon to Nîmes; the *rues des pasteurs* were to be found on both sides of the river, with crossings at Avignon for Provence and at Pont-Saint-Esprit for the Cévennes.

By 1560 the geographical contours of Calvinism were emerging clearly. There was a wide scattering of churches, with a constellation in Normandy and a thick clustering south of the Loire forming a crescent which curved to the south of the high plateau of the Auvergne and had Lyon and La Rochelle

[15] Garrisson-Estèbe, 52.
[16] A. Molinier (see Further Reading), 249; E. Le Roy Ladurie, 'Huguenots contre papistes' (see Further Reading), 321; id., *Paysans* (see Further Reading) i. 348–51.

at its tips.[17] It had taken a remarkably short time to break through the crust of local habit and custom. Lucien Romier long ago warned against giving undue emphasis to the importance of commercial contacts in the diffusion of Calvinism. He considered that local studies might well reveal a more basic cause, particularly in the greater or lesser degree of incapacity or negligence in the clergy, taken in conjunction with the forces of tradition and habit.[18] But if some of the Catholics were flabby and ineffective, this was a negative factor; on the positive side the conversion of priests and friars commonly brought to the pulpits trained theologians and practised preachers with missionary fervour and, often, a readiness to accept martyrdom.[19] Renegade friars evangelized in the Dordogne valley and in the Cévennes, while Dauphiné saw a massive defection of *curés* who became pastors in their villages.

In accounting for the spread of ideas in the Middle Ages C. H. Haskins drew attention to what he termed stations of high tension, representing different social strata, universities, cathedral centres, courts, and towns, which communicated with other similar stations rapidly and over wide distances.[20] This is applicable to the diffusion of Calvinism in sixteenth-century France, where, although the peasantry remained largely insulated, Haskin's stations were still available and new ones were created. The earliest of these was Meaux, where the bishop, Guillaume Briçonnet, brought in his friend, Lefèvre d'Étaples, to help in making the diocese a humanist and Lutheran centre. Lefèvre was joined by, among others, Gérard Roussel, and also by Farel, who reported jubilantly in 1524 that all France was most joyfully receiving the word of God.[21]

The station at Meaux closed down in 1526 after an attack upon it by the *Parlement* of Paris, but this served only to free its staff for service elsewhere. An attempt to capture the university of Paris resulted in defeat and Calvin's hurried departure. Provincial universities became reception centres: Calvin himself stayed in Poitiers and Orléans after he left Paris. The importance of the universities was emphasized by Beza, who wrote that 'God began to make his voice heard at Orléans, which was with Bourges the fountain from which all the waters surged over the kingdom.' This view was echoed by Hauser, who considered that 'dans une forte mesure, la Réforme est une fille des collèges et des universités', citing Caen, whose professors he considered to be largely responsible for making Normandy a province notorious for heresy.[22]

Civic wealth and pride in this period of the French Renaissance

[17] Estèbe, 55.
[18] Romier, *Royaume*, ii. 182.
[19] Ibid. 206–8; Imbart de La Tour, iv. 275–8.
[20] *Studies in Mediaeval Culture* (Oxford, 1929), 94–104.
[21] É. G. Léonard, *Histoire Générale* (see Further Reading), i. 203.
[22] Constant, op. cit., 327; Hauser, *Naissance*, 62, 64.

stimulated the foundation of humanist colleges, which were rapidly infiltrated by the Reformers. The college of Guyenne, founded in Bordeaux in 1533, immediately attracted a colony of Parisian scholars. Florimond de Raemond, who wrote a history of the rise and decline of heresy in his day, described how he and other pupils at this college were told not to make the sign of the cross, 'a monkey trick', at the start of lessons, and were covertly instructed in the new ideas. Such children, when they grew up, may well have helped to make the valley of the Garonne a highway for Reformation ideas.[23] Montpellier, a university of international fame, was penetrated, and it was a vital centre for countering the influence of the *parlement* of Toulouse. Nîmes also was a station of high tension in Languedoc. The college there, founded in 1534 and upgraded into a university in 1539, was instrumental in the conversion of the city. The first rector, Imbert Pecolet, who had also been active in Montpellier, was accused of heresy in 1537, the year in which he was engaged in founding the first Calvinist church in Nîmes. His successor was the humanist, Claude Baduel, who had met Calvin in Strasburg. He spoke of the saintliness which made Nîmes shine out in the encircling gloom, and he praised Calvin for his piety, erudition, and spiritual energy, which 'console us through the medium of his weighty and frequent letters'.[24] The influence of Calvin was such that by 1540 lower Languedoc had reached the point of no return.

The court could be the most powerful station of all, and this was Calvin's view, for he always put his trust in the conversion of princes. The French court was divided, since Marguerite d'Angoulême, the sister of Francis I, gave her support to the Reformers. She combined personal piety of a mystical kind with a taste for exercising patronage. She corresponded with Erasmus, was the patron of Lefèvre, and had Briçonnet, bishop of Meaux, as her spiritual director. When she was duchess there, Alençon flourished as a Reformation centre, and when she became duchess of Anjou with Bourges as her capital, she busied herself with university appointments. In 1527 she married Henri d'Albret and became queen of Navarre. Her court at Nérac sheltered the refugees from Meaux. Lefèvre pursued his scholarship there; Roussel, for whom Marguerite obtained the see of Oloron, devoted his energies to the conversion of Béarn; while Calvin and Clément Marot stayed at Nérac. Marguerite found fresh fields for her patronage in the Midi. Her nominees became bishops in Languedoc and her protégé, Baduel, became rector of the university of Nîmes.[25] Although Marguerite herself remained an Erasmian Catholic, the undermining of orthodoxy in France owed much to her activities, and among her legacies can be counted

---

[23] L. Fèbvre, *Le Problème de l'Incroyance au XVIe siècle* (Paris, 1942), 30–1; Garrisson-Estèbe, 36.

[24] D. Sauzet, 'Huguenots et papistes, du XVIe au XVIIIe siècle', in R. Huard (ed.), *Histoire de Nîmes* (Aix-en-Provençe, 1982), 150–1.

[25] Molinier, 251.

her daughter, Jeanne d'Albret, the Calvinist queen of Navarre, and her grandson, Henri IV.

The court of Ferrara, presided over by Renée de France, daughter of Louis XII, who did not, unlike Marguerite, remain ambivalent, supplied yet another centre for French Calvinists. Clément Marot went to Ferrara after Nérac, and Calvin also stayed there. His stay was important, for he converted the duchess and two fellow-guests, Antoine de Pons, who possessed estates in Saintonge and in the Limousin, and his wife, Anne de Parthenay-Soubise, whose family was to be active in the west from the first civil wars until the fall of La Rochelle in 1628. The château at Pons became a centre for disseminating Calvinism in Saintonge, which therefore did not receive the new faith from geographical or trading contacts.[26]

Lucien Romier considered that the massive conversions among the nobility between 1558 and 1562 changed the character of French Calvinism. The conversions, often coloured by material and sometimes even cynical considerations, reflected social strains and the immediate tensions caused by demobilization after the Peace of Cateau-Cambrésis. Hauser, who had described Calvinism before 1559 as a 'religion des petites gens', christened the new brand 'protestantisme seigneurial', since churches and nobles were linked by chains of protection. Michelet himself drew attention to the paucity of noble names before 1555, for Crespin's *Martyrologe* mentions only three.[27] Yet the nobility were represented in the Reformation movement before the mid-sixteenth century, while the examples of Languedoc show that *protestantisme seigneurial* was no new arrival in 1559.

The Paris church founded in 1555 had two noblemen as pastors, François de Morel and Antoine de la Roche-Chandieu. It was a noble, the sieur de Ferrière, who particularly pressed for the foundation of the church, since he wished his baby son to be christened according to Calvinist rites. 130 arrests were made after a Calvinist service in the rue Saint-Jacques in 1557, of whom thirty were nobles, and not all newly converted. The nobility of Picardy, Calvin's own province, was affected, and the Calvinists of Laon in 1552 sought the protection of a nobleman, the comte de Roucy.[28]

In Languedoc an equivalent for the Pons family of Saintonge can be found in the Crussols. Charles de Crussol, vicomte d'Uzès, who died in 1547, was the most powerful noble in eastern Languedoc, having thirty vassals between Pont-Saint-Esprit and the lower Cévennes, besides a barony in the Vivarais, close to Valence. He had sympathies with the Reformation, and married Jeanne de Genouillac, who was in the household of Marguerite d'Angoulême and whose château at Assier was a centre for Protestant gentlemen from Quercy and Périgord. The Vivarais barony

[26] É. G. Léonard, *Le Protestant français* (Paris, 1955), II, 14.
[27] Romier, *Royaume*, ii. 255-62; Hauser, *La Prépondérance espagnole* (Paris, 1933), 45.
[28] Léonard, *Histoire générale*, ii. 90; Léonard, *Le Protestant français*, 48, 13.

became a Calvinist area owing to the efforts of the Crussols, father and son, and also of Jean de Monluc, the Erasmian bishop of Valence. Crussol as seneschal of Nîmes-Beaucaire protected Protestants from harassment by the *parlement* of Toulouse. Seigneurial Protestantism was also to be found in the Cévennes among the lesser nobility. The merchants of Nîmes took Calvinism to the areas around Anduze, but Anduze also had a Calvinist noble family, admittedly of recent vintage, which furnished sons who trained in Geneva and who served as pastors in Lyon, Uzès and Nîmes. In the mountains behind Anduze it was the squires who converted their peasantry, and seigneurial Calvinism found a most successful practitioner in Charles de Taulignon, an early convert, who was elected pastor of his church at Barre in 1561.[29]

When we turn to the towns and indeed Calvinism in France has been termed a religion of towns, it is apparent that those attracted to Reformation ideas were merchants, shopkeepers, craftsmen, and artisans, together with professional men, schoolmasters, lawyers, and doctors. Hobbes was to write in the *Leviathan* that 'it is manifest that the instruction of the people dependeth wholly on the right teaching of youth in the universities', a view anticipated by an Italian observer in 1559 who reported that in Guyenne 'heresy is propagated by the students returned from the universities, which are themselves highly contaminated.'[30] The *parlements* of Bordeaux and Toulouse reiterated injunctions against schoolmasters. In Rouen in 1546 a doctor invited a preacher who proceeded to hold weekly meetings in a field. In Montauban the conventicle of five members was started by a young man of the town who had studied law at Paris and picked up his Calvinism there. From Montauban comes the pleasing story of the schoolmaster whose pupils sang the psalms of Marot under the trees in the evenings and who was arrested and imprisoned by the bishop. The devotion of the boys was such that they rescued their schoolmaster, and they in their turn were shielded by the town authorities, which blocked investigations by the outraged *parlement* of Toulouse.[31]

The growing strength of Calvinism stemmed partly from its success in recruiting local élites, the town notables, especially lawyers and notaries, often employed in local courts. The *parlements*, stuffed with tradition and legal lore, were in general hostile, but the 1550s saw them wavering. The *Parlement* of Paris became affected, as the trial in 1559 of Anne du Bourg with six other councillors showed. In 1562 it was rumoured, admittedly on the principle of guilt by association, that up to a third of the members were

---

[29] Molinier, 250–2; Garrisson-Estèbe, 26–7; P. Joutard, *Les Cévennes entrent dans l'histoire* (Toulouse, n.d.) i. 111.

[30] Romier, *Royaume*, ii. 271.

[31] P. Benedict, *Rouen* (see Further Reading), 51; Gaston Serr, *Une Église protestante au XVIe siècle: Montauban* (Aix-en-Provence, 1958), 9, 11–12.

tinged with Calvinism. The *parlement* of Rouen remained largely impervious, but there were Calvinist sympathizers in the *parlements* of Grenoble and Bordeaux and in 1562 thirty out of the eighty members of the *parlement* of Toulouse were said to be Calvinist.[32]

The élites of the towns overlapped with the civic authorities. Hauser held that although the municipalities showed no more than a mild interest in the Reformation, even this negative attitude stimulated the 'prodigious development of Protestantism in the Midi and in the south-west at the start of the Wars of Religion.' But the attitude of the magistrate was much more positive and the towns were power-stations of the Reformation, generating the current for the resistance of the Midi in the Religious Wars. The local courts also played an essential role in the survival of Calvinism threatened by the persecuting edicts, and they simultaneously weakened the authority of the crown. Blaise de Monluc, lieutenant-governor of Guyenne, reported in 1561 that the root of disorder had lain with the local judicial and financial officials who favoured the new religion. The *présidial*, established in 1552 to hive off lesser offences from the *parlements*, were particularly affected, which may be partially explained by their jealousy of the latter bodies. The attraction of Calvinism for the notaries was especially important for the running of the consistories, for they had the skills of numeracy and accountancy, and in the Midi their knowledge of French was an added qualification.[33]

Calvinism infiltrated all levels of society in the mid sixteenth century, but artisans predominated numerically. The social composition of Calvinism was thus contrasted with the general pattern of French society, since it failed to capture the peasantry, some 80 per cent of the population. The Cévennes stand out as an exception, since commercial links with Nîmes stimulated rural industry. The peasants were engaged in the textile and leather trades and were receptive to Calvinism. The particular character of the Cévennes led Le Roy Ladurie to coin his aphorism 'cardeurs huguenots, laboureurs papistes', and to agree with Hauser that Calvinism in France was largely a religion of artisans. In a census of Calvinist congregations made at Montpellier in 1569 for fiscal purposes, 69 per cent were artisans and shopkeepers and 15.4 per cent were drawn from the professional classes.[34] The list of martyrs, beginning with the fourteen carders of Meaux in 1546 and going up to 1559, is composed predominantly of artisans. The statistics for the refugees in Geneva in the same period, though they need to be used cautiously, also show a majority of artisans. Two-thirds of the refugees

[32] Estèbe, 61; Benedict, 78.

[33] Garrison-Estèbe, 31–5; H. Hauser, *Études* (see Further Reading) 202. Romier, *Royaume*, ii. 277–83; Estèbe, 61–2; J. K. Powis, 'Order, Religion and the Magistrates of a Provincial Parlement in Sixteenth-century France', *Archiv für Reformations geschichte* (1980), 187–8.

[34] Le Roy Ladurie, *Paysans*, i. 341–3.

there were French; the majority came from two areas, Languedoc (especially the Cévennes) and Normandy (especially Rouen), and of these two-thirds were artisans.[35]

Yet the Genevan picture is not a true reflection of the situation inside France, since it was easier for artisans to emigrate than other groups. On the other hand, the figures are more reliable for detecting which trades favoured the Reform most. It is not surprising to find a high proportion of textile workers, the single largest industry in France, but it is of interest to discover that the shoemakers had an absolute majority over all the other trades represented in the exile. Indeed, the shoemaker's shop, 'where the artisan read the Bible while using his awl', has been described as 'the agency for the diffusion of heresy in Languedoc'.[36] Inns and taverns were other recognized centres of diffusion. Hauser wrote that 'in Rouen in 1560 the working man's cause and the cause of Reform were one and the same', and the taverns can be regarded as working mens' clubs.[37] Discussion in the taverns underpinned the sermon. The oral transmission of ideas was especially important in the Midi, where there were few printing presses and scarcely any publications in Occitan. The link between printing and the Reformation is not simple. The shoemakers were the least literate among the artisans of Nîmes. Yet the Calvinist emphasis on the pre-eminent importance of the Bible created an incentive and a demand for books. Bernard Palissy made the point by implication when he described the early days of the church at Saintes when he and five other artisans took turns to compose sermons, grappling with the problems of literacy, and on Sundays walking in the fields singing psalms.

The artisans in the Calvinist movement were not unskilled workers but craftsmen, journeymen, and shopkeepers. Florimond de Raemond, a convert who subsequently recanted, wrote satirically that 'the first to hear the truth (this was the password which they whispered in each other's ears) were goldsmiths, masons, carpenters and other miserable wage-earners, who became overnight excellent theologians'. But he also wrote that the exiles in Geneva, the 'painters, clockmakers, goldsmiths, booksellers, and printers', were all members of 'crafts possessing a nobility of spirit'. Such craftsmen could rise into the merchant class, as they did in Vienne and Toulouse, where Calvinist merchant-drapers and goldsmiths figured among the commercial élites, as the master-printers did at Lyon. In Paris during the Massacre of St Bartholomew the Catholic mob looted the wealthy shops of the Huguenot drapers, goldsmiths, and furriers, as alluring as 'the caves of Ali Baba'.[38]

[35] R. Mandrou, 'Les Français hors de France au XVIᵉ et XVIIᵉ siècles, *Annales ESC*, 1959, 662–6; Le Roy Ladurie, *Paysans*, i. 349.

[36] Le Roy Ladurie, 'Huguenots contre papistes', 321.

[37] H. Hauser, 'La Réforme et les classes populaires', *Rev. d'hist. moderne et contemporaine* 1899, 31; Garrisson-Estèbe, 45.

[38] Garrisson-Estèbe, 15, 39.

By the mid century, although Protestantism was widely diffused and had a broad base in society, there was as yet no structured Calvinism. The conventicles or 'gathered churches' met secretly and often at night for Bible-readings, but there were neither pastors nor sacraments. It was possible for the timid and the cautious to combine these pious meetings with outward conformity to Catholic rites, particularly in the case of infant baptism. But Calvin scented danger and in 1543 and in the the following year condemned *Messieurs les Nicodémites*, comparing the conformists to the cowardly Nicodemus who had visited Christ secretly by night. French Nicodemites expressed their total consternation when given the choice of imprisonment, death, or exile by Calvin; but he was unmoved. Some indeed followed his counsel of non-resistance, choosing exile or facing martyrdom. The winter of persecution began with the horrific massacre of the Vaudois in 1545, and in 1551 came the martyrdom of the five students of Lyon, exhorted by Calvin himself to take courage since not a drop of their blood would be shed in vain. In 1554 Jean Crespin's *Livre des Martyrs* was published in Geneva, coincidentally with Foxe's *Book of Martyrs*, both publicizing the cult. By 1559 an understandable preference for resistance appeared, but Calvin continued to urge the persecuted not to shrink from making the supreme sacrifice.

Erasmianism withered in this climate. In 1557, when Beza and Farel visited Basle, both denounced Erasmus. At a dinner Farel spat out that Erasmus had been 'le pire des charlatans, archi-déshonnête, archi-scélérat, archi-débauché'.[39] The Interim of Augsburg in 1548 ratified the Lutheran mass, but Calvinism took its stand on *Scriptura sola* and the rejection of magic in the sacrament. Guillaume Bigot, a humanist who had dabbled in Protestantism but then returned to his old religion, was startled to find on his return from Germany in 1550 how different France was. In Lutheran Germany he had retained old friendships because belief in the Real Presence presented no problem, but in France the 'sectaries' shunned him.[40] Calvinist dislike of superstition was apparent in the calendars published in Geneva which commemorated not the myths of saints but historical events, such as Luther's attack upon indulgences and the death of Edward VI.[41]

Calvin neutralized the Nicodemites, but he faced another danger for his movement in iconoclasm, violence, and street demonstrations. Trained in the law and a humanist scholar, Calvin deplored the violence which erupted in the attacks upon the statues of saints and Virgins and maintained that actions against idolatry should be undertaken only by those whom God had put in authority to do so. He was warned by Baduel, the humanist professor

[39] P.-F. Geisendorf, *Théodore de Bèze* (Geneva, 1967), 89.
[40] Imbart de La Tour, iv. 307–8.
[41] N. Z. Davis, *Society and Culture* (see Further Reading), 204.

at Nîmes, against the journeymen of Lyon who sought 'carnal liberty under the false title of the Gospel'.[42] Action was required from Geneva both to exert pressure upon the French government to get the edicts against heresy cancelled and also to control radical elements which could so easily associate Calvinism with social subversion.

The world of humanism had been the world of the court, and it was to courts that Calvin turned by preference, penning elegant exhortations to princes and noblemen. He appealed to Francis I on behalf of the Vaudois and to Henri II on behalf of the prisoners taken after the raid upon the rue Saint-Jacques in 1557. His correspondents ranged from Protector Somerset and Edward VI—hailed as the new Joshua—to the kings of Sweden and Poland, German princes and the duchess of Ferrara. Calvin was thus initiating a policy of international Calvinism, but totally ineffectively as far as the victims of persecution were concerned. In contrast, he was successful in giving cohesion to the churches in France. From 1555 the structure of the consistory with elders and deacons was made obligatory, and trustworthy ministers were made available on request by the Company of Pastors in Geneva. The consistory became the mark of a true church, termed an *église dressée*, in contrast to the amorphous Bible gatherings, known as *églises plantées*. Pierre Viret explained at the inception of the consistory of Lyon in 1560 that the special vocation in the church enjoyed by elders and deacons was not meant to disturb rank and order in the secular sphere, while Beza in 1571 wrote to Bullinger that the French churches had always had in common with Geneva 'the aristocratic principle of the consistory'.[43]

Calvin by this time had immense authority, but how did he exercise it and what were his aims? In 1547 there were rumours that the church in Nîmes, without a consistory, was administering the sacraments, which stimulated Calvin to write a general directive to the congregations of France warning them against such ambitions and advising the faithful to pack up their belongings and to come to Geneva, where they could enjoy the true usage of the sacraments.[44] In 1555 the church in Paris complete with a consistory, was founded and was served by a succession of outstanding pastors from Geneva, including Gaspard Carmel, the nephew of Farel, and Nicolas Des Gallars, a nobleman, who as a student in Geneva had been one of the official scribes of Calvin's sermons and who was to be transferred to the French congregation in London in 1560.

Once the Paris church was founded, consistories were rapidly estab-lished, and the Genevan Company of Pastors sent out on requests from France eighty-eight pastors between 1555 and 1562.[45] The old centres of

[42] Ibid. 11.
[43] Ibid.; R. M. Kingdon, *Geneva and the French Protestant Movement* (see Further Reading), 103.
[44] Léonard, *Histoire générale*, ii. 88–9.
[45] R. M. Kingdon, *Geneva and the Coming of the Wars* (see Further Reading), preface.

Poitiers and Orléans had consistories in 1555 and 1557. In the next year the congregation of fifty at La Rochelle formed a consistory with eight elders and deacons, and sent to Geneva for a pastor. By 1560 it had two pastors and wanted more, but Calvin had none to send.[46] The church at Nîmes became a consistory in March 1561, and by the end of the year Pierre Viret was preaching to 8,000 communicants.[47] By then the number of consistories in France had risen to 1,785, and Calvin's supply of pastors fell far short of the demand.

How far was this great increase due to Calvin's initiative and direction? Was he the organizing genius responsible for sending out pastors nerved to danger and martyrdom? Imbart de la Tour held that Calvin's genius lay in his grasp of the right moment to organize religious revolution, and in his recruiting of secret agents, packmen, merchants, and pastors.[48] Professor Kingdon has illuminated both the work of the Company of Pastors and the shadowy activities of the ministers sent to France, resulting in a 'Geneva-created French ecclesiastical organization'. Although recognizing that pastors were despatched in response to formal requests from France, he stressed the tight discipline of the Genevan mother-church in Reformed France. He held that for the faithful in France, as in other countries, Geneva was both the 'organizing centre' and the 'final authority', the Moscow of the sixteenth century.[49]

No-one would deny that the connections between Geneva and the French Reformed Church were very close in the time of Calvin and Beza, while Calvin's foundation of his Academy in 1559 set the seal upon Geneva's role as the leading European centre of high tension. But it is difficult to ascribe solely to Calvin and the pastors from Geneva the French Calvinist explosion of the years from 1555 to 1562. Calvin's own policy was to wait upon the court and Providence, and Providence took a hand with the deaths of Henri II and of the boy-king Francis II, described by Beza as a 'miserable child' whose 'horrible death' was 'no less wonderful and even more opportune' than that of his father.[50] Calvin's anxiety for an understanding with the court explains why he discouraged organized churches until 1555 and continued thereafter to advocate secrecy, prudence, and passive obedience. It was Paris, not Geneva, which ignited the explosion. The huge service in the rue Saint-Jacques, the demonstrations at the Pré-aux-Clercs, and, most important of all, the meeting in 1559 of the first synod of the Reformed Church, which issued the Discipline and Confession of Faith, were all Parisian events. Calvin deprecated the meeting

[46] E. Trocmé, 'La Rochelle de 1560 à 1628. Tableau d'une société réformée au temps des guerres de religion' (unpublished thesis, Strasburg, 1950), 208–19.
[47] Sauzet, *Histoire de Nîmes*, 151–2.
[48] Imbart de La Tour, iv. 264–5, 186–7, 448–9.
[49] Kingdon, *Geneva and the Coming of the Wars*, 110, 128.
[50] Geisendorf, 124.

of the synod and his envoy arrived late, enabling the representatives of the seventy-two churches to show their independence by issuing a Confession which was a mild variant upon that of Geneva.[51]

It can be argued that Calvin, rather than showing a sense of the moment to organize revolution, mistimed matters and underestimated the gale-force of the movement, while his hopes of securing diplomatic intervention by the Elector Palatine and the duke of Württemberg were soon dashed. If Calvin is to be regarded as an organizer of revolution, he failed lamentably, for La Rochelle was not the only town to find Genevan pastors in short supply. In his letter to Bullinger in May 1561 Calvin showed a lack of fervour and a failure of planning, writing; 'It is unbelievable to see how impetuously our brothers are rushing forward. Pastors are demanded from all parts. The title of pastor is solicited with as much avidity as the efforts made to obtain benefices in the Roman Church. My door is besieged like that of a king. Vacant posts are fought over as if the reign of Christ had been peaceably established in France . . . But our resources are exhausted. We are reduced to searching everywhere, even in the artisan's workshop, to find men with some smattering of doctrine and of piety as candidates for the ministry.'[52] The distaste of the humanist scholar for recruiting at the artisan level is plain, but it was the failure to found the Geneva Academy until 1559 which helps to explain the critical shortage of pastors. That shortage in its turn is a reason for the ease with which seigneurial Protestantism became grafted onto the consistory structure. The influence of Geneva upon France was very great and there was active correspondence between Calvin, the pastors and the consistories, but Calvin, as Professor Trocmé has cogently argued, worked in favour of restraint, not expansion.[53]

Calvin failed to capture the court as such, but there were some important conversions which added to the tensions at the court and gave the Calvinist movement its political muscle. The death of Henri II, which entailed a regency, left three families contending for power. The Guises, who had invested heavily in church offices, led the Catholic party. The Bourbons, Princes of the Blood, headed the reversionary interest. Antoine de Bourbon was king of Navarre through his marriage to Jeanne d'Albret. He was an unsatisfactory convert, intent on his personal ambitions, but his presence at the Pré-aux-Clercs demonstrations gave the Huguenots encouragement. On his wife's public conversion in 1560, Calvinism became the official religion of Béarn and spread widely in the west, for d'Albret fiefs stretched from Guyenne to the Limousin. The marriage between politics and religion

---

[51] Léonard, Histoire générale, ii. 98–103; J. D. Benoît, 'L'Année 1559 dans les années calviniennes', Rev. d'Hist. et de philosophie religieuses (1959); J. Poujol, 'De la confession de foi de 1559 à la conjuration d'Amboise', BSHPF (1973).

[52] BSHPF (1872), 538.

[53] E. Trocmé, 'Une révolution mal conduite' (see Further Reading).

was solemnized when his younger brother, Condé, described by Calvin as debauched by ambition, was elected Protector-General of the Churches of France in 1562 on the eve of civil war.

The third family, the Montmorencis, produced in the Châtillon brothers, François d'Andelot, Colonel-General of the Infantry, and Gaspard de Coligny, Admiral of France, converts whose religion was as sincere as their services were invaluable to the Calvinist cause. D'Andelot's conversion illustrates the regional effect of the religion of a great noble, for in 1558 he went on an evangelizing tour of his wife's lands on the Loire and in lower Brittany, founding twelve churches and making successful conversions, especially among the squirearchy. Nor were these converts of necessity merely clients anxious to ingratiate themselves with a patron. Among those converted after a service in Nantes cathedral was François de La Noue, from then onwards a client of the Châtillons, who never wavered in his faith and whose career and writings provide insight into the social and political outlook of a Huguenot noble, anxious to combine loyalty to his religion with loyalty to his country. In the mid seventeenth century Moïse Amyraut, the renowned professor at Saumur, chose La Noue as the subject for a biography designed to illustrate the finest qualities of a Huguenot gentleman.[54]

The short period between the death of Henri II in 1559 and the start of the Wars of Religion in 1562 was as decisive for French Protestantism as the Massacre of St Bartholomew ten years later. These years saw Calvinism, impelled by a new offensive spirit, moving towards victory. Basements and cellars could no longer hold the faithful, who came out into the daylight, taking over churches and cathedrals. The high tide of conversion even rose to the level of the *parlements*. The *Grande Chambre* of the *Parlement* of Paris had invariably condemned heretics to the flames, and Anne du Bourg was martyred in 1559, but in that year four Huguenots were sentenced merely to exile, while debates in the *Parlement* showed that minds were not totally closed to toleration.[55] The Calvinist churches and nobility had two courses open. They could pursue an eirenical path in the hope that ecumenical formulae would plaster over differences, or they could show their strength in demonstrations and open-air services.

But Calvin did not lead an offensive; he limited his objectives to toleration and warned the faithful against provocative behaviour. In the brief reign of Francis II the court was dominated by his uncles the Guises, whose forcible removal was attempted by the Conspiracy of Amboise, instigated by Condé. Calvin and Beza were accused of involvement, and the charge cannot be lightly dismissed. But even if they are exonerated, it can be

[54] H. Hauser, *François de La Noue* (Paris, 1892), 7–8 and *passim*; F. E. Sutcliffe (ed.), *Discours politiques et militaires* (Geneva, 1967); Moïse Amyraut, *Vie de François de La Noue* (Leiden, 1661).
[55] Richet, 770.

held that Calvin's hesitation helped to bring about the failure of the plot. The plot was a coup that failed, but nevertheless the resort to arms helped to convince Catherine de Médicis of the strength of the Huguenots and therefore of the need for conciliation, a policy which she initiated when she became regent. For the Huguenots, the reprisals after Amboise mark the point at which it became clear that survival spelt resistance. Agrippa d'Aubigné, the most uncompromising of Calvinists, whose powerful pen was devoted to the Huguenot cause, was the son of a Protestant noble of Saintonge. He recalled that at the age of eight he was taken to Paris by his father, their route taking them through Amboise where the heads of those executed were on display. In an emotional scene the boy was adjured to remember and to avenge these deaths or be for ever cursed.[56]

The first year of Catherine's regency saw intensified Calvinist activity with continued occupation of churches and iconoclasm leading to inevitable Catholic retaliation. Catherine made her bid for reconciliation by summoning a conference at Poissy of bishops and twelve Calvinist ministers. One of her favourite bishops at the court was Monluc, bishop of Valence, who had been active in bringing Protestantism to the Vivarais and who as an Erasmian survivor thought that the abolition of the worship of saints and images would be a small price to pay for the French translation of the Bible and the psalms.[57] Not surprisingly the public summit meeting at Poissy between theologians exacerbated differences and the meeting broke up in disarray after Beza's unequivocal stand against transubstantiation. Catherine kept Beza at the court and, convinced that Huguenot strength required concessions, issued an edict of toleration in January 1562. This was welcomed by the Huguenots as a victory, for by it they were given the right of holding public services outside the towns and of private worship inside the towns, together with the right to have consistories and ministers, and to hold synods. They saw the edict as the first of victories to come, but instead it was the climax of Huguenot fortunes. Only after thirty-six years of civil war did the Huguenots regain by the Edict of Nantes the position they had held in 1562, and the Edict of Nantes was an end of concessions by the monarchy, not a beginning.

The immediate consequence of the Edict of January was civil war in the spring. The *Parlement* refused to accept the edict, violence grew worse, and breaking-point was reached when the duke of Guise massacred a congregation assembled for a service at Vassy. Condé and a reluctant Coligny agreed on a resort to arms. The first civil war ended a year later in Huguenot defeat. The Peace of Amboise in March 1563 restricted services in the towns, but favoured the nobility by giving seigneurs the right to hold services on their estates. Condé's sacrifice of the towns, the centres of high

[56] Agrippa d'Aubigné, *Œuvres* (Pléiade edn., Paris, 1969), 'Sa vie à ses enfants', 385–6.
[57] L. Romier, *Catholiques et huguenots à la cour de Charles IX* (Paris, 1924), 100–1.

tension, was deplored by Coligny, who considered that more harm had been done by a stroke of the pen than could have been done in ten years of war.[58] The geographical consequences of the war were equally important. Defeat in Normandy drove the Huguenots south of the Loire, where the majority of their churches were already. The 'United Provinces of the South' began to take shape from 1562 when the institutions of Calvinism became part of the society of the Midi.

The first civil war had lasted less than a year but its legacy was militarized Calvinism and sectarian fury. The Conspiracy of Amboise had not received the backing of the churches, but now the synod of Clairac gave a paramilitary structure to the churches of Guyenne.[59] The system was adopted in southern France and Condé's title of Protector-General of the churches of France fitted the facts. When war came Beza acted as chaplain to the psalm-singing troops of Condé and orders were despatched by both to the churches for men and money. Political assemblies, adjuncts of the synods, came into existence to co-ordinate the war-effort. Antoine de Crussol was nominated as head of the Calvinist forces in Languedoc and Dauphiné. Two subordinate councils issued in 1563 a detailed directive of 136 articles, which covered the enforcement of the Discipline, salaries of ministers, charity for the poor and for the war victims, inventories of church property and plate, a loan to be raised from nobles and wealthy citizens, and a scale of payment for troops, starting with 6,000 livres for Crussol.[60]

Condé was alert to the military importance of the towns, and the Calvinists responded enthusiastically to his call for a takeover of urban government. Municipalities fell with astonishing ease into the hands of Calvinist minorities. In Nîmes, the capital of Protestant Languedoc, the city militia was Calvinist-controlled and the town council was captured in 1561. There was also a council of twenty-four, nominated by the consistory and in charge of defence, collection of rates and tithes, payment of salaries to ministers, and poor relief.[61] A citizen of Millau, a small town of some 4,000 inhabitants on the edge of the Cévennes, recorded in his diary the Calvinist takeover, typical of what happened elsewhere. A consistory was formed, a pastor requested from Geneva, new magistrates installed, churches sacked, and inventories made of the plate. Priests and friars were driven out and by 1562 no one mentioned the word mass. Condé appointed a governor, the town walls were strengthened, workshops set up for making cannon and muskets, and troops hired from the Cévennes, then a reservoir of

[58] Geisendorf, 222.

[59] Romier, *Royaume* ii. 264–6.

[60] P. H. Chaix, 'Promotion sociale et Réforme: Charles du Puy de Montbrun', *BSHPF* (1975), 456–60.

[61] A. Guggenheim, 'The Calvinist Notables of Nîmes during the Era of the Religious Wars', *Sixteenth Century Journal* (1972).

manpower, to reinforce the urban militia.[62] Millau became a Huguenot citadel and a conference centre for the political assemblies of the churches of France.

Rouen, where the Calvinists formed 21 per cent of the population, and Lyon, where they formed 33 per cent, were transformed against a dramatic backcloth of riots and image-breaking in the spring of 1562 into little Genevas with consistories backed by nominated assemblies and Calvinist magistrates.[63] But Rouen surrendered to a royalist siege and peace in 1563 brought the Calvinist regime in Lyon to an end. Nor were Calvinist attempts to obtain control of towns always successful; the towns of Provence stood out, as did Bordeaux. The most serious blow in the Midi came from the fiasco in Toulouse which occurred simultaneously with the temporary successes in Rouen and Lyon. Toulouse was extremely important strategically, because it controlled the route to Bordeaux and the Atlantic and the routes to the Cévennes, Languedoc, and the Mediterranean. The Huguenots formed only 14 per cent of the population of Toulouse, but, responding to the call of Condé, there was an attempted coup, accompanied by image-breaking and desecration of churches. Retaliation by a Catholic mob with support from notables and the *parlement* culminated in street fighting, looting, and mass executions until peace was restored, leaving some 300 dead.[64]

After the Peace of Amboise the Huguenots continued to present a formidable challenge. They had their power-base in the South, from which troops were drawn for campaigns in the North, and established a new area of control in Saintonge with a base at La Rochelle. The town became the Huguenot capital from 1568 when the Bourbon court of Jeanne d'Albret and her son, Henri of Navarre, moved there from Nérac. The Huguenot defeat at Jarnac in 1569 when Condé was killed was followed by a brilliant recovery. Coligny's cavalry swoop on the South and Crussol's campaign in Saintonge enabled the Huguenots to negotiate very favourable terms at the Peace of Saint Germain in 1570. They were given the right to hold services in a larger number of towns and were ceded four fortified towns, La Rochelle, Cognac, Montauban, and La Charité-sur-Loire, the first indication of a division between a Catholic North and a Protestant South.

The Huguenot momentum of the years 1559 to 1562 was never recovered, but the two years between 1570 and 1572 saw renewed optimism. The synod held at La Rochelle in 1571 was the first to be given legal status by letters patent and Beza came from Geneva to preside. All the Huguenot grandees

[62] *Mémoires d'un calviniste de Millau* ed. J. L. Rigal (Rodez, 1911), 20–30.

[63] Benedict, 78; Davis, 1.

[64] J. Estèbe, 'Les Saint-Barthélemy des villes du Midi', in *L'Amiral de Coligny* (see Further Reading), 718–20; M. Greengrass, 'The Anatomy of a Religious Riot in Toulouse in May 1562', *Journal of Eccles. History* 1983.

were present, and also Louis of Nassau, younger brother of William of Orange. The Calvinists at the synod of Paris in 1559 had not bowed to Geneva, but in 1571 they needed the imprimatur of Beza. Peter Ramus, that persuasive and truculent philosopher, not content with attacking Aristotle, was campaigning for less power for the ministers and more for the congregations, a proposal which appealed as little to seigneurial Calvinism in France as it did to clerical Geneva.[65] The Confession of Faith of La Rochelle was eminently orthodox and served as a basis for the Confession of the Flemish and Walloon churches enacted at Emden later in the year, a demonstration of an international Calvinist front.[66]

Secondly, Coligny was invited to take his seat once again on the royal council and the marriage was arranged between Henri of Navarre and Marguerite de Valois, designed to bring peace to the warring religions and factions. Coligny was not a cipher but a man of policy. He wanted French national interests and Protestant international interests to be linked by a war against Spain in the Netherlands. A war in Flanders would occupy the nobility and give them new fields to plunder; alliances with England and the Palatinate would form a Protestant bloc in Europe; and France while freeing the Netherlands would regain possessions in the north-east, lost at the disastrous Treaty of Cateau-Cambrésis.

The plan was smashed by the Massacre of St Bartholomew which occurred on 24 August 1572, six days after the royal wedding. A contract had been put out by the duke of Guise for the murder of Coligny, and this botched but ultimately successful crime triggered off a massacre, which lasted for three days in a Paris crowded with Huguenots who had come to the wedding. Coligny's murder was the culmination of a mafia-like feud between the Guises and the Montmorencis, while there was court involvement in the events of St Bartholomew, since Catherine de Médicis was nervous of the projected war and disliked, as her younger son the duc d'Anjou also did, the influence of Coligny. But the collective murder of some 200 Huguenot nobles lodging in and around the Louvre pales beside the massacre by the Paris mob of some two to three thousand victims, which in its violence can be compared to the September massacres of 1792. The bells rang out to mobilize the mob, which, when it was tiring of the slaughter, was reanimated by a convenient miracle, for a withered thorn tree suddenly flowered in front of a statue of the Virgin in a cemetery in the centre of the area worst affected by killing and looting.[67]

The accounts written after the event by both Catholics and Protestants saw the massacre as premeditated. Protestant writers gave Coligny the

[65] For the synod see Kingdon, *Geneva and the French Protestant Movement* and J. R. Armogathe, 'Quelques réflexions sur la Confession de foi de la Rochelle', *BSHPF*, 1971.

[66] D. Nantua, 'Les Réformés aux Pays-Bas et les Huguenots spécialement à propos du synode d'Emden (1571)', *L'Amiral de Coligny*, 577–600.

[67] J. Estèbe, *Tocsin pour un massacre: La saison des Saint-Barthélemy* (Paris, 1968).

lineaments of a martyr, a role into which he fitted easily, since he had an austere piety and a Calvinist belief in the hand of Providence, enhanced by a gloomy predilection for the Book of Job. Coligny's policies were rejected by the court; Calvinism in France was rejected by the Paris mob. Michelet was the first to emphasize the phenomenon of crowd violence. He wrote of the clanging of the church bells, the orchestral background to the massacre, and saw behind the frenzy a ritual element in the violence, something 'de primitif et de sacré à la fois'.

The Massacre of St Bartholomew was not solely a Paris event; it began, as Michelet wrote, 'a season of massacres', which occurred in the early autumn in twelve towns in the provinces.[68] When couriers brought the news from Paris, massacres took place in the northern towns of Meaux, Orléans, Troyes, Bourges, and Saumur, all towns with Protestant histories. Lyon had its Vespers, while Rouen with its large Protestant minority had a four-day massacre with a total of 400 to 500 victims. The Jesuit, Émond Auger, preached an emotive sermon in Bordeaux, reproaching the authorities for their failure to match Paris and Orléans, and the mayor dutifully unleashed a mob which despatched 200 to 300 victims. Toulouse had a massacre with roughly the same number of victims, putting it in the same league as Bordeaux. In Toulouse, Protestant magistrates implicated in the abortive coup of 1562 were hanged in their red robes. In Bordeaux there had also been an attempted coup in 1562, and these urban vendettas played their part in the settling of accounts in 1572.[69]

The violence of St Bartholomew was not new but more intensive, for rioting and lynch-law had been pervasive from 1562. The Huguenots had desecrated churches and shrines, and defaced statues and paintings. Their preachers had thundered out the commands of that dangerous book, the Old Testament, urging them to overthrow altars, to hew down graven images, and to smite the inhabitants of idolatrous cities with the edge of the sword. Calvinists fulfilling these commands were engaged, as they saw it, on a work of re-education, and were unaware of, or indifferent to, the emotional shock aroused by crumbling the wafer, dragging the bones of revered saints around their home towns, beating up priests, or demolishing Nîmes cathedral. Calvinist tradition held that 'those of the Reformed religion made war only on images and altars, which did not bleed', whereas Catholics spilt blood, and there is some substance in the claim. Calvinists were concerned with the pollution that came from objects rather than from people, apart from their hatred of priests who dealt in magic. Secondly, since they were drawn from the more respectable sections of society, Calvinist crowds in France were less liable to loot and plunder on a major scale. Looting was a

[68] J. Michelet, *Histoire de France*, ix. 330–1 (Paris, 1876).

[69] Benedict, 126–8; Estèbe, 'Les Saint-Barthélemy', *L'Amiral de Coligny*; H. Hauser, 'Le père Émond Auger et le massacre à Bordeaux', *BSHPF*, 1911.

disciplined affair when methodical inventories were made of church plate, as at Millau in 1562.

The anger of the Catholic mob was aroused not by objects, apart from Genevan Bibles, but by people. Calvinists were seen as endangering traditional religion and local customs, thus putting the community at risk and making killing and desecration of corpses defensible. As in the case of the seventeenth century popular revolts, questions of instigation, connivance, or spontaneity arise, but whatever the answers, fanaticism remains a constant factor in these religious massacres. As in the case of race riots, the inhumanity and lynch-law of the mob arose from the sense of outrage, real or imaginary, felt by a community towards an alien body within it, which needed to be purged to restore health to the community.[70]

Resentments and fears had been built up over the years, and the clash of cultures raises the question of the nature and impact of the Calvinist consistory. This was the most original of Calvin's institutions and has been seen as giving birth to a new type of man, *l'homme protestant*, said to be Calvin's greatest creation for the modern world.[71] The consistory substituted for the old order of the confessional (a one-to-one relationship of priest and sinner) a community relationship of the congregation, within which ruled the consistory of elders and ministers, both elected. The French Discipline of 1559 defined the office of the elder as consisting in 'watching over the flock with the pastors to see that the people come to services, and reporting on scandals and faults. . .', and in being generally concerned with the order, upkeep, and government of the Church'.[72] The consistory was a new social unit, disruptive of the old communities, and one which introduced new behavioural patterns and prescribed a different code for Calvinists. But the consistories, even if disruptive, were not subversive of society, though this charge was easily made in the atmosphere of riot in the early 1560s, particularly in Guyenne.[73] There was a large overlap between the elders of a church and the notables of a town or a village. An investigation of the social background of 300 elders in thirteen localities in the Midi over forty years reveals that less than one-sixth of the elders were artisans or peasants and that the overwhelming majority was drawn from office-holders, lawyers, merchants, and in the country, from seigneurs.[74]

---

[70] For full discussions of mob violence, see Davis, 'The Rites of Violence', *op. cit.* 152–87, repr. from *P & P* (1973); J. Estèbe, *Tocsin pour un massacre*; J. Estèbe and N. Z. Davis, 'Debate', *P & P* (1975); Garrisson-Estèbe, 163–4; Richet, 770–4.

[71] Léonard, *Histoire générale*, i. 307; Le Roy Ladurie, *Paysans*, i. 356.

[72] Garrisson-Estèbe, 90.

[73] The charge that Calvinism was socially subversive was made by Monluc, the Lieutenant-Governor, and gained credence following the murder of the baron de Fumel on his estates in the valley of the Lot. Fears of Protestant disorder coincided with the temporizing policies of the crown and led in Bordeaux to Catholic notables forming a union to defend the interests of those who claimed their property had been damaged by Protestants. Powis, 193–4; Garrisson-Estèbe, 166–7.

[74] Ibid. 94.

This interlocking of the consistory with local institutions strengthened Huguenotism, but also narrowed its popular base, because re-election and co-option, as in municipal elections, led to oligarchy and helped to check the momentum of conversion.

The reformation of manners and morals, which it was the duty of the elders to enforce, made the consistory a highly successful medium of social control. But Calvin also saw the unit of the family as another vital element in his Church. The family reinforced the consistory but was also supposed to be a little church on its own.[75] The father was responsible for upholding standards of piety and behaviour. Calvinists advertised their separateness in their choice of Old Testament names for their children, which É. G. Léonard illustrated with the story of the peasant from the Tarn who, summoning his children to dinner, called: 'Abraham, Isaac and Jacob, come to the table at once. Joshua, close the door and if Joshua doesn't, then Melchizedek shall.'[76] Calvinists in the confines of family and consistory breathed a rarefied air and their rectitude drew them apart from the local community. Beza himself recorded with satisfaction that the carnival in Rouen disappeared when the Huguenots gained control in 1562.[77] Sir Walter Ralegh's view that the court of Elizabeth I 'glows and shines like rotten wood' was far more applicable to the court of Catherine de Médicis, which was especially luminous if compared with Coligny's household, which with its morning and evening prayers, sermons, and psalm-singing was the model of a Calvinist family unit. The country gentleman, Olivier de Serres from the Vivarais, who had been in Geneva, both practised and preached the virtues of piety, hard work, and efficiency, ruled his household as a patriarch, and in his standard work, *Le Théâtre d'Agriculture*, entitled a chapter 'De l'Office du Père de famille envers ses domestiques'.[78]

Calvinism was an ascetic religion and never more so than in the mid-sixteenth century when it spread with such explosive force across France. The appeal of austerity was very great in itself, but Calvinists also were fortified by their belief in being of the elect. In his *Méditations sur les Psaumes* d'Aubigné wrote that Heaven had chosen the Huguenots to be 'the soldiers and followers of the God of armies', and God had bestowed upon them as the price of his love 'their hatred of idolatry and of the devil's jargon used in the polluted sacrifice of the mass'.[79] Biblical themes, such as leaving Babylon, the deliverance from Egypt, the march across the Desert, and the conquest of Canaan, were transposed into contemporary reality. The Bible gave proof of the election of God's people in the events of the Flood and of

[75] Ibid. 318.
[76] Léonard, *L'Homme protestant*, 119 n. 2.
[77] Richet, 786, n. 44.
[78] Garrisson-Estèbe, 278, 331.
[79] D'Aubigné, 561.

the flight from Sodom, together with the accounts of Moses leading the Chosen People and Joshua taking his followers across the Jordan. Coligny's passage of the Loire in 1568 by an unexpected ford was immediately seen as another miraculous crossing of the Red Sea, and his troops knelt to sing Ps. 114.[80] A calamity was a call to repentance and St Bartholomew's Day became 'le jour du Seigneur', who had chastised his people. From 1572 the theme of the long march across the Desert was invoked more frequently as a morale-raiser for the elect on their way to the Promised Land.[81]

The elders were the guardians against lapses into the ways of Babylon. These lapses, such as dancing, games of chance, and sexual misconduct, incurred the disapprobation of the elders, who could ban the guilty from the Lord's Supper—which was celebrated four times a year—unless pardon for the fault had been sought by appearing before the consistory or the congregation. The consistory could employ moral sanctions only, but its strength lay in the weight of community disapproval and in the public avowal of transgressions in contrast to the privacy of the confessional. Heavy drinking was condemned, and so were taverns, which is interesting in view of the importance attached to the tavern in the dissemination of Protestantism.[82] Fathers were supposed to eat at home, for dining in taverns carried temptation. Women and girls might arouse unchaste thoughts and the flow of wine might lead to dancing, that most dangerous of social pastimes. Alcoholism comprised only 4 per cent of consistory offences in the Midi, far less than in the bibulous Palatinate, but even so the vineyard-workers of Languedoc were highly sensitive to the threat of falling consumption—as they are today to the import of Italian and Spanish wines.[83] In Montpellier for three Sundays running a mob of around 600 vineyard-workers, together with their wives and daughters, who according to a disapproving Calvinist had long hair falling over their bare shoulders, paraded with shouts of 'We will dance in spite of the Huguenots.' There was violence in Gaillac where the vineyard workers threw Calvinist notables into the Tarn to teach them to eat fish in Lent, while those unfortunate enough to surface were cut up on butchers' slabs.[84]

The Calvinist Establishment in the synods proscribed all 'dancing, mummery, games, and plays'. Huguenots opted out when they shunned carnivals and fêtes, for the denunciation of dancing as smacking of 'papist pollution' and lascivious struck at a traditional feature of urban and rural life. Colbert a century later was to instruct an intendant that one way of detecting the degree of rural poverty was to see whether the peasants danced

[80] P. Bourguet, 'L'Amiral de Coligny, chrétien réformé', L'Amiral de Coligny, 36–7.

[81] M. Soulié, 'Y a-t-il une "Symbolique du Désert"?', BSHPF (1975).

[82] Garrisson-Estèbe, (45, 293).

[83] Ibid. 294; J. Estèbe and B. Vogler, 'La genèse d'une société protestante; étude comparée de quelques registres consistoriaux languedociens et palatins vers 1600', Annales ESC (1976).

[84] Romier, Royaume, ii. 232; Le Roy Ladurie, Paysans, i. 344.

on Sundays and feast days.[85] In Calvinist-controlled towns the equivalent of the Welsh Sunday was imposed, with shops and taverns closed and the afternoon devoted to the exercise of the catechism.[86] The consistory in Montauban in 1597 asked the town council to forbid strolling players, whose performances would entail 'curiosity, debauchery, waste of time and money' and fail to edify. Prostitutes were naturally anathema and everywhere run out of town. Elders in Montauban showed the keenness of detectives in sniffing out moral lapses, especially dancing, and reliable members of the flock were sent off to listen for the tell-tale sounds of violins tuning up for parties.[87]

Twenty-one per cent of the regulations of provincial synods were concerned with feminine frivolity—towering hair-styles, plunging neck-lines, wide farthingales, and alluring cosmetics.[88] Sobriety in dress was expected, and de la Noue castigated both men and women for wearing fashionable clothes, encrusted with pearls and jewels like chalices, and involving debt and mortgages.[89] Obedience to her husband was considered a woman's first duty by Beza, who stressed what may perhaps be termed a Calvinist work-ethic for women. They were to engage tirelessly in household duties, but they were also enjoined to add to family earnings by engaging in crafts and selling the products. Modesty and chastity were the first of Calvinist feminine virtues, but in the matter of clothes it is reassuring to find the women of Nîmes so undisciplined that in 1592 the consistory took action. It ruled that a pastor and an elder should go from house to house to request women to dress modestly 'as was fitting for those who made a profession of serving God'.[90] The aristocratic Madame Duplessis-Mornay, whose husband, the reputed author of the *Vindiciae contra Tyrannos*, was in the service of Henri of Navarre, was barred from communion by the bourgeois consistory of Montauban because of her fashionably piled-up hair. This she refused to change, and appealed to the national synod, taking refuge in the argument that she had to obey her husband according to the Scriptures.[91] Various reasons have been suggested for the attraction of Calvinism for women, among others that they needed relief from the domestic round and that they discovered a new purpose and identity.[92] In matters of dress, however, that identity seems to have been found as much in revolt against the consistory as in submission to it.

---

[85] Romier, *Royaume*, ii. 230–1; *Correspondance administrative sous le règne de Louis XIV*, ed. G. B. Depping (Paris, 1855), iii. 85.

[86] Trocmé, 'La Rochelle', 152–4.

[87] Serr, 31–2.

[88] Garrisson-Estèbe, 306.

[89] Ibid. 191–2.

[90] Garrisson-Estèbe, 307.

[91] Ibid. 307–8. Mme Duplessis-Mornay was a sincere Calvinist, who had fled from Paris during the massacre of Saint Bartholomew with her three year-old child in spite of family pressure to abjure.

[92] Davis, 'City Women and Religious change', op. cit. 66–7, R. Mandrou, *Introduction a la France Moderne, 1500–1640*, (Paris, 1961) 117.

The consistory records of Ganges in the valley of the Hérault illustrate life in one of these little Genevas. Ganges had, besides a consistory, a political council, Calvinist magistrates, and a Calvinist seigneur, who was himself an elder. The reports of unseemly incidents alleged to have taken place behind orchard walls or in bedrooms have an affinity with malicious gossip-columns. The baron de Ganges was censured for attending dances, but respect for the social hierarchy was preserved, since he was not required to go to the consistory: the consistory went to his château. Although repentance and anxiety to be readmitted to the congregation were the norm, offenders could be recalcitrant. Pierre Boudon for a space of five years was forbidden to attend the Lord's Supper because of his affair with the delightfully named Étienne Amoureuse. He firmly refused to acknowledge the paternity of a son and even the liaison itself, nor was he prepared to appear before the consistory, saying that he would prefer to change his religion. Dancers came on to the streets of Ganges only at night and for greater anonymity wore masks to the fury of the elders, while in a nearby village a charivari at night turned into a murderous attack on the pastor who rashly emerged from his house to remonstrate.[93]

There were inevitable frictions, but the consistories were the foundation of the Calvinist system. The consistories gave the Calvinists their separate identity and strength, but also their alien and suspect status. The behavioural patterns imposed made the Huguenots a conspicuous minority, as the Moriscos were in Spain. The Massacre of St Bartholomew was a turning-point for the Huguenots. The momentum of conversion had already slowed down by 1570, but in Normandy, Picardy, and the Île-de-France the effects of the massacre were dramatic and permanent. Calvinism had struck deeper roots in the South and a major effect of the massacre was a sharper demarcation of an existing frontier. Some refugees crossed the dividing line, but the great majority proceeded to the traditional areas of the diaspora, England, the Netherlands, and Geneva, which was so crowded a reception centre that the clerk could not write down the names properly. Beza despaired, more especially because of the number of abjurations, writing at the close of 1572 that with the exception of the South, 'these have been and still are unbelievable'.[94] The massive abjurations in the North were caused both by the immediate shock and also by the cumulative effects of years of insecurity. The churches in Normandy were crowded out by those who abjured, for whom the Promised Land was now only a mirage in the desert. A cloth merchant of Paris, writing to two colleagues in Albi on business shortly after the massacre, reported that there had been 5,000 conversions already in the capital and urged them not to indulge in false

[93] M. Oudot de Dainville (see Further Reading), 468, 474.
[94] Garrisson-Estèbe, 71–2, 177; Benedict, ch. ix.

hopes when only abjuration would save their lives and keep their families from poverty.[95]

The immediate reaction to the massacre in the South was one of consternation. Beza was informed in September that the Calvinists in Nîmes, some 20,000, were planning a mass emigration to Geneva.[96] The Gascon nobles had suffered heavy losses, since, as clients of the d'Albrets, so many had gone to the royal wedding and been murdered in Paris. Leadership was lacking since Jacques de Crussol, the commander in western Languedoc and in Saintonge, had abjured to save his life, while Henri of Navarre and the Prince of Condé had also abjured and were in custody. In the temporary vacuum it was the towns and lesser nobility which rallied and which could mobilize for defence the more quickly because of the political councils and assemblies which had been a feature of Condé's wars. In Languedoc there had been heavy investment in church land, either put up for sale by the monarchy or expropriated by notables and nobles.[97] Calvinism was therefore an economic investment to be protected.

Resistance was also organized in the south-west. Consistory and municipality worked together in La Rochelle to withstand a royalist siege, contacted London for a loan, and in an address to Elizabeth I invoked Guyenne's past as an English province and recognized her as 'leur Reine souveraine et Princesse naturelle'. This was deplored by La Noue, governor of the town, but the precedent was set for the disastrous English alliance in 1626.[98] Montauban took steps to control the Garonne, and commando raids from Nîmes secured the Cévennes. De Thou was later to comment that the success of the Huguenots in the South after the murder of so many of their military leaders and the initial disarray was astonishing, for in less than a year they had re-established control, and without enlisting foreign aid.[99]

Crown efforts to recover control of the South were met by a Huguenot confederation, which included the provinces of Dauphiné, Languedoc, Guyenne, Gascony, Périgord, and Saintonge. The dominant provinces were Languedoc and Gascony with twin capitals at Nîmes and Montauban. The confederation never had solid control of the South given Calvinist failure to capture control of Bordeaux, Toulouse, and Marseille. Even so, this federal structure, the United Provinces of the Midi, gave a new coherence and a changed outlook to Huguenotism. The federation saw in the Midi the first attempt at coexistence, an empirical response to military needs and peaceable daily life. The governor of Languedoc, Montmorenci-Damville, a Catholic, anxious to carve out a sphere of influence for himself,

---

[95] Richet, 777, where the letter is printed in full.
[96] Geisendorf, 307.
[97] Le Roy Ladurie, *Paysans*, i. 360–71.
[98] Hauser, *De La Noue*, 50.
[99] Garrisson-Estèbe, 178–9.

needed the support of the Huguenots as much as they needed his. Nîmes had seen Protestant excesses in 1567, but there were no Catholic retaliations after the massacre in Paris, while in 1574 Damville summoned a mixed Assembly of Catholics and Protestants there, which had as President the vicomte de Paulin, a Huguenot.

What was the nature of this Huguenot federation? The anonymous diarist of Millau wrote a fictional account of an interview set in 1573 between the Queen Mother and a delegate from the federal Assembly of the South, which is evocative of hopes and dreams not far below the surface. The Queen Mother was told; 'You no longer have business with a prince, an admiral, or other great lords. You are now dealing with younger sons and poor gentlemen, or with a cobbler, a mason, a locksmith, or others of small estate, who will, Madame, take great pleasure in taking up arms and going to war.' De Thou wrote that the South constituted 'une nouvelle espèce de république' and Damville found the Huguenots, 'ennemis de toute noblesse', uncomfortable allies. This was the classic period of Huguenot monarchomach theories, of the *Vindiciae contra Tyrannos* and of the *Réveil-matin des Français*, which adumbrated a constitution that was translated into practice by the Assembly of Millau at the close of 1573.[100]

The basic unit was the town, while at the regional level there were assemblies of nobles and notables on the pattern of the provincial estates. Innovation came in the judicial and federal spheres. There were substituted for the *parlements*, the *chambres mi-parties*, another attempt at coexistence, while the *présidial* courts, those rivals of the *parlements* and hotbeds of Calvinism in Guyenne, were given wider jurisdiction. At the federal level there was a political assembly, composed of three representatives from each province, and endowed with regalian powers of government and taxation. Novelty lay in the appointment of a Protector: the Assembly of Millau in 1574 nominated the prince of Condé to the office, 'as a true judge of Israel elected by God', and in 1577 Henri of Navarre, no longer a prisoner of the court, replaced him.

There were inevitable tensions between nobility and notables, but war determined that the nobles reasserted themselves. Guerrilla units were always officered by nobles, even if civilian advisers were attached. Henri of Navarre, the so-called king of Gascony, found that the office of Protector resembled that of the first magistrate of a republic rather than that of an absolute monarch, though deputies at the Assembly of la Rochelle in 1588 talked of the tyranny of the Protector.

The state of Israel was never realized in practice. The Huguenot guerilla units indulged in pillage. In 1581 the diarist of Millau, who had taken pride in the measures adopted to protect its citizens, wrote that anyone going out to the fields was liable to be either murdered or taken prisoner, and that it

[100] Delumeau, 181; Garrisson-Estèbe, 209, 219–20.

was better to be dead than taken prisoner.[101] The Assembly of Millau had directed that ministers should be paid state stipends, but war made this impossible and ministers, as in Ganges, continued to squabble with their congregations over payment. The United Provinces of the Midi were a product of war, and their federal arrangements played a vital part both in maintaining the armies of Henri of Navarre in the field and in preserving a strong defensive base. The bastion of the South and the Huguenot political assemblies were key factors in extracting from Henri of Navarre, when he became king, the Edict of Nantes in 1598.

The Edict was hammered out over two years between Henry IV's government and a Huguenot Assembly representing the whole of France and not merely the South. In addition, the great Huguenot nobles brought pressure by refusing to fight with the royal armies and threatening to choose a new Protector. The final settlement produced what Léonard called 'a disadvantaged religious confession and a privileged social and political body'.[102] Liberty of conscience was accorded, but the vital right to have services was restricted to where there were churches in 1597. This acceptance of minority status was far removed from the triumphant hopes of the mid-sixteenth century. Yet that minority acquired privileged status. The four fortresses granted in 1570 were increased to over a hundred, ranging from important towns to fortified villages and castles, a reflection of the bargaining power of the nobility. Moreover, the Crown promised a subsidy towards the payment of the garrisons and the stipends of ministers. There was to be no discrimination against Protestants holding office, while the *chambres mi-parties* were retained and were to function side by side with the *parlements*. The Huguenots for their part agreed to pay tithes and to contribute towards the rebuilding of Catholic churches.

The Edict of Nantes introduced a dualism into France, which now contained both a Catholic state and a Protestant state. The king was a Catholic, but Henri IV was also Protector of the Protestant churches. The Protestant state had its political assemblies, its fortresses, and its delegates or ambassadors to represent its interests at court. It had also international standing, for the Protestant interest was a live factor in diplomacy in a Europe still haunted by the threat of Spanish domination. The question was whether this dualism was practicable and whether coexistence was workable. The English ambassador, Sir George Carew, in his perceptive account of France at this time said of Henri IV that 'the body of those of the reformed religion is a great thorn in his foot'; and that if force should be used against the Protestants they seemed determined to 'cantonize themselves in Guienne'. However, in Carew's view Henri's policy was to observe the Edict, to conciliate the Protestants by offering pensions and

---

[101] Garrisson-Estèbe, 216–17, 210–20.
[102] Léonard, *Le Protestant français*, 32.

offices to the most eminent among them, and to work for a union of the churches, or at least 'a common liturgy'.[103]

Henri IV himself had decided that Paris was worth a mass, and for some Huguenots so might a place or pension at the court, which is how that rigorous Huguenot, d'Aubigné, explained the conversions that followed Henri's abjuration in 1593, in itself unforgivable in his view. D'Aubigné's especial wrath was poured out upon 'le grand convertisseur', Jacques Du Perron, the son of a Calvinist minister and himself a convert, who had eased the path of Henri's conversion and been rewarded by becoming bishop of Évreux and a cardinal. He satirized Du Perron as an expert angler, who pulled in, among other fish, Nicolas de Harlay, seigneur de Sancy, who had hoped that his conversion would enable him to get ahead of Rosny (later Sully) in the race for office. Another was Palma Cayet, whose conversion made a sensation, since he was chaplain to Catherine de Bourbon, the king's sister, whose court in the Louvre was the main Protestant centre in Paris.[104] A reinvigorated Catholic church, infused with Counter-Reformation piety and zeal for proselytizing, put the Huguenots on the defensive, and whereas in the mid sixteenth century popular works of piety had poured in from Geneva, between the Edict of Nantes and the Peace of Alès there was a flood of conversion literature.[105] Conversion became fashionable, and for many it was combined with the emotive feelings of loyalty which the Bourbon monarchy of Henri IV evoked. When Tallemant Des Réaux described the conversion of his uncle, mayor of La Rochelle, he wrote aptly that 'il se fit catholique, ou du moins il fit profession de la religion du prince'.[106]

Yet Catholics felt disquiet. The Edict of Nantes had been forced upon the *parlements* and the court contained far too many Protestants. Sully, Henri's loyal servant and a firm, though not a pious, Huguenot, accumulated offices and utilized Protestant talent in the departments which he controlled. Among his chief auxiliaries in the Treasury were the four Arnauld brothers, of the family which later headed the Jansenist movement. In the king's immediate household, though he had a Jesuit confessor, Protestants clustered. The first gentleman of the bedchamber, Pierre de Beringhen, was a Protestant and so were the king's four doctors, who included Théodore Turquet de Mayerne, later to practise at the court of James I. Barthélemy de Laffemas became *contrôleur-général du commerce*, and it was he who invited Olivier de Serres to come to Paris and to introduce the silk industry there. Antoine de Montchrétien, later famous for his *Traicté de l'économie politique*, which advocated protectionist economics, was head of the iron

[103] *A Relation of the State of France under Henry IV in 1609*, ed. T. Birch (London, 1749), 441-2.
[104] D'Aubigné, *Confession catholique du sieur de Sancy*, Pléiade edn. 575-666; M. Yardeni, 'Ésoterisme, religion et histoire dans l'œuvre de Palma Cayet', *Rev. de l'histoire des religions*, 1981.
[105] L. Desgraves, 'Un aspect des controverses entre catholiques et protestants, les récits de conversion (1598-1628)', *Actes du XIIᵉ Colloque de Marseille, 1982* (Marseille, 1983), 89-111.
[106] *Historiettes* Pléiade edn., 1960, ii. 557.

industry, while royal patronage was given to the tapestry factory of the Gobelin family.[107]

These appointments illustrate how much talent there was to be tapped among the Huguenots, and nowhere is this more apparent than in the architectural sphere. Henri IV saw Paris as the stage setting for the Bourbon monarchy. He was the second creator of Fontainebleau; he extended the Louvre and the Tuileries, while he was also the patron of imaginative urban development in Paris. The painter Jacob Bunel and the sculptor Barthélemy Prieur, both Huguenots, worked in the Louvre, but Henri's spectacular success was to call upon a brilliant group of Calvinist architects originating from the little Protestant town of Verneuil-sur-Oise. He invited back to Paris the two Cerceau brothers, who had fled rather than go to mass, and employed their nephew, Salomon de Brosse, who in his turn recruited his brother-in-law, Charles Du Ry. The Calvinism of the sixteenth century is associated with austerity, but de Brosse designed magnificent palaces for the king and the aristocracy, using the classical orders and composing splendidly in mass, deriving much inspiration from Vignola, the creator of the Gesù, the prototype of Jesuit churches.

Marie de Médicis when regent chose de Brosse to be the architect for the Luxembourg Palace. He designed the gallery to house the paintings of Rubens, who had been commissioned to commemorate the achievements of Henri IV, and the resulting magnificence testifies to the successful collaboration between a Calvinist and a Catholic. De Brosse saw buildings and gardens as a unity, and at the Luxembourg he worked in association with Jacques Boyceau, a Calvinist noble from Saintonge who became under Henri IV *intendant des jardins du roi*. Le Vau, Le Brun, and Le Nôtre created Versailles; de Brosse, Rubens, and Boyceau created the Luxembourg—two Calvinists and a Catholic.

De Brosse was besieged with commissions for châteaux and prestigious hôtels in Paris, and he also worked for the Church, rightly earning acclaim for his classical façade of Saint-Gervais. The canons of Orléans, engaged on rebuilding their cathedral battered during the Religious Wars and wishing to modernize its Gothic fabric, choosing de Brosse in preference to the Jesuit architect, Martellange. Yet like the Cerceaus and the Du Rys, de Brosse remained firm in his Calvinism, and indeed a Geneva Bible was listed among his possessions after his death, while he was buried in the Protestant cemetery in the rue des Saints-Pères.[108]

The Huguenots of Paris had their church at Charenton, easy of access by river, which helps to explain the number who lived in the faubourg Saint-

[107] Léonard, *Le Protestant français*, 50–1.
[108] R. Coope, *Salomon de Brosse* (London, 1972); Menna Prestwich, 'Patronage and the Protestants in France: Architects and Painters', in J. Mesnard and R. Mousnier (eds.), *L'Âge d'or du mécénat, 1598–1601* (Paris, 1985).

Germain, known as 'little Geneva'. The temple at Charenton with its congregation of nobles, office-holders, architects, and craftsmen was practically an annexe of the court and shows not only coexistence but the assimilation of Huguenots on the cultural level. In 1623 de Brosse built a new temple at Charenton on the design of a Vitruvian basilica, for the first temple, the creation of his uncle, Jacques II du Cerceau, had been burned down in 1621 by a Paris mob. The event produced fears of a second St Bartholomew and Protestants left Paris. This time, however, it was not a case of Paris influencing the provinces, but of the provinces influencing Paris. The mob at Charenton was reacting to a Huguenot war south of the Loire, where Montauban was withstanding a royal siege.

The two religions remained largely estranged from each other in the provinces. There was constant friction over the application of the Edict of Nantes, especially over clause 27, which upheld the right of Calvinists to hold offices, but which the *parlements* applied restrictively.[109] In the Protestant towns the local councils and consistories were interdependent. La Rochelle had a proud record of civic achievement with its temple which accommodated 3,500, its public library, its printing press, its scholarships for ordinands to study at Saumur or abroad, but its consistory upheld the Discipline as strictly as did the elders of Montauban.[110] Nîmes had a tradition of coexistence since the time when Damville was governor and had an expositor in Anne Rulman, a Protestant lawyer and a professor at the Nîmes university. In a speech of welcome to the lieutenant-general of Languedoc in 1604 he spoke of the two religions being contrary in themselves but united in their love for the king, and a year later he spoke of a new Augustan age. Rulman was, however, a firm Calvinist, for he defended in the courts the third consul of Nîmes, charged with breaking the violin of a dancing-master newly arrived in the town, and he denounced dancing as the 'devil's pimp', because of the 'intimacies of contact' that it encouraged.[111]

Both confessions were aggressive and suspicious in Nîmes. In 1598 the diocese acquired a reforming bishop, Pierre de Valernod, who sent Jesuit missionaries into the Cévennes, established a Jesuit college in Nîmes, and began rebuilding a new cathedral in a city overwhelmingly Calvinist. His visitation of the western half of his diocese in 1611 revealed a trail of destruction as a result of the Religious Wars. Out of sixty-six churches, twenty-two were ruined, twenty-four were partially ruined, and of these five were in Protestant hands. Reconstruction and the reclaiming of churches and church land produced tension. Meanwhile the consistory stood for Huguenot values, deprecating mixed marriages and deploring the conversions which occurred in the upper echelons of Nîmes society. Despite these,

[109] R. Mousnier, *La Vénalité des offices sous Henri IV et Louis XIII* (2nd edn., Paris, 1971), 638–45.
[110] Trocmé, 'La Rochelle', 308, 304–5, 282, 274.
[111] R. Sauzet (see Further Reading), 171, 177.

Calvinism showed a vitality lacking in the North. In Nîmes, far from a fall in Huguenot numbers, there were 450 conversions from Catholicism in the first two decades of the seventeenth century. In Paris matters were different, but in Nîmes a goldsmith was reprimanded by the consistory for 'working on idols, images, and the equipment of the mass' and an apothecary was exhorted not to sell wax candles to Papists. The municipal hospital was run by a Protestant town council and the sick of both confessions were admitted, which led to a running battle between pastors and priests to capture the souls of the dying. In 1614 a *curé* going to administer the last rites to a converted shoemaker was chased away and kicked in the stomach (so that he nearly died) by the pastor, the Protestant wife, and angry neighbours.[112]

The crisis which set off the second cycle of religious wars resulted from Louis XIII's decision to apply the clauses of the Edict of Nantes to Béarn and to enforce Catholicism there. The Huguenots viewed his victory in Béarn as the shape of things to come and could organize resistance through their political assemblies. In 1621 the Assembly of La Rochelle divided France into eight circles, nominating a military governor chosen from the great nobility for each. The pattern of the past was being repeated, for Condé had been proclaimed Protector-General of the Churches of France, but now the prospective war was a defensive one, fought to preserve privileged minority status.

This second phase of the religious wars lasted intermittently for seven years, and the tenacious resistance can be attributed to the strength of Calvinist fervour in towns such as Montauban, La Rochelle, and Nîmes and to the leadership of the duc de Rohan. Rohan combined military and political skills and he evoked a loyalty which made him a folk-hero after his death. Those nobles chosen to lead the circles either refused their commands or rapidly defected and converted. Conformity paid more handsome dividends than rebellion, while the propaganda in favour of royal absolutism and non-resistance, not least that conducted by Calvinist ministers, had its effect. Gaspard de Coligny, governor in Lower Languedoc, declared for the king in 1623 and became a marshal of France. The duc de La Trémoille, a grandson of William of Orange, declared his apostasy when serving in the royal army before La Rochelle. The conversion of Lesdiguières, governor of Dauphiné and the friend of Henri IV, produced consternation, but he became Constable of France. Only Rohan responded to the Huguenot call and thus, as É.-G. Léonard said, saved the honour of French Protestantism. He was the obvious leader, since through his grandfather's marriage into the d'Albret family he was a second cousin of Henri IV and he had a claim to Béarn should Louis XIII have no male heirs. His younger brother, Soubise, devoted his energies to

---

[112] Ibid. 54–65, 72–3, 168, 184.

the defence of La Rochelle and Saintonge, while his formidable mother, Catherine de Parthenay, moved into La Rochelle during the siege of 1628 and became a Resistance heroine, stoically living on her meagre ration of bread and horsemeat.[113]

Rohan had international standing. He was the friend of Maurice of Nassau and the godfather of Charles I. The aid which had been secured in the sixteenth century from England and the Palatinate had been ineffective and damaging to the Huguenot cause. English intervention during the siege of La Rochelle was disastrous in every way. Rohan drew his strength from the towns of Languedoc, while the resistance of Montauban and, above all, of La Rochelle had an epic quality. Even so, there were divisions in the towns between magistrates and merchants, who looked to peace, and the artisans and shopkeepers, or in the case of La Rochelle the fishermen, who were militant Calvinists. Once La Rochelle fell the royal armies moved against the south, where the troops Rohan raised from the Cévennes did not compensate for localism and a failure of united resistance. The Peace of Alès in 1629 registered the fall of the United Provinces of the Midi and the end of the privileged political status of the Huguenot minority.

The questions raised at the outset of this essay should now be reconsidered. Had Calvinism, although its adherents comprised only 6 or 7 per cent of the population, remained so strong that, as Chaunu held, the Catholic future of France was not secured until the fall of La Rochelle in 1628? Or was Léonard right in contending that in the 1620s Rohan was fighting for a cause already lost? Here it is necessary to draw some simple distinctions. If 'the cause' is taken to mean the creation of a solidly Calvinist France—and it had meant this for the sixteenth-century Huguenots—then the cause had been lost by the time of the massacre of St Bartholomew at the latest, and probably as early as 1562. Control of Paris and of France north of the Loire was essential to the cause in this sense. But if 'the cause' is understood to mean the 'kingdom of the south', the continued existence of a Huguenot minority with the political and military strength to enforce its acceptance and guarantee its security, this was not lost until the Peace of Alès; and was, most unexpectedly, to be revived over seventy years later by the Camisards. For Léonard, taking a general view of France, the Peace of Alès was followed by a long period of 'le protestantisme en léthargie'.[114] But the most recent study of the diocese of Nîmes gives convincing evidence in support of the conclusion that there at least 'après 1629, la Réforme resta conquérante'.[115] If 'the cause' is taken in a third sense to mean the

---

[113] For a detailed study of Rohan see J. A. Clarke (see Further Reading). See too J. Pannier, L'Église Réformée de Paris sous Louis XIII (see Further Reading), 579, 567–77; Léonard, 'Le protestantisme français', 166.

[114] Léonard, ii. 331.

[115] Sauzet, 179, 255.

continued presence within French society of men and women with strong Calvinist convictions, this survived both the first and the second of the Wars of Religion and was to confute the calculations of the framers of the Revocation of the Edict of Nantes.

Finally it may be asked how much the French Huguenots had owed to international Calvinism during this period. An adequate answer to this large and complex question cannot be given in a few sentences. It appears, however, that while the indebtedness of the Huguenots to Geneva during the years of Calvin's dominance there (1541–64) is undoubted, it has sometimes been exaggerated. The first national synod of the French Reformed Church was held in Paris in 1559, while it was only in that year that the Academy of Geneva was founded. Calvin was urging caution and restraint on the Huguenots during the crucial years in which they believed themselves to be moving to complete victory in France. By 1629 the Huguenot movement was one which in two senses had been 'made in France'. Calvin and Beza had been born and educated in France; and the achievements of the Huguenots, not least in the fields of letters, learning, and the arts, cannot be regarded merely or mainly as the product of docile obedience to directives from Geneva.

Further Reading

Basic books

Delumeau, J., *Naissance et affirmation de la Réforme* (Paris, 1965).
Garrisson-Estèbe, J., *Protestants du Midi, 1559–1598* (Toulouse, 1980).
Imbart de La Tour, P., *Origines de la Réforme*, iii. (Paris, 1916); iv. (Paris, 1935).
Léonard, É. G., *Histoire générale du protestantisme* (2 vols., Paris, 1961; tr., London, 1967).
Romier, L., *Le Royaume de Catherine de Médicis: La France à la veille des guerres de religion* (2 vols., Paris, 1925).

Books dealing with particular regions or problems

L'Amiral de Coligny et son temps (Supplement to *BHSPF*, 1974).
Benedict, P., *Rouen during the Wars of Religion* (Cambridge, 1981).
Clarke, J. A., *Huguenot Warrior: the Life and Times of Henri de Rohan, 1579–1638* (The Hague, 1966).
Davis, N. Z., *Society and Culture in Early Modern France* (London, 1975).
Estèbe, J., *Tocsin pour un massacre: La saison des Saint-Barthélemy* (Paris, 1968).
Hauser, H., *Études sur la Réforme française* (Paris, 1909).
—— *La Naissance du protestantisme* (Paris, 1940).
Kingdon, R. M. *Geneva and the Coming of the Wars of Religion in France 1555–1563* (Geneva, 1956).
—— *Geneva and the French Protestant Movement 1564–1572* (Geneva, 1967).
Le Roy Ladurie, E., *Les Paysans de Languedoc*, i. 3 (Paris, 1966).

—— 'Huguenots contre papistes', in P. Wolff (ed.), *Histoire de Languedoc* (Toulouse, 1967), ch. 3.

Pannier, J., *L'Église réformée de Paris sous Henri IV* (Paris, 1911).

—— *L'Église réformée de Paris sous Louis XIII de 1611 à 1629 environ* (Paris, 1932).

Parker, D., *La Rochelle and the French Monarchy: Conflict and Order in Seventeenth-Century France* (London, 1980).

Salmon, J. H. M., *Society in Crisis: France in the Sixteenth Century* (London, 1975).

Sauzet, R., *Contre-Réforme et Réforme catholique en Bas-Languedoc: Le diocèse de Nîmes au XVIIᵉ siècle* (Paris, 1979).

Wolff, P. (ed.), *Histoire des Protestants en France* (Toulouse, 1977), essays 1–3.

Articles

Chaunu, P., 'Le XVIIᵉ siècle religieux. Réflexions préalables', *Annales ESC* (1967).

Léonard, É. G., 'Le protestantisme français au XVIIᵉ siècle', *Rev. hist.* 1948.

Molinier, A., 'Aux origines de la Réformation cévenole', *Annales ESC* (1984).

Richet, D., 'Les conflits religieux à Paris dans la seconde moitié du XVIᵉ siècle', *Annales ESC* (1977).

Trocmé, E., 'Une révolution mal conduite', *Rev. d'hist. et de philosophie religieuses* (1959).

Oudot de Dainville, M., 'Le consistoire de Ganges à la fin du XVIᵉ siècle', *Rev. d'hist. de l'Église de France*, (1932).

In addition, the admirably indexed *Bulletin de la Société de l'Histoire du Protestantisme Français* (*BSHPF*) is an absolute mine of information.

IV

The Ambivalent Face of Calvinism in the Netherlands, 1561–1618

ALASTAIR DUKE

Seeing it has pleased the Lord God to set apart from the whole human race and to gather together . . . a people and a church through the preaching of the Word of God . . . He will grant to that church quite undeservedly (as the beloved bride of His son Jesus Christ, not having spot or wrinkle) eternal salvation and blessed everlasting life.

> From the preamble to the 'Acta van de classis Zuid-Beveland, 1579–1581',
> ed. J. P. van Dooren, in *De nationale synode te Middelburg in 1581. Calvinisme
> in opbouw in de noordelijke en zuidelijke Nederlanden* (Middelburg, 1981), 218.

But in my opinion . . . the evangelical net should be cast as far and as widely as possible in order that many people may be gathered to the Lord.

> From a speech made by Cornelis Pieterszoon Hooft on 16 August 1617.
> *Memoriën en adviezen van Cornelis Pietersz. Hooft* (Utrecht, 1871), 202.

WHEN the States of Holland finally outlawed the mass in March 1581, shortly before the States-General declared that Philip II had forfeited his sovereignty over the United Netherlands, only a small fraction of that province professed the Reformed faith. In 1587 the provincial States, incensed by the pulpit tirades directed against the magistrats, pointedly reminded some leading ministers that fewer than one in ten Hollanders belonged to the Reformed Church.[1] Though support for the new religion grew, the French ambassador to the United Provinces reported in 1600 that Roman Catholics still formed the majority of the population,[2] and less than two years before the national synod of Dort, Oldenbarnevelt, the Advocate of Holland, informed Dudley Carleton, the English diplomat, that the Protestants made up only one-third of the population: 'la plus saine et plus riche partie' had remained loyal to the Catholic Church.[3]

Recent local studies have confirmed the accuracy of these contemporary estimates, although the religious complexion varied greatly between one

---

[1] P. Bor, *Oorsprongk, begin ende vervolgh der nederlantscher oorlogen*, ii (Amsterdam, 1679), 975–6.
[2] J. Briels, *De nederlandse emigratie, 1572–1630* (Haarlem, 1978), 98 n. 13.
[3] J. den Tex, *Oldenbarnevelt*, (see Further Reading), ii. 574.

town and another. By comparing the sporadic information about the membership of some Reformed congregations in the early seventeenth century with the census of 1622 we can discover the relative strength of the Calvinist community in a few towns. At Den Briel, a small fishing-port at the mouth of the Maas, about one-fifth of the entire population belonged to the Reformed church at this time, while at Enkhuizen, then at the peak of its prosperity with almost 21,000 inhabitants, the Reformed church had a membership of 3,000.[4] At Alkmaar, however, the Calvinists accounted for a meagre 5 per cent of the 12,000 townspeople.[5] Despite the continued expansion of the towns in the province of Holland, in 1622 almost half the population still lived in the countryside. Here the disparities between the Calvinist communities were even more striking. In a handful of villages the Reformed church drew considerable support, while in many others only three or four came to the Lord's Supper, the focal point of Reformed worship. For a dozen villages, with a total population of over 12,000 in 1622, the number of Reformed members is known from casual entries made between 1590 and 1620. Taking the figure closest to 1622, we find a total of 700 Calvinists, or almost 6 per cent of the entire population.[6]

Outside Holland and Zeeland support for the Reformed church grew even more slowly. Catholic services ceased, at least officially, in June 1580 in the adjoining province of Utrecht, yet returns from the rural parishes in 1606 show that the Reformed churches had made little headway. In that year forty-one ministers from the countryside reported to the provincial synod on the state of religion in their parishes. In only five villages had the new religion secured a measure of popular support, and in only half the parishes had the Lord's Supper been held, often attended by fewer than a dozen communicants.[7] Calvinist *predikanten* strove to convince their bemused parishioners of the superior virtues of metrical psalm-singing, the Heidelberg catechism, and public baptisms. But they continued to display a wayward affection for pilgrimages, crucifixes, and votive offerings. To keep the devil at bay during thunderstorms they still resorted to the 'superstitious' ringing of the church bells. If it was difficult to build

[4] A. Th. van Deursen, *Bavianen en slijkgeuzen* (see Further Reading), 133.

[5] H. E. van Gelder, 'Hervorming en hervormden te Alkmaar' in *Alkmaarse opstellen* (Alkmaar, 1960), 67. First published in *Oud-Holland*, 40 (1922). This figure omits the Remonstrants who formed a separate congregation.

[6] Derived from data in van Deursen, *Bavianen*, 132.

[7] For the religious condition in the countryside of Utrecht see 'Visitatie der kerken ten platten lande in het sticht van Utrecht ten jare 1593', *Bijdragen en mededeelingen van het Historisch Genootschap*, 7 (1884), 186–267; J. P. van Dooren, 'Kerkelijke toestanden in de provincie Utrecht omstreeks 1600', *Nederlands archief voor kerkgeschiedenis*, n.s. 49 (1969), 183–93; *Acta der provinciale en particuliere synoden . . . 1572–1620*, ed. J. Reitsma and S. D. van Veen, vi (Groningen, 1897), 294–328. Even in East Friesland, where the ruler had not opposed Protestantism, the Reformed church reported in 1576 that in many villages the Lord's Supper was never or only rarely held, and then with as few as four or five communicants, *Die evangelischen Kirchenordnungen des XVI. Jahrhunderts*, vii *Niedersachsen*, ed. E. Sehling (Tübingen, 1963), 437.

Jerusalem in Amsterdam, it was still more difficult to win the inhabitants in the remoter parts of northern Brabant to 'the pure doctrine'. Here the ministers, often from Holland, appeared to the overwhelmingly Catholic villagers as carpet-baggers, their earliest congregations composed of deserters and opportunists.[8] Sometimes the task exhausted the patience of the most diligent minister. In 1588 Ds. Johannes Hartmanni left his charge at Heusden, a fortified town on the Maas, because he had become so discouraged by the godless conduct of its inhabitants and their 'great contempt for the Word of God'. Hartmanni moved to a village in south Holland, but though it is not known how he fared there, the correspondence of a *predikant* in the neighbourhood, with its litany of complaints about the disregard for the sabbath and fast-days and the insolence of the papists, suggests that he would find himself once more casting his pearls before swine.[9]

Scholars of the Reformation in Germany and England have recently discovered that even with the backing of the prince the inhabitants in these countries accepted Protestantism slowly, and then only partially. But as long ago as 1930 the late Pieter Geyl alerted Dutch historians to the 'slow reformation', when he drew attention to the tardy reception of Calvinism in rural Utrecht and the lack of enthusiasm for the Sea Beggars in the towns of Holland in 1572.[10] At one stroke Geyl disposed of the myth that the Dutch had embraced Calvinism spontaneously: insofar as they adopted the Reformed religion, they did so under duress; in other words, they had been 'Protestantized'. L. J. Rogier (1894–1974), the foremost historian of Dutch Catholicism, demonstrated the resilience of the old church by combining the evidence from the Reformed synods with the returns made by missionary priests.[11] The population in large parts of the Republic, especially in the eastern Netherlands and in the 'conquered' lands of the Generality in the south, but also in parts of Holland itself had remained loyal to the Catholic church throughout the period of the Calvinist ascendancy. The first ministers in most villages resembled, in Rogier's vivid phrase, 'generals without an army'.[12] By establishing the continuity of the Catholic tradition, Rogier subtly shifted the emphasis of the debate on the Reformation. The successes achieved by the Calvinists were attributed to the intervention of a particular set of circumstances. Only where the

---

[8] The exceptionally well-documented historical novel by A. Roothaert, *Die verkeerde weereldt* (Utrecht, n.d.) gives an evocative account of the religious tensions in the Peelland of north Brabant.

[9] G. Hamoen, *Het begin van de reformatie in de ring Heusden* (Heusden, 1980), 16; L. Knappert, 'Stukken uit den stichtingstijd der Nederlandsch Hervormde Kerk', *Nederlandsch archief voor kerkgeschiedenis*, n.s. 7 (1910), 246–61.

[10] P. Geyl, 'De protestantisering van Noord-Nederland', *Leiding*, 1 (1930), 111–23; the substance of this article appears in his *History of the Low Countries: Episodes and Problems* (London, 1964), 32–42.

[11] L. J. Rogier (see Further Reading).

[12] Ibid., i. 442.

misconduct of the late medieval clergy had brought the Church into local disrepute, where the civil authorities staunchly supported the new religion after 1572, or where the Catholic cure of souls had been interrupted as a result of the fighting for a prolonged period did the course of 'Protestantization' run smoothly.[13]

Rogier's history of Dutch Catholicism in the early modern period first appeared almost forty years ago, but the discussion he provoked continues, though less stridently. In two respects our understanding of the Reformation in the Low Countries has changed significantly. Historians no longer write about the Reformation there as though it were a three-stage rocket, with distinct Lutheran, Anabaptist, and Calvinist phases. The pluriform character of both Catholicism and Reformed Protestantism is better understood, while the importance of the middle groups, the *politiques*, the *neutrales* as they were sometimes known, is generally recognized.[14] Secondly, the support given to the Reformed by the provincial States and the magistracies appears to have been rather less whole-hearted than Rogier supposed. In so far as these had a coherent religious policy, it stemmed from their fear of Spain (and therefore their concern not to drive Dutch Catholics into association with the enemy), their wish to maintain harmony in the local community, and their understanding of the demands of commerce. The Catholic religion was considered politically dangerous, whereas to the Reformed synods 'popery' was idolatrous, to be abolished lock, stock, and barrel. In practice the impact of the ostensibly repressive and numerous anti-Catholic edicts and ordinances was blunted by the connivance of those in authority. These were less concerned to further the Calvinization of Dutch society, than to render Dutch Catholicism politically docile.[15] But neither of these revisions has invalidated Rogier's conclusion that in the northern Netherlands, at least, the Calvinist churches originally lacked popular support.

No student of the Dutch Reformation would dissent from this conclusion: the evidence for the small size and slow growth of the early Reformed congregations is unassailable. There is, however, less agreement about the reasons for the sluggish response to Calvinism. For many historians the failures of the Reformed church stem from the continuing vitality of the traditional forms of piety. In this respect the evidence from the rural parts speaks eloquently. Then, too, we should not forget that the fluctuating fortunes of the rebel provinces in their war with Spain may well have deterred many from entering into membership of the Reformed church. As late as 1629 the Imperialist army under Montecuculi invaded

[13] Ibid., i. 444.

[14] The importance of the middle groups is well illustrated by J. J. Woltjer, 'De vrede-makers', *Tijdschrift voor geschiedenis*, 89 (1976), 299–321.

[15] O. J. de Jong, 'Is Nederland geprotestantiseerd?' *Rondom het Woord*, 9 (1967), 65–7.

the heart of the Republic: Catholic worship was restored at Amersfoort and Holland itself threatened.

But an important, and rather neglected, obstacle to the rapid growth of the Reformed churches in the northern Netherlands was self-imposed, for the Dutch Calvinists insisted that access to Communion should be restricted to those who had placed themselves under the 'discipline of Christ'. In this way they drew a distinction between 'those of the Church' and the 'children of the world'.[16] And the patriotism of the diehard Calvinist was tempered by his conviction that the cause of the Gospel should take precedence over 'the restoration of the Netherlands'. As Gaspar van der Heyden, who had been the first Reformed minister at Antwerp, put it in a letter to a colleague in 1573, 'what profits us the possession of many towns and walled places, if Jerusalem be not built there, for that is more pleasing to the Lord than all Jacob's dwellings'.[17]

By then the Reformation in the Low Countries had been in ferment for fifty years. The protracted gestation of Dutch Protestantism affected the subsequent development of the Reformed churches in ways which were still apparent in the early seventeenth century. To begin with, the evangelicals in the Low Countries drew their inspiration from Germany. Without question the *auctor intellectualis* here, as elsewhere, was Luther.[18] In the 1520s evangelicals in the Netherlands had no quarrel with Luther, the Wittenberger, whose eucharistic theology was still evolving.[19] Support for the new doctrines came above all from the *mediocriter litterati*—the clerics, schoolmasters, printers, and skilled craftsmen. Such men flocked to Wittenberg to hear Luther, while at home they found spiritual comfort from reading his works, as well as others by lesser-known German Evangelicals, including Urbanus Rhegius, Otto Brunfels, and Caspar Huberinus. But Charles V's hostility to the new ideas led in the Netherlands to the savage repression of their proponents. As a result the evangelical movements in Germany and the Low Countries began to draw apart in the 1530s and 1540s.

After the Peasants' War, which had gravely compromised the Reformation, the evangelical theologians and jurists in Germany drew up the church orders, catechisms, and liturgies in order to ensure a measure of

---

[16] From chronicle of the Groninger Calvinist Abel Eppens, cited by W. Bergsma, 'Zestiende-eeuwse godsdienstig pluriformiteit. Overwegingen naar aanleiding van Abel Eppens', *Historisch bewogen. Opstellen over de radicale reformatie . . . aangeboden aan Prof. dr. A. F. Mellink* (Groningen, 1984), 9.

[17] M. F. van Lennep, *Gaspar van der Heyden, 1530–1586* (Amsterdam, 1884), 208.

[18] C. Ch. G. Visser, *Luther's geschriften in de Nederlanden tot 1546* (Assen, 1969). Andrew Johnston, who is preparing a Ph.D thesis for the University of Southampton on early Dutch evangelical writing has been able to show that this debt to Luther was even greater than has been supposed. I wish to acknowledge his help in this field.

[19] Explicit denials of the Real Presence among evangelicals in the Low Countries do not occur before 1525, see J. Trapman, 'Le rôle des "sacramentaires" des origines de la réforme jusqu'en 1530 aux Pays-Bas', *Nederlands archief voor kerkgeschiedenis*, 63 (1983), 1–24.

doctrinal stability and institutional permanence. In this way Luther's religious revolution was secured against the Romanists, but equally against the blandishments of the *Schwärmer* and the *Sakramentslästerer*, as the Anabaptists and the Zwinglians were known. Eucharistic theology among German evangelicals came to be defined by the standard of the *Confessio Augustana* and this, in turn, ensured adherence to Luther's emphasis on the Real Presence. In this process the Schmalkaldic League, which the evangelical princes set up in 1531 in self-defence against the emperor, played some part. Subscription to the Augsburg Confession was not required by the members, but the League's domination by the Lutheran princes and the dependence of the south German cities, which had previously been influenced by Zwingli, on their protection made it difficult for them to maintain their distinctive theology. The religious peace of Augsburg (1555) sealed the Lutheran triumph in Germany by denying recognition to Reformed Protestantism. But in the Habsburg Netherlands, where the religious agreements reached in Germany had no legal validity, Lutheranism had no such entrée. This may explain why, despite Luther's immense influence, his eucharistic theology seems to have aroused little or no interest amongst Dutch evangelicals.[20]

Moreover, as Lutheranism edged towards respectability in the Empire, orthodox Lutherans found it hard to minister to the 'good Christians' living 'under the cross' in the Low Countries. As early as 1531 Luther had apparently warned evangelicals at Antwerp not to meet in secret assemblies.[21] However, the estrangement between Protestants in Germany and the Low Countries only became obvious in the early 1550s, with the outbreak of the second sacramentarian controversy. The rift came to light when the Lutherans of north Germany pointedly refused hospitality during the winter of 1553–4 to a company of Reformed Protestants from the Netherlands, who had been in exile at London until the accession of Mary Tudor caused them to leave. Between the colloquy of Marburg in 1529 and the religious peace of Augsburg the Reformation in the Low Countries slipped out of the Lutheran orbit. When the sacramentarian controversy broke out again the Dutch evangelicals found themselves in opposition to leading Lutheran spokesmen such as Westphal. And when in 1566 the Lutherans did organize a church at Antwerp, they brought in German theologians, who provided the congregation with a church order and liturgy based on German models. Confessional Lutheranism consequently appeared to be an exotic growth in the Low Countries.

Evangelicals who abhorred the Roman church as the abode of Antichrist were bound, for salvation's sake, to withdraw from this 'congregation of evil-doers'. By 1531 the previously informal conventicles had begun among

---

[20] J. W. Pont, *Geschiedenis van het lutheranisme in de Nederlanden tot 1618* (Haarlem, 1911), 41.
[21] Ibid., 42–3, 330.

the Anabaptists at Amsterdam to acquire the features of a gathered church. As well as reading the Scripture, they commemorated the Lord's Supper,[22] and deacons dispensed alms. Moreover, those admitted to baptism first promised not to go to mass, or to indulge in drinking or gossiping. By baptism they bid farewell to the world, including the Roman church, and entered the covenant; they therefore called themselves 'covenanters'.[23]

The Dutch Anabaptists defined the church as a voluntary fellowship of holy beings, 'an assembly of the righteous', as Menno Simons said,[24] at odds with the world. This notion of the church as a remnant in conflict with the forces of Antichrist chimed with their own experience as a persecuted minority and gave meaning to their present tribulation. Their sufferings put their faith to the test: as a result the saints would be purified and the dross purged.[25] But the Anabaptists did not rely only on the external instrument of persecution in order to keep holy the congregation of God. Discipline was also necessary. 'As a city without walls and gates, or as a field without ditches or fences,' wrote Menno, 'so also is a church which has not the apostolic exclusion or ban.'[26] Following in the wake of the Swiss Brethren, the Dutch Anabaptists insisted that 'without discipline there could be no church'.[27] At first they used excommunication to bring the sinner to repentance, but before long their concern shifted to the preservation of the congregation. Both Menno Simons and Dirk Philips yearned to bring about the church 'having no spot or wrinkle' and discipline was indispensable for this purpose.[28] The rigorists among them went so far as to demand that in order to keep the congregation unblemished the excommunicant should be shunned even by his spouse.[29]

The Anabaptists chided the magisterial reformers for the lax discipline in their churches. Among the Reformed this reproach did not pass unheeded. The Polish Reformer John à Lasco responded, when he was superintendent of the evangelical church in East Friesland, to the Anabaptists' complaint about the absence of discipline in the territorial church by appointing laymen in 1544 to oversee the conduct of the people.[30] In the Low Countries the Anabaptists remained a thorn in the flesh of the Reformed throughout the sixteenth century and beyond. Disaffected Calvinists, offended by the

[22] A. Mellink, *Amsterdam en de wederdopers in de zestiende eeuw* (Nijmegen, 1978), 21.

[23] G. Grosheide, *Bijdrage tot de geschiedenis der anabaptisten in Amsterdam* (Hilversum, 1938), 95. The religious dissidents distinguished themselves between 'covenanters' and 'evangelicals'. J. G. de Hoop Scheffer, *Geschiedenis der kerkhervorming in Nederland van haar ontstaan tot 1531* (Amsterdam, 1873), 110.

[24] Menno Simons, *Complete Writings* (Scottdale, Pa., 1956), 234.

[25] W. E. Keeney, *Dutch Anabaptist Thought and Practice, 1539–1564* (Nieuwkoop, 1968), 182.

[26] Simons, *Complete Writings*, 962.

[27] K. R. Davis, 'No discipline, no church: an Anabaptist contribution to the Reformed tradition', *Sixteenth Century Journal*, 13 (1982), 45–9.

[28] Keeney, *Dutch Anabaptist Thought*, 150.

[29] Ibid. 163–5.

[30] A. van Ginkel (see Further Reading), 164.

'disorderly conduct . . . and the lax discipline' in their own ranks, might well be drawn to the gathered Anabaptist congregations.[31] Theologians and church historians have remarked on the affinities between the Calvinist and Anabaptist doctrine of the church.[32] But as the Anabaptists made almost no headway in the French-speaking world, the Calvinists there were not confronted in practice with this challenge; by contrast, in the Netherlands the Anabaptists' reputation for virtuous living put the Reformed on their mettle. In this respect the presence of the Anabaptists probably reinforced the sectarian tendencies latent in Dutch Calvinism.

On the other hand, the disintegration of Dutch Anabaptism after 1555 into a host of splinter congregations served as a warning of what might happen if authority depended on the subjective judgement of strong-willed leaders. The first Dutch Anabaptist confession of faith was not drawn up until 1577. With this example before them the Dutch Reformed churches were perhaps more willing to be bound by the presbyterian system of church government than were the French churches. Certainly the violent quarrel between the presbyterian and congregationalist parties which troubled the French Reformed church in the decade before the massacre of St Bartholomew seems not to have greatly affected the Calvinists in the Low Countries.[33] But the Reformed theologians working in the Low Countries were obliged to repudiate explicitly certain doctrines characteristic of the Dutch Anabaptists. The debate held at Wismar between Martin Micronius and Menno Simons in 1554 on the Incarnation inaugurated a polemic which was to be pursued in formal disputations and in doctrinal refutations for the rest of the century.[34] This preoccupation with the Anabaptists sets the Netherlands Confession of Faith apart from the French or Scots Confessions. The authors of the Netherlands Confession condemned the teaching of the Anabaptists on the Incarnation, baptism, and the civil powers.[35] In matters both of doctrine and discipline the radical Reformation provoked a sharp response from the Reformed churches in the Netherlands and so indirectly exerted an influence on the character of Dutch Calvinism.

[31] A. C. Duke and R. L. Jones, 'Towards a Reformed Polity in Holland, 1572–1578', *Tijdschrift voor geschiedenis*, (1976), 89, 384; A. Th. van Deursen *Het kopergeld van de Gouden Eeuw* iv. *Hel en hemel* (Assen, 1980) 118; J. H. Wessel, *De leerstellige strijd tusschen nederlandsche gereformeerden en doopsgezinden in de zestiende eeuw* (Assen, 1945), 22–9.

[32] See esp. W. Balke, *Calvijn en de doperse radikalen* (Amsterdam, 1973); English tr. *Calvin and the Anabaptist Radicals* (Grand Rapids, 1982).

[33] R. M. Kingdon, *Geneva and the Consolidation of the French Protestant Movement, 1564–1572* (Geneva, 1967), 62–137; Kingdon's suggestion that synodal government had its critics among Netherlands Protestants at this time receives some support from W. van 't Spijker, 'Stromingen onder de reformatorische gezinden te Emden' in D. Nauta *et al.* (eds.), *De synode van Emden, 1571–1971* (Kampen, 1971), 63–6. However, the main attack on synods came from the Erastians, not from the 'congregationalists'.

[34] Wessel, *Leerstellige strijd.*

[35] J. N. Bakhuizen van den Brink (see Further Reading) arts. XVIII, XXXIV, XXXVI.

Apart from the Anabaptists, the evangelicals in the Low Countries did not begin to form counter-churches until the mid-sixteenth century. To be sure, they denounced certain doctrines of the Church, and some engaged in blatantly anti-Catholic acts. But the sporadic attacks on the clergy and on the objects of Catholic ritual were carried out by isolated individuals, whereas the iconoclastic riots of 1566 were concerted by the hedge-preachers and the consistories. Most evangelicals supplemented their attendance at mass by reading scriptures and edifying literature, usually of a Lutheran provenance, at home and in conventicles, where the religious issues of the day were discussed. Often evangelically minded priests led these gatherings, while continuing to preach in the churches. Though eucharistic theology was discussed, the sacraments were almost certainly not administered, nor was there any sort of organization beyond a rudimentary common chest to relieve those in need in their circle.[36]

The transition from dissent within the Church to open schism accelerated in the 1540s. The colloquy at Regensburg (1541) seems to have precipitated a debate in evangelical circles about the status of the Roman church. Evidently the counsel of Capito, one of the Strasburg reformers, to the effect that evangelical Christians should not quit the Roman church for all its defects, circulated at this time in the northern Netherlands.[37] Calvin, on the other hand, regarded the mass as an abomination. He therefore advised evangelicals dwelling 'in the midst of Papists' either to withdraw completely from idolatry (thereby risking persecution) or to leave for some place where the gospel was openly professed. In 1543 Calvin's *Petit traicté* brought consternation to evangelicals at Tournai and elsewhere in the Walloon provinces.[38] For the next generation this problem continued to exercise evangelicals in the Low Countries. Around 1550 à Lasco wrote in much the same vein: Christians might only go to mass if they were willing to bear witness there to their faith![39] Anguished Protestants in Holland asked the church at Emden in 1558 whether they might attend 'Papist sermons' while 'the brethren' from Middelburg sought guidance from the Dutch stranger-church at London a few years later.[40] Usually they were warned against making any compromises. To fortify their resolve the heroic

[36] The evangelicals at Tournai had such a 'boette' by 1531; G. Moreau, *Histoire* (see Further Reading), 70 n. 1.

[37] P. Fraenkel, 'Bucer's Memorandum of 1541 and a "Lettera nicodemitica" of Capito's', *BHR* 36 (1974), 575–6.

[38] Moreau, *Histoire*, 90–1. Significantly this was the first of Calvin's writings to be translated into English and Dutch and one of the earliest to be translated into Italian.

[39] The Latin version had been written by August 1550. *De fugiendis papatus illicitis sacris* appeared in Dutch in 1557. The French text may be found in F. Droz, 'Musculus, Poullain et les temporiseurs' in *Chemins de l'hérésie*, i (Geneva, 1970), 234–47. Bertrand le Blas (1554) and Hans Tuscaens (1566) caused a sensation by desecrating the host at mass!

[40] Emden, Archiv der Evangelisch-Reformierten Gemeinde 329/1, 18 Apr. 1558; *Kerkeraads-protocollen der nederduitsche vluchtelingen-kerk te Londen, 1560–1563*, ed. A. A. van Schelven (Amsterdam, 1921), 224.

conduct of the martyrs was set before them in Micronius' account of the
execution of Hoste van der Katelyne in 1555 and in the Reformed
martyrologies of Crespin and van Haemstede, the first editions of which
appeared in 1554 and 1559. For good measure Karel de Coninck, an
erstwhile Carmelite from Ghent and himself to die a martyr's death at
Bruges in 1557, translated the cautionary tale of Francesco Spiera, the
Italian evangelical who had died in despair in 1548, having forsaken his
faith two years earlier.[41] The moral could not have been plainer.

By no means all evangelicals looked on the Roman church as 'the church
of Antichrist'. In 1557 a certain Jan Daelman, in a debate with the
Reformed minister van Haemstede, maintained 'that the Roman church, for
all its corrupt practices, is the Church of Christ; that whoever leaves the
Roman church, leaves the Church of Christ; that a Christian may use all the
Romanist superstitions and idolatry, without committing sin, provided he
does not seek his salvation in such practices'.[42] Among the well-educated
urban élites, whose piety had been coloured by the *Enchiridion*, such
attitudes were not uncommon. Confessional boundaries also mattered
rather less in the newly incorporated provinces of Friesland, Groningen,
and Gelderland. Here evangelically disposed priests might cease to
celebrate mass, attend Lutheran universities, and still return to preach in
the Catholic churches![43]

But those evangelicals who broke with the Roman church, while
remaining in the Netherlands, were bound sooner or later to erect privy
churches, where the Word might be preached purely and the sacraments
rightly administered. For, as Calvin told the Walloon congregation of
Antwerp in 1556, 'it is not enough to read and to hear (the Word)'.[44] The
inchoate Scripture-meetings became church services, the place of the
gadabout hedge-preacher was taken by a properly called minister, who was
charged with the care of specific congregations, and discipline was
introduced. The first Reformed church of this sort came into being at
Antwerp in 1555, the same year as the Protestant church at Paris was
constituted.[45] Yet we should not jump to the conclusion that by this time the
Protestants in the Low Countries took their theology and church order from
Geneva. Luther's influence had indeed receded, but other reformers
besides Calvin were looked to for guidance.

Joannes Uytenbogaert (1557–1644), whose Remonstrance in 1610 set out
the doctrinal position of the Arminian party, tells us that in his youth at

---

[41] A. L. F. Verheyden, *Het brugsch martyrologium* (Brussels, n.d.), 40.

[42] J. Decavele (see Further Reading), i. 383.

[43] J. J. Woltjer (see Further Reading), chs. vi, viii, ix; F. van Dijk, 'Dr. Johannes Eelts, *c.*1528–1588, persona te Groningen, en de tegenstelling katholicisme/protestantisme in zijn tijd', *Groningse volksalmanak* (1970–1), 16–48.

[44] Cited by F. L. Rutgers (see Further Reading), 223.

[45] A. J. Jelsma, *Adriaen van Haemstede en zijn martelaarsboek* (The Hague, 1970), 22.

Utrecht he had studied a wide range of evangelical literature. These included works by Luther, Melanchthon, and Bullinger, not to mention the writings of several lesser-known Dutch evangelicals.[46] Given the unofficial nature of the Reformation in the Low Countries and the lack of any central direction, such eclecticism was only natural. Netherlanders had encountered Protestantism in many different guises as they travelled to Wittenberg, Marburg, Strasburg,[47] and Zürich or across the North German Plain, though East Friesland, Bremen, and eastwards to the Baltic. In East Friesland they found a hybrid Reformation. Here à Lasco had superimposed on the basically Lutheran church order of 1535 a discipline and liturgy more in keeping with Strasburg than Wittenberg. In the town of Norden Lutheran and Reformed liturgies were both in use in the 1550s.[48] The church at Emden fulfilled certain of the roles played by Geneva in the organization of French Protestantism. Large numbers of religious refugees from the Low Countries joined the town church, whose consistory ministered as best it could to the needs of the churches 'under the cross', giving advice and sometimes sending ministers. Emden, too, became the base for the Reformed printing industry in north-western Europe after 1553. From the presses of the Netherlands, émigré printers issued a stream of Bibles, metrical psalms, catechisms, consolation-literature, and anti-Catholic polemic for the Dutch Protestants in exile or still dwelling 'amidst the Papists'. Nor was Emden the only haven. The accession of Mary Tudor cut short the first wave of stranger churches in England. But the church-order devised for the Dutch church in London under Edward VI left its mark on Reformed Protestantism in the Low Countries for a long time to come.[49] Dutch- and French-speaking communities of exiles settled in the Lower Rhineland and at Frankfurt, each with its own ethos.

In the Walloon provinces the Reformation moved in step with the evolution of French Protestantism. When French evangelicals began after 1550 to prefer Geneva to Strasburg as a place of refuge, their counterparts from Tournai, Valenciennes, and Arras followed suit. Likewise, the religious literature then coming off the Genevan presses found a market in the francophone provinces.[50] By 1553 French-speaking artisans, who had

[46] A. J. van 't Hooft, *De theologie van Heinrich Bullinger in betrekking tot de nederlandsche reformatie* (Amsterdam, 1888) 100.

[47] L. F. Halkin, 'Protestants des Pays-Bas et de la principauté de Liège réfugiés à Strasbourg' in *Strasbourg au cœur religieux de XVIe siècle* (Strasburg, 1977), 297–307.

[48] M. Smid, *Ostfriesische Kirchengeschichte* (Pewsum, 1974) 179–82.

[49] The London stranger-churches have been the subject of two recent theses: P. Denis, 'Les églises étrangères à Londres jusqu'à la mort de Calvin. De l'église de Jean Lasco à l'établissement du calvinisme' (Liège, Licence 1973–4) and A. Pettegree, 'The Strangers and their Churches in London, 1550–1580' (Oxford Univ. D. Phil. thesis, 1983). I am indebted to Dr Pettegree for allowing me to consult his thesis.

[50] G. Moreau, 'Un colporteur calviniste en 1563', *BSHPF* 118 (1972), 1–21. The Calvinist influence in the Walloon provinces is confirmed by id., 'Catalogue des livres brûlés à Tournai par order du duc d'Albe (16 juin 1569)', *Horae Tornacenses* (1971), 194–213.

probably drifted to Flanders proper in search of employment, were trying to win over their fellow workers to the teachings of Calvin.[51] Through the French-speaking minorities in the Flemish towns and the close connections between the French and Dutch stranger churches in London and Emden, Calvinism *pur sang* surmounted the language barrier, which Anabaptism had failed to break in the other direction. By 1560 Calvin was well enough known in Flanders for a Protestant barber-surgeon to include him in his pantheon of great reformers along with Zwingli, à Lasco, and Micronius.[52]

But Reformed Protestants in the Low Countries, and especially in the Dutch-speaking parts, never depended on Geneva as closely as their co-religionists in France. Whereas the Genevan church formally despatched at least eighty-eight pastors to French congregations between 1555 and 1562, only a dozen of the eighty-four preachers active in the southern Netherlands before 1566 had ties with Geneva, of whom four had matriculated at the Academy.[53] Netherlanders certainly resided in Geneva: seventy indeed enrolled as *habitants* between 1549 and 1560, and therefore took an oath to live 'selon la Sainte Religion évangelique ici purement annoncée', but most of these hailed from the Walloon provinces.[54] Translations are not necessarily an accurate reflection of the popularity of their authors with the public, but translations may create a readership where none existed before. The Dutch evangelical without any Latin or French would have had limited opportunities to read Calvin for himself. By the Reformer's death in 1564 only four of his writings had appeared in Dutch, far fewer than had been translated by this time into English, German, or even Italian.[55] Though the evidence is circumstantial, it suggests that the Genevan church had not as yet impinged deeply on the consciousness of Protestants in the Low Countries, above all those in the Dutch-speaking parts.

Yet the foremost Netherlands Protestants were well aware that Calvin's star was in the ascendant. By the later 1550s Cornelis Cooltuyn, Guilielmus Gnapheus, and Anastasius Veluanus, were evidently familiar with the *Institutes*.[56] And the leading ministers bracketed Calvin with Bullinger and

---

[51] Decavele, op. cit. i. 339.

[52] Ibid., i. 630.

[53] P. M. Crew, (see Further Reading), 84–7. Cf. R. M. Kingdon, *Geneva and the Coming of the Wars of Religion in France, 1555–1563* (Geneva, 1956) 135–7.

[54] *Livre des habitants de Genève*, i. *1549–1560*, ed. P. F. Geisendorf (Geneva, 1957). Only five Flemings and two Hollanders enrolled. On the other hand, twelve inhabitants of Ghent obtained burgher status at Emden between 1553 and 1560.

[55] Based on A. Erichson, *Bibliographia Calviniana* (repr. Nieuwkoop, 1960) and *Index Aureliensis*, vi s.n. Calvin, Jean. Books by Calvin began to appear in the northern Netherlands from 1557, when some were found at Culemborg, near Utrecht.

[56] Joannes Anastasius Veluanus cites Calvin in *Der leken wechwyser* (1554); Gnapheus borrowed material from *Institutes*, bk. iv for the dedicatory epistle in *Tobias ende Lazarus* (1557); Cooltuyn's denunciation of the mass as a sacrifice in *Dat evangeli der armen* (1559) leans heavily on Calvin's treatment of this matter in the *Institutes*. Andrew Johnston drew my attention to the Cooltuyn parallel.

Melanchthon and sought his opinion. Exiles from the Low Countries at Frankfurt turned to Calvin to resolve their internal conflicts and to guide them in their delicate negotiations with the Lutheran clergy.[57] The growing respect for the Genevan church among Dutch Protestants is brought out by the decision of the Reformed in Holland to enlist the aid of Calvin, and later Beza, in the early 1560s in order to refute the spiritualist views advanced by Dirk Volkertsz Coornhert.[58] One might otherwise have expected the Dutch Reformed still to seek guidance from the church at Emden, which had called the first ministers to serve in Holland only a few years earlier.

But familiarity with the *Institutes* and respect for the Genevan divines are no guarantee of Calvinist orthodoxy. The later careers of Arminius, Uytenbogaert, and Vorstius provide a timely warning, for these Remonstrant theologians had enjoyed Beza's favour as students at Geneva. And several of the earlier Dutch evangelicals who thought well of Calvin, including Veluanus and Cooltuyn, disagreed with him on the doctrines of the Real Presence and election. But the pluriformity of the Reformation in the Netherlands, to which we have already referred, did not hinder Reformed Protestants with differing opinions about predestination from working together in order to build up a Reformed church in very trying circumstances.[59] These unresolved differences lay buried like a time-bomb with a long fuse in Reformed Protestantism until it exploded in the last decade of the sixteenth century. Only with the decision to expel the Remonstrants at the synod of Dort was the controversy within the Reformed church checked. In no time the publicists from both the Remonstrant and contra-Remonstrant camps were laying claim to be the authentic heirs of the Dutch Reformation—and such was diversity of the Reformed inheritance that, by careful selection of the evidence, they could both advance plausible cases.

The Reformed Protestants in the Low Countries, like the French Calvinists, eventually adopted a presbyterian church order. This polity was intended to prevent any revival of 'proud prelacy'. The synod held at Emden in 1571 opened by affirming the cardinal principle of presbyterianism, namely that 'no church shall exercise dominion over another church'.[60] This church came to be governed through a hierarchy of assemblies, beginning with the consistory or *kerkeraad*, and ascending through the *classis* (the Scottish presbytery), the provincial synods to the

---

[57] Rutgers, op. cit., 129–34, 137–40.

[58] H. de Vries Heekelingen, *Genève pépinière du calvinisme hollandais*, ii (The Hague, 1924), 263–86.

[59] W. Nijenhuis, 'Variants within Dutch Calvinism in the Sixteenth Century', *The Low Countries History Yearbook*, 12 (1979), 48–64.

[60] *Acta van de nederlandsche synoden der zestiende eeuw*, ed. F. L. Rutgers, Werken der Marnix-Vereeniging, Serie II, deel III (Utrecht, 1889), 55. This gives the text in Latin and Dutch; for a modern German translation of the acts see D. Perlich, 'Die Akten der Synoden der niederländischen Gemeinden ... gehalten in Emden, den 4 Oktober 1571' in *Emder Synode 1571–1971* (Neukirchen, 1973), 49–66.

highest court, the national or general synod. This pattern accorded in many respects with the decentralized political tradition in the Habsburg Netherlands, where the prince's authority had been curtailed by the town corporations and provincial States. The consistory corresponded to the municipal corporations and the provincial synods to the states. On the other hand the biennial national synod envisaged at Emden remained a pious hope during the lifetime of the Republic. The provinces guarded their sovereign powers in the ecclesiastical, as well as in the political sphere, too jealously to allow this supra-provincial body to flourish.

But when the first consistory came into being at Antwerp in 1555, this all-embracing synodal hierarchy still lay some years ahead. Our immediate concern is to examine the purpose and antecedents of this institution. Clearly the Reformed church order at this stage in the Low Countries did not stem directly from the Genevan *Ecclesiastical Ordinances*. Though these had been drawn up in 1541, they were not published for another twenty years. Besides, this order had been framed for a small city-state, whose magistrates, citizens, and *habitants* had professed publicly their allegiance to the Reformation: in other words, for a Christian commonwealth. It was therefore quite unfitted for a church 'under the cross', where the magistrates remained Papists. Orders which had been devised for stranger-churches, however, lent themselves more readily to such circumstances.

Calvin himself had developed piecemeal one such 'order' during his stay at Strasburg between 1538 and 1541. The magistrates of that city had given him 'pleins pouvoirs' to weld the French-speaking evangelicals, who numbered some hundreds, into a church. As the minister to this congregation Calvin was not under the same restraints as were the ministers of the parish churches. Here, for example, discipline could be closely linked to the Lord's Supper. And Calvin denied unrepentant sinners admission to the Table lest these by their presence profane the solemn event. All those intending to communicate were expected to intimate their decision beforehand to Calvin.[61] In a revised form the order and liturgy of this *ecclesiola gallicana* was later published by Valérand Poullain, who had served the French exiles at Strasburg since 1544. Quite shortly after coming to England he published his *Liturgia sacra* in order to inform the revisers of the Prayer Book about the practice of the Strasburg church.[62] As one might expect discipline was here explicitly tied to the Lord's Supper.

Bucer too had advocated a stricter discipline in the Strasburg church, partly in order to answer his Anabaptist critics. But not until the crisis provoked by the Interim in 1548, and then only briefly, did he have an opportunity to realize at Strasburg the *christliche Gemeinschaft*. The

---

[61] J. Plomp, *De kerkelijke tucht bij Calvijn* (Kampen, 1969), 156–66.
[62] V. Pollanus, *Liturgia sacra (1551–1555)*, ed. A. C. Honders (Leiden, 1970).

members of this community voluntarily placed themselves under the supervision of *Seelsorgediener*, in effect elders. Those who refused to join these *corpora christianorum* were eventually to be asked to abstain from the Lord's Supper. However, these voluntary congregations did not long survive Bucer's departure from Strasburg in 1549.[63]

In Emden too the Anabaptists spurred on the magisterial reformers to strengthen discipline. In 1544 John à Lasco introduced the *Kirchenrat* for this purpose. Originally the four ministers sat with four lay assistants-the *cives*—who doubled as church-wardens and as elders.[64] À Lasco seems to have derived the notion of the lay helper from the church-order Bucer had drafted shortly before for Hermann von Wied, the evangelical prince-bishop of Cologne.[65] After the Interim, à Lasco left East Friesland to become the superintendent of the stranger churches at London. And it was he who devised the church-order for them, though it was revised by Jan Utenhove and Micronius, before being first published in Dutch by the latter in 1554. Cognate orders in Latin, French, and German appeared in the succeeding decade.[66] No doubt John à Lasco imported features characteristic of the church he had known at Emden, but he probably also drew on Poullain's *Liturgia sacra*. Either way the antecedents of the London church may be traced, at least in part, to the *ecclesiola gallicana* at Strasburg and to Martin Bucer.[67]

By no means all the features of the London order derive from Strasburg. Micronius and Jan Utenhove both knew the church at Zürich at first hand and would therefore have been familiar with the *Prophezei* there, which recur in the London order.[68] But in the specific matter of discipline à Lasco's order stood in a tradition which had originated in Strasburg. At Zürich the exercise of discipline fell to the Christian magistracy: they had the task of punishing publicly recalcitrant sinners. According to Bullinger excommunication had no place in the church. Not only did the practice lack adequate scriptural warrant, it defeated the purpose of the Lord's Supper, which had been instituted to give sinners an opportunity to render thanks to the Lord, not to remove the tares from the wheat.[69] At Geneva the consistory maintained discipline and barred unrepentant sinners from the

[63] Van Ginkel, op. cit. 99–101.

[64] Smid, *Ostfriesische Kirchengeschichte*, 166.

[65] Van Ginkel, op. cit. 164–6.

[66] M. Micron, *De christlicke ordinancien der nederlantscher ghemeinten te Londen (1554)*, ed. W. F. Dankbaar (The Hague, 1956). À Lasco published the Latin version later as *Forma ac ratio tota ecclesiastici Ministerii* at Frankfurt in 1555.

[67] Van Ginkel, op. cit. 115.

[68] P. Denis, 'La prophétie dans les églises de la réforme au XVIᵉ siècle', *Revue d'histoire ecclésiastique*, 72 (1977), 300–4; Pettegree, 'Strangers and their Churches', 63–4.

[69] Plomp, op. cit. 28–9; J. Wayne Baker, 'In Defense of magisterial discipline: Bullinger's "Tractatus de excommunicatione" of 1568' in U. Gäbler and F. Herkenrath (eds.), *Heinrich Bullinger 1504–1578. Gesammelte Aufsätze zum 400. Todestag* (Zürich, 1975), 147–9.

Table. But since the Genevan elders were chosen annually from the municipal councils, their position differed from that held by their namesakes in the stranger-churches or the churches 'under the cross' in the Netherlands: in the latter the elders acted solely on behalf of the church. This difference did not pass unremarked. In the early seventeenth century the anti-Calvinist regent of Amsterdam, Cornelis Pietersz. Hooft, hoped to embarrass the Contra-Remonstrants when he pointed out that the elders in Holland were still chosen by the consistories, unlike the practice in Geneva![70] To which his opponents might have retorted that Amsterdam scarcely resembled the Christian commonwealth of Geneva.

According to Luther the true Church was to be found wherever the Word was preached faithfully and the sacraments properly administered, and the Lutherans never swerved from this definition.[71] Calvin came close to making discipline the third mark, but he stopped short.[72] Discipline, however, assured the safety of the Church: 'for to hang together, the body of Christ must be bound together by discipline as with sinews.'[73] In Calvin's teaching on the Church a tension develops between his concern lest the Lord's Table be polluted by the attendance of shameless sinners and his abhorrence of schismatics, who broke the Church's unity. When Reformed exiles at Wesel sought Calvin's advice in 1554 as to whether they should set up their own congregation on account of the objectionable Lutheran ceremonies used in the town church he warned them that separation on those grounds could not be justified.[74] For the same reason he considered the rigorism characteristic of the Anabaptists as a threat to the Church's unity and to evangelical freedom.[75] Probably he was prevented from including discipline as the third mark of the church by such fears.

Yet it was precisely the challenge presented by the Anabaptists which induced the Strasburg theologians to add discipline to the *notae ecclesiae*.[76] In 1538 Bucer succeeded in persuading a large number of Anabaptists in Hesse to return to the territorial church by conceding the principle that 'there cannot be a Church without discipline'.[77] And this principle, which Bucer also maintained in his apologia for the church order of Cologne

---

[70] Cornelius Pietersz. Hooft, *Memoriën en adviezen*, i (Utrecht, 1871), 131, 157, 207, 296. In fact, of course, the corporations exercised a good deal of influence over consistorial appointments, but it suited Hooft's book to emphasize that the Dutch Calvinists had in this respect been unfaithful to the Genevan model.

[71] Plomp, op. cit. 22.

[72] Ibid., 124.

[73] Ibid., 125–7. Quotation from 'Calvin's Reply to Cardinal Sadolet', in *Calvin: Theological Treatises*, ed. J. K. S. Reid (London, 1954), 245.

[74] G. R. Potter and M. Greengrass, *John Calvin* (London, 1983), 139.

[75] Balke, *Calvijn en de doperse radikalen*, 225–40; Plomp, op. cit. 100–15.

[76] Davis, 'No Discipline', 50. Poullain reflected the Strasburg traditions when he included discipline as one of the three marks of the church in the confession he composed for the congregation at Glastonbury. Pollanus, *Liturgia sacra*, 207.

[77] Davis, 'No Discipline', 54.

(c.1543),[78] was to be put into practice by the influential stranger churches at London. In 1551 Jan Utenhove boasted that 'our Netherlands nation never before had a congregation where the Word of God was so purely preached, the Sacraments so uprightly administered and the Christian discipline so diligently and faithfully exercised.'[79] And this threefold definition of the Church recurs in the *Christlicke ordinancien*.[80] From London Dutch exiles like Jacob Dieussart carried it back to Flanders.[81] In 1561 the Netherlands Confession of faith duly included 'la discipline ecclesiastique' among the signs of the Church.[82]

Discipline became essential to the Reformed churches in the Low Countries. Without discipline the Lord's Supper could not be properly administered, as Calvin himself reminded a French congregation in 1554.[83] But the process by which the clandestine Bible-reading assemblies became transformed into fully fledged Reformed congregations with consistories was gradual and liable to be interrupted by the arrest of the principals. The metamorphosis took place in secrecy, the historian has to piece together the evidence from the trial proceedings of those unfortunate enough to fall into the hands of the magistrates, and from stray remarks passed in the correspondence of the underground congregations and the consistory minutes of the stranger churches. By 1566 churches had been *dressées*, as the French Calvinists described congregations with discipline, in the chief Walloon towns[84] as well as at Ghent, Bruges, and Hondschoote in Flanders. In Brabant, apart from Antwerp, which acted as the mother-church for the duchy, only Breda certainly had a consistory by then,[85] though the 'brethren' at Brussels appear to have been quite precocious. In the records of the Dutch church at London there are passing references to the Calvinist communities on the island of Walcheren in Zeeland, which suggest that they, too, had a church order of sorts before 1566.[86] Holland lagged behind: there the embryonic congregations were served by a minister with a roving commission from the church at Emden.

[78] B. Hall, 'Diakonia in Martin Butzer' in *Service in Christ. Essays Presented to Karl Barth on his 80th Birthday*, ed. J. I. McCord and T. H. L. Parker (London, 1966), 96.

[79] Micron, *Christlicke ordinancien*, 1.

[80] Ibid., 89.

[81] Dieussart had been a member of the London church before his arrest in Flanders in 1560; see Decavele, op. cit. i. 411–12. For his martyr's testimony see (A. van Haemstede), *Geschiedenis der martelaren . . . tot het jaar 1655* (Arnhem, 1868), 719.

[82] Bakhuizen van den Brink, art. XXIX. Significantly the French confession, drawn up in 1559, omits discipline as a true mark of the Church.

[83] Potter and Greengrass, *John Calvin*, 152.

[84] Brully's ministry to the Walloon towns in 1544 ended after less than two months, giving him too little time to organize the churches. Though charged with preaching and teaching heretical doctrine about the real presence, he was not charged with administering Communion, see C. Paillard, *Le Procès de Pierre Brully* (Paris and The Hague, 1878), 80.

[85] A. J. M. Beenakker, *Breda in de eerste storm van de opstand. Van ketterij tot beeldenstorm, 1545–1569* (Tilburg, 1971), 41.

[86] From *Kerkeraads-protocollen . . . 1560–1563*, 121, 200, 224, 229–30, 236, 347, 349, 436.

Perforce the Calvinist churches in the Low Countries, as in France, came into existence as individual congregations: the presbyterian or synodal framework followed. Since 1562 meetings of the churches in the southern provinces had occurred at Antwerp.[87] In this development the French-speaking churches seem to have taken the lead, though these meetings were almost certainly also attended by the Dutch churches: the division of the French and Dutch Calvinist churches into separate synods did not take place until 1577. In the 1560s the Reformed churches in the Netherlands hitched their wagon to the French Protestant Church for the simple reason that the synodal system of government had been first introduced in France in 1559. In the matter of synods the church-orders of the gathered churches could no more provide a model than those of the Reformed city states. This explains why the earliest synods held in the Low Countries set their course by the *Discipline ecclésiastique* of the French Calvinists.[88] But in following the French example, the Reformed churches in the Netherlands may thereby have fallen more directly under the influence of Calvin and Beza, who watched so vigilantly over the affairs of the French churches, than has been suspected. À Lasco deliberately included in his church order certain features which were intended to check the growth of clerical domination. These included congregational participation in the election of church officers and the institution of prophecy, by which the ministers could be called to account by the members for their preaching.[89] Yet by the synod of Emden in 1571 these practices had apparently fallen into a desuetude among the Reformed Protestants in the Low Countries. Beza, for one, would surely not have regretted their passing!

The arrival of Alva in the summer of 1567 forced many Protestants to flee the country. In the diaspora the need for closer liason between the communities scattered through England and Germany and those in hiding in the Netherlands became more urgent. The campaigns orchestrated by William of Orange in 1568, 1570, and 1572 underlined the importance of

[87] G. Moreau, 'Les synodes des églises wallonnes des Pays-Bas en 1563', *Nederlands archief voor kerkgeschiedenis*, n.s. 47 (1965), 10.

[88] F. R. J. Knetsch, 'De nationale synode te Dordrecht 1578 en de positie der waalse kerken' in D. Nauta *et al.* (eds.), *De nationale synode van Dordrecht 1578* (Amsterdam, 1978), 55–60; id., 'Kerkordelijke bepalingen van de nederlandse synoden "onder het kruis" (1563–1566) vergeleken met die van de franse (1559–1564)' in J. Fabius *et al.* (eds.), *Kerkhistorische studiën* (Leiden, 1982), 29–44.

[89] In France Jean Morély's support for the practice had been brought into disrepute with the triumphant clericalist party in France; in the stranger churches prophecy continued, albeit in an attenuated form, until the 1570s. At the so-called Convent of Wesel, which probably took place at Antwerp in 1567, the institution was discussed at length, but Emden made no mention of the practice. The memory, however, lingered on. The classis of the Neder-Veluwe discussed a proposal to revive prophecy in 1606, *Acta van de classis Neder-Veluwe (Harderwijk) van 1592–1620*, ed. G. van der Zee (Goes, n.d.) 108. According to this the *exercitium prophetiae* still continued in East Friesland. Note the alarm of the Reformed church in the *classis* Alkmaar in 1587 about 'the great assemblings of young people' who met to expound 'some passage in Scripture by way of a sermon'. G. Brandt (see Further Reading), i. 728.

concerted action. In the entourage of the prince the Calvinist consistories were regarded as a means of obtaining information about the enemy and raising money for the recruitment of troops. But this, in turn, presupposed a greater coherence than had hitherto marked the Reformed churches. It was significantly the Calvinist scholar-stateman, Philippe Marnix de Sainte-Aldegonde, at Orange's side by 1571, who championed the plan to 'incorporate all the congregations of the Netherlands into a single body'.[90] And it was the example of the French church he had in mind when he invited the Dutch church at London to attend the national synod at Emden in 1571.[91] The decision reached at Emden to subscribe to both the French and Netherlands confessions of faith was intended to seal the doctrinal unity of the two Reformed churches.[92] But it also symbolized the triumph of the Calvinist church-order among the Reformed in the Low Countries, a triumph about which a minority of Protestants had some nagging doubts.

In 1572 the Lord, as it appeared to the Calvinists, opened 'the door for the proclamation of his Word in the Netherlands'. But, like the Israelites under Joshua, they were not to wrest control of the Promised Land without a struggle. When considering the slow advance of the Reformed church in Holland after 1572, we need to bear in mind how few of the inhabitants of Holland had any inkling of the Reformed church-order. Because of this lack of experience the Reformed church at Dordrecht appealed in 1572 to the Dutch church at London for ministers 'who were reasonably familiar with the regiment of the church'.[93] Moreover, the existing political order did not immediately collapse when the Sea Beggars entered the towns. Some magistrates went into the wilderness in the first years of the revolt in Holland, but especially in the smaller towns, where the supply of men with the requisite political experience and wealth was limited, the families in control of the corporations under Alva retained their grip.[94] Even at Amsterdam, whose magistrates were drastically purged in 1578, ten Catholics sat on the revised town corporation.[95] The governing classes in Holland could not then easily slough off traditional political habits or old religious loyalties.

On that account, however, the convinced Calvinists in the Reformed church had difficulty in deciding whether they had indeed a truly 'Christian

[90] Ph. Marnix de Saint-Aldegonde, *Godsdienstige en kerkelijke geschriften. Aanhangsel*, (The Hague, 1878), 16.

[91] W. van 't Spijker, 'Stromingen', 62–3.

[92] *Acta van de nederlandsche synoden*, 56.

[93] Briels, *Zuidnederlandse emigratie*, 26.

[94] C. C. Hibben, *Gouda in Revolt. Particularism and Pacificism in the Revolt of the Netherlands, 1572–1588* (Utrecht, 1983), 67–76; S. A. Lamet, 'The *Vroedschap* of Leiden 1550–1600: the Impact of Tradition and Change on the Governing Elite of a Dutch City', *Sixteenth Century Journal* 12 (1981), 19–20.

[95] H. A. Enno van Gelder, 'Nederland geprotestantiseerd?', *Tijdschrift voor geschiedenis*, 81 (1968), 457.

magistracy'. They knew how few whole-heartedly endorsed the political objectives of Orange or showed any zeal for the Calvinist cause. In 1572 the magistrates pointedly ignored the Beggars' demand that the Reformed should be allowed to worship in the principal church in the towns.[96] Instead the town corporations did all in their powers to secure the Catholic establishment by writing into their agreements with the Beggars clauses designed to safeguard the clergy and the churches from attack. Freedom of religion might be guaranteed, but no formal provision for Reformed worship was made. In a few towns the magistrates cast about in search of some sort of anodyne Catholicism, purged of those 'superstitious' ceremonies many humanist Catholics found objectionable. But these attempts to find a middle road between Rome and Geneva came to nothing, with the exception of Huibert Duifhuis' congregation at Utrecht, which flourished with magisterial approval from 1578 until its demise in 1586.[97]

Sooner or later Catholic worship ceased in the parish churches, and then in the religious houses, in most cases by the spring of 1573 in the rebel-held towns in Holland. And the magistrates came to realize the need for them to work out a *modus vivendi* with the Reformed churches, of whose doctrine, catechisms, and church-orders they had little knowledge. More or less willingly the civil authorities—the magistrates and the provincial States—lent their authority to the Reformed church. They paid the ministers' salaries from the revenues which formerly belonged to the Roman Catholic church. Indeed the income from the famous Benedictine abbey at Egmond was diverted in order to pay the professors of the new university founded at Leiden in 1575 for the education of the rising generation of political and religious leaders. Calvinist ministers were engaged to serve as chaplains to the army and the fleet, pilgrimages were forbidden by placards and local ordinances, and schoolmasters were required to use the Heidelberg catechism. In all these ways the civil authorities fulfilled, as they believed, the requirements of Christian magistrates.

To the Erastians among the civil authorities the Reformed church no longer had any need of consistories now that it lived under a Christian magistracy. Caspar Coolhaes, a minister at Leiden between 1574 and 1582, supported this opinion. In a treatise written in 1582 he argued 'wherever the Christian magistracy discharges the office of guardian towards the church . . . there is no need for any consistory' and he pointed to the example of the church at Zürich.[98] In the early seventeenth century Cornelis Pietersz.

[96] Duke and Jones, 'Towards a Reformed Polity', 377–8.
[97] E.g. at Gouda, Hibben, *Gouda*, 86; at Goes (Zeeland) in 1578, H. A. Enno van Gelder, *Revolutionnaire reformatie* (see Further Reading), 45 and possibly also at Amersfoort in 1579, C. A. van Kalveen, ' "Een vast gelove, ende Christus vrede si met ons ende alle onse vianden mede." De definitieve vestiging van de reformatie te Amersfoort, 1579–1581', *Nederlands archief voor kerkgeschiedenis*, 62 (1982), 38; for Duifhuis at Utrecht, see Brandt, *History of the Reformation*, 346–50, 370–1, 378–80.
[98] H. C. Rogge, *Caspar Janszoon Coolhaes, de voorloper van Arminius en der Remonstranten*, i (Amsterdam, 1858), 230.

Hooft complained that the contemporary Calvinist ministers had failed to distinguish between the circumstances 'of a church which is under the protection of a Christian magistracy and one which is under the cross'.[99] In other words, the consistory was only required by the church during persecution; otherwise, it served no purpose.

But when Hooft wrote of a Christian magistracy he was, at least as far as his opponents were concerned, merely begging the question. In 1607 a minister in a synod at Delft declared that he would not acknowledge the civil powers as 'Christian' until they had expelled from the country everyone who refused to join the Reformed church![100] An uncharacteristically extreme statement, no doubt, but it demonstrates the problem contemporaries had in reaching a consensus on the qualities expected of a Christian magistracy. The Calvinists had their own definitions. The authors of the Netherlands confession of faith laid on the magistrates the responsibility for the uprooting of all idolatry and false religion 'so that the kingdom of Antichrist may be overthrown and the kingdom of Christ Jesus advanced'.[101] The problems for the Reformed were twofold. Could magistrates, who themselves declined to submit to the Reformed discipline, fulfil such a charge? And secondly, should the Christian discipline be maintained, even where a Christian magistracy occurred?[102]

Even 'under the cross' there had been disagreements among the Reformed concerning the nature of the Church. In 1557–8 a heated controversy broke out among the brethren at Antwerp. The consistory condemned as reckless and divisive the decision of one of their ministers to preach to the rich, who had not as yet entered the congregation and forsworn the Roman church. In their letter to Emden the elders and deacons explained their point of view.

. . . as we live in a place where the people, in their blindness, speak ill of the way of God, there must be a separation between the children of God and those of the world. This is most conveniently accomplished through the profession of faith and submission to the discipline of Christ.

The signatories did, however, preface these observations by saying that this problem would not exist if they dwelt 'in a free country'. Then all who wished might hear the Word.[103]

After 1572 the Reformed found themselves 'in a free country' and they

[99] Hooft, *Memoriën*, i. 81, 222; Rogge, *Coolhaes*, i. 126 n. 45. See also R. H. Bremmer, *Reformatie en rebellie, Willem von Orange, de calvinisten en het recht van opstand. Tien onstuimige jaren: 1572–1581* (Franeker, 1984), 133–4.

[100] Briels, *Zuidnederlandse emigratie*, 27.

[101] Bakhuizen van den Brink, 141; cf. also R. B. Evenhuis, *Ook dat was Amsterdam. De kerk der hervorming in de gouden eeuw*, i (Amsterdam, 1965), 182.

[102] *Classicale acta 1573–1620. Particuliere synoden Zuid-Holland*, i. *Classis Dordrecht, 1573–1600*, ed. J. P. van Dooren (The Hague, 1980), 20.

[103] *Brieven uit onderscheidene kerkelijke archieven*, ed. H. Q. Janssen and J. J. van Toorenenbergen, (Werken der Marnix-Vereeniging, serie III), deel II (1ᵉ stuk) (Utrecht, 1877), 71–2.

acknowledged that they had responsibilities to those outside the congregation. Petrus Dathenus, who was noted for his Calvinist fervour, confessed
in a letter to Bullinger in 1570 that it would be unrealistic to expect the same
strict discipline in a territorial church, such as was then being established in
the Palatinate, as could be maintained in Geneva or in the Dutch stranger-
church at London. As a minister who would be required to answer before
the Lord for those committed to his care, he was satisfied if he could clearly
distinguish his flock and if the sacraments could be protected against open
profanation.[104] After 1572 the Reformed churches in Holland were quite
prepared to make concessions to accomodate tender consciences 'in the youth
of this church'. Wafers might be used at Communion instead of bread, the
custom of reading the Sunday gospel continued, the elderly permitted to
make their profession of faith before the minister and two elders instead of
in the face of the full consistory. Aware that the singing of the metrical
psalms did not always catch on with village congregations, the national
synod of Middelburg in 1581 permitted the church at Deventer to choose a
dozen or so of the 'lightest' psalms and to publish these along with some
carefully-chosen hymns in the local dialect. In this way the synod hoped to
accustom Overijsselaars to Dathenus's psalms.[105] A much more significant
response to the new circumstances came with the decision, reached not
without much heart-searching, to administer baptism to all children,
including the offspring of 'Papists'.[106] In this respect the Reformed *dominee*
took the place vacated by the parish priest.

But on one point the Dutch Calvinists remained inflexible. They would
not surrender consistorial discipline. Admission to the Lord's Supper was
to remain carefully supervised to ensure that those who sat at the Table ate
'worthily'. That was only possible with consistorial discipline: in the
absence of discipline the Lord's Supper could not take place. In the early
years in the countryside the minister might be the only member and
arrangements had to be made so that he sat at the Lord's Table in a
neighbouring church which had discipline.[107] In the province of Utrecht
the necessary discipline was provided to begin with by the consistory in the
city of Utrecht. So the distinction which had existed 'under the cross'
between the *prudents* and the *fidèles*, between those 'outside' and those
'within' the congregation, gave way after 1572 to one between the
liefhebbers, who came to the sermons, and the *lidmaten*, or members, who
had placed themselves 'under the sweet yoke of our chief shepherd Jesus
Christ'. But the fundamental distinction between 'the children of God' and

---

[104] Van 't Spijker, 'Stromingen', 61.
[105] *Acta van de nederlandsche synoden*, 372, 444.
[106] van Deursen, *Bavianen*, 135–9.
[107] e.g. *Acta van de classis Neder-Veluwe*, 37.

'the children of the world' did not change, for that was quintessential to Dutch Calvinism.

Ranged on the other side in this debate about the nature of the church were those for whom the Reformation had, above all else, put an end to the tyranny of penance, which had brought despair to sinners, and restored evangelical liberty. This was of course an outlook shared by all the reformers, including Calvin and the Reformed Protestants. But no sooner had the reformers begun to give permanent institutional expression to the new theology, than they laid themselves open to the charge of reviving that very tyranny they had formerly denounced. Already by 1526 Erasmus compared the Lutheran yoke unfavourably with the burdens imposed by the papists.[108] Milton's familiar denunciation of the Presbyterians as the 'new forcers of conscience' has an ancestry which goes back to the earliest years of the Reformation.

In the Low Countries the Calvinists were accused by other evangelicals of forging a 'new monkery' and of setting up 'the Genevan inquisition', on account of the strict discipline which surrounded the Lord's Supper. To Duifhuis, for whom church orders belonged to the category of matters indifferent, any other sort of discipline than that exercised by the magistrates represented a 'tyrannizing over consciences, and a remnant of the Popish yoke'.[109] Herman Herberts, another minister influenced by the spiritualists, once shocked the Calvinists by describing the Heidelberg catechism as 'a new monstrance in which they (sc. the Calvinists) want to incarcerate Christ', because of the Reformed practice of expounding some portion of the catechism each Sunday.[110] Others, like Coolhaes and Hooft, likened the visitation conducted by the Calvinist elders on the eve of the Lord's Supper to auricular confession in the Roman church.[111]

These critics of the Calvinists wanted a comprehensive church. In the church orders drafted by the States of Holland in 1576 and 1591 the Lord's Table would have been opened to all who wished to come. Preparations were to have been limited to an exhortation by the minister to remind the communicants to search their own consciences.[112] At Utrecht Duifhuis allowed all who wished to sit at the Supper to come: no profession of faith was required, no roll of members kept.[113] Oldenbarnevelt at his trial urged the public church to attract to its services Lutherans, Mennonites, even

---

[108] P. Denis, 'Jean Laski et le retour au papisme' in *Les Eglises et leurs institutions au XVIᵉ siècle*, ed. M. Perronet (Montpellier, 1978), 14.

[109] Brandt, i., 349.

[110] Rogge, *Coolhaes*, ii. 180–1.

[111] Hooft, *Memoriën*, ii. 126; Rogge, op. cit. 52.

[112] C. Hooijer, *Oude kerkordeningen der Nederlandsche hervormde gemeenten, 1563–1638* (Zaltbommel, 1865), 124, 344–5.

[113] Brandt, loc. cit.

Papists,[114] while Hooft, who stood in this as in other respects close to the Advocate, wanted the 'evangelical net' to catch as many as possible. To this end the rigid insistence on binding confessions, catechisms, consistorial discipline, in fact the whole Calvinist paraphernalia, should be relaxed. With some, especially among the magistrates, there was a natural desire to retain control of the new church, but one may also detect an irritation at the refusal of the Reformed churches to fulfil the part of a comprehensive church to which all patriotic Dutchmen might belong. From the standpoint of the civil powers the Calvinists' separation of society into two camps was politically very inconvenient. No wonder some magistrates, notably at Leiden, looked enviously on the Reformed church at Zürich, where discipline remained unambiguously in the hands of the lay powers and where consistories were unknown.[115]

But the Calvinists were not convinced. They believed themselves to belong to a people whom it had pleased God to call forth from the nations. That they found themselves, at least for a time, in a small minority caused them no surprise. After all, as their confession of faith declared, the Church might appear to the world to be 'very small', as in the time of Ahab, yet even then the Lord had reserved to Himself seven thousand, who had not bowed down to Baal.[116] In their trials the vicissitudes of God's people in the Old Testament remained a consistent source of comfort, as also did the doctrine of election. The state of their own society confirmed their reading of the scriptures. From this perspective success, as measured in terms of numerical support, was unimportant. Keeping faith with the Lord in prosperity, no less than in adversity, was what counted.

By the early seventeenth century the size and influence of the Reformed church grew and gradually the magistrates, who had tended to stand aloof in the early years of the Revolt, began to enter the congregation and to take their places in the consistory. The national synod of Dort in 1618 marked the triumph of Calvinist theology within Dutch Protestantism and the church became increasingly preoccupied with the creation of a Christian society. Yet the Reformed church never became the church of all, or even a majority, of Dutchmen. Many reasons have been offered for this failure, as we have already observed, but the search for the *purior ecclesia*, to which many Calvinists in the seventeenth century remained faithful, was surely a restraint on the popularity of the Reformed churches. The sense of being a chosen people, 'set apart from the human race', which had inspired the Calvinists in their tribulations under Philip II, could not entirely be blotted out by the worldly prosperity they came to enjoy. And so the Dutch Calvinists in the seventeenth century remained in a debate with themselves,

---

[114] J. den Tex, *Oldenbarnevelt*, iii. *Bestand* (Haarlem, 1966), 31.

[115] Rogge, *Coolhaes*, i. 62–86.

[116] Bakhuizen van den Brink, *Nederlandse belijdenisgeschriften* art. XXVII.

in which one party, by now the smaller, looked back with nostalgia to the heroic age of the Reformation.

Further Reading

Bakhuizen van den Brink, J. N. *De nederlandse belijdenisgeschriften in authentieke teksten* (2nd edn. Amsterdam, 1976).

Brandt, G., *The History of the Reformation and other Ecclesiastical Transactions in and about the Low Countries* (4 vols., London, 1720–3).

Carter, A. C., *The English Reformed Church in Amsterdam in the Seventeenth Century* (Amsterdam, 1964).

Crew, P. M., *Calvinist Preaching and Iconoclasm in the Netherlands, 1544–1569* (Cambridge, 1978).

Decavele, J., *De dageraad van de reformatie in Vlaanderen, 1520–1565* (2 vols., Brussels, 1975).

Deursen, A. T. van *Bavianen en slijkgeuzen. Kerk en kerkvolk ten tijde van Maurits en Oldenbarnevelt* (Assen, 1974).

—— *Het kopergeld van de Gouden Eeuw*, iv. *Hel en hemel* (Assen, 1980).

Deyon, S. and Lottin, A., *Les Casseurs de l'été 1566: l'iconoclasme dans le Nord de la France* (Paris, 1981).

Enno van Gelder, H. A., *Revolutionnaire reformatie. De vestiging van de Gereformeerde Kerk in de nederlandse gewesten . . . 1575–1585* (Amsterdam, 1943).

—— *Vrijheid en onvrijheid in de Republiek. Geschiedenis der vrijheid van drukpers en godsdienst . . . van 1572 tot 1619* (Haarlem, 1947).

—— *Getemperde vrijheid. Een verhandeling over de verhouding van Kerk en Staat in de Republiek . . . en de vrijheid van meningsuiting in zake godsdienst, drukpers en onderwijs gedurende de 17e eeuw* (Groningen, 1972).

Ginkel, A. van, *De ouderling. Oorsprong en ontwikkeling van het ambt van ouderling en de functie daarvan in de gereformeerde kerk der Nederlanden in de 16e en 17e eeuw* (Amsterdam, 1975); summary in English.

Groenhuis, G., *De predikanten. De sociale positie van de gereformeerde predikanten in de Republiek der Verenigde Nederlanden voor ±1700* (Groningen, 1977); summary in English.

Kok, J. A. de, *Nederland op de breuklijn Rome-Reformatie. Numerieke aspecten van protestantisering en katholieke herleving in de noordelijke Nederlanden, 1580–1880* (Assen, 1964), summary in English.

Moreau, G., *Histoire du protestantisme à Tournai jusqu'a à la veille de la Révolution des Pays-Bas* (Paris, 1962).

Nijenhuis, W., *Adrianus Saravia (c.1532–1613). Dutch Calvinist, first Reformed defender of the English Episcopal Church on the basis of the ius divinum* (Leiden, 1980).

Parker, G., *The Dutch Revolt* (London, 1977).

Rogier, L. J., *Geschiedenis van het katholicisme in Noord-Nederland in de zestiende en zeventiende eeuw* (3 vols., Amsterdam, 1947).

Rutgers, F. L., *Calvijns invloed op de reformatie in de Nederlanden voor zooveel die door hemzelven is uitgeoefend* (2nd edn., Leiden, 1901).

Smitskamp, H., *Calvinistisch nationaal besef in Nederland vóór het midden der 17e eeuw* (The Hague, 1947).

Tex, J. den, *Oldenbarnevelt* (2 vols., Cambridge, 1973).

Tukker, C. A., *De classis Dordrecht van 1573 tot 1609* (Leiden, 1965).

Woltjer, J. J., *Friesland in hervormingstijd* (Leiden, 1962).

V

The Territorial Princes in Germany's Second Reformation, 1559–1622[1]

HENRY J. COHN

IN his autobiography, written at the beginning of the Thirty Years' War, the former Heidelberg court preacher Abraham Scultetus reflected on the vaunting political ambitions which Calvinists in Europe had entertained thirty years earlier:

I cannot fail to recall the optimistic mood which I and many others felt when we considered the condition of the Reformed churches in 1591. In France there ruled the valiant King Henri IV, in England the mighty Queen Elizabeth, in Scotland the learned King James, in the Palatinate the bold hero John Casimir, in Saxony the courageous and powerful Elector Christian I, in Hesse the clever and prudent Landgrave William, who were all inclined to the Reformed religion. In the Netherlands everything went as Prince Maurice of Orange wished, when he took Breda, Zutphen, Hulst, and Nijmegen. But what entered our heads? We imagined that *aureum seculum*, a golden age, had dawned. But this was folly, for within twelve months the elector of Saxony, the count palatine, and the landgrave of Hesse all died, King Henri of France deserted the true faith, and all our golden hopes went up in smoke. Since then God has marvellously protected and preserved the churches in France and Germany, so that we have learned from this that all the trust that one places in the most courageous, the richest, or the most skilled princes is fruitless and foolish, because the honour of preserving churches is due not to this world, but to heaven; not to men, but to the Lord God.[2]

Yet Scultetus did less than justice to the historical role of rulers in Germany, both before and after 1591, in establishing churches with Calvinizing tendencies. By 1620 two out of the four lay electors of the Empire, those of Brandenburg and the Palatinate, were Calvinist, as were, or until recently had been, five dukes in Silesia and one in Anhalt, the landgrave of Hesse-Cassel, seventeen imperial counts, the imperial cities of Bremen and Colmar, and the semi-autonomous territorial town of Emden.[3] These states had sponsored the three Reformed universities of Heidelberg,

[1] Assisted by a British Academy grant for research in Germany.
[2] *Die Selbstbiographie des Heidelberger Theologen und Hofpredigers Abraham Scultetus (1566–1624)*, ed. G. A. Benrath (Karlsruhe, 1966), 30–1.
[3] J. I. Good (see Further Reading), 435.

SCHLESWIG-
HOLSTEIN

E. FRISIA
Emden
1589
•Hamburg

•Bremen
1581

NETHERLANDS

BENTHEIM
1592
TECKLENBURG
1586
STEINFURT
1591   Lemgo   LIPPE
CLEVES   •   1601

•Wesel
1564
MÖRS〇   MARK
1574
BERG   WITTGENSTEIN
Cologne   1567
•   NASSAU
JÜLICH   SAYN   1577
1565   •Herborn
WETTERAU
WIED   YSENBURG
1580   1583

SOLMS
1580
HANAU-
1598   Frankfurt   MÜNZENBERG
SIMMERN   PALATINATE   1591
1561

ZWEIBRÜCKEN   Neustadt •Heidelberg   Amberg
1588   •   •

ANHALT
1596

UPPER PALATINATE
1561

WÜRTTEMBERG

Strasburg
•

Colmar ⌐ᔆ⌐
1589   ⌐BADEN-
⌐¬DURLACH
Basle

•Zürich

SWITZERLAND

Map. 2. The Second Reformation in Germany, 1559–1622

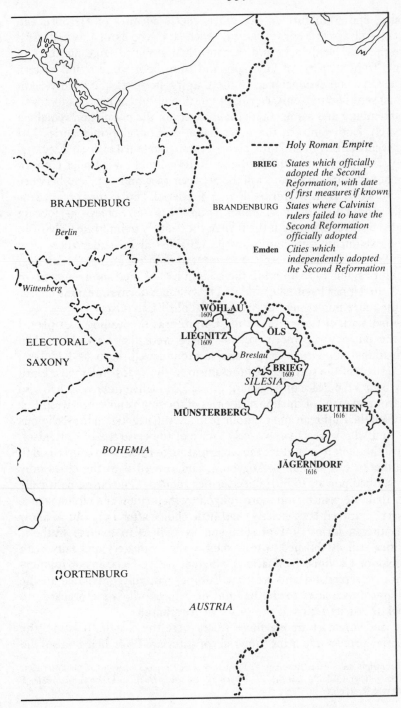

Holy Roman Empire

BRIEG States which officially adopted the Second Reformation, with date of first measures if known

BRANDENBURG States where Calvinist rulers failed to have the Second Reformation officially adopted

Emden Cities which independently adopted the Second Reformation

BRANDENBURG

Berlin

Wittenberg

ELECTORAL
SAXONY

WOHLAU
1609

LIEGNITZ
1609

ÖLS

Breslau

BRIEG
1609

SILESIA

MÜNSTERBERG

BEUTHEN
1616

BOHEMIA

JÄGERNDORF
1616

ORTENBURG

AUSTRIA

Marburg, and Frankfurt an der Oder, the Academies of Herborn and Bremen, and a score of *Gymnasien*, secondary schools of the first rank. Before the war Heidelberg and Herborn had attracted large numbers of students from all parts of Germany and from both western and eastern Europe. On a confessional map of the Empire, however, the twenty-eight Calvinist states occupy only a small proportion of the land mass; moreover, in Brandenburg and some others the majority of the population remained obstinately Lutheran. On the other hand, additional principalities had earlier seemed likely to join the Calvinist camp, but failed to do so. Electoral Saxony, the heartland of the Lutheran Reformation, came under Crypto-Calvinist influence on two occasions, between 1571 and 1574 and between 1586 and 1591. Both Margrave Ernest Frederick (1584–1604) of Baden-Durlach and Duke John Adolphus (1590–1616) of Schleswig-Holstein struggled for over a decade at the turn of the century to infiltrate Calvinism into their staunchly Lutheran countries.[4] Stable Calvinist allegiances were not confined to Rhineland centres adjacent to the west European Calvinist communities, but were found in the eastern half of the Empire as well, in Anhalt, the Upper Palatinate, and several Silesian duchies, regions not far from the more numerous Bohemian and Polish Calvinists.

The hallmark of Calvinism in the Empire was the leading part played from the outset by princely rulers. There were few Calvinist 'urban Reformations' supported by a popular groundswell, such as had been characteristic of the spread of Lutheranism in the 1520s and 1530s. Until shortly before the Peace of Augsburg in 1555 Zwinglian influences had also been strong in many of the imperial cities of the south and south-west. For that reason the Lutheran and Catholic princes who negotiated the Religious Peace, and who were as yet scarcely aware of the existence of Calvinism, confined the right to introduce the Reformation to rulers who subscribed to the Lutheran Confession of Augsburg, and conceded to the cities only circumscribed powers to introduce further changes. The cities, politically weaker than the princes and more obliged by inclination and circumstance to observe imperial laws strictly, had little choice after 1555 but to allow only Lutheran forms of Protestantism, as well as to tolerate Catholic minorities still established within their walls. Ministers and laity with Zwinglian or Calvinist inclinations, whether native Germans or immigrants from Switzerland and western Europe, naturally gravitated to the courts and universities of the handful of princes who were prepared to overlook the strict terms of the Peace of Augsburg.

First and foremost among these rulers were the electors palatine, the premier lay princes under the imperial constitution. From being one of the

4 W Baumann, (see Further Reading); E. Feddersen, 'Der Kryptocalvinismus am Gottorfer Hofe unter Herzog Johann Adolf', *Schriften des Vereins für Schleswig-Holsteinische Kirchengeschichte*, 2. Reihe, 8 (1926/8), 344–91.

last of the major principalities to adopt Lutheranism, in 1546, the Rhine Palatinate emerged with the succession of Elector Frederick III (1559–76) as the principal centre of inspiration for German Calvinists seeking both theological guidance and political leadership. Only the defeat of Elector Frederick V at the battle of White Mountain in 1620, the loss of his Bohemian crown, and the fall of Heidelberg to the Spanish army in 1622 put an end to this era. For sixty years, with a brief interruption under the Lutheran Elector Louis VI (1576–83), German Calvinists looked to Heidelberg university as their chief source of intellectual inspiration, to its famous library, the *Bibliotheca Palatina*, and to the city's prolific printing-presses. The Heidelberg church order of 1563 was that most frequently copied or adapted in other German states. The Heidelberg Catechism of the same year, although influenced by Zwinglian views on faith and the sacraments, was widely subscribed to in place of or alongside other Calvinist confessions both in Germany and abroad, in several Swiss cantons, at the Synod of Dort in 1618–19, and later in North America.

The court of the electors palatine was not only a major opportunity for preferment to the exiled Calvinist pastors and officials of all Germany, but through it ran the threads of European diplomacy. Personal and family ties bound the electors to leading figures on the European scene. Several members of the ruling Wittelsbach family had spent many years of their youth at French and other European courts. Frederick III married the widow of the Netherlands noble Henry of Brederode in 1569, Frederick IV the daughter of William of Orange in 1594, and Frederick V Elizabeth Stuart, daughter of James I, in 1613. From the 1560s the Calvinist electors shared the belief of the French Huguenots, the Netherlands rebels, and English Puritans in a European-wide, papally inspired ideological conspiracy to subvert Protestantism. In the eyes of western European Protestants, international Protestant solidarity in the face of this supposed threat required alliances with the German princes, most of whom were, however, reluctant to commit themselves. The eagerly accepted role of the Palatinate was to persuade other princes to overcome their scruples, though only with the foundation of the Evangelical Union of 1608 did Heidelberg achieve a measure of success in these endeavours. The electors had, however, assisted with troops and money in the conflicts of France and the Netherlands. Their poor military showing scarcely warranted the Roman triumph with which Frederick III's son John Casimir was greeted in Heidelberg on his return from France in 1576, but at least these interventions did divert the Catholic forces from devoting all their attention to the hard-pressed west-European Calvinists.

Yet it would be wrong to see the Palatinate as the sole source of inspiration for either Calvinist churches or Calvinist political initiatives within the Empire. Four main centres of Calvinist influence radiated outwards between 1560 and 1620: Heidelberg, Wittenberg (until 1591), Nassau, and the scores of communities in and near the Lower Rhenish duchies of Jülich, Cleves, Berg, and Mark. This last group included not only refugee churches of Flemings, Walloons, and Frenchmen, but sizeable native German ones which took over the existing synodal organization of Jülich and Cleves when most of the Netherlands exiles returned home from 1575 onwards.[5] It was not merely because of the proximity of the Netherlands that Calvinists congregated most thickly in the centre and west of the duchies; there they could also enjoy the protection of noble landed families like the counts of Mörs-Neuenahr and Dhaun-Falkenstein, and the lords of Quadt and Hardenberg. From the 1520s onwards the dukes had attempted humanist reforms within the church, but between 1566 and the end of the century harsh Counter-Reformation policies were implemented by the advisers to dukes now debilitated by insanity. The nobles, therefore, gravitated to the Calvinist cause and received political support from the Estates, as did the more independent Cleves towns Wesel and Duisburg where Calvinism was to gain the upper hand.

Yet many Calvinist communities in the Rhineland long remained, as they had begun, churches under the cross, or at best uneasily tolerated minorities, not unlike the early French and Netherlands communities. Independent but co-operating synods, sometimes confusingly called *classes* or quarters, developed in Jülich (1570), Cleves (1572) and Berg (1589). They provided a source of strength for the scattered and harassed urban presbyteries, on the lines of the system operated in France and stipulated for the Netherlands and the Empire at the Synod of Emden in 1571. The substantial Calvinist minorities in the imperial cities of Aachen and Cologne, when not themselves under severe pressure from the municipal authorities, gave valuable spiritual and other aid to the synods. Despite all handicaps, the number of Calvinists grew. Once toleration was declared in all four duchies in 1609, a general synod was established the following year for the now openly proclaimed communities.[6] Since the great majority had hitherto been voluntary churches, like those in East Friesland and Emden, and often half-secret churches as well, their relations with the state were far removed from the experience of Calvinism in German territorial states where it was introduced, even imposed, from above.

Before considering what impact Calvinism had on the German principalities, it may be asked why rulers, who as Lutherans already controlled former church lands and the organization of their churches, and

---

[5] H. Frost, 'Der Konvent von Wesel im Jahre 1568 und sein Einfluß auf das Entstehen eines deutschen evangelischen Kirchenverfassungsrechtes', *ZSS*, Kan. Abt., 56 (1970), 374.

[6] H. Forsthoff (see Further Reading), 435–6, 472–5, 498–501, 544–6, 556–7; E. Simons, *Niederrheinisches Synodal- und Gemeindeleben "unter dem Kreuz"* (Freiburg and Leipzig, 1897), 2–3, 5–8, 15–20; H. Frost, 'Gedanken' (see Further Reading), 2–10, 14–17, 20–2, 27–35.

who enjoyed the protection of the Religious Peace of 1555, should choose
the Calvinist faith and therefore the dangers not only of imperial outlawry
but of ostracism by fellow Protestant rulers. In the age of increasingly rigid
confessional orthodoxy in the second half of the sixteenth century,
Lutheran and Catholic rulers alike succeeded in concentrating ecclesiastical
powers into their own hands. Did Calvinism strengthen or weaken state
authority in ways unknown to other Protestant rulers? What was the
response of Calvinist rulers and their Lutheran subjects, in practice and in
political theory, to the issue of whether resistance to monarchical authority
was justified? How could Calvinist discipline and institutions be reconciled
with authoritarian princely rule; and how successful were they in
inculcating Calvinist teachings? The place of the German Calvinist
principalities in the constellation of international power politics, and the
development of politico-religious parties within the Empire, were the
essential framework for the growth of Calvinism in the territories, but
cannot be considered fully in a survey principally concerned with the role
of Calvinist churches within the individual states.

The German Reformed churches, as the rulers preferred to call them, or
the Second Reformation, a phrase used by historians during the last twenty-
five years, had certain features shared by Calvinist churches elsewhere in
Europe and others which were not. Characteristic of Germany was that the
change, or attempted change, from the Lutheran to the Reformed faith was
imposed by fiat of the ruler.[7] The Second Reformation was in this respect
distinct from the late Lutheran Reformations attempted after 1555 either
unsuccessfully by popular pressure, as in the episcopal cities of Bamberg,
Trier, and Würzburg, or successfully, and mainly by the efforts of the city
authorities, in Aachen, Dortmund, Essen, Colmar, and Hagenau.[8] The
Second Reformation was also accompanied by a reorientation to a more
aggressive and international stance in foreign policy, and therefore
ultimately, towards 1600, by a change in defence arrangements under the
influence of the militia schemes of the house of Nassau. Gerhard Zschäbitz
interpreted the Second Reformation entirely in terms of power-blocs

[7] H. Schilling, *Konfessionspolitik* (see Further Reading), 47–50.

[8] K. von Greyerz, *The Late City Reformation in Germany: the Case of Colmar, 1522–1628*
(Wiesbaden, 1980), 196–203. Ignoring long-established usage of the term 'Second Reformation',
Richard Gawthorp and Gerald Strauss, in 'Protestantism and Literacy in Early Modern Germany',
P & P, 104 (1984), 43–5, apply it to the Pietist offshoot from Lutheranism in the late seventeenth and
eighteenth centuries. Since Pietism shared the earlier Second Reformation's aim of completing the
Lutheran Reformation, it might be called the 'Third Reformation' by any historian so inclined. In *Piety
and Politics: Religion and the Rise of Absolutism in England, Württemberg and Prussia* (Cambridge, 1983),
Mary Fulbrook avoids any false nomenclature, but in comparing the role of Pietism in the state with that
of Puritanism, she fails to consider that Puritanism might more appropriately be contrasted with the
Second Reformation than with Pietism. However, further confusion is provided by C. Lindberg, *The
Third Reformation? Charismatic Movements and the Lutheran Tradition* (Macon, Ga., 1983), who calls
Pietism the second Reformation and uses 'Third Reformation' for modern Pentacostalism and the
charismatic renewal movement among Lutherans.

among the Protestant princes: those who sided with the modern nation-state and wanted to modernize their feudal states were ranged against the supporters of the old Empire.[9] Yet the foreign Calvinists with whom German rulers allied were chiefly the French and Netherlands opponents of powerful centralizing monarchies. Only for the house of Nassau was involvement with the interests of international Calvinism great enough to outweigh the disadvantages of dubious minority religious status within the Empire.

Above all the Second Reformation was marked not just by certain shifts in doctrine from the Lutheran position, but by the reform of Christian life through the systematic reordering of the Church, education, and even the state on the principles of biblical evangelism.[10] Between 1530 and 1560 the Lutheran theologians had become disillusioned at their own failure to improve the quality of religious observance and understanding. Ecclesiastical visitations in the latter part of the century revealed gross ignorance about the fundamentals of faith and widespread non-attendance at church.[11] The work of the Lutheran Reformation still had to be completed; in this sense the Elector Frederick III of the Palatinate used the word 'reformiert' at the imperial diet of 1566. The Nassau confession of 1578, drafted by the theologian Christoph Pezel, an exile from Wittenberg, declared the need for the continuation of the Wittenberg Reformation by means of a further 'Reformation', 'emendation' or 'improvement', since the challenge of the Counter-Reformation, especially the activity of the Jesuits, required the purging of all remaining superstitious ceremonies.[12] Lastly, the thoroughgoing reform of Christian life also brought a new revival of humanist learning and a different relationship between secular and ecclesiastical authorities.

The irenic writings of German Calvinists, from the *Admonitio* of Zacharius Ursinus in 1581 to the *Irenicum* of David Pareus in 1614, stressed their points of agreement with the Lutherans and tried to win them over by persuasion, but the Lutherans rejected any overtures at co-operation in the harshest terms, for which already the Formula of Concord of 1577 had set the tone. The Formula, which won the allegiance of some two-thirds of the squabbling Lutheran theologians and churches, destroyed any opportunity of occupying the middle ground and forced all theologians to choose sides.

---

[9] G. Zschäbitz, 'Zur Problematik der sogenannten "Zweiten Reformation" in Deutschland', *Wissenschaftliche Zeitschrift der Universität Leipzig, Gesellschafts- und sozialwissenschaftliche Reihe*, 14. iii (1965), 505–9. For a more balanced Marxist summary, see M. Steinmetz, *Deutschland von 1476 bis 1648* (2nd edn., Berlin, 1978), 256–60.

[10] T. Klein (see Further Reading), 70–1.

[11] G. Strauss, *Luther's House of Learning: the Indoctrination of the Young in the German Reformation* (Baltimore, 1979), 249, 300–2; id., 'Success and Failure in the German Reformation' *P & P*, 67 (1975), 30–63.

[12] C. Andresen (ed.), *Handbuch der Dogmengeschichte*, ii (Göttingen, 1980), 295.

Indeed, fundamental differences of belief and practice divided the two churches, despite Calvinist attempts to gloss over them. Divergent interpretations of the nature of the sacraments and of Christ, though not of predestination, were the major issues in Germany. The Second Reformation rejected the physical presence of Christ in the elements of bread and wine in the sense that the recipient, even if an unbeliever, partook of his body. It also ridiculed the concomitant Lutheran belief in the ubiquity of Christ in the world, stressing instead his humanity. Much turned on which version of the Confession of Augsburg was accepted as binding, the original published in 1531, the *Invariata*, or Melanchthon's revision of 1540, the *Variata*. The issue was complicated by further variations between Latin and German texts of the *Invariata* and between different printings. The most important change in the *Variata* was Melanchthon's rewording of the article on the Real Presence in the sacraments; the formula that 'with' the bread and wine were administered the body and blood of Christ was more acceptable to the South German Reformers.

The fiercest disputes, especially among laymen, were over matters of outward observance which may seem trivial but reflected either doctrinal differences or the Calvinist convictions that Luther had left much papal idolatry intact and that there were no adiaphora, no religious customs that were a matter of choice. Rulers were often unwilling, or unable, to introduce the whole gamut of recommended changes, but among the Calvinist demands more usually acceded to were that the eating of the whole host at communion should give way to the breaking of plain white bread, stone altars to wooden tables, and stone fonts with consecrated water to tin basins with ordinary water. The breaking of bread became for German Calvinists the symbol which the chalice had been for Bohemian Hussites. Readily grasped by laymen who wished to express their 'church patriotism', the breaking of bread embodied for theologians the imitation of Christ's action at the Last Supper, the need for visual symbols of his passion and death, and the denial of the Real Presence in the sacraments.[13] The number of church festivals was drastically reduced from over thirty to under ten, but a monthly day of penitence and prayer often added. A wholesale assault was launched on the remnants in Lutheran observance of images, saint-worship, vestments, fasting, organ music, graveside funeral services, and above all the practice of exorcizing the devil in baptism.

The ruler's responsibility in this work is best outlined in the torso of a Calvinist commentary on Luther's German Bible left behind by Christian I of Saxony's theologians at his death in 1591. Its central theme was the need to implement a Christian Reformation not only in theology, but in every

---

[13] B. Nischan (see Further Reading), 18, 20.

sphere of spiritual and political life. The Lutherans were condemned as neither Evangelical nor Papist. Since all Christian subjects are contracted to fulfil God's Word, the Christian magistrate as God's deputy is answerable that services are attended, the Lord's Day observed, and blasphemy severely punished. Because some of the clergy and many of the people oppose God's work, the ruler is obliged to compel them to their duty. The prince should also help to ensure victory for God's commands in the lands of his neighbours, while an active foreign policy against Catholics was likewise justified from the Bible.[14]

In Saxony, as elsewhere, such ideas should not be seen as a foreign importation, but essentially as a native growth. Certainly many Swiss, Italian, French, and Netherlands theologians found their way to the Empire, particularly to Heidelberg, but in the south and south west of the country a strong tradition went back to the 1520s of Zwinglian and Bucerian Churches, the south German urban Reformed. When through political circumstances after the defeat of the League of Schmalkalden in 1547 most southern imperial cities donned a straitjacket of Lutheranism, their leading humanists, clergy, and lay officials sought refuge with sympathetic rulers.[15] Although the electors palatine Frederick II (1544–56) and Otto Henry (1556–9) were Lutherans, they allowed a wide variety of opinions among their subjects and at the university of Heidelberg. Frederick was the only prince at the negotiations for the Religious Peace of 1555 to speak up for freedom of worship for all inhabitants of the Empire, not just the freedom of rulers to introduce Lutheranism to their principalities. This policy was urged by his successors at imperial diets until Frederick III dropped it during the course of the Augsburg Diet in 1566.[16]

The other native mainstream of the Second Reformation consisted of the Philippists, the pupils and friends of Philip Melanchthon, who from the 1550s onwards became Crypto-Calvinists and later Calvinists in Wittenberg itself, Hamburg, Bremen, Heidelberg, and Breslau. Among the many gradations of Philippist viewpoints, the Crypto-Calvinists, like those in Wittenberg since 1571, held to the Calvinist doctrine of the sacraments. The two expulsions from Wittenberg of Crypto-Calvinists in 1574 and Calvinists in 1591 scattered them to Nassau-Dillenburg, Heidelberg, Zweibrücken and other welcoming centres in western Germany.[17] Already in the 1560s a dozen or so Silesian Philippists fled from persecution to the haven of Heidelberg, where men like Ursinus and Pareus were to play a leading role in Calvinizing the Palatinate and the lands of other rulers. By no

---

[14] Klein, op. cit. 167–80.

[15] V. Press, 'Stadt und territoriale Konfessionsbildung' (see Further Reading), 258–60.

[16] E. F. P. Güss, *Die kurpfälzische Regierung und das Täufertum bis zum Dreißigjährigen Krieg* (Stuttgart, 1960), 36; W. Hollweg *Augsburger Reichstag* (see Further Reading), 291, 315.

[17] J. Moltmann (see Further Reading), 9–13.

means all the swirling mass of internal German exiles were theologians or clerics. Many were influential lawyers, civil servants, university professors of all faculties, booksellers and other laymen who regularly met and corresponded with one another.

A new wave was set in motion when the Lutheran Elector Palatine Louis VI (1576–83) instituted a purge at Heidelberg. During the ensuing 'seven lean years', as Pareus later called them, only the small enclave about Neustadt, left to the elector's younger brother John Casimir in their father's will, remained Calvinist in the Palatinate. Burggrave Fabian von Dohna, the East Prussian humanist-educated Junker who served in John Casimir's wars and in his administration, later claimed that during the reign of Louis VI Calvinists from all over the Empire came to serve John Casimir, even without pay, as he was the only German Calvinist prince.[18] John Casimir and John VI (1559–1606) of Nassau subsequently encouraged the clerics and lay advisers who had taken refuge with them to assist the Second Reformation in the territories of the Wetterau counts (to the west and south of Hesse), Lippe, Bremen, and elsewhere. Several of the leading figures, like Christoph Pezel, had three or more staging posts. Scultetus' career spanned more than fifty years and a dozen centres.[19] The widely travelled Westphalian nobleman Johann von Münster wrote thirty-seven polemical and educational books on religious subjects. He served the Calvinist cause at the courts of Dillenburg, Schleswig-Holstein, and Tecklenburg, among others, but failed to get a post in the Palatinate in 1603 because he had written a treatise against dancing.[20] The enthusiasm of these men for the work in hand was epitomized in 1586 by the Saxon nobleman Otto von Grünrade, president of the ecclesiastical council of the Palatinate: 'God be praised that my earthly fatherland [Saxony] is not so dear that I would not rather live in a Reformed Church which is my true fatherland'.[21]

While Calvinist rulers could draw on the services of clergy and officials from all parts of the Empire, they had to work within the constraints of the Peace of Augsburg, which only allowed rulers who adhered to the Confession of Augsburg to determine the religion of their subjects. The true interpretation of that confession assumed all the greater importance. After 1561 many Lutheran princes were influenced by their theologians no longer to accept Melanchthon's *Variata*, to which alone Calvinists could consent. At the diet of 1566 Duke Christopher of Württemberg and Count Palatine Wolfgang of Zweibrücken tried to persuade other Lutheran rulers to accede to Emperor Maximilian II's demand that the diet condemn Frederick III of

---

[18] *Selbstbiographie des Burggrafen Fabian von Dohna (1550–1621)*, ed. C. Krollmann (Leipzig, 1905), 26.

[19] M. Smid, *Ostfriesische Kirchengeschichte* (Leer, 1974), 279.

[20] H. Richter, 'Johann von Münster', *Westfälische Lebensbilder*, 4 (1933), 114–19, 124.

[21] P. Münch (see Further Reading), 83.

the Palatinate as a Calvinist. At the last moment they drew back from the brink. The moderating influence of Elector Augustus I of Saxony prevailed, as did the consideration that the Lutherans could not afford to weaken Protestant unity by alienating the most senior Protestant elector under the constitution. Moreover, as Duke Christopher later admitted, if they had proceeded to a condemnation, '. . . the persecutions in France, Spain, the Netherlands and other similar places would grow at once by heaps, and by that condemnation we should be guilty of shedding their blood.'[22] For the rest of the century diets neither condemned nor approved of Calvinism. The Calvinist rulers always professed themselves bound by the Confession of Augsburg and therefore protected by the Religious Peace. Inevitably this involved a measure of deceit. The Elector Frederick III and Count Simon VI (1563–1613) of Lippe claimed that they based their own beliefs and their Churches only on the Bible, not on the works of named theologians, but Simon had a large library containing many Philippist and Calvinist works, while Frederick III was familiar with the theological controversies of the day and had the Calvinist confessions and major theological works systematically published at Heidelberg.[23]

The religious preoccupations of many German Calvinist rulers, especially those who first introduced the Second Reformation, and of their lay and clerical advisers, cast doubt on any purely political explanation of the Second Reformation, though undoubtedly political motives had some weight. John VI of Nassau-Dillenburg's gradual conversion took place from 1572 to 1574, but was consistent with his much earlier preference for simple services and his dislike for myth, magic, and especially exorcism, which he had already banned from the Church. He was influenced by his brothers William of Orange and Louis of Nassau, as well as by nobles associated with them in the Netherlands enterprise. Nevertheless, that enterprise could only succeed in association with the Calvinist ideology that in turn spiritualized and justified their political actions. Subjectively, at least, John's conversion was an act of conviction. Even then, a fully Calvinist Church was established only by slow stages in Nassau-Dillenburg during the next twelve years.[24]

The Calvinist rulers were to a large extent related by marriage to one another, and frequently to Netherlands nobles, but more often than not these marriages were concluded after they became committed to the Calvinist cause or had fought in the Netherlands. Family connections and political influence from the Palatinate contributed to Count Palatine John I (1569–1604) of Zweibrücken becoming a Calvinist in 1588. Similar

[22] Hollweg, op. cit. 387.
[23] Ibid. 157, 160–1; G. Schormann, 'Simon VI. und seine Bibliothek', *Jahrbuch für westfälische Kirchengeschichte*, 70 (1977), 76–81, 87, 92–3.
[24] R. Glawischnig (see Further Reading), 125–6; Münch, op. cit. 73–95.

influences were exerted on some of the Wetterau counts by John VI of Nassau and on Simon VI of Lippe from Hesse and the Wetterau counts. Yet education also played its part, as it had done for the first generation of Lutheran princes. A vital role was filled by the Academy at Strasburg, heavily patronized by young scions of the Bentheim, Lippe, Zweibrücken, Ysenburg, Solms, and other princely and noble families. From the mid-century the Strasburg city council encouraged the Lutheran faction in the school opposed to the influence of Johann Sturm and other teachers inclined towards Calvinism, but most of the students supported the Calvinists.[25] For many of the counts who attended the Strasburg Academy and in some instances then spent time at Heidelberg university, education and family connections reinforced one another and were buttressed by correspondence with Calvinist theologians. Typical of rulers was the career of the Elector Christian I of Saxony (1586–91), who had a Philippist tutor, then continued his theological studies on his own, and was finally brought to the Reformed faith by his father's councillor Dr Nikolaus Krell.[26] John I of Zweibrücken was a learned intellectual of no mean theological accomplishments whose conscience was torn for years between the contradictory advice of a Lutheran court preacher and a Crypto-Calvinist superintendent before he resolved his doubts about the Formula of Concord in favour of Calvinism.[27]

The political impulses towards Calvinism were more evident in the five Wetterau counties of Solms-Braunfels, Ysenburg-Büdingen, Wied-Runkel, Sayn-Wittgenstein, and Hanau-Münzenberg, and in the landgraviate of Hesse-Cassel, all of which John VI of Nassau wished to gain for his planned political union to uphold the cause of Calvinism in the Empire and western Europe.[28] Succession disputes within a ruling dynasty propelled Landgrave Maurice of Lower Hesse towards Calvinism after 1592 and Count John of East Friesland until his death in 1591.[29] Elector John Sigismund of Brandenburg might easily be written off as a ruler who adopted Calvinism in 1613 simply as a means to ensure the loyalty of his subjects in the Rhenish duchies and Dutch aid against the rival claimant to this disputed succession. John Sigismund had, however, been educated at the Strasburg Academy and the university of Heidelberg, where the Calvinist elector palatine, the ruling family, and the theologians made a great impression on him. Political circumstances merely encouraged him to

---

[25] A. Schindling, *Humanistische Hochschule und freie Reichsstadt, Gymnasium und Akademie in Straßburg, 1538–1621* (Mainz, 1977), 34–6, 135–9, 335–68, 382–3.

[26] Klein, op. cit. 8, 11.

[27] W.-U. Deetjen, 'Das Ende der Entente cordiale zwischen den Bruderkirchen und Bruderdynastien Pfalz-Zweibrücken, Württemberg und Pfalz-Neuburg', *Blätter für württembergische Kirchengeschichte*, 82 (1982), 39–43, 62–5, 88–93.

[28] G. Menk, '"Qui trop embrasse peu estreind." Politik und Persönlichkeit Graf Johannes VI. von Nassau-Dillenburg, 1580–1606', *Jahrbuch für westdeutsche Landesgeschichte*, 7 (1981), 131–4.

[29] K. E. Demandt, *Geschichte des Landes Hessen* (2nd edn., Kassel, 1972), 244–5; H. Schmidt (see Further Reading), 191–2.

proclaim his faith openly in spite of the strong Lutheran allegiances in his own family and in Brandenburg.[30] For all these princes conviction was from the outset as deeply engrained as the political considerations with which it was associated. Elsewhere, commitment to the Calvinist cause even outran what was politically feasible. Count Arnold II of Bentheim-Tecklenburg had to proceed with utmost caution in introducing the Second Reformation after 1586 because of the proximity of marauding Spanish troops from the Netherlands. In Anhalt, sandwiched between Brandenburg and Saxony, the princes for many years from 1596 onwards considered it prudent to profess loyalty to Lutheranism while implementing several measures characteristic of the Second Reformation.[31]

The key conversion of a ruler was the earliest. Frederick III of the Palatinate became Calvinist well before his more active intervention on behalf of French and Netherlands Calvinists. To the alarm of his wife Mary of Brandenburg-Ansbach, who had originally converted him to Lutheranism, he spent the years between 1559 and 1561 agonizing over his decision.[32] A fierce theological debate was already raging in the university and pulpits at Heidelberg when Frederick came to the electorate but, like Frederick the Wise earlier, he preferred to deal with Ursinus, Olevian, and their fellow theologians through his own lawyers and advisers rather than directly. The most influential of these advisers were the three brothers and counts of Erbach who had contacts with Strasburg and the Reformers Calvin and Bullinger. They were never to accept Calvinism themselves, but played a part as the elector's councillors in encouraging him to go at least half-way along the road. Thereafter a letter from Melanchthon towards the end of 1559 eventually convinced Frederick during 1560 to see the sacraments in Calvinist terms.[33] The elector immersed himself in biblical study, in the middle of which he declared in April 1560 to his son-in-law, the elector of Saxony, that he would 'first seek the kingdom of God and afterwards worry the less about temporal matters, since everything of that kind will then be granted us'.[34] The notion that obedience to God would bring rewards on earth was common even among princes. The elector's

[30] W. Delius, 'Der Konfessionswechsel des brandenburgischen Kurfürsten Johann Sigismund', *Jahrbuch für berlin-brandenburgische Kirchengeschichte*, 50 (1975/7), 125–6.

[31] K. G. Döhmann, *Das Leben des Grafen Arnold von Bentheim, 1554–1606* (Burgsteinfurt, 1903), 14, 17, 23–4, 30, 41, 47–8; H. Duncker, *Anhalts Bekenntnisstand . . . 1570–1606* (Dessau, 1892), 82, 100–12; *Die evangelischen Kirchenordnungen* (see Further Reading), ii (1904), 530–8.

[32] A. Kluckhohn, 'Wie ist Kurfürst Friedrich III. von der Pfalz Calvinist geworden?', *Münchner historisches Jahrbuch* (1866), 434–8, 451–7; Hollweg, op. cit. 4–7, 15–30.

[33] V. Press, 'Die Grafen von Erbach und die Anfänge des reformierten Bekenntnisses in Deutschland', in H. Bannach and H.-P. Lachmann, (eds.) *Aus Geschichte und ihren Hilfswissenschaften* (Marburg, 1979), 667–78; W. Hollweg, *Neue Untersuchungen zur Geschichte und Lehre des Heidelberger Katechismus* (Neukirchen, 1962), 36–7; R. Lossen, *Die Glaubensspaltung in der Kurpfalz* (2nd edn., Heidelberg, 1930), 55–6.

[34] Kluckhohn, op. cit. 459.

denial that he was too greatly influenced by his advisers in reaching his decision receives support from the circumstance that already late in 1561, without consulting them, he replaced the host by white bread in the churches of the Palatinate. The theological arguments persuaded him to take this step less than did his own experience that the common folk worshipped the host as if it were God himself. Thomas Erastus' classic statement of the Calvinist view on the breaking of bread, *Das Büchlein vom Brotbrechen*, was published in Heidelberg in 1563 concurrently with the Heidelberg Catechism.[35]

One advantage of both religious and political significance in adopting Calvinism may have been in the elector's mind. A thorough visitation under Lutheran auspices of the Palatinate in 1556 had revealed not only ignorance, non-attendance at services, and disrespect for the sacraments, but on the one hand a clinging to 'Papist ceremonies' by clergy and laity, and on the other considerable Anabaptist penetration in at least the two administrative districts of Kreuznach and Neustadt. The remedy proposed was good Christian discipline as at the time of the primitive church.[36]

Especially since the indecisiveness of Frederick II's reign had left even villages in the turmoil of religious disputes, the Lutheran reform measures of Otto Henry had had too little time to take effect, and anyway could only have added to the confusion by allowing use of the catechisms of both Luther and the Württemberg Reformer Johannes Brenz. Frederick III's preface to the Heidelberg Catechism stressed the need for unity and uniformity.[37] These might be expected to arise more effectively from Calvinist discipline and institutions than from their Lutheran counterparts. At the end of 1564 Frederick expressed admiration for the unity in belief among the Huguenot churches in France and for their strictly enforced Christian discipline, which had not failed to punish the transgressions even of a Condé. He commented equally favourably on the Netherlands Calvinists.[38] The spread of Anabaptism was blamed in an edict of 1568 not only on poor preaching but on godless behaviour which offended the simple. Therefore the local officials were to set the elector's subjects a good example of church attendance and Christian conduct, and appoint God-fearing men in every parish to supervise behaviour at church and reprimand

[35] Hollweg, *Neue Untersuchungen*, 182–3; Nischan, op. cit. 20.

[36] G. Biundo, 'Bericht und Bedenken über die erste kurpfälzische Visitation im Jahre 1556', *Jahrbuch der Hessischen Kirchengeschichtlichen Vereinigung*, 10 (1959), 1–41; G. A. Benrath, 'Les visites pastorales dans le Palatinat electoral au XVIᵉ siècle', in *Sensibilité religieuse et discipline écclesiastique* (see Further Reading), 70–2.

[37] W. Hollweg, *Neue Untersuchungen zur Geschichte und Lehre des Heidelberger Katechismus. Zweite Folge* (Neukirchen, 1968), 14–15.

[38] *Briefe Friedrichs des Frommen*, ed. A. Kluckhohn (2 vols., Braunschweig, 1868–72), i. 538–9; A. Kluckhohn, *Friedrich der Fromme* (see Further Reading), 312–13; G. A. Benrath, 'Die Eigenart der pfälzischen Reformation und die Vorgeschichte des Heidelberger Katechismus', *Heidelberger Jahrbücher*, 7 (1963), 20.

public misdemeanours.[39] Frederick believed that the Anabaptists should be converted by persuasion and the example of a model church, but that model could only be achieved by measures which went beyond what even the stricter Lutheran Churches accomplished with their rudimentary parish discipline.

Frederick III was merely the foremost of those Calvinist rulers who became directly involved in every stage of the Second Reformation, leaving far less to be implemented independently by their theologians than was usual among Lutheran princes at this time. Frederick himself welcomed the small colony of Netherlanders settled at Frankenthal in 1562, insisted that the church ordinance of 1563 conform to the Heidelberg Catechism and the Bible,[40] and took part in an iconoclastic tour of churches in the provinces during 1565. By one account his own fist smashed through a painted crucifixion in the cell of the prioress of Liebenau.[41] His grandson Frederick IV (1583–1610), although much more under the influence of his officials, addressed the citizens of Heidelberg on their shortcomings on several occasions during the visitations of 1593–5 and then went to the Upper Palatinate to enforce similar measures between 1596 and 1598. Margrave Ernest Frederick of Baden-Durlach, familiar in Latin with the Church Fathers as well as the Bible, wrote his own Calvinist confession, which was published in 1599 as an appendix to his theologians' refutation of the Formula of Concord.[42] From 1605 onwards Maurice of Hesse (1592–1627) sermonized his subjects and conducted hearings to make them accept his 'Three Points of Improvement' directed against the doctrine of ubiquity, images, and use of the host. The tenor of his message was clear: 'Christ did not say I am custom, but I am the truth.' One historian has commented that the landgrave held out biblical phrases to individual subjects like a pistol, so that the answers rarely reflected true opinions.[43] The impatient Calvinist bureaucracy which divided Marburg backsliders into twelve categories proved as likely to be self-defeating in Hesse as elsewhere. Count Wolfgang Ernest of Ysenburg deliberately tricked his subjects between 1596 and 1598 by secretly removing Lutheran pastors on trumped-up moral charges. He told their replacements to present the new teachings as if they were the old Lutheran ones, had his officials interrogate subjects on their beliefs in the presence of armed guards, and himself

[39] Güss, op. cit. 61–6.
[40] Die evangelischen Kirchenordnungen, xiv, Kurpfalz, ed. J. F. G. Goeters (1969), 47.
[41] H. Rott, 'Kirchen- und Bildersturm bei der Einführung der Reformation in der Pfalz', Neues Archiv für die Geschichte der Stadt Heidelberg und der rheinischen Pfalz, 6 (1905), 243–53.
[42] Baumann, op. cit. 163–8.
[43] T. Griewank (see Further Reading), 54, cf. ibid. 49, 53, 60; E. Hofsommer, Die kirchlichen Verbesserungspunkte des Landgrafen Moritz des Gelehrten von Hessen (Marburg, 1910), 69–71, 81, 93; H. Heppe, Die Einführung der Verbesserungspunkte in Hessen von 1604–1610 (Kassel, 1849), 85.

delivered a long speech urging the clergy to cleanse the Church of all mistaken doctrine.[44]

Another aspect of princely intervention was the founding of *Gymnasien* and the reform and purging of universities, not only for the usual purpose of training loyal officials for church and state, but also to cultivate Calvinist late humanism by attracting the best teachers. These men and their pupils were often sent to aid fellow princes embarking on the same course. Not only were advanced Latin schools established or reformed on the initiative of larger cities like Bremen, Emden, and Wesel or medium-sized ones like Duisburg and Düsseldorf, but quite modest towns came through princely initiative to harbour schools of considerably more than regional significance: Hanau, Hornbach in the Zweibrücken territories, (Burg)Steinfurt in the county of Bentheim-Tecklenburg, and Zerbst in Anhalt. Many of the schools modelled their curricula on the Strasburg Academy. The outstanding example, and the one which had the greatest impact on other Calvinist high schools, was the Academy at Herborn. Established in 1584 by John VI of Nassau to educate his sons and speed the Calvinization of his lands and those of the Wetterau counts, it soon came to outshine Heidelberg as a centre for innovative Calvinist thought and synthesis in many fields of learning. Herborn was the prime centre disseminating in Germany the Ramist logic and dialectic which were so valuable in training Calvinist preachers for the confessional disputes. Ramism had direct practical application in Christian education and in popularizing the theology of the Christian life. The publications of Herborn's professors represented the pinnacles of Calvinist late humanist achievement: Johann Piscator's literal Bible translation and commentaries, Kaspar Olevian's covenant theology, Wilhelm Zepper's ecclesiology, Johannes Althusius' *Politics*, and Johann Alsted's encyclopaedias and writings on homiletics and education that were to influence Comenius, a one-time Herborn pupil.[45] The Calvinist principalities and cities of the Empire, although a scattered minority, benefited from a threefold interchange of intellectual ideas, of personnel, and of major statements of the faith and measures for its implementation, of which the Heidelberg Catechism and church order were by far the most influential. Both the creation and the diffusion of these instruments of the Calvinist mission were taken directly in hand by the rulers.

Rulers were well aware that control over religion strengthened state authority. Frederick IV declared the maintenance of churches and schools in the Palatinate to be 'the foremost part of our rule as elector and the basis of all temporal and heavenly welfare'.[46] Later discussion of Calvinist

---

[44] G. Hanle (see Further Reading), 27-30.

[45] G. Menk (see Further Reading), 13-14, 34, 53-4, 116-18, 174-9, 197-216, and *passim*; R. J. W. Evans, *The Wechsel Presses: Humanism and Calvinism in Central Europe, 1572-1627* (Oxford, 1975), 17-19; Andresen, op. cit. 329-30.

[46] V. Press, *Calvinismus und Territorialstaat* (see Further Reading), 128.

institutions will examine how they could fill that role within the principalities. In frontier areas of the Palatinate Calvinism was ruthlessly imposed as early at 1564–5 on towns and villages ruled jointly with the bishops of Worms and Speyer and the margrave of Baden. Implementation of the true faith here flouted the legal rights of patrons to benefices and the conventions of imperial law in a manner that also extended the territorial influence of a state lacking clearly demarcated boundaries.[47] The standing in imperial politics of lesser Calvinist states like Lippe and Nassau improved as their commitment to a minority faith adhered to by few rulers promoted them into the league of major principalities.[48]

Political advantage could thus be gained from the adoption of Calvinism, but the economic returns proved less than anticipated. Policies favourable to west European exiles were at best of marginal economic benefit for the principalities before the Thirty Years War. The economic advantage accrued instead to Aachen, Cologne, Frankfurt, Hamburg, and the few other already flourishing imperial or territorial cities which admitted sizeable Calvinist minorities with a wealthy mercantile element. The privileged Palatinate settlements at Frankenthal, Lambrecht, Schönau, and Otterberg attracted a few thousand textile workers, Gobelin weavers, goldsmiths, and painters, but overall these remained relatively poor communities even when compared with the nearby towns of the electorate. The ambitious new town of Neu-Hanau, founded in 1606 by Count Philip Louis II (1595–1612) of Hanau-Münzenberg to attract more merchants and artisans from neighbouring Frankfurt, where Calvinists were being harassed, was for both political and practical reasons slow to get off the ground and failed in its objectives.[49]

Foreign-policy interests were more closely linked than economic ones to the ascendancy of Calvinism in the Palatinate and Nassau. Yet the expectations raised abroad and the ambitions which rulers entertained of aiding persecuted foreign Calvinists could only in small part be fulfilled because of the constraints under which they operated. The small principality of Nassau-Dillenburg came close to bankruptcy under the burden of large contributions to the Netherlands cause during the four decades from 1566. In the Palatinate Frederick III devoted considerable financial resources to aiding the Huguenots, the expeditions of his son John Casimir, and William of Orange, but since very little of his outlay was reimbursed, his successors felt obliged to adopt a more mercenary

---

[47] Hollweg, *Augsburger Reichstag*, 48–50.
[48] Schilling, op. cit. 202.
[49] W. Alter, *Pfalzatlas. Textband* (2 vols., Speyer, 1964–80), ii. 1050–5; G. Kaller, 'Bevölkerung und Gewerbe in Frankenthal, Neustadt und Lambrecht am Ende des 16. Jahrhunderts', in E. Facius and J. Sydow (eds.), *Aus Stadt- und Wirtschaftsgeschichte Südwestdeutschlands* (Stuttgart, 1975), 152, 166–7; H. Bott, *Gründung und Anfänge der Neustadt Hanau, 1596–1620* (2 vols., Marburg, 1970), ii. 407–14, 418–20; H. Schilling, 'Innovation through Migration', *Histoire sociale*, 16 (1983), 18.

approach. John Casimir in particular had only a small principality of his own between 1576 and 1583.

The political limitations were even more compelling. After initial hesitation until 1566, Frederick III was never in doubt about the justice of military aid for threatened Protestants, but wished to avoid both imperial stricture and isolation from the Lutheran princes. He clandestinely supported John Casimir's expeditions to France in 1567–8 and 1575–6, and sought English aid for him in 1568, but denied to the Emperor that his son's actions were any responsibility of his.[50] John Casimir has been perhaps too easily dismissed as nothing but a mercenary without deep religious conviction and selfishly intent on securing the bishoprics of Metz, Toul, and Verdun, or else alternative lands in France or the southern Netherlands. He was not the only or the first person to propose the forcible recovery of the lost bishoprics for the Empire; Frederick III had done so in 1560, the Strasburg schoolteacher and active partisan for the Huguenots, Johann Sturm, in 1564, and the Emperor's adviser Lazarus von Schwendi in 1577.[51] John Casimir also had grounds for grievance that the Huguenots and King Henri III of France had not implemented earlier treaty obligations to pay the costs of his expeditions. He even had some justification in expressing mistrust for Henri of Navarre 'because of "machiavilliards" which were about him'.[52] The poor relationships between John Casimir and both Navarre and Orange were not just the result of personal quarrels and financial pique. The count palatine, while undeserving of the reputation of a fanatical Calvinist which his services to the radicals of Ghent gave him in the Netherlands, nevertheless looked askance at French and Netherlands *Politiques* prepared to change faith and ally with Catholics.

Not only during the reign of the Lutheran Louis VI did the electoral Palatinate fail to further the Calvinist cause on the international stage. For the next twenty years the intermittent problems of minorities and regencies again threatened the continuance of Calvinism at home and created distractions from an active foreign policy. In his first years as regent for Frederick IV from 1583, John Casimir had to tread cautiously while strengthening his position against his Lutheran co-regents. On John Casimir's death in 1592 it took two years, the concerted efforts of the councillors of the Palatinate, and the intervention of John VI of Nassau and his army to make the country safe from the pretensions of the Lutheran

---

[50] B. Vogler, 'Le rôle des Électeurs palatins dans les guerres de religion en France (1559–1592)', *Cahiers d'histoire*, 10 (1965), 58–68; P. Krüger, *Die Beziehungen der rheinischen Pfalz zu Westeuropa, 1576–82* (Munich, 1964), 3; C.-P. Clasen (see Further Reading), 5, 8–11.

[51] Vogler, op. cit. 57; J. Rott, 'Le recteur strasbourgeois Jean Sturm et les Protestants français', *Actes du Colloque 'L'amiral de Coligny et son temps'* (Paris, 1974), 422; Krüger, op. cit. 126.

[52] *Calendar of State Papers, Foreign. Elisabeth*, xii (London, 1901), 229; Krüger, op. cit. 36, 45, 95, 131.

Count Palatine Reichard of Simmern to the regency. A similar crisis threatened the succession when Frederick IV became gravely ill in 1602. In his will he replaced the rightful regent, the Lutheran Count Palatine Philip Louis of Neuburg, by John I of Zweibrücken and a fistful of five other highborn Calvinists. As a further guarantee for the survival of the Calvinist church the supreme council was reorganized and purged of all non-Calvinists in 1604, incidentally removing any possibility of serious opposition to the more aggressive policies of Christian of Anhalt in the period leading to the Thirty Years War.[53]

Nassau was long spared dynastic troubles, but the fivefold partition of the county in 1606 and subsequent quarrels with his brothers made it impossible for John VII (1606–23) to assume the leading role in Calvinist counsels which his father had held for forty years. By contrast with John Casimir, John VI could never have been accused of being a political adventurer. During his governorship of Guelders between 1578 and 1580 this earnest missionary helped to convert much of the province from Catholicism to Calvinism. He worked tirelessly, but by 1584 in vain, to resist Bavarian designs on the strategically important prince-bishoprics of Cologne and Münster. Until the end of the century he and his son developed in numerous memoranda, one of the earliest of which was presented to Sir Philip Sidney at Cologne in 1577, a coherent and rationally argued analysis of the Protestant predicament in the face of conspiracy among the Counter-Reformation powers. The task which the counts conceived for Calvinist rulers was to secure a threefold unity—in religion, defence, and 'correspondence'—against an enemy seeking ascendancy by exploiting Protestant divisions. Their defensive militias, organized along similar lines and with provision for reciprocal aid, would be a preliminary to the long-sought Protestant alliance. By 'correspondence' was understood the exchange of political news and opinions with a view to formulating common action that might or might not lead to an alliance, but could also go beyond the terms of any alliance. Correspondence was to be conducted simultaneously at three levels, among the imperial counts (Nassau being the leader of the league of Wetterau counts), the German Protestant states, and West European Protestants. Little of this went beyond the planning stage, but the ideas were adopted with modifications by Christian of Anhalt in his policies for the Palatinate and the Evangelical Union.[54]

Within the principalities, no less than in the wider political sphere, the fortunes of Calvinism were not simply a product of the ruler's wishes, but depended in good measure on the response of the nobles and of the representative estates which they usually dominated. The extent to which

---

[53] Press, *Calvinismus*, 324–5, 374–90, 420–5, 440, 449–52.
[54] Glawischnig, op. cit. 128, 146–50; L. Paul, *Nassauische Unionspläne. Untersuchungen zum politischen Programm des deutschen Calvinismus im Zeitalter der Gegenreformation* (Münster, 1966), 6–9, 23–7, 65–76, 239–43, 259–61.

the nobles feared inroads into their rights as patrons of ecclesiastical benefices often proved crucial. Owning little patronage, the nobles in Lippe helped the count to enforce the Second Reformation against recalcitrant towns and villages. The Hessian nobility, however, might well object to Landgrave Maurice's claim that God had given him his 'bishop's crozier' and with it the nobles' right to fill benefices. The Lutheran nobles of the Upper Palatinate for decades reacted strongly against an intermittent policy of forcible Calvinization by administrations owing allegiance to the distant Rhineland, but by the 1590s they had been bought off by concessions for their own lands to the extent that they were no longer in the van of resistance. In the southern part of the Rhenish Palatinate the Lutheran imperial knights, many of them traditionally loyal servitors of the state, were with few exceptions alienated and had to be replaced in the central government by Calvinist counts from the Wetterau and by patrician and other officials from south German imperial cities.[55]

Albeit with mixed success, Calvinism was thus partly instrumental in creating a more absolutist style of government in relations with the nobles and officials. It did not, however, lead to that other feature of absolutism, the creation of a standing army. Counts John VI and John VII of Nassau fervently believed that the need for protection against Spanish troops in the Rhineland could best be assured by a system of well-disciplined and co-operating militias supplied by the allied Calvinist rulers of the area. Their attempts at the turn of the century to introduce this *Landesdefension* in the strongest of these powers, the Palatinate, even though supported by Christian of Anhalt, did not proceed very far against the opposition of the imperial knights in the south of the country and the quarrelling factions within the council of the weak-willed Elector Frederick IV: the counts themselves were ousted from the administration by 1604.[56]

Altogether, as Heinz Schilling has argued, the imposition of religious uniformity could serve either to strengthen or to weaken the state according to circumstances. In small states like Lippe, Bentheim, or Nassau, where the other central institutions had not yet, or only recently, been formed according to the more centralized pattern established in larger principalities since the late fifteenth century, ecclesiastical councils and superintendents could become the leading edge of the bureaucratization of princely rule. The highly able Calvinist lawyers and theologians who introduced the Second Reformation, and might otherwise not have been attracted to serve in such small states, also justified princely absolutism with their theoretical writings because it was the sole means for introducing the new faith to an

---

[55] Schilling, *Konfessionspolitik*, 205–9; Heppe, op. cit. 100–2, 109; J. B. Götz, *Die religiösen Wirren* (see Further Reading), 146, 156–8, 213–8, 259–60; V. Press, 'Die Grundlagen der kurpfälzischen Herrschaft in der Oberpfalz, 1499–1621', *Verhandlungen des Historischen Vereins von Oberpfalz und Regensburg*, 117 (1977), 45–62; Press, 'Stadt und territoriale Konfessionsbildung', 253, 259.

[56] Press, *Calvinismus*, 406–19.

often hostile population. Whereas the Lutheran princes of the early sixteenth century had easily won their subjects to at least nominal Protestant allegiance, and could therefore use the new ecclesiastical institutions without hindrance to reinforce their authority, countries in which Lutheranism had already been established only reluctantly received the more radical Calvinist reform later on. Their populations could resist effectively if they had either strong Estates or independent-minded cities.

Lemgo in Lippe was a Hanseatic town enjoying traditional medieval autonomy under the count and had adopted the Lutheran Reformation before its rulers, a process which strengthened the city's sense of communal solidarity. Count Simon VI's introduction of the Second Reformation at the turn of the century coincided with his determination to become master within his own territories. Lemgo's struggle over the next two decades to retain the Lutheran faith subsumed all political and economic issues at stake between the city and the count. Through the mediation of neighbouring powers and the Emperor, who were anxious to avoid war, Lemgo was by 1617 largely successful in its aims.[57] The case of Lutheran Lemgo was similar in its issues, length, foreign involvement, and successful outcome to the resistance by Calvinist Emden against the Lutheran counts of East Friesland.[58]

Lemgo was not the only Lutheran city in a Calvinist state to cast doubt on the stereotype of passive Lutheran obedience to the ruler. Some cities appealed to the Emperor to uphold the Religious Peace of 1555 in defence of the Augsburg Confession, but the Peace of Augsburg had also given rulers the right to impose the Augsburg Confession, to which Calvinist princes clung by claiming to act in conformity with the *Variata*. Even without imperial protection, Lutheran Marburg and Schmalkalden were bold enough to resist the troops of the landgrave of Hesse, Pforzheim the margrave of Baden, and Berlin the elector of Brandenburg in 1615. The most persistent and on occasion bloodily violent resistance was by Amberg and other towns in the Upper Palatinate. Almost continuously between 1563 and the outbreak of the Thirty Years War Amberg, like Lemgo a city which had introduced the Reformation before its rulers, held out against the electors palatine. The capital city of the Upper Palatinate was aided by some members of the princely family, notably Louis VI when regent there for his father, and by the nobles who sat with Amberg in the diet. Even when the resistance of the Estates subsided towards 1600, the common people in town and country stayed away in droves from communion services for which the breaking of bread had been imposed.[59]

Almost nowhere was the Second Reformation introduced without at least

---

[57] Schilling, *Konfessionspolitik*, 35–6, 176–80, 203, 350–4, 365–9, 386, 390.

[58] Schmidt, op. cit. 205–35; Smid, op. cit. 249–74; H. Schilling, 'Reformation und Bürgerfreiheit' (see Further Reading), 149–61.

[59] Götz, op. cit. 194–208, 248, 252–5, 258, 275; *Die evangelische Kirchenordnungen*, xiii, M. Simon (ed.), *Altbayern* (1966), 264, 275.

initial large-scale popular Lutheran rejection, but it was only likely to persist where strong cities led the way, or at least the Estates as in Anhalt, where it was also easy to attend alternative Lutheran services across the borders in Brandenburg or Saxony. In rural parishes of the county of Ysenburg the communities loyal to Lutheranism met secretly, proposed boycotting any of their members who would not abide by the old religion, locked the churches to prevent Calvinist sermons, and when they were reopened stayed away.[60] Such resistance was greeted with supercilious mockery by Calvinist propagandists. A treatise of 1596 justified the purging of Lutheran ceremonies in Anhalt, even though it angered the populace, on the grounds that ill customs could not be kept for the evil and the stubborn; church services would be changed in Anhalt in the same way as Moses had destroyed the golden calf.[61] When Calvinism was introduced by force in so many formerly Lutheran states, it was not surprising that Lutheran writers looked askance at attempts at reconciliation by Calvinist eirenists. Popular resistance can be largely explained as adherence to old customs and the semi-magical rites of popular religion, but these attachments were probably heightened by resentment at the confusion caused by frequent decreed changes in confession. By reintroducing Catholicism to a greater or lesser degree for a few years after 1548 in most Protestant principalities, the Interim of Augsburg had a disorientating effect comparable to the Marian reaction. England experienced six major changes in religion in the space of twenty-three years, the Palatinate and Upper Palatinate the same number in thirty-nine years. One Upper Palatinate peasant complained that he found it difficult to 'bend like a reed in the wind'.[62]

Despite the tendency of Calvinist rulers towards absolute rule over their subjects in religious and secular matters, all the major ones seem to have fully received the common currency of Calvinist resistance theories at a relatively early date. Already in 1567 Frederick III's envoy to Catherine de Medici, Zuleger, argued, in an early anticipation of the final section of the *Vindiciae contra Tyrannos*, that 'the subjects owe more obedience to God than to Your Royal Majesty, and when they defend themselves in a matter affecting the honour of God, German princes may also aid them'.[63] In 1572 Paul von Welsberg, steward to Count Philip Louis I of Hanau-Münzenberg (who had barely escaped from the Massacre of St Bartholomew), gave an oration full of monarchomach sentiment at the university of Basle.[64] In 1591

---

[60] Hanle, op. cit. 37–40.

[61] H. Leube, *Kalvinismus und Luthertum im Zeitalter der Orthodoxie* (Leipzig, 1928), 104–5; Good, op. cit. 346–50.

[62] Götz, op. cit. 89.

[63] A. Kluckhohn, 'Zwei pfälzische Gesandschaftsberichte über den französischen Hof und die Hugenotten von 1567 und 1574', *Abhandlungen der Historischen Classe der Königlich Bayerischen Akademie der Wissenschaften*, 11. ii (1869), 194; for further instances of the rulers and politicians of the Palatinate subscribing to resistance theories, see Clasen, op. cit. 17–19.

[64] G. Menk, 'Philipp Ludwig I. von Hanau-Münzenberg (1553–1580)', *Hessisches Jahrbuch für Landesgeschichte*, 32 (1982), 146–8.

the Saxon chancellor Nikolaus Krell in one breath exalted the supremacy of the ruler as God's deputy in religious matters and said that a tyrannical one could be resisted, not by the subjects, but by those who are also appointed by God to government, i.e. the inferior magistrates of Calvinist teaching.[65] John VI of Nassau recommended Beza's *De jure magistratuum* to the duke of Brunswick as useful for the circumstances in which persecuted Calvinists found themselves in 1577. From the 1580s the counts of Nassau and their theologians advocated a contractual covenant theology under the name of *mutua obligatio*. The double contract in the state, religious and political, was received by Zepper and Piscator before 1600. Althusius had spent nearly twenty years at Herborn before he assembled in his *Politics* these and other ideas which he had absorbed at the Academy, notably federalist theories which dovetailed with the abortive Nassau plans for a Calvinist political union in the Empire and Europe. From 1604 Althusius was able as syndic in the city of Emden to put into practice against the counts of East Friesland the resistance theories that had been nurtured by princes of William of Orange's German family and their professors.[66]

To overcome the numerous obstacles in the way of religious uniformity, all the German Calvinist states constantly refined their ecclesiastical institutions in successive edicts which grew longer and more detailed. Their churches emerged with a hybrid structure combining Lutheran and Calvinist elements. The centralized Lutheran ecclesiastical council, sometimes confusingly called consistory, was taken over, as were the superintendents, later given the Calvinist name of inspectors. Calvinist *classes* flourished in several places, as did synods that were either independent of the state or subordinate to it. Presbyteries were in working order during the sixteenth century in Nassau, Zweibrücken, and the Palatinate, but not until the early seventeenth century in Anhalt, Bentheim, Hesse, and Lippe. Calvinist Bremen went furthest in retaining the control over church discipline by the magistrates established in the imperial city's Lutheran period. Bremen exemplified the church as agent of the Christian state as so ably justified by the Swiss Zwinglians Gualter, Musculus, and Erastus.

Towards the other end of the spectrum Nassau, after several years of debate and experimentation, adopted in 1582 the full presbyterial system as revised for western European Calvinists in the Middelburg church order of the previous year. At the Herborn Synod of 1586 theologians from Nassau and three of the other Wetterau counties completed this church system and adopted it for their lands. All four grades of Calvinist

---

[65] Klein, op. cit. 178.

[66] L. Hatzfeld, 'Moses und die Kriegskunst. Eine Studie zur Piscatorbibel', *Nassauische Annalen*, 68 (1957), 286–7; G. Oestreich, *Geist und Gestalt des modernen Staates* (Berlin, 1969), 170, 342–5; Menk, *Herborn*, 258–63.

ecclesiastical office were instituted; the pastors were elected by the *classis* and some of the elders, and merely formally approved by the community and the ruler. By making the count of Nassau answerable to the synod a false appearance was given of a Church independent of the state. On John VI's insistence he effectively continued to control the church through his ecclesiastical council, superintendents, and visitations; and he also financed the church and regulated marriages. Zepper supplied this indirect management by the ruler with its theological coping-stone in *De politia ecclesiastica* (1595), which assigned to the civil authority a leading role, as deacon alongside the ministers, within an otherwise thoroughly Calvinist church polity.[67]

In the Palatinate church order, about the working of which most is known, the synodal-presbyterial system was introduced less fully and piecemeal. After the church ordinance of 1563 the ecclesiastical council became the most centralized institution of the whole electoral administration and one of the most powerful. Through its regulation of the pre-university schools, Heidelberg university, and censorship it had entire responsibility for creating the future élite in church and state. Its inspectors and visitations penetrated more deeply into the local administrative districts than did the treasury or any other central body. As a new council it could develop its administrative practices unfettered by tradition; thus it had no native noble members. Although the administration of secularized church lands was separate, the ecclesiastical council was occasionally used for secular purposes like enquiring into the state of readiness of the country's defences in 1600.[68] After all, half of its members were laymen; Frederick III's will insisted that this balance be maintained, as otherwise church government would again acquire an oppressive primacy as under the Papacy.[69] Through the Heidelberg Catechism and the church ordinance of 1563, as well as the influence of clergy who had been trained and had served in the Palatinate, its system was widely copied in other German states. Although the county of Bentheim was adjacent to the Netherlands, between 1588 and 1613 its rulers adopted the church order of the distant Palatinate for their lands.[70]

Church discipline in the Palatinate was at first entrusted to the lay local

[67] Münch, op. cit. 85–96, 117, 199–206; W. H. Neuser, 'Die Einführung der presbyterial-synodalen Kirchenordnung in den Grafschaften Nassau-Dillenburg, Wittgenstein, Solms und Wied im Jahre 1586', *Jahrbuch für westfälische Kirchengeschichte*, 71 (1978), 49–56; Menk, *Herborn*, 239–42; P. Münch, 'Contribution à la théorie de la visite pastorale au Nassau-Dillenbourg au XVIᵉ siècle', in *Sensibilité religieuse*, 85–8. Analysis is still awaited of the vast mass of Nassau visitation protocols, which would shed much light on the operation of the system.

[68] Press, *Calvinismus*, 116, 123, 127–8, 138.

[69] A. Kluckhohn, 'Das Testament Friedrichs des Frommen', *Abhandlungen der Historischen Classe der Königlich Bayerischen Akademie der Wissenschaften*, 12. iii (1874), 77.

[70] H. Smend, *Kirchenverfassung der Grafschaft Bentheim* (Borna nr. Leipzig, 1908), 5–6, 14–15, 24, 27–35.

officials, who even supervised the pastors. In 1568 the Englishman George Withers initiated at Heidelberg the fierce debate over a new form of discipline conducted by the Calvinist theologians against the adherents of Erastus. The elector's compromise edict of 1570 allowed the ecclesiastical council and the elector to continue controlling excommunication, but the local officials were now to appoint elders (though under the name of 'supervisors') to assist the pastors in reporting breaches of the country's police ordinances, which included some religious matters. Nevertheless, in the wake of the Synod of Emden, which recommended the full presbyterial system for all German Calvinist churches, *classes* and presbyteries were introduced in 1571. As in his increasingly interventionist foreign policy, Frederick III followed the advice of the minority of staunch Calvinists among his councillors to accept the full Calvinist system. Here the immigrant communities may have been exemplary, notably the Netherlanders at Frankenthal with their minister Peter Dathenus. Although half of the elders continued to be appointed and half were co-opted, the local lay officials and superintendents were largely withdrawn from the work of the presbyteries and *classes*. Frederick IV's edict of 1601 set out the all-embracing duties of presbyteries after the manner of consistories elsewhere in Europe: the presbytery was designed to make the Church holy by suppressing all scandal on the name of God; to ensure piety, discipline, and honour; and to maintain members of the community in unity of faith and brotherly love, as well as in just, pious and wise conduct.[71]

What this meant in practice during the early decades of Calvinism in Geneva and for the Huguenot churches of France, the Emden Calvinists, the native community in Cologne, or the exiles in Frankfurt, was that at least a third and in some places nearer half of the cases which came before the consistories were not concerned with doctrine or ecclesiastical and moral discipline, but with reconciling members of the community who had fallen out with one another, husbands with wives, parents with children, masters with servants, neighbours with neighbours.[72] To be on good terms with the rest of the community was for Calvinists an essential part of worthiness to receive the sacraments. The encroachment on secular jurisdiction is evident, especially as the cases sometimes concerned

[71] *Die evangelischen Kirchenordnungen*, xiv 48–9, 52–6, 83–4, 87, 436–41, 448–50, 593–603; R. Wesel-Roth, *Thomas Erastus* (Lahr, 1954), 47, 54, 61; Press, *Calvinismus*, 247–54; B. Vogler, *Vie religieuse* (see Further Reading), i. 637–8, 640–1.

[72] E. W. Monter, 'The Consistory of Geneva, 1559–1569', in P. de Clerk (ed.), *Renaissance, Reformation, Resurgence* (Grand Rapids, Mich., 1976), 67, 72; R. M. Kingdon, 'The Control of Morals by the earliest Calvinists', ibid. 102–3; H. Schilling, 'Reformierte Kirchenzucht als Sozialdisziplinierung? Die Tätigkeit des Emder Presbyteriums in den Jahren 1557–1562', in W. Ehbrecht and H. Schilling (eds.), *Niederlande und Nordwestdeutschland* (Cologne, 1983), 272–5, 301–2, 310–16, 325; *Kölnische Konsistorial-Beschlüsse . . . 1572–1596*, ed. E. Simons (Bonn, 1905), 503–8; *Das Protokollbuch der Niederländischen Reformierten Gemeinde zu Frankfurt am Main. 1570–81*, ed. H. Meinert (Frankfurt, 1977), *passim*.

economic disputes or acts of violence. Likewise the presbyteries administered poor relief, normally the responsibility of urban authorities. Of
the four presbyteries in the Palatinate with protocols for periods of between
twenty-five and forty years until 1619, those of Germersheim and Neustadt
dealt with a preponderance of issues that were not religious in the strictest
sense, whereas in Neckarelz and especially Bacharach secular cases were
fewer but still numerous; physical violence was, however, rarely dealt with
in any of these presbyteries.[73] Presbyteries and local officials usually co-
operated amicably to enforce both police ordinances and religious edicts.
The elector's reserve powers of excommunication were hardly called on,
since the communities effectively employed the lesser weapons of
admonition, fine, or temporary exclusion from the sacraments. Except in
the small Westphalian lordships which feared the competition to their
authority and forbade presbyteries, presbyterial supervision was compatible with centralized state authority, and indeed carried out some tasks for
which central governments lacked resources.

The effectiveness of church discipline and Calvinist education may be
gauged with the aid of visitation records. Few of the records of Calvinist
visitations in Germany have yet been rigorously examined, but Lutheran
and Catholic ones portray, at least in rural parts, an almost uniform picture
of gross underachievement. The theologians and ecclesiastical councils
naturally viewed their task as to pick out faults rather than lavish praise;
legal training often made them skilled fault-finders. Even discounting such
bias, the Heidelberg visitations reflect badly on the impact which Calvinism
had on townsmen who might be considered better educated. Whereas the
Lutheran visitation of 1582 under Louis VI had recorded many citizens still
clinging to Calvinism, those of 1593–5 were designed to test actual religious
knowledge in the capital and throughout the country. Not disputed
theological issues, but the five main points of Christian doctrine were
examined: the Ten Commandments, the Apostles' Creed, the Lord's
Prayer, and the nature of baptism and the eucharist. The elector and his
advisers were horrified at the findings. Even in Heidelberg scarcely one in
three heads of households could repeat the five main points without error,
while many did not know the Lord's Prayer, how salvation came, or what
was understood by faith.

The remedy was to introduce a comprehensive scheme for private
catechistical instruction for adults. The noon sermon on Sundays was also
turned into an exposition of the catechism. In 1595 the instruction was
prolonged, as even those who now knew the five points by heart still did not

[73] J. Estèbe and B. Vogler, 'La Genèse d'une société protestante: étude comparée de quelques
registres consistoriaux languedociens et palatins vers 1600', *Annales* 31 (1976), 363, 367, 376–9; G. A.
Benrath, 'Reformation und Calvinismus', in K.-P. Westrich (ed.), *Neustadt an der Weinstraße*
(Neustadt, 1975), 504–7.

grasp their meaning. Further schemes had meanwhile been added to catechize the rural population and young people beyond school age. Abbreviated versions of the complex Heidelberg Catechism were now published to aid understanding. In Heidelberg daily prayers at home were urged and Sunday observance reinforced. Frederick IV declared that he wanted the capital to become an example to the rest of the Palatinate, 'a holy city, blessed and honoured by God'; its inhabitants would eventually be rewarded with eternal salvation, but in the meantime with material well-being. The presbyteries assisted in the programme of catechistical instruction for at least the next fifteen years.[74] The electors seemed willing to subscribe to the objective of the theologians and of Otto von Grünrade, president of the ecclesiastical council, to reproduce in Heidelberg the holy city of Geneva, itself already part myth.

The discipline and order, *Zucht und Ordnung*, instilled by the ecclesiastical ordinances of the Calvinist principalities chimed in with the social discipline which rulers sought in the secular sphere. Police ordinances and ecclesiastical edicts complemented one another, and the lay and ecclesiastical officials co-operated in enforcing them. Success was limited, even where organized resistance was lacking or had been broken. Human frailty and stubbornness could—and can—triumph over most well-meaning attempts at educational improvement. Nevertheless, the potential prize seemed attractive to rulers; it added a further political incentive for persisting, even against the odds, in upholding Calvinism, a policy which anyway was the only one that they could square with their consciences.

The attempt to perfect a model Calvinist state had been heightened during the years just before the Palatinate embarked on ambitious Calvinist policies on a wider front. Frederick IV and Frederick V were electors who, even when they reached their majority, left most decisions of state to their councillors. Apart from periods when a more moderate policy was pursued under the influence of Lutheran imperial knights between 1592 and 1597 and of the Regent John II of Zweibrücken between 1610 and 1614, the star of Christian of Anhalt was in the ascendant. As a young man in 1591 he had gone to the aid of Henri of Navarre at the head of the most successful German Protestant army to participate in the French conflicts. Soon after becoming regent in the Upper Palatinate in 1595 he became recognized as the effective leader of the Protestant party in the Empire. While conducting his diplomacy from Amberg, he pulled the strings in the Heidelberg council through men like Ludwig Camerarius and Michael Loefenius. Although gifted with many personal talents and statesmanlike qualities, he pursued adventurous objectives more characteristic of a John Casimir, and made no allowance for the restricted financial resources of the Palatinate.

[74] G. A. Benrath, 'Das kirchliche Leben Heidelbergs' (see Further Reading), 56–73, 80; Benrath, 'Visites pastorales', 72–7; Vogler, *Vie religieuse*, ii. 794–9.

In connection with the Jülich-Cleves succession dispute and Protestant grievances in the Empire, Anhalt made alliances and conceived rash projects which extended to every corner of Europe. Under French influence he helped to give the Heidelberg court an international complexion and a new royal polish. The implicit Wittelsbach claim from medieval times to be a rival kinglike power to the Habsburgs emerged once more and was strengthened by the English marriage. Already from 1605 draft schemes had circulated in Heidelberg to the effect that if Bohemia broke loose from Habsburg rule, the elector palatine might become king.[75] As a result of Anhalt's discussions with the Bohemian nobility, Frederick V was eventually offered the crown in 1619 after the deposition of Ferdinand I. Since, when their advice was sought, the Heidelberg council, the Evangelical Union, and James I of England all failed to express unambiguously their opinion that the offer should be declined, Anhalt's urgings prevailed on the elector.

In the event international Calvinism, and England in particular, failed to come to the rescue of Bohemia or the Palatinate. The ensuing conflagration brought the destruction by the victors of the would-be model Calvinist states in the Palatinate and Upper Palatinate, although they survived in many of the lesser principalities. As Calvinism had been established through the goodwill and fervour of dynastic rulers and their advisers, so it fell through their overweening ambition. Yet scarcely anywhere had the Second Reformation won popular support before the collapse. The future seemed to lie with the compromise sketched out already before 1618 in Brandenburg, where, on the foothills of toleration, a Calvinist court was to rule over a Lutheran Church and people.

[75] F. H. Schubert, 'Christian I. von Anhalt-Bernburg', *Neue Deutsche Biographie*, iii (Berlin, 1957), 221–3; Press, *Calvinismus*, 489–91; M. Ritter, *Deutsche Geschichte im Zeitalter der Gegenreformation und des Dreißigjährigen Krieges (1555–1648)* (3 vols., Stuttgart and Berlin, 1889–1908), ii. 201–5, 260–3; V. Press, 'Bayerns Wittelsbachische Gegenspieler—Die Heidelberger Kurfürsten, 1505–1685', in H. Glaser (ed.), *Um Glauben und Reich. Kurfürst Maximilian I.* (Munich, 1980), 31–2.

Further Reading

Baumann, W., *Ernst Friedrich von Baden-Durlach. Die Bedeutung der Religion für Leben und Politik eines süddeutschen Fürsten im Zeitalter der Gegenreformation* (Stuttgart, 1962).

Benrath, G. A., 'Das kirchliche Leben Heidelbergs in den Jahren 1593 bis 1595', *Heidelberger Jahrbücher*, 10 (1966) 49–82.

Chadwick, O., 'The Making of a Reforming prince: Frederick III, Elector Palatine', in R. Buick Knox (ed.), *Reformation, Conformity and Dissent* (London, 1977), 44–69.

Clasen, C.-P., *The Palatinate in European History 1555–1618* (2nd edn., Oxford, 1966).

Die evangelischen Kirchenordnungen des 16. Jahrhunderts, ed. E. Sehling (15 vols., Leipzig and Tübingen, 1902–77).

Forsthoff, H., *Rheinische Kirchengeschichte*, i, *Die Reformation am Niederrhein* (Essen, 1929).

Frost, H., 'Gedanken über das reformierte Kirchenverfassungsrecht am Niederrhein zwischen Emden (1571) und Duisburg (1610)', *Monatshefte für evangelische Kirchengeschichte des Rheinlandes*, 23 (1974), 1–49.

Glawischnig, R., *Niederlande, Calvinismus und Reichsgrafentum, 1559–1584. Nassau-Dillenburg unter Graf Johann VI.* (Marburg, 1973).

Good, J. I., *The Origin of the Reformed Church in Germany* (Reading, Pa., 1887).

Götz, J. B., *Die erste Einführung des Kalvinismus in der Oberpfalz, 1559–1576* (Münster, 1933).

—— *Die religiösen Wirren in der Oberpfalz von 1576–1620* (Münster, 1937).

Griewank, T., 'Das "christliche Verbesserungswerk" des Landgrafen Moritz und seine Bedeutung für die Bekenntnisentwicklung der kurhessischen Kirche', *Jahrbuch der Hessischen Kirchengeschichtlichen Vereinigung*, 4 (1953), 38–73.

Hanle, G., *Graf Wolfgang Ernst von Ysenburg und die Einführung des Calvinismus in der Grafschaft Büdingen* (Grünstadt, 1966).

Hollweg, W., *Der Augsburger Reichstag von 1566 und seine Bedeutung für die Entstehung der Reformierten Kirche und ihres Bekenntnisses* (Neukirchen, 1964).

Klein, T., *Der Kampf um die zweite Reformation in Kursachsen 1586–1591* (Cologne, 1962).

Kluckhohn, A., *Friedrich der Fromme, Kurfürst von der Pfalz, der Schützer der Reformierten Kirche, 1559–76* (Nördlingen, 1879).

Menk, G., *Die Hohe Schule Herborn in ihrer Frühzeit (1584–1660). Ein Beitrag zum Hochschulwesen des deutschen Kalvinismus im Zeitalter der Gegenreformation* (Wiesbaden, 1981).

Moltmann, J., *Christoph Pezel (1539–1604) und der Calvinismus in Bremen* (Bremen, 1968).

Münch, P., *Zucht und Ordnung. Reformierte Kirchenverfassung im 16. und 17. Jahrhundert (Nassau-Dillenburg, Kurpfalz, Hessen-Kassel)* (Stuttgart, 1978).

Nischan, B., 'The "Fractio Panis": A Reformed Communion Practice in late Reformation Germany', *Church History*, 53 (1984), 17–29.

Press, V., *Calvinismus und Territorialstaat. Regierung und Zentralbehörden der Kurpfalz 1559–1619* (Stuttgart, 1970).

—— 'Stadt und territoriale Konfessionsbildung' in F. Petri (ed.), *Kirche und gesellschaftlicher Wandel in deutschen und niederländischen Städten der werdenden Neuzeit* (Cologne, 1980), 251–96.

Schilling, H., *Niederländische Exulanten im 16. Jahrhundert: ihre Stellung im Sozialgefüge und im religiösen Leben deutscher und englischer Städte* (Gütersloh, 1972).

—— 'Reformation und Bürgerfreiheit. Emdens Weg zur calvinistischen Stadtrepublik', in B. Moeller (ed.), *Stadt und Kirche im 16. Jahrhundert* (Gütersloh, 1978), 128–61.

—— *Konfessionspolitik und Staatsbildung. Eine Fallstudie über das Verhältnis von religiösem und sozialem Wandel in der Frühneuzeit am Beispiel der Grafschaft Lippe* (Gütersloh, 1981).

Schmidt, Heinrich, *Politische Geschichte Ostfrieslands* (Leer, 1975).

Sensibilité religieuse et discipline ecclésiastique Recherches et Documents, XXI (Strasburg, 1975).

Vogler, B., *Vie religieuse en pays rhénan dans la seconde moitié du XVI^c siècle (1555–1619)* (3 vols., Lille, 1974).

—— *Le Clergé protestant rhénan au siècle de la Réforme (1555–1619)* (Paris, 1976).

Wesel-Roth, R., *Thomas Erastus: Ein Beitrag zur Geschichte der Reformierten Kirche und zur Lehre von der Staatssouveränität* (Lahr, 1954).

VI

Calvinism in East Central Europe: Hungary and Her Neighbours

R. J. W. EVANS

THE evolution of Calvinism in East Central Europe presents some basic puzzles which historians have still done little to resolve. Why did the Reformed faith spread so rapidly in the middle of the sixteenth century? Why did it prove especially attractive to the non-German peoples of the area? How did it achieve such differing degrees of penetration and ultimate success? Only in Hungary, and there only amongst Magyars, did Calvinism endure. But the Hungarian Reformed Church—today one of four substantial Calvinist Churches on the continent—played a crucial role, informing and sustaining a tenacious view of national culture and political mission. This introductory essay will therefore naturally concentrate on the growth of that role, the more so as one important constitutive element within it, the fascinating Puritan movement of the seventeenth century, cries out for analysis in a European context. But I shall try to indicate salient comparisons with neighbouring lands.

One factor which shaped the religious contours of the region from the 1540s is quite simply a delayed response to Luther's Reformation. Whereas many of the Germans settled in Bohemia, Hungary, and Poland took up the new message as quickly as their fellows in the *Reich* other nationalities remained largely ignorant of the issues for a further twenty years or so. This was a matter of geography and communications rather than of ethnic allegiance. As a result their exposure to Protestantism came just as the northern German version of it lost its initial dynamic, and rival Swabian and Swiss expositors began to make the running.

At the same time a further, more fundamental consideration came into play: the intimate links already forged by humanism between intellectual élites in the East and centres of printing and education in the southern Rhineland. Thus (to cite a few examples) the Bohemian scholar Hrubý z Jelení (Gelenius) became chief collaborator at the Froben press; Hungarian letters owed much to editions at Strasburg and Basle, while the learned reformer of the latter city, Simon Grynaeus, spent several years in Buda;

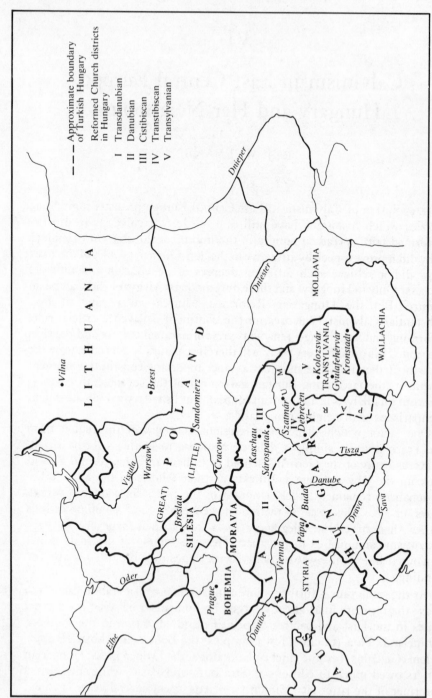

Map 3. Hungary and her Neighbours, *c.*1600

Erasmus cultivated admirers throughout the area, and sold his library to the Polish family of Laski. Not that domestic Germans were immune to such influences: indeed, Johann Honter combined intellectual direction of the Transylvanian Saxons with an Evangelical churchmanship which was arguably tinged deeply by his experience of Switzerland. Nor that non-Germans avoided Wittenberg: Czechs, Slovaks, and Magyars flocked there, and sat at the feet especially of the undoctrinaire Melanchthon. Yet when decision was necessary, Protestant Germans tended to rally behind Lutheran orthodoxy, as Honter eventually did at Kronstadt; whereas non-Germans were swayed, however marginally, in the opposite direction, looking to other sources of the new faith, more moderate and reasonable perhaps, set into an existing mould of learned discourse and personal contact.[1]

While until 1550, and even a little afterwards, the situation remained almost wholly inchoate, prospects for fully fledged Calvinism might have been accounted rosier in Bohemia and Poland than in Hungary. Bohemia was the home of the *Jednota bratrská* (Brotherly Unity), the sect of Czech Brethren, most radical survival of the Hussite movement, whose theology earned them (albeit from later commentators) the title of 'Calviniani ante Calvinum'. The Brethren formed a network of gathered congregations, tightly disciplined, ruled by elected seniors, directed to practical ideals, and hardened in adversity since they still stood under nominal proscription. By the 1530s the *Jednota* had begun to widen its horizons, accepting the need for schools at home and higher education abroad, admitting approved members of the nobility to membership, publishing a confession of faith (which appeared simultaneously at Zürich, in a quasi-Zwinglian, and at Wittenberg, in a quasi-Lutheran redaction), and turning to the king for approval of it. There was now scope for the Reformation to confirm its secular but austere priorities. In 1540 Matěj Červenka visited Calvin and Bucer in Strasburg, while Blahoslav, a future leader, studied soon afterwards at Basle. Meanwhile the Utraquist majority of the Bohemian population likewise came under Protestant influence, and its extremer spirits moved to a confrontation with the crown by 1547, though the

[1] The literature on Erasmian humanism in the area is too extensive and diverse for even summary indication here. Recent studies of Melanchthon's influence are R. Říčan and E. Kovács in *Philipp Melanchthon 1497–1560*, i (Berlin, 1963), 237–69 (Bohemia and Hungary); O. Bartel in *Odrodzenie i Reformacja w Polsce* 6 (1961), 73–89 (Poland); I. Borzsák in *Irodalomtörténeti Közlemények* 69 (1965), 433–46; W. H. Neuser in *Zeitschrift für Kirchengeschichte* 84 (1973), 49–59 (both Hungary). For Honter see K. Reinerth, *Die Reformation der siebenbürgisch-sächsischen Kirche* (Gütersloh, 1956), and *Die Gründung der evangelischen Kirchen in Siebenbürgen* (Cologne and Vienna, 1979); E. Roth, *Die Reformation in Siebenbürgen*, i–ii (Cologne and Graz, 1962–4). I. Schlégl in *Zwingliana* 12. 5 (1966), 330–70, is more sceptical of Swiss influence on him. I. Juhász in *Zeitschrift für Kirchengeschichte*, 81 (1970), 308–33, adds little.

immediate outcome of that was discomfiture and some persecution.[2]

The failure of Bohemia's contribution to the Schmalkaldic war caused thousands of Brethren to seek exile in Great Poland, where they exerted considerable impact on the local nobility because of their Slavonic speech and exemplary, ordered conduct of life.[3] Their arrival coincided with an intensified and increasingly radical religious debate in the country at large, made possibly by the accession of the open-minded Sigismund II. In 1555 Geneva began a pugnacious campaign to win Poland over. A former Franciscan called Lismanini, sent by the new king to sound out religious opinion abroad, came back as Calvin's convinced lieutenant in order to co-ordinate it. Others arrived too, men like Peter Statorius, who later called himself Stojeński and compiled the first Polish grammar. The following year the celebrated reformer Jan Łaski (John à Lasco) returned from organizing the strangers' church of Edwardian London to launch a mission in his homeland (cut short by his death in 1560). Swiss ideas found a quick foothold particularly in the south, around Cracow, and in widely scattered parts of Lithuania. They soon engendered an extensive theological literature, notably the great vernacular Bible printed at Brest in 1563 under the patronage of the magnate family of Radziwiłł, and even a catechism in White Russian dialect, translated by the Young Szymon Budny.[4]

Yet limits were set to this advance, in part precisely because it faced little entrenched opposition and therefore had little need for close definition. Moves towards broad-based Protestant solidarity started in Poland as early as 1555, with a limited alliance at Koźminek between Calvinist sympathizers and the *Jednota*. Sustained by Łaski, they led in 1570 to the deliberately loose form of agreement known as *Consensus Sandomiriensis* (after the town of Sandomierz). The Reformed Church did not appear to require strong leaders of its own; certainly it found none, beyond the active and versatile Trzecieski (Trecesius) and Tretius, both petty nobles from the Cracow

[2] For general works on the *Jednota* see bibliography. On its theology: M. Strupl in *Church History* 33 (1964), 279–93. On its pedagogy: Joseph Müller, *Die deutschen Katechismen der Böhmischen Brüder* (Berlin, 1887), esp. pt. 4; A. Molnár, *Českobratrská výchova před Komenským* (Prague, 1956). On Blahoslav see, most recently, S. Bimka and P. Floss (eds.), *Jan Blahoslav, předchůdce J. A. Komenského 1571–1971* (Uherský Brod, ?1974), esp. 36–41, 50–61. K. Oberdorffer conveniently surveys Utraquist attitudes in *Bohemia, Jahrbuch des Collegium Carolinum* 6 (1965), 123–45.

[3] Jobert (for title, see Further Reading, Section C), 114, suggests these reasons. See, in general, J. Bidlo, *Jednota bratrská v prvním vyhnanství*, i–iv (Prague, 1900–32).

[4] The campaign is well documented in the correspondence of Calvin and his friends: T. Wotschke, *Der Briefwechsel der Schweizer mit den Polen* (Leipzig, 1908); E. W. Zeeden in *Syntagma Friburgense, historische Studien H. Aubin dargebracht* (Lindau and Constance, 1956), 323–59. Standard on Łaski are still the works of a German born in England and pastor in Russia: H. Dalton, *Johannes a Lasco* (Gotha, 1881), the Eng. tr. (London, 1886) absurdly breaks off in 1550, even before Łaski's main residence in London, and *Lasciana nebst den ältesten evangelischen Synodalprotokollen Polens 1555–61* (Berlin, 1898); cf. now H. Kowalska, *Działalność reformatorska J. Łaskiego w Polsce* (Wrocław etc., 1969). For Calvinist printing see the fine general study by A. Kawecka-Gryczowa, *Z dziejów polskiej książki w okresie Renesansu* (Wrocław, 1975), 7–163.

region.[5] It could not stem a secession from its own ranks of more extreme elements who turned to Antitrinitarianism, led by émigrés such as Statorius and natives such as Budny.

Bohemia likewise moved towards a *modus vivendi* which reduced the need for any advanced doctrinal stance. Ferdinand I could not repress dissent in the manner of his Spanish nephew, Philip II; his successor Maximilian, like Poland's Sigismund II, had no desire to do so. Ferdinand's stealthy takeover of the traditional Utraquist consistory only helped to strengthen noble dominance of the new religious movements, while Maximilian's willingness to abolish the Utraquist *Compactata*, the old agreements between the Hussites and Rome, left scope for new arrangements, though not for full-scale Protestant organization. In 1575 the estates gained royal sanction for their so-called *Confessio Bohemica*, a loose Protestant association based on Sandomierz, mainly Lutheran in its theology, but reflecting the workaday values of the Brethren, who continued to indulge Hussite loyalties and a fiercely separate identity. Swiss teaching remained inconspicuous (and nominally forbidden in print), but more and more it acted as a leaven. One of the *Jednota* seniors, Jiří Strejc, ensured that the *Confessio Bohemica* did not condemn it, and the simultaneous purge of Melanchthonian moderates in neighbouring Saxony made it seem an increasingly attractive option.[6]

In Hungary Calvinism came late and homespun. No reformers espoused it unequivocally in the 1540s—the convictions of the pioneering Dévai Bíró are still a matter for debate—though the diet found it necessary to prohibit 'sacramentarian' (meaning radically anti-sacramental) ideas in 1548. The country had strikingly little contact with Geneva: apart from Gergely Belényesi and one or two equally obscure figures, no Hungarian met or even corresponded with Calvin himself. But closer connections were established with Zürich from 1549, when Bullinger sent the *Consensus Tigurinus*, negotiated between him and Calvin, by which a united Reformed front was achieved, to eastern Europe for approval.[7] Then during the 1550s threats to the Hungarian political nation—more pressing than elsewhere in the

---

[5] These two exact contemporaries are easily confused. Andrzej Trzecieski was a humanist and poet; see the life by J. Krókowski (Warsaw, 1954) and his *Carmina*, ed. Krókowski (Wrocław, 1958). Christoph Tretius was director of the Reformed college in Cracow; see T. Wotschke in *Altpreußische Monatsschrift*, 44 (1907), 1–42, 151–210. On the *Consensus*: O. Halecki, *Zgoda Sandomierska 1570 r.* (Warsaw, 1915).

[6] Hrejsa, *Česká Konfesse* (see Further Reading B; cf. discussion there), esp. 286ff.

[7] For Genevan links: G. Loesche and József S. Szabó, *Kálvin hatása és a kálvinizmus Európa keleti országaiban* (Debrecen, 1912), 111–73; M. Bucsay, *Belényesi Gergely* (Budapest, 1944). If, as Bucsay claims, 'Belényesi' is identical with Gergely Szegedi (cf. below), then he was not so obscure. For Bullinger: E. Zsindely in T. Bartha (ed.), *A Második Helvét Hitvallás Magyarországon és Méliusz életműve* (Budapest, 1967), 55–86, and in T. Bartha (ed.), *Tanulmányok és szövegek a magyarországi református egyház 16. századi történetéből* (Budapest, 1973), 931–1001 (documents); Schlégl, art. cit. C. d'Eszlary summarizes and exaggerates these contacts in *BSHPF* 110 (1964), 74–99.

region—helped to establish and secure the Reformed Church. Of course the trauma of Ottoman conquest since 1526 had brought wholesale discredit upon the old ecclesiastical establishment and perhaps a spiritual-cum-emotional predisposition towards the purity of Calvin's untrammelled faith. But the political configurations of the mid-century were probably more decisive: fears of Counter-Reformation under the vengeful Cardinal Martinuzzi; insecurity *vis-à-vis* the Turks; an embattled population reduced to constitutional self-help, and sustained—as the Dutch were to be—by extensive internal migration of the enterprising.[8]

Thus anti-Habsburg sentiments among the nobility (as in Bohemia, but stronger) gave the edge to a clerical Reformation which could proceed most easily in the east, and especially in Transylvania, that region whose medieval semi-autonomy hardened with the breakdown of the old kingdom into full separation under loose Ottoman suzerainty. The vigorous but wayward Kálmáncsehi preached the Swiss doctrine of the Eucharist around Debrecen, and his message was confirmed by Péter Méliusz, who inspired the confession of Marosvásárhely in 1559, reprinted in German at Heidelberg four years later. Now the final break with Lutheran influence proceeded alongside a further factor (as in Poland, but more clear-cut) of confrontation with antitrinitarian extremists. Méliusz drew on moral support from abroad: on Tretius, on the Palatine doctors and Bucer, above all on Bullinger, who wrote a lengthy epistle to the Hungarians and whose Second Helvetic Confession, promulgated at Debrecen in 1567, set the seal on a process already largely accomplished by the synods of Tarcal and Torda (1562–3). In a series of dramatic disputations he challenged local Arians, at first the vernacular heterodoxy of Tamás Arany, then the powerful intellectualized arguments of his former associates. Dávid and Blandrata.[9]

It is hardly too much to say that Méliusz, this tough, relentless, eclectic, highly productive organizer, formulator, and polemicist, created in Hungary a church suited to the needs of the predominantly Magyar political nation, squarely located between Counter-Reformation hierarchy and sectarian anarchy. That church was Reformed, to employ the least invidious term, and quasi-Calvinist, like Méliusz's own hybrid theology (not for nothing did he compile the most verbose of all 'Calvinist' professions of faith). But its largest tendency remained humanistic, fed as it was by a continuous stream of divinity students who imbibed the Melanchthonian

---

[8] One important example are the exiles from Szeged in Debrecen; cf. S. Bálint in *Debreceni Déri Múzeum Évkönyve* (1967), 215–25.

[9] All the standard accounts (see Further Reading) give detailed treatment to the key decade of the 1560s. See also the documents in Lampe (ed.) (see Further Reading A), 125–274, and the important article by I. Révész in *Századok*, 70 (1936), 38–75, 163–203. On Méliusz: Bartha (ed.), *Második Helvét Hitvallás*, esp. 9–53 (E. Tóth) and 103–92 (G. Kathona); Bartha (ed.), *Tanulmányok*, esp. 405–98 (L. Makkai); Wotschke, *Briefwechsel*, 320.

tradition at Wittenberg (at least till the 1570s) and elsewhere. And the new edifice would hardly have survived without backing from the first powerful prince of independent Transylvania, the Catholic Stephen Báthory, and his confessionally mixed advisers with their Italianate and Renaissance culture.[10] The legislation from 1568, which ensured religious toleration in the principality, so long as the four existing Churches should introduce no doctrinal innovation, came too late to sustain Roman Catholic or Lutheran dominance, too early to satisfy the still questing and unstable Unitarians, but just at the right moment for Méliusz.

The rest of the century saw some consolidation of this situation throughout East Central Europe, but no dramatic advance. Everywhere Calvinism was directed by clerics and professional men, physicians providing especial sustenance. Everywhere it enjoyed significant noble protection. Yet social factors alone can explain little: the response even among intellectuals and gentry was very mixed, while the incidence of magnate, merchant, and artisan support appears quite uneven.[11] Much depended both on the political situation and on cultural, particularly ethnic and linguistic traditions. Equally important was the driving force of foreign contacts, if not necessarily of foreign models. Students and their tutors increasingly attended universities at Heidelberg and Altdorf, Leiden and Herborn, Basle and Geneva, the more so as Saxony became less congenial; thus they were still often led to new religious experiences by humanist curiosity rather than by existing confessional commitment. Learned contacts with some Rhineland printing centres pointed in the same direction.[12]

That is clearest in the Bohemian case. There, although the absence of serious religious polemic[13] bears witness as much to lack of fervour as to the mediating aegis of the 1575 Confession, moderate Calvinist ideas grew in favour, especially among educated members of the *Jednota*. The schools of

---

[10] On Méliusz's theology: I. Révész, *Méliusz és Kálvin* (Cluj, 1936); M. Bucsay in Bartha (ed.), *Második Helvét Hitvallás*, 303–51, and in Bartha (ed.), *Tanulmányok*, 219–77. His *Confessio catholica de praecipuis fidei articulis* is printed in E. F. K. Müller, *Die Bekenntnisschriften der reformierten Kirche* (Leipzig, 1903), 265–376. Wittenberg's importance is stressed by Pokoly (see Further Reading A) i. 120 and *passim*. More than a thousand Hungarians attended during the sixteenth century (compare 870 or so Bohemians and many fewer Poles). For Báthory's court see L. Szádeczky, *Kovacsóczy Farkas, kanczellár 1576–94* (Budapest, 1891), esp. 19 f.; E. Veress, *Berzeviczy Márton 1538–96* (Budapest, 1911), esp. 169 f.; and most recently T. Klaniczay in *Cheiron* 1.2 (Brescia, 1982), 31–58.

[11] The best treatment of socio-political issues is in Schramm (see Further Reading C), with some comparative material. Moderate Calvinist sympathies are particularly evident among medical men in Bohemia (Monau, Jordán, Lavín, Timín, Aragosius . . . above all Crato); cf. R. J. W. Evans, *Rudolf II and his World* (Oxford, 1973), 92 ff., esp. 99, and *passim*.

[12] R. J. W. Evans, *The Wechel Presses: Humanism and Calvinism in Central Europe 1572–1627* (Oxford, 1975), for the world of publishing. Some of the main literature on university attendance is indicated in my *The Making of the Habsburg Monarchy 1550–1700* (Oxford, 1979), 26 ff.

[13] An exception to prove the rule is J. Heidenreich (Hedericus), *Examinatio Capitum Doctrinae Fratrum . . . in Bohemia et Moravia, vulgo Picardorum* (Frankfurt an der Oder [1580]), which gave rise to other tracts; cf. Gindely (see Further Reading B), 2. 260 ff.

the Brethren fostered them, notably the model *Gymnasium* at Eibenschütz which was run by the celebrated Esrom Rüdiger, expelled from Wittenberg for his liberal and conciliatory views. So did their theological activity. The Bible translation of Kralice, completed in the 1590s by an erudite team in which Strejc figures prominently, carries markedly Calvinist glosses; while the sect's practice seems to have acknowledged the Genevan liturgy for the Eucharist by the early years of the next century. It is a telling fact that the Brethren's credo was included, albeit without permission, in various editions of the *Harmonia Confessionum*, first published at Basle in 1581.[14]

Leadership of the *Jednota* fell increasingly to a band of well-travelled and cultivated noble families, especially from Moravia—Žerotíns, Kounices, Hodices—which had established intimate links with Beza's Geneva and Grynaeus's Basle. Beza's library at length found its way to the castle of the Zástřizlýs (recall the destination of Erasmus's!), while Grynaeus' right-hand man and son-in-law was a Silesian, Amandus Polanus, who while achieving fame as a theologian maintained close contact with his homeland.[15] But the *Jednota* was a small minority: perhaps no more than 1 per cent of the population in Bohemia and 3 per cent in Moravia. Among Protestants at large such tendencies had less scope. The bulk of the country by now followed roughly Lutheran practices. Only in the sister province of Moravia again, where clearer entrenched Catholic positions engendered a somewhat purer Evangelical response, do a few fully organized Reformed congregations seem to have grown up in the remote south-east.[16]

Poland had considerably more Calvinists than Bohemia by the late sixteenth century: about 200 churches in Little Poland and 200 more in Lithuania, representing some 25 per cent of the total number in those areas. At least one-tenth of the whole nobility was sympathetic, though many fewer townsmen and peasants. They enjoyed settled circumstances, helped by the semi-official letter of toleration enunciated in the Warsaw Confederation of 1573 and by reaffirmation of the Sandomierz agreement with the Brethren and the Lutherans. They made a real cultural impact: witness, for example, the pungent moralizing prose of the nation's first great

[14] Hrejsa, op. cit. 314 ff., 389 ff.; Říčan (see Further Reading B), 155 f., 178 ff. Cf. F. M. Bartoš in R. Říčan (ed.), *Jednota bratrská 1457–1957* (Prague, 1956), 111–45; O. Odložilík in *Festschrift E. Winter* (Berlin, 1966), 106–18 (Rüdiger); F. Hrubý in *Sborník J. Pekař*, i–ii (Prague, 1930), ii. 39–69, at 49 ff. (Eucharist). M. Daňková, *Bratrské tisky ivančické a kralické 1564–1619* (Prague, 1951), covers the *Jednota*'s publishing enterprises.

[15] Hrubý (ed.), *Étudiants tchèques* (see Further Reading B); O. Odložilík, *Jednota bratrská a reformovaní francouzského jazyka* (Philadelphia, 1964), for Geneva; E. Staehelin, *Amandus Polanus von Polansdorf* (Basle, 1955). Even royal officials might belong to such circles in the 1590s: J. Müldner, *Jan Myllner z Milhauzu*, ii only (Prague, 1934), *passim*.

[16] How purely Lutheran was this Protestantism in Moravia (and by implication in Bohemia too) became a matter of lively debate between Hrejsa and Hrubý (see Further Reading B), with Hrubý inclined to believe in full Lutheran, and some Calvinist organization, (specific discussion of the latter in Hrejsa, *Česká konfesse*, 373–5, and in *Český časopis historický*, 41 (1935), 35 ff.; 44 (1938), 321 ff.; 45 (1939) 41). There is some new material in *Archiv für Reformationsgeschichte*, 73 (1982), 255–83 (I. Burian).

vernacular writer and social observer, Mikułaj Rej.[17] Yet something was missing; in the absence of either internal cohesion or external pressure Poland's Reformed Church began to stagnate. It lacked any proper co-ordination between regions, and the peak of Swiss contacts was past. More seriously, the Catholic crown retained much essential authority, both political and religious, and the magnates—despite various Radziwiłłs and Chodkiewiczes, Leszczyńskis and Ostrorógs—never felt truly alienated from it. Their enthusiasm for spiritual novelties could prove very short-lived, as was soon demonstrated by the reversion to Rome of young Mikułaj 'the orphan' Radziwiłł, son of the Maecenas of the Brest Bible.

That was the greatest difference between the Polish and Hungarian situations (Bohemia represents an intermediate case). Hungary's protean but assertive Reformation, while still outside the mainstream, achieved firmer clerical and political organization by 1600 and a somewhat stronger sense of purpose. In the east, Calvinists profited from the fierce struggle for control of the antitrinitarian movement in the 1570s, and led successful resistance to any Jesuit presence in Transylvania. But they had to accept all sorts of awkward local compromises, with the rule of the *maior pars* in mixed parishes only a palliative. At Zetelaka, in the remote eastern marches, the Reformed congregation as late as 1610 accepted a Roman Catholic priest, provided he officiated in Magyar and did not say Mass. Evidence of image-breaking seems very sparse.[18]

Elsewhere things moved more slowly still. The west and north-west possessed no Protestant organization at all until 1576, while further definition came only after a colloquy at Csepreg in 1591 had failed to reconcile differences over the Eucharist, whereupon followers of the prominent preacher, István Beythe, found themselves accounted Calvinists. In Upper Hungary landowners took the ecclesiastical law into their own hands and Calvinism fell on to the defensive: by the synods of Žilina and Spišské Podhradie Lutheran arrangements predominated, perhaps because of the strength of German burgher influence in that area.[19] The heart of the country, now under more or less effective Turkish control, presents a confusing picture, but there is no doubt of some effective Calvinist organization from a comparatively early stage, notably along the lower Danube, in Baranya and Tolna.[20]

[17] Figures in Schramm, op. cit. 27 ff., 137 ff.; Jobert, op. cit. 135 ff. For the cultural contribution see T. Grabowski in *Rozprawy Akademii Umiejętności. Wyzdiał filologiczny*, ser. 2, 28 (Cracow, 1906), 250–488.

[18] I. Juhász, *A székelyföldi református egyházmegyék* (Cluj, 1947), 37 f. (Zetelaka) and *passim*. Pokoly, op. cit. i. 171 ff. (images), and *passim*.

[19] On Transdanubia: A. Fabó, *Beythe István életrajza* (Pest, 1866); Thury (see Further Reading A). J. Mocko, *Eliáš Láni . . . a jeho doba* (Liptovský Sv. Mikuláš, 1902), is a biography of the chief (Slovak) Lutheran organizer in the north; cf. D. P. Daniel in *Archiv für Reformationsgeschichte*, 70 (1979), 260–76, and in *Church History*, 49 (1980), 387–400.

[20] See, most recently, G. Kathona, *Fejezetek a török hódoltsági reformáció történetéből* (Budapest, 1974), on Tolna.

Yet how authentically 'Calvinist' was all this? The label was useful mainly to enemies, and links with Geneva remained strictly limited: Beza knew no one in Hungary when he appealed for funds on behalf of his beleagured city in 1592 (it is interesting that in the event he secured finance from Lutherans too). One of the faith's foremost lay protectors, István Báthory of Ecsed, denied that he had 'ever served János Kalviny', while Méliusz hardly cites the great man at all.[21] Other theologians, from Dévai to the superbly excoriatory Bornemisza, are equally difficult to classify. Even the most rigorous of them, Szegedi Kis, compiled his *Loci Communes* from a multiplicity of sources, particularly from Musculus of Berne. That did not mean the product was inferior: indeed, Szegedi's oeuvre, including the *Speculum Pontificum Romanorum*, which owed much to John Bale, appeared in numerous West European editions, while the *Enchiridion* of Izsák Fegyverneki was printed at least nine times at Basle between 1586 and 1628.[22] Magyar Protestants could be proud of other things as well: domestic publishing, above all the earthily inspired Bible translation completed after many vicissitudes by Gáspár Károlyi in 1590, and a much improved educational system. This extended to burgeoning collegiate foundations, especially at Debrecen and Sárospatak, where Fegyverneki was rector, but its roots lay in the simpler verities of the catechism of Heidelberg, which passed through dozens of editions by the end of the seventeenth century.[23]

Hungary's fuzzy-edged Reformation yielded a similarly imperfect fit with Western counterparts in administrative matters. Its inner organization was squarely clerical. From the 1550s local ecclesiastical districts (*tractūs*— the (later) Magyar term is *egyházmegyék*) under seniors (*esperesek*), preserving the outlines of late medieval priestly fraternities, banded together into six, subsequently five, provinces (*egyházkerületek*), which each—with one exception—chose a superintendent to wield highest authority.[24] Hungary's Calvinists, like her Lutherans and Unitarians, regularly described the latter official as a bishop (with the quaint result that in Transylvania the only Church which now lacked a bishop was the Roman Catholic one). Synods of ministers regulated the doings of their flocks

---

[21] M. Bucsay in *Kirche im Osten* 17 (1974), 163–79 (Beza in 1592); cf. Roth, op. cit. ii, and Reinerth, *Gründung, passim*, on continuing 'syncretism' among the Saxons. Loesche and Szabó, op. cit. 159 ff., examine earlier contacts with Beza. I. Révész in *Theológiai Szemle*, 10 (1934), 75–108, esp. 87 (Báthory).

[22] On Szegedi Kis: G. Kathona and M. Bucsay in Bartha (ed.), *Tanulmányok*, 13–174.

[23] T. Bartha (ed.), *A Heidelbergi Káté története Magyarországon* (Budapest, 1965), esp. 19–91 (B. Nagy). For iconoclasm about the founding of Sárospatak see J. Szűcs in *A Ráday Gyűjtemény Évkönyve* 2 (1981), 7–56; and on schooling in general: I. Mészáros, *Az iskolaügy története Magyarországon 996–1777 között* (Budapest, 1981).

[24] The provinces were—and are—Transdanubia (*Dunántúl*), united in 1734 with Upper Danubia (*Felsődunamellék*); Danubia (*Dunamellék*); two provinces astride the river Tisza, one Cistibiscan (*Tiszáninnen*), the other Transtibiscan (*Tiszántúl*); and Transylvania (*Erdély*). They are named on the map. The *Tiszáninnen* had no superintendent until 1734. Most perceptive on the organizational development is Ö Miklós, *A magyar protestáns egyházalkotmány kialakulása a Reformáció századában* (Pápa, 1942).

through canons operative mainly at district level, and correspondingly diverse. Thus Debreceners, following Zürich, were brought to forswear bells, funeral services, and vestments, but sang lustily to the tunes in Gergely Szegedi's hymn-book and later Szenczi Molnár's psalter. At the same time the Reformed clergy had to acknowledge substantial lay control. Church property nominally belonged to the congregation, while Church courts enjoyed little respect unless sustained by the *brachium saeculare*, and ecclesiastical visitations revealed some hair-raising abuses. Most importantly there grew up the custom that an incumbent should be not only elected, but annually re-elected by his parishioners (the so-called *papmarasztás*, 'priest-keeping'), in practice a licence for arbitrary interference from landowners, as well as from urban magistrates who might prohibit visitation altogether.[25]

Sixteenth-century Calvinism thus made gains in East Central Europe which were comparatively bloodless, but which by the same token we might equally call anaemic. A catalyst was necessary to take the Church any further in Hungary, as also to deprive it of its more limited attainments in the other two countries. The test came with the years immediately after 1600, as constitutional conflicts exploded throughout the area. Hungary experienced them first. Habsburg pressure for Counter-Reformation, in the context of a protracted Turkish war, widespread devastation, and political confusion, provoked a rising in 1604 under István Bocskai. Besides securing himself as the first Reformed prince of Transylvania, Bocskai was able to dictate terms in the rest of Hungary, and by 1608 Protestants had won full constitutional recognition, even—ostensibly—for peasants on the lands of a Catholic lord.[26] The Bohemians promptly extorted similar, more modest guarantees by the Letter of Majesty of 1609, which made possible the open profession of Calvinism, particularly by Dutch immigrants, perhaps even the bones of a new Reformed Church.[27] A decade later renewed Protestant-led rebellion there expelled the Habsburgs altogether, along with their

[25] Lampe (ed.), op. cit., cites a number of these synods and their canons; a completer listing in Á. Kiss (ed.), *A 16.században tartott magyar református zsinatok végzései* (Budapest, 1881). Bucsay (see Further Reading A), i. 121–3 (Debrecen). E. Illyés, *Egyházfegyelem a magyar református egyházban* (Debrecen, 1941), detailed on the workings of Church discipline. There is valuable evidence of the conscientious visitations carried out by István Miskolci Csulyak in *Történelmi Tár* (1906), 48 ff., 266 ff., 368 ff. (J. Zoványi); and much on all these matters from a Transylvanian standpoint in Pokoly, op. cit. iv.

[26] There were two stages: the Vienna settlement of 1606 applied only to the estates (nobles and burghers) and 'without prejudice to the Catholic religion'; the Pressburg diet of 1608, summoned to ratify this settlement, held out for larger concessions, including self-determination for village communities. We have adequate political account, but K. Benda in *Südostforschungen*, 33 (1974), 85–124, provides a good summary, and cf. now A. Molnár, *Fürst Stefan Bocskay als Staatsmann und Persönlichkeit* (Munich, 1983). For some further literature on the whole period of crisis: Evans, *Habsburg Monarchy*, 41 ff.

[27] A. Gindely, *Geschichte der Ertheilung des böhmischen Majestätsbriefes von 1609* (Prague, 1868); Hrejsa, op. cit. 433 ff.; M. E. H. N. Mout, *Bohemen en de Nederlanden in de zestiende eeuw* (Leiden, 1975), 118–49 (Dutch church); Hrubý in *Sborník Pekař*, 56–8, 66.

Catholic supporters, until the battle of the White Mountain dramatically reversed the position. Meanwhile between 1606 and 1609 a domestic contest worked itself out in Poland which bore some similarity to the imminent clash in the lands of St Wenceslas and had a similar, if less spectacular outcome. The abortive *rokosz* (revolt) of Sandomierz—the name itself a potent symbol—was directed against centralization, arbitrary royal powers, and Jesuit influence.[28]

Calvinism undoubtedly made a major contribution to these movements of estates' opposition. The international contacts fashioned by generations of students underlay attempts both at confederation within the region and at co-ordination with the programmes of Huguenot, Dutch, and Palatine politicians. We can find them documented above all in the vast correspondence, much of it published, yet still largely unexplored, of Karel Žerotín and Václav Budovec, secular leaders of the *Jednota* in Moravia and Bohemia respectively. Links subsisted not only with Swiss, but increasingly with German Calvinist centres: Amberg, Zerbst, Altdorf, Herborn, Heidelberg, Kassel, Hanau, where scholars and diplomats like Ancel, Bongars, Lingelsheim, Rem, and Christian of Anhalt evinced a reciprocal concern about events further east.[29] Two of the most-travelled intellectuals, the Moravian Opsimathes and the Hungarian Szenczi Molnár, now saw to the publication of Calvin's *Institutes* in Czech and Magyar, and each sought the same international backing for his enterprise, including copies for the English political leadership.[30]

Moreover, Calvinist commitment was reinforced by elements of its renowned resistance theory. First Polanus exhorted the citizens of his native Troppau to self-defence against royal interference in 1603. The following year Péter Alvinczi emerged as spokesman for the opposition when a similar *démarche* took place at Kaschau in Upper Hungary; later he wrote sustained apologies for Bethlen Gábor against Ferdinand II. Bocskai appeared to

[28] J. Maciszewski, *Wojna domowa w Polsce*, i only (Wrocław, 1960) deals with 1606; there is nothing recent on subsequent events. This revolt has often, but misleadingly, been called after one of its Catholic sponsors, Zebrzydowski.

[29] P. von Chlumecky, *Karl von Zierotin und seine Zeit*, i–ii (Brünn [Brno], 1862–79), ii; K. Žerotín, *Listy psané jazykem českým*, ed. V. Brandl, i–iii (Brno, 1870–2); id., *Dopisy 1591–1610*, ed. F. Dvorský (Prague, 1904); V. Budovec, *Korrespondence z let 1579–1619*, ed. J. Glücklich (Prague, 1908); id., *Nová korrespondence z let 1580–1616*, ed. Glücklich (Prague, 1912). Examples of Western interest ibid., and in J. Bongars and G. M. Lingelsheim, *Epistolae* (Strasburg, 1660); H. Kunstmann, *Die Nürnberger Universität Altdorf und Böhmen* (Cologne and Graz, 1963), 29–33, 88 ff. (Rem); G. Menk, *Die Hohe Schule Herborn in ihrer Frühzeit, 1584–1660* (Wiesbaden, 1981), *passim*. A. van Schelven in *Archiv für Reformationsgeschichte*, 36 (1939), 117–41, is stimulating but slight. Polish contacts do not seem to have been properly investigated, but see T. Wotschke in *Archiv für Reformationsgeschichte*, 33 (1936), 145–64; Hrubý in *Sborník Pekař*; and below n. 35.

[30] On Opsimathes' rare edition of the translation begun by Strejc, with a dedication to King James I, see Odložilík, *Jednota bratrská*, 59–62, and M. Bohatcová in *Gutenberg-Jahrbuch* (1974), 163–5. A. Szenczi Molnár, *Az Keresztyeni Religiora és Igaz Hitre valo Tanítás* (Hanau, 1624), ded. and epilogue; cf. Evans, *Wechel Presses*, 51, and R. Dán in *Magyar Könyvszemle* 95 (1979), 226 n. 3, on a copy sent to Archbishop Abbot (for whose interest in Hungary cf. S. L. Adams in K. M. Sharpe (ed.), *Faction and Parliament* (Oxford, 1978), 146 f.).

contemporaries as the deliverer promised by Calvin against tyranny, and he features as such on the Reformation memorial in Geneva.[31] The freebooting soldiery (*hajdúk*) of the military frontier actively responded to the invitation. The ideology of insurrection in Poland has been linked with the Calvinism professed by several leaders of the *rokosz*, while the most formidable of the rebels of 1618, the outspoken Austrian Tschernembl, who even retired to die in Geneva, seems to have derived his ideas from a wide reading of the monarchomach literature. His fellow-organizers in Bohemia and Moravia, Budovec and Ladislav Velen Žerotín (Karel's cousin), the former an active polemicist against the Lutherans, the latter a sumptuous magnate but convinced Calvinist, directed the campaign to dethrone the Habsburgs in favour of the elector palatine.[32] Now Christian of Anhalt, together with the hawkish Camerarius—already editor of a work on the *Jednota*—and the court preacher Scultetus, a native of Silesia, brought Heidelberg's militant doctrine to Prague, pouring political content into the old channels of humanist intercourse. Their symbolic purification of the cathedral of St Vitus represented a deliberate liturgical revolution, the climax of the whole revolt. At the same time moves were afoot, both in Bohemia and in Hungary, to seal an alliance with the Ottomans, a notorious policy anathematized elsewhere as 'Calvino-Turcism'.[33]

Yet we must beware of exaggeration. Troppau and Kaschau were, after all, predominantly Lutheran cities, as were many leaders of resistance: Illésházy and Thurzó in Hungary, Thurn and Schlick in Bohemia, and the academic tribune Jessenius, who mediated between the two countries. Where Lutherans failed to respond to the anti-Habsburg summons, as in Styria, the causes of their inaction were not necessarily confessional in the first instance.[34] Bocskai's *Apology* makes no mention of Calvin, and his rebellion triumphed in Hungary because of temporary solidarity—religious

[31] F. Hrubý in *Český Časopis Historický*, 37 (1931), 593–600 (Polanus). S. Imre, *Alvinczi Péter . . . élete* (Hódmezővásárhely, 1898); Alvinczi was probably the author of the *Querela Hungariae* (1619) and *Machiavellizatio* (1620). Benda, art. cit. 115–21 (also in *Études européennes. Mélanges V. L. Tapié* (Paris, 1973), 235–43); Bocskai has a statue at Geneva thanks mainly to the Hungarian connections, including a wife, of Alexandre Claparède (1858–1913).

[32] Poland: Cz. Chowaniec in *Reformacja w Polsce*, 3 (1924), 256–66; A. Strzelecki ibid. 7/8 (1935–6), 101–84; J. Tazbir, *A State without Stakes* (Eng. tr. New York and Warsaw 1973), 55 f.; J. Tichý in *Česko-polský sborník* i (Prague, 1955), 293–307. Sturmberger (see Further Reading B), esp. 32, 36 ff., 90 ff., 336 ff. (Tschernembl). Budovec needs a biography. F. Hrubý, *Ladislav Velen z Žerotína* (Prague, 1930), 12 ff., 52–6, and *passim*.

[33] F. H. Schubert, *Ludwig Camerarius 1573–1651* (Kallmünz in der Oberpfalz, 1955). On Scultetus: V. Press, *Calvinismus und Territorialstaat* (Stuttgart, 1970), 509 ff. For the events of 1619–20 in Prague see [C. A. Pescheck], *The Reformation and Anti-Reformation in Bohemia*, i–ii (London, 1845), i. 356 ff.; Hrejsa, op. cit. 543 ff.; J. Hemmerle in *Stifter-Jahrbuch*, 8 (1964), 243–76. On 'Calvino-Turcism' (first so called by the English recusants Rainolds and Gifford in 1597): M. E. H. N. Mout in *Tijdschrift voor Geschiedenis*, 91 (1978), 576–607; cf. *Oratio Apologetica pro serenissimo Gabriele Bethleno* ('Pozsony', 1624), 7 ff., 29 ff.

[34] W. Schulze in *Zeitschrift des Historischen Vereins für Steiermark*, 62 (1971), 33–48, who goes beyond I. Lindeck-Pozza in *Jahrbuch der Gesellschaft für Geschichte des Protestantismus in Österreich*, 60 (1939), 81 ff.; 61 (1940), 15 ff.

and social—among the Protestant estates; when his unruly soldiers sallied into neighbouring Moravia or Austria they did much to achieve an opposite result. The directors of the *rokosz* concentrated on historic and Catholic grievances, recognizing that any call for a Calvinist king in Poland would be political suicide. There is no serious evidence of foreign Protestant involvement in it; indeed, Sigismund III's court appears to have been able to play on fears of Bocskai as a bogeyman.[35] Vilém Rožmberk, first nobleman in Bohemia and prime contact of Christian of Anhalt, remained an eccentric and unreliable *grand seigneur* despite his favour towards the *Jednota*, which he had joined against all family tradition. Karel Žerotín, tormented by political responsibility and troubled by the dogma of predestination, retired at length into private life. Even in Tschernembl the linkage between belief and action is not entirely clear.[36] Faced with its greatest trial, Calvinism in East Central Europe proved simply too weak and variegated to yield any broadly acceptable political precepts. Its brief takeover of the Bohemian state in 1619–20 demonstrated only its lack of international coherence.

That should not surprise us, since we have already seen that the attraction of the faith was always as much cultural as doctrinal or political. Even during the crisis years after 1600 a number of Reformed churchmen clung to eirenical ideas, the fruit both of a humanist education and of local traditions of tolerance—Hussite *Compactata* and *Confessio Bohemica*, Transylvanian statute of Torda and Confederation of Warsaw, coexistence with Orthodox communities in Poland and Hungary—which bespoke generations of political necessity and divided power.[37] The Heidelberg theologian, David Pareus, won a particular following with his schemes for Protestant unity; whatever German historians have made of his motives, East European supporters found the message of his *Irenicum* of 1614 genuine enough. They included Alvinczi, who as minister at Kaschau cheerfully accepted Lutheran usage over organization, feast-days, images, altars, and the wafer (rejecting only auricular confession and wearing of the alb), and the attractive János Samarjai, who sought to prolong an era of good feelings in western Hungary. Samarjai issued a noteworthy appeal for harmony between the Augsburg and Helvetic Confessions—earning

---

[35] Maciszewski, op. cit. 136–8, 219 f., and *passim*: cf. Schramm, op. cit. 291–314. A contemporary Polish indictment of Bohemian Protestantism (Hrubý in *Sborník Pekař*) is also revealing.

[36] On Rožmberk and the Brethren cf. J. Salaba in *Věstník Královské České Společnosti Nauk* (1900), no. ix. For Žerotín see Chlumecky, op. cit. i, esp. 258 f., 273 ff., 376 ff. *passim*; ii, no. cxix. Sturmberger admits (op. cit. 244–8 and *passim*) that his conclusions in this area remain speculative, pending groundwork on other Austrian Calvinists or quasi-Calvinists.

[37] Tazbir, op. cit., offers the best recent summary, for Poland, though a full comparative view is still needed. Cf. the general arguments of Hrejsa, op. cit., and F. M. Bartoš, *Bojovníci a mučedníci* (2nd edn., Prague, 1946), for Bohemia. L. Binder, *Grundlagen und Formen der Toleranz in Siebenbürgen bis zur Mitte des 17.Jahrhunderts* (Cologne and Vienna, 1976), rehearses some of the Transylvanian issues. See also Menk, op. cit., on the cultural cohesiveness of Central European Calvinism.

himself the vitriolic response of a cloddish Lutheran rival—while his Reformed *Agenda* (the first full Magyar liturgy of any kind) demonstrates as late as 1636 a peculiar native mix of ecclesiastical ceremonies, not excluding Catholic ones.[38]

After the White Mountain Calvinism was extirpated from Bohemia. Reformed preachers suffered banishment before any other group, and Comenius, prophet of many progressive causes, above all of popular education, was foremost in carrying the best of earlier *Jednota* ideals into emigration. Only one or two of the semi-independent Silesian duchies, where Protestants were still tolerated, sustained small Calvinist minorities in contact with Germany. Meanwhile in Poland too, where some of the Brethren now betook themselves as in 1547, the movement had begun to fade since the *rokosz*, even without significant persecution. Its values came to appear ignoble and unpatriotic, and what remained of its oppositional thought was subsumed in the increasingly reactionary ethos of the estates' body politic (the egregious Siciński, first wielder of the devastating *liberum veto*, was a Calvinist). By 1700 hardly more than a quarter of former congregations survived; a century later only a handful. Lively minds slipped away westwards, including two eristic professors of Franeker in Friesland: Jan Makowski and his pupil Nicholas Arnold. The last, vestigial Calvinist politician, Andrzej Piotrowski, was expelled from the *sejm* in 1717.[39]

In Hungary things were different. There events from 1604 served to delimit and confirm existing Church structures, and the Calvinist faith gained extra stimulus from the adherence to it of successive princes of an autonomous Transylvania. The mantle of Bocskai fell upon Bethlen Gábor (ruled 1613–29) who, without impugning the status of the other received religions, raised the Reformed interest to the level of an ecclesiastical

---

[38] G. Brinkmann, *Die Irenik des David Pareus* (Hildesheim, 1972), minute and myopic, aims to refute the scepticism of H. Leube, *Kalvinismus und Luthertum im Zeitalter der Orthodoxie*, i only (Leipzig, 1928), esp. 39 ff.; cf. W. Holtmann, *Die pfälzische Irenik* (Göttingen, 1960), and H.-J. Schönstädt, *Antichrist, Weltheilsgeschehen und Gottes Werkzeug . . . im Spiegel des Reformationsjubiläums 1617* (Wiesbaden, 1978), *passim*. Pareus himself (on whom see also above pp. 3, 6, 142) came from Silesia and cites the examples of Sandomierz and the *Confessio Bohemica*. For Alvinczi see Imre, op. cit.; K. Révész, *Százéves küzdelem a kassai református egyház megalakulásáért 1550–1650* (Budapest, 1894), 18 ff.; I. Révész, art. cit. (n. 21), 90 ('I am neither a Lutherist nor a Calvinist'). J. Samarjai, *Magyar-Harmonia. Az az Augustana es az Helvetica Confessio Articulussinac eggyező ertelme* (Pápa, 1628); attacked by I. Lethenyei, *Az Calvinistac Magyar Harmoniaianac . . . meg-hamisétása* (Csepreg, 1633). On his *Agenda*: G. Kathona, *Samarjai János gyakorlati theologiája* (Debrecen, 1939); cf. Thury, op. cit. 379 ff. Other Pareus links with Hungary: I. Újfalvi Katona, *Tractatus de Patrum . . . Authoritate . . .* (Frankfurt am Main, 1611), pref.; A. Fabó (ed.), *Codex evangelicus diplomaticus*, i only (Pest, 1869), 116–18; Bartha (ed.), *Heidelbergi Káté*, 35 f.; cf. L. Dézsi (ed.), *Szenczi Molnár Albert naplója, levelezése és irományai* (Budapest, 1898), 76–8.

[39] Figures from J. Tazbir in J. K. Fedorowicz (ed.), *A Republic of Nobles: Studies in Polish History to 1864* (Cambridge, 1982), 201–17. For Makowski, Arnold, and Piotrowski see *Polski Słownik Biograficzny*, in progress (Warsaw, 1937–), s.v.

establishment. Its clergy, though they hardly figured, either now or later, in the government of the principality, gained confidence and purpose, as well as material rewards: a guarantee of full tax exemption in 1614, and the grant of hereditary nobility in 1629.[40] By turns ruthless and temporizing, combining crude ambition with genuine creative vision, Bethlen achieved for his fledgling state a power-base with which to protect co-religionists in Hungary proper and a modestly comfortable, if increasingly isolated, vantage-point from which to survey the discomfiture of Calvinists elsewhere in the 1620s and 1630s.

Thus newly consolidated and embattled, Hungarian Calvinism promptly faced a serious challenge from within. Since the late sixteenth century a ferment had swept through Germany, mainly in the smaller states—reaching Bohemia momentarily in 1619—which may best be described as a 'Second Reformation'.[41] It involved tightening of discipline and cleansing of conduct and belief in the face of lax observance and recidivist Catholic threats. It tended to reject the classical (or 'pagan') legacy of the Renaissance in favour of Christian encyclopaedism and the Ramist striving after logical directness and simplified method. It demanded a moral and organizational crusade, an end to sterile doctrinal wrangling. It preached broad popular commitment, and encouraged some chiliastic enthusiasm. Hungary, with her very incomplete 'first Reformation', more like a transfer of authority inside the clerical sector; with her many survivals, including a freshly sanctified episcopal hierarchy, and her growing vulnerability to the Romanizing wiles of Cardinal Pázmány (was she not living on borrowed time *vis-à-vis* both Habsburgs and Turks?) Hungary formed an obvious target. There alone, where such ideas took longest to strike root, did they explicitly attract the same name current for them in England, where they had emerged first of all. Their exponents styled themselves 'Puritans'.

The movement had some domestic precursors. The sixteenth century produced fierce moralists: Heltai, Károlyi, Bornemisza, who indulged occasional apocalyptic visions. Méliusz introduced elements of social criticism, even of social contract, into his polemics of the inflammatory

---

[40] Zs. Trócsányi, *Erdély központi kormányzata 1540–1690* (Budapest, 1980), 39, 219 f., on government and Church; evidently seventeenth-century princes relied on informal methods both to favour and to control their Calvinist hierarchy (contrast the later public role of Catholic bishops under the Habsburgs). J. Barcza, *Bethlen Gábor, a református fejedelem* (Budapest, 1980), is useful, though starry-eyed; all denominations received these clerical privileges, though Reformed ministers were best placed to benefit from them. For the background: Pokoly, op. cit. ii. 53ff.; iv. 64 ff., *passim*.

[41] This term has been freely used by recent German historians to describe the establishment of new Calvinist Churches. Cf. T. Klein, *Der Kampf um die zweite Reformation in Kursachsen 1586–91* (Cologne and Graz, 1962); H. Schilling, *Konfessionskonflikt und Staatsbildung* (Gütersloh, 1981); Menk, op. cit.; and above pp. 141–2. Though seen in part as an initiative towards the process of state-building from above, it may serve to denote a broader phenomenon which embraced also early pre-Pietism and also (perhaps) such things as Rosicrucian aspirations.

1560s.[42] But it drew especially on foreign experiences. In 1609 a senior called Újfalvi, who had travelled widely in the humanist circles of Germany and the Low Countries, made a public attack on the powers of his local Transtibiscan bishop. Bitter controversy ensued, during which (significantly) the issues were referred to Pareus in the Palatinate, before Újfalvi was condemned, defrocked, and severely punished.[43] West of the Danube, in 1617, another critical pastor had better success. János Pálfy, fresh from studies at Heidelberg, painlessly introduced into his small-town parish of Pápa the country's first lay presbytery: six burghers, four councillors (including the chief magistrate), and six soldiers from the local garrison. Within a few years his example spread, even though the initial elective principle suffered some dilution. Meanwhile the most footloose Hungarian humanist of their generation, Szenczi Molnár, was also a notable representative of spiritual transition. While his editions of the *Institutes* and the Bible demonstrate intellectual rigour and orthodoxy, other projects are evidence of a rising austerity: versions of Stoic and pious texts, besides the dictionary which reflects his burning commitment to vernacular culture.[44]

The decisive steps which brought Puritanism to Hungary were taken by Bethlen Gábor, himself no kind of ascetic and no friend of religious innovation. Bethlen spent generously to send promising Calvinist students abroad, and also patronized learning at home. In the last year of his life he founded a high-school at his capital of Gyulafehérvár and gained professors from war-torn Herborn to launch it. Johann Heinrich Alsted and Henrich Bisterfeld were swept to Transylvania by a conflict which had fundamentalized their late-humanist engagement with universal learning and filled it with a quasi-puritan spirit. Alsted, like that earlier émigré, Rüdiger in Moravia, held sway until his death in 1639, operating on a firmly biblical and pedagogic base, compiling compendia of godly science and philosophy suitable to the needs of his academy. The younger Bisterfeld became an active princely adviser, diplomat, and intriguer.[45]

[42] G. Heltai, *A részegségnek és tobzódásnak veszedelmes voltáról* (1552), ed. B. Stoll (Budapest, 1951); G. Károlyi, *Két könyv minden országoknak és királyoknak jó és gonosz szerencséjeknek okairul* (1563), ed. A. Harsányi (Budapest, 1940); P. Bornemisza, *Ördögi Kisirtetekről* (1578), ed. S. Eckhardt (Budapest, 1955). On Méliusz: Makkai in Bartha (ed.), *Tanulmányok*, esp. 421, 494–6. Eschatological inclinations may have been curbed by the open millenarianism of some Unitarians (Pokoly, op. cit. i. 205–7; Révész, art. cit. (n. 9), 163 ff.).

[43] On the affair: Lampe (ed.), op. cit. 337–55; S. Kiss in *Egyháztörténet* (1959), 218–41. On the background of Újfalvi, also known as Szilvásújfalvi Anderkó, see B. Keserű in *Irodalomtörténeti Dolgozatok*, 41 and 54 (Szeged 1968, 1969).

[44] Pálfy: Thury, op. cit. 177–87, 218 ff.; J. Makár, *Kanizsai Pálfy János élete és munkássága* (New Brunswick, N.J., 1961). For Szenczi Molnár see the diary and correspondence ed. Dézsi, op. cit., and, most recently, S. Csanda and B. Keserű (eds.), *Szenci Molnár Albert és a magyar késő-renesánsz* (Szeged, 1978); cf. his *Discursus de Summo Bono* (1630), ed. J. Vásárhelyi (Budapest, 1975).

[45] On the circumstances of the invitation: G. Menk in *Jahrbuch der Hessischen Kirchengeschichtlichen Vereinigung*, 31 (1979), 29–63; on its intellectual background: R. J. W. Evans in *Korunk*, 32 (1973), 1908–16, where I argue that Alsted had retreated by 1629 from the speculative adventures of his earlier career. On Bisterfeld see J. Kvacsala in *Századok*, 25 (1891), 447–78, 545–77.

Much about the same time English influence began. Some contacts proceeded at an official ecclesiastical level: in 1634 Bisterfeld and the chief ministers of the Church drafted a thoughtful and pious response to the eirenical overtures of the Scotsman, John Dury, which continued those of Pareus.[46] But the main impact was more subversive, albeit at first indirect. In 1620 a pioneering Magyar translation of William Perkins appeared, via Spanish(!) and Latin according to its preface; several others were to follow. During the next decade some Hungarian students, displaced from Germany to the Netherlands by war, sat at the feet of the stern William Ames at Franeker. An increasing number slipped across the Channel for shorter or longer periods.[47] Among them was Pál Medgyesi, who soon returned to Debrecen to publish in 1636 his translation (begun by Szenczi Molnár) of Lewis Bayly's *Practice of Piety*. This Magyar *Praxis Pietatis* became the most-read seventeenth-century book in Protestant Hungary.[48]

Another pupil of Ames, János Tolnai Dali, stayed several years in England and established closer links with Puritan circles. In February 1638 (the very same month as the Scottish Covenant) he and a number of like-minded compatriots subscribed in London to a 'Formula Singularitatis' or League of Virtue, which bound them to return home and serve the cause of militant spiritual renewal. Their provocative dress and demeanour initiated twenty years of turbulence among the Calvinists of Transylvania and eastern Hungary, while their religious principles made for confusion precisely because it was Puritan strictures which did much to form a clearer self-perception on the part of orthodox churchmen. At first the newcomers were actually condemned as 'Arminians'.[49]

What was the Puritan challenge? It did not lie in political radicalism: Medgyesi and Tolnai Dali were both protégés of the Transylvanian prince György I Rákóczi (ruled 1630–48) and his family, the former as court preacher, the latter as professor at Sárospatak. With the help of Bisterfeld they aimed to build on the godly authority of a reforming ruler in the mould of Bethlen Gábor. Nor did it lie in social revolution, though Puritans

---

[46] General surveys of English influence are Berg (see Further Reading D), and for the doctrinal-spiritual side J. Bodonhelyi, *Az angol puritánizmus lelki élete és magyar hatásai* (Debrecen, 1942). The reply to Dury was published in 1654 as *Concordiae inter Evangelicos quaerendae Consilia quae ab Ecclesia in Transylvania Evangelicae Pastoribus ... Professoribus ... approbata fuerunt.*

[47] János C. Kecskeméti (tr.), *Catholicus Reformatus az az Egynehany vetelködes ala vettetet hitnek agazatinak magyarázattya* (n.p., 1620); other Perkins translations in Berg, op. cit. 87–91. I. Czegle considers Ames' early Hungarian pupils in *Irodalomtörténeti Dolgozatok*, 77 (Szeged, 1971). Hungarians in England are listed by Trócsányi (see Further Reading D); some additions by G. Kathona and Gy. Gömöri in *Irodalomtörténeti Közlemények*, 80 (1976), 92–7; 82 (1978), 459–62.

[48] P. Medgyesi (tr.), *Praxis Pietatis. Az az: Kegyesseg-Gyakorlas* (Debrecen, 1636 and six further edns.); cf. T. Esze in *Könyv és Könyvtár*, 3 (1963), 43–77. There were also (Czecho-)Slovak translations. On Medgyesi's life: K. Császár, *Medgyesi Pál élete és működése* (Budapest, 1911).

[49] Zoványi (see Further Reading D), with a detailed account of the activities of Tolnai Dali and the first phase of Puritan awakening (ibid. 25 f. the 1638 document and its ten original signatories). Géza Szabó, *A magyar református orthodoxia* (Budapest, 1943), is helpful on the emergence of 'orthodoxy'.

inveighed against the arbitrary power of the nobility (a cause not without attraction for the prince), and the peculiar circumstances of the east Hungarian borderlands, temporarily and insecurely attached to the Transylvanian state, contributed to a special popular appeal there. Shifting political allegiances and economic uncertainty, factors which had earlier conduced to the growth of Calvinism in the first place, now helped to make the semi-peasant, semi-urbanized inhabitants of Debrecen and other boroughs sympathetic to the Puritan message.[50]

Above all, surely, the Puritans were what they claimed to be: moral reformers, with a programme for the removal of superstition and establishment of a godly polity regulated by an alliance of intellectuals, lesser clergy, and common citizenry. This cause demanded the abolition of the episcopate and the full and immediate introduction of a presbyterial system, as elaborated by Medgyesi in two Magyar dialogues—one with learned citations, the other boiled down for popular consumption. For years the issue remained on the table: the hierarchy, led by Bishop Geleji Katona, accused the Puritans of sowing anarchy and insubordination; Puritans countered by claiming that only presbyteries and disciplined devotion could protect the country from Counter-Reformation. Geleji Katona took the exceptional step of convening a national synod at Szatmár in 1646 (though it is revelatory of the disparate character of Hungarian Calvinism that neither side invoked the example of Pálfy across the Danube). Its conclusions were fairly even-handed, admitting in theory that the Church should provide for more lay involvement, while chastising hotheads who thought the time ripe for a major transformation.[51]

By 1648 the dangers of excess appeared very evident to the new Rákóczi prince, György II. England, having exported the stimulus for Puritanism, also exported its crisis. György II now sought to mobilize lay influence within the Church for his own purposes, and he sponsored razzias against 'Independentists', which roughly meant the extremer faction led by Tolnai Dali. That issue in its turn aroused furious polemic, both at home and in the Netherlands, which harboured large numbers of Hungarian students at the time (many were pupils of the Polish professor Arnold whom we have already encountered). It was characterized by Puritan attempts to distance themselves from 'separatist' tendencies, while asserting their sole pos-

---

[50] Makkai (see Further Reading D; cf. discussion there). The areas in question formed the so-called *Partium* (see map). Debrecen was on the very edge of this zone. During 1621–9 and 1645–8 the *Partium* extended to embrace seven further counties of north-east Hungary, stretching as far west as Kaschau and Miskolc. Since the Rákóczi dynasty owned vast possessions in those counties anyway, they fell into the Transylvanian sphere of influence throughout the period from the 1620s to 1650s.

[51] P. Medgyesi, *Dialogus Politico-Ecclesiasticus* (Bártfa, 1650); id., *Rövid Tanitás az Presbyteriumrol* (Sárospatak, 1653), with refutation of the argument that presbyteries will dissolve society or weaken the Church. Révész, *Szatmárnémeti zsinat* (see Further Reading D) on Szatmár; Zoványi, *Puritánus mozgalmak*, 141–204, with good coverage of the whole altercation.

session of true religion, typically the teachings of Ames.[52] Only a few students and artisans, mainly in the town of Nagyvárad, agitated for radical levelling.

In the 1650s the prince's adventurous foreign policy, with its designs on Poland and talk of a renewed anti-Habsburg alliance, gave Puritans a fresh chance to fish in troubled waters. At this point chiliasm became a motive force. It had always been present among spiritual radicals, at least since the arrival of Alsted, who acquired a European reputation for his prophecies (they appeared in English in 1643), and Bisterfeld. Further encouragement came, here too, from England—witness the bizarre eschatological fantasies of John Stoughton, sent back to Hungary with Tolnai Dali.[53] Similar 'arcana imperii pietatis' (as Stoughton called them) were proclaimed from nearby Moravia by Mikuláš Drabík: what appear to us the muddiest vaticinatory bleatings possessed a heady appeal for beleaguered enthusiasts around the Transylvanian court. They seem to underlie both Rákóczi's summons in 1650 to Jan Comenius to reform schooling in the principality and the latter's acceptance of it. Bisterfeld's contribution was the attempt to resuscitate a 'Calvinist international', under Cromwell's leadership, co-ordinated again by Dury's ideals of Protestant eirenism.[54]

In 1657 György II Rákóczi suffered defeat in Poland and these aspirations collapsed. A desperate imbroglio ensued. Puritans rallied to the princely candidate—Ákos Barcsay—who seemed to offer them most (a kind of Transylvanian 1619), but were discountenanced by a rival claimant, János Kemény, for all that Kemény himself, in common with other Hungarian aristocrats of the day, had felt the influence of their moral and pietistic precepts.[55] By the end of the 1650s English influence ran the other way: now the exiled Isaac Basire, former chaplain to King Charles I, emerged as the foremost spokesman for hierarchy and decorum. Soon both

[52] On György II Rákóczi and the Church see Pokoly, op. cit. ii. 209–53. Nicholas Arnold's Hungarian pupils, 'qui cos sunt ingeniorum in facultate nostra, perpetuumque Academiae nostrae decus . . . Patriotis nostris, pietatis, diligentiae, acuminis, in disputando dexteritatis, facem praeferunt', co-operated to produce his *Heinrici Echardi Lutherani Scopae Dissolutae* (Franeker, 1654). Thoughtful defences of 'mainstream' Puritanism, English and Hungarian: Péter Bacca, *Defensio Simplicitatis Ecclesiae* (Franeker, 1649; 2nd edn. much expanded, Franeker, 1653); G. Miskolci Csulyak, *Angliai Independentismus*, with I. Telkibányai, *Angliai Puritanismus* (both Utrecht, 1654).

[53] J. Stoughton, *Felicitas Ultimi Saeculi* (London, 1640), with ded. (to Rákóczi) and pref. by Samuel Hartlib. None of Hungary's apocalyptic writers (e.g. Andreas Horváth, *De Judaeorum ante novissimum diem conversione futura* (Kaschau, 1658); I. Szathmári Ötvös, *Titkok Jelenése* (Nagyszeben, 1668)) were as far gone as Stoughton.

[54] *Prophecies of Christopher Kotterus, Christiana Poniatovia, Nicholas Drabicius . . .* (2nd edn., London, 1664), 91–115; cf., most recently, F. Hýbl et al. in *Studia Comeniana et Historica* 17 (Uherský Brod, 1977 [really 1980]), and below, n. 62 on Comenius. 1654 saw the publication of Dury's earlier message from the Hungarians (above, n. 46); for his activities in the 1650s see J. Kvacsala in *Századok*, 26 (1892), 709–19, 793–810, and from the Western side: K. Brauer, *Die Unionstätigkeit J. Duries unter dem Protektorat Cromwells* (Marburg, 1907); J. M. Batten, *John Dury* (Chicago, 1944).

[55] J. Kemény, *Önéletírása és válogatott levelei*, ed. E. V. Windisch (Budapest, 1959), 78 f., 89 f., 94 ff., 110, 151, 176 f. Cf. the still more revealing memoirs of Miklós Bethlen, *Önéletírása*, ed. E. V. Windisch, i–ii (Budapest, 1955).

he and his Puritan opponents fell into the political maelstrom already predicted by Medgyesi, in sermons full of apocalyptic woe, as retribution for the blindness and folly of his countrymen.[56] The Turks destroyed Nagyvárad and occupied Transylvania, though they left a feebler Calvinist, Mihály Apafi, as its vassal ruler. Hungary now saw a restoration—ironically coincidental with the English one—of immediate Ottoman controls and longer-term Habsburg ambitions.

The greatest contribution of Hungarian Puritans lay in popular education and national culture. It began with a commitment to translation itself: numerous prefaces worry about orthography, the nature of the literary language, and the problems of mass communication.[57] Not only the Magyar tongue benefited from their concern. Transylvania's Romanians too, wooed by the princes for political purposes, gained some vernacular religious works and felt some attempts at Protestant persuasion, though the response was slight.[58] Puritan texts called for a recovery of grace and a rebirth of the nation from disaster and disunity by the exercise of simple piety. Hungarians were urged to forsake immorality and ungodly behaviour, especially their particular sins (as it appeared) of peasant inebriation and over-indulgence in the *csárdás*. Parallels with the fate of the Jews were regularly drawn.[59] Of course higher truths mattered too, and they should be approached by the famous method of Peter Ramus, whose schematic and deductive course of universal logic began to be introduced into Reformed schools during the 1640s. In 1658—very belatedly by the standards of Calvinist educators further west—his *Dialectics* appeared in a Hungarian version by György Martonfalvi.[60]

Such an ordering extended ultimately to the whole scheme of creation,

[56] W. N. Darnell (ed.), *The Correspondence of Isaac Basire* (London, 1831); cf. F. Babinger (ed.), *Conrad Jacob Hiltebrandt's dreifache schwedische Gesandschaftsreise . . . 1656–8* (Leiden, 1937), 47, 51–3, 130, 143 f. P. Medgyesi, *Sok Jajjokban . . . szegény igaz Magyaroknak . . . Siralmi* (Sárospatak, 1658); id., *Magyarok hatodik jajja . . .* (Sárospatak, 1660).

[57] Examples: J. Mikolai Hegedűs, *Az mennyei igasságnak Tüzes Oszlopa* (Utrecht, 1648), 134–8; id., *Biblia Tanui kiket a Bilia* [sic] *állatott elő* (Utrecht 1648), ded. and pref.; Medgyesi, *Dialogus*, ded.; Apáczai (below p. 188), pref.

[58] These efforts had been started in the sixteenth century, by both Calvinists and Lutherans (cf. the work of Budny and others in Poland). See Pokoly, op. cit. ii. 164–79, 276 ff.; I. Révész, *La Réforme et les Roumains de Transylvanie* (Budapest, 1937); B. Kelemen in E. Csetri *et al.* (eds.), *Művelődéstörténeti tanulmányok* (Bucharest, 1979), 116–20.

[59] Interesting examples from the pre-1660 period: Christoph Darholcz (tr.), *Novissima Tuba . . .* (Kassa, 1639), cf. J. Jankovics in *Irodalomtörténeti Közlemények*, 86 (1982), 303–12; M. Dioszegi Bónis (tr.), *Az Részegesnek Gyülölseges . . . állapotya* (Leiden, 1649), drink; Mihály Felső-Bányai (tr.), *A'Leleknek Uti Költsege* (Utrecht, 1651); Benedek Nagy-Ari, *Orthodoxus Christianus az az Igaz Vallasu Keresztyen* (Nagyvárad, 1651), rather more sophisticated; Fülöp J. Bökenyi (tr.), *Mennyei Lampas . . .* (Utrecht, 1652); J. Somosi Petkó, *Igaz és Tökéletes bodogságra Vezérlő Ut* (Sárospatak, 1656), with intriguing ded.; László Gyöngyösi (tr.), *A'keresztyén Vallásnak fundamentumi* (Utrecht, 1657); István Czeglédi, *Az Orszagok Romlasarul* (Kassa, 1659), in the Medgyesi mould. The parallel between Hungarian and Jewish tribulations dates back at least to András Farkas, *Az zsidó és magyar nemzetről* (1538).

[60] Gy. Martonfalvi (ed.), *Petri Rami Dialecticae libri duo* (Utrecht, 1658, 2nd expanded edn. Debrecen, 1664). Cf. the discussion by B. Tóth in *Könyv és Könyvtár*, 12 (1979), 85–105.

and the greatest Hungarian spokesman for these pedagogical ideals was the most talented disciple of Alsted and Bisterfeld, the short-lived but dynamic János Apáczai Csere. In 1655, on completing his studies at Harderwijk (where he attained the first doctorate at the new university) and Utrecht, Apáczai issued there his *Magyar Encyclopaedia* with the explanatory subtitle: 'A fair arrangement of all wisdom hitherto discovered, true and useful'.[61] The work is plainly derivative and Apáczai does not claim otherwise. Subject by subject he acknowledges the authority of Descartes (starting out from the Cartesian *cogito*), Ramus, Alsted, Ames, Regius, Althusius (on resistance, *inter alia*), and so forth. Yet it is also something extra: the first vernacular encyclopaedia *eo nomine* in any language, with some strikingly up-to-date passages and a remarkably progressive overall intention. We sense the author's desperate urgency to propagate his panacea of universal education. That accorded with the mission of Comenius to Hungary. In the event, Comenius felt out of his depth in the local struggles, alienated by radical sectarians, suspicious it seems even of Medgyesi, certainly of Bisterfeld. After four years he left dissatisfied. Yet his programmatic statement of 1654, *Gentis Felicitas*, summarized the essential Puritan aim of a harmonious society instructed in true personal and social discipline under the guidance of a godly prince; while the experiences of his difficult years at Sárospatak soon left their traces in his masterly practical textbook, the *Orbis Pictus*.[62]

This process of vulgarization—in the original, positive sense of the word—represents the principal claim of Hungary's Puritans to be reckoned modern spirits. Advanced intellectuals in their way, fortified by lengthy travels in distant lands (compare the impact of exile on their English equivalents), they preached a message which was intended to be simple and direct, though in fact often found peculiar and dangerous. In some measure Puritanism grew out of socio-economic pressures, and many of its propagators came from comparatively humble backgrounds. But equally it was the product of speculative *déracinés*, emotionally radicalized by the tense realities of the eastern Hungarian borders, where many of them were strangers. Thus their movement had something in common with sixteenth-century Antitrinitarianism, though now the context was one of 'Second Reformation' rather than of international humanism; moral fervour took precedence over rational dissent, and its arch-prophet was a real English expatriate, Ames, whose writings exercised vast influence from the 1650s. Ames' most important interpreter, the Ramist Martonfalvi, displays some

---

[61] The important preface to the *Encyclopaedia* is in Latin, the main text in Hungarian. For Apáczai's life see I. Bán, *Apáczai Csere János* (Budapest, 1958).

[62] Lajos Rácz, *Comenius Sárospatakon* (Budapest, 1931); some new perceptions in É. Földes and I. Mészáros (eds.), *Comenius and Hungary* (ibid. 1973). Comenius' attitude to Medgyesi appears from V. Petráčková and M. Steiner in *Studia Comeniana et Historica*, 25 (1983), 45–60; his attitude to Bisterfeld from Kvacsala, art. cit. (n. 45), 551 ff.

criticism of serfdom, some sense of the democratic implications of the presbyterian order; yet the contemporary mind must have been held far more powerfully by the fierce and terrifying logic of an unwavering predestinarian theology.[63]

The half-frustrated movement for reform of Hungarian Calvinism in the mid seventeenth century left a mixed, even contradictory legacy. Its tight pursuit of moral rectitude continued to set a censorious tone for the future. Further translations of English classics and passionate denunciations of the dance accompanied a strengthening of Church courts, which had started in 1619 with Bethlen's *Articles* and gained precision from the canons formulated by Geleji Katona in the aftermath of the synod of Szatmár. To judge by visitation reports, new sins often outran new punishments, and the clergy did not always help (when a synod of 1705 prohibited the wearing of wigs and pontificated about beards, its decision was vigorously contested by one maverick who thought himself exempt on the grounds of prior consecration as an Anglican priest).[64] At the same time the intellectual influence of Puritanism remained generally innovatory and liberating. Cartesian ideas, accepted first by Apáczai, spread rapidly, if at a fairly crude level, and led to a hesitant dismantling of Aristotelian categories. Szilágyi's philosophy textbook of 1678, written in a mildly Cartesian spirit and sent abroad for publication, proved too much for the theology censors of Zürich.[65] Cartesianism blended with a gradual reception of Copernican cosmology, again following Apáczai's initiative, and of the covenant theology taught by Coccejus in the Netherlands. Coccejans fuelled a major row in the Hungarian academies, whose contours—like those of the contentious doctrinal issues of the day—are not now easily plotted. Most remarkable of all, perhaps, the practice of piety taught a psychological awareness which yielded a rich vein of native autobiography.[66]

On the institutional front the outcome was likewise double-edged.

---

[63] Gy. Martonfalvi, *Exegesis . . . Medullae Amesianae*, i–ii (Debrecen, 1670–5), in Latin; id., *Taneto és Czafolo Theologiaja . . .* (Debrecen, 1679) in Hungarian; cf. Berg, op. cit. 108–19, for other works based on Ames, whose own *Medulla Theologica* and *De Conscientia* appeared at Debrecen in 1685. Révész, *Társadalmi és politikai eszmék* (see Further Reading D), seems to pitch his claims for Martonfalvi too high. Cf. also pp. 4–5, 259 on Ames.

[64] Examples: Mihály Gyulai, *Fertelmeskedő s'bujálkodó Tancz Jutalma* (Debrecen, 1681); János Pathai, *Tancz felbonczolasa* (Debrecen, 1683); István Szentpéteri, *Tancz pestise* (Debrecen, 1697); all condemnations of dancing. Szentpéteri extended his execrations to drinking and swearing in his *Hangos Trombita* (Debrecen, 1698) and *Ördög Szigonnya* (Debrecen, 1699). On discipline: Illyés, op. cit. 88 ff.; Juhász, *Székelyföldi egyházmegyék*, 81 ff.; Zoványi, *Tiszántúl* (see Further Reading A) i. 44 (Anglican orders).

[65] The latest summary of Cartesian influence is by Z. Tordai in *Magyar Filozófiai Szemle* 6 (1962), 54–77; cf. Szabó, op. cit. 99 ff.; I. Bán in *Századok* 110 (1976), 1052–69, esp. 1055 ff. B. Tóth in *Magyar Könyvszemle*, 93 (1977), 313–23 (Szilágyi).

[66] J. Zoványi, *A Coccejanismus története* (Budapest, 1890). Cf. E. Makkai, *Pósaházi János élete és filozófiája* (Kolozsvár, 1942), for an interesting transitional thinker who was semi-Cartesian but very anti-Coccejan. Two famous autobiographies are listed above, n. 55; another, rather later one is Kata Bethlen, *Önéletírása*, ed. M. Sükösd (Budapest, 1963).

Puritan pressure secured more and more lay involvement. Presbyteries were progressively instituted both in towns (especially where Calvinists constituted a minority) and in the countryside. Along the remote valleys of the Küküllő rivers in Transylvania they sprang up like mushrooms under the protection of an enthusiastic senior.[67] Yet the evolution brought little popular participation. Instead it tended to be captured by the forces of the secular establishment in ways foreshadowed by György II Rákóczi's strong-arm tactics of the 1650s. In the now firmly Reformed towns on the eastern plain municipal authorities sought to use the presbyterial system in order to manage stiff-necked ministers. In Transylvania Prince Apafi inaugurated a curatorial board, with five lay and five clerical members, to direct the affairs of the Church. Such moves went with a clearer distinction between noble and commoner in matters of ecclesiastical jurisdiction: whereas the *Articuli Bethleniani* had stressed the obligations of social status (they provided for nobles to be fined three times as much as others for non-attendance), later practice found ways of reintroducing privilege.[68]

The pretensions of notables were much helped by political circumstances from the 1660s. With Transylvania reduced to impotence, the Habsburgs could launch an assault on heresy in Hungary proper, particularly given the constitutional pretext of a futile conspiracy uncovered in 1670 (whose ringleaders were in fact mostly Catholics). A brutal campaign during the next decade ripened a crop of mainly Calvinist martyrs; the affair of the ministers condemned to toil as galley-slaves in the Mediterranean until they were rescued by a Dutch admiral became a European *cause célèbre*. In the 1680s the frontal assault had to be abandoned, but legal chicanery continued, and Protestant worship was restricted to a limited number of approved ('articulated') localities.[69]

Emperor Leopold I's endeavours bear a striking similarity to the exactly contemporary ones of Louis XIV: only in Hungary the (abortive) 'Revocation' came first and various native versions of dragonnades and ecclesiastical *réunions* followed. But Hungarian Protestants enjoyed what Huguenots now lacked: noble support, increasingly integrated into Church government. Grievances could still fuel a grand insurrection in the Bocskai tradition (though neither of the new malcontent leaders, Imre Thököly and Ferenc II Rákóczi, was Calvinist); even the last throes of a Calvinist international may be detected in the embarrassed posture of English and Dutch emissaries during the war of Spanish Succession, seeking to mediate

---

[67] Pokoly, op. cit. iii. 284 f.; iv. 197 ff.

[68] Ibid. iv. 179 ff., v. 16 ff.; Illyés, op. cit., esp. 95 f., 99.

[69] Sketch of this Habsburg policy in Evans, *Habsburg Monarchy*, 121 f., 237 f., 249 f., and *passim*. Much documentation in Okolicsányi (see Further Reading A) esp. appendix, 153–250; Lampe (ed.), op. cit. 447 ff., 746–919; Bod (see Further Reading A) ii. 52 ff. The crude B. Obál, *Die Religionspolitik in Ungarn . . . während der Regierung Leopold I.* (Halle, 1910), is still often cited. See also, most recently, P. F. Barton and L. Makkai (eds.), *Rebellion oder Religion?* (Budapest, 1977).

between their Austrian allies and their oppressed co-religionists.[70] At the local level a Reformed squirearchy sustained religion as a prime badge of county liberties, and many a little town could take shelter under the same aegis. After the Habsburgs acquired Transylvania at the beginning of the 1690s Calvinism fell back on the defensive there too. Apafi's mixed curatorium was confirmed and strengthened in 1709, and the institution soon spread to the four provinces further west, though they still fought shy of any unified structure of authority.[71] Certain families, like the Telekis and Rádays, founded their eighteenth-century prominence in no little measure on services to the Reformed Church.

Thus in Hungary the Calvinist faith survived both the kind of constitutional shock which had forced it into exile from Bohemia and the ebbing of credibility which had caused it to wither away in Poland. It survived with something in hand, as a semi-official confession, never lacking sufficient support from above to forestall possible sectarian criticism from below. Thanks to its humanist inheritance and its Puritan infusions the Church sustained respectable levels of debate and a continuing literary output—Bibles, sermons, funerary orations, cate-chisms, tracts of various kinds—much of which had to be carried abroad for printing by the rising number of students at Dutch and Swiss universities, and was subject to periodic confiscation by the authorities. There is vernacular craft too in the artistic values it created, above all the finely elaborated, colourful wood-panelled ceilings which remain the pride of many village churches. And adversity provided the stimulus to historiography for a European audience: the most important documen-tation was smuggled out to be published at Utrecht in 1728 (the manuscript later found its way to Oxford).[72]

Isolation also brought penalties, with some loss of vision and intellectual ambition, especially among the clergy. Certainly the perception of other Calvinist destinies grew dim: one of the first Hungarian journalists, Reformed in background, could tell his readers exactly a century after the Revocation that the Huguenots had been expelled from France in 1598 and readmitted in 1685.[73] But the restriction most significant for the future lay

[70] There is religion and much else in the reports of George Stepney and others for the years 1703–11, printed in English by E. Simonyi (ed.), *Angol diplomatiai iratok II Rákóczi Ferencz korára*, i–iii (Pest–Budapest, 1871–77).

[71] J. Zoványi, *Egyetemes főgondnok és főconsistorium a magyarországi református egyházban* (Budapest, 1903). After the Rákóczi rebellion Pál Ráday was chief curator (*főkurátor*) *ad hominem* until his death in 1733. Then from the synod of Bodrogkeresztúr (1734) each province had a chief guardian (*főgondnok*), though the whole Church retained a single agent to the Habsburg government in Vienna.

[72] Lampe (ed.), op. cit. Professor Lampe merely saw through the press a work which in substance had already been completed by Pál Ember of Debrecen twenty years earlier. Bodleian Library, Oxford, MS. Add. A 57–8; cf. Á Ritoók in *Magyar Könyvszemle*, 89 (1973), 175–85, 364–76.

[73] Gy. Kókay (ed.), *Magyar Hírmondó . . . válogatás* (Budapest, 1981), 275 (an article by Sándor Szacsvay).

implicit in the whole evolution we have been examining. When national sentiment began to be more clearly articulated, it became a capital fact of politics that Hungary's Calvinists spoke Magyar. Ecclesiastical community could provide a vehicle for the goals of national cohesion.

As I indicated at the outset, this phenomenon allows of no simple explanation. The very lack of doctrinal purity in the crucial later sixteenth-century phase may have encouraged a gradual organization of Protestant Churches on lines of existing differentiation, partly ecclesiastical, but also cultural and linguistic, so that they found themselves in the end more or less ethnically watertight. Manifestly the process on the Calvinist side was not simply anti-German. It is by no means clear, as some have argued,[74] that the Habsburg threat tended to discredit all German religious influence (and what then of Counter-Reformation?) or that disillusion with Wittenberg—where many Magyars still studied till the end of the sixteenth century—was cause rather than consequence of their gradually espousing a different doctrine. Evidence from Turkish Hungary hardly supports such a view, unless we explain the growth of Calvinism among Magyars there as determined by initiatives across the frontier, or as being more acceptable to Ottoman authorities. Nor does the continued presence of a remnant of Magyar-speaking Lutherans: those in Transylvania, mainly at Kolozsvár and around Kronstadt, seem to bespeak precisely the strength of local German influences (oddly enough Apáczai came from one such village), whereas the larger survival in Upper Hungary invites a more regional explanation, to cover the Lutheran persuasion of a substantial minority of Slovaks too.[75]

What took place between the 1540s and the late seventeenth century was at most a semi-conscious deepening of communal values through confessional solidarity. Contemporaries betray only an occasional awareness that religion might possess ethnic implications. The greatest printer of Transylvanian Calvinism, Heltai, and its most restless leader, Dávid (both later Unitarians) came of Saxon stock and ended by largely forswearing their German allegiance, but we can only speculate as to the nature of the

---

[74] Usually no better than a textbook assumption, but more seriously sustained by M. Asztalos in *A Bécsi Magyar Történeti Intézet Évkönyve*, 2 (1932), 81–94, and in *Egyetemes Filológiai Közlöny*, 58 (1934), 1–11; criticized by I. Révész in *Századok*, 68 (1934), 257–75. G. Szabó, *Geschichte des ungarischen Coetus an der Universität Wittenberg 1555–1613* (Halle, 1941), gives a balanced account of students at Wittenberg until the crypto-Calvinist breach in 1592.

[75] In the later nineteenth century accurate statistics of both religious and national allegiance became available and recorded some 300,000 Magyar Lutherans (against 450,000 Slovak Lutherans and 400,000 German Lutherans). At that time there were approximately 2,200,000 Calvinists in Hungary, Magyars almost to a man/woman, and about 4,200,000 Magyar Roman Catholics (against 1,300,000 Slovak Catholics and the same number of German Catholics, these latter being mainly descended from post-1700 immigrants). Lutherans would be a leading sector in the early nineteenth-century contest to assert both Magyar and Slovak identities (Kossuth and Petőfi, Kollár and Štúr, were all Lutheran), thereby demonstrating both their full membership of the national body and also probably their special need to make that membership explicit.

attractions or pressures which accompanied their transition. The conciliatory Samarjai addressed his work to 'sage persons of every nation', though he also suggested that a Magyar Lutheran might have more in common with a Calvinist like himself than with any other Lutheran.[76] Most of his co-religionists (like Reformed Czechs and Poles in their time) were content with a vague sense of rectitude in the defence of constitutional liberties and in resistance to what were seen as alien impositions.

Subsequent patriotic commitment to—or distaste for—Calvinism as the 'Magyar religion', though fortified by the movement's disappearance elsewhere in East Central Europe, involved a misunderstanding of its origins which has not yet been wholly repaired.[77] But the historian of these events too should remember that his very use of the term 'Calvinism', however unavoidable, carries with it anachronistic associations, at least until the end of our period. Ironically indeed, an identification which represented the fruit of a century's Western influence upon Hungarian Protestantism, culminating in the Puritans (who were made, as one judgment had it, 'by Christ and Calvin'), later contributed to that closing of cultural frontiers which Magyar and rival nationalisms, for all their incidental virtues, rendered inevitable.

[76] Samarjai, op. cit., sig. (i)2. See Reinerth, *Gründung*, 229 ff., for reflections on Heltai and Dávid.

[77] Révész, art. cit. (n. 21), esp. 101 ff. The idea of Debrecen as the 'Calvinist Rome' came still later, in 1864, bred by the tercentenary of Calvin's death out of the fierce contemporary agitation against Habsburg absolutism.

Further Reading

East Central Europe has been grievously neglected in standard accounts of Calvinism. Only A. van Schelven, *Het Calvinisme gedurende zijn bloeitijd*, i–iii (Amsterdam, 1943–64), vol. iii, began to give it adequate coverage, and his work remained a torso. Most Western historians have had to rely on outdated and heavily simplified material, often in mediocre translation. What follows is an indication of the most important general and background literature for Hungary, Bohemia, and Poland, some of it already touched on in the preceding notes.

A.   Hungary's Reformed historiography is naturally the strongest of the three, and continuous since the early eighteenth century. The political documentation of a broad Protestant kind in P. Okolicsányi, *Historia Diplomatica de Statu Religionis Evangelicae in Hungaria* (n.p., 1710), printed in Germany, was followed by F. A. Lampe (ed.), *Historia Ecclesiae Reformatae in Hungaria et Transylvania* (Utrecht 1728, cf. n. 72), printed in the Netherlands, and by the vast compilation of the Transylvanian pastor-*littérateur*, Péter Bod, *Historia Hungarorum Ecclesiastica*, ed. L. W. E. Rauwenhoff *et al.*, i–iii (Leiden, 1888–90), published—likewise in the Netherlands—long after his death. Over the last hundred years two outstanding scholars have dominated the field: Jenő Zoványi (1865–1958), uneasy blend of

Calvinist convert and radical liberal, iconoclastic and controversial (cf. Révész's appreciation in *Századok*, 99 (1965), 1393–1403); and Imre Révész (1889–1967), last member of a dynasty of Reformed churchmen and teachers. Zoványi's *A reformáció Magyarországon 1565-ig* (Budapest, 1921) and *A magyarországi protestantizmus 1565-től 1600-ig* (op. posth., Budapest, 1977) afford the largest survey of the sixteenth-century Hungarian Reformation as a whole; while his *Magyarországi protestáns egyháztörténeti lexikon* (again op. posth., Budapest, 1977), is indispensable as a work of reference. Révész's *Magyar református egyháztörténet*, i only (Debrecen, 1938), carries the story of Calvinism to 1608; many of his smaller contributions have already been mentioned. More recently M. Bucsay has provided an excellent short account, with splended bibliography: *Geschichte des Protestantismus in Ungarn*, i–ii (2nd edn. Vienna etc., 1977–9, revised and much enlarged from the 1st edn., Stuttgart, 1959). The best histories of the five ecclesiastical provinces are E. Thury, *A dunántúli református egyházkerület története*, i only (Pápa, 1908), J. Zoványi, *A tiszántúli református egyházkerület története*, i–ii (Debrecen, 1939), and J. Pokoly, *Az erdélyi református egyház története*, i–v (Budapest, 1904–5), this last painting a lively, though highly patriotic picture of Transylvanian developments. The most substantial recent venture is the three volumes edited by T. Bartha and published under the series title *Studia et Acta Ecclesiastica* (Budapest, 1965–73, cf. nn. 7, 23) on the occasion of Calvinism's quatercentenary in Hungary. None of these authors offers a convincing explanation of the attractiveness of Calvinism to Magyars in particular. Révész is perhaps most thoughtful: for an accessible introduction to some of his views see *BSHPF* 84 (1935), 91–103 (though his article in *Századok*, 68 (1934), 257–75, has more coherence). I. Kónya, *Tanulmányok a kálvinizmusról* (Budapest, 1975), esp. 117–25, and *Kálvinizmus és társadalomelmélet* (Budapest, 1979), shows the bankruptcy of a crude Marxist interpretation. Foreign coverage of these matters is almost non-existent, although E. Doumergue, *La Hongrie calviniste* (Toulouse, 1912), deserves mention because of the writer's standing as an authority on Calvin himself.

B. Calvinism in Bohemia has been treated largely as a subordinate dimension of the *Jednota bratrská*, from the old political history by A. Gindely, *Geschichte der Böhmischen Brüder*, i–ii (Prague, 1868, originally issued (Prague 1857–8) with the alternative title *Böhmen und Mähren im Zeitalter der Reformation*), through the sound but apologetic J. T. Müller, *Geschichte der Böhmischen Brüder*, i–iii (Herrnhut, 1922–31), to the very capable, if still slightly apologetic survey by R. Říčan, *Die Böhmischen Brüder* (Berlin, 1961, somewhat abbreviated from the Czech original of 1957; the chapter on theology, 283–321, is by A. Molnár). There is a mass of material for religious history in general in Z. Winter, *Život církevní v Čechách*, i–ii (Prague, 1895–6), and F. Hrejsa, *Dějiny křest'anství v Čechách*, v–vi (Prague, 1948–50). The classic work of interpretation is an earlier study by Hrejsa. His *Česká konfesse: její vznik, podstata a dějiny* (Prague, 1912), far broader than the title suggests, amounts to an elaborate *plaidoyer* for a distinctive Bohemian Protestant tradition. The debate on this issue between him and F. Hrubý in *Český Časopis Historický* 40 (1934), 265–309; 41 (1935), 1–40, 237–68; 44 (1938), 296–326, 474–85; 45 (1939), 31–44, represents also the most important contribution to the difficult problem of the ethnic complexion of religious allegiance in Bohemia and Moravia. Hardly any recent work exists at all on Calvinist trends in the country, as K. Richter in K. Bosl (ed.), *Handbuch zur Geschichte der böhmischen Länder*, i–iv (Stuttgart, 1966–74), ii, esp. 111 ff., 167 ff., and J. Purš and M. Kropilák (eds.), *Přehled dějin Československa*, in progress (Prague, 1981–), i/2, 56 ff., serve to indicate. Indeed, the most important recent publication is still a work from that inter-war generation, the posthumous collection of correspondence edited by F. Hrubý, *Étudiants tchèques aux écoles protestantes de l'Europe occidentale à la fin du 16e et au début du 17e siècle* (Brno, 1970). Little is available in English, though O. Odložilík in *Journal of World History*, 13 (1971), 172–203, can help as a first orientation; I have not seen J. K. Zeman, 'Responses to Calvin and Calvinism among the Czech Brethren 1540–1605' in *American Society for Reformation Research*, Occasional Papers, I (1977), 41–52. Despite the authoritative biography by H. Sturmberger, *George Erasmus Tschernembl* (Linz, 1953), the related problem of Calvinist trends within the predominantly Lutheran body of Austrian Protestantism, especially in Upper Austria, awaits its historian.

C. Polish Calvinism, always overshadowed in scholarship by the Catholic tradition, found a contemporary chronicler in another pupil of Makowski at Franeker, Andrzej Węgierski (pseud. Regenvolscius), *Systema historico-chronologicum Ecclesiarum Slavonicarum* (Utrecht, 1652, reprinted as *Libri IV Slavoniae Reformatae* (Amsterdam, 1679)); id., *Kronika zboru ewangelickiego krakowskiego* (Cracow, 1817) deals with Cracow. J. Łukaszewicz, *Dzieje kościołów wyznania helweckiego w Litwie*, i–ii (Poznań, 1842–3), and id., *Dzieje kościołów wyznania helweckiego w dawnej Małej Polsce* (ibid. 1853), are still fundamental. Much can be found about Calvinist evolution in the émigré Protestant V. Krasinski's classic *Historical sketch of the . . . Reformation in Poland*, i–ii (London, 1838–40), and in two later standard works on the period of Protestant advance: W. Zakrzewski, *Powstanie i wzrost reformacji w Polsce 1520–72* (Leipzig, 1870), and T. Wotschke, *Geschichte der Reformation in Polen* (Leipzig, 1911). Subsequent Reformation scholars, particularly since 1945, have concentrated heavily on the Arians or 'Polish Brethren', but there is much material in the journal *Reformacja w Polsce* (from 1921, since 1956 renamed *Odrodzenie i Reformacja w Polsce*). Useful studies have been written of aspects of Calvinist society and culture, especially S. Konarski, *Szlachta kalwińska w Polsce* (Warsaw, 1936), on the nobility, and S. Tworek, *Działalność oświatowo-kulturalna kalwinizmu małopolskiego* (Lublin, 1970), on schools; but there is no work of synthesis. The best modern Western accounts: a survey by B. Stasiewski, *Reformation und Gegenreformation in Polen, neue Forschungsergebnisse* (Münster, 1960), the convincing socio-economic analysis of G. Schramm, *Der polnische Adel und die Reformation* (Wiesbaden, 1965), and the attractive broad canvas of A. Jobert, *De Luther à Mohila: La Pologne dans la crise de la chrétienté 1517–1648* (Paris, 1974), go some way to remedy that deficiency; but these too abstain from any real inquiry into the ethnic issue of Polish susceptibility to Swiss rather than German doctrine.

D. A long tendency to disparage and belittle the Hungarian Puritan movement, evident from 'Lampe' through to the generation of Pokoly, was challenged (like so much else) by J. Zoványi, *Puritánus mozgalmak a magyar református egyházban* (Budapest, 1911), a work concentrating heavily on ecclesiology and clerical politics. The other sustained treatment, stimulated by shorter contributions from I. Révész, *A szatmárnémeti nemzeti zsinat és az első magyar református ébredés* (Budapest, 1947), and *Társadalmi és politikai eszmék a magyar puritánizmusban* (Budapest, 1948), has come from L. Makkai, *A magyar puritánusok harca a feudalizmus ellen* (ibid. 1952; English abstract in *Acta Historica*, 5 (Budapest, 1958), 13–44). This is an ingenious, even virtuoso attempt at a heavily socio-economic interpretation; yet although Makkai pays some attention to the political situation and to the English connection, his failure to acknowledge the spiritual dynamic of Puritanism, in either England or Hungary, diminishes his insights. While much biographical and bibliographical spadework has been accomplished, particularly by B. Trócsányi, *Magyar református theológusok Angliában a 16. és 17. században* (Debrecen, 1944), P. Berg, *Angol hatások 17. századi irodalmunkban* (Budapest, 1946), and G. Borsa *et al.* (eds.), *Régi magyarországi nyomtatványok*, in progress (Budapest, 1971–   ; superseding Károly Szabó (ed.), *Régi magyar könyvtár*, i–iii (Budapest, 1879–98)), the subject of Anglo-Hungarian seventeenth-century religious links deserves further study. I hope to return to it as an aspect of the 'Second Reformation' in Protestant Europe as a whole.

VII

England and International Calvinism
1558–1640[1]

PATRICK COLLINSON

I

IN 1569, Jan van der Noot, a native of Antwerp, had occasion[2] to reflect on his own distracted times, when most European states were full of tumult and, 'more is the pitie', with the shedding of Christian blood. But God had raised up godly princes and certain safe places 'where the elect and faithfull have resorted and bene preserved'. Such was the Rhenish Palatinate and its Prince Elector Frederick, a veritable Daniel or Josiah. But Noot was addressing not Daniel but Deborah, for he was one of those who had chosen to take refuge in England, 'a moste safe and sure harborough, where we live (God be thanked) under your Maiesties protection and safegarde in great libertie to serve God in eyther language, the French or the Dutche . . .'. And not only in French and Dutch. 'The worde of God is purely preached here in six or seven languages.' Counting on the fingers of two hands, one confirms the accuracy of the arithmetic. In Elizabethan London one could hear Protestant sermons not only in English and Latin but in French, Flemish, Italian, and even Spanish. And so Noot congratulated Queen Elizabeth on her blessed state, 'maugre the beards' of her enemies, and designated her 'specially elect of God'.

These were not everyone's perceptions, perhaps not entirely those of the queen with whom they were shared. Noot's fellow-countryman Emanuel van Meteren reported, plausibly enough, that the English were very suspicious of foreigners, 'whom they despise'. Elizabeth's lord keeper, Sir Nicholas Bacon, had once said (admittedly in the aftermath of the fall of Calais): 'That there be in England to many Frenchmen and that it were

---

[1] The tenure of an Andrew C. Mellon Fellowship at the Huntington Library, San Marino, Calif. provided the opportunity to write this essay. I am grateful to Dr Simon Adams for having read this essay in draft and for his helpful criticisms.
[2] The occasion was the dedication of a literary work of seminal importance, the English version of the book of poems and emblems called *Het Theatre* (earlier printed in London in Dutch and French), translated by the young Edmund Spenser as *A Theatre . . . [of] Worldlings* (1569). See J. van Dorsten, *The Radical Arts: First Decade of an Elizabethan Renaissance* (Leiden and London, 1970), 75–85. Van Dorsten suspects Noot of having been a member of the Family of Love.

much better yf ther wer none at all I cannot perceive that anie man denieth.'[3] Nor, from where they stood, were all foreign Calvinists as delighted with the Elizabethan dispensation as Noot. Theodore Beza had to explain to Heinrich Bullinger why Geneva was hated in England and on another occasion exclaimed: 'Quae talis unquam Babylon extitit?' The English church settlement rested primarily on the principles of autonomy from Rome and royal supremacy, not on the reception of true doctrine and conformity with the community of Reformed churches. Consequently, relations between England and the centres of continental Reform were never secure and always subject to political arbitrariness. As early as 1568, Bullinger wrote: 'Expectabimus ergo non ex Anglia sed ex coelo liberationem.'[4] Nevertheless, we may begin by investigating the substance behind Jan van der Noot's sanguine vision of an England where Word, sacraments, and discipline were all received in acceptable forms; where the ruler was an elect instrument of divine purpose; where the faithful of all nations were welcome; and where a common religious identity transcended differences of language and national culture.

A recent writer has rightly insisted that 'the English Reformation was uncompromisingly Protestant' and has demonstrated that at the heart of its Protestantism was the Swiss or Reformed theology of grace, which emphasized predestination. This was 'the fundamental theology of English Protestantism'.[5] From the earliest moment at which one can discern a formal and political alignment of the English Church in this direction, which is early in the reign of Edward VI, the local fortunes of Calvinism (as it is distinctly anachronistic to describe the theology and ecclesiology of the 1550s) and the place of England in international Calvinism were matters inseparably intertwined. The adoption of Reform on the Swiss–South German pattern was favoured by the presence in Edwardian England of the leading non-Lutheran Protestant divines, of whom Martin Bucer of Strasburg, the Italians Pietro Martire Vermigli (Peter Martyr) and Bernardino Ochino, and the learned Pole Jan Łaski (John à Lasco) were the most distinguished. It was also aggressively insisted upon by Englishmen who knew 'the best reformed churches' from the inside, of whom the most prominent was John Hooper, called by the Dutchman Maarten Micron 'the future Zwingli of England', but in fact a future bishop and martyr. For a time Hooper had lodgings with Micron who was one of the founders of the

---

[3] W. B. Rye, *England as Seen by Foreigners in the Days of Elizabeth and James I* (1865), p. 70; BL MS Add. 33271 fol. 15ᵛ. I am grateful to Professor G. R. Elton for helping with the dating of Bacon's speech, which was made in the House of Commons in Mary's last parliament.

[4] Beza to Bullinger, 3 September (1566), *Correspondance de Théodore de Bèze*, vii (1566), ed. H. Meylan *et al.* (Geneva, 1973), no. 500; Beza to Bullinger, 29 July 1567, *Correspondance*, viii (1567) (Geneva, 1976), no. 566; Bullinger to Beza, 11 February 1568, *Correspondance*, ix (1568) (Geneva, 1978), no. 587.

[5] Dewey D. Wallace Jr., *Puritans and Predestination* (see Further Reading).

'stranger-church' which in 1550 received its royal charter and the use of the large church building of the Austin Friars. This foundation was seen by its sponsors as much more than a home from home for foreign Protestant refugees. Like Zürich itself, and presently Geneva, it was an example which both the Church of England and the embryonic Reformed Church in the Netherlands were encouraged to emulate: a model church, presided over by a superintendent who was a pioneering modeller of churches, à Lasco.[6]

With Mary's accession, foreign and native Protestants alike scattered to continental cities of refuge, where the experience of the English exiles completed their assimilation into the Reformed camp at a time of worsening relations with the Lutherans. The colonies at Frankfurt, Strasburg, Zürich, Geneva, and Emden were all of seminal importance for the immediate future of the English Church and English Protestantism. Emden, another of Łaski's churches and a mother church for the Dutch Reform, was a launching pad for anti-Marian propaganda. Strasburg and Zürich nurtured the episcopal leadership of the future. At Frankfurt there were portents of an alternative churchmanship, critical and opportunistic, the germ of Elizabethan Puritanism. The leading light of this tendency was the first Englishman who can be called a Calvinist (rather than Zwinglian) internationalist: William Whittingham, a future dean of Durham. Whittingham was an expatriated Francophone with long experience in the universities of Orléans and Paris, who was corresponding with Calvin before the death of Edward VI. He was the first Englishman to receive ordination within the non-episcopal, reformed ministry, indeed at the hands of Calvin himself. But he was not, in spite of a hoary tradition, the reformer's brother-in-law.[7] After the 'troubles' of Frankfurt, which were proleptic of later convulsions in the Elizabethan Church, Whittingham's party and its sympathizers, together with their principal pastor John Knox, made a second migration to Geneva, where the church was founded which was joined to the future of English Calvinism by a kind of umbilical cord, and out of which came an invaluable asset of that future: Whittingham's Geneva Bible of 1560.

On Elizabeth's accession, roles were again reversed. Beza could now address the English Church as 'vos Anglos suo tempore dispersos, qui nunc

[6] The most recent account is A. D. M. Pettegree, 'The Strangers and their Churches in London, 1550–1580' (unpubl. Oxford D. Phil. thesis, Oxford, 1983). See also Ph. Denis, 'Les Églises d'étrangers à Londres jusqu'á la mort de Calvin: de l'Eglise de Jean Lasco à l'établissement du calvinisme' (unpubl. *mémoire de licence*, Liège, 1974); and Frederick A. Norwood, 'The Strangers' "Model Churches" in Sixteenth-Century England', in *Reformation Studies: Essays in Honor of R. H. Bainton*, ed. F. H. Littell (Richmond, Va., 1962) and his *Strangers and Exiles: A History of Religious Refugees* (Nashville and New York, 1969), i. 263–308. The magisterial study is still Baron F. de Schickler, *Les Églises du Refuge* (see Further Reading). J. Lindeboom, *Austin Friars: History of the Dutch Reformed Church in London, 1550–1950*, English Tr. D. de Iongh (The Hague, 1950) is a slighter work.

[7] Émile Doumergue, *Jean Calvin: Les hommes et les choses de son temps* (repr. Geneva, 1969), iii. App. V. 'Whitingham, le prétendu beau-frère de Calvin', 666–75.

per Dei gratiam estis dispersorum hospites.'[8] In London the stranger-churches—the Dutch in Austin Friars, the French in Threadneedle Street, together with an Italian and, for a time, a Spanish congregation—were refounded under a modified constitution which placed them more immediately under the surveillance of the bishop of London, now their superintendent *ex officio*. Under the first Elizabethan bishop, Edmund Grindal, a recently repatriated Strasburg exile, this imposed few restrictions on the autonomy of the congregations, although it did help to prevent their infiltration by Anabaptists and other undesirables.[9]

From the outset, Geneva recognized, as any foreign observer would, the strategic importance of Protestant England. Englishmen in Geneva who were reluctant to commit themselves to a still uncertain future under Elizabeth were urged by Calvin himself to return.[10] As for the stranger-churches, they had a double value both as resources of relief and recuperation for embattled French and Dutch Protestants and as a means of correcting any errant tendency on the part of the English state. Calvin made this second motive abundantly clear when he told Grindal that he deeply regretted the fact that things had not gone as well as all good men had hoped and at first expected, doubtless a reference to the queen's taste for popish ceremonial and her appetite for church lands. On the other hand, there was a real danger that the stranger-churches would themselves become reservoirs of infection. Geneva had some experience of the proclivity of refugee communities to fall into disarray, prey to doctrinal error and human failing, and especially to that most reprehensible of all weaknesses for a Calvinist, 'ambition'. The best prophylactic against such dangers was to reduce the participation in church affairs of 'the people' and to locate authority with 'the best' in a carefully modelled consistory.

The prime instrument of this policy was Nicolas Des Gallars, sieur de Saules, a senior colleague of Calvin who in 1551 had acted as his ambassador to the Edwardian Court and in 1559 had played a signal role in the first national synod of the French Reformed Church, held secretly in Paris. That Calvin was willing to spare the pedigree and diplomatic gifts of such a man, 'non sine acerbo dolore', is some indication of London's importance in his perception. Calvin, Des Gallars, and Grindal made a troika. Calvin told the London French that Grindal was their friend and protector. Grindal assured Calvin that des Gallars had been of the greatest assistance to himself 'and to our own churches'. Des Gallars assured Calvin that without Grindal he would not have been able to cope.

[8] Beza to Bishop Edmund Grindal, 8 Mar. 1569, *Correspondance de Théodore de Beze*, x (1569). ed. A. Dufour *et al.* (Geneva, 1980), no. 658.

[9] Full references for much of what follows will be found in my essay 'Calvinism with an Anglican Face' (see Further Reading) and in id., *Archbishop Grindal 1519–1583: the Struggle for a Reformed Church* (1979), 125–52.

[10] *The Seconde Parte of a Register*, ed. A. Peel (Cambridge, 1915), i. 58.

Although Grindal was not always at ease with the ruthlessness with which Geneva imposed its will and its own, narrowly conceived orthodoxy, he was mostly willing to serve as its ally and agent. First, Des Gallars was enabled to overcome the resistance to his leadership of rival claimants to the pastorate. Then the authority of the bishop, assisted by Des Gallar's polemical talents, was invoked to suppress a challenge to the consistory of the Dutch church made by the Dutch martyrologist Adriaen van Haemstede, assisted by the Italian libertine Giacomo Aconcio (Acontius). Haemstede's offence was to speak up for the Anabaptists as weak and deluded members of Christ, and it was compounded by the very Acontian proposition that the heretical doctrine of Christ's nature entertained by these dissidents was merely circumstantial, not fundamental. There followed a protracted *cause célèbre*, described by its historian as 'un combat aux frontières de l'orthodoxie'[11] and a matter of international interest and report. Eventually, Grindal had no choice but to ratify the sentences of excommunication passed against Haemstede and his supporters by the Dutch consistory, and to repeat the sentence when Haemstede, having fled to Emden, returned to Austin Friars in the spirit of Michael Servetus' provocative appearance in Geneva in 1555.

In 1561 Des Gallars was a spokesman with Beza at the Colloquy of Poissy and in 1562, after burying his wife and several children in plague-stricken London, he left for Orléans. Further troubles followed in the Dutch congregation, and more battles royal in defence of Calvinist integrity (or, as seen from the other side, in defence of religious liberty) involving the Spanish evangelicals Casiodoro de la Reina and Antonio del Corro. In these episodes Grindal proved a more reluctant executioner. Soon the international Calvinist telegraph would hum with complaints about the complacency of the English bishops. The sentences which counted in these circles were not those pronounced by the bishop-superintendent but the view of Beza that Reina and Corro were probably crypto-Servetan antitrinitarians, which appeared in his published *Epistolae* (1573). This publication contained a chilling reminder of the probable fate of free-thinkers in a truly godly commonwealth, in Beza's endorsement of the public execution of the Heidelberg dissident, Johannes Sylvanus.[12] That Corro was given a hearing in London and Oxford for many years and was protected by powerful patrons is indicative of the qualification which the historian must at once make if he is to call Elizabethan England a Calvinist state. Yet when Des Gallars returned to Geneva from war-ravaged Orléans in 1569, he took occasion to remind Grindal of the notable role which the bishop-

[11] Ph. Denis, 'Un combat aux frontières de l'orthodoxie: la controverse entre Acontius et Des Gallars sur la question du fondement et des circonstances de l'Église', *BHR*, 38 (1976), 55–72.

[12] This letter was suppressed in the 1575 edition. See P. G. Bietenholz, 'Limits to Intolerance: the Two Editions of Beza's *Epistolae Theologicae*, 1573', *BHR* 35 (1973), 311–13.

superintendent had played in the defence of the truth. In the dedicatory epistle to his edition of the anti-heretical writings of the early Latin Father Irenaeus, Grindal was told that he was Irenaeus reborn: 'Merito igitur te Irenaeo comparo.'[13]

II

For a Des Gallars or a Beza, heresy was meat and drink. If it had been found not to exist it would have been necessary to invent it. There was no lack of resistance to Calvinism in Elizabethan England. But much of it was the sullen rejection of ordinary people, instinctive Pelagians who found predestination an unacceptable proposition and many of whom were still Papists at heart. This inertia, embedded in what one writer called *The Countrie Divinitie*,[14] was inarticulate and would be all but inaccessible to us but for the publicity accorded it by Calvinist and Puritan critics. Even in academic circles there seems to have been little investigation of altèrnative theologies of a provocative kind, apart from the activities of Corro at Oxford and, a little later, the teaching of the Frenchman Peter Baro in Cambridge. So for the time being the talents of an Irenaeus were not in great demand. What was required was the converting, missionary energy of a new and Protestant Augustine. In the conservative English north country, Archbishop Grindal would soon have to take upon him the role of an apostle. As for international Calvinism, so far as English involvement was concerned this had more to do with diplomacy, money, and cultural cross-fertilization (which is to say, with Sir Philip Sidney)[15] than with heresy-hunting.

Perforce, this essay has to be Hamlet without the prince: by which is meant the Protestant foreign policy[16] first envisaged by Sir Nicholas Throckmorton, 'the first true Puritan politician', and then, in the 1570s and

[13] Des Gallars to Grindal, 31 January (1569 or 1570) (Preface to *Divi Irenaei Graeci scriptoris . . . libri quinque Adversus portentosas haereses Valentini et aliorum* (Geneva, 1570), *Correspondance de Théodore de Bèze*, x, App. III, 267–73. In dispensing the funds left for charity by their brother Robert Nowell, Alexander Nowell, dean of St Paul's and author of the standard catechism of the English Church, and Lawrence Nowell, dean of Lichfield, made payments to the most dissident of the learned strangers, Corro, Reina, and the French theologian Peter Baro, as to impeccable Calvinists (*The Spending of the Money of Robert Nowell*, ed. A. B. Grosart (London, 1877), 62–5, 100–6).

[14] George Gifford, *A briefe discourse of certaine points of the religion which is among the common sort of christians which may bee termed the Countrie Divinitie* (1581).

[15] J. A. van Dorsten, *Poets, Patrons, and Professors: Sir Philip Sidney, Daniel Rogers, and the Leiden Humanists* (Leiden, 1962); James M. Osborn, *Young Philip Sidney 1572–1577* (New Haven, 1972); R. C. Strong and J. A. van Dorsten, *Leicester's Triumph* (Leiden, 1964).

[16] This paragraph follows and quotes from S. L. Adams, 'The Protestant Cause: Religious Alliance with the European Calvinist Communities as a Political Issue in England, 1585–1630' (unpubl. D. Phil. thesis, Oxford, 1973). I am grateful to Dr Adams for his permission to cite his thesis. See also his essays 'The Road to La Rochelle: English Foreign Policy and the Huguenots, 1610–1629', *PHSL*, 22 (1975), 414–29, and 'Foreign Policy and the Parliaments of 1621 and 1624', in *Faction and Parliament: Essays on Early Stuart History*, Kevin Sharpe (ed.) (Oxford, 1978), 139–71.

1580s, elaborated by the secretary of state Sir Francis Walsingham and his staff, under the potent patronage of Robert Dudley, earl of Leicester. Dr Simon Adams has called this a policy of 'political Puritanism' defined as 'the advocacy of assistance to the Church abroad, rather than rapprochement with the Catholic powers or *Realpolitik*, as the guide for English policy'. The ardent religious conviction at its heart and one which Walsingham evidently shared was expressed by the Puritan lawyer and pamphleteer John Stubbs: 'We have the Lord's right hand on our side and all the hearts and hands of those of the religion.'[17] 'For the common citties of God there ought to be a common defence', wrote an anonymous Puritan diplomat. This apparently naïve ideal, not so much a substitute for policy as a guiding light through the complexity of policy, was first attempted in the military expedition to Le Havre (Newhaven) in 1562-3, frequently advocated in the late 1570s but as constantly frustrated by the queen's opposition and other factors. Finally it was somewhat ingloriously allowed its head in Leicester's Netherlands expedition and governorship of 1585-7, 'primarily a Puritan enterprise' both in inspiration and participation. At this moment England came closer than at any other time in history to undertaking that active leadership of the international Calvinist cause which enthusiastic publicists so often attributed to her. Stubbs exclaimed: 'These wars are holy.'

After that it was downhill all the way. For a full half-century there was more of fantasy and nostalgia in 'the protestant cause' than substance, given the reluctance of the monarchy to identify with it. Under James I, who favoured eirenical solutions to the problem of European security, much of the political aid which had been rendered to internationally militant Calvinism in Elizabeth's name was withdrawn. Meanwhile, efforts to discover in a succession of aristocrats, from the second earl of Essex through Prince Henry to the third earl of Pembroke, what Dr Adams has called 'an *ersatz* Leicester' were not very successful. In the 1620s the contortions of the duke of Buckingham's dealings with the French Huguenots involved some cynical manipulation of the tattered fragments of the good old cause, as well as what a preacher denounced as 'taking part against our own religion'. Nevertheless, the importance, even the negative importance, of the impossible dream can scarcely be exaggerated. However, this is a subject for the wide screen, too vast to be accommodated in this essay and so, except for these brief remarks, omitted.

Fund-raising in aid of the international Calvinist cause still awaits the historian with the heroic capacity of a Braudel to draw together a mass of scattered evidence and the vision to see the topic whole. We may then discover a motivation, a network, and a methodology reminiscent of the 'third world' charities of our own time, with their particular concerns for refugees, for the sustenance of both persecuted and militant groups in

[17] *John Stubbe's Gaping Gulf*, ed. L. E. Berry (Washington, DC, 1968), 86.

revolutionary situations, for education and the preparation of leadership cadres, and even for the purchase of military hardware and the mounting of guerrilla operations. Until this work has been done, we must make do with a debris of fragments, although the bits and pieces can be so arranged as to suggest regularities and continuities.[18] 'To the afflicted churches, either of the strangers or of our own, tenne pounds', runs the modest will of Robert Smith, servant to the Northamptonshire MP and active Puritan, George Carleton. Learned and impoverished strangers were one of the principal subjects of the posthumous charity of the government attorney Robert Nowell, as distributed by his brothers, the deans of St Paul's and Lichfield. A total of £221. 11s. 4d. was dispensed out of this fund to the Italian, Dutch, and French churches in London and the provinces and to many individual strangers. In disposing of another estate, the London mercer Richard Culverwell, uncle of a famous Puritan preacher, bequeathed a gold chain which he had received from the queen of Navarre and spoke of 'manye other her jewells of greate value' which had come into the possession of others, 'for the furtherance and defence of the Ghospell and suche as sincerely professe the same'. Although Culverwell describes these treasures as 'franckly' given, they seem to have been pledges. In 1582, an agent of the Geneva government estimated that La Rochelle was in debt to the city of London to the tune of £40,000.[19]

An important element in the rhythm of religious life among English Calvinists and Puritans was the public fast, kept as a whole day of humiliation, prayer, and preaching and often related to some special 'occasions'. In 1586 in Suffolk these included 'the state of the Frenche church' and two years later the London French related their own fast to the afflictions of the Church, 'tant en France que au pais bas, ensemble l'estat de ce Royaume'. It seems to have been common practice on these special days of assembly to collect money for some specific purpose, perhaps linked with the occasion of the fast. According to a cryptic report from the anti-Puritan sleuth Richard Bancroft, the money collected by Puritans in this way 'for their brethren that travell for them beyond the seas' was forwarded to Culverwell and to the London preacher John Field.

So it was that when a conference of Puritan ministers in the country, the so-called Dedham Classis, received a request from the Threadneedle Street church for aid and relief, it was decided not to make a public collection but 'to deale privately with the best affected'. To gather funds publicly but without due authorization was sometimes attempted but it was irregular if not illegal. Partly for this reason, partly for reasons of ideological

---

[18] To the references to be found in my essay 'The Elizabethan Puritans and the Foreign Reformed Churches in London', *PHSL*, 20 (1964), 528–55, repr. in Collinson, *Godly People*, 245–72, add *The Spending of the Money of Robert Nowell*, 62–5, 100–6.

[19] Archives d'État, Geneva, Pièces Historiques 2066. See p. 205, n. 22 below.

commitment, we can be sure that much of the money raised in the cause of international Calvinism came from the pockets of 'the best affected'. The 'contes des deniers des pauvres' of the French church in London have been preserved for the period November 1572 to December 1573[20] (and no other accounts until the late seventeenth century), presumably because they contain a creditable record of English benevolence in the aftermath of the St Bartholomew massacres, when scores of refugee pastors poured into the south of England. But much of the generosity was that of 'the best affected', including Calvinist notables like the countess of Sussex and Sir Francis Hastings, brother of the earl of Huntingdon, who brought £10. 4s. 'venant des gentils hommes du conté de Lecestre'; and famous preachers and divines, among them Thomas Cartwright, Thomas Lever, William Whittingham, and old colleagues of Whittingham from the English consistory in Geneva, William Williams, Thomas Wood, and John Bodley. We also find the names of the wealthy Puritan goldsmith with whom Cartwright was staying at this time, Richard Martin, and of a young law student called Nicholas Fuller, who was destined to become a vociferous Puritan attorney and Parliament man.

In 1582–3, the greatest of all such 'gatherings' was launched in order to relieve the city of Geneva itself from the threat posed by the duke of Savoy, Charles Emmanuel. This was no hole-in-the-corner affair but a public collection supported by the Privy Council and duly licensed. In the diocese of Canterbury, the contributors whose names were recorded were numbered in hundreds (but not in thousands) and represented a cross-section of provincial society.[21] But even in these auspicious circumstances the response had clear ideological overtones, as we learn from almost every page of the journal kept by the agent of the Geneva government, Jean Maillet, who cooled his heels in London from November 1582 until September 1583.[22] Alderman Richard Martin (whom we have already met and whose personal contribution on this occasion was £20) told Maillet that it was the government's opinion that Papists should not contribute but only those whose sympathies were engaged as co-religionists—which was why those who were of that sort contributed more largely, so that they might not appear suspect and of a contrary religion.[23] Evidently subscribing to the

[20] Archives of the French Protestant Church of London, MS 194.

[21] PRO SP 12/161/21.

[22] The journal is in Archives d'État, Geneva, Pièces Historiques 2066. I am most grateful to Simon Adams for allowing me to use his transcript of this remarkable source, which he intends to publish. On Maillet's mission, see L. Cramer, *La Seigneurie de Genève et la maison de Savoie de 1559 à 1603* (2 vols., Geneva and Paris, 1912) and in *Bulletin de la Société d'histoire et d'archéolgie de Genève*, iii (1905), 385–404. Part of a letter from Beza to Walsingham introducing Maillet is printed in Paul-F. Geisendorf, *Théodore de Bèze* (Geneva, 1967), p. 369.

[23] 'Qui estoit cause que ceux qui estoyent tels, contribuyoient plus largement afin de n'estre suspects et de religion contraire.'

Geneva fund had some of the same significance as taking the Bond of Association a year later.[24]

The queen had no such need to pretend to a sympathy which she did not feel. When the agent first met the secretary of state, Sir Francis Walsingham warned him not to expect much from that quarter, since he foresaw 'grands empeschements': notably 'la mauvaise opinion' which the queen had always entertained of Geneva on account of John Knox's *First Blast of the Trumpet Against the Monstrous Regiment of Women*. (One of Des Gallar's rivals in Threadneedle Street had suggested in 1560 that Elizabeth might refuse to confirm the appointment of a pastor sent 'by those who have greatly offended her'.) In any case, Walsingham suggested, better wait for the return to Court of the earl of Leicester. When Leicester came he told the agent that his mistress regarded Geneva as 'une lampe qui a servi pour esclairer presque toutes les Églises de l'Europe.' Such words cost nothing. The agent was not granted an audience, but Walsingham reported back that the queen doubted whether the city was in any serious danger and thought that she was probably more in need of money than Geneva was. Walsingham, expecting this outcome, had asked Maillet how much he was looking for. He had replied that beggars could not be choosers.

After delays and elusive promises, the Council placed the responsibility for raising the money on the City and the Church, employing the standard procedure for charitable collections beyond the locality under the device of letters patent. By late April, £1,434 had been collected in the province of Canterbury, although some bishops were defaulters, including John Scory of Hereford, whose exile in Emden was now a distant memory. (But Edwin Sandys of York said that he would stake his all, 'engager sa chemise', in the cause.) In these circumstances the agent was tempted to do business with an unofficial committee of leading Puritan ministers, headed by Walter Travers, Cartwright's right-hand man: but was advised that it would be prudent to work through more regular channels. In the event, the church collections produced a satisfying response. A vicar in Hertfordshire pleaded poverty ('I fare full sad') but still sent ten shillings 'to helpe these godlie people, troubled for the gospel of Jesus Christ': a widow's mite indeed, since Walsingham himself gave only twenty times as much.[25] Eventually the machinery set in motion managed to raise not far short of £6,000. Subsequently (and there were further collections for Geneva in 1590 and 1603) it became accepted practice for the government to call upon the

---

[24] David Cressy, 'Binding the Nation: the Bonds of Association, 1584 and 1696', in *Tudor Rule and Revolution: Essays for G. R. Elton from his American Friends*, ed. Delloyd G. Gutha and John W. McKenna (Cambridge, 1982), 217–34.

[25] Patrick Collinson, *The Religion of Protestants* (see Further Reading) 126–7; information supplied by Simon Adams.

official Church to arrange voluntary contributions from the faithful, presumably on a parochial basis.[26]

But the success of the 1582–3 operation depended critically on the patronage of Calvinists in the upper echelons of government. Sir Walter Mildmay, who in times past had wished that he could join the English exiles in Geneva,[27] was cordial. Philip Sidney promised that his father would arrange a collection in Wales. The earl of Bedford recalled the hospitality of Geneva in Mary's days and thought that this debt should now be paid. For three hours he enquired minutely into the condition of the city, protested that it was as dear to him as his native country and swore that the representative of such a republic was equal in his estimation to the ambassador of the greatest monarch under Heaven. Back from his estates three months later, Bedford brought more money than he had expected. The 'bonnes gens du pays' had paid two, three, four pounds without compulsion. He had never seen them better disposed. But was it done for Geneva, or for the name of Russell? The Protestant councillors and courtiers all made substantial contributions, from Bedford's £40 and Leicester's £30 to ten pounds each from Sidney, Walsingham, and Mildmay and twenty from Francis Bacon's enthusiastically religious mother. The conservatives, Sir Christopher Hatton, Sir James Croft, Lord Hunsdon, seem to have given nothing. The moral is clear. The response to Geneva in her hour of need had come spontaneously from certain old Geneva hands like John Bodley, who acted as Geneva's banker on this occasion; and from a small Puritan clique. Only the patronage of the Protestant earls stimulated the respectable appearance of a groundswell of national sympathy and support.

The experience of 1582–3 was closely paralleled more than forty years later in the English reaction to the disaster of the Rhenish Palatinate, and in particular to that aspect of the crisis which most engaged the hearts of Calvinists: the destitution of Calvinist ministers and schoolmasters and their wives, families, and widows: at least eight hundred souls, not to count 'sundrie thousands of godly private persons' who had fled as refugees from the Habsburg onslaught on their homeland.[28] Between 1626 and 1633, the English contribution to the Palatinate relief fund far outstripped the help which came from the Swiss, French, and Dutch, or so the Palatine ministers themselves were prepared to testify to 'the whole sympathyzing Christian

---

[26] PRO SP 14/4/8, SP 15/36/29. On the evolution of the procedures for conducting charitable collections or 'briefs' see C. J. Kitching, 'Fire Disasters and Fire Relief in sixteenth-century England: the Nantwich Fire of 1583', *BIHR* 54 (1981), 171–87.

[27] *Secondé Parte of a Register*, ii. 58.

[28] With what follows I have been helped by Dr O. P. Grell's unpublished doctoral dissertation (European University Institute, Florence, 1983): 'Austin Friars and the Puritan Revolution. The Dutch Church in London, 1603–1642: and in particular by ch. 5: The Collections for the Palatinate'.

world'.[29] The recovery of the Palatinate was the occasion for a charitable collection in 1620 and then, after the failure of the 1621 Parliament to deliver a subsidy or an effectively compulsory 'benevolence', again in 1623.[30] The relief of refugees was a distinct issue and considered wholly an object of Christian charity. Once again, although seventy years separated these events from the reign of Mary, there were those who remembered the Exile and regarded English generosity on this occasion as payment of an old debt.[31] And once more, just as the Puritan preachers of London had concerned themselves with the relief of Geneva in 1582–3, so in 1626 an early initiative was taken by their successors, the ranking godly ministers of this later generation: John Davenport of St Stephen's Coleman Street, William Gouge of Blackfriars, Richard Sibbes of Gray's Inn and Thomas Taylor, lecturer at St Mary Aldermanbury, where John Field had once preached. In a circular letter addressed to 'all godly christians', these ministers dramatized the plight of their Palatine brethren, who would be 'very thankfull for course bread and drink if they could gett it' and called for a 'gathering'. This was to discard the caution which Travers (characteristically) had shown in 1583 and the subscribers to this letter were prosecuted in the High Commission, presumably for their temerity in organizing an unauthorized, semi-public collection.[32]

The subscribing ministers said that they knew 'a sure and safe way' to get help into the hands of those for whom it was intended. These men usually did know a way, for Davenport, Gouge, and Sibbes were part of that extraordinary Puritan enterprise known as the Feoffees for the Purchase of Impropriations which began operations in this same year, 1626. Another famous cleric associated with both the Feoffees and the Palatinate gathering was the so-called 'patriarch of Dorchester', John White, who had already raised large sums for the Palatinate in his own town and parish. One senses that talent for almost conspiratorial wheeling and dealing which in 1629 would carry over into the Providence Island Company and the Massachusetts Bay Company, enterprises partly inspired by John White's writings. Just as the Feoffees included merchants and lawyers as well as divines, so the Palatinate collection involved the close co-operation of preachers and prominent Puritan laymen, like Alderman Isaac Pennington, whose home in the Whitefriars served as an 'ordinary' for Puritan visitors to the city.[33]

The 'safe and sure' way which the London preachers knew for channeling

---

[29] Ecclesiae Londino-Batavae Archivum, ed. J. H. Hessels, iii (Cambridge, 1897), no. 2239.

[30] John Rushworth, Historical Collections, i (1862), 60–1; Ecclesiae Londino-Batavae Archivum, iii, no. 1805. See Marc L. Schwarz, 'Lord Saye and Sele's Objections to the Palatinate Benevolence of 1622: Some New Evidence and its Significance', Albion, 4 (1972), 12–22.

[31] Ecclesiae Londino-Batavae Archivum, iii. nos. 1985, 2100, 2239, 2262, 2263, 2276, 2281.

[32] Letters of John Davenport, Puritan Divine, ed. I. M. Calder (New Haven, 1937), 26–7, 29–30.

[33] I. M. Calder, Activities of the Puritan Faction of the Church of England 1625–33 (1957); R. P. Stearns, The Strenuous Puritan: Hugh Peter 1598–1660 (Urbana, 1954), 34, 40; Frances Rose-Troup,

funds to the Palatine refugees was the Dutch church in London through its 'politicke mannen', merchants with appropriate resources and contacts and much experience in fund-raising. (Austin Friars found the vast sum of £33,000 for the relief of its own poor in only sixteen years.)[34] Close co-operation between the strangers and English Calvinists in the Edwardian and Elizabethan tradition continued and was assisted by a partial merging of the two communities. One of the elders at Austin Friars, John de la Motte, had been born in Colchester to Flemish parents. He was a wealthy and pious London businessman who found his way into Samuel Clarke's catalogue of modern English saints, with special commendation for his '*Sympathizing* bowels' shown towards the persecutions and troubles 'in *France*, at *Rochel*, in the *Valtoline*, in *Bohemia*, in *Germany*: And more particularly in the *Lower* and *Upper Palatinate*.'[35] When, in 1628, Charles I ordered general collections for the Palatine refugees his proclamation referred to information received from the Dutch church in London. Both on this occasion and in the second collection ordered in 1630 centralized administration and transmission of the funds was delegated to the Austin Friars consistory. According to the refugees themselves, the king had been persuaded to take these steps by the intercession and labour both of the London Dutch and 'cordatiorum quorundam Anglorum'.[36] The archives of the Dutch church, which contain well over a hundred items of correspondence between Austin Friars and the refugee groups, record the diligent thoroughness with which the money was doled out and accounted for; while in England the Dutch consistory was engaged in an endless round of letter-writing to bishops and other clergy, of visits to Lambeth House, and of frequent meetings.[37]

The royal collection was to be commended in every parish in England and Wales and taken up either in church services or from door to door. But once more, as in 1572 and 1583, the names of those who gave generously reads like a selective rollcall of what a seventeenth-century Puritan would have called 'notable private Christians'.[38] In a way the Palatines were

---

John White the Patriarch of Dorchester (1930), 43–4; A. P. Newton, *The Colonising Activities of the English Puritans* (New Haven, 1914); Valerie Pearl, *London and the Outbreak of the Puritan Revolution: City Government and National Politics, 1625–43* (Oxford, 1961), 179.

[34] Grell, op. cit.

[35] Samuel Clarke, *The Lives of Sundry Eminent Persons in this Later Age* (1683), ii. 102–4.

[36] *Cal. SP Dom. Charles I 1627–1628*, 532; *Cal. SP Dom. Charles I 1629–1631* 205; *Ecclesiae Londino-Batavae Archivum*, iii, nos. 1906, 2045, 2046.

[37] Ibid. iii, scattered between nos. 1851 and 2426. See especially no. 2191.

[38] Grell, op. cit. The largest single contributor was apparently the Puritan civil lawyer Dr Henry Hawkins who in his will left £300 'to the distressed ministers of the disturbed protestant churches in Germanie' and an equivalent sum to the Feoffees for Impropriations, part of which was diverted to the Palatinate fund after the suppression of the Feoffees, according to the terms of his will. William Gouge was an executor. (PRO HCA 1/32/1, fol. 90, cited by Grell; B. P. Levack, *The Civil Lawyers in England 1603–1641* (Oxford, 1973), 186–7, 237; *Ecclesiae Londino-Batavae Archivum*, iii. nos. 2158, 2160, 2179, 2267.)

drawing attention to this ideologically motivated response to their needs when they pointed out that Camden's *Britannia* told them that there were 8,700 parishes in England and that it seemed unlikely that all of them could have contributed to their uttermost!

III

Our investigation of Protestant fund-raising has suggested that English Calvinism, like English humanitarianism or English Communism in later generations, was the cause of an inner circle, well known to one another and somewhat estranged from the generality of society. That degree of estrangement is pin-pointed in the stigma of 'Puritan' which, from the 1560s to the 1660s, was commonly attached to such people, indicating not only the unusual warmth of their attachment to religion, but their dissatisfaction with the extent of the reformation achieved in the English Church within the terms of the Elizabethan religious settlement. In the most outspoken manifesto of Elizabethan Puritanism, *An Admonition to the Parliament*, composed in 1572 by two young London preachers, Thomas Wilcox and John Field, these questions were put: 'Is a reformation good for France? and can it be evyl for England? Is discipline meete for Scotland? and can it be unprofitable for this Realme?'[39] This sense of solidarity with international Protestant community was demonstrated by Puritans in London (and perhaps in provincial towns like Norwich, Colchester, and Canterbury, although this has yet to be investigated) in their active involvement in the affairs of the stranger churches, which they continued to regard as models of the 'church rightly reformed' such as they hoped to see established in England.[40] An obscure London parson, suspended from his cure for nonconformity, wrote plaintively: 'Yt semethe ryghtfull that subiects naturall receve soe muche favoure as the churches of natyonall straungers here with us. But we can not once be harde so to obtayne.' On more than one occasion, Puritan agitators and politicians pointed out that Parliament had no need to look beyond the forms of worship employed in the stranger-churches in order to find an acceptable alternative to the Book of Common Prayer. The *Admonition to the Parliament* was published only after the failure of a parliamentary bill which would have legalized the use of these liturgies in parish churches.

This led an opponent of the Puritans to complain that all the troubles in the English Church were attributable to the 'strange churches, as well beyond the seas as here among us remaining'. There was some truth in this. In the course of the 1560s, the Geneva pastorate, inspired and taught by Beza, was hardening its attitude with respect to 'the discipline', insisting on

[39] *Puritan Manifestoes* ed. W. H. Frere and C. E. Douglas (1954 edn.), p. 19.

[40] References for what follows will be found in my essay 'The Elizabethan Puritans and the Foreign Reformed Churches in London' already noted.

the necessity of that element in the life of the Church and in the hands of its own officers, and defining it according to a narrow exegesis of certain New Testament texts. Presently Geneva took exception to the view, defended in Heidelberg by Thomas Erastus, that under a Christian magistracy there was no need for discipline in this sense; and found itself at odds with the mentors of Erastus and the true home of 'Erastianism', Zürich. As for England, Beza moved from a cautious familiarity with the Elizabethan bishops, Grindal in particular whom he knew personally, to a largely negative appraisal of English religious conditions as falling victim to 'avarice' and 'ambition'. In this he was encouraged by the pessimistic reports carried to Geneva by Puritan emissaries. The critical shift in his attitudes can be traced through Beza's *Correspondance*, especially with Bullinger in Zürich, and it accompanies a hardening contempt for diocesan episcopacy as lordly 'domination'.[41]

But Beza was not lacking in diplomacy and like Agag he contrived to tread delicately. When the Puritans urged him to intervene directly in the English controversies he declined, knowing that letters from Geneva were more likely to hinder than help.[42] In 1568 he dedicated his New Testament to the queen and two years later chose Sir Walter Mildmay as the recipient of his *Tractatae Theologicae*, apologizing for their acerbic tone. When the *Admonition* appeared he attempted to detach himself from 'such very indiscreet proceedings', which were liable to prejudice his own dealings with certain English 'seigneurs'.[43] That was said in a letter to Threadneedle Street. Correspondence between Geneva and the English Puritans was commonly directed through the French church in London, 'a thing they do very frequently', according to one report.[44]

The recipients of these letters seem to have moved in and out of the foreign congregations with ease and familiarity. Some, especially merchants with a command of foreign languages and relevant business contacts, served as officers. For example, that inveterate internationalist John Bodley was an elder of the French church. When Sir Thomas Middleton became Lord Mayor of London in 1613 he had been a member of the Dutch church for more than thirty years.[45] Early in Elizabeth's reign, the communicants at

[41] *Correspondance*, vii, nos. 472, 476, 479, 500; viii, nos. 524, 534, 544, 547, 554, 557, 559, 560, 566, 573; ix, no. 615.

[42] Thomas Sampson to Beza, 20 July 1567, *Correspondance*, viii. no. 565; Beza to Bullinger, 19 June 1566, *Correspondance*, vii. no. 476. A singularly unhelpful letter, as it transpired, was the one which Beza wrote to Grindal on 27 June 1566, which was pirated by the authors of the *Admonition*. (*Correspondance*, vii, no. 479; *Puritan Manifestoes*, 43–55.)

[43] Beza's dedication to Mildmay was dated 27 February 1570. (*Correspondance*, xi, no. 744.) For Beza and the *Admonition*, see Patrick Collinson, *The Elizabethan Puritan Movement* (1967), 121. Beza's later relations with the Church of England, and especially with Archbishop John Whitgift, are documented in John Strype, *Life of John Whitgift* (Oxford, 1822), ii. 105–6, 160–73, iii. 300–4.

[44] *The Zurich Letters*, ed. H. Robinson, Parker Society LII (Cambridge, 1846), 291.

[45] Grell, op. cit.

Threadneedle Street were joined by veterans of the English Geneva congregation, Whittingham and his French wife among them, 'et plusieurs aultres englois'. From time to time more distinguished guests flashed what were doubtless calculated signals by ostentatiously taking the sacrament with the French: in 1565 William Cecil's brother-in-law, the diplomat Henry Killigrew, and in 1568 no less a personage than the earl of Leicester. Ten years later, at a time when he was hoping to find an active and commanding role in the Low countries, Leicester heard a sermon from the Dutch minister in Norwich and wrote: 'Me thinkes I hear every day the voyce of that people.'[46]

Grindal had to ask the French to exercise discretion in admitting English visitors to their services, and to distinguish between those who merely wished to make an ecumenical gesture and others who were effectively schismatics and had deserted their own parish churches. Later, with the worsening of conflict in the Church of England, the authorities became increasingly anxious that the stranger churches should not provide a bolt-hole for disaffected Puritans. The strangers, who were glad to welcome English communicants 'a cause qu'ils son unis de fois avec nous', were obliged to give undertakings not to encourage dissidents. On the other hand John King, bishop of London from 1611 to 1621, followed the earlier example of Grindal in instructing the London parish clergy not to give sanctuary to strangers who were in flight from the discipline of their own congregations. In Grindal's time that was regarded in Threadneedle Street as 'acte de levesque remarquable'.[47]

Not only Geneva veterans like Bodley and Whittingham but Puritans who had never crossed the sea and had never met Calvin or Beza seem to have felt more affinity with their foreign co-religionists than with fellow Englishmen who were of a contrary religious persuasion or of none. In 1584 this sense of international brotherhood was demonstrated in the streets of London when the funeral of a Scottish minister, one of a group of Presbyterian exiles, was accompanied by a procession of more than five hundred 'godlie brethren, ministers and citicens', including three French pastors with 'manie Frenchmen'. Old Sir Nicholas Bacon, with his talk of eradicating Frenchmen, would have been flabbergasted. But the twentieth century, which is experienced in its own manifestations of international ideological solidarity, finds itself on familiar ground. In Edinburgh, a Scottish minister who received on consecutive days letters from La Rochelle and from John Field in London wrote to Field: 'It is no small comfort brother . . . to brethren of one natione to understand the state of the brethren in other

---

[46] Quoted, Adams, 'The Protestant Cause', p. 80.

[47] Commission of Bishop King to the Dutch congregations of London and Colchester, 9 August 1615; *Ecclesiae Londino-Batavae Archivum*, iii no. 1758. For other references, see my 'The Elizabethan Puritans and the Foreign Reformed Churches in London'.

nationes.' 'Touching the word *forreyne*', wrote William Bradshaw, 'those Churches being all the same houshold of faith that we are, they are not aptly called forreyne . . . So all Churches and all members of the Church, in what Country so ever they be, are not to be accounted Forreyners one to another, because they are all Citizens of heaven, and we all make one family or body.'[48]

IV

In this essay, English Calvinism and Calvinists have so far been defined narrowly as a partisan cause and a coterie somewhat out of the main stream of English society and drawing closer to the international Calvinist community. A volume with the title *International Calvinism* has beckoned in that direction. But the time has come to acknowledge that there was a more broadly-based reception of Calvinism in the Elizabethan and Jacobean Church of England, amounting to 'the received interpretation of the Church's doctrine'.[49] The 'English Creed', as an Elizabethan author styled the Articles of Religion,[50] was different in form and application from the confessions of faith of the national Reformed churches. So it has often been said that the Church of England is not a confessional church. Nevertheless, the account of salvation, faith, grace, and predestination rendered by the Articles was broadly consistent with the Reformed consensus on these matters and directly indebted to specific Reformed sources at some points.[51] The consequence was a public sense, rarely challenged before the time of Archbishop Laud, that the English Church and nation were in essential harmony with other Reformed churches, their sacraments and ministries interchangeable for migrants and foreign travellers. Episcopacy, which other Reformed churches lacked, was of the *bene esse* rather than the *esse* of the Church.[52]

So English Calvinism was not equivalent to Puritanism. Few Elizabethan religious controversialists referred more frequently to Calvin than the Puritans' most doughty opponent, Archbishop John Whitgift. And Whitgift was only one of many English divines conventionally classified as 'Anglicans' rather than 'Puritans' who expressed their regard for Calvin on

[48] BL MS Add. 4736, fol. 166ᵛ; R. M. Gillon, *John Davidson of Prestonpans* (1936), 262–3; William Bradshaw, *A myld and iust defence of certeyne arguments* (1606), 5.

[49] I owe this careful phrase to an unpublished paper by Dr F. H. Shriver, 'The Character of Jacobean Anglicanism: Arminians, Calvinists and the Via Media'.

[50] Thomas Rogers, *The Faith Doctrine and Religion Professed and Protected in the Realm of England* (1607, repr. Parker Society, XL (Cambridge, 1854)) was entitled in the original version of 1584 *The English creede, consenting with the true, auncient, catholique, and apostolique church.*

[51] Wallace, *Puritans and Predestination*, 16–17.

[52] Norman Sykes, *The Church of England & Non-Episcopal Churches in the Sixteenth & Seventeenth Centuries: An Essay Towards the Historical Interpretation of the Anglican Tradition from Whitgift to Wake* (1949); Norman Sykes, *Old Priest and New Presbyter* (1956).

many occasions. Yet a distinction may be drawn between intellectual debts of this kind, which admitted Calvin into the controversial arena, and an absorption of Calvinist divinity which was so complete as to structure and furnish a world-view, an intellectual system, and a rule of life. This was the difference between a merely theoretical Calvinism and the applied, practical, and highly combative Calvinism of some puritan divines, and it distinguishes Whitgift from the dominant theological force in late Elizabethan Cambridge, William Whitaker, whose powerful mind turned and spun its syllogisms within the concepts of the exclusive truth and authority of Scripture, the sovereignty of God's predestinate grace, and the Antichristian falsity of the pope's Church.[53]

Hence, the extent to which English Protestantism in the age of its maturity can be properly called Calvinist is one of some delicacy and difficulty. 'Calvinist' is a stereotype and too blunt an instrument for any discriminating purpose. English Protestants were not disposed to surrender their theological judgement to some Genevan *magisterium*. 'Calvin herein grants more than I would grant', was the marginal comment of an unknown reader on a particular point encountered in his reading of the *Institutes* in Thomas Norton's English translation. John Whitgift and his Puritan opponent Thomas Cartwright freely quoted Calvin the one against the other, but each met with the same response: we reverence Mr Calvin but we do not believe anything to be true simply on the basis of his say-so. Later Whitgift warned against giving more credence to the 'bare names and authoritie' of Calvin and Beza than was given to the ancient Fathers; and even declared that the Church of England 'doth in no respect depend upon them'.[54] But these were debating points, and to quote the last remark out of context would be particularly misleading. There was considerable dependence.

But at the same time, the student who has only heard of 'Calvinism' must learn that English theologians were as likely to lean on Bullinger of Zürich, Musculus of Berne, or Peter Martyr as on Calvin or Beza, while they accorded a higher measure of authority to Ambrose, Athanasius, Augustine, Chrysostom, and Cyprian, for the apologetics of the Church of England (and not only the English Church) always rested on a patristic foundation. Such names were the missile weaponry of Elizabethan divinity, so much of which was polemical. But if we were to identify one author and one book which represented the centre of theological gravity of the Elizabethan Church it would not be Calvin's *Institutes* but the *Common Places* of Peter Martyr, described by his translator, Anthony Marten, as 'a verie Apostle'.

[53] Peter Lake, *Moderate Puritans and the Elizabethan Church* (Cambridge, 1982).
[54] Collinson, *Elizabethan Puritan Movement*, 104; *The Works of John Whitgift*, ed. J. Ayre, i. Parker Society, XLVI (Cambridge, 1851), 247–8, 436; H. C. Porter, *Reformation and Reaction in Tudor Cambridge* (Cambridge, 1958), 359–60, 350–1.

And at least equally influential was Bullinger, whose view of the religious role of Christian magistracy was well adapted to political reality in Elizabethan England.[55]

Even when their purposes were different, Elizabethan protestant writers were eclectic. To take the martyrologist John Foxe as an example: in the works of religious edification and spiritual comfort which he wrote or edited and brought to the press it would be hard to apply any limiting label and we must pause before defining Foxe as a Calvinist—or anything else. He found much of value in the writings of Martin Luther (although he was not a Lutheran) and especially in those works which reveal Luther as a physician of the wounded conscience. It was due almost entirely to Foxe that Luther lived on in the English religious consciousness, above all as the author of the ever-popular *Commentary on Galatians*.[56]

A generation after Foxe, 'Calvinism', if it meant anything, no longer signified Geneva and the churches that looked to Geneva for guidance but a loose and free alliance of churches, universities, academies, and other intellectual, political, and spiritual resources located in France, the Netherlands, South-West Germany, England, and Scotland, not to speak of more distant outposts. New names began to count: Beza for one, but also Junius, Danaeus, the Heidelberg doctors and their influential Catechism, Ursinus, and above all Zanchius, called by an early seventeenth-century Oxford professor 'clarissimus superioris seculi theologus'.[57] The very names, let alone the voluminous works, of these second-generation Calvinist theologians are now unknown to all but a few specialists. Yet at the turn of the century they were studied not only in Oxford and Cambridge but by the erudite country clergy of East Anglia.[58] These authors were all in a sense 'Calvinists', but whether their Calvinism was a legitimate implementation of Calvin's own programme or a departure from the spirit and method of his theology is still a matter of debate.

All this must be borne in mind as we concede that the Church of England was putting down its anchors in the outer roads of the broad harbour of the Calvinist or (better) Reformed Tradition. The anchors sometimes shifted

---

[55] *The Common Places of the most famous and renowned Divine Doctor Peter Martyr* (1583), Anthonie Marten's dedicatory epistle to Elizabeth I; David J. Keep, 'Theology as a Basis for Policy in the Elizabethan Church', in *The Materials Sources and Methods of Ecclesiastical History*, SCH, xi, ed. D. Baker (Oxford, 1975), 263–8, and Dr. Keep's 1970 Sheffield Ph.D. thesis, 'Henry Bullinger and the Elizabethan Church'.

[56] The prefaces to the following English editions of Luther, all printed by the Huguenot printer Vautrouiller, establish Foxe's prime responsibility for the whole enterprise: *A commentarie . . . upon the epistle to the Galatians* (1575), *A commentarie upon the fiftene psalsms, called psalmi graduum* (1577), *A right comfortable treatise containing fourteene pointes of consolation for them that labor* (1578), *Special and chosen sermons* (1578).

[57] C. M. Dent, *Protestant Reformers* (see Further Reading) 100–1.

[58] Patrick Collinson, 'The Beginnings of English Sabbatarianism', in Collinson, *Godly People*, 429–43.

but they did not drag until the late 1620s. The anchor-chains were the magisterial theologians who made themselves masters of the schools and of half the colleges in Oxford and Cambridge in the second half of Elizabeth's reign: in Cambridge, William Whitaker, William Fulke, Laurence Chaderton, and, in a rather different and more popular vein, William Perkins; in Oxford the formidable John Reynolds, who as an expositor of the Calvinist scheme of grace had cut his teeth on the free-thinking Spaniard, del Corro. Reynolds, as a recent study has emphasized, almost epitomized in his own person the Reformed Church of England, 'not narrowly Calvinist and Genevan, but inspired by a variety of continental protestant centres', expressing 'a hybrid and broadly-based theological tradition.'[59]

As they pursue the developing and changing fortunes of that tradition into the early decades of the seventeenth century, historians of doctrine encounter and sometimes fail to agree on three related questions which will be briefly rehearsed in conclusion. To what extent was that version of Calvinism which we find elaborated by the prolific English school of 'experimental predestinarians', with its penchant for the concept of covenanting with God ('federal theology'), an original outgrowth with a manifest destiny in North America?[60] What, in its English version, was that radical variant of Calvinism, a sucker as it were growing from the root, known as Arminianism? What was its derivation and at what point did it seriously and successfully challenge the Reformed or Calvinist ascendancy? The final question concerns the nature of that challenge. Was the anti-Calvinist, Arminian backlash a fundamental repudiation of the doctrinal heart of the Reformation itself, a denial of what had been taken for orthodoxy, as its opponents claimed? Or was it little more than a reaffirmation of religious and ethical values which were authentically Protestant, entrenched in the Thirty-Nine Articles, and never lacking defenders within the native tradition of the Reformed Church of England? In this perspective 'Arminianism' was simply a salutary correction of distortions perpetrated by the extreme Calvinism which had triumphed at the Synod of Dort (1618). After all, Calvin himself (unlike Beza) took no exception to the proposition that Christ died for all men, which later became a hallmark of 'Arminianism'.[61] Each of these problems could comfortably occupy a large volume and in a few paragraphs it is possible only to review the present state of these difficult and still controversial questions.

'Calvin against the Calvinists' has been an attractive slogan, drawing

---

[59] Dent, *Protestant Reformers*, 1–2, 91–102.

[60] Amid a plethora of literature, two salient points: R. T. Kendall, *Calvin and English Calvinism* (see Further Reading); Perry Miller, *The New England Mind: the Seventeenth Century* (New York, 1939).

[61] Kendall, *Calvin and English Calvinism*, 13–15.

attention to the significant changes in theological method which are detectable in the work of Beza, Zanchius, and Perkins, and thereafter in much English and New English divinity. And it makes a useful point which has some general validity, as indicating the difference which necessarily exists between a religious founder and the movement which acquires his name. Calvin had no intention of creating a system of thought called Calvinism.[62] And his theology was one of equipoise, in which predestination was not, as it was for later Calvinists, the major organizing principle. Nevertheless, to mean by 'Calvinist' something other than a follower of Calvin will always seem a trifle perverse, while the extent to which Calvin's legacy was falsified by his immediate successors has been exaggerated.[63] It is possible to speak of a 'giant leap' across the 'chasm' separating Calvin, the biblical humanist, from seventeenth-century Calvinist scholasticism while regarding Beza as a transitional and bridging figure, a systematizer but scarcely a Protestant scholastic. The Aristotelian rot, if that is what it was, seems to have begun not with Beza but with the Italians Peter Martyr and Girolamo Zanchi.[64]

As for English Calvinism, it may be simple ignorance of concurrent developments in continental theology which has sometimes led to undue stress on the particular deviance of the English school. These writers were such attentive students of the whole body of Reformed divinity that their treatment of the life of the individual Christian, or of such topics as the 'conscionable' keeping of the Sabbath, sometimes regarded as an English peculiarity, may represent a practical application of what they had learned rather than any conspicuous departure from it.[65]

However, those who emphasize a peculiar 'English Calvinism' are right in one important respect. Calvinist doctrine was far from shaping the institutional fabric of the English Church, as to a large extent it was able to do elsewhere, where the Reformed religion was not politically established, or where the political establishment was amenable. On the contrary, that fabric thwarted and redirected the forward thrust of doctrine, diverting its implementation away from the objectivity of church order, sacraments, and

[62] Basil Hall, 'Calvin Against the Calvinists', in G. Duffield (ed.), *John Calvin*, Courtenay Studies in Reformation Theology, I (Appleford, 1966), 19–37: B. G. Armstrong, *Calvinism and the Amyraut Heresy* (Madison, 1969); *The Work of William Perkins*, ed. I. Breward, The Courtenay Library of Reformation Classics, III (Appleford, 1970); Kendall, *Calvin and English Calvinism*.

[63] Perry Miller misrepresented 'federal' theology as a radical departure from Calvinism in *The New England Mind*. Among other critics, see Jens G. Møller, 'The Beginnings of Puritan Covenant Theology', *Journal of Ecclesiastical History*, 14 (1963), 46–67.

[64] Jill Raitt, *The Eucharistic Theology of Theodore Beza: Development of the Reformed Doctrine* (Chambersburg, 1972); John S. Bray, *Theodore Beza's Doctrine of Predestination* (Nieuwkoop, 1975); Wallace, *Puritans and Predestination*: J. P. Donnelly, *Calvinism and Scholasticism in Vermigli's Doctrine of Man and Grace* (Leiden, 1976); C. J. M. Burchill, 'Girolamo Zanchi in Strasbourg, 1553–1563' unpubl. Ph.D. thesis, Cambridge, 1980.

[65] This is an evident weakness of Kendall's *Calvin and English Calvinism*.

discipline, which before the 1640s English Calvinists were powerless to alter, towards the subjectivity of personal piety. Consequently, English Calvinism both fed into and fed upon that devout anxiety about eternal destinies which Perkins expressed in the title of a casuistical treatise: *A case of conscience, the greatest that ever was: How a man may know whether he be the child of God or no* (1592). More and more the 'practical syllogism' of godly living was brought into play to provide not only the comfort but the instrumentality of assurance. But the intense scrutiny of self and of the difference between true and counterfeit faith may have actually reinforced what threatened among devout Calvinists, and especially Calvinist women, to become an enervating obsession. It also drew ever more odious attention to the conflict between the godly lives of the elect and the profane lives of the reprobate which in the public sector was socially divisive. A reaction against these damaging excesses was readily forthcoming, precisely because the reception of Calvinist doctrine in England had never been so complete as to exclude other theological tendencies which found space to live within the latitude of the Articles of Religion and which were nourished by elements of a more catholic tradition, preserved in the principal resource of the Reformed Church of England, the Book of Common Prayer.

In England, as in the Netherlands and elsewhere, the worm in the apple was presently identified as 'Arminianism', belief in the potential universality of divine redemption and in the capacity of man's free will to appropriate God's grace or to spurn it.[66] This doctrine was not so much 'the spawn of a papist', as an English critic put it, as a residuum of Lutheran teaching on these matters. In mid-Elizabethan England, a reviving preference for the optimistic evangelicalism of the Lutheran tradition was revealed in the popularity in some quarters of the writings of the Danish syncretist, Niel Hemmingsen.[67] But not only were aspects of the Calvinist scheme of strictly predestinate grace under fire in England some years before the views of Arminius of Leiden became notorious. There was a capacity within the Church of England to set up a more fundamental and broadly based reaction against Calvinism than was implied in the Arminian onslaught on the predestinarians. For the English liturgy implied in its undertones and ethos as much as in any explicitly dogmatic statement the universal availability of grace through the sacraments and the use of petitionary prayer. It surrounded prayer and sacraments with a potential richness of ceremonial devotion which was anything but Calvinist. And it stimulated a revived sense of the ministry of word and sacraments as a holy

---

[66] A. W. Harrison, *Arminianism* (1937); N. R. N. Tyacke, 'Arminianism in England in Religion and Politics, 1604–1640', (unpubl. D.Phil thesis, Oxford, 1968); N. Tyacke, 'Arminianism and English Culture' (see Further Reading); Wallace, *Puritans and Predestination*, ch. 3 'The Arminian Controversies, 1610–1650'.

[67] Six of Hemmingsen's works were published in English between 1569 and 1581 (*STC* nos. 13057–68). See especially his *A learned and fruitful commentarie upon the epistle of James the Apostle* (1577) and *A postil or exposition of the Gospels* (edns. 1569(2), 1574, 1578).

priesthood, deriving its validity not from the Christian community (as Luther said) or from its political head (as Henry VIII would have it) but from Christ and his apostles, through a divinely commissioned episcopate. An important and provocative aspect of this revived clericalism was to confront directly the material interests of lay society by reaffirming the sacrosanctity of ecclesiastical property. The Arminian disputes in the Netherlands between Remonstrants and Contra-Remonstrants were of a radical nature, but they remained disputes within the Reformed tradition. English 'Arminianism' threatened to step out of that tradition altogether.

The implications of what may be regarded as a portmanteau of religious attitudes[68] may not have reached as far as the total subversion of the Protestant Reformation itself. But it has been said that they threatened the essence of the Protestant religious experience. William Prynne (a lawyer) thought that the very title-deeds of salvation were at stake.[69] Moreover the circumstances of its promotion were such that many, perhaps most, informed Protestants feared a conspiracy to bring back Popery in transparent disguise. It used to be thought that the *fin de siècle* attack mounted on Calvinism in late Elizabethan Cambridge heralded the natural wasting of a foreign body in the English Church and a return to sanity in the form of a balanced and normative Anglican theology of the middle way. But this is incorrect. Archbishop Whitgift's ruling in the Cambridge controversy, contained in the Lambeth Articles (1595), was an endorsement of the substance of the position staked out by Whitaker and other Calvinists, although in Whitgift's recension tending to favour the biblical and cautious Calvinism of Calvin himself. After all, as Whitgift assured his brother Hutton of York, these were 'matters never doubted of by any professors of the Gospell during all the tyme of your aboade and myne in the universitie.'[70] If the Lambeth Articles had been officially endorsed and imposed, English Calvinists would have had little more to fear. Although this did not happen, high Calvinism continued to prevail, dominating the universities and the religious press throughout the reign of James I, a monarch who was at ease with the moderate Calvinist consensus,[71] and for much of Archbishop George Abbot's long tenure of the primacy.

[68] However, Dr Tyacke has voiced a *caveat* against the notion that Arminianism was 'a catch-all term of abuse', insisting that contemporaries had an exact sense of what it was ('Arminianism and English Culture', 94–5).

[69] Wallace, *Puritans and Predestination*, 101; Tyacke, 'Arminianism and English Culture', 94.

[70] Quoted by N. R. N. Tyacke, *History*, 69 (1984), 135. Compare Porter, *Reformation and Reaction in Tudor Cambridge* with Lake, *Moderate Puritans*, 218–26, and with Wallace, *Puritans and Predestination*, 66–8.

[71] Tyacke, 'Arminianism in England'; id. 'Puritanism, Arminianism and Counter-Revolution' (see Further Reading). On the complexities of the political and other motives for James's theological preference, which cannot be labelled simply 'Calvinist', see F. H. Shriver, 'Orthodoxy and Diplomacy' (see Further Reading); Christopher Grayson, 'James I and the Religious Crisis in the United Provinces 1613–19', and John Platt, 'Eirenical Anglicans at the Synod of Dort', in *Reform and Reformation: England and the Continent, c.1500–c.1750, SCH*, Subsidia 2, ed. D. Baker (1979), 195–219, 221–43.

This was not necessarily a reflection of free opinion, since both academic debate and scholarly publication were biased by regulation and even censorship. By the same token, when fashions changed it was not a consequence of the natural attenuation and exhaustion of Calvinism. That might have occurred by 1650 but not in 1630. It was a sudden and politically contrived *renversement* which toppled Calvinism from its throne. The contrivers were the so-called 'Arminian' churchmen themselves: principally Richard Neile and secondarily William Laud; the duke of Buckingham who leant increasingly in that direction; and above all King Charles I. As late as 1628 Charles was still viewed as orthodox by the godly Sir Robert Harley and in 1629 he was lauded by the Palatine exiles as 'Orthodoxae fidei strenuus defensor'.[72] But his contrary religious preferences had been clear to those with eyes to see soon after his accession and his actions now represented, according to some observers, an unprecedented invasion of the realm of theological definition by the royal governor. When the issues were debated at York House in 1626, in the presence of Buckingham, it was obvious which way the wind would now blow. Within months further discussion was stifled by the royal declaration which to this day prefaces the Thirty-Nine Articles. Ostensibly this maintained the officially agnostic reticence of the Church of England on 'curious points'. But since its effect was to silence the Calvinist moral majority and to prevent them not only from coercing the Arminian minority but from preaching on matters considered of vital importance in the salvation of God's elect children, the royal proclamation made the Church safe for anti-Calvinists and even outlawed Calvinism. The stage was set for William Laud's assumption of ecclesiastical primacy and his implementation of the Caroline ecclesiastical policy in the 1630s. Dr Tyacke has written: 'The Arminians and their patron King Charles were undoubtedly the religious revolutionaries in the first instance.' 'The result was a polarization of extremes unknown since the Reformation.'[73]

But how to characterize one of these two extremes remains a problem. To call it 'Arminian', as contemporaries increasingly did, is to stigmatize, to define the whole in terms of one of its parts and to distract and falsify by importing the name of a foreign theologian whose authority in England was uncertain. 'Anglican' anachronistically obscures the important truth that Calvinists too were members of the Anglican Church who could justly claim to have the weight of recent tradition on their side. And 'High Church' will not do at all, since Calvinists too had occupied the heights and often embraced the principles of *jure divino* episcopacy. As for 'Laudian', this term not only imposes the views of one man on a party whose opinions were by no means monolithic or even coherent. It has led some critics to ask

[72] Collinson, *The Religion of Protestants*, 168–9; *Ecclesiae Londino-Batavae Archivum*, iii. 1414.
[73] Tyacke, 'Puritanism, Arminianism and Counter-Revolution', 121, 129.

whether the religious reaction and polarization described by Dr Tyacke was really as drastic as he has suggested, since Laud was careful (if only for tactical reasons) to distance himself from the dogmatic excess of Arminianism in the strict sense and was more overtly concerned with 'decent' and stately ceremonial than with controversial doctrine.[74]

There was a spectrum of theological opinion in the early seventeenth-century Church, and some finely adjusted positions with respect to grace and predestination. Many ranking churchmen were deliberately eclectic, the biographer of Laud's bitter enemy Bishop John Williams remarking: 'He that is discreet will make his Profit out of every side, or every Faction, if you like to call it so.'[75] There was a strong polemical disposition to avoid the excesses of both sides in the Dutch controversy and at Dort the English delegation (itself divided on some matters) adopted an eirenical stance which lay between, although by no means midway between, the Remonstrant and Contra-Remonstrant positions. But the centre of gravity, 'orthodoxy', was still Calvinist and the desire of the English delegation at Dort to draw back from the extremities of hyper-Calvinism implied no weakening with respect to that orthodoxy but rather a concern which was as much pastoral as polemical and political to avoid what the bishop of Bath and Wells, Arthur Lake, renowned for his exemplary piety, called 'distasteful accessories'. This would deprive the unorthodox (the Remonstrants) of 'all excuse' not to submit.[76]

Yet to conclude that a kind of moderation really prevailed, even after 1626, or that the English Church was swinging back to a traditional *via media* which only external pressures had disturbed, or that Archbishop Laud merely corrected the rudder and set his course by the lodestar of the Thirty-Nine Articles is to be deceived by the subtle conventions of contentious debate. The fact is that there were two sides, both given to the language of moderation and consensus, both deeply dyed in the mentality of divisive faction.[77] Whatever else animated and motivated the Laudians we may confidently attribute to them a perfect hatred not only of Puritanism but of what they chose to call Puritanism, which their opponents defended as the orthodox faith of the Church. The suggestion by Richard Montagu in his book *A new gagg for an old goose* that Popery and Puritanism were Scylla and Charybdis and that the Church of England stood in the gap between

[74] Kevin Sharpe, 'Archbishop Laud and the University of Oxford', in *History and Imagination*, ed. Hugh Lloyd-Jones, Valerie Pearl and Blair Worden (London, 1981), pp. 146–64; Peter White, 'The Rise of Arminianism Reconsidered', *P & P* 101 (1983), 34–54. I have benefited from discussing these issues with Dr F. H. Shriver.

[75] Quoted, Collinson, *The Religion of Protestants*, 82.

[76] Platt, 'Eirenical Anglicans'; Bishop Lake's correspondence with Samuel Ward, Bodleian Library, MS Tanner 74, fols. 174, 190; for Lake, see Collinson, *The Religion of Protestants*, 85–88.

[77] I am indebted for several points to Dr Peter Lake's forthcoming article, 'Calvinism in the English Church, 1570–1635' in *P & P*.

them, which was also Laud's view, was totally unacceptable to the religious majority. Earlier in the century, Archbishop Richard Bancroft had been called by a loud-mouthed Scot 'the capital enemy of all Reformed churches in Europe'.[78] Laud really was such an enemy and would have been proud of the label. 'To think well of the Reformed Religion', wrote the earl of Northumberland in 1639 'is enough to make the Archbishop one's enemy.' At Laud's trial it was alleged that in 1634 he had insisted on altering the Letters Patent for the third Palatinate collection so as to exclude the words 'the true Religion which we together with them do professe' and William Prynne (a hostile witness) alleged that the archbishop had expressed his distaste for a cause which he only supported for the sake of the queen of Bohemia. Laud denied these circumstances, stated that 'we may be, and are of the same religion', though differing in some points; and whether for the sake of the winter queen or from any other motives, actively supported all three collections: 'What I may further do for that cause shall not be wanting.'[79] But what Laud could do to make life unbearable for the stranger churches in his own diocese and in London was also not wanting.[80] Not only Prynne and his kind but that extreme moderate, Lord Falkland of Great Tew, would condemn as both 'unpoliticke' and 'ungodly' the archbishop's evident breach of 'that union which was formerly betweene us and those of our religion beyond the sea.'[81]

Laud's triumph was transient, and where we leave the story the climax of English Calvinism was still to come, in the Westminster Confession of 1647. Thereafter it would fall victim not to sudden assassination but to its own contradictions, and to the morbid processes which eventually overtake all systematic achievements of the human mind and spirit. But before that happened the ancient debt to Geneva was repaid: not so much in money (although relief was as readily available in 1685 as it had been in 1572, 1583, and 1626) as in the currency of that pragmatic, pious divinity of the English Puritan school which had been nurtured in the unusual ecclesiastical conditions prevailing in post-Reformation England and which was to be the perdurable product of English Calvinism. By 1640, English Calvinism was making its way back to its continental source, especially in the works of the most widely read of English divines, William Perkins. In the early seventeenth century, his books were to be found as far afield as Hungary. In

[78] Quoted, R. G. Usher, *The Reconstruction of the English Church* (1910), ii. 165.

[79] H. R. Trevor-Roper, *Archbishop Laud 1573–1645* (1940), 376; William Prynne, *Canterburies Doome* (1646), 391–3; *The Works of William Laud*, iv (Oxford, 1854), 312–13, vi (Oxford, 1857), 417–18, vii (Oxford, 1860), 22, 126–7, 151. For what the queen of Bohemia thought of Laud's 'cold compliments', see *Cal. SP Dom. 1634–1635*, 509.

[80] This relatively familiar aspect of the Laudian religious reaction is extensively documented in Hessels, *Ecclesiae Londino-Batavae Archivum*, and covered in Schickler's *Les Églises du Refuge*, Lindeboom's *Austin Friars*, and most recently by Dr Grell.

[81] Quoted, Marc L. Schwarz, 'Lay Anglicanism and the Crisis of the English Church in the Early Seventeenth Century', *Albion* (1982), 2.

1648 his *The whole treatise of the cases of conscience* was translated into Hungarian, where it joined Bishop Lewis Bayly's best-seller *The Practice of Piety*. By then, Perkins had been translated into Czech, Dutch, French, German, and Spanish, and as a posthumously international Calvinist he made his contribution to the next chapter of Protestant history as a father, or rather stepfather, of Pietism.[82]

[82] Information communicated by Dr György E. Szönyi in a forthcoming paper, 'English Books in Hungary (1575–1714)'; Breward, *Work of Perkins*, 106–7, 130.

Further Reading

Adams, Simon, *The Protestant Cause*: a forthcoming book deriving from Dr Adams' 1973 Oxford D.Phil. thesis 'The Protestant Cause: Religious Alliance with the European Calvinist Communities as a Political Issue in England 1585–1630'.

Collinson, Patrick, *The Elizabethan Puritan Movement* (1967).

—— *The Religion of Protestants: the Church in English Society 1559–1625: the Ford Lectures 1979* (Oxford, 1982).

—— 'Calvinism with an Anglican Face: the Stranger Churches in Early Elizabethan London and their Superintendent', 'The Elizabethan Puritans and the Foreign Reformed Churches in London', in *Godly People: Essays on English Protestantism and Puritanism* (1983), 213–44, 245–72.

Dent, C. M., *Protestant Reformers in Elizabethan Oxford* (Oxford, 1983).

Kendall, R. T., *Calvin and English Calvinism to 1649* (Oxford, 1979).

Lake, Peter, *Moderate Puritans and the Elizabethan Church* (Cambridge 1982).

Perkins, William, *The Work of William Perkins*, ed. I Breward, Courtenay Library of Reformation Classics, III (Appleford, 1970).

Porter, H. C., *Reformation and Reaction in Tudor Cambridge* (Cambridge, 1958).

Schickler, Baron F. de, *Les Églises du refuge en Angleterre* (3 vols., Paris, 1892).

Shriver, F. H., 'Orthodoxy and Diplomacy: James I and the Vorstius Affair', *EHR* 85 (1970), 449–74.

Tyacke, N. R. N., 'Puritanism, Arminianism and Counter-Revolution', in Conrad Russell (ed.), *The Origins of the English Civil War* (1973), 119–43.

—— 'Arminianism and English Culture', in A. C. Duke and C. A. Tamse (eds.), *Britain and the Netherlands*, vii. *Church and State since the Reformation*, ed. (The Hague, 1981), 94–117.

Wallace, Dewey D. Jr., *Puritans and Predestination: Grace in English Protestant Theology, 1525–1695* (Chapel Hill, 1982).

VIII

Calvinism in Scotland, 1559–1638

MICHAEL LYNCH

IN the summer of 1559 the earl of Argyll and Lord James Stewart, the two leading nobles in the Protestant Lords of the Congregation in revolt against the regent, Mary of Guise, wrote to William Cecil, secretary to the English privy council:

We are sorry to be judged slow, negligent and cold in our proceedings . . . You know, sir, how difficult it is to persuade a multitude to revolt of established authority.[1]

Protestantism, although it had been infiltrating Scottish society since the mid-1520s, was still a minority movement. Its origins were tangled and many of its aims still unclear. It lacked clear intellectual leadership and was still striving to achieve respectability. The greatest problem for Scottish Protestantism was to escape the series of false starts which had bestrewn its past.

Scotland had already had a Lutheran Reformation a generation earlier which had failed. By 1540 sizeable numbers of Lutheran preachers and intellectuals had already left Scotland for England or the continent and most never returned. The movement reached its apogee in 1543 when parliament, under the influence of the earl of Arran, head of the house of Hamilton and heir presumptive to the throne, had passed an act allowing all subjects access to the scriptures in the vernacular. The Tyndale Bible, it was reported, was to be seen 'lying almost upon every gentleman's table'. A wave of popular iconoclasm directed against religious houses swept through a number of the larger towns. Yet the Reformation of 1543 was short-lived and premature. Its excesses provoked a backlash, especially amongst townspeople. Its political backing evaporated when Arran's 'godly fit' came to an abrupt halt at the end of 1543 in a complicated palace coup.[2] Protestantism throughout the rest of the 1540s was tainted by its involvement with English ambitions in Scotland. Its momentum and its

[1] Cal. State Papers, Scot. i, no. 516.

[2] J. Durkan, 'Scottish "Evangelicals" in the Patronage of Thomas Cromwell', Records of the Scot. Church Hist. Soc., 21 (1982), 127–46. [RSCHS]; John Knox's History of the Reformation in Scotland, ed. W. C. Dickinson (Edinburgh, 1949), i. 45; G. Donaldson, Scotland: James V to James VII (Edinburgh, 1965), 64–8.

links with Zwinglian reform were further weakened by the death in 1546 of its natural leader, George Wishart. The Protestant party in Scottish politics collapsed after the fall of the Castle of St Andrews in 1547, which sent John Knox to the French galleys and induced the Protestant movement to go to ground. Yet Protestantism, now fuelled by English pamphlets and service-books as well as Bibles, became more difficult for the authorities to root out as it retreated into the household, mostly of middling and lesser lairds (or gentry) in rural areas and of merchants and professional men in the towns. There were signs from about 1556 onwards, perhaps as a result of a brief return visit to Scotland by Knox, that these house cells were being put on a more formal footing in the form of 'privy kirks', in which passages from Scripture were read and preached upon and communion administered. Yet the initiative had passed in the meantime to a Catholic reform movement. A series of provincial councils of the church met between 1547 and 1559, inducing a searching, if not always productive, self-examination. The church proved increasingly willing to resort to the evangelical tools of preaching and catechizing. A vernacular catechism was printed in 1552 and short abstracts of parts of it were issued to the parish clergy in 1559. The structural faults of the church remained, especially at parish level, but it was a more formidable opponent in 1559 than it had been earlier.[3]

Protestantism needed to regroup and reconsider its position. The first step in this direction was taken in December 1557 in the form of a 'common bond' in which 'the Lords and Barons professing Jesus Christ' promised to 'apply our whole power, substance and our very lives to maintain, set forward and establish the most blessed word of God'. The 'First Bond' was the first of many religious covenants in the history of Scottish Protestantism. Although its language was robust its specific aims were modest and cast so as to be acceptable to all shades of Protestant opinion: it was against sin, 'Satan and all wicked power' and for the establishing through their own efforts of 'faithful ministers purely and truly to minister Christ's Evangel and sacraments to His people'.[4] It was designed to induce Protestantism out of the household and to restore a political dimension to the movement. By 1559 it seemed to have succeeded in both its aims. The marriage of Mary, Queen of Scots to the Dauphin in April 1558 had heightened the nobility's fears of an increasingly French-dominated administration headed by the queen-mother, Mary of Guise. The burning

---

[3] The character of the Catholic reform movement is in dispute. Catholic historians, such as T. Winning, 'Church Councils in Sixteenth-century Scotland', in D. McRoberts (ed.), *Essays on the Scottish Reformation* (Glasgow, 1962), 337–58, stress its orthodoxy and how much it anticipated the second session at Trent. J. K. Cameron, '"Catholic Reform" in Germany and in the pre-1560 Church in Scotland', *RSCHS* 20 (1979), 111–15, shows how much it imitated some of the compromises made with Lutheranism by Catholic reformers at Cologne in the 1540s. The proceedings of the councils are printed in *Statutes of the Scottish Church*, ed. D. Patrick (Scot. Hist. Soc., 1907).

[4] *Scottish Historical Documents*, ed. G. Donaldson (Edinburgh, 1970), 116–17.

of an obscure Protestant schoolmaster four days later, seemingly presaging a new campaign against heresy, had prompted more open protection of Protestant preachers by Protestant notables and induced the first serious manifestation of popular Protestantism since 1543. Protestant piety and politics were being drawn closer together as were the different constituent parts of Protestant feeling.[5]

The Reformation crisis itself was sparked off by a riot at Perth in which the town's religious houses were sacked within days of Knox's return from Geneva in May 1559. By July the 'Congregation', now comprising a cross-section of society from nobles to lairds and townspeople, had purged a series of towns in central Scotland and entered the capital, Edinburgh, where Knox was installed as its first Protestant minister. The regent was deposed in October 1559 and a provisional government established, which turned to England for military aid while still protesting its loyalty to the Scottish crown. The arrival of an English army in Scotland in March 1560 proved to be the decisive factor and the Treaty of Edinburgh in July, concluded between English and French commissioners, arranged the removal of all foreign troops from Scottish soil. The Congregation had won—or had been given victory. The Reformation itself had still to be defined and authorized. This was done by the 'Reformation parliament' which met in August 1560 and voted to abolish papal authority, proscribe the mass, and adopt a Protestant Confession of Faith.[6]

In outline the course of events between 1557 and 1560 seems straightforward and their outcome decisive. Yet the dilemma which faced the Congregation in the summer of 1559 had been genuine and its consequences were far-reaching. The revolt had started as a religious crusade but had failed to find sufficient support. A number of seemingly convinced Protestant notables had behaved ambivalently; others had changed their minds at the first sight of the dangers of social insurrection. By October 1559 the Congregation had been forced to change tack. Appeals for support had been made, in increasing desperation, not only to wavering Protestants but even to staunch Catholics to fight, if not for religion, for 'the liberty of this your native country'. The Protestant revolt had become by degrees a conservative reaction on behalf of the 'born counsellors' of the realm against allegedly undue French influence in government. The language of the covenant had been replaced by a more seductive image—the commonweal.[7]

It was a rather odd revolution. Not a single major office in either the

---

[5] For further information see G. Donaldson, *All the Queen's Men* (see Further Reading), 27–9, and J. Wormald, *Court, Kirk and Community* (see Further Reading), 109–16

[6] See Donaldson, *James V*, 92–102, and Wormald, *Scotland*, 115–20, for detailed accounts.

[7] *Scottish Correspondence of Mary of Lorraine, 1543–1560* (Scot. Hist. Soc., 1927), 429; R. Mason, 'Covenant and Commonweal: the Language of Politics in Reformation Scotland', in N. Macdougall (ed.), *Church, Politics and Society 1408–1929* (Edinburgh, 1983), 100–12.

executive or judicial functions of government changed hands. The earl of Huntly, the greatest Catholic magnate in Scotland, remained as chancellor because even he had briefly joined the Congregation. Most town-councils continued as before; purges were generally avoided outside the capital. Bishops of the old church continued to enjoy the fruits of their benefices along with the rest of the secular clergy and some had even attended the Reformation parliament. Nothing was done to phase out the structure of the old church and little to phase in that of the new. There was no act of uniformity and no test act before 1573 to bind clergy or office-holders to the new religion. There was as yet not even a detailed Protestant manifesto.[8]

That programme emerged fully four months after the close of the Reformation parliament. A 'Book of Reformation' had been commissioned by the provisional government in April 1560 and was ready within three weeks. That draft, much of it the work of Knox, had not proved acceptable and an enlarged committee of ministers—the 'six Johns'—was set up to revise it. The result, after much internal disagreement and numerous further revisions, was the *First Book of Discipline*, which was presented to a thinly attended convention of nobility and lairds in January 1561.[9] It was an impressive but untidy document, which mirrored many of the strengths and weaknesses of the Protestant movement itself. It was as much concerned with a vision of a new society infused by the spirit of God as it was with church polity. For both the active co-operation of the nobility, the 'chief pillars' of the Reformation as Knox called them, was necessary. That was, as will be seen, given only fitfully and usually on the nobility's own terms. The convention of 1561 rejected the new church's claims to the revenues of the old and in doing so not only undermined much of the programme in the *First Book* but also cast doubt on the authority and status of the godly magistrate in the continuing work of reformation.

The main emphasis of the *Book*—and the one which most distinguished it from the Catholic reforming efforts of the 1550s—lay in the emphasis given to a parish reformation. But the blueprint was remarkably permissive: the arrangements for poor relief, to which the Reformed Church gave high priority, were left to each locality to decide upon as 'God will show you wisdom and the means'; each congregation was allowed to organize elections to the kirk session (or consistory) 'as best seems them'. The *Book of Discipline* recognized the need for a continuing reformation but did not provide effective means or direction. Amongst the casualties of the failure in 1560–1 to find adequate endowment was a scheme for ten superintendents to replace and rationalize the old episcopate. Only five were ever appointed and they were obliged to seek the co-operation of three Catholic bishops

[8] Donaldson, *Queen's Men*, 51, 66; M. Lynch, *Edinburgh* (see Further Reading), 76–80; G. Donaldson, *The Scottish Reformation* (Cambridge, 1960), 54–61.

[9] *The First Book of Discipline*, ed. J. K. Cameron (Edinburgh, 1972), 3–14.

who converted in 1560. The result was that in many respects the progress of the Reformed Church after 1560 depended on a series of local reformations, each moving at its own pace and with its own distinctive problems to surmount.[10]

The key figures in this parish reformation were of course the ministers. But the failure to endow the church properly cast in doubt the Reformers' scheme to raise the stipends and status of the parish clergy for more than a generation after 1560. The inequities and divisions in the old church were as a result visited in part upon the new: the gap between the unbeneficed curate and the pre-Reformation bishop was replaced by that between the reader, licensed to read the common prayers but to do little else, and the minister or superintendent, paid anything up to twenty times as much. There were other natural divisions within the reformed ministry in the generation of 1560. The bulk of the readers and about half of the ministry as a whole were comprised of ex-Catholic clergy, whose conversion for the most part came only in 1560 or after.[11]

The 'six Johns' who composed the *Book of Discipline* themselves amply demonstrated the diversity of background and experience which characterized the first generation. Two of its compilers, Douglas and Winram, had been important Catholic reformers throughout the 1550s. These two late converts from St Andrews argued for the pre-eminent role their own university should have in the construction of the new godly commonwealth to such effect that the Book had more to say about the universities than any other single subject. Row was until the autumn of 1558 a well-connected canon lawyer resident in Rome. The other three—Knox, Willock, and Spottiswoode—had come to Protestantism much earlier and each had served in the Edwardian church. Their paths had, however, diverged since then. Spottiswoode, who had been ordained in England by Archbishop Cranmer, returned to Scotland in 1550, falling under the patronage of a family of West Lothian lairds, one of whom visited Geneva in the mid 1550s. Willock, who had enjoyed the patronage of the duchess of Suffolk, fled to Emden after 1553; his experience there reinforced his Zwinglian sympathies and was influential in the passages in the *Book* describing the exercise and the duties of superintendents.

Knox had fled with the mainstream of English Marian exiles to Frankfurt before going on to Geneva after the internal dissension within the English Congregation came to a head in 1555. He was the only one of the six with direct experience of Genevan or French Calvinism. Although Knox later

[10] Ibid. 113, 175. See also Donaldson, *Scottish Reformation*, 59–66; M. Lynch, 'From Privy Kirk to Burgh Church: An Alternative View of the Process of Protestantization', in Macdougall (ed.), *Church and Society*, 94.

[11] Donaldson, *Scottish Reformation*, 90, 126–7. See *Thirds of Benefices, 1561–1572*, ed. G. Donaldson (Scot. Hist. Soc., 1949), for details of the financial settlement. See C. H. Haws (ed.), *Scottish Parish Clergy at the Reformation, 1540–1574* (Scot. Record Soc., 1972), for the provenance of the parish clergy.

seemingly came to epitomize the Scottish Reformation, it is striking how tenuous his connections were with Scotland before 1559. It is doubtful if he should be cast in the role of leader in exile of Scottish Protestantism in the 1550s. It was Willock, not Knox, who was recognized by his Catholic opponents as the 'primate' of the reformers early in 1559. Although Knox was appointed minister of Scotland's capital in July 1559 he was temporarily withdrawn within the month to be replaced by Willock. The change of personnel also manifested itself in different Reformed traditions: Knox had used the Genevan prayer book of 1556; Willock reverted to the Edwardian prayer-book of 1552 which the town's Protestants had hitherto used in their privy kirk. The different experiences of the 1550s—ranging from reforming Catholicism to exilic Calvinism—left different marks on the Reformers of 1560.[12]

Doctrine proved, however, to be less of a problem to surmount than polity. A confession of faith, skilfully drafted in vernacular Scots mainly by Knox, managed to collate the various non-Calvinist theological influences playing on the Reformers whilst retaining distinct echoes of the French *Confession* of 1559.[13] The *Book of Discipline*, which took months rather than weeks to prepare, did not, however, adopt the ready-made Calvinist primer of the French *Discipline*. Although there were traces in it of both the French *Discipline* and Calvin's *Ecclesiastical Ordinances* of 1541, the Scottish *Book of Discipline* was more obviously a work of many tongues. The complicated story of its compilation illustrated how much Scottish Protestantism lacked uniformity and direction despite its political victory in 1560. There was no detailed Protestant programme produced before the revolt or during it. The course of the revolt had confused rather than clarified many issues. It did not bring to power a committed or united Calvinist party. It had not come about, as in France, as the result of a sudden increase of Calvinist pastors or propaganda but by the widening of the aims of the rebels to the point where they claimed to be the patriotic party which could protect all interests, including those of Catholic magnates such as the earl of Huntly. The revolt had become, even before it ended, a quest for settlement.

The internal inconsistencies within the Protestant movement were exposed still further by the return of Queen Mary from France in August 1561. She refused throughout the six years of her personal reign to ratify the legislation of 1560. Her religious policy of a standstill, enforced by a proclamation issued within a week of her return, compounded the ambiguities of the Reformation settlement. The mass remained proscribed

[12]   R. Keith, *History of Church and State in Scotland* (Spottiswoode Soc., 1850), iii. 395. The most detailed biography of Knox is J. Ridley, *John Knox* (Oxford, 1968). Convenient biographies of the five others are available in K. Hewat, *Makers of the Scottish Church at the Reformation* (Edinburgh, 1920); see esp. pp. 141, 177, 185, 285. For Willock see also Durkan, 'Scottish "Evangelicals"', 153–6, and the essay on him in D. Shaw (ed.), *Reformation and Revolution* (Edinburgh, 1967), 47–61.

[13]   J. Kirk, 'The Influence of Calvinism' (see Further Reading), 157–61.

but other Catholic sacraments such as baptism and marriage were not illegal. The Reformed Church, shorn of its claims for full endowment, was forced to turn to the crown rather than the nobility for patronage; it accepted a compromise financial settlement in 1562 by which it and the crown shared a third of the fruits of the benefices of the old church. Knox and his ministerial colleagues became virtual state pensioners of a Catholic queen whose financial concessions gave the reformed church a quasi-official but precarious status. The national synod of the church, not surprisingly, remained unsure of its position, evidenced by the different names by which it referred to itself in the 1560s; the term 'General Assembly' came into acceptance only in 1563. By then an attempt had been made by the Assembly to revise the *Book of Discipline* in the light of changed circumstances. It was significant that none from the original committees of 1560 took part. Control of the affairs of the church at national level was in the early 1560s passing into the hands of what Knox cuttingly called the 'courtiers'—nobles like Lord James Stewart, who was granted the earldom of Moray by the queen in 1562.[14]

The unstable coalition of the Lords of the Congregation had also been affected by the queen's return. The major issue in Scottish politics for fully a decade after 1561 proved to be not the settlement of Protestantism but the sovereignty of the crown. The Protestant party of 1559-60 dissolved amidst the new complexities of the Marian period. Two successive attempts were made to stage a Protestant coup: the first, in 1565, was led by Moray in an effort to counter the threat posed by the prospective marriage of the queen to her cousin, Henry Stewart, Lord Darnley; the second, in 1566, was a more overtly Protestant demonstration against the seemingly Catholic drift of Mary's policies and focused on the hapless figure of her servant, David Riccio. Each foundered on a division of opinion within the Protestant nobility, who habitually put loyalty to the crown or self-interest above religion.

The eventual revolution of 1567 which resulted in the forcible deposing of the queen was less clear-cut than it seems at first sight. This time a broad coalition of nobles had successfully formed, but only to remove Mary from the influence of her third husband, the earl of Bothwell. There was considerably less support for the more drastic action which followed of putting her infant son, James, on the throne and appointing her half-brother, Moray, as regent. An ultra-Protestant coup had taken place within a coup. The result was a bitter civil war which lasted almost seven years, despite Mary's flight to England in 1568. It was not a war of religion despite overtly sectarian propaganda used by the king's party. The bulk of the

[14] Donaldson, *James V*, 110-13, 125; D. Shaw, *General Assemblies of the Church of Scotland* (Edinburgh, 1964), 19; *The Booke of the Universall Kirk* (Bannatyne Club, 1839), i. 41 [*BUK*]; Knox, *History*, ii. 5, 107.

greater nobility backed the queen until her cause became untenable because of her continuing absence. The regent found ranged against him in the queen's party many of his most trusted Protestant allies in the campaign of 1559–60. By 1570 Moray, the most important Protestant noble patron of the Reformation generation, was dead, shot by an assassin's bullet; it was characteristic of the times that his murderer was not a Catholic but a member of a rival family which was predominantly Protestant.[15] Two more short-lived regencies followed before the earl of Morton came to power in 1572 and brought the civil war to a close with English military aid. He became regent on the day Knox died—a double symbol of the passing of an era. A largely new generation, both in church and state, was left to put in order the confused legacy of the Reformation of 1560 and the decade which followed it.

How much real progress had the Reformed Church made since 1560? It had planted some 250 ministers and perhaps three times as many readers or exhorters in Scotland's thousand parishes.[16] There were, as will be seen, a number of paradoxes or ambiguities within this parish-based reformation but it was nonetheless a remarkable achievement seen against a background of political instability and the uncertainty of the church's finances. The church's other significant achievement lay in a growing sense of its own distinctive identity. The Scottish Reformation underwent a process of Calvinization, not in the build-up to the Reformation crisis nor even during it, but in the first half of the 1560s. This was all the more remarkable since it took place at the time when political Calvinism was in retreat. The church, compromised by its financial dependence on the crown, took refuge in a new and largely Calvinist uniformity of liturgy and discipline. Its new Calvinist identity compensated for its deficiencies as an ecclesiastical institution.

The new church had gained enough self-confidence to add a tart rider to its endorsement in 1566 of the Second Helvetic Confession to the effect that it could not approve the retention of saints' days, which in Scotland had been abolished in 1560.[17] In the same year Knox in the preface to Book IV of his *History* went so far as to claim:

As touching the doctrine taught by our ministers and . . . the administration of Sacraments used in our Churches, we are bold to affirm that there is no realm this day upon the face of the earth that hath them in greater purity; yea (we must speak the truth whomsoever we offend), there is none . . . that hath them in the like purity.[18]

The myth of the perfection of the Scottish kirk was born.

[15] An important reassessment of Protestant politics in the 1560s and civil war period is given in Donaldson, *Queen's Men*; see esp. pp. 55–6, 85–6, 100, 117.

[16] An abstract of the number of ministers and readers in 1574 is given in *Wodrow Miscellany*, ed. D. Laing (Wodrow Soc., 1844), i. 396.

[17] Knox, *Works*, ed. D. Laing (Wodrow Soc., 1846), vi. 544–50.

[18] Knox, *History*, ii. 3.

There was a certain amount of truth to it—saints' days had been abolished along with the use of the organ, the sign of the cross, and much else[19]—but also much exaggeration and self-delusion. Knox in this passage was writing about the period before the return of Queen Mary complicated loyalties. Yet at Easter 1561 less than a fifth of Edinburgh's adult population took communion by the new rite.[20] However perfect the new church might have been there was no magical mass conversion to it in 1560 or immediately afterwards. There was also a good deal more variety of practice in its early days than Knox made out. The Genevan Book, the *Book of Common Order*, was formally adopted by the General Assembly in 1562 but there were often deviations from it, especially in the administration of the sacraments. It prescribed no ceremony for burials other than an exhortation in church, but at Montrose a burial service was followed for some time after 1560 which included readings from the Tyndale Bible rather than the Genevan and prayers to be said at the graveside from the English 1552 Book.[21] It was often the areas or individuals with the longest experience of Protestantism which proved the most resistant to the new Calvinist uniformity. Copies of the Genevan liturgy were fairly scarce in any case and copies of Calvin's printed works scarcer still; ministers borrowed and lent what few volumes they had to make do with. Few Calvinist works were reprinted on native presses—Beza's *Oration* was one exception which went into two editions in 1561–2.[22] The most profound Calvinist influence came in a form which had virtually no rivals—the catechism. Calvin's *Catechism* was bound up with every edition of the Book of Common Order printed in Scotland between 1562 and 1611. There was no vernacular catechism of Scots origin to rival it until 1581 and the General Assembly was still unsuccessfully looking for a short catechism to replace it in 1616.[23] It was Calvin's *Catechism* which became the crucial tool used in the weekly exercise from the early 1560s onwards. The exercise was not a means of mass conversion although some laymen did attend its meetings; it was an instrument to secure the ideological uniformity of the ministers, very necessary in a church where nearly half of the first generation of ministers were late converts from the pre-Reformation clergy. By 1580 a genuine Calvinist consensus had emerged. The ministry had very real differences over ecclesiastical polity and relations with the state but it was united—from Archbishop Adamson to his

[19] See J. Kirk, '"The polities of the best reformed kirks": Scottish Achievements and English Aspirations in Church Government after the Reformation', *SHR* 59 (1980), 25–8.

[20] Lynch, 'Privy Kirk', 93.

[21] *BUK* i. 30, 54; *Wodrow Misc.* 295–300; I. B. Cowan, *The Scottish Reformation* (London, 1982), 134, 146.

[22] See H. G. Aldis (ed.), *A List of Books printed in Scotland before 1700* (rev. edn., 1970), nos. 30, 34; Cowan, *Reformation*, 204.

[23] W. R. Foster, *The Church before the Covenants* (Edinburgh, 1975), 130; W. McMillan, *The Worship of the Scottish Reformed Church, 1550–1638* (London, 1931), 133–4.

bitter critic, Andrew Melville—on doctrine, discipline, and the vehemence of its anti-papistry.

The basic—and divisive—problem of the period from 1567 onwards, when Scotland had at last a godly prince or a godly regent acting on his behalf, was the sorting-out of the boundaries between a Calvinist church and a Calvinist state. Certain topics were not contentious. Parliament proved willing to lend its authority to the new rigour of Calvinist moral discipline by making adultery punishable by death in 1563. It was glad to rid itself of the growing problem of poor relief by devolving responsibility for it to the kirk session and parish in 1574.[24] But these were comparatively minor matters; the two battlegrounds proved to be ecclesiastical polity and education.

The General Assembly had begun to move away from the state as soon as government took on an explicitly Protestant hue—during Moray's brief regency. The civil war postponed the dilemma until Morton's regency. Morton, however, was intent on not letting things drift any longer: 'religion and government', he argued, 'being so joined in many respects . . . it is very requisite that in this time of repose we be careful for the good order and provision of the policy of the kirk in things ambiguous and irresolute'[25] The 1570s and 1580s saw a struggle between an increasingly Erastian government and a church increasingly anxious to assert and extend its independence of the state. This was, in one sense, a conflict between broad Protestantism and strict Calvinism. That tension had existed in the 1560s—and was seen at the coronation of James VI in 1567, when Knox preached the sermon from the Book of Kings but the ex-Catholic bishop of Orkney performed the anointing of the king in accordance with ancient ritual[26]—but it had usually been latent. It was given added impetus by two developments in the 1570s. Government under Morton became more interventionist—in secular affairs as well as ecclesiastical—and was fond of imitating English practices, most notably in its attempts to reconstitute episcopacy and in royal patronage of the church.[27] The disquiet felt within the church over these developments was heightened by the emergence of a new breed of ministers, educated in the 1560s and conditioned in their thinking by the shortcomings of the church in that decade.

Once again, however, as in 1559, the leadership of the forward ministers passed to a returning exile from Geneva—Andrew Melville. Melville, the son of an Angus laird, had had strangely little contact with his homeland since he had left to pursue his education in Paris in 1564 or during the six years after 1568 when he taught in Geneva. He returned to Scotland in 1574 as a scholar with an international reputation appointed to resuscitate the moribund University of Glasgow rather than as a Calvinist ideologue intent

[24] Wormald, *Scotland*, 100, 167–8.   [26] Ridley, *John Knox*, 472–3.
[25] *Wodrow Misc.* 289.   [27] Donaldson, *Scottish Reformation*, 177–81.

on recasting the mould of the Scottish Reformed Church. By 1580, when he moved to St Andrews as principal of St Mary's College, he was the acknowledged 'light and leader' of the 'schools and kirk of Scotland'.[28]

Melville's most significant contribution lay in the reorganization of St Mary's as the major seminary in Scotland for the training of ministers. Designed as an 'anti-seminary' to counter the Jesuit menace, St Mary's quickly came to be acknowledged as the 'temple' of the new Jerusalem. Melville was also involved with the simultaneous attempt to found a similar university in Edinburgh. Yet both there and in St Andrews itself he encountered bitter opposition. The three colleges of St Andrews saw an academic version of the struggle between strict Calvinism, as represented by Melville and his Ramist curriculum at St Mary's, and broad Protestantism, seen both in the more conservative curriculum of the two other colleges and in the university's chancellor, Archbishop Adamson. The battle raged on throughout the 1580s and 1590s in much the same way as at St John's College, Cambridge. In Edinburgh the struggle to found a university became part of a seesawing struggle in the early 1580s between pro-court and radical factions on the town council. By 1583 the court itself intervened, on the very eve of the opening of the new town college, to wrest the project from the radical ministers and turn the planned seminary into a safer, conservative college of humanity. 1583 was the climax of a growing interest taken by the state in higher education. Commissions had visited the universities in the 1560s, but these had been authorized by the General Assembly. Morton had set up commissions under the authority of the privy council to reshape both higher and grammar school education in the 1570s. The Erastian solution was explicit by the mid 1580s and it came into direct conflict with the academic ambitions of Melvillianism.[29]

Melville played a prominent rather than dominant part in the systematic attempts made to recast the programme of the church in the changed circumstances of the 1570s. A series of committees of the General Assembly, involving more than thirty ministers, produced the *Second Book of Discipline* in 1578 after two years of deliberations. The second *Book* was a more even and considered document than the first, reflecting the growing cohesion of the ministry. But it, like the *First Book*, served only as a signpost for the church's developing vision of itself rather than as a major step forward in the Calvinist mission. The *Book*'s financial claims remained unrealized and its view of the relations of church and state were specifically rebutted by parliament in 1578. A modest beginning in the overhaul of the

[28] There is considerable dispute over Melville's standing and influence. Cf. Kirk, 'Polities of best reformed kirks', 39–42, and Donaldson, *Scottish Reformation*, 191–3. His reputation undoubtedly owed something to the hagiography written by his nephew; see *The Autobiography and Diary of Mr. James Melville* (Wodrow Soc., 1842), 143.

[29] Melville, *Diary*, 254; M. Lynch, 'The Origins of Edinburgh's "Town College": A Revision Article', *Innes Review*, 33 (1982), 4–11; T. McCrie, *Andrew Melville* (2nd edn., 1846), 76–9, 203–7.

church's organization was made in 1581 when thirteen presbyteries were set up, mainly in the Melvillian heartland of the east coast and lowlands, 'to be exemplars to the rest which may be established hereafter'. Most, in fact, were a reconstructed exercise now given new responsibilities of oversight and discipline rather than a wholly new institution.[30]

It was the church's misfortune that these modest beginnings became entangled with the complex feuding which engulfed Scottish politics after the fall and execution of Morton in 1581. The arrival of James VI's cousin, Esmé Stuart, from France in 1579 and his preferment at court had caused resentment amongst many of the nobility; his alleged Catholic leanings provoked the ministers into a frenzied bout of anti-papistry. The stage was set for a *rapprochement* between ministers and nobility and for a palace coup, which came with the Ruthven raid of 1582, which took its name from the ultra-Protestant magnate, Lord Ruthven, earl of Gowrie. It was fear—of papistry, and a new 'opinion of absolute power'[31] put in the young king's head by evil advisers—which reconstituted a Calvinist party in the early 1580s. The actions of the Ruthven regime were specifically endorsed by the General Assembly and its period in power coincided with the publication of George Buchanan's monumental justification of the revolution of 1567, his *Rerum Scoticarum Historia*. The Ruthven regime was short-lived. But its fall in 1583 and the retribution which followed in the parliament of 1584 with the 'Black Acts' reasserting the authority of the crown over all estates, ecclesiastical as well as temporal, provided the setting for the major confrontation between church and state in the reign of James VI. It was hardly surprising that the crown should detect a Calvinist conspiracy in the tangled web of the politics of the 1580s or that it should seek to ban 'that form late invented in this land',[32] the presbytery. Yet there is some doubt about how real the conspiracy was. Although the Calvinist party seemed more united and organized in the 1580s than ever before, the Ruthven conspirators contained dissidents with a chequered past as well as ultra-Protestants; there was still suspicion amongst many ministers of the nobles' motives; the nobles' spokesman, the historian David Hume of Godscroft, was in turn wary of the popular enthusiasm of the towns.[33] Calvinism, despite the advances it had made in other areas, still found it difficult to consolidate itself on an organized political footing.

The crisis of the 'Black Acts' precipitated the flight into England of a

[30] *The Second Book of Discipline*, ed. J. Kirk (Edinburgh, 1980), 44–51; Cowan, *Reformation*, 132; Donaldson, *Scottish Reformation*, 207; *BUK*, ii. 480.
[31] Melville, *Diary*, 119.
[32] *The Historie and Life of King James the Sext* (Bannatyne Club, 1825), 186.
[33] Donaldson, *Queen's Men*, 141–3; David Hume, *History of the House and Race of Douglas and Angus* (Edinburgh, 1743), 200. Suspicion of the populace was a recurrent theme in Scottish Calvinism. The prominent minister, John Davidson, declared in 1594 that he feared 'the multitude of Edinburgh' more than the court (D. Calderwood, *History of the Kirk of Scotland* (Wodrow Soc., 1842–9), v. 339).

substantial number of Melvillian ministers; they were followed by a smaller rump of nobles who had compromised themselves in the Ruthven Raid. Their brief exile—for most were allowed to return to Scotland by the end of 1585—represented the high-water mark in the Scottish consciousness of a sense of the Calvinist international. Scotland, so the exiles argued, was the cockpit of a Tridentine conspiracy against the whole church; the next target would be England. They were in close contact with the Walsingham circle and the French church in London in their efforts to set up a similar Scots church; their manifesto was sent to Geneva and Zürich; elaborate attempts were set in train to link what was claimed to be the Scottish church in exile with other Reformed Churches.[34]

These efforts evaporated, as did the wider sense of a Calvinist international, with the end of the exile in 1585. The nobles, once restored to favour, cast off the mantle of ultra-Protestant politics. The ministers, encouraged by a series of studied concessions from the crown between 1585 and 1592 which allowed the return of presbyteries, redirected their efforts towards the continuing problem of the evangelization of the many dark corners of the land. By the 1590s the Scottish church had turned inwards, resurrecting the myth of its own perfection which was, it was claimed, 'admirable to foreign kirks'.[35] The growing interference in the affairs of the church by James VI—by the manipulation of General Assemblies and the gradual restoration to influence of bishops between 1596 and 1610— deepened the mood of introspection and defensiveness. The spectre haunting Scottish Calvinism after James' succession to the English throne in 1603, was of 'the midden of the corruption of the kirk of England coming upon us'.[36]

The fear of creeping anglicization took on a fresh urgency with the forcing of the Five Articles, which included an instruction to kneel at communion, through both General Assembly and parliament between 1618 and 1621. The growing disquiet over the liturgy and the activity of bishops came to a head in the reign of Charles I with his attempt to force a service book on the Scottish church in 1637. The opposition to the prayer book, evidenced by the widespread support throughout Scotland for the National Covenant of 1638, brought into alliance many strands of grievance. Archibald Johnston of Wariston, an Edinburgh lawyer and principal author of the Covenant, marvelled that God had drawn 'so great unity out of appearances of division amongst us'. What was particularly significant was that the condition of the church was widely taken as a metaphor for the state of the country. What began in 1637 as a protest movement co-ordinated

34 Calderwood, *History*, iv. 38–45; *Wodrow Misc.* 416–17, 429; G. Donaldson, 'Scottish Presbyterian Exiles in England, 1584–8', *RSCHS* 14 (1962), 69–72, 76–8.
35 Calderwood, *History*, v. 387.
36 John Row, *History of the Kirk of Scotland* (Wodrow Soc., 1842), 437.

through the presbyteries became open revolt when the General Assembly called at Glasgow in November 1638 continued sitting in defiance of Charles' wishes and proceeded to abolish bishops and undo much of the royal-inspired innovations of the previous thirty years. Church and state, nobles and ministers, town and country were at last united as of one mind—against Charles I and his bishops.[37]

The victorious Protestant reformers of 1560 faced two major problems as well as a host of minor ones. The virtually complete failure of the financial schemes of the *First Book of Discipline* forced the Reformed Church into an ambivalent relationship with the state and an uncertain dependence on the nobility. The Reformers had come to power as a minority movement, even in the towns; the narrowness of their support set limits on both the pace and comprehensiveness of Protestant reform. Protestantism had been infiltrating the east coast towns for more than quarter of a century before 1559. Yet Protestants in most towns—with the possible exceptions of Perth and Dundee—were still in the 1540s and early 1550s to be counted in handfuls.[38] Urban Protestantism first took root in an influential coterie of wealthy merchants, professional men, and intellectuals, who dominated the movement until the mid 1550s. Their wives, notably Knox's 'dear sisters' of Edinburgh, played a forthright role in the Protestant household from early on. By about 1556 these house cells were taking on a more formal structure in the guise of 'privy kirks' although they continued to meet in the private houses of the richer merchants among them. These clandestine meetings partly took the form of an exercise in which teachers expounded on passages from Scripture. They were also a virtual miniature consistory in which elders and deacons were appointed by election from within the congregation. A number of the teachers in the Edinburgh privy kirk, including John Erskine of Dun and Willock, later gained prominent positions in the Reformed Church once established. Yet a number of the elders and deacons whose names are known in Edinburgh came from well beneath the social status expected, for example, of a member of the town council. They included minor merchants, ordinary master craftsmen, and, remarkably, journeymen or apprentices. This particular privy kirk provides a tantalizingly brief glimpse just before the Reformation crisis broke of the changing nature of urban Protestantism in Scotland.[39]

Knox had forecast in his tract of 1558, *A Letter addressed to the*

[37] Donaldson, *James V*, 200–11, 306–10; I. B. Cowan, 'The Five Articles of Perth', in Shaw (ed.), *Reformation and Revolution*, 160–77; D. Stevenson, *The Scottish Revolution* (Newton Abbot, 1973), 56–87; *Diary of Sir Archibald Johnston of Wariston* (Scot. Hist. Soc., 1911), i. 352. The text of the National Covenant is conveniently printed in *Scottish Historical Documents*, 194–201.

[38] Cowan, *Reformation*, 107–14, 119.

[39] Lynch, *Edinburgh*, 38, 83, 276–80. Although Protestantism had by the 1550s made a forceful impact on women at the top of urban society there was curiously little trace of it among Scottish noblewomen—in sharp contrast to France.

Commonalty of Scotland, that no distinction would be made between rich and poor in the new godly society. This tract has conventionally been seen as a manifesto for a future Calvinist revolution; much of it should be seen rather as an attempt to justify what had already taken place in the privy kirks.[40] A new godly and classless society, albeit in miniature, had already come into being. The worshippers and even the office-holders in Edinburgh were not only drawn from a bourgeois élite, as they had undoubtedly been up until the mid 1550s; they ranged from apprentices to merchant princes or highly placed servants in royal government. It was a most unlikely assembly in a society so conscious of rank and privilege and it must have been taken by some as an indicator that religious enthusiasm might indeed transcend the customs and conventions of existing society.

The advance of Protestantism in most of the Scottish towns was not a story of triumphant and uncompromising progress towards a Calvinist society even after 1560; it was usually a stop-go affair shot through with ambiguities and compromises. In Edinburgh one-half of the town establishment proved willing by November 1562, when a subscription list of 160 'faithful brethren' was drawn up to raise funds for a new poor hospital, to subscribe to Protestantism. The subsequent behaviour of a number of the faithful—who were in reality closet Catholics—makes it clear that theirs was at best a civic and eirenic Protestantism. There were Catholics too amongst the town's leading craftsmen who petitioned the council in 1560 'to establish such a kirk' as would be 'a mirror and example to all the rest of this realm'. The strength of their motivation should not be underestimated; a godly society with a learned preaching ministry, proper discipline and decent provision for all its members, rich and poor, was the goal of 'civility' which could capture Catholic imaginations as well as Calvinist. Yet in practice Scottish towns, unaccustomed to direct taxation, proved remarkably reluctant to meet the bill for their godly ideals. Eight different fund-raising schemes were tried and failed in Edinburgh in the 1560s; a parliamentary statute of 1574 for a compulsory poor rate throughout Scotland foundered. Scotland muddled on into the seventeenth century with a voluntary system of poor relief; and the role of the kirk-session steadily evolved from that of being the nagging conscience of the civil power to the point where by 1600 it had complete control of the problem of the poor.[41]

It is clear from the Edinburgh subscription list that by 1562 the social

---

[40] Knox, *Works*, iv. 528–30. The *Letter* was circumspect as to the role of the common people in resisting tyranny. It was more concerned with exhorting them to withdraw from the mass and withold the tithe, as had already been done in towns where a privy kirk had been set up. See *Works*, iv. 527–9; cf. Ridley, *Knox*, 276–8.

[41] Lynch, *Edinburgh*, 31–4, 181–2, 265–6; Lynch, 'Privy Kirk', 91–2; cf. P. Collinson, *The Religion of Protestants* (Oxford, 1982), 171; *Edinburgh Burgh Records*, iii. 90–2; *Acts of Parliaments of Scotland*, iv. 232–3.

mould of urban Protestantism had firmly set there. The populist streak, which had been so marked in the later 1550s, had disappeared. The subscribers were overwhelmingly drawn from the larger merchants, lawyers, who made up fully a fifth of the list, and a craft aristocracy in the wealthier guilds. Conspicuous by their absence were the urban lower classes who had held office in the later 1550s. The privy kirk in taking on a 'public face', as Knox described its official establishment, had taken on respectability as well. The new faith needed to gain popular support but that would take time. It was more necessary that Calvinism gained converts or at least acceptability within the urban élite. As a result, the inner core of the new Protestant regime brought to power almost by accident in 1560 remained for some time in the same family circles as had dominated the movement up to the mid-1550s. In the kirk-session preference was given in the election of elders to those who, in Knox's words, had been 'of good conversation and honest fame *in the privy kirk*'.[42] For some time after 1560 the chief criterion of Protestant respectability continued to be how long one had held a party card. The Reformation of 1559–60 had had the effect, not of broadening the Protestant movement in the towns, but of narrowing its power-base and perhaps also, temporarily, its appeal as well.

The towns were clearly envisaged by the Reformers who drew up the *First Book of Discipline* as providing the growth-points for the Reformed Church. By 1580 this policy was beginning to produce real and lasting returns. A new grass-roots enthusiasm with certain unwelcome social consequences had emerged in a number of towns by the early 1580s. The Reformation and its repercussions had largely been debated within the privileged confines of town-councils or kirk-sessions. The debates of the Melvillian period were conducted in a much wider forum: the Edinburgh town-council was openly criticized by its ministers in the pulpit as was the court. The kirk-session, under pressure from the crown to condemn the excesses of its strident ministers, threatened to split along the lines of wealthy élitist elders against *nouveaux* Calvinists, who were mostly drawn from the deacons and of humbler social origins. The symbolic confrontation of the 1560s had been the interviews between Mary, a Catholic queen, and Knox, the uncompromising Calvinist minister, on the question of the authority of Scripture and the royal prerogative. In the 1580s the question was much the same but the confrontation was between the godly but Erastian prince, James VI, and a lay 'Scripturar', John Blackburn, a minor Edinburgh merchant and elder, who was summoned to the royal palace at Falkland to subscribe to a letter condemning the town's Melvillian ministers who had fled into exile in England following the passage through

---

[42] Lynch, *Edinburgh*, 179–81; Knox, *History*, ii. 277–8. The italics are mine. Much of this analysis depends on the evidence for Edinburgh. Research in progress may reveal a more consistently populist strain of Protestantism in Perth; see Lynch, 'Privy Kirk', 88.

parliament of the 'Black Acts'. Knox had moral certainty on his side. Blackburn, the archetype of the new wave of Calvinism which swept over urban society a generation after the Reformation was equally resolute but less able to bandy biblical texts. He asked to consult a Bible before he gave his king an answer but a night spent in irons did not produce more than his assertion that the letter was 'against the Word of God and his conscience'.[43]

The pressure from James VI on the church tightened in the 1590s and after his move to London in 1603. The divisions, both social and political, within the Edinburgh kirk-session became more open and acrimonious, especially after the king's attempts from 1618 onwards to introduce quasi-Anglican liturgical practices such as kneeling at communion. By then the 'giddy-headed' radicals on the session were more expert in reciting passages from Scripture; the target was now their own ministers, the despised mouthpieces of the crown and burgh establishment. The threat posed by this brand of outspoken radicalism could not be ignored; in 1618 the Edinburgh town-council took steps to swamp kirk-session elections in an attempt to blunt the influence of what had become a platform for protest. A new-style urban Calvinist, fuelled by an inner conviction verging on antinomianism as much as by political animus, endangered the broad Calvinist consensus which had marked the Reformed Church since the late 1570s. Scripture or the individual conscience was brought into play against what was seen as an increasingly corrupt, Erastian church, arguing that on issues such as kneeling it was 'a point of papistry . . . to believe as the kirk believes'.[44] By the early 1620s substantial parts of congregations in Edinburgh and Fife had withdrawn from communion. The issue had moved on from the corruptness of the new liturgy to virtual separatism. Scottish Calvinism, however bitter its internal wranglings over ecclesiastical polity, could until 1620 have fairly claimed to be a seamless robe. It approached the reign of Charles I uneasily stretched between the established church and the conventicle.

The nobility had commissioned the *First Book of Discipline* and the *Confession of Faith* had acknowledged that the civil magistrate had a role in the 'conservation' as well as the 'purgation' of religion. Yet there was from the very beginning a serious division of opinion within the reformed church on the question of the godly magistrate. John Knox had appealed from abroad throughout 1557 and 1558 to the nobles' 'office and duty' as inferior magistrates 'to vindicate and deliver your subjects and brethren from all violence and oppression to the uttermost of your power'. A quite different view had been put forward by the Lutheran-influenced laird from Angus, John Erskine of Dun, whose career in the history of Scottish Protestantism

[43] Lynch, *Edinburgh*, 162–3, 366–72; W. H. Makey, *Church* (see Further Reading), 155–6; Calderwood, *History*, iv. 123–4.

[44] Calderwood, *History*, vii. 35–64, 436–7; Makey, *Church*, 157–9.

lasted twice as long as that of Knox. This convert of the 1530s, who continued as superintendent of Angus into the 1580s, was the chosen spokesman of the 'professors of Christ's Evangel' who petitioned Mary of Guise in May 1559. He, in distinct contrast to Knox, was anxious to make a sharp distinction between 'the government of mortal men' and 'the government of the spiritual and heavenly kingdom, the kirk of God we mean'. There were certain oddities about this. Knox, the Genevan Calvinist, advanced a view of the 'office' or 'vocation' of the magistrate which had strong Lutheran overtones; Erskine, the Lutheran and later bitter critic of Andrew Melville, was closer to the classic Calvinist insistence on a separation of the two kingdoms. Knox appealed to Scottish nobility in much the same terms as to the English; he made no concession to the conventional flattery of Scotland's great noble houses seen in the work of both Buchanan and David Hume of Godscroft. If Knox was the prophet of the nobility, he did not write in terms which they would readily have understood or welcomed. Erskine, by contrast, had long experience of the interference of the nobles in the affairs of the pre-Reformation church; his petition of 1559 was concerned to warn the nobles as much as the regent that they had 'no pre-eminence nor authority above the kirk'.[45]

It was more usual for ministers' attitudes to turn on their personal connections, sometimes long established, with noble or lairdly patrons. The translation into Gaelic made by John Carswell, superintendent of Argyll, of the *Book of Common Order* was dedicated to the 'mighty just-judging, gentle-speaking lord', the earl of Argyll, whose family had acted as patrons of Carswell since at least 1550. Carswell also paid due deference to 'the Christian brethren who were at Geneva' and the title of his work rendered precisely into Gaelic the proper title of the Geneva Book, *The Form of Prayers*. Yet this was Calvinism which had undergone a drastic process of naturalization: the reformed church in Argyll acknowledged that 'it ought to have a lord or secular noble over it, called . . . *magistratus civilis*', which put it at the opposite end of the religious spectrum from the church in Angus, whose superintendent was Erskine of Dun.[46] Yet Erskine indeed provides a striking example of the mixing of the two kingdoms. He was a laird and also provost of the burgh of Montrose as well as a superintendent who liked to call himself a bishop; no doubt he felt that he had more than one vocation.

Ecclesiastical appearances were often deceptive. More important was the fact that Scotland was a country where power was highly devolved. Central power, whether in the shape of the privy council or General Assembly of the

[45] See Knox, *Works*, i. 272, and iv. 465–520, for his 'Appellation to the Nobility' of 1558, and *Spalding Miscellany* (Spalding Club, 1849), iv. 88–92, for Erskine's petition. The contrast is suggestively drawn in A. H. Williamson, *Scottish National Consciousness* (see Further Reading) 8, 16–18, 150 n. The *Confession of Faith* is conveniently printed in Knox, *History*, ii. 257–72.
[46] *Foirm na n-Urrnuidheadh* (Scot. Gaelic Texts Soc., 1970), 173; D. E. Meek and J. Kirk, 'John Carswell, Superintendent of Argyll: a Reassessment', *RSCHS* 19 (1975), 10, 18, 20.

church, had to find a measure of consent in the localities to implement its will. What the new church needed above all else was leadership, but as much in the localities as at the centre. This was provided in its first generation by a loose combination of a few nobles and a much larger collage of lairds along with Knox, the five superintendents, and the handful of prominent Catholic churchmen who conformed in 1560. Their leadership took different forms. Argyll acted as a territorial magnate and was until his death in 1573 virtually the sole patron of Protestantism in the far west. His family enjoyed as much control over the benefices and personnel of the new church as it had over the old. But in Scotland noble power and patronage over the church was usually diffuse and indirect. Power tended to be personal rather than territorial and nobles lacked specific rights of ecclesiastical patronage.[47] The influence of the Hamiltons, headed by the earl of Arran, the prince of the blood who lent respectability to the rebels in 1559 and had earlier been given the French duchy of Châtelherault, was widespread; but it stemmed from the large number of greater and lesser barons carrying the Hamilton name rather than the family's sizeable but scattered landed possessions or the forty-odd parishes notionally in their control. Yet the Hamilton nexus did not follow Châtelherault *en masse* when he joined Moray in an abortive Protestant *putsch* in 1565. Noble power, like that of burgh magistrates, operated through a measure of consent rather than *Diktat*. The result was often a blurring of motives or issues, not least the religious. Although Châtelherault never quite cast off his Protestant mantle, he and his house clearly put the interests of family above religious conviction throughout the 1560s and beyond. After the abysmal attempt at a coup in 1565 they turned away from Protestant politics as a means of promoting their dynastic interests and went in search of new allies. By 1568 they shared with the largely Catholic family of the Gordons the leadership of the party which supported Queen Mary after her deposition in direct opposition to the rival king's party backing the infant James VI and headed by Châtelherault's fellow Protestant conspirator of both 1559 and 1565, Moray. Châtelherault did not have the means to act as a Protestant patron like the earls of Huntingdon or Leicester in England. But, although a prince of the blood, he was no Condé either and his house was not the noble dynasty to give either security or unity to the Protestant movement in the difficult decade of the 1560s.

The most influential Protestant noble throughout the 1560s was undoubtedly Lord James Stewart, who wrested the earldom of Moray from the Catholic 'pope' of the north-east, the earl of Huntly, when he fell from royal favour in 1562. The new earl boasted that he would bring the north-east to Protestantism but it is difficult to detect much progress in that direction by the time he was assassinated in 1570. Although Huntly had

[47] Wormald, *Scotland*, 20–6, 131; Wormald, '"Princes" and the Regions in the Scottish Reformation', in Macdougall (ed.), *Church and Society*, 68–9.

been killed while in rebellion against the crown in 1562, the tentacles of the elaborate Gordon kinship network proved capable of surviving the removal of its head: Huntly's cousin remained entrenched in Old Aberdeen as the Catholic bishop of the diocese and chancellor of the university; a client family continued to hold the royal burgh of Aberdeen in its grip. Moray's patchy record in the north-east demonstrated the limitations of central power in trying to implement its will in the localities and the fact that Catholicism and Catholic magnates could not be eliminated by transplant surgery. There was no forced plantation of Protestantism in the localities; it had to find consent to allow it to grow. This took time, not least because Scottish nobles had a distressing habit, when no middle ground existed between Catholicism and Calvinism, of slipping from one to the other and back again, so that by the 1590s various reports estimated that as many as a third of the nobility had Catholic sympathies.

Moray was an unusual figure in many ways. He had studied briefly under Ramus at Paris and corresponded with Calvin. He was on intimate terms with Leicester and had an extensive network of contacts in France, including some of the Huguenot nobility whom he visited again in 1565 *en route* for Geneva. Yet he was as well connected with the Catholic reformers—like Douglas and Winram—who joined the Reformed Church as he was with the Genevans, like Knox and Christopher Goodman. As a royal bastard he lacked the traditional loyalties enjoyed by most Scottish magnates in their own localities. The hub of his influence lay in St Andrews, both in the university and the Augustinian priory secured for him by James V. He secured the appointment of Douglas as rector of the university in 1550 and of George Buchanan, whom he had met in France, as principal of St Leonard's in 1566. Numbers attending St Leonard's increased sharply in the 1560s and it became the chief seminary for the production of ministers until Andrew Melville went to St Mary's in 1579. Many prominent so-called 'Melvillian' ministers actually attended St Leonard's after 1560 but before Melville's return to Scotland in 1574. Moray's priory provided more than a score of canons who became ministers or readers in the new church. One of them became the luckless minister of Aberdeen in Moray's ill-fated venture in the north-east. Another collaborated in the production of 1566 of a metrical psalter which bore distinct traces of Huguenot influence. The full extent of Moray's literary patronage remains unclear. He almost certainly arranged the printing of the *Book of Common Order* in 1564 through a client, Alexander Clerk, whom he had met in France in the 1550s. After Moray became regent his client was rewarded by being made the head of a consortium licensed in 1568 to strip lead from the two most prestigious cathedrals in the north-east, Elgin and Old Aberdeen. Moray remains an enigma—a Renaissance scholar and humanist by training but also a witch-hunter whose hand lay behind the first Scottish statute against witchcraft of 1563; a literary patron but also a promoter of professional iconoclasts. Yet it was Moray as much as any of the ministers—including John Knox—who helped to give a Calvinist tone and emphasis to the Scottish Reformation in the course of the 1560s.[48]

Moray was one of very few Scottish nobles who acted as if he believed in a Calvinist international. His misfortune lay in the fact that, apart from a brief period in the summer of 1559, there was never a 'revolutionary party' in Scotland. His allies of 1559 steadily deserted him. Châtelherault did so after 1565 and other nobles who had been prominent in the Congregation during the Reformation crisis slipped away as the 1560s progressed. Most of the nobility, when pressed, put their own interests or loyalty to the crown above religion. The result was that a striking number of magnates, both Protestant and Catholic, joined the Marian party in order to reverse the revolution of 1567. Prominent among them was another of the former leaders of the Congregation, the earl of Argyll. The resulting civil war engulfed Scottish society and politics between 1567 and 1573 and propaganda was sharper than during the Reformation crisis. The king's party cast scorn on the unholy alliance of Catholics and 'feigned Protestants that have no God but gear' in the queen's party. Yet it ignored the presence in the supposedly ultra-Protestant king's party of at least two major Catholic magnates. This was not a war of religion but a civil war which followed the confused pattern of many civil wars, with issues changing as the war went on and men changing sides in both directions in response. So confused were the issues that the Edinburgh establishment, despite the explicit support given to the king's party by its minister, John Knox, was split in two in its loyalties.[49]

The civil war ended as it began—with an explicitly Protestant regency in control, but that of Morton, head of the house of Douglas, rather than Moray. The most serious effect of the war was ironical indeed: the king's party, in order to bolster its flagging fortunes, had after 1570 resorted to the episcopal temporalities as a campaign fund.[50] The king's party would have liked to have fought the war as a Protestant crusade as in France; it ended by

[48] M. Lee, *James Stewart, Earl of Moray* (New York, 1953), 206; Hewat, *Makers of the Scottish Church*, 185, 316–17; J. Kirk, 'Royal and Lay Patronage in the Jacobean Kirk, 1572–1600', in Macdougall (ed.), *Church and Society*, 141–2; P. H. Brown, *George Buchanan* (Edinburgh, 1890), 241; Kirk, 'The Influence of Calvinism', 174; D. Laing, 'An Account of the Scottish Psalter of 1566', *Procs. Soc. Antiqs. Scot.* 7 (1867–8), 448–9; J. Durkan, 'Contract between Clerk and Lekpreuik for printing the Book of Common Order, 1564', *The Bibliotheck*, 11 (1983), 131; *Reg. Privy Co.* i. 608–10.

[49] H. G. Koenigsberger, 'Organization of Revolutionary Parties in France and the Netherlands during the Sixteenth Century', *J. of Modern History*, 27 (1955), 335, tried to extend his thesis to Scotland only in an aside and to a 'lesser degree'. It is difficult, even so, to see any party organization, however rudimentary, in Scotland before the 1580s and then only briefly. The real 'revolutionary party' belonged to the Covenanting period. See Donaldson, *Queen's Men*, 83–116; *Cal. State Papers Scot.* iii, no. 123; Lynch, *Edinburgh*, 200–11.

[50] Kirk, 'Royal Patronage', 129–30.

engineering the most severe blow to the independence of the Reformed Church in the first generation of its existence. the The noble raid on the resources of the church towards the end of the civil war was more important than the return of Andrew Melville from Geneva in 1574 or any refuelling of Calvinist sensibilities amongst the ministers as the trigger for the increasingly explicit dissatisfaction within the church in the 1570s which resulted in the uncompromising reforms set down in the *Second Book of Discipline*. Well before Melville returned threats were made to appeal on the matter of the new bishops to 'all reformed kirks within Europe' in order to preserve the integrity of the kirk. By 1578 the continuing abuse of patronage and the evasive tactics of the civil power had resulted in direct criticism of lay patronage itself as an undesirable legacy of papistry.[51]

Criticism of the conduct and greed of the nobility grew louder and more outspoken as the 1570s went on. By the early 1580s it was the crown itself or the court which became the focus of resentment, although few ministers as yet went as far as John Davidson, who forecast, from the precedent of Mannaseh, that James VI would 'close that race' of kings if he did not mend his ways.[52] The increasing antagonism between the crown and a vociferous section of Melvillian ministers in the 1580s provided an opportunity for a brief *rapprochement* between the Melvillians and the nobles still willing to play the ultra-Protestant card in Scottish politics. The perennial difficulty remained that a number of nobles were willing to risk a single turn of the cards, as in the short-lived Ruthven regime which came to power in 1582 by the tried and trusted method of capturing the person of the king but which fell by the equally sure method of letting him escape. Few, however, were prepared to stay longer in the game, as Scottish kings were usually inclined to overlook one error of judgement but not two in close succession. There were few voices raised in defence of that 'pearl of godliness', the earl of Gowrie, the architect of the Ruthven raid, when he was executed in 1584 for attempting a second coup.

The other chief hope of the ministers in the 1580s was the earl of Angus, leader of the ministers and nobles who fled into exile in England in 1584. The nobles settled at Newcastle, and Angus was instrumental in drawing them together as a reformed congregation with its own ministers and kirk-session. A complete programme was devised of daily prayers and exercise, weekly lecture, twice-weekly meeting of elders and deacons, four sermons a week, and monthly fast and communion, all to be supplemented by individual contemplation of 'the miserable estate of our kirk and country' along with that 'of France and Flanders'. Seldom can Scottish nobles have

---

[51] Calderwood, *History*, iii. 156–62; *Second Book of Discipline*, 33–5, 234.

[52] Calderwood, *History*, viii. 257. The sin of Mannaseh, who made 'Judah and the inhabitants of Jerusalem to err', was a favourite text of Scottish ministers to illustrate the wilful defection of their rulers from the pristine purity of the Scottish Reformation. See Knox, *History*, ii. 108–9.

reached such heights of godliness. Yet within a year of their return to Scotland late in 1585 the Newcastle exiles had all, except for Angus, reverted to type. His death in 1588 removed the last hope amongst the ministers for a truly godly magistrate.[53]

By the 1590s criticism had extended beyond the individual conduct or patronage of nobles. Some began to see them as the new Antichrist, blocking further reform of the church. Robert Bruce, who was in the van of the fashionable new twist beginning to be given Calvinist theology of a double covenant, took the assault on noble privilege a stage further in the 1590s by sharply distinguishing between the true 'spiritual bonds' which held together men and Christ and the 'carnal bond of blood or alliance' which constituted the basis of the kinship network. Bruce predicted that the new 'celestial glue', as he called it, of faith and grace would replace the traditional ties of kinship. It was a startling vision of a Calvinist future, transcending rather than solving the problem which the *First Book of Discipline* had so conspicuously ignored, the godly magistrate. The Reformed Church had sought to recast society in its own image in 1560 but had failed, at least by its own impossibly high standards. It tried again in the 1590s, this time recasting its ambitions in the language of millenarian expectation. It seemed for a time that it might enjoy the support of James VI but before the decade was over found itself outbid by a rival millenarian gospel, centring on the promotion of Scotland's king as a contemporary David, not only 'nursing father' of the Scottish kirk but potential protector of Calvinist Europe.[54] The godly prince, so late in entering the Scottish scene, had hijacked not only the language of the clerical party wanting further reform of the church but also their newly adopted symbol itself, the national covenant. There was certainly growing opposition to James' liturgical reforms as well as increasing resentment of absentee kingship after James left Scotland in 1603, but one of the main reasons why the different strands of opposition took so long to develop or join together was the belief that the king of Scots was on a divine mission.

It is often said that the major achievement of the reformed church was to restore a resident, qualified parish ministry in contrast to a pre-Reformation church of under-paid and overworked curates.[55] Yet this achievement, remarkable as it was, took the better part of forty years after 1560 and was almost as much a stop-go process as the spread of Protestantism before 1560. It also had its ambiguities and paradoxes. It is difficult, as has been seen, to make firm pronouncements about the spread of Protestantism in Scotland, either before or after the Reformation of 1560. The evidence is

53 Melville, *Diary*, 181–5; Donaldson, 'Presbyterian Exiles', 76.
54 Williamson, *National Consciousness*, 39–43, 69–70; Robert Bruce, *Sermons* (Wodrow Soc., 1843), 66, 154.
55 See e.g. Donaldson, *Scottish Reformation*, 87–95.

scattered and often lacks precision. It has recently been argued that the
surest guide to charting the progress of the Reformers, indeed at times the
only guide, is the data available for tracing the settlement of a parish
ministry. This evidence is itself often incomplete and comes in the form of
occasional snapshots, as in 1563, 1567, and 1574. Often it helps confirm and
quantify what might have been expected: in Angus and the Mearns, which
had strong traces of early Protestantism, a majority of parishes had acquired
a reformed ministry by 1563 and all but a handful by 1567; in the more
remote deanery of Inverness, only two of the twelve parishes had a
Protestant incumbent before 1568. The church had about 1,080 parishes;
by 1567 they were served by about 850 clergy and by 1574 just over 1,000,
who were heavily concentrated in the east coast, central lowlands, and less
remote parts of the south-west and Borders.[56]

Yet the counting of ministers, it might be said, has much in common with
the counting of sheep and has at times the same hallucinatory effects.
Although Erskine of Dun was remarkably successful in settling a ministry
he was sharply attacked in the General Assembly for admitting poorly
qualified candidates. If the old church was a church of curates the new one
in its first generation was largely a church of readers and exhorters; less than
a quarter of the parishes had a minister even by 1574. There was, however, a
paradox within this. The *First Book of Discipline* was highly sceptical of the
office of reader, which it viewed as a temporary expedient and of strictly
limited value: this 'vain shadow' of a minister could not dispense the
sacraments or preach. When the most militant General Assembly since the
Reformation met in 1567, in an atmosphere of heady excitement at the
imminent downfall of Scotland's Catholic queen, it intended a second
Reformation: idolatry should be hunted down and a true church set up by
the planting of superintendents, ministers, and 'other needful members of
the kirk'. Needs had changed since 1560. By 1574 an appreciable increase in
the numbers serving in the ministry had resulted but most were readers or
exhorters, not ministers. And ironically the hawks of the 1567 Assembly had
been forced to turn to the religious houses of the old church to effect an
improvement in the numbers of their own clergy. Four of the monks of the
Benedictine abbey at Dunfermline were appointed as readers after 1567.
Three of them continued to live in the monastery and, according to a Jesuit
report of 1580, also continued to recite the offices of their order. The sight of
Calvinist readers who were part-time Benedictine monks may seem bizarre
but outside the burghs it is difficult to see what else but the convent or abbey
might act as a growth-point for the organization of the ministry if the
secular parish clergy of the old church would not conform. This example
illustrates the dangers of being too confident about the convictions or

[56] Cowan, *Reformation*, 159, 162, 170; *Wodrow Misc.* 396.

motives of many of the ministry of the new church when so many of its personnel were drawn from that of the old. Many who did conform did not do so immediately after 1560 and a number of those admitted after 1567 had already been convicted of illegally saying mass. The late 1560s were desperate times which called for desperate measures.[57]

In some areas, such as Kyle, where there was already a core of convinced Protestantism amongst nobles or lairds, the inadequacy of provision made by the established church seems to have induced a retreat into the Protestant household; Knox's old friend, Campbell of Kinzeancleuch, virtually set up an exercise in his own home to examine his family nightly and his servants weekly.[58] Even in the burghs, where the new church had concentrated its most talented ministers, the raw statistics of ministerial appointments hide a more ambiguous reality. All the major burghs had only a single minister in the 1560s except Edinburgh, which had two from 1562, and Dundee two from 1569. Most of these burgh ministers were assisted only by a reader who had often been a chaplain in the pre-Reformation burgh church. The vicar of one London parish in the 1630s felt himself to be ineffective with a congregation of 1,400 adult parishioners. The two Edinburgh ministers of the 1560s had to deal with an adult congregation in the region of 7,500. The ministers of Perth and Aberdeen were only marginally better off and the minister of the much smaller burgh of Culross complained of his 'intolerable' burden of 2,000 communicants. It was only after Perth appointed a second minister in 1595 that it instituted weekly catechizing in place of a fairly perfunctory system of an annual examination of parishioners before communion. It may be that limitations of clerical manpower threw greater weight on the eldership in Scottsh Calvinism than elsewhere but there were few signs that it could act as an evangelizing agency. The vital element remained the minister and in Scotland as a whole the church had not improved on a ratio of one minister to four parishes by the end of the 1570s. Some of the burghs became oases of pastoral excellence but few did so before 1600.[59]

A further crisis of manpower hit the church about the end of the 1570s as significant numbers of the clergy who had conformed from the pre-Reformation church began to die off. The *Second Book of Discipline* was more than a reassessment of the continuing problems of establishing the church; it was a response to a major organizational crisis. The *Book* proposed, not the typical Calvinist fourfold organization, but one on three

[57] *First Book of Discipline*, 22, 104; *BUK*, i. 106–10; M. Sanderson, 'Catholic Recusancy in Scotland in 16th Century', *Innes Review*, 21 (1970), 89; M. Dilworth, 'Monks and Ministers after 1560', *RSCHS* 18 (1974), 216–20.

[58] Calderwood, *History*, iii. 312.

[59] Collinson, *Protestants*, 212; Lynch, *Edinburgh*, 9–14; Row, *History*, 473; *Spottiswoode Misc.* (Spottiswoode Club, 1845), ii. 272–4.

levels—General Assembly, provincial synod and communal eldership, which was intended to group together the individual kirk-sessions in a district to form a body somewhere between colloquy and consistory. The assumption lying behind this scheme was that the way forward lay in a reduction in the number of parishes from over 1,000 to 600, each to be served by a resident minister. The plan aborted largely for want of finance and a more conventional fourfold system gradually emerged after 1581 containing both presbyteries and kirk-sessions.[60] But even presbyteries were slow to establish themselves: fifty were planned in 1581 but only thirteen were set up, mostly in or near towns in the lowlands; it took a further thirty years for the original target to be met. By 1638, sixty-six were represented in the General Assembly.[61]

The medieval parish system continued with minor alterations and the church struggled on. By 1596 there were 539 ministers and by 1648 there were 838. It is clear that by the 1620s virtually all lowland parishes had ministers and the breakthrough had been made. The ministry was by now virtually an all-graduate profession. Complaints about the level of stipends faded away after 1625. New churches began to be built after 1610.[62] Yet all was not well within the ministry. James VI's series of interventions in the affairs of the church had forced the General Assembly to meet outside Edinburgh. The clerical party, largely drawn from Fife and Lothian, which had been accustomed to dominating Assemblies, did not appreciate the resulting influx of ministers from remoter parts; James Melville lampooned 'the drunken Orkney ass' who in 1596 led the subservient rabble from the north happy to accommodate the crown. The Melvillian ministers were increasingly exposed for what they had always been—élitist, better paid and educated, as well as more influential in the corridors of power within the church.[63]

One minister who died in 1609 left as his epitaph an explicit warning of the 'distraction of minds' within the clergy. Between then and 1636 a series of influences, both external and internal, threatened to tear the fabric of the ministry. The dichotomy in the mind of the church—which had existed since Knoxian days—between a Calvinist international and the myth of the unrivalled perfection of the Scottish church began to widen. The meddling of James VI and the recasting of some Calvinist expectations around him induced a new wave of introspection and disillusionment.[64] A number of ministers went to France, the Netherlands, and Ulster in these years and

---

[60] *Second Book of Discipline*, 101–8.

[61] W. R. Foster, 'The Operation of Presbyteries in Scotland, 1600–1638', *RSCHS* 15 (1963), 21–2.

[62] Foster, *Church*, 133, 153–4, 174; Makey, *Church*, 96, 102.

[63] Melville, *Diary*, 440; cf. Collinson, *Protestants*, 131, on similar tendencies amongst Elizabethan Presbyterian ministers.

[64] See Williamson, *National Consciousness*, 39–41; Row, *History*, 12, 412.

returned with extra influences working upon them.[65] Some taught in Huguenot academies like Saumur, Sedan, and Montauban until evicted by Richelieu; the experience gave a new edge to their dislike of bishops and suspicion of kneeling. Several ministers who had gone to Ulster were similarly ousted in 1636 and returned, often to parishes in the south-west, with a particular dislike of episcopacy and were prominent amongst those who disliked any form of set prayers, including even the Lord's Prayer. The result amounted to something approaching liturgical anarchy which would not have been tolerated in other Calvinist churches, as John Welsh, son-in-law of Knox, discovered when he was reprimanded by the French National Synod for departing from set forms while pastor at St Jean d'Angély.

The influence of the Netherlands, to whose universities Scots graduates increasingly turned rather than those in France after 1625, was more complicated. A number of leading ministers had a comprehensive knowledge of developments in Dutch theology and Samuel Rutherford was offered chairs of theology at Utrecht and Harderwyck. There were Scots—rather than English—congregations set up at Veere and Rotterdam and much of the Calvinist literature read in Scotland came off Dutch printing presses. The Synod of Dort had come as 'a great comfort' after the forcing of the Five Articles through the General Assembly by the king in 1618 and the decisions taken at Dort became the touchstone of Calvinist orthodoxy in Scotland for much of the seventeenth century. A more significant influence came in the deep suspicion of sectaries and separatists felt by some of the ministers who had experience of the Netherlands, like David Calderwood; Brownism became the lurking fear of many otherwise radical ministers. A series of rifts, social and geographical as well as doctrinal or liturgical, threatened the unity of the ministry in the early seventeenth century.

The social structure of the ministry of the reformed church was in almost constant evolution in this period. This was hardly surprising as Scottish society as a whole was in process of significant readjustment in the century after 1550. A number of overlapping groups had for various reasons profited from new acquisitions of wealth or land, or come to a new prominence in office in either ecclesiastical or civil administration, as centre and localities, in both church and state, drew closer together. The rise of the ministers was paralleled by—and indeed part of—the rise of a new gentry and new professions. Early modern Scotland was very far from being a static society controlled by a clerical caste. The apparent triumph of the ministers needs to be set against the triumph of various sections of the laity. The new neo-clericalism went side by side with the growing influence of lairds, lawyers,

---

[65] See *Wodrow Misc.* 569-90; W. A. Campbell, 'Robert Boyd of Trochrigg', *RSCHS* 12 (1956), 222, 234; A. L. Drummond, *The Kirk and the Continent* (Edinburgh, 1956), 28-41, 80, 99, 126-7; Row, *History*, 317, 465; McMillan, *Worship*, 71-2; G. D. Henderson, *Religious Life* (see Further Reading), 73, 77-9, 84-6, 94-5.

feuars, and urban oligarchies.[66] It would take the turmoil of the 1640s to reveal their respective standing and the ultimate but ambivalent dependence of each on the nobility.

The ministers shared many of the characteristics of these other rising groups. Their families tended to intermarry and increasingly they developed the hallmarks of a hereditary caste. Andrew and James Melville were only two of a race of Melvilles in the kirk. At least 17 per cent of the ministers serving in the church between 1616 and 1638 had followed their fathers into the profession; by 1648 it had risen to 27 per cent or, if only known fathers are brought into the calculation, to a little over 50 per cent. Sons of nobles were not totally unknown in the Reformed Church but were rare indeed; there was only one in 1648 and he was illegitimate. There had been a number of ministers in the first and second generations of the new church who had come from baronial families—Erskine of Dun was himself a laird—or from the upper reaches of the urban bourgeoisie but such connections became rarer or more slender as time passed. It has been estimated that by the 1640s less than one in twenty of the ministry came from the upper reaches of Scottish society, whether rural or urban. The typical minister—if he was not from a minister's family—was the son of a modest merchant or craftsman or small landed proprietor beneath the status of a laird.[67]

This clear pattern of recruitment is all the more striking as there had been murmurings as early as the 1590s that ministers 'live like lairds'. They enjoyed a steady rise in income over the next thirty years; by the late 1620s their stipends seldom sunk beneath £30 sterling in sharp contrast to some English rural vicars on £5 a year. By the 1640s the upper crust of the profession, the ministers of Edinburgh, were earning £100. The result of this new-found prosperity, which gives a novel twist to the Weber thesis, was that the ordinary rural minister, earning something like ten times the average income of his congregation, had money to spare in a society usually acutely short of cash; so he lent it, at interest, to his flock. The Edinburgh ministers, ranging from Knox in the 1560s to Alexander Henderson in the 1640s, lent to the nobility.[68]

The ministers also enjoyed considerable perquisites; it was expected that ministers' children would have their education paid for by their

---

[66] Wormald, *Scotland*, 160–76. The secularization of church lands in Scotland took the form of setting them in feu-ferm, mostly between 1550 and 1570. The major beneficiaries amongst the new class of feuars were the existing tenants, given a new security of tenure in return for payment of a fixed annual fee, which was progressively eroded by price inflation (see M. Sanderson, *Scottish Rural Society in 16th Century* (Edinburgh, 1982), 124–33, 188–90; Makey, *Church*, 1–15). A rather different view of Scottish society can be seen in H. R. Trevor-Roper, 'Scotland and the Puritan Revolution', in *Religion, the Reformation and Social Change* (London, 1967), 395–8.

[67] Makey, *Church*, 94–105.

[68] Calderwood, *History*, v. 177 n; Makey, *Church*, 106–22; Foster, *Church*, 164–5.

congregations. One presbytery agreed in 1642 to grant a bursary to send a laird's son to St Mary's College only because there was no minister's son suitable. Like the lawyers, the ministers stressed their new professional status and clung to the special privileges which kept them apart from the rest of society; only three species escaped taxation in Jacobean Scotland— the poor, the lawyers, and the ministry. Their collective self-consciousness was fostered even before their admission to the ministry; the universities remained largely clerical seminaries where bursars had to 'live collegialiter' and remain answerable to the home presbytery. The collegiality of the ministers, when ordained, was underpinned by the exercise and presbytery, which, even if they notionally existed as mixed bodies, both in time became virtual closed meetings of clergy. By the 1630s almost fifty years of experience had induced some ministers to declare the attendance of the laity at the presbytery as unprofitable.[69] The ministers' *esprit de corps* had never been greater, yet the locus of authority within the church was being increasingly called into question. The twin hubs of the ministry, at least in the minds of the Melvillians, had by the 1580s become the Melvillian seminary of St Mary's and the joint lodging of the Edinburgh ministers— until James VI had forcibly disbanded the lodging in 1596.[70] After that influence seeped slowly away from Fife and Lothian to the south-west, where Samuel Rutherford was in the 1630s building up a chain of virtual conventicles, which would reveal a new breed of radicalism and radical ministers before the end of the 1640s.

Seventeenth-century Scotland was in a real sense a Calvinist nation but it was not a society in the grip of its Calvinist ministers. There is little doubt in the minds of most Scottish historians—though perhaps still confusion elsewhere[71]—that the nobility rather than the clergy were the key instruments in the course of the Scottish Revolution. Even the most forward of the ministers, like Rutherford, acknowledged them as the natural patrons of a second Reformation. The National Covenant of 1638 was also known as 'the noblemen's covenant' since they would protect both church and nation from the effects of absentee kingship and its agents, the anglicizing bishops. By 1641, when Charles I and the Covenanters agreed on a constitutional settlement along highly traditional lines, the nobility had regained much of the pre-eminence in the governing of Scotland which they had enjoyed before 1603. Their influence over the kirk was demonstrably increasing rather than declining over much of the course of the Revolution and this was symbolized in 1638 by their reclaiming seats in both presbytery

[69] Row, *History*, p. xx; Foster, *Church*, 134–5; Makey, *Church*, 132; Collinson, *Protestants*, 114–16, detects much the same *esprit de corps* in England.

[70] Melville, *Diary*, 254, 330.

[71] The effects of the idiosyncratic excursion made into seventeenth-century Scotland by Trevor-Roper, 'Scotland and the Puritan Revolution' are discussed in D. Stevenson, 'Professor Trevor-Roper and the Scottish Revolution', *History Today*, 30 (1980), 34–40.

and General Assembly, much to the displeasure of many ministers. The drafting of the National Covenant had been carefully controlled by the nobles, working in league with a small circle of the most radical of the ministers, and it was a document which surprised and alarmed much of the ministry. The abolition of bishops by the Glasgow Assembly of 1638 represented the removal, at the insistence of the nobility, of their chief rivals for power in privy council and parliament rather than the final stage in a long campaign by a section of ministers to purge a corrupt church of its unscriptural elements. The capacity of the ministers themselves to influence events was hampered in turn by the agreement of the General Assembly in 1638 that they should not hold civil office or power. The boundaries between church and state, which had been vaguely drawn ever since the earliest days of the Reformed Church, were being redrawn—albeit still with elements of ambiguity—in favour of the laity.[72]

The Scottish Revolution brought to a climax a number of recurrent themes in Scottish Calvinism. Sixteenth-century Scotland had not had a genuine revolutionary party or a group of Huguenot monarchomachs to justify its actions. By 1638 a party had come into existence with a formal organization, linked by the 'Tables', standing committees representing the nobles, barons, burgesses, and ministers and linking the capital with the localities. John Knox had acted as secretary to the loose coalition of the Lords of the Congregation in the revolt of 1559–60; it was significant that the organizing secretary of the party of 1638 and the author of its revolutionary manifesto was not a minister but a well-connected Edinburgh lawyer, Johnston of Wariston. He epitomized the rise to a new prominence of the middle orders of Scottish society anxious to stake out a clearer political role for themselves. The Revolution brought together the Calvinist or Knoxian canon with the revolutionary but secular tradition of George Buchanan; the ministers who rode to war with the armies of the Covenant had, it was said, the Geneva Bible in one saddlebag and Buchanan's *History* in the other. It completed the process which had been going on since the 1590s of a merging identity in the form of a covenanted nation of church and state.[73]

The day of the signing of the National Covenant was hailed by Wariston as 'the marriage day of the kingdom with God'. Scotland was acclaimed as the new Israel, they being 'the only two sworn nations of the Lord'. The renewal of Scotland's covenant with God was also for him 'the gloriousest day that ever Scotland saw since the Reformation' because it signalled the

---

[72] See D. Stevenson, *Revolution and Counter-Revolution in Scotland, 1644–51* (London, 1977), 106–7, 218, 224.

[73] Williamson, *National Consciousness*, 143–5; S. A. Burrell, 'The Covenant Idea as a Revolutionary Symbol: Scotland 1597–1637', *Church History*, 27 (1958), 339–43, 348; W. A. Gatherer (ed.), *The Tyrannous Reign of Mary Stewart* (Edinburgh, 1958), 5 n.

final—and successful—attempt to restore the Scottish church to the pristine perfection of its early years. The intervening years had been characterized by the church's 'gadding after strange lovers', but the revolt against Charles I took place during 'the honeymoon betuix the Lord and his runaway spouse'. As often before, Scottish Calvinist insularity shaded incongruously into an idiosyncratic sense of the Calvinist international: the Scottish church in its rediscovered perfection would 'be a pattern to other nations' to imitate. by 1639 the British context, which had been absent from Scottish Calvinist thinking since James VI had borrowed it in the 1590s, had returned to Scottish politics. The union of 1603 was recast as 'the greatest blessing that God hath bestowed on this isle . . . next to the Christian faith'. The Scottish apocalypse was to be found in England, but only as the first step towards a greater Calvinist Reformation 'to be propagated from Island to Continent'.[74] Scottish Calvinism had from its beginnings been a missionary faith. By the 1630s the Scottish mission was more or less complete—at least in lowland Scotland. It sought new fields to evangelize—in England and Ireland—but with disastrous results.

[74] *Diary of Sir Archibald Johnston of Wariston, 1632–1639* (Scot. Hist. Soc., 1911), 321–2, 336, 344, 347–8.

Further Reading

Cowan, I. B., *The Scottish Reformation: Church and Society in Sixteenth-Century Scotland* (London, 1982).

Donaldson, G., *All the Queen's Men: Power and Politics in Mary Stewart's Scotland* (London, 1983).

The First Book of Discipline, ed. J. K. Cameron (Edinburgh, 1972).

Henderson, G. D., *Religious Life in Seventeenth Century Scotland* (Cambridge, 1937).

Kirk, J., 'The Influence of Calvinism on the Scottish Reformation', *RSCHS*, 18 (1974), 157–79.

—— (ed.), *The Second Book of Discipline* (Edinburgh, 1980).

Lynch, M., *Edinburgh and the Reformation* (Edinburgh, 1981).

Makey, W. H., *The Church of the Covenant, 1637–1651: Revolution and Social Change in Scotland* (Edinburgh, 1979).

Stevenson, D., *Revolution and Counter-Revolution in Scotland, 1644–51* (Royal Historical Society Monographs, London, 1977).

Williamson, A. H., *Scottish National Consciousness in the Age of James VI* (Edinburgh, 1979).

Wormald, J., *Court, Kirk and Community: Scotland, 1470–1625*, New History of Scotland, iv (London, 1981).

IX

Calvinism in Colonial North America, 1630–1715

W. A. SPECK AND L. BILLINGTON

THE topic of Calvinism in colonial North America conjures up visions of the Pilgrim Fathers sailing to Plymouth in the *Mayflower* in 1620; of John Winthrop following them across the Atlantic a decade later to found Massachusetts; of the expulsions from the 'City upon a Hill' which was Winthrop's vision of Boston, leading to the settlement of Rhode Island; and of the colonization of the Connecticut River valley and of New Haven from the base in the Bay. In short, colonial Calvinism seems synonymous with Puritan New England. Certainly the Puritans in New England drew considerable attention to themselves, and have kept it ever since. The literature on almost every conceivable aspect of their attitudes, activities, and beliefs is by now immense.

Yet they were by no means the only Calvinists in the colonies which eventually became British America. On the contrary, the Dutch had settled New Amsterdam, which the British renamed New York, before the great migration from England to Massachusetts; French Huguenots fled to North America from the repressive regime of Louis XIV; and by the end of the seventeenth century Presbyterians, by no means unknown in New England, were firmly established in the middle colonies. While the Dutch and French contributions to American religious life were minor in comparison with that of the Congregationalists, as New England Puritans came to be called, that of the Presbyterians was arguably as important. Yet they have been relatively neglected by historians.

This essay therefore seeks to redress the balance. Inevitably, since so much has been written on the Puritans, the emphasis given to New England in the literature is reflected in the space devoted to it in the following discussion. Nevertheless, the aim is to provide an overview of Calvinism in the whole of colonial North America before 1715. Consequently, after a synthesis of current scholarship on the doctrine, discipline, and social history of Congregationalism in New England, there follows an account of the contributions of Dutch, French, and Presbyterian Calvinists to the development of colonial society.

Towards the end of the seventeenth century Cotton Mather (1663–1728), third in the line of a prominent Puritan family in Massachusetts, composed his *Magnalia Christi Americana: or, The Ecclesiastical History of New England*. He introduced the work by recounting attempts made by some French Huguenots to settle a colony in the New World. Villegagnon, the leader of the expedition, wrote to Coligny requesting 'that Geneva might supply them with Pastors', a request answered by none other than 'the blessed Calvin' himself. Although this attempt at colonization was abortive, Mather reassured his readers 'that in our age there has been another essay made not by French, but by English Protestants, to fill a certain country in America with Reformed Churches; nothing in doctrine, little in discipline, different from that of Geneva'.[1] It seems appropriate in a study of Calvin's influence in colonial North America to test the validity of this claim.

Any investigation into the nature of religious doctrine in seventeenth-century New England must start with the monumental contribution of Perry Miller. The subtitle he gave to the second volume of his major work, *The New England Mind*, 'From Colony to Province', summed up his theme that Puritanism in North America began as a current in the mainstream of the Reformation in Europe, only to become a backwater by the third generation or so. 'Leaders of the first generation were participants in a great world . . . in international Calvinism' maintained Miller. 'They were not colonials, and never would become colonial; though they died in America, they were never to be Americanized.'[2] Albeit, the Calvinism which they upheld had become considerably Anglicized before it was exported to America.

At the heart of the doctrines which the Puritans took with them to New England were the Calvinist concepts of salvation and justification. An American version of these found expression in the Confession of Faith adopted at the Boston Synod of 1680: 'By the decree of God, for the manifestation of his glory, some men and angels are predestinated unto everlasting life, and others fore-ordained unto everlasting death'; 'those whom God effectually calleth, he also freely justifieth, not by infusing righteousness into them, but by pardoning their sins, and by accounting and accepting their persons as righteous, not for any thing wrought in them or done by them, but for Christ's sake alone.'[3]

As Miller observed, these stark doctrines begged two vital questions. How were men to know that they were saved? What was the point of good works if they were irrelevant to justification? Calvin's English disciples developed the concept of federal theology as a solution to these problems. William Perkins (1558–1602), the leading divine of Elizabethan

---

[1] Cotton Mather, *Magnalia Christi Americana* (New York, 1967), i. 40.
[2] Perry Miller, *The New England Mind* (see Further Reading), ii. 6.
[3] Williston Walker, *The Creeds and Platforms of Congregationalism* (Boston, 1960), 371, 378–9.

Cambridge, addressed himself to the first question in *A Treatise tending unto a declaration whether a man be in the estate of damnation or in the estate of grace: and if he be in the first, how he may in time come out of it: if in the second, how he may discern it and persevere in the same to the end* (1589). Perkins found answers to these problems in the covenant of grace, or God's 'contract with man, concerning the obtaining of life eternal, upon a certain condition'. This had replaced the covenant of works, or God's contract with Adam, guaranteeing him eternal life if he upheld divine law. Adam's breaking of the law had also broken the contract. Thereafter God had offered a fresh covenant to men whereby he guaranteed them eternal life if they had faith in him. It was this idea that there were two parties involved which gave man a role, however slight, in his own salvation.

The nature of this role was examined by Cambridge disciples of Perkins, such as William Ames (1578–1633), author of the *Medulla sacrae theologicae or Marrow of sacred divinity* (1623), whom Miller called 'the father of the New England church polity', and John Preston (1587–1628), whose *New Covenant* (1629) he extolled as 'prerequisite to any understanding of thought and theology in seventeenth-century New England'. Ames's puritanism offended the university authorities, and he was suspended from his ecclesiastical duties. Thereupon he left Cambridge and travelled widely until he became Professor of Theology at Franeker in the United Provinces in 1622. After his death his widow took herself and his books to New England. Though Preston's orthodoxy was also suspect he managed to retain his university post, partly by virtue of the protection of the Duke of Buckingham. In the *New Covenant* he wrote 'if thou beleeve, it is certaine then, thou art in the covenant'. All that the believer had to prove was that he had 'saving faith' in order to be assured of salvation. Although in strict Calvinist theology such faith was the unmerited gift of God's grace alone, as Miller noted 'in practical life the dogmatic rigors of absolute predestination are materially softened. A juridical relationship is slyly substituted for the divine decree.'[4]

Proving that one had 'saving faith' provided an answer to the second question. Although God justified those he effectually called without anything being done by them, he still expected them to obey the moral law. Those in the covenant of grace were held to be 'free from the Covenant of the Law; but not from the commandment of it'. Good works were not necessary for salvation, but they were a concomitant of grace. Justification in federal theology was succeeded by sanctification, so that those with an effectual calling became literally 'visible saints'.[5]

The doctrine of the covenant of grace therefore gave man a much more

---

[4] Perry Miller, 'The Marrow of Puritan Divinity', *Errand into the Wilderness* (Boston, Mass., 1955), 58, 59, 71, 79.
[5] See E. S. Morgan, *Visible Saints* (see Further Reading).

active role in securing his own salvation than Calvinism is usually allowed to have advocated. Perhaps the ultimate extent of this in New England was the notion entertained by some Puritans there that men could even prepare themselves to receive grace, so that they would be ready to accept the covenant when it was offered to them. Amongst those who took it this far was Thomas Hooker (1586–1647). Like so many Puritan divines Hooker had been educated at Cambridge University. In 1626 he became lecturer at Chelmsford, but fled to Holland after Archbishop Laud deprived him of the post and haled him before the High Commission. In 1633 he sailed to Massachusetts. He took issue with those who held that preparation for the reception of grace was impossible, maintaining that 'Christ is marvellously ready to come, only he watcheth the time till your heart be ready to receive and entertain him.' Miller observed of this that 'in many passages describing the extent to which an unregenerate man may go in the work of preparation, some of these writers passed beyond any limits that could be reconciled with Calvinism'.[6] This was to overlook the ambiguities in Calvin's own writings, and the various interpretations which could be put on them. It was to assume that there was an unambiguous orthodoxy prescribed by Calvin, deviations from which could be described, and even denounced, as unorthodox. In reality Calvinism stood towards Calvin as Marxism towards Marx, a dynamic not a static theology, and an elastic not a rigid creed. Just as Marxism can contain the works of Lenin and the thoughts of Chairman Mao, so Calvinism could stretch to the boundaries of Arminianism on the one hand, and the borders of Antinomianism on the other.

Those who urged that the elect were not merely passive recipients of grace but were active partners to a covenant were not far removed from Arminius. As R. T. Kendall has shown, both accepted that people with an apparently effectual calling could fall from grace. The only major difference was that the 'experimental predestinarians', as he calls them, explained this as temporary rather than saving faith, while Arminius accounted for it by claiming that the apostate had resisted grace, which they regarded as irresistible.[7]

Their opponents in New England, led by Anne Hutchinson, insisted that they were preaching a covenant of works, and that only two preachers were truly upholding the covenant of grace. Mrs Hutchinson arrived in Massachusetts in 1634 from Boston, Lincs., where she had been a parishioner of John Cotton (1585–1653), one of the two she excepted from her general stricture on New England clergymen. He was yet another Cambridge clergyman who fled to America after being arraigned by Laud before the Court of High Commission. While in England Cotton had

6 P. Miller, *Errand into the Wilderness*, 87 n. 154.
7 R. T. Kendall, *Calvin and English Calvinism to 1649* (Oxford, 1979), *passim*.

believed that the unregenerate could prepare themselves to receive grace, and had stressed the importance of repentance before faith. In Massachusetts, however, he changed his mind, and agreed that there was nothing a man could do to hasten faith. This encouraged Mrs Hutchinson, who had followed him to New England, to develop her views as having his authority, to the point where she claimed that the elect enjoyed a personal revelation from God that they were saved, and was accused of Antinomianism. When she was interrogated by ministers in 1636, Cotton was also questioned. He placed great store on the authority of Calvin in his defence, replying to one question 'Let Calvin answer for me.'[8] At this stage he refused to disown Mrs Hutchinson, but the matter grew more serious in 1637 when the General Court convened the first synod to be held in New England, for the express purpose of trying her for heresy. The synod, after condemning some eighty-two errors, sentenced her to banishment, and as it transpired to death, for she was killed by Indians in 1643, a fate which Winthrop recorded with grim satisfaction as a providential judgment. Though Cotton refused to sign a document which listed the errors, during the course of the trial he jumped off the fence to become Mrs Hutchinson's main prosecutor.

Cotton thereafter became the leading theologian among the first generation of colonists in New England. His principal adversary, Thomas Hooker, who accused him of advocating 'a fair and easy way to Heaven', took himself off to Connecticut.[9] Although there may not have been room enough in Massachusetts for two charismatic divines with such divergent views, there certainly was within New England Calvinism.[10]

The doctrinal flexibility of Calvinism as it developed in seventeenth-century New England stretched beyond the covenant of grace to sacramental theology. Like Calvin, New England theologians recognized only two sacraments, baptism and communion. Their attitudes towards both, however, were highly ambivalent. On the one hand they were not means of grace necessary to salvation, as Catholics insisted. Yet on the other hand they had a sacramental role. Upholders of New England orthodoxy maintained against Antinomians and Baptists that the two sacraments were seals to the covenant. They did not create, but they endorsed membership of the church.[11]

---

[8] N. Pettit, *The Heart Prepared: Grace and Conversion in Puritan Spiritual Life* (New Haven, Conn., 1966), 145.

[9] William B. Stoever, 'A Faire and Easy Way to Heaven': *Covenant Theology and Antinomianism in Early Massachusetts* (Middletown, Conn., 1978). See also Larzer Ziff, *The Career of John Cotton* (Princeton, NJ, 1962).

[10] For the diversity of views among New England divines see James W. Jones, *The Shattered Synthesis: New England Puritanism before the Great Awakening* (London, 1973).

[11] C. E. Hambrick-Stowe, *The Practice of Piety: Puritan Devotional Disciplines in Seventeenth-century New England* (1982), 125; E. Brooks Hollifield, *The Covenant Sealed: The Development of Puritan Sacramental Theology in Old and New England 1570–1720* (New Haven, Conn., 1974).

Attitudes towards the ministry also smacked of having it both ways. Since episcopacy was eschewed, then episcopal ordination, setting priests apart from the laity as a separate sacerdotal order, was denounced. Yet this did not entail acceptance of the priesthood of all believers, with ministers merely exercising an evangelical function. They were pastors, set apart from their flocks even if chosen by them.[12]

Despite the dynamism and flexibility of New England doctrines, Cotton Mather's claim that they did not differ from those of Calvin was not far-fetched. He was perhaps disingenuous, however, in asserting that church discipline in New England differed little from that of Calvinist churches in Europe.

Nineteenth-century historians, seeing the origins of religious denominations in the sectarian squabbles of sixteenth- and seventeenth-century Protestants, distinguished churches in Massachusetts as being Congregationalist rather than Presbyterian in their genesis. This distinction apparently explained why the New England colonists accepted the Confessions of Faith of the Westminster Assembly in 1646, but preferred their own system of church government as defined by the Platform adopted by a Synod held at Cambridge, Mass., in 1648.

Such a distinction is anachronistic. Perry Miller placed the Massachusetts churches in an historical setting when he drew a crucial distinction between the separatist congregation which settled in Plymouth in 1620, and the non-separating communities established at Salem and Boston a decade later. The colonists at Plymouth were in schism with the Anglican church, having left England to reside in Holland before setting out for North America. Those in Massachusetts Bay, by contrast, claimed to be still in communion with the Church of England.[13]

Though the distinction seems academic now, the settlers in the Bay took it seriously. One of their many objections to Roger Williams was that he denounced them for communicating with Anglicans, and called upon them to repudiate the Church of England. Not surprisingly he was more welcome, at least initially, in Plymouth than in Boston. Roger Williams (c.1604–83) was yet another Cambridge man who migrated to New England. From his arrival in 1631 until his banishment to Rhode Island in 1635 he was a thorn in the flesh of the visible saints. His typological interpretation of Scripture led him to reject the notion that they were in a covenant of grace with God. He also denied that they could enforce conformity upon those they regarded as being unregenerate. This was the main charge brought against him for which he was banished.[14] The

[12] David D. Hall, *The Faithful Shepherd: A History of the New England Ministry in the Seventeenth Century* (Chapel Hill, NC, 1972), 113.

[13] Perry Miller, *Orthodoxy* (see Further Reading).

[14] For Williams see Perry Miller, *Roger Williams: His Contribution to the American Tradition* (New York, 1953), and E. S. Morgan, *Roger Williams: The State and the Church* (New York, 1967).

Congregationalists, who suppressed nonconformity far more ruthlessly than Laud ever did, claimed the authority of Calvin for their actions. This prompted Williams to reply that respect for Calvin as a great theologian did not necessitate slavish subscription to his intolerance.[15] Williams's plea for toleration was, however, lost on the rulers of Massachusetts, who resisted the arrival of the Quakers in the 1650s with draconian legislation, including the death penalty for defying a sentence of banishment. Puritans in New England thus retained their integrity against 'innovations in religion' from whatever source they came.

In Massachusetts they realized the ideal of the gathered church. By 1636 church membership there was restricted to 'visible saints' who covenanted with one another to form a congregation. Only those who could provide convincing evidence of having 'saving faith' were admitted to full communion. During the 1630s applicants were interviewed by the gathered church in a body: pastors, elders, and brethren. Thereafter, however, they tended to be scrutinized by the ministers alone.

There were not wanting critics of this exclusiveness. Thomas Hooker objected to its strictness, and relaxed the requirement in Connecticut. Applicants for church membership in the Valley were not subject to the same severe scrutiny as they were in the Bay. Nevertheless 'Presbyterians' such as John Noyes and Thomas Parker in Massachusetts, and John Watman in Connecticut, accused their congregationalist colleagues of hypocrisy in seeking evidence of saving faith, and admitted all but notorious sinners to church membership.[16] They received support from fellow Presbyterians in England who rose to power after the first civil war. It was partly to answer such critics in Massachusetts and England that the Cambridge synod was convened in 1646. By the time the Cambridge Platform had been constructed in 1648, however, the triumph of the New Model Army had brought more sympathetic men to the fore in England, so that the restrictive nature of admission to full communion in Massachusetts was not questioned from the mother country again until after the Restoration. Meanwhile John Davenport had implemented an even more stringent test of eligibility in New Haven after its foundation in 1639. That colony, unlike Connecticut, fully endorsed the Cambridge Platform's reaffirmation of the requirement for evidence of saving faith.

The requirement was deterrent enough to ensure that church membership became confined to a minority of the inhabitants of New England, perhaps only 20 per cent, by the second generation. This caused problems, for while the children of 'visible saints' were regarded as covenanted church

---

[15] G. Spini, 'Remarques sur la Réforme française dans l'historiographie puritaine de la Nouvelle Angleterre', in P. Joutard (ed.), *Historiographie de la Réforme* (Paris, 1977), 103.

[16] For the disputes between Congregationalists and 'Presbyterians' in Connecticut see Paul R. Lucas, *Valley of Discord: Church and Society along the Connecticut River, 1636–1725* (Hanover, NH, 1976).

members, their baptisms being seals of their subscription to the covenant, they could not become full members until they had experienced regeneration. What, then, was the status of their children, the grand-children of the original settlers, to be?

As early as 1648 Richard Mather tried to get a proposal incorporated in the Cambridge Platform that children of unregenerate church members should at least be baptized, but this was defeated. Nevertheless this proposal, known as the Half Way Covenant, was gradually adopted as the solution to the problem. In 1662 a synod convened by the General Court of Massachusetts sanctioned this process, which several churches had already adopted. It ruled 'that church members who were admitted in minority, understanding the Doctrine of faith, and publicly professing their assent thereto; not scandalous in life, and solemnly owning the covenant before the church, wherein they give up themselves and their children to the Lord, and subject themselves to the Government of Christ in the Church, their children are to be baptized.' The synod's rulings were not, however, accepted by Connecticut, while several ministers in Massachusetts resisted them. Since the recommendations of New England synods were advisory rather than mandatory, it took some time for the Half Way Covenant to be widely practised.[17]

The various synods which met to thrash out doctrines were not the apex of a system of consistories, presbyteries, and colloquies such as Calvinist churches in Europe established. On the contrary, there were no consistories or provincial synods in seventeenth-century New England. There were some meetings of ministers in district associations during the first few decades in Massachusetts, but these were discontinued, probably because, as Winthrop noted, they were objected to 'as fearing it might grow in time to a presbytery'.[18]

Towards the end of the seventeenth century, however, many clergymen though it desirable to re-establish such associations. They were concerned that the clergy seemed to have less authority than they had exercised in the first years of settlement, and were anxious to reassert it. Not that New England was ever a theocracy in the sense of being ruled by its preachers. At the local level the General Court, comprising Governor, Deputy Governor, assistants, and elected deputies, was composed of laymen. Church and state were not altogether separate in Massachusetts and New Haven, since the franchise for voting in provincial elections was restricted to church members, dominion being thus founded in grace. Nevertheless this did not give the clergy special leverage in the state.

Indeed, as far as settling religious disputes was concerned, the state tended to take the lead. Synods were convened by the General Court, and not by the General Convention of ministers, which usually met simultan-

---

[17] Robert G. Pope, *The Half Way Covenant* (Princeton, NJ, 1969).   [18] Walker, 469.

eously with the Court's annual session. The first synod to be held, that which resolved the Antinomian controversy, was to some extent more the product of a struggle for power between lay politicians than of a contention between ministers. Anne Hutchinson's cause was assisted in the short run from having the support of the younger Henry Vane, who was elected as Governor in 1635. But in the long run she suffered when the colony dropped Vane in 1637 and elected in his place John Winthrop, who was violently opposed to both of them. Vane (1615–60), the son of Sir Henry Vane, an office-holder and secretary of state, was only twenty when the freemen chose him for their Governor. At first they were delighted to have the son of an English Privy Councillor as their leader. But their delight turned to dismay when he took up the Antinomian cause, even going so far 'as to maintain a personal union with the Holy Ghost'. Among the most shocked was John Winthrop (1588–1649), founder of Massachusetts Bay, himself a former country gentleman in Suffolk and official in the Court of Wards. He stood against Vane in the gubernatorial elections of 1637, determined to assert Congregationalist orthodoxy in the state as well as in the Church.

Yet as long as church membership remained the basis of the provincial franchise, the church could scarcely feel subordinate to the state. When a new charter was issued to Massachusetts in 1691, however, replacing the old one revoked in 1684, the right to vote in colonial elections was vested not in a religious but in an economic qualification, the ownership of a freehold worth forty shillings a year. Meanwhile New Haven had been incorporated into Connecticut, which had never confined the vote to church members. These changes alarmed some clergymen, who considered them a blow to the authority of the church in New England. Other developments in these years also caused them concern. They detected declension from the standards set by the first generation, as Mammon came to dispute with God for the worship of the colonists. They were shaken by the outbreak of witchcraft at Salem in 1692, regarding it as a 'visitation from Hell'. They were dismayed by the vigorous attempts to introduce Episcopacy during the 1680s. They were more disturbed still when some of their own number, notably Thomas Brattle and Solomon Stoddard, showed signs of being influenced by Presbyterian and even episcopal notions.

Feeling that the New England Way was in danger, they revived the local associations of clergymen shortly after the Glorious Revolution. When Brattle set up a church in Boston in 1698, and appointed a minister who had been ordained in England, without seeking the advice of other churches, the self-appointed guardians of orthodoxy decided that the time had come to make a stand. In 1701 Increase Mather published his *Order of the Gospel*, challenging the recent developments as a threat to Congregationalism:

If we espouse such principles as these, namely that churches are not to enquire into the regeneration of those whom they admit unto their communion; that admission to sacraments is to be left wholly to the prudence and conscience of the minister; that explicit covenanting with God and with the Church is needless; that persons not qualified for communion in special ordinances shall elect pastors of churches; that all professed Christians have right to baptism; that brethren are to have no voice in Ecclesiastical Councils; that the essence of a minister's call is not in the election of the people, but in the ceremony of imposing hands; that persons may be established in the pastoral office without the approbation of neighbouring churches or elders, We then give away the whole Congregational cause at once . . .

To preserve 'the Congregational cause' the General Convention of ministers at their meeting in 1704 issued a circular letter to churches, urging their pastors to discourse with young members of their congregations 'to win their consent unto the covenant of grace, in all the glorious articles of it'. This received the approval of local associations, which agreed to consociate for the support of traditional practices. The outcome was the promulgation of proposals in 1705 for formal machinery to monitor orthodoxy in individual churches. Although they were approved by the General Convention in 1706 they failed to obtain the approval of the General Court, largely because of the opposition of the Governor. Where under the old Massachusetts charter Governors had been elected, by the new one they were royal appointees. In Anne's reign the Governorship was held by Joseph Dudley, a staunch Anglican and avowed enemy of Congregationalism.

Similar proposals were more successful in Connecticut. There the Governors were still elected, and in 1707 the colony made the rare choice of a Congregational minister, Gurdon Saltonstall. He gave his approval to the convening of a synod at Saybrook. When it met in 1708 the synod adopted articles for the administration of church discipline which were incorporated in the Saybrook Platform. Among its resolutions were provisions for the establishment of consociations of churches and Councils of elders, to determine disputes within churches, which had been particularly bitter in Connecticut, and to censure those which did not accept their decisions. The ultimate penalty was that of non-communion, which fell just short of excommunication, a sentence anathema to Congregationalists as being a violation of the autonomy of individual churches. The Saybrook Platform nevertheless went further in encroaching on that autonomy than any previous synod. The General Court expressed its approval of the synod's proceedings by authorizing their publication in 1710, and by distributing them throughout Connecticut in 1714.[19]

Supporters of the Saybrook Platform were clearly convinced that it was necessary in order to re-establish contact with the rising generation, with whom the churches were allegedly losing touch. This begs the question of the social impact of Calvinism on colonial New England.

[19] Ibid. 478–523; Lucas, 169–187.

In turn this presents a major methodological problem. Perry Miller inspired a whole generation of historians to study the intellectual history of Puritanism. Since 1960 there has also been a considerable amount of research into the social history of New England, influenced by the French *Annales* school.[20] By and large these investigations have been conducted independently, along parallel rather than converging lines. The upshot is that there is one set of monographs analysing Puritan thought, and another reconstructing social realities, concerning such diverse topics as the family, social structure, urban development, and economic change. Those writing in the Miller tradition tend to assume, as he himself did, that Puritan ideology was so all-pervasive that the history of New England society in the seventeenth century could be written from the diaries, pamphlets, and sermons inspired by it. The new social historians, by contrast, basing their conclusions on quantifiable sources, are more inclined to assume that Puritanism had relatively little impact on most colonists outside a predominantly clerical élite. There were, after all, some 93,000 people in New England by 1700, of whom perhaps only a fifth were church members. Many if not most of the rest possibly shared the attitudes of those who settled North-East of Boston, as recorded by Cotton Mather.[21]

I have heard that one of our ministers once preaching to a congregation there, urged them to approve themselves a religious people from this consideration, that otherwise they would contradict the main end of planting this wilderness; whereupon a well-known person, then in the Assembly, cry'd out, Sir, you are mistaken, you think you are preaching to the people at the Bay; our main end was to catch fish.

Since the history of the impact of Calvinism on New England society has yet to be written, it would be rash in this essay to go far beyond puritan attempts to regulate social activity. Certainly they tried to exercise control over all aspects of life, however far short of success their efforts came.

Because they were instrumental in creating a new society in the wilderness, the Puritans were in a unique position to draw up a blueprint of how they wanted that society to develop. And because they have too often been seen as the pioneers not only of New England but also of the American way of life, that blueprint has persistently been misrepresented. It was not, for instance, a design for democracy, liberty, or capitalism.

The men who settled Plymouth and Massachusetts were no democrats. John Winthrop, while aboard the *Arbella* en route for America, preached a celebrated lay sermon in which he emphasized the importance of the social

[20] For a survey of the 'new history of the early modern era' see Jack P. Greene and J. R. Pole (eds.), *Colonial British America* (London, 1984).
[21] *Magnalia*; For a recent discussion of the relationship between Puritan ideas and New England society see the essays by George Selement, David D. Hall, and Darrett B. Rutman in *William and Mary Quarterly* 41 (1984), 32–61.

hierarchy: 'God Almighty in his most holy and wise providence, hath so disposed of the condition of mankind, as in all times some must be rich, some poor; some high and eminent in power and dignity; others mean and in submission.' When lots were allocated in the nascent townships of the new colonies they were not equal, but differed in size according to the status of the colonists concerned. As we have seen, participation in political life was restricted in Massachusetts to church members. Even in Connecticut, where the restriction was not adopted, the franchise was vested in a property qualification, and not given to all adult males.

Nor were the upholders of orthodoxy noted for their libertarian views. On the contrary, they upheld it to the point of rigorously suppressing deviations from it. In this respect they came to be out of step with co-religionists in England. When the Independents rose to power under Cromwell they tolerated Presbyterians, Baptists, Fifth Monarchists, Quakers, indeed any group which was not held to be a threat to the regime. Religious toleration came much later in New England, and then it was largely imposed from outside.

It could be argued that the Puritans who went to North America remained locked in a sixteenth-century mentality in other respects, too. So far from being at the cutting edge of economic change in England, the bourgeois vanguard of a capitalist revolution, they can be seen as social reactionaries, who, disliking trends in English society, fled across the Atlantic to preserve traditional ways of life. Thus, though many were craftsmen and tradesmen before they left, they adapted themselves to a mainly agricultural economy upon their arrival. Preachers upheld the virtues of rural life and criticized the growth of commerce. They also attacked usury, and the courts supported them. In 1639 the General Court fined Robert Keayne, a Boston merchant, £200 for making excessive profits. John Cotton tried to persuade the church to add the spiritual penalty of excommunication to the fine, while another clergyman demanded a law to make such extortion a capital offence.

Yet, as Stephen Foster has argued, it would be much too easy 'to develop from this case an irrepressible conflict between the 'medieval' oligarchy of magistrates and ministers, who prized piety, stability, and order, and a 'modern' class of merchant capitalists, who valued mobility and material acquisition'. Keayne had been making between 50 and 100 per cent profit, which it did not take a Puritan preacher to denounce as excessive. Moreover in his attack on usury Cotton accepted the notion of a just price. Although he castigated covetousness, he accepted that prosperity in secular affairs could be a sign of an effectual calling. 'Looke at thy wordly business, art thou diligent in thy calling', he wrote, 'it is well, and you say, cursed is he that doth the work of the Lord negligently, and work of his calling, is the worke of the Lord'. Cotton Mather's *A Christian at his Calling* emphasized the same point, as did Samuel Willard, (1640–1707), president of Harvard College in Anne's reign, when he wrote '*riches* are consistent with *godliness*, and the more a man hath the more advantage he hath to do good with it, if God give him an heart to it'. Where the condemnation of covetousness was inimical to the development of capitalism, the advocacy of diligence in business as a sign of effectual calling was consistent with the Weberian Protestant ethic. As Foster concludes 'much of what Weber theorized does help to explain the development of New England and the true nature of the peculiar tension that inhered in Puritan economic life.'[22]

Among the developments apparently eroding traditional society which troubled those who emigrated from England was the growth in the numbers of landless labourers and masterless men, which threatened social order. As Larzer Ziff puts it[23]

Puritanism emerged as a way of coping with the threatening conditions of masterlessness and landlessness in sixteenth century England. In developing responses to these conditions that would enable men to make something of themselves, the Puritans developed a particular way of living the common life and developed a pattern of reaction to the problems they confronted in their daily reality.

Landlessness virtually ceased to be a problem with the unlimited resources initially available in North America. Not that all New Englanders became farmers. There was plenty of scope for fishing and fur trapping even at the time of the first settlements, while the development of the colonies, together with the rapid growth of Boston, created demand and opportunities for tradesmen and merchants. Nevertheless New England remained overwhelmingly agricultural, and landownership was significantly more widespread there than in the mother-country.

Indeed the abundance of space for expansion on the apparently limitless frontier has been seen as posing a new challenge, the problem of maintaining shared values in a potentially widely diffused population. One answer to this alleged problem has been perceived in the provision of a system of public education to inculcate and preserve the puritan ideal in the wilderness. Whether or not the colonists did regard the frontier as a threat to be contained by education is debatable, but that an educational system was rapidly established cannot be denied.[24] The foundation of Harvard College in 1636 ensured the steady recruitment of an educated clergy which, as we shall see, gave Calvinists in Massachusetts and adjacent colonies a considerable advantage over their brethren elsewhere in North America. By

---

[22] Stephen Foster, *Their Solitary Way: The Puritan Social Ethic in the first century of settlement in New England* (New Haven, 1971), 99–126.

[23] Larzer Ziff, *Puritanism in America* (London, 1973), p. x.

[24] B. Bailyn, *Education in the Forming of American Society* (New York, 1972); K. E. Lockridge, *Literacy in Colonial New England* (New York, 1974), 103–8.

the time Yale was founded in the 1701 New England had provision for University education comparable with any in the Old World. Meanwhile it had also developed a secondary school system second to none.

A solution to the question of masterlessness was found in the enforcement of subordination to the head of a family. Strictly speaking unmarried people were not allowed to live alone, but either had to establish a household with servants of their own, or lodge with a family.

The family, indeed, was held to be the foundation of social order in New England. 'Well-ordered families', according to Cotton Mather, 'naturally produce a good order in other societies.' As in England the family embraced all members of the household, servants as well as kin: not as in the mother country, in New England it also included slaves. Although blacks never became more than 3 per cent of the population, unlike parts of the South where they formed a majority, chattel slavery was by no means unknown in the puritan commonwealth. Nor was racial prejudice.

In 1705 an Act was passed in Massachusetts 'for the better preventing of a spurious and mixt issue' prohibiting sexual relations between the races. Other forms of prejudice could be more subtle. One slave complained that his master called him Cotton Mather 'designing to put an indignity upon me'. Yet there was not the same degree of legal discrimination as existed in the slave codes of southern colonies. 'In general the negro held the rights of Englishmen before the courts. The legal apparatus did not undergo subtle shifts when negroes came before it'.[25]

Legislation was probably the most effective way by which the Puritans tried to enforce their ideology on New England society. In 1648 the laws of Massachusetts were incorporated into a legal code. 'The first compilation of its kind in the English-speaking world', as G. L. Haskins observes, it 'stands as a monument to the elements of tradition and design from which the early law of Massachusetts was fashioned.' Where it has sometimes been assumed that the code was based on the Bible, and especially on the Pentateuch, Haskins stresses that it drew on the traditions of English customary and common law. Nevertheless there was a strong emphasis on biblical authority too. Thus capital punishment was prescribed for blasphemy, idolatry, cursing or smiting of parents, and reviling of magistrates. The death penalty was also imposed for such moral offences as adultery, bestiality, incest, rape, and sodomy.[26] As there was no distinction between sin and crime in colonial New England, offenders in cases of this kind were tried by church as well as by secular courts. Indeed they were more likely to be excommunicated than executed, though some adulterers were hanged,

[25] R. C. Twombly and Robert H. Moore, 'Black Puritan: The Negro in seventeenth-century Massachusetts', *William and Mary Quarterly* 24 (1967), 224–42.
[26] G. L. Haskins, *Law and Authority in Early Massachusetts: a Study in Tradition and Design* (New York, 1960), 2 and *passim*.

while one Potter was put to death in New Haven in 1662 along with 'a cow, two heifers, three sheep and two sows, with all of which he had committed his brutalities.'[27]

Lesser sins, like drunkenness and swearing, were punished by public confession in church, and by fines in the lay courts. In 1675 a specific office of tithingman was established in Massachusetts to enforce sobriety. Each was to 'take the charge of ten or twelve families of his neighbourhood' and report any offences against the drink laws. In 1677 their authority was extended to control Sunday drinking.[28]

Not that the puritans were opposed to the consumption of alcohol in itself, merely to the abuse of it. They were not the killjoys of legend. As Edmund Morgan puts it:[29]

Contrary to popular impression the Puritan was no ascetic. If he continually warned against the vanity of the creatures as misused by fallen man, he never praised hair shirts or dry crusts. He liked good food, good drink and homely comforts; and while he laughed at mosquitoes, he found it a real hardship to drink water when the beer gave out.

The one exception which they made to the general acceptance of alcoholic beverages was that they did not allow them to be sold to Indians. This was because their legendary low tolerance to alcohol produced alarming drunken behaviour in native North Americans. At least it alarmed the Puritan, though whether he considered that drink extinguished reason or revealed diabolical possession it is difficult to decide.[30]

That some puritans originally held the Indians to be children of God and capable of salvation is clear from the stated objective of the Massachusetts Bay Company that its 'principal end' was to 'win and incite the natives . . . to the knowledge and obedience of the only true God and Saviour of mankind, and the Christian faith'. The Great Seal of the General Court depicted a scantily clad native with the words 'come over and help us' issuing from his lips. Some missionaries went over to convert them, and were particularly successful on the islands of Martha's Vineyard and Nantucket. On the mainland, however, more modest efforts met with a meagre reward. Indeed several 'converts' joined their fellow Indians to fight the white colonists when King Philip's War broke out in 1675.

The barbarities committed by both sides in this and the earlier Pequot war of 1636 confirmed the view held by many if not most Puritans that the

[27] E. Oberholzer Jr., *Delinquent Saints: Disciplinary Action in the Early Congregational Churches of Massachusetts* (New York, 1968), 127–51; Cotton Mather, *Magnalia*, ii. 406.

[28] Morgan, *The Puritan Family* (Boston, 1966), 148–9.

[29] Ibid. 16: see also Hans-Peter Wagner, *Puritan Attitudes towards Recreation in Early New England* (Frankfurt am Main, 1982).

[30] William S. Simmons, 'Cultural Bias in the New England Puritans' Perception of Indians', *William and Mary Quarterly* 38 (1981), 56–72.

natives of North America were inhuman savages. Few were more outspoken than Cotton Mather, who introduced his discussion of wars with 'the Indian salvages' by observing:[31]

These parts were then [1636] covered with nations of barbarous Indians and infidels, in whom the 'prince of the power of the air' did 'work in a spirit'; nor could it be expected that nations of wretches, whose whole religion was the most explicit sort of devil-worship, should not be acted by the devil to engage in some early and bloody action, for the extinction of a plantation so contrary to his interests, as that of New England was.

In Mather's view the colonists and natives were cast as actors in a gigantic struggle of good against evil. God's providence was working in the wilderness, testing his chosen people by many trials and vicissitudes. Parallels with the biblical story of the children of Israel were consciously drawn. Among the afflictions which the elect had to endure in North America were the Indians. God cleared the way for the colonists by wiping out the natives of the coastal region with disease before the great migration from England took place. He also ensured that the Puritans triumphed in the Pequot and King Philip's wars. At the same time these were providential warnings to the colonists that they were falling from grace.

Over the seventeenth century a significant change took place in the nature of events which preachers cited as afflicting providences. In the early decades of colonization they took the form of external threats; Indian raids, adverse weather conditions, harvest failures, outbreaks of sickness. These culminated in the devastating Indian attacks of 1675–6 known as King Philip's War, a godsend for Jeremiahs. By the third generation, however, they were increasingly concerned with failings in the colonists themselves; apostasy, declension, luxury. These secular themes illustrate the growing fear that by 1700 Calvinism was losing its mission in New England.

By contrast with the Puritans, the Dutch did not look to America to fulfil ideological or religious dreams. They enjoyed sufficient religious liberty at home not to need a refuge overseas, and the promoters of New Netherland were no Winthrops trying to establish a city upon a hill. Earliest Dutch activity in the Hudson river valley was motivated by the desire for quick profts from furs, and even when the Dutch West India Company ousted these freebooters in 1621 and established a monopoly in the region, furs were still their primary interest. The first permanent settlement at Fort Orange, later Albany, far up the Hudson river, was intended to open up the fur trade of the interior, while the village established in 1626 on the lower tip of Manhattan island was to serve as a shipping centre and headquarters for the colony. The whole enterprise was only a tiny fraction of the West India Company's operations, and an unprofitable fraction at that. By 1629,

[31] *Magnalia*, ii. 552.

the Company had switched to promoting colonization, but it jealously guarded its trading monopoly, and vacillated between concentrating on the fur trade and developing the agricultural potential of the region. Few Dutch could be persuaded to leave their prosperous farms and workshops in the most advanced economy in Europe for the uncertain and harsh existence of pioneering. Even the Company's officials were men of poor quality, quarrelsome and drunken, and little good came of the abandonment of the Company's trading monopoly in 1638. Profit-seeking private merchants, and the slow but threatening advance of Dutch farms provoked the Indians into raid after raid until by 1650 there were barely four thousand people in the impoverished colony. The New England settlements to the north, which then numbered 23,000 inhabitants, encroached on territory claimed by the Dutch, while both French and English competed for the fur trade. Moreover, the majority of the settlers drawn to New Netherland were not Dutch but Walloons, Germans, Jews, Scandinavians and dissenting English from Connecticut drawn by the generous land grants offered by the West India Company. In this unstable world the early representatives of the Reformed Church faced massive difficulties.[32]

Yet in contrast to the traders and settlers, Reformed ministers, frustrated in their attempts to establish a religious monopoly at home, hoped to develop an ideal Calvinist society in the New World. The West India Company agreed to appoint only Reformed clergy in their settlement, and shortly after the founding of New Netherland sought suitable chaplains. Unfortunately the rapidly growing Dutch overseas empire created a demand for clergy which far outstripped the supply. In the Netherlands itself, there was already a shortage of good ministers, and few men of talent were willing to volunteer for service overseas. The Reformed Church, therefore, relied heavily on *ziekentroosters* (visitor of the sick), lay officials who read prayers, chapters from the Bible, and the occasional sermon from an approved book. Although not permitted to minister the Lord's Supper, they were allowed by special permission to baptize and perform marriages. One high ranking Dutch colonial official called these *ziekentroosters* 'clownish, uncircumcised idiots', and while he wildly exaggerated, many of these men were from humble backgrounds and poorly educated.[33] It was only men of this type that the Reformed Church could initially find to go to New Netherland. Two *ziekentroosters* were sent out, but their religious work was very limited. One man, Bastiaen Jansz. Krol, a barely literate former silk worker arrived in the spring of 1624, but gradually saw other

[32] Thomas J. Condon, *New York Beginnings: The Commercial Origins of New Netherland* (New York, 1968); Van Cleaf Bachman, *Peltries or Plantations: The Dutch West India Company in New Netherland, 1623–1639* (Baltimore, Md., 1969).
[33] George L. Smith, *Religion and Trade in New Netherland: Dutch Origins and American Development* (Ithaca, NY, 1973), 77, 160–8.

openings for his talents than the lay ministry. By 1626 Krol was storekeeper at the Company's post at Fort Orange, and he went on to manage one of the first large land grants and act as temporary director-general of the colony. Krol saw little prospect in New Netherland of establishing an ideal Reformed society, but he showed a ready talent for getting ahead in a rough pioneering world.[34]

The first minister in the colony, Jonas Michaelis, was a man of different education and outlook from Krol. A university graduate, Michaelis was an ultra-Calvinist, who supported Reformist hardliners against the Dutch policy of religious tolerance. He arrived in Manhattan in the spring of 1628 with two small daughters, having lost his wife on the voyage, and was shocked by what he found. Michaelis hoped for a large and stable agricultural population amongst whom he could establish the elaborate governmental apparatus of the Reformed Church. He had clear views of what constituted proper spheres of authority for church and state, but his plans seemed irrelevant in a hard-pressed trading-post of 200 people, where serious farming had hardly begun. Even those few people were divided between Dutch- and French-speakers with many regarding the colony as only a temporary location. There was surprise that an attempt was being made to organize a church, and the busy director-general had little time for a dreamer like Michaelis, who complained of poor and scanty food and lack of servants. Ignored and disillusioned, he returned to Holland in 1632.[35]

His successor, Everardus Bogardus, stayed much longer in America, but did little more. A former *ziekentrooster*, who had served in Guinea, he was ordained for the ministry although never completing a university education. Very conscious of his status and anxious to assert the authority of his office, he clashed with Director-general Twiller and his successor, Kieft, neither of whom could cope with the problems besetting the colony. Bogardus preached ferocious sermons comparing Twiller unfavourably with his goats and Kieft with an African monster. They responded by disrupting religious services, calling Bogardus a drunkard and accusing him of stirring the people to mutiny and rebellion. Indian attacks were weakening the colony and destroying the Reformed Church's dream of a successful mission to the native population. Settlers of many nationalities and religions attracted by business prospects or land grants showed little cohesion. By 1647 the West India Company resolved to make a new start, and Kieft was dismissed. It was perhaps ironic that he and Bogardus, having been locked in combat for so long, were drowned in the wreck of the same ship while returning to the Netherlands. Although other Reformed ministers remained in the colony, the Reformed Church was no nearer to

[34] Ibid. 160–1; Gerald F. De Jong, *The Dutch in America, 1609–1974* (Boston, Mass., 1975), 88.
[35] *Narratives of New Netherland, 1609–1664*, ed. J. Franklin Jameson (Boston, Mass., 1909), 119–33; Smith, *Religion and Trade*, 162–7.

establishing a stable Calvinist society, after twenty years of work, than the West India Company was to striking a successful balance between fur trading and farming.[36]

Between 1647 and 1663, when he surrendered to the British, Peter Stuyvesant came close to fulfilling the plans of the Company. He established a successful colony in which agriculture was well established and order maintained. In that work, Stuyvesant gave sympathy and practical support to the Reformed faith, which he saw as a major ally in his bid to develop a more unified society. The special position granted to the Reformed Church in the colony from the beginning was formally confirmed as early as 1640. The relevant section of the charter reads:

No other Religion shall be publically admitted to New Netherland except the Reformed, as it is at present preached and practised by the public authority in the United Netherlands; and for this purpose the Company shall provide and maintain good and suitable preachers, schoolmasters, and comforters of the sick.[37]

Exception was made for English Calvinists, both Congregational and Presbyterian, who often came as organized groups from New England, settling on Long Island and other areas. They were allowed to elect their own magistrates and levy town rates for the support of their ministers and churches. Church attendance was compulsory in their communities on the basis of local laws confirmed by Stuyvesant. He also issued general moral codes for the colony, attacking Sabbath-breaking and drunkenness. The Reformed Church was given additional financial aid when income from tithes proved inadequate. Ministers like Johannes Megapolensis, who served in the colony from 1643 until his death in 1673, and Samuel Drisius, who could preach in Dutch, French, and English, were men of greater talent and adaptability than Michaelis and Bogardus.[38] Pastors remained in short supply, however, even at the end of the century, when the Reformed Church had only six ministers, although the number of congregations had increased to twenty-three. There were few likely candidates in America and they faced the cost and hazard of returning to Europe for ordination. The reluctance of Dutch ministers to leave the Netherlands remained high.[39]

In New Netherland, the Reformed Church placed the same emphasis on creeds and doctrine as at home. Attention was especially given to the decrees of the Synod of Dort of 1618/19, which had taken an uncompromising stand against Arminianism. The Heidelberg Catechism was used as a statement of

[36] Jameson, *Narratives*, 186–7, 320–37; Smith, *Religion and Trade*, 168–73; Allen W. Trelease, *Indian Affairs in Colonial New York: The Seventeenth Century* (Ithaca, NY, 1960).

[37] John W. Pratt, *Religion, Politics and Diversity: The Church-State Theme in New York History* (Ithaca NY, 1967), 11; Smith, *Religion and Trade*, 179–89.

[38] *Ecclesiastical Records, State of New York*, ed. Hugh Hastings (Albany, NY), i. 192, 334–562; De Jong, *The Dutch in America*, 88–9.

[39] De Jong, *The Dutch in America*, 92–6.

Calvinist orthodoxy, and its tenets were taught children before they became communicant members of the Church. Worship consisted of Scripture-reading, prayers, psalm-singing, and a sermon, of which the last was the most important.[40] In New Amsterdam, Fort Orange, and a few other centres, stone or well-built wooden churches existed, but many of the smaller farming communities held occasional services in private homes and barns. Although the Reformed Church, like New Netherland itself, improved dramatically under Stuyvesant's capable rule, neither he nor his ministerial allies were able to establish the Calvinist monopoly of religious faith which the law called for. Megapolensis bemoaned the presence of Jews, who had 'no other God than the Mammon of unrighteousness', and urged that 'these godless rascals' be sent away. He and his Reformed colleagues attacked Quaker shoemaker-preachers, together with the Lutherans and the 'wild, drunken, unmannerly clown' who administered to them. Even many of the New England Congregationalists, who had moved into Dutch territory, were viewed with suspicion as irregularly trained or ordained. Only their fellow Presbyterians amongst the English on Long Island were regarded as pious, learned, and godly.[41]

Stuyvesant tried hard to suppress religious dissent. The Lutherans in New Amsterdam were prevented from retaining their minister, who was expelled from the colony. Quakers were also driven away, and village officials fined for allowing them to preach.[42] This policy, however, ran contrary to the tolerant practices of the Netherlands, and more importantly, it directly opposed the efforts of the West India Company to attract settlers to the colony, which had become more important to the Company's fortunes by the 1650s with the loss of Brazil and commercial problems in Europe. Without a larger population and agricultural staples as an alternative to the fur trade, New Netherland had little prospect of surviving. In 1661 the Company issued an appeal to religious dissenters in England urging them to settle in New Netherland, promising that 'they shall have full liberty to live in fear of the Lord . . . and shall be likewise courteously used'. Two years later, on the eve of the first English conquest, the Company wrote to Stuyvesant condemning his expulsion of Quakers and other sectarians:

. . . We doubt very much whether we can proceed against them rigorously without diminishing the population and stopping immigration which must be favoured at a so tender stage of the country's existence. You may therefore shut your eyes, at least not force people's consciences, but allow every one to have his own belief, so long as he behaves quietly and legally, gives no offence to his neighbours, and does not oppose the government'[43]

[40] Ibid. 92–3.   [41] Jameson, *Narratives*, 392–400.
    [42] Pratt, *Religion, Politics and Diversity*, 18–21; Harry J. Kreider, *Lutheranism in Colonial New York* (New York, 1942), 14–21.
    [43] *Ecclesiastical Records*, i. 530; Smith, *Religion and Trade*, 230–5.

After the conquest, the English authorities accepted and extended this policy, granting the Lutherans, for example, the right to have ordained ministers. The Reformed Church was also guaranteed religious freedom, although it faced competition from an Anglican establishment from 1695. This created few difficulties until the administration of the eccentric and overbearing Lord Cornbury, who attempted to subordinate all denominations to an enlarged Anglican Church. The Reformed Church had long followed the policy of seeking approval of the appointment of new ministers, which had never been refused until Cornbury's regime. The governor even attempted to introduce an Anglican minister into the vacant Reformed church at Kingston, NY. The Dutch were outraged, and pointed out to Cornbury that he was acting contrary to English policy since the capitulation of 1663. The Kingston church acquired a Reformed pastor from the Netherlands, whom Cornbury refused to license. This produced a crisis in which leaders of the Dutch community made plain their total opposition to this policy. Cornbury backed down but failed to win Dutch support because of his continued persecution of Presbyterians. By 1709 his policies were so discredited that his opponents, including the Dutch, brought about his downfall.[44]

Apart from the Cornbury regime, the Reformed Church faced few political problems. Ministering to prosperous farmers and merchants in Manhattan, Long Island, the Hudson river valley, and adjacent areas of New Jersey, it remained rigidly Calvinist and set in its ways. All respectable adults were admitted to communion and the Church became identified with the maintenance of Dutch language and culture. Still linked to the *classis* of Amsterdam, and totally dependent on Holland for ministers, the Church was scarcely able to provide clergy for newer settlements like the Raritan Valley, where Dutch farmers received communion from Presbyterians in a language they could only half understand.[45] Reformed ministers opposed all Pietists, whether they came from Rhode Island ('the sewer of New England'), or the Netherlands. In 1685 the minister, Henricus Selyns complained to the *classis* of Amsterdam about tailors, cobblers, and others who were coming from Holland and endeavouring to be appointed as lay readers and schoolteachers:

They speak against the church, public prayers, and the liturgy of the church. True believers are grieved at these things and look forward to very great trouble therefrom to the church of God.[46]

The most important of these lay readers, whose position was very similar to that of the *ziekentrooster* in early New Netherland, was William Bartholf.

[44] Pratt, *Religion, Politics and Diversity*, 49–58; *Ecclesiastical Records*, iii. 1574–672.

[45] Jacob Tanis, *Dutch Calvinistic Pietism in the Middle Colonies: A Study of the Life and Theology of Theodorus Jacobus Frelinghuysen* (The Hague, 1967), 42–57.

[46] *Ecclesiastical Records*, i. 400, 907–8.

Bartholf came to America about 1685 as a cooper. He settled in New Jersey, where there were no Reformed clergy, and acted as lay reader. Bartholf had been influenced by the teaching of Jacobus Koelman, the Dutch Pietist scholar, who was deeply versed in English Puritan thought. Koelman was distressed by what he saw as decline in the Reformed Church and shocked by the number of unregenerate ministers and church members. Bartholf brought these views to his teaching and was opposed by the more formalistic ministers of New York. They could not, however, block his ordination on his return to Holland or prevent him returning to America and becoming the first settled Reformed pastor in New Jersey. Bartholf had sought ordination from the *classis* of Walcheren, not Amsterdam, because he regarded more than half the ministers of the latter as unregenerate. In America, Bartholf was long viewed as a 'schismatic' or a 'restless spirit' by the ministers of New York, but his zeal and untiring labours in preaching and establishing new churches gradually won their respect as 'a very honourable and pious man'. Fortunately for the avoidance of conflict, Bartholf concentrated his efforts in New Jersey, and did not attempt to spread his views among the older churches of New York. It was left to the young Theodore Frelinghuysen in the 1720s to open the divide between seekers for a more experimental divinity and the formalist leaders of the Dutch Reformed Church in America.[47]

Although the Reformed Church in the middle colonies included French-speaking Walloon congregations, these established few links with the 2,000 Huguenot refugees who crossed the Atlantic before 1700. Coming in increasing number after the Revocation of 1685 and settling mostly in New York, South Carolina, and Massachusetts, these Huguenots did well in a rapidly expanding colonial economy, but they made little permanent contribution to the Reformed tradition in America. Lacking a national synod in France since 1659, the Huguenots showed little sense of how to organize beyond local congregations. The exiles also failed to develop a regular pattern of correspondence between churches in America and Europe, such as existed between the Dutch Church and Amsterdam. The French laity were also over-reliant on ministers, many of whom showed little taste for the hardships of America, were disreputable, or speedily advocated conformity to Anglicanism. Everywhere, as their most recent historian shows, the Huguenots were submissive to established authority, and willing to marry outside their group with a speed which quickly destroyed refugee cohesion.[48]

In Massachusetts, the Huguenots received an exceptionally warm

---

[47] Tanis, *Dutch Calvinistic Pietism*, 44–7; James Tanis, 'Reformed Pietism in Colonial America' in F. Ernest Stoeffler (ed.), *Continental Pietism and Early American Christianity* (Grand Rapids, Mich., 1976), 44–5.

[48] Jon Butler, *The Huguenots in America: A Refugee People in New World Society* (Cambridge, Mass., 1983).

welcome from fellow Calvinists who had long followed the process of Protestants' being persecuted and expelled from France. Early attempts at rural settlement quickly collapsed, and by 1700 the only substantial Huguenot community in Massachusetts was at Boston. The first two ministers serving the French congregation there were so unsatisfactory that some Huguenots began to drift into the Congregational Church. The third French minister was well regarded but soon returned to England, and it was not until 1697 that a pastor was obtained, who enjoyed a long period of service. Although Pierre Daillé was well regarded in Boston society, his salary was irregularly paid, and by the time his successor, Andrew Le Mercier, was appointed in 1716, Huguenots in the city were being assimilated into the wider community and denominational structure, most joining the Congregationalists in a colony where Anglicanism had limited appeal.[49] Le Mercier did get a small stone church built with the aid of wealthy Bostonians, and he played an active part in the religious and intellectual life of the city. A Presbyterian by conviction, he took an active part, with Ulster Scots, in organizing the Presbytery of New England in 1745. By then, however, the French religious tradition in Boston was almost dead, and Le Mercier's church closed three years later from lack of support.[50]

In South Carolina, a much larger Huguenot population established a network of French Reformed congregations served by three ministers in 1700, the largest denomination in the colony. But this was a false beginning. An increasingly assertive Anglican Church was attractive to some French ministers and lay people, who hoped to obtain financial aid, identification with political authority, and a French version of the Anglican liturgy. By 1715, some rural congregations had conformed to Anglicanism, and others disbanded. As in Boston, Huguenots in South Carolina mixed easily with the English, and marriage-records show a high level of assimilation from 1720. In Charlestown, a single French congregation continued, but it was in 'dissolution and decay' by the eve of the Revolution. Those Huguenots who became Anglicans failed to preserve a significant French influence in that Church. Not even the language survived many years. Many Huguenots joined other denominations, but also failed to carry a distinct French element into their new churches.[51]

The same pattern occurred in New York, where the government made a determined effort to press Anglicanism on the French newcomers. Huguenot ministers were compliant, and one, Élie Neu, went so far as to justify Lord Cornbury in his attack on Presbyterians. Key French churches

[49] Ibid. 71–88; Cotton Mather, *Diary* (New York, 1911), i. 134–5.

[50] Butler, 83–90; Jonathan Greenleaf, *Sketches of the Ecclesiastical History of Maine* (Portsmouth, NH, 1821), 94–5.

[51] Butler, 94–5, 107–20.

were won over to Anglicianism, even though dissenting minorities tried to preserve the Reformed tradition, either by preserving a French congregation or joining the Dutch. Some French congregations drifted slowly into Anglicanism, reflecting the high level of Huguenot assimilation that was taking place. Soon the only surviving French Reformed church was in New York city, and its minister, Louis Rou, was an Anglican sympathizer. Rou created a scandal by marrying a fourteen-year-old girl, and although his congregation survived this ordeal and drifted on until closed by the Revolution, it had ceased to play a major role in a city where there was no longer a distinct Huguenot community.[52]

New England Puritans and British Presbyterians of the early seventeenth century shared many elements of faith and practice. Their neo-Calvinism stressed election, saving grace, diligence in one's calling, and a covenant theology which, while not abandoning predestination, moderated its harshness. They recognized two sacraments, baptism and communion. They agreed on the need for an educated ministry and for all inhabitants of a parish, not just church members, to conform to a rigid moral code, not as a means of regeneration but to avoid scandalous neglect of God's law that would breach the covenant.

Where Puritans and Presbyterians disagreed was in their conception of the Church and to a lesser degree the ministry. To the Puritans, the Church of Christ on earth was essentially composed of individual, autonomous congregations, whose members had given public testimony to the work of God in their hearts. Each church heard these conversion accounts of prospective members, and while not claiming infallibility, judged whether they had received a genuine call. The Presbyterians took a broader view of the Church and favoured a more complex hierarchical structure of government with presbyteries, synods, and a general assembly above each congregation. Ministers and elders exercised disciplinary powers which in New England were the function of all male members including the minister. Among Presbyterians, applications for church membership were heard only by ministers and elders, and members probably made up a higher percentage of those attending church than in New England. Members were also admitted to the whole Church of Christ and not just to a particular congregation in the same way that ministers were ordained to the Universal Church and not just to a specific congregation as in New England.[53]

Although the majority favoured the Congregational way, early New England contained a vociferous minority who supported the Presbyterian model of the Church, and conflict was common in both Massachusetts and the Connecticut valley. Since the government of New Netherland

---

[52] Ibid. 189–197; Hastings, *Ecclesiastical Records*, iii. 1493 and *passim*; Stoeffler, *Continental Pietism*, 26–7; Boyd S. Schlenther, *Life of Makemie* (see Further Reading) 216.

[53] Leonard J. Trinterud, *Forming of an American Tradition* (see Further Reading), 16–20.

recognized Presbyterians as identical with the Dutch Reformed Church in faith and government, dissident Presbyterians from New England moved readily into Dutch territory, where land was also available. The Revd Francis Doughty, who had lived in the Netherlands and had a Dutch son-in-law, came to Massachusetts in 1637, but was forced to leave Taunton because of his advocacy of Presbyterianism. He and his followers settled on Long Island in 1642, but were driven out by the Indians. Doughty came to Manhattan, where he preached to the English and the Dutch, and later ministered to a congregation at Flushing, Long Island. Unlike Dutch Reformed ministers, Doughty was not entitled to state support, and his congregation was very tardy in paying his salary. By 1650 he was indebted to the West India company for about 1100 guilders for 'goods and necessaries of life', and although Stuyvesant tried to compel the inhabitants of Flushing to maintain their minister, they refused to honour the contract. Some time in the late 1650s Doughty left New Netherland for Maryland and Virginia, where he served for a decade as an itinerant Presbyterian minister.[54]

Another Presbyterian pioneer under Dutch auspices was Richard Denton, who came over to New England with Winthrop in 1630. After ministering in Massachusetts and Connecticut, Denton's Presbyterian views led him and his followers to leave for Long Island in 1644. The Dutch described him as 'a Presbyterian preacher . . . a pious, godly, and learned man . . . in agreement with our church in every thing'. In 1658 Denton returned to England to recover a legacy and his congregation dwindled. Many other New Englanders followed Doughty and Denton into Dutch territory, but only a minority were convinced Presbyterians. Most were seeking generous land grants or trading opportunities, and were either Congregationalist or indifferent to religion.[55] By the time of the English conquest of New Netherland, scattered Presbyterians existed in many parts of New York and New Jersey, but they lacked a regular supply of ministers and formal organization. Some congregations switched from Presbyterianism to Congregationalism and back again according to the preference of the minister available, the people being glad to have regular religious worship and showing limited interest in details of church government. The arrival of Scots and Ulstermen in the region gradually strengthened the Presbyterian element, and the same was true in Maryland and Virginia, where Doughty was joined first by an English Presbyterian minister, Matthew Hill, and later by William Traill, who was sent out by the presbytery of Laggan in Ireland in answer to an appeal from the colonies. In 1683 Traill was followed by Francis Makemie, a young minister

---

[54] Lucas, 59–70; Jameson, *Narratives*, 334–5, 343, 366–8, 397–401; Trinterud, *Forming of an American Tradition*, 26.
[55] Jameson, *Narratives*, 397, 401; Trinterud, *Forming of an American Tradition*, 22–3.

from Ireland, who became the best-known of the founders of American Presbyterianism.[56]

Makemie itinerated from North Carolina to New York, and opened up a friendly correspondence with Increase Mather and other New Englanders. By the early eighteenth century with the move toward consociation in Massachusetts and the Saybrook Platform in Connecticut, Congregationalism was shifting closer to the Presbyterian model. Makemie was aware of a similar movement in England, and returning to London gained the support of the United Brethren, a joint Congregationalist-Presbyterian committee, which was later to provide financial aid and ministers for the infant Presbyterian cause in America. A fierce controversialist, Makemie constantly defended Calvinist orthodoxy against Quakers, Papists and other critics. Like many early Presbyterian ministers, the financial limitations of pioneer congregations also forced Makemie into business enterprises, which led his opponents to label him a 'Jack of all Trades'.[57]

By 1706 there were sufficient Presbyterian churches for ministers to form the presbytery of Philadelphia with Makemie as moderator. Three ministers from New England were among the founders and the remainder were from Scotland or Scots from Ulster. It was a loosely structured arrangement at the beginning, with many congregations lacking ministers, and with finances stretched to serve a growing and scattered population. Outside Pennsylvania and New England, they faced harassment from Anglicans in the middle colonies and the South. In New York and New Jersey, Lord Cornbury was particularly high-handed in asserting Anglican supremacy, arresting Makemie and others for preaching without a licence. Overplaying his hand, Cornbury provoked a spirited defence by Makemie, and the combined opposition of Presbyterians, Dutch Reformed leaders, and their allies in Europe and New England. During the first decade of its existence, the presbytery of Philadelphia remained orientated towards New England and the United Brethren in London, but the number of migrants from Scotland and Ireland was growing. In 1717 a synod was organized in Philadelphia with three effective presbyteries.[58]

By the second decade of the eighteenth century, therefore, a Presbyterian church had become entrenched in North America which would eventually make as significant a contribution to Calvinism on that continent as did the Congregationalists of New England. The Puritans of Plymouth, Massachusetts, Connecticut, and New Haven, though in the first century of

[56] Trinterud, *Forming of an American Tradition*, 26–7, and Schlenther, *Life of Makemie*, 1–20.
[57] Schlenther, *Life of Makemie*, 15–24 and *passim*.
[58] *Records of the Presbyterian Church in America . . . 1706–1788*, (New York, 1904, repr. 1969), 9–29, 47–55; Schlenther, *Life of Makemie*, 189–244; Trinterud, *Forming of an American Tradition*, 29–45; Richard Webster, *A History of the Presbyterian Church in America from its Origins until the Year 1760* (Philadelphia, Pa., 1858), 97 ff.

colonization they contributed more to the Calvinist tradition than the Dutch, the Huguenots, or the Presbyterians, were not the sole keepers of the ark of the covenant in the New World.

Further Reading

Butler, Jon, *The Huguenots in America: A Refugee People in New World Society* (Cambridge, Mass., 1983).

Hall, David D., 'Religion and Society', *Colonial British America*, ed. Jack P. Greene and J. R. Pole (London, 1984).

Miller, Perry, *Orthodoxy in Massachusetts* (Gloucester, Mass., 1933).

—— *The New England Mind* (2 vols., Cambridge, Mass., 1939–53).

Morgan, E. S., *Visible Saints: The History of a Puritan Idea* (New York, 1963).

Pratt, John W., *Religion, Politics and Diversity: The Church-State Theme in New York History* (Ithaca, NY, 1967).

Schlenther, Boyd S., *The Life and Writings of Francis Makemie* (Philadelphia, Pa., 1971).

Smith, George L., *Religion and Trade in New Netherland: Dutch Origins and American Development* (Ithaca, NY, 1973).

Trinterud, Leonard J., *The Forming of an American Tradition: A Re-Examination of Colonial Presbyterianism* (New York, 1949 repr. Freepost, NY, 1970).

X

Calvinism in France, 1598–1685

ÉLISABETH LABROUSSE

I. *The organization of the French Protestant Churches*

THE Edict of Nantes (1598) can be seen as the last in a series of royal decrees aimed at putting an end to the Wars of Religion. Its peculiarity is that it was to remain in force—at least on paper—for eighty-seven years. As an edict of pacification, it displeased extremists in both camps; however, the more sensible Protestants realized that Henri IV could hardly have achieved a better settlement for churches that included barely 6 or 7 per cent of his subjects,[1] and the (Catholic) *Parlements*, after sulking, all eventually had to give way and include it in their records.

The Edict gave leave to profess the Reformed religion in the kingdom, that is, the Calvinist doctrines and church organization, with its presbyterian-synodal pyramid, as defined by two documents in 1559, the Confession of Faith and the Discipline. As a guarantee for the Huguenot minority, the Edict established what has been called 'a state within the state', that is the right, for some years, to hold political assemblies and control a certain number of towns and fortresses.

But the Edict did not put the ERF[2] on an equal footing with the Roman church. It re-established Catholicism in those few places where its practice had been discontinued and it provided everywhere for the rebuilding of Catholic churches which had been destroyed, the reopening of monasteries and convents, and, above all, the restoration of property to the Catholic clergy. A tight, unbroken network of parishes again covered the kingdom and all were obliged to pay tithes to the Roman Church, while its religious festivals were compulsory days of idleness for everybody.[3] On the other hand, Protestant temples and ministers were allowed to function only in

---

[1] S. Mours, *Les Églises réformées en France* (Paris, 1968), 157–67. Even if approximate, the figure is broadly accurate. In about 1570 the proportion was much greater, but the Wars of Religion had substantially reduced it, through deaths, irreversible emigration, and the falling-off of the lukewarm.

[2] Protestants described their churches (the plural is significant) as *Églises réformées de France* ERF; but their legal appellation was *Religion prétendue réformée*, RPR.

[3] The problems created by the obligation (not everywhere legal in the beginning) to decorate façades of houses for the Corpus Christi procession, and to show respect to the Holy Sacrament by kneeling when it was carried through the streets to the dying, occurred throughout the century causing ceaseless and increasingly thorny difficulties to the Huguenots.

certain well-defined localities. This involved three kinds of privilege; first, *possession*, when in existence in 1596 or 1597; secondly *concession* of one or two places in each *bailliage* throughout the kingdom;[4] thirdly, *exercices de fief*, which were restricted to the manors of Huguenot nobles with tenurial rights of justice. The clue to these arrangements lay in the highly uneven distribution of Protestantism in France at the time of the Edict of Nantes, as an outcome of the successes of the League north of the Loire. More than 80 per cent of the Huguenots lived in western and, above all, in southern France. Elsewhere Protestantism had been so reduced that only small and scattered groups survived. Royal commissioners presided in each province over the implementation of the Edict's clauses, a laborious proceeding which took years to complete.

By letters-patent attached to the Edict, the King had undertaken to allocate considerable sums each year, to be apportioned to the Churches by the provincial synods, to compensate for the payment of tithes by Protestants in rural areas, for the return of Catholic Church property, and for the costs involved by their military institutions. After the death of Henri IV in 1610 however, these allowances soon ceased to be paid regularly, and became only occasional payments after 1630.[5]

The Edict loosened the former monopoly enjoyed by the Roman Church in allowing Frenchmen to adopt whichever of the two accepted forms of Christianity it recognized; thus it implemented a restricted freedom of conscience. The Reformed Churches were granted explicit privileges—first and foremost the right to legal existence. Theoretically, all offices of state, professions and occupations were open to the Huguenots, and special courts—*Chambres de l'Édit* or *mi-parties*[6]—would settle any dispute in which a Huguenot was involved.

Yet, whereas being a Protestant was no longer a serious flaw, it was nonetheless still a handicap. After the conversion of Henri IV to Catholicism (1593) a shift towards the King's religion began to appear among the nobility and this gathered momentum throughout the next century. From 1629 onward, at any rate, the weight of the aristocracy, once so powerful in the Huguenot party, became negligible. This withdrawal distinctly weakened the minority both politically and financially. On the other hand, the churches were relieved from the schemes of unreliable and

---

[4] A number of Ligue towns on surrendering to Henri IV stipulated that Protestant worship should never be established within their walls. This applied also to cathedral cities and explains why Protestant temples came to be built outside the walls, in the suburbs. Thus the Parisian Huguenots went to Charenton to worship, those of Rouen, to Quévilly, etc.

[5] They were provided, for example, when national synods were convened, as these entailed heavy expenses on travel and accommodation for the participants.

[6] One should not be misled by the appellation 'mi-parties': they had Huguenot judges, but they were outnumbered by the Catholic ones. The *Chambres de l'Édit* established in Paris and in Rouen were abolished in 1669 and those for Languedoc, Guyenne, and Dauphiné ten years later.

troublesome members, and the ministers, as a body, were able to play the dominant role in the communities.

The Edict of Nantes froze the ERF in the positions they had held or won shortly before 1598. It brought welcome security to Protestant communities whose situation had until then been precarious. But as a grave counter-balance, the Edict debarred any proselytism on the Protestant side. The Edict provided a protective rampart to the Churches, yet it circumscribed their influence. From then on, a great deal of energy was devoted to the safeguarding and piecemeal defence of the privileges granted by the Edict, which nevertheless were being constantly eroded. The militant dynamic of the sixteenth century gave way to concentration on survival and self-defence. Open war was replaced by cold war. The tens of thousands of cases which the *Chambres de l'Édit* had to deal with during the seventeenth century, while showing how hard it was for the two communities to reach peaceful coexistence, testify nevertheless to the relative success of the Edict, since the opposing parties now resorted to the courts and no longer to acts of violence.

The presbyterian-synodal form of organization established by the Discipline had been drawn up in the sixteenth century; it was supposed to follow the practice of the apostolic age. Besides, its compilers had tacitly assumed a church enjoying a monopoly, and therefore with a mass membership,—a different situation from that which confronted the ERF in the seventeenth century. Yet the Discipline remained the revered charter of their organization.

Each congregation was governed by its own consistory, which normally grouped about a dozen elders around the minister. These elders were men of acknowledged piety, two of whom generally resided in each of the 'districts' of the town or area concerned. They were renewed annually by co-option, the 'people' being required merely to ratify the elders' decision or, though this seldom happened, to challenge it. Self-government such as this was fairly similar to that enjoyed by many towns in the Midi. In both cases those chosen were generally notables—men who knew French, and who could often read and write, frequently lawyers, notaries, doctors, apothecaries, or rich merchants.

The Protestant churches had chosen a policy of financial autonomy. They were organized federally at several levels, being grouped into 'colloquies' which formed part of 'provinces', each with a yearly meeting of its own synod to which every church was supposed to send its minister and two of its elders; in practice, the poorer churches found it hard to meet the travelling-expenses of a full deputation and often their minister was their only representative. Of capital importance for the working of the ERF, the provincial synods were also courts of appeal against the decisions of the consistories. In addition, this annual assembly examined candidates for the ministry, assigned churches to them, or presided over transfers of pastors within the province. Finally, it discussed questions of common interest, such as the allocation of quotas for the subsidies to maintain the academies, or the choice of provincial deputies to a national synod.

National synods functioned as the highest courts in the governmental system of the ERF. They met every three years until 1626, after which they became less and less frequent, there being only four, in 1631, 1637, 1645, and 1659. A national synod had as its members two ministers and two elders from each synodal province. It was empowered to settle any doctrinal dispute that might have arisen; a responsibility which Catholic polemicists did not fail to emphasize, arguing that, despite their claim to the contrary, the Protestants could not do without 'infallible' authority. A national synod, as the highest court of appeal, could definitively suspend or excommunicate a minister. It had to make a choice—later, to confirm the choice made by the court—of the *Députés généraux* (after 1644, the single *Député général*) entrusted with representing the ERF before the King.[7] Finally, national synods supervised the functioning of the academies and allocated the amount that each province had to pay to the appropriate academy. The three main academies (to which that of Sedan was added after the annexation of the Principality by France) were at Saumur, Montauban, and Die (in Dauphiné).[8] Each academy had a grammar-school associated with it. The academies themselves consisted only of a faculty of arts (the two years spent studying philosophy which were common to all European institutions of higher education at this time) and a faculty of divinity, which trained future ministers. Though the three years' teaching was brilliant at Saumur, where many of the professors were renowned theologians (whose doctrinal originality evoked suspicion and engendered polemic), it was probably commonplace elsewhere, partly because the meagre resources entailed heavy teaching loads.

Although the contributions from the churches to the expenses of the academies were levied strictly, they were also adjusted to the very different capacities of the congregations, the large communities being assessed much more heavily than the small country churches. However, following French fiscal usage of the time, the basis for assessment was not the actual resources of the taxpayer, but the amount needed to meet expenses, quotas for the raising of this sum being then allocated. The same procedure operated at the level of each church: householders were asked for contributions proportionate to the taxes paid to the king. Consequently, the smaller and poorer communities sometimes expected from their members sums which they were quite unable to spare, and hence those small churches suffered

---

[7] Solange Deyon, *Du loyalisme au refus* (see Further Reading).

[8] To which can be added, for the first part of the seventeenth century those of Nîmes and of Orthez (in Béarn).

perpetual and heavy deficits. The financial autonomy of each Reformed church led to wide variations. Whereas most of those north of the Loire had a healthy budget, as also the large churches in the important towns of the South, rural churches with a small membership could rarely make ends meet.

When the allowances from the king became increasingly uncertain, money problems became acute in many of the small churches in the South, where the recantation of a single nobleman (and the disappearance of his substantial subscription) would hopelessly unbalance a church's budget. In many small towns of the Midi the minister's salary (400 or 500 livres a year) was paid only in part, and arrears mounted astronomically. Among the Huguenots of the Midi, a credit arrangement went some way towards easing this situation, by making the churches' recognizances for debt the equivalent of promissory notes among the Protestants. This device proved more or less adequate, especially as the ministers were recruited from among the notables and often were tolerably well off. But their painful or tricky financial position did not escape the notice of the political authorities, always keen to secure informers among the pastors or to encourage defections. However, successes remained sporadic.

The financial difficulties of the communities of the Midi often loom large in the acts of their consistories. They sometimes embittered relations between a minister and his church, described as 'ungrateful' because it failed to ensure the promised salary. The consistories did not go so far as to invoke the law in order to seize the meagre property of those faithful who were in arrears with their contributions, but, as a last resort, they did sometimes threaten the defaulter with refusal of the *méreau*, the token which proved his right to participate in the Lord's Supper. Obviously, those who failed to contribute were not lukewarm in their faith, for they would have merely needed to abjure a religion that they found so burdensome. Protestants had, in any case, to pay tithes to the Roman clergy. Finally, since the contributions paid by the Protestants to their church were assessed on a footing with the royal taxes, they could, psychologically, inspire the same dislike—but without the benefit of sanctions against non-payment which ensured receipt of the *taille*.

The way in which the consistories tackled the financial problems that so often bedevilled them reveals a certain degree of incompetence and an astonishing lack of realism. When a minister threatened to leave (as the provincial synods allowed when his salary had not been paid over a long period), the elders of the church, in a panic, would hold meeting after meeting, resorting to various shifts to raise the money and storing up rash promises for the future. Then everything would calm down—until the next crisis. Yet these men were often officials of their towns, whose financial management was not so deplorable as their church's. But it would be wrong to see the consistories as negligent, for it should be recognized that their essential function, as defined by the Discipline, was a spiritual one.

Their prime task, in fact, was to constitute a religious court responsible for watching over the behaviour of the faithful. The sanctions they imposed, lacking civil consequences, were effective only in proportion to the goodwill—the repentance—of the persons subjected to them. Obedience towards the consistory was far from universal, and quick response even less so: often, the accused would present himself only after a third warning. It was especially during the weeks preceding the four annual Lord's Suppers that delinquents surrendered *en masse* before the prospect of suffering deprivation of the *méreau*, a severe sanction inflicted only for grave offences, but hovering over all who failed to submit to the consistory's authority. Once the offender appeared before the panel of elders, this was usually satisfied with hearing him express his regret for having behaved badly for example, by dancing, playing cards, or wearing a mask during Carnival. Sinners often sinned again, but the consistories continued to be indulgent towards them, as they were also towards another type of offence, being present at a Papist ceremony. A severer punishment, consisting of the obligation to express regret not just before the elders but in church, on Sunday, before the whole congregation, awaited the person who had contracted a mixed marriage (described picturesquely as *bigarré*, 'parti-coloured') and not only the offender, but the parents as well. It was exceptional for the consistories to inflict a temporary exclusion from the Lord's Supper (this happened in cases of sexual offences or of witchcraft), and excommunication was rarer still: it was used against the 'rebel' who had embraced Catholicism, and was therefore proclaimed *in absentia*.

The main beneficent activity carried out by the consistories was that of settling quarrels. In a society strongly attached to points of honour, the existence of the consistory offered an amicable solution to brawls: by obeying its injunctions one could be conciliatory without losing face. Acts of reconciliation and arbitration absorbed all the effort of the consistories in the periods leading up to the Communions, when every elder reported the disputes or fights that had occurred in his area of surveillance.[9] Another of the consistory's basic activities was the distribution of relief to the poor and the sick, to widows, orphans, and old people and to *passants de la religion*.[10] Money from Sunday collections went to fill the poor-box,[11] but in periods of

---

[9] It should be noted that the consistories, in keeping with the society of the time, appear to have been remarkably indulgent towards men in cases of sexual offences (true, a confession was needed and when coping with obstinate denials, the elders were powerless); on the other hand, curiously enough, they were firmly on the side of wives beaten by their husbands.

[10] Travellers equipped with a certificate from their minister or consistory showing where they come from, where they were going, and on what purpose.

[11] The Discipline provided, along with elders, for deacons who were to be especially concerned with charity. Actually the distinction between the two roles often became blurred, except that one elder would administer the poor-box, while the allotment of aid would be decided by the whole consistory.

crisis (epidemics and harvest-failures) the consistories excelled themselves and contracted debts in order to relieve wretchedness.

The French consistories thus bore only a remote resemblance to their equivalents in the Calvinist countries of Europe. Their authority, which was wholly moral, required considerable dexterity in its exercise. A stubborn church-member could always appeal to the next provincial synod—and appeal entailed suspension of the punishment imposed. Then, if the sanction was confirmed by the provincial synod, he could appeal to the national synod. After the synod of 1644, this meant waiting for fifteen years, until the Loudun synod in 1659! Moreover, when Mazarin eventually authorized that meeting, he made known that it would be the last the government would permit. The Protestant organization was thus deprived of its central authority and the Discipline left headless by the removal of its supreme tribunal. But, above all, it was always open to a discontented Huguenot to abjure his Protestantism. In France, being a Protestant meant *choosing to remain one*. The consistories and the faithful were all the more aware of this possible outcome of excessively acute conflicts, in that more than one hot-tempered Huguenot threatened to resort to it, and even carried it out in a momentary impulsive act, which would be cancelled a little later by a contrite repentance. This permanent possibility accounts for the indulgence and forbearance shown by the French consistories to inveterate backsliders. Their mildness should not be ascribed to weakness, but resulted from the practical situation. It would therefore be futile to describe their working on the basis of the textual content of the Discipline. The consistory registers of seventeenth-century France survive in sufficient quantity[12] for us to measure the degree of distortion imposed on the theoretical rules when these were applied in conditions very different from those envisaged by the writers of the Discipline. A salute has to be paid to the devotion and prudence so often shown by the consistories, torn between the strict requirements of a revered text—the Discipline—and the obstacles that reality put in the way of translating these requirements into practice.

We can therefore observe the existence in seventeenth-century France of a Protestant sub-culture nourished by an obstinate particularism that in very many respects went beyond what was strictly religious. Religion was of course central, and the Huguenot was constantly reminded of this by the demands laid upon him by his faith—but also, to no less an extent, by the second-class citizenship that it entailed in the realm of the Most Christian King.

[12] See E. Labrousse, 'L'Église réformée du Carla en 1672-3', *BSHPF* (1960-1). See also the thesis of Béatrice Causse on Die in Dauphiné (deposited in the Bibliothèque de l'Histoire du Protestantisme français, 54 rue des Saints-Pères, Paris); J. Estèbe and B. Vogler, 'La Genèse d'une société protestante. Étude comparée de quelques registres consistoriaux languedociens et palatins vers 1600', in *Annales ESC*, 31 (1976), 362-88 (perhaps somewhat over-idealized).

The cardinal importance of preaching (for Calvinists almost a third sacrament) and the educational level of the ministers, which was incomparably higher than that of most *curés* in the villages and market-towns, made a significant contribution to the spreading of the French language in the *pays d'Oc*. French was the language of the Bible, of the Discipline, of sermons, and of consistorial registers. Indeed in the Midi to know French was to rise above the level of the masses. The preaching of the Calvinist ministers also raised the educational level of the Huguenots in another way. An illiterate countryman heard so many sermons in the course of his life, that he might well derive from them not only, of course, reasonably precise religious ideas, but also some glimpses of cosmology, history, geography, and medicine, for these lengthy discourses were quite regularly punctuated by digressions, full of a variety of information. Protestantism did not succeed in completely uprooting popular superstitions, but it went a long way towards it, and greatly reduced belief in astrology and witchcraft, while also stimulating a lively and often mocking incredulity towards Popish miracles, thereby sowing the seed of a criticial attitude of mind. In principle, every Protestant church had an infant school attached to it, and illiteracy was apparently less widespread among the Huguenots than among their Catholic neighbours in the same social milieu and geographical area. Although the Bible was still expensive, editions of the New Testament and the Psalms were widely circulated among the Protestants. We know, moreover, how fond they were of singing the Psalms, which came almost to oust any other repertoire.

It would be gratuitous to assume that genuine Christian piety was more frequent among Protestants'than among Catholics. Nevertheless, the mere fact that they formed an active minority and were subject to forms of discrimination which did not allow them to forget it nourished an inexhaustible spring of resistance to the Catholicism which surrounded them. Calvinists had the arrogance and the spiritual pride which stem from the conviction of belonging to an élite. Above all, most certainly there was the belief that they were sheep in the 'little flock' of the redeemed, and indeed Huguenots applied to themselves the verse of Luke 12: 32. After all, election means selection. Here we perceive another capital difference between the Huguenots and the other Protestants of Europe. From a sociological standpoint, the Huguenots present some of the features of sectaries. There was a voluntarist aspect to adherence to the ERF, which involved a choice that was made afresh every day, even if subconsciously. Furthermore, the importance ascribed to doctrine, to salvation by faith (which marked off the Huguenots from their Catholic countrymen far more than any difference in their way of life), led them to regard as saved all those who professed their dogmas, that is to say, all Protestants. When a religious denomination embraces an entire population, it is obvious to the more pious that some of their coreligionists, who lead scandalous lives, are in a state of perdition. Not so in France, where one could confidently foresee the salvation of anyone and everyone who professed the pure doctrine, even if his behaviour was not wholly above reproach. From this angle, it appears that the Huguenots were far removed from the Puritans. They probably did tend towards a certain austerity, such as could also be found among the Jansenists but, all the same, French Protestants were not obsessed by scruples. They found proof that they were among the elect in that they belonged to a community which was subjected to disabilities and, soon, to oppression. This said, it remains true that, subjectively, the Huguenots saw themselves as members of a Church. It is only in certain aspects and from the standpoint of the present-day historian that sectarian features can be observed among them. Even if these features were only secondary, however, they marked off French Protestantism from the Calvinism of other countries.

II. *The relations of the Huguenots with French society and with European Protestantism*

How did the Huguenot communities fit into a society which, as a whole, was so strongly coloured by Catholicism? When put in such a general way, this is a meaningless question, because the local situations were so different. Only in Poitou and Languedoc did the Protestant communities constitute social pyramids similar to those of the population at large, that is, incorporating a mass of peasantry, craftsmen, bourgeois, and lesser nobles. Elsewhere, Protestantism had above all affected urban circles—craftsmen, tradesmen, bourgeois. To put it roughly, Protestantism north of the Loire was of the latter type, whereas, in the 'Bible Belt' of the South, the urban elements dominated a mass of peasants, whom, however, they did not always control.[13]

The position of each of the two religions in relation to the other was very different. Because they were dispersed throughout the kingdom, the Huguenots could not ignore their Catholic countrymen, whereas some of the latter might never have rubbed shoulders with a heretic, and therefore had only their always hostile and often fantastic prejudices to go by.

At the same time, the ferocious conflicts of the sixteenth century had not been enough to obliterate the time-honoured solidarity of kinship and community. As a result, the religious pluralism established by the Edict of Nantes achieved some undeniable successes. In France, conversion to Protestantism had been, in most cases, the outcome of individual

[13] During the troubles of the 1620s the poorer classes joined with the nobles in armed resistance to the royal forces, whereas a considerable section of the Southern bourgeoisie disapproved of what they regarded as an adventurist tactic.

decisions.[14] Consequently, families in the wider sense, were often—at least, in the beginning of the seventeenth century—of mixed religion. When we observe the consistories imposing only light penalties on the faithful who had attended a Papist service on the occasion of the christening or the wedding of a Catholic relative, we can guess that the elders were being indulgent towards an 'offence' which they themselves often had good reason to understand.

The ministers very early on denounced mixed marriages, but the traditions which dictated the choice of a bride or a bridegroom were not easily renounced, at least among the less militant Huguenots and in places where they were not very numerous. In any case, it is far from certain that the marriage of a Huguenot girl into a Catholic family was invariably detrimental to the Protestant community. The religious ardour of women and their decisive role in education at the nursery-stage sometimes led to their children embracing Protestantism when they grew up. Generally speaking, there did not exist among laymen that watertight division between the two confessions which the most fervent elements on both sides, and especially their clergy, strove to create. Comings and goings between one Church and the other were not uncommon in places where a socio-economic and numerical equilibrium dissuaded both sides from the ambition to dominate. In other words, the system established by the Edict of Nantes favoured a peaceful coexistence, which meant, on the doctrinal plane, that for many people 'the other church' (called by polemicists 'opposed' or 'false') did not figure as 'Satan's synagogue', but merely as an inferior form of Christianity. Everyone appreciated that christening was a sacrament common to both. The religious toleration implied by the implementation of the Edict of Nantes began, hesitantly, to become part of the everyday life of some Frenchmen and its insidious progress was probably not halted until the 1660s.[15]

At the other end of the social scale, at Court and in literary, learned, and artistic circles, everyday relations between Catholics and Protestants were courteous: while it was still eccentric and rather ridiculous to be a Huguenot, this was no longer a monstrous blemish among the social élites.[16]

Nevertheless, there were still powerful pressure-groups in France which, having reluctantly accepted the Edict of Nantes as a temporary expedient,

[14] Béarn, the domain of the Queen of Navarre, Jeanne d'Albret, became Protestant by the sovereign's decision, and in some towns in the Midi Protestantism had been adopted as a result of the decision of the municipal authorities. Even in these exceptional cases, however, a substantial minority of the population had stayed loyal to Catholicism, more or less openly.

[15] Even the Revocation did not end this eirenicism at the popular level. Memoirs written by Huguenots about their adventurous journeys to join the Refuge often contains expressions of gratitude for help received from Catholic neighbours at the time of their clandestine departure, help which had indeed been risky to give.

[16] See pp. 11–13, 101–3.

fervently desired to see the country return to religious uniformity, though not through warfare. The Counter-Reformation was at its height and gave dynamism and vitality to French Catholicism. Naturally, the most relentless adversaries of the Protestants were to be found among the Catholic clergy. Many of these, both secular and regular, saw the re-establishment of religious unity in France as their prime task, and it is not surprising that the convocations of the Catholic clergy, which met every five years, should have constantly voiced their disapproval of the Edict of Nantes and tried, with increasing success, to restrict its sphere of application, while looking forward to one day securing its cancellation.

The activity of the Catholic clergy was deployed on several planes. Controversy conducted by the pen doubtless bore little fruit: the Huguenots, despite their small numbers, did not lack good writers and they rarely let an attack go unanswered. Furthermore, there is reason to believe that, in these technical debates, the literate laymen on both sides only read the champions of their own cause. Abjurations exclusively decided by these discussions were strictly reserved to a few intellectuals.

Controversy took place also on a level more accessible to the masses; namely the missions of Catholic priests or friars in regions with a large number of Huguenots. Though these missions were sometimes conducted by Jesuits in the cities, in the country areas they were above all carried out by the Capuchin friars. Everywhere they constituted an exasperating and harmful harassment of the Protestants,[17] and from the middle of the seventeenth century onwards they enjoyed the scarcely concealed, and soon quite open, backing of the civil authorities. Since they possessed incomparably smaller resources in men and money than their opponents the Huguenots could only remain on the defensive.

Last, but not least, the Catholic clergy were able to exploit the extensive scope for legal quibbling for which the 'concessional' privileges granted to the Protestants offered endless opportunities as also did the frequent everyday incidents that could provide the occasion for lawsuits against consistories and individuals.[18]

Although the Catholic clergy were, by their very vocation, opposed to the Edict of Nantes, they were not its only opponents, nor even, perhaps, the most dangerous. The hostility of the *robe* and, in particular, of the

---

[17] Sometimes in these debates a local minister who was not necessarily a distinguished dialectician was confronted by an experienced Catholic controversialist. Sometimes the Capuchin preaching electrified the humble Catholics and incited them to acts of violence against their Huguenot neighbours, depicted as enemies of God and deserving of Heaven's vengeance. It could also happen that some Protestants who had come initially out of curiosity were won over by the emotive impact of the Capuchin sermons, filled with stories of amazing miracles and terrifying descriptions of hell. See B. Dompnier, 'Missions de l'intérieur et réforme catholique en Dauphiné au xviiᵉ siècle' (Third Cycle Thesis, University of Paris I) reviewed, *BSHPF* (1982), 117–19.

[18] For example, the temple had to be rebuilt elsewhere if it was too close to a Catholic building, or if it had been erected on a site which had formerly belonged to the Catholic Church. See also above, n. 3.

parlements was focused not so much on the Protestants themselves, as on the charter which gave them legal existence. The Edict of Nantes, not without justification, seemed to these lawyers an unprecedented piece of legislation, which amounted to a sort of treaty between the king of France and a small section of his subjects. Therefore, it was for them an outrageous document which ought, one day, to be eliminated from French law. The factor of personal competition also played its part here: if the profession of Catholicism was to become once more a necessary qualification for offices, Protestants would be eliminated from the race for appointments. Either covertly or overtly, the same considerations applied in other professions and trades as well, and the decrees of the royal Council which, from 1670 onward, closed a steadily increasing number of occupations and trades to the Huguenots were undoubtedly welcomed by many who were not necessarily fervent Catholics, but who were relieved to see some competitors removed.

However intense economic rivalry with regard to the Huguenots may have been, seventeenth-century culture would have deemed it unbecoming to base any open dislike on this. What was more serious for French Protestants was, perhaps, not so much the number of their declared adversaries as the indifference of everyone else. Their only hope, after the loss in 1629 of the illusory guarantees constituted by the *places de sûreté*, lay in the king's good will. Some protection was enjoyed by the ERF when war gave the Crown more pressing concerns than the restoration of religious uniformity in the kingdom. Besides, this legal existence of the minority in France served more than once as trump-card in foreign policy.[19] Yet a saying attributed to Louis XIV is highly suggestive; he is said to have remarked of the Huguenots that his grandfather (Henri IV) loved them and his father (Louis XIII) feared them, but, for his part, he neither loved nor feared them. The historic disaster that lay in wait for French Protestantism is implicit in these haughty and glacial words.

They can serve, besides, to outline schematically the contrasting tactics (which in fact cancelled each other out) that were pursued by the 'firm' Huguenots (the hawks) on the one hand, and the 'prudent' Huguenots (the doves) on the other. The former (almost all Southerners) sought to make the sovereign fear them by threatening to take up arms, while the latter hoped to win his love or, at least, to appear harmless to him, by submitting dutifully to his commands. Probably neither of these two methods would have produced much result, but their simultaneous practice cancelled any advantage they might have gained separately. From the middle of the century onward, the best the Huguenots could hope for was, pathetically, to

---

[19] Both in relation to the Protestant princes of Germany, the United Provinces, and England (diplomatic appointments more than once given to Huguenots), and in relation to the Holy See (in this case the king of France used the pretext of the presence of heretics in his realm as a reason for rejecting certain requests).

be ignored, but their enemies were not prepared to grant them this modest favour.

Lacking any ally in French society[20] and very much in a minority, the Huguenots were isolated, peculiar, and therefore quickly considered as suspect. The Catholic polemicists attacked not only their theological tenets but also their church organization—their Discipline—and depicted in the blackest colours the historical events of the recent past and the malign role played by the Protestants. In this type of controversy, in short, it was not so much the heretical views of the Huguenots as the fact of the schism which came under attack. The organization of their churches was depicted, with indignation and horror, as 'republican' in the seventeenth-century sense of the word. Disapproving emphasis was laid upon the principle of equality between the ministers, which implied rejection of hierarchy and of bishops. The role assigned to the elders—laymen!—was underlined as an enormity. The system of assemblies which governed the ERF gave off a whiff of 'democracy', anathema to seventeenth-century Frenchmen.

The culture of the time mingled religion inextricably with politics, and so it seemed deviant and dangerous that the Huguenots, as subjects of an absolute monarchy, should organize their churches on a model which looked republican. In contrast, the hierarchy of the Catholic church, a pyramid culminating in the Roman pontiff, was hailed as the only form of religious organization capable of harmonizing with a monarchical regime. 'No bishop, no king', the Protestant James I of England had once pithily observed.

While political theory was supposed to demonstrate the incompatibility of the Protestant Discipline with a monarchy, concrete arguments drawn from the past were to harm the Huguenot cause even more damagingly. Tendentious narratives of the Wars of Religion portrayed the Protestants as having been innovating troublemakers, rebels, disturbers of the peace, promotors of revolution. Was not a monarchy cherishing vipers in its bosom if it allowed their continued presence among its subjects? The Huguenots were, for the time being perhaps, peaceable and inoffensive, but their ancestors and co-religionists abroad had shown and were showing the potentialities for disorder and subversion latent in their religion.

To be sure, since 1584, when their leader, Henri of Navarre, had become heir to the throne, the French Protestants had discovered the virtue of the divine right of kings, and their adherence to this doctrine soon went deep and became a matter of sincere conviction. As anti-Papists first and foremost, the Huguenots congratulated themselves on being the only fully consistent Gallicans. According to them, they alone, through their break

---

[20] The Augustinian theology of the Jansenists brought them close to the Calvinists in some respects and so, in order to refute the amalgam which their Jesuit opponents tried to establish between Port-Royal and the heretics, they showed themselves specially active and sharp in the polemic against the Protestants.

with Rome, were able to stand unreservedly for the jealous defence of the prerogatives of the king of France. However Erastian where the Catholic church was concerned, and wishing to see that Church properly controlled by the Crown, the Huguenots departed from this attitude, of course, as soon as they found their own churches impeded by royal interference. Erastianism makes sense only if the sovereign himself belongs to the church whose functioning he supervises. The peculiar situation of the ERF under the thumb of a civil power hostile, and in any case alien, to their faith, doomed them to a self-contradictory position: in theory, their absolutist beliefs led them to grant extensive rights to the monarch, but, in practice, they deplored his exercise of these rights in dealing with them.

Their absolutist beliefs, based primarily upon several passages in the Scriptures,[21] were naturally reinforced by their dependence on the Crown, which after 1629 was the only bulwark capable of holding back their enemies. Article 40 of the Huguenot Confession of Faith was, at first sight, comforting for the king, had it not been for the conditional clause at the end: 'provided that the sovereignty of God remains intact'. Indeed these few words seriously weakened the entire submission to the king's authority which was required from the faithful in the preceding passage. And all the more so because Catholic scholars took care to remind people that the first monarchomachs of the sixteenth century had been Protestants. The Huguenot writers of the seventeenth century vied with each other in condemning the theory of tyrannicide advanced by certain Jesuit authors, but these obvious attempts to shift the opprobrium for a contractual theory of political power scarcely succeeded in making the well-informed forget the *Vindiciae contra tyrannos*, Hotman and Beza, not to mention foreign Calvinists, such as Knox, Goodman, and Buchanan.

The Catholic polemicists saw in the Huguenots an outpost of the Protestant hydra and, in particular, of that 'Calvinist International' whose supposed internal solidarity terrified its enemies. The support given by Elizabeth of England to the Sea-Beggars in the Netherlands and to the French Huguenots was remembered. Buckingham's unfortunate expedition to La Rochelle had not been forgotten either. And the links of the ERF with the other Calvinist churches of Europe were still apparent—links with Geneva, the United Provinces, the Palatinate, and, to a lesser degree, with Scotland and England. The Court strove systematically to thwart such relations, for instance by forbidding foreigners to serve as ministers or professors in France.[22] But the Walloon churches—of French-speaking

---

[21] In particular Rom., 13. 1–6 and 1 Pet. 2.13.

[22] In 1618 the French Government forbade the Huguenot deputies who had been elected to attend the Synod of Dordt to participate in its proceedings. For a long time the special status of the city of Geneva in its relations with France enabled its citizens to be ministers in France, but in 1669 the French Government put an end to this privilege. The French synods were not allowed to carry on any official correspondence with Calvinist churches abroad, but this obstacle could be circumvented up to a point by means of apparently private letters exchanged between ministers.

Protestants established in the Netherlands and in England—were in many cases serviced by pastors of French birth, several of whom occupied one of the chairs of theology in the distinguished university of Leiden, while French ordinands, when sufficiently well off to enjoy a *peregrinatio academica*, never failed to spend a year or two in Geneva and in Holland.

Contact between the Huguenot élites and their co-religionists abroad often went so far as the formation of ties of kinship[23] and the Protestants of the frontier regions traded readily with their nearby fellow Protestants. those of Dauphiné and the Pays de Gex had commercial ties with Geneva, those of the East and North with the Palatinate and, especially, the United Provinces, and those of the 'maritime provinces', from Calais to Bordeaux, with the British Isles.[24]

In the event of an acute conflict between allegiance to the King of France and Protestant solidarity, past events (so often recalled by Catholic polemicists) gave reason to expect that political loyalty would yield to the priorities of religion, and the Gallicanism that the Huguenots proclaimed so loudly was not enough to wipe out memories of their cosmopolitan leanings.

It would, however, be misleading to overstate these inclinations anachronistically. A Huguenot remained fundamentally and naïvely French, sharing in the arrogant ethnocentrism of his country's culture. The size of their membership—about a million—made the ERF, even though 'under the cross' (that is, deprived of a religious monopoly and of the protection of a Protestant 'magistrate') feel that they were on an equal footing with the Calvinists of the Netherlands and they no longer had as great a deference towards Geneva as in Calvin's time. Furthermore, the French were prone to imagine that their own habits and modes of thought were shared by their co-religionists abroad. From this followed illusions which were sometimes ludicrous. Thus they misunderstood the specific character of the Church of England and had a very inadequate idea of what differentiated it from the Nonconformists. *A fortiori*, the distinctive features of German and Scandinavian Lutheranism were beyond them,

[23] An extreme case of this is provided by one of the great Protestant families of France north of the Loire, the Du Moulins. The theologian Pierre I (1568–1658) taught at Leiden in his youth and subsequently established with King James I such close relations that the French Government objected. Two of his numerous sons, Pierre II and Louis, settled in England. Another, Cyrus, was a minister in France after almost becoming one in the Netherlands, and it was in Zeeland that the youngest of them, Henri, ended his career as a minister. Furthermore, Pierre I's brother-in-law, André Rivet, who began as a minister in France, became professor of divinity at Leiden and then tutor to William II of Orange. One of Pierre I's grandsons, Pierre III, whose father was Cyrus, after holding a subordinate post in the foreign affairs department in Paris, entered the service of Charles II, but left it in 1672 to become one of the secretaries of William III of Orange, when the United Provinces were at war with France and England. Pierre Jurieu, the leading exponent of resistance in the *Refuge*, was the grandson of Pierre I Du Moulin and the brother-in-law of Pierre III Du Moulin.

[24] It was no accident that most of the few Frenchmen who knew English in the mid-seventeenth century were Huguenots from Normandy. The Protestant merchants of Rouen often arranged exchange-visits for their sons with their opposite numbers in London, so that these young men could become bilingual.

even though the ministers had a glimpse of the different theological options.[25]

The fellow-feeling of the Huguenots towards other Protestants, however little they understood their peculiarities, and, above all, their constant contact with Catholicism, encouraged their ministers to view with favour oecumenical projects for the Protestant confessions, such as that discussed at the national synod of Tonneins in 1614, to which James I had given his patronage. These Huguenots, who were a minority in their own country, had everything to gain from a less divided European Protestantism.

Besides, there were always among the Huguenots some eirenicists who dreamt of conciliation, not of course with 'Popery', but, at least, with Gallican Catholicism. The historic example of England seemed to show that a break with Rome was the key to everything. In that hope and on that condition—both chimerical—they were prepared to make considerable adjustments in their practices, and at times the French authorities, Richelieu in particular, seemed favourable to projects which, in their minds, would have meant a rallying of the Huguenots to Catholicism at the price of a few trivial concessions coming from the majority Church. This was well understood by the less utopian of the ministers, who looked unkindly upon those who were called, derisively, *accommodeurs de religion*. Some of the latter, indeed, were secretly pensioned by the Court, but the vigilant synods always, in the end, tracked down these black sheep.

Not all the *accommodeurs de religion*, however, were venal, and, especially in the years preceding the Revocation, these men tried to save something from the storm they felt was approaching. We can surmise that they had another motive as well. It is clear that the religious pluralism of the kingdom of France was always looked upon in the seventeenth century as an unfortunate anomaly. The itch for polemics in the culture of the time plainly shows people to have believed that, to a very great extent, religious truths were capable of being proved. In a sense, there was at least *one* attitude common to Catholics and Protestants alike, and that was intolerance, the confident certainty of possessing a truth so obvious that it could not fail to be acknowledged except through bad faith, cupidity, pride, or crass ignorance. Relativism was uncommon in the seventeenth century. Peaceful coexistence at the popular level remained inarticulate and was viewed askance by the leading theologians. After 1629, the Huguenots were able to give play to their fundamental intolerance only here and there, in minor incidents, few and far between, whereas the Catholics had a latitude which only increased with time. But if we consider the doctrinal roots, we

[25] The national synod held at Charenton in 1631 resolved to allow communion to Lutherans travelling in France, if they should ask to take it. After 1685, however, it came as a painful shock to some Huguenot refugees to discover that, for many Lutherans, a Calvinist did not count for more than a Roman Catholic.

see that intolerance was pervasive in the Calvinism of the time,[26] and was not at all a peculiarly Catholic characteristic. Both Protestants and Catholics wanted their own confession to triumph through the elimination of all other forms of Christianity. The weak position of the Huguenots in France simply caused their dogmatism to lie beneath the surface. They had accepted the Edict of Nantes politically and clung to it passionately, but theologically, just as with the Catholics, the Edict remained for them merely an expedient; their ideal was still a national church with a mass membership and assured, by the support of the secular arm, of a monopoly of Christian truth. In this sense, the Revocation of the Edict of Nantes, seen as an attempt to restore the religious unity of France, although it evoked indignant condemnation on the part of the Huguenots, was perhaps better understood by those who were harmed by it than by many subsequent historians. It was the way the Revocation was put into effect, much more than the principle behind it, that shocked its victims.

III. *The historical stages*

If we examine the eighty-seven years from the Edict of Nantes to its Revocation, three main phases can be picked out. Between 1598 and 1629, revocation was only one possibility among others. In the following thirty years, between the Peace of Alès in 1629 and the Treaty of the Pyrenees in 1659, revocation seemed probable. But in the quarter-century after that, this probability grew and grew, until it became a certainty for an ever more imminent future, to take effect in October 1685—by which time the Edict had for several years already been in nearly every way a dead letter and the ERF was disabled and dying.

The military and political safeguards granted for a period by the letters-patent accompanying the Edict were shown to be illusory thirty-one years later. Thanks to the peace, the settled condition of the Huguenots had allowed the diversity of their secular interests, which varied between provinces and social groups, to emerge and weaken the solidarity which had been the strength of the 'Party' during the Wars of Religion. The Protestants north of the Loire, together with a significant number of middle-class Southerners, refused to consider rebellion justified by the extension of the regime of the Edict of Nantes to Béarn, a move which implied the re-establishment of Catholicism there. Many ministers and town notables detected a spirit of adventurism in taking up arms and resented the personal ambitions and rivalries of many a Protestant nobleman.

[26] For example, the condemnation of Arminianism by the Synod of Dort (1618–19), or the harsh, even venomous criticisms directed from Holland at the divines of Saumur. Then later there was the *Consensus Helveticus* adopted at Geneva in 1675: subscription to its rigid articles condemning all exegetical research was made obligatory on all ordinands wishing to become ministers, at the Geneva Academy as in the universities of Switzerland.

Richelieu's political wisdom rewarded the loyalty to the monarchy of the majority of Protestants by confirming, at the Peace of Alès in 1629, all the religious articles of the Edict of 1598. These articles, however, had henceforth no guarantee other than the king's word. The curious 'state within the state' sanctioned by the letters-patent attached to the Edict of Nantes was now at an end, and, with it, the Protestant 'Party'. All those whose adherence to the cause had been due above all to a spirit of particularist resistance, imbued with a stale flavour of feudalism and opposed to the centralizing policies of the Crown, no longer had any ground not to renounce a religion which entailed disabilities while lacking, from now on, any political attraction. As a result, French Protestantism became politically very much weaker, and in this respect the year 1629 marks the real end of the Wars of Religion. The situation thereafter recalls the early period of Protestantism in France before 1560, when religious considerations were paramount. By disappearing, the Protestant 'Party' left the field clear for the Protestant *churches*, now relieved of the embarrassing burden of the rivalries of the Huguenot nobility, although at the same time, deprived of their protection. From then on the ministers were to enjoy a position of unrivalled pre-eminence at the head of French Protestantism. The period could be called a 'clerical' phase in the history of the ERF, during which— moving at cruising speed, without any catastrophic jolts, and enjoying comparative security—a normal life opened up for the Protestant faithful.

The Academy of Saumur prospered in this relatively golden age. Its professors strove to strike a balance between Arminianism, condemned at Dort, and the more uncompromising expressions used by Calvin on predestination. Amyraut's 'hypothetical universalism' can be seen as a theology which was both 'enlightened' and flexible in its presentation of the classical dogmas of Calvinism, leaving room for a moderate infusion of rationalistic humanism. The peculiar situation of the French Protestants prohibited them from having any violent internal disputes, and even though the men of Saumur were regarded as heretics by many in Geneva and in Holland, the national synods of France could not afford to condemn them.[27] The Saumur theses, although far from obtaining support from all the French ministers, won over some of the best known among them: thus, in 1685, three of the four ministers at Charenton favoured the doctrine of 'hypothetical universalism'.

The Huguenot of the mid-seventeenth century (unlike his co-religionists in other countries) has to be described, broadly speaking, by reference to the Papists among whom he lived. His behaviour was, apparently, somewhat

---

[27] Indeed, the Edict of Nantes would be no longer applicable to an institution declared 'heretical' by a national synod: the Saumur Academy would have had to close its doors and its professors would have been prosecuted. Even the hard-liner Pierre I Du Moulin thought twice about the matter and agreed to 'extend the hand of fellowship' to Amyraut.

more austere than theirs, except in the case of the Catholic *dévots*, who were equally sober and opposed to swearing. In the field of doctrine, the Huguenot rejected with horror all forms of 'idolatry' and ridiculed 'superstition'. His watchful monotheism explains the mocking irony of his attitude to many Catholic beliefs and practices. This disposition, oddly enough, brought the Huguenots for a moment close to the *libertins*, since both groups jeered at medieval miracles, the cult of relics, and the tales of diabolical possession.[28] This gave rise to a feeling of spiritual superiority over the Catholics which was of decisive importance psychologically. The Huguenot knew that he belonged to the best of the Christian churches. Nevertheless, the idea of divine election, which denies all merit in the person who benefits from it (for to be a Huguenot was a gift of God's grace), combined with all the handicaps inflicted on the French Protestant by the majority community to ensure that his sense of superiority was free from the more sickening kind of triumphant complacency.

While it would be going too far to describe as precarious the situation of the French Protestants in the period between the Peace of Alès and the Treaty of the Pyrenees, it was at least fragile, and they knew it.[29] The fervent support given by the Huguenots to the absolutism of divine right was, in part, a way of warding off the dangers that threatened them. Their loyalty to the Crown during the Frondes (1648–51), duly acknowledged by a Royal Declaration in May 1652, might, perhaps have reduced the mistrust felt by the political authorities, had it not been for the English Great Rebellion, which revived with such intensity the image of the Protestant as someone essentially 'seditious' and 'republican'.

The Huguenots tried to mitigate this ricochet effect upon them of the English Revolution by desperately identifying themselves with the Church of England, by emphasizing the royalism of the English Presbyterians, and by furiously denouncing the baseness and heresy of the Independents and sectaries.

As regards the first point, the English royalist refugees in France did nothing to help the Huguenots.[30] Identifying the latter with the Nonconformists at home, they cold-shouldered them, especially as the semi-official envoys of the Parliamentary party in England regularly attended services at Charenton! This antipathy often shown by most of the

---

[28] During the famous case of diabolical possession at the Ursulines' convent in Loudun, a town where there were many Protestants, the latter gave voice to their scepticism and laughed at the efforts of the exorcists.

[29] This is shown, for example, by the dismay and anxiety over the future observable in the correspondence between Rivet (at Leiden) and the Parisian Huguenot lawyer Sarrau. Cf. *Correspondance intégrale d'André Rivet et de Claude Sarrau* (1641–1650), ed. and annotated by Hans Bots and Pierre Leroy, (3 vols., Amsterdam, 1978–82), ii. 342 (Sarrau to Rivet, 20 Dec. 1642).

[30] Some English royalists, however, were more discerning, such as John Cosin, future bishop of Durham, who had cordial relations with a number of French pastors.

English refugees towards the ERF encouraged the French Catholics to equate the Huguenots with the English regicides.

Besides, the royalism of the Presbyterians was not grasped by a poorly informed French public opinion. It was known that the Scottish Presbyterians had been responsible for Charles I's original misfortunes, and, without looking more closely into the facts, they were blamed for the whole series of setbacks which culminated in his execution, the greatest crime committed since the Crucifixion, according to the pastor Baux de l'Angle.[31] Huguenot writers sought, indeed, to outdo each other in protesting their execration of the English regicide 'monsters', in the hope of drowning the few indiscreet Huguenot voices that were raised in favour of the Parliamentary party by persons who failed to see how dangerous such a stance was for the ERF.[32]

Although the Independents advocated a form of church organization that was vigorously rejected by the Huguenots, devoted to their presbyterian-synodal Discipline, nevertheless the theology of many of these Congregationalists was that of Calvinism. Yet the national synod held at Charenton in 1644 took care expressly to condemn the Independents and such sympathisers as they had found among the Huguenots of the maritime provinces, open to English influence. All these efforts proved futile. The French Catholics and, in the first place, the political authorities, did not concern themselves with such nuances, but were satisfied with simplistic propositions, such as that the English revolutionaries were Protestants, therefore Protestants were dangerous persons to have in a monarchical country.

Furthermore, the protection which Cromwell saw fit to extend to the ERF was highly damaging to them. Mazarin needed an alliance with England in order to put an end to the interminable conflict between France and Spain. The Cardinal therefore took care to satisfy the Protector, and the French Protestants were never so well treated[33] as during the short period when Mazarin was not yet sure that the English Commonwealth would side with France. But the Huguenots had only a brief respite. The Declaration of

---

[31] He was most probably the translator into French of a late Remonstrance to Fairfax (18 January 1649) from the presbyterian clergy of London, to which he added a preface. Ten years later he used a similar expression in a *Lettre . . . à feu M. de Saumaise sur son Apologie du roi d'Angleterre* (i.e. the *Defensio regia pro Carolo I*). To this latter Milton replied with his *Pro populo anglicano defensio*, in 1651.

[32] In a sermon preached at Alençon on 24 February 1649 (and published much later) the minister, Hérault, naïvely urged his audience to think ill of the English revolutionaries and, in any case, not to say anything good about them, especially when Catholics were present. The preacher was ardently royalist, but knew that all his parishioners did not share his views. There are other indications of sympathy among the Huguenots of Normandy for the English Parliamentarians.

[33] In one case even scandalously, when the murder of a servant of the bishop of Nîmes, during a scuffle with Huguenots who attacked him, was not followed by a prosecution, thanks to intervention by Cromwell.

May 1652, which had been so favourable to them, was succeeded by that of 1656, which was less advantageous. Besides, it gave notice for the future of a new degree of supervision over the implementation of the Edict of Nantes, which rightly seemed to the Huguenots to imply a sinister threat. Finally, when in 1659 Mazarin authorized the holding of a national synod, he made it clear that it would be the last. This meant a disastrous blow for the organization of the ERF.

Under Mazarin, therefore, Huguenot liberties were eroded, but not in a dramatic way. The Huguenots had been on the defensive since the death of Henri IV. Under Richelieu, religious controversy no longer featured the Homeric invectives of the earlier period, but the change was far from being entirely reassuring for the Huguenots. When they were seen as heretics, the Protestants were simply monsters to be avoided, if they could not be burnt; but if they were envisaged as schismatics, then tradition assigned to the secular arm the task of bringing them back into the flock.

When Mazarin died in 1661, the personal rule of Louis XIV began. The young king lost no time in dissolving the *Compagnie du Saint Sacrement*, a semi-secret society of Catholic notables, founded in 1630, one of whose aims (which also included charitable works) had been to seize every opportunity to harm the Huguenots. Needless to say, what had influenced the king had only been his horror of 'cabals' and 'factions', something of which the Jansenists were to have harsh experience, to say nothing of the ERF.

The Declaration of 1656 was put into effect. Two commissioners were nominated for each province, the Protestant one being selected, so far as possible, from among those thought to be cowardly or venal, and the Catholic one being often the Intendant. In any case, the Intendant was also empowered to resolve their disagreements, and the effect of these judicial proceedings was to inflict severe losses on the ERF, many temples being in jeopardy or suppressed.[34] Certainly, some of these temples had, here and there, been erected in excess of those authorized by the Edict, but the review carried out by the commissions was systematically biased, and most of the *usurpations* and *attentats* laid at the Protestant door were fraudulent inventions. In Poitou, where there were many Huguenot lesser nobles, the availability of *exercices de fief* mitigated matters for a time.[35] But the actively anti-Protestant line being taken by the Court could not but be apparent, even if a declaration of 1669 seemed to take a step backward. In that same year, moreover, a decree of the council forbade Protestants to leave France without special permission. Although it was difficult to apply, the decree showed that the government, aware of the damage inflicted upon Spain by

[34] This frequently happened in the case of temples of *possession* when the consistories concerned could not produce written proof of existence in 1596 and 1597. Having confidence in the Edict of Nantes, they had failed to preserve the documents which had justified the building of the temple when the Edict was first introduced.

[35] After 1679 numerous restrictions were imposed on *exercices de fief* by a series of Council decrees.

the expulsion of the Jews and Moriscos, aimed at the extinction of the ERF, but without wishing to see the faithful emigrate.

A Council decree of 1663 forbade a Protestant who had turned Catholic to go back to his former religion. This showed clearly that, in France, the RPR was suffered rather than authorized; the decree was subsequently to provide a pretext for suppressing numerous temples, on the grounds that a relapsed Catholic had been allowed to attend a service there. In populous urban communities it was not easy to prevent an *agent provocateur* from being present, and, besides, from the theological standpoint, it would have been unthinkable to rebuff those who, in good faith, were asking to become Protestants once more. Another betrayal of the Edict was the permission granted to diocesan officials to being lawsuits against the Protestant consistories in their jurisdiction. The officials seized any and every pretext: the cost of the legal proceedings ruined the Protestant communities, and when the final judgement was given it was regularly to their detriment.[36]

Two main lines of attack can be discerned. The first aimed at destroying Protestant institutions, temples above all, but also schools and academies. A shower of Council decrees multiplied the chances of Protestants' finding themselves in breach of the law, and being immediately punished by the suppression of the church concerned and the banishment of its pastor from the province. Courage began to be needed to become an elder, since, legally, the consistories were the targets *par excellence* for all this chicanery. Nevertheless, until the very end, the last academies to remain open welcomed their normal number of ordinands and the consistories kept up their usual membership.

The second method was directed at individuals, and, above all, at notables: ministers, noblemen, rich bourgeois. Care was taken, in the first place, to draw them towards the king's religion by linking possible abjuration with favours such as pensions, moratoria on their debts, and tax-rebates. The *Caisse des Économats*, which the Huguenots called the *caisse des conversions* and which was administered by a former Protestant, Pellisson, was to be described by Bayle as a *'foire aux âmes'*. In this case, the objects of attention were Huguenots of lower status: every recantation qualified for the gift of a sum of money, often very small. We need to remember the crude psychology derived from Augustinian teaching which justified procedures such as this. Should a man not perceive the truth (by definition, the truth of the Catholic religion), it followed that he was blinded by his passions. By manipulating his greed in favour of the 'true' religion it was claimed that his previous vicious leanings were neutralized so that his impartiality thus

---

[36] In 1683 the barrister Claude Brousson urged the Protestant consistories in the South to rebuff the *Parlement* of Toulouse out of hand and not to attempt any more a legal defence whose futility had become obvious. Cf. p. 308 for another of his initiatives. Later on Brousson took holy orders abroad and returned to France to carry on a clandestine ministry: he died a martyr for his faith, executed in 1698.

recovered might enable him to recognize the truth. Moreover, should the convert's abjuration be insincere, it meant that he was heading for damnation, which made him no worse off, since, as a heretic, he was already subject to that fate. Morally and theologically, the efforts made to attract the Huguenots to the old religion were neither absurd nor objectionable in the eyes of their initiators. But the results achieved remained meagre.[37]

Hence the authorities turned to making the profession of Protestantism as uncomfortable, humiliating, and burdensome as possible. Gradually, niggling vexations were succeeded by open persecution. In the years that followed the Peace of Nijmegen (1678), the Edict of Nantes was casuistically applied: what was not explicitly allowed was forbidden. Decrees framed on this principle were so numerous that they constituted a sword of Damocles hanging over the Huguenots, even though they were far from being systematically implemented. In consequence, in the years just before the Revocation, there were few Protestants who were not in breach of the law, often without knowing it.

More terrible still than the regulations which had gradually closed to the Huguenots all occupations and professions other than agriculture and trade were those which struck at their family life. A Huguenot woman could no longer be a midwife, and Catholic midwives were encouraged to baptize new-born babies, thereby making them *ipso facto* Catholics. Priests and judges were enjoined to attend the deathbeds of Protestants in order to invite recantation *in extremis*; families which opposed this cruel intrusion were liable to severe penalties. Midwives, priests, and judges were not, of course, uniformly lacking in humanity, but, nevertheless the Huguenots lay at their mercy.

As part of the one-sided lawmaking which made it illegal for persons to go over to Protestantism (in formal contradiction with the letter of the Edict of Nantes), a Council decree lowered to seven the legal age at which a Huguenot child could abandon the religion into which he was born. This decree seems to have shocked the acute sense of paternal authority possessed by the French jurists and never to have been applied. It was connected with what became one of the most effective methods for making the obstinate give in, namely, the kidnapping of children, who were taken away from their stubborn Protestant parents by *lettre de cachet* to be brought up (at their parents' expense) in convents or Jesuit colleges. The humbler Protestants were not exposed to this kind of distress, but, as against that, these simple souls were less able than the notables to prepare an escape from France and to play the game of dissimulation, either temporarily (so as to facilitate their

---

[37] Some wretched creatures, who may or may not have begun life as Huguenots, hastened from diocese to diocese to repeat an alleged abjuration which earned them some money. The converters eventually grew wise and took steps to check on clients of this sort more carefully.

eventual departure) or over a long period, like the Nicodemites of the sixteenth century.[38]

During the summer of 1681 Poitou was subjected to the notorious *dragonnades*, the billeting of soldiers in Protestant homes, an unbearable and ruinous procedure which was kept up until the family abjured. This classic method of punishing disobedient elements[39] procured a large number of abjurations in the province. Perhaps with a view to retaining the goodwill of the Protestant princes of Germany, however, the authorities ceased for a time to resort to this brutal proceeding and tried a different tack. A formal *Avertissement* from the Catholic clergy, calling upon the Huguenots to go over to Catholicism, couched in language both unctuous and menacing, was presented to most of the surviving consistories. This amounted to a snare, for the document was presented jointly by the Intendant (or one of his *subdélégués*) and the bishop (or his representative), so that any purely negative reaction by a consistory would be classed as seditious. The Protestant lawyers composed a subtle reply which, after it had been given at Charenton,[40] was imitated by the provincial consistories with slight variations. It was a fervent assertion of absolute submission to the Crown, accompanied by a rejection, respectful but firm, of the spiritual authority claimed by the bishops over the Huguenots, those supposed lost sheep, living in their dioceses. Some time passed before Versailles realized that the *Avertissement* was everywhere receiving the same clever and dilatory type of reply, and then it became necessary to resort again to the *dragonnades*, which had demonstrated their effectiveness in Poitou. During the summer of 1685 this method was applied throughout southern France.

The Court was very close to achieving its first objective. The demolition of temples and the banishment or imprisonment of ministers meant that nothing was left of the Huguenot religious organization. In 1683, at the initiative of Brousson, outdoor services were held in Dauphiné and Vivarais in the places where the temples had been pulled down. This touching reaction, intended to be non-violent, provoked a terrible repression; and, to make matters worse, it was firmly disavowed by the ministers of Charenton and the *Député général*, who thought that only silent and abject submission might, perhaps, postpone the total destruction of French Protestantism.

[38] This term was made up by Calvin to signify those persons who had been won over to the Protestant faith but whom fear of reprisals caused to keep up an outward appearance of Catholicism. He was inspired by the story of Nicodemus, who came to visit Jesus only by night, so as not to compromise his position (John 3:2).

[39] It had been employed, for example, in Brittany to inflict punishment after the fiscal revolt of 1675 and in Pamiers, against the Jansenists hostile to the *Régale*. The depredations of the soldiers billeted on their reluctant hosts soon reduced them to destitution when the military presence went on for more than a few days.

[40] After the last national synod in 1659, the four or five ministers of Charenton constitued *de facto* the sole central body possessed by the ERF. They collected and circulated information, suggested defensive tactics, and were the first to be warned of the Government's anti-Huguenot measures. But their role lacked any legal basis and was wholly unofficial.

The authorities had, however, foolishly supposed that wherever the temples had been demolished the Huguenots, for want of anything else, would attend mass on Sundays. But this did not happen at all. The Government thus found itself faced with an unexpected situation of apparent de-Christianization. Were tens of thousands of subjects of the Most Christian King to live like beasts or heathens? Immensely long journeys to one of the few temples still left standing made possible belated Protestant christenings, marriages, and occasional participation in the Lord's Supper, but these were impracticable for many Huguenots. At that time, in France, the registration of births, marriages and deaths was the responsibility of the clergy after the Edict of Nantes: the *curés* and the pastors. The banishment of the latter created a void. A curious Council decree of September 1685—which was never applied—provided for the appointment, in each province, of an itinerant minister who was to be paid by the king and who was to perform christenings and marriages of those Huguenots deprived of temples and therefore of resident pastors; he was also supposed to keep the deaths registered. This decree plainly exposes the confusion of the civil authorities in face of the disconcerting situation their anti-Protestant policy had created.

At this point, the Court had either to beat a retreat or else go on to the bitter end. The latter solution was the one adopted, and indeed, there were many arguments in its favour. The widespread *dragonnades* of the summer of 1685 had induced many abjurations, and the tax-exemptions given latterly to facilitate them were affecting fiscal returns adversely. It was expedient to stop distinguishing between those Frenchmen who were old Catholics, those who were '*nouveaux catholiques*' (recent converts), and obstinate Huguenots. Under the specious pretext that there were no more Huguenots in France—which enabled Louis XIV, who had confirmed the Edict after his majority, to avoid breaking his word too obviously—the Edict of Nantes was revoked in October 1685. No more than a score of temples (there had been over nine hundred initially) were left standing, while the organization of the ERF, their schools, hospitals, and academies, had disappeared several years earlier. But hundreds of thousands of Huguenots had abjured under coercion or by involuntary proxy (when a few notables had recanted in the name of the whole community), or else had succeeded in not abjuring by abandoning their homes and going into hiding.

Having officially become, once more, *toute catholique*,[41] France could now deal severely (and did not fail to do so!) with those French who did not attend mass on Sundays. For a while, the Court could flatter itself with the thought that the RPR had vanished forever from the kingdom. But disenchantment followed quickly. At least 200,000 Huguenots, perhaps

[41] See Pierre Bayle, *Ce que c'est que la France toute catholique* (see Further Reading).

more, managed to escape abroad, despite the prohibition and the very heavy penalties incurred by those caught in the act. As for the Protestants left in France, the majority of them put up a stubborn and cunning resistance to forced Catholicization. Even if their children were baptized by a priest and even if they themselves were unable, for several years, to evade going to mass, at least they obstinately refused to take Communion *à la papauté*, as they called it among themselves. Consequently, marriage in church became impossible for them, and, as a result, there were eventually tens of thousands of Protestant couples in the Midi who were 'living in concubinage', which created awkward legal situations. The Revocation had not solved a problem, it had merely given rise to several new ones, which persisted until 1787, when an Edict of Toleration for Protestants acknowledged officially that the Revocation had failed.

How are we to understand the policy of the French Court, which too many earlier historians have been content to condemn? Rooting out religious pluralism from the kingdom was the equivalent of making prevail in France the famous principle *cuius regio, eius religio*, which was seen as an essential rule of sound policy.[42] Religious pluralism spelt anarchy and sedition, and looked like a signal weakness in any country that allowed it. Conversely, religious uniformity was considered to be the best bond of national unity. The old Gallican slogan, *Une foi, une loi, un roi* was taken to embody an essential political truth; it would be wrong to view the religious policy of Versailles merely in terms of crude Catholic devotionalism. The text of the Edict of Nantes itself had expressed the pious hope that all Frenchmen might one day be reunited in one faith, and the Crown never ceased, all through the century, to desire the eventual accomplishment of a project, which, even if it was not given permanent priority, continued to be a constant objective of internal policy.

The actual date of the Revocation was not dictated solely by developments inside the kingdom. A number of external circumstances contribute to explaining it. There was not only the accession to the English throne of the Catholic James II, but there were also the bad relations between the French King and the Vatican. Louis XIV hoped to force the Pope to congratulate him on the Revocation, but in fact Innocent XI took his time over this. In addition, 1683 had seen the victory of the Emperor, aided by John Sobieski, over the Turks. The king of France had expected a Turkish victory, after which, having carefully refrained from helping to defend Vienna, he intended to intervene as saviour of Christendom. Events

[42] The Treaty of Westphalia in 1648, like that of Augsburg in 1555, had applied this principle. Even so, however, it had allowed the right of *beneficium emigrandi* to the minority communities, just as this had been allowed to the Socinians of Poland a little earlier. It is quite possible that the better-informed among the French Protestants had counted on being allowed to realize their property and leave the country, if ever the Edict of Nantes should be abrogated. In any case, the formal ban on Huguenot laymen leaving France seemed to some to be one of the most disgraceful features of the Revocation.

had spoilt his calculations, and he needed to regild his tarnished escutcheon as the Most Christian King.

Certainly, subsequent events proved to the full that the Revocation (and, more generally, the crushing of the ERF, of which it was the culmination) was an appalling political mistake. But it is hard to see how Louis XIV, given the man he was, could have avoided it. The Revocation resulted from a fatal misunderstanding of the real factors in the problem, leading him inevitably to adopt an illusory solution. The conception of the RPR that prevailed at the Court was disastrously wrong. It was seen as a sort of Catholicism gone astray, and it seemed therefore that with the Protestant notables won over and the pastors banished, then, being deprived of leaders and 'agitators', the Huguenot people, a passive mass, would rally obediently to the king's religion. This meant ignoring the sense of personal responsibility cultivated through Protestantism, in short, the staunch individualism of the faithful. Though poison for the strong, pride is the strength of the weak. The practice of Calvinism had, in a way, instilled into the humble something of the abstract principle of the priesthood of all believers, the sense of being adult and the view that the first religious duty was no longer to submit to priests or Prince, but to obey the commands of God. With the institutions of the RPR dismantled and the pastors driven away, the Protestant people filled their place. It was their sense of personal identity, their gut refusal to be manipulated by others, as much, perhaps, as their concern for their eternal salvation, that the Huguenots expressed in their loyalty to their faith.

Before their departure into exile,[43] the pastors had explained to their flocks that the misfortunes which had come upon them were a punishment from God for their sins. Brought up on the Old Testament, the Huguenots—the New Israel—knew that God chastises his elect for their good and that ordeals have a positive role. From this religious standpoint, the French Court was only the secondary cause unwittingly executing the designs of Providence. This analysis of the situation, though seemingly masochistic, was in reality stimulating. The Huguenots did not feel that they were being sacrificed to the Moloch of *raison d'État*, but rather that they were being tested by a God who still saw them as his favourite children. If their resistance had been politically based, it would soon have petered out on encountering a reality that proved the futility of their efforts and made emigration the best course to take. But that resistance was based on the

---

[43] Unlike the laymen, ministers were allowed to choose between recantation and exile. They were given only fifteen days to make up their minds and had to leave behind their property and also any of their children over seven years old. The fact that under these conditions between 75 and 78 per cent of the ministers chose exile bears witness to the strength of their beliefs. The authorities cherished no illusion, of course, regarding the sincerity of abjurations extorted under duress, but comforted themselves with the hope that the children and grandchildren of the 'new Catholics' would eventually become true Catholics, as happened in more than one case.

intention to obey God rather than men: and in such cases 'it is not necessary to hope in order to undertake, nor to succeed in order to persevere'.[44] Furthermore, several years of a persecution both petty and iniquitous had supplemented the condescending contempt traditionally felt for 'Papist idolatry' with a virulent hatred which by itself would have constituted a major obstacle to successful catholicization.[45] What the Court, imprisoned in its self-blinding arrogance, had failed to foresee was the resistance of the Huguenot common people, against which a sovereign of those days could bring to bear only the ineffective weapon of a repression that, though ferocious, was necessarily intermittent.

How are we to assess the role played by the Catholic Church in all this? There has possibly been a tendency to exaggerate it. Perhaps the Church was not so much the driving force as the fifth wheel on the coach. Certainly it supplied the respectable justifications, the propaganda, and quite often the personnel employed in implementing a policy which it had outlined and for which it had suggested several of the methods. But one may doubt whether it had been able to determine the adoption of such a policy and to unleash it. The Church was happy to ascribe to itself a decisive role in the developments that led to the Revocation, but the fact remains that what the dragoons said to the Huguenots was 'le Roi le veut'.

The indictments composed by Protestant writers against the fate inflicted on their confession (in books printed in Holland) helped to overstate the role played by the Catholic Church in the misfortunes of the Huguenots. The monarchical loyalism of these writers prevented them from directly indicting the Crown; in any case, it would have been highly tactless to do so. They therefore blamed exclusively the abominable counsels given to the Prince by their sworn enemy, the Roman Church, and, without delving deeply into the reasons for the policy that struck at them, they stigmatized the methods employed to enforce it and the pharisaical propaganda orchestrated by the Church. To consider the Revocation as, above all, a last spasm of the Counter-Reformation is perhaps a mistake, thereby attributing to a misconceived piety what is to be ascribed to *raison d'État*— itself also misconceived.

The Huguenot writers assembled overwhelming evidence of the inhumanity of the methods used by their persecutors, but, on the theoretical plane, they merely clung to the legal formalism which desperately recalled the 'perpetual' character given to the Edict of Nantes by Henri IV. Down to the Revocation itself their trials had not yet caused their attachment to absolutism to waver, any more than they had estranged them from a

---

[44] This is supposed to have been the motto of William the Silent.

[45] It is instructive that this failed to happen only in the few dioceses where the bishop had refused to allow the dragoons to come in and had relied exclusively on persevering with persuasion, as for instance Percin de Montgaillard in his tiny diocese of Saint Pons.

dogmatism which forbade any programme of toleration; indeed, in principle they accorded liberty to 'the true religion' only, that is, to their own. However, there began to emerge, at the level of polemics, in opposition to the argument of authority, invoked in its purest form by the 'converters', a reference to an authority no less ultimate than the alleged infallibility of the Catholic, Apostolic, and Roman Church. This was an authority that was atomized and no longer institutional, namely, the dictate of the individual conscience, even if that individual was a very humble person, such as, for example, an illiterate old woman.[46] There is a suggestive parallelism between the hesitant beginnings of this doctrinal position (which spread rapidly in the *Refuge*) and the fact that, because all corporate action had been temporarily made impossible for the Huguenots, resistance to Catholicization had become the personal responsibility of each French Protestant.

[46] In the *Conférence* of Jean Claude with Bossuet, the former chose this extreme case to set against the authority of Councils and of Tradition. A minister at Charenton since 1666, Claude, who died at the Hague in 1687, was one of the leading figures in the French Protestant community of his time. Bossuet, Bishop of Condom and later of Meaux, was the great Court preacher and an eminent controversialist, for whom the Revocation of the Edict of Nantes meant the fulfilment of his heart's desire.

Further Reading

Contemporary sources

[Bayle, Pierre], *Ce que c'est que la France toute catholique sous le règne de Louis le Grand* (Saint-Omer [=Amsterdam], 1686); ed. É. Labrousse (Paris, 1973).

[Benoît, Élie], *Histoire de l'Édit de Nantes, contenant les choses les plus remarquables qui se sont passées depuis sa publication, jusqu'à l'Édit de Révocation* (5 vols., Delft, 1693-5).

[Brousson, Claude], *État des réformés en France* (3 vols., Cologne [=Holland], 1684).

[Claude, Jean], *Relation succincte de l'estat où sont maintenant les églises réformées de France* (n.p., 1666); tr., *A brief Relation of the persecution and sufferings of the reformed Churches in France* (London, 1668).

[——], *Considérations sur les Lettres circulaires de l'Assemblée du Clergé de France de l'année 1682* (The Hague, 1683).

[——], *Les plaintes des Protestans cruellement opprimez dans le royaume de France* (Cologne [=Holland], 1686); ed. with introduction and notes by Frank Puaux (Paris, 1885). The abridged English version, *An Account of the persecutions and oppressions of the Protestants in France* (1686), was publicly burnt to appease the French Ambassador. The full translation did not appear until 1707: *A short account of the Complaints . . . of the Protestants in . . . France* (London, 1707).

The works listed above were written by Protestants and are not impartial, but they provide much evidence from original sources.

Vol. v of the *Catalogue de l'Histoire de France* (Bibliothèque Nationale, Paris, 1968) gives under the heading Ld^{176} a very full bibliography of pamphlets concerning seventeenth-century France.

Short list of modern works

Léonard, É.-G., *Histoire générale du protestantisme*, ii (Paris, 1961), chs. iii, vii, with a full bibliography; English tr., ed. H. H. Rowley (London, 1967).

Ligou, Daniel, *Le Protestantisme en France de 1598 à 1715* (Paris, 1968).

Mours, Samuel, *Le Protestantisme en France au XVIIe siècle* (Paris, 1967).

Two excellent discussions of particular issues are provided by:

Deyon, Solange, *Du loyalisme au refus: les protestants français et leur député général entre la Fronde et la Révocation* (Lille, 1976).

Stauffer, Richard, *L'Affaire d'Huisseau, Une controverse protestante au sujet de la réunion des chrétiens (1670–1671)* (Paris, 1969).

XI

French Calvinist Political Thought, 1534–1715

MYRIAM YARDENI

IT is no accident that, although there are excellent studies of particular phases in French Calvinist political thought, there is no comprehensive study covering the whole period from its appearance in 1534 until 1715. Indeed, from the beginning, and even after 1715, two apparently opposed tendencies characterized the political thought of the Reformed religion in France. On the one hand, there was fidelity to Calvin's ideas, and on the other hand, there was an unfailing pragmatism; the two together make it hard to take a general view. The explanation of this paradox probably lies with Calvin himself. It is too easily forgotten that the first edition of the *Institutes of the Christian Religion* was not only the product of an exceptional logic, brilliance, and intellectual honesty, but was also a work written for a specific occasion,[1] a point made very clear in the preface of 1535, the *Epistle to the King*. After the affair of the Placards in 1534, when manifestos ridiculing the mass were prominently displayed, the stigmas of rebellion and republicanism were ineffaceably imprinted on the image of French Calvinism as far as French public opinion was concerned. in his *Institutes* Calvin sought to give the lie to these charges, describing his preface as being 'a complete defence'.[2]

The preface, which is not lacking in genuine French patriotism, underlines the absolute loyalty of the Reformed religion to the king. As is well known, the *Institutes*, using purely religious arguments, condemn all rebellion, for according to Calvin, all authority, including that exercised by a tyrant, is of divine origin. Yet a close examination of the *Institutes* reveals ambiguities, and sometimes the work seems to be written by a citizen rather than by a subject. In the first place, the total submission due to the civil authorities is essentially political, while on the religious plane the subject is absolutely free to be guided by his conscience. Calvin naturally rejected the edict of 1540 which defined heresy as a crime of *lèse-majesté*.

There was for Calvin in the spiritual sphere, a Church of God, that is, the

---

[1] P. Mesnard (see Further Reading), 276–7.
[2] Jean Calvin, *Institution de la religion chrétienne*, ed. J. Pannier (Paris, 1961), i. 35 (Epistre).

church of the elect. In the temporal sphere, so to speak, there were churches which, although Christian, disputed over dogma, thus demonstrating the disappearance of Christian unity. In differing degrees, these churches represented parts of the truth, and even of the ideal church; the choice of belonging to one of these churches was a matter of liberty of conscience. The choice did not conflict with total submission to the civil and political authority as willed and commanded by God. The submission and even the martyrdom of the early Christians constituted in Calvin's eyes a striking illustration of this thesis. Society and, in this instance, the state, were for Calvin absolute necessities, since human justice and equity were exercised through their mediation. The magistrate who was not a private person, was expected to exercise his powers within the limits of the laws. Obviously, the magistrate or the ruling authority almost always departed from these principles, but the duty of the people was nevertheless to obey.

Most of these themes, included in the famous ch. XVI (on *Civil government*) of the edition of 1541 (a reworking of ch. VI in that of 1536), underwent no alteration in the various Latin and French editions, continually revised by Calvin down to 1559. One may wonder whether the citizen's part consists in blind loyalty or in total resignation, since all that remains for him is to pray to God. Nevertheless, this terrible Calvinist, and in this respect Lutheran, doctrine of non-resistance was qualified by some reservations. First, on the religious plane there was room for civil disobedience. Again, should there be a conflict between the divine will and the royal will there was room for pacific intervention by the inferior magistrates, who themselves also partook of divine authority. The Estates and the *parlements* should probably be added to the authorities competent to intervene.[3] Moreover, after 1560, the date of the conspiracy of Amboise, some significant changes can be discerned on the part of Calvin himself, even though he condemned the conspiracy unequivocally. There had already appeared in the 1559 Latin edition of the *Institutes* the much-discussed phrase according to which the ruler who exceeded the bounds of his authority by setting himself against God had abrogated his own power';[4] and in Calvin's *Homily on the First Book of Samuel* (1560)[5] the intervention of the inferior magistrates became a form of control.

To be sure only the inferior magistrates and neither the people nor groups of individuals had the right to intervene, to correct, or even to oppose. And for Calvin, opposing certainly did not mean rebelling, even against a tyrant, since tyranny was also installed by God's will and it was necessary to wait upon that same divine will for its end. History was full of examples of tyrants punished and tyrannies destroyed. All the people

---

[3] J. W. Allen (see Further Reading), 59.
[4] Ind. iv. 20; (see Further Reading), ii. 219.
[5] Skinner, 214.

could do was to express themselves not directly but through their 'ephors', and it remains a question whether for Calvin such 'ephors' existed in the monarchies of his time and were the 'Princes of the Blood'.

At the outset of the Wars of Religion there were thus three breaches in Calvinist teaching through which revolutionary theses could burst in. First, there was the Lutheran theory of the right and even the duty of the inferior magistrates to oppose tyranny.[6] Secondly, there was Calvin's thesis concerning the ephors; and thirdly, the possibility that a ruler who had abrogated his own power became a private citizen, deprived of the aura of divine authority. Nevertheless, Calvin was very careful not to enlarge this breach by referring to the biblical examples of Moses or of the revolt of Othniel in the Book of Judges, which for him remained exceptional cases.

The period of the Wars of Religion

Political thought deals with the institution and organization of the bonds which exist, or ought to exist, between the individual and the state, through the medium of society. Calvinist political thought in France is no exception. However, although it originated in what was peculiar to and typical of sixteenth-century France, it has universal implications. Indeed, its great novelty and modernity lay in the fact that it was called upon to confront problems that were unprecedented and to find original answers in the form of theoretical as well as practical solutions. The problems were modern and the responses were modern, even though wrapped, according to the fashion of the time, in an aura of false antiquity and medieval constitutionalism, especially in the sixteenth century.

Three principal and separate phases can easily be distinguished in the development of French Calvinist political thought down to 1715: the period of the Wars of Religion, the period of the Edict of Nantes, and that of the *Refuge*. Undoubtedly, the most innovatory phase, sometimes even termed revolutionary, was that of the Wars of Religion, a phase which lasted at least into the 1580s. The two later periods saw, in the main, only variations on the theses formulated during the Wars of Religion which provided an almost inexhaustible arsenal of weapons that could be easily adapted to varied historical situations.

The political thought of the Huguenots during the Wars of Religion proceeded by a very long and uncertain road, which led from Calvin's limited monarchy to the popular sovereignty of the monarchomachs and then to absolutism sanctioned by divine right. The first two stages were particularly innovatory, even revolutionary. Although there are antecedents for each of the great changes undergone by Calvinist political thought

---

[6] O. K. Olson, 'Theology and Revolution; Magdeburg, 1550–1551', *The Sixteenth Century Journal*, 3 (1972), 56–79; E. Wolgast, *Die Religionsfrage als Problem des Widerstandrechts im 16 Jahrhundert* (Heidelberg, 1980), 25–7.

during the Wars of Religion, there can be no doubt that the three conceptions, a strong but limited monarchy of the Renaissance type,[7] that of the monarchomachs, and that of divine-right absolutism, are difficult to reconcile. Furthermore, the political theories of the Huguenots in this period were readily adapted to historical circumstances which were themselves changing at an accelerating pace, without concern for coherence or continuity.

The end of the 1550s and, above all, the beginning of the Religious Wars, are significant for the politicization of French Protestantism, or, in other words, for the seizure of control of the 'Huguenot party' by the aristocracy. For, as soon as the Huguenots took the road to war the influence of the military—of the aristocracy—gained momentum.

Meanwhile, during the Religious Wars, the French Calvinists adapted and elaborated the organization and structures which were to be theirs until the revocation of the Edict of Nantes and the diaspora. The presbyterian and synodal structure dates from 1559. From this date, each church was directed by a consistory formed of a pastor and elders. A group of churches formed a colloquy. France was divided into synodal provinces which held regular synods. Above these was the national synod. This was a form of organization, simultaneously very democratic and very centralized, from which the Calvinist spirit of order excluded any tendency to anarchy.

This institutional system in part explains the inconsistencies and the great changes which occurred within such a brief period in French Calvinist political theory, even though some of the first pastors trained in Geneva were of noble origin.[8] Yet the institutional explanation is insufficient, making it necessary to return to Huguenot pragmatism, with its gift for propaganda adapted to the needs of the moment, combined with a conspicuous capacity for evolving theories and concepts, due probably to the joint influence of lawyers and theologians on the political thought of the years 1559 to 1598.

Down to the first war of religion, the chief problem occupying Calvinist theorists was religious toleration, or, to use the language of the time, the problem of liberty of conscience. At the beginning of the 1560s the great Huguenot thesis was still that there should be no interference, no contradiction between the religion of subjects and their fidelity and loyalty to the king. But once the king took a different view this beautiful logic collapsed, as became more and more obvious as the massacre of St Bartholomew drew closer.

The first breach in this convenient evasion of the problem of French Protestants' relations with their king and with France, in a political context,

---

[7] Cf. J. Russell Major, *Representative Institutions of Renaissance France* (Madison, 1960).

[8] R. M. Kingdon, *Geneva and the Coming of the Wars of Religion in France, 1555–1563* (Geneva, 1956), 12, 138.

was the Conspiracy of Amboise in May 1560. The aim of the conspiracy, led by La Renaudie, was to seize the person of the young King Francis II, and thus to eliminate by physical force the baneful and 'illegal' influence of the Guises. Calvin denounced the conspiracy unequivocally, but two of his close followers, Hotman and Beza, the future theorists of monarchomach thought, supported it, at least morally.

The aristocratic stamp of this conspiracy, behind which Condé's figure can be discerned, is beyond doubt. Politically, the conspiracy can be put into the tradition of noble claims to rights of supervision and of giving counsel. It was easy to slide from this position towards claiming the right of intervention by the magistrates—and the nobles, especially the princes of the blood.

It was in the wake of the urgent need to explain the Conspiracy of Amboise to the French that the distinctively French form of Calvinist political thought originated. This is not to say that ties with Geneva did not remain strong nor that inspiration did not sometimes come from there. But in future Calvinist thought had to respond to questions and situations that arose from French realities and to give replies accordingly.

The first task for those who wished to justify, or at least to explain the Conspiracy of Amboise was to present it as an action undertaken to rescue the king from the hands of those who held him prisoner. For the king was still if not absolute then at least inviolable in the popular view of the Huguenots no less than of Catholics. He represented the highest interests of the kingdom. From this there followed that Protestants should suffer martyrdom for their faith, but it was also their duty to intervene when the kingdom was at stake as was made plain in an anonymous pamphlet of 1560, an early echo of the Magdeburg theses.[9] Hence the patriotic tone of all the apologies for the Conspiracy of Amboise, presented as a spontaneous uprising of true Frenchmen against foreign usurpers, in this case the Guises. In the *Histoire du Tumulte d'Amboise* (Strasburg, 1560), the 'Estates' in whose name the nobility had taken up arms made their entry into Huguenot political thought, presaging Hotman's *Franco-Gallia* of 1573.

All these themes were taken up again and developed after the massacre of Vassy in 1562, which together with the armed rising of Condé marked the beginning of the Wars of Religion. On all sides the role of the nobility in the defence of kingdom and king was extolled. The view, too, was expressed that if the country was suffering from financial difficulties, these could be solved by confiscating the property of foreigners, that is, of the clergy.

What characterized French Calvinist political thought between the Conspiracy of Amboise and the massacre of St Bartholomew was a slide from the *right* to resist to the *duty* to resist, whenever the fatherland, France,

[9] *Briève remonstrance des estats de France au roy leur souverain seigneur* . . . (Rouen, 1560).

the kingdom, or the state was in danger. The number of factors held to endanger France kept on increasing. Among these, the Italian queen-mother, Catherine de Médicis, held a place of honour.

During these years a slow and almost imperceptible movement towards a new type of constitutionalism became apparent. This new character stemmed from the combination of the traditional and continuing demands of the nobility with the aspirations of the patriotic humanism of scholars and intellectuals, interwoven with the problems and needs of liberty of conscience. Besides the weighty noble presence, there intruded an element which, by the standards of the time was undoubtedly democratic. The state was no longer regarded as uniquely the king's affair, at least once he ceased to care for the interests of his faithful subjects, Catholic or Protestant, that is, once he oppressed them: or, expressed differently, once he was no longer capable of representing and personifying the good of all. It is true that the democratic element here is of a religious, not a social character. Nevertheless, it is possible to perceive the possibility that the king would not be able or willing to represent or defend with impartial equity the interests of all his subjects. Yet the king, kingdom, and subjects formed an indivisible unity.

The presence of all these elements latent in Huguenot thought before St Bartholomew makes it easier to understand the growing radicalism of Calvinist political theory. But a certain vagueness still persists because these elements were wrapped up in a language of loyalty, of submission to the king, and of patriotism, concealing the slide into monarchomachism after St Bartholomew. An evolution in ways of thinking, opportunism, and a need to adapt all probably played their part in these slow mutations. But it must also be appreciated that forms and modes of expression were much more than an attempt to conceal realities.

After St Bartholomew there was no more camouflage, but an explosion of revolutionary theses. Psychological shock, consternation, the physical need to defend life and property swept away all restraint. This was a real revolution not only in the theses propounded, but also in mentality and outlook. It saw too the birth of a profoundly original kind of political thought. Certainly it is possible to take the great representative works of this period, along with innumerable pamphlets, and to link them with antecedent writings. Thus Duplessis-Mornay's *Vindiciae contra Tyrannos*, published in 1579, offers many similarities with the *Discours de la servitude volontaire* of Étienne de La Boétie, a Catholic and a friend of Montaigne. This was written before 1550 but published only in 1576 by Simon Goulart, a Protestant doctor from Dauphiné, in his celebrated collection of pamphlets, *Mémoires de l' Estat de France*, Produced after the massacre of St Bartholomew.[10] Much has been written about the scholastic origins of the

[10] *Mémoires de l'Estat de France sous Charles IX* (3 vols, Meidelbourg, 1578).

theory of resistance and of popular sovereignty. It is easy to detect the theses of Pierre d'Ailly, of William of Ockham, and even of Thomas Aquinas in the writings of Beza, Hotman, and Duplessis-Mornay. The great—and the less great—theorists, jurists, theologians, and historians of these years, all highly educated, certainly knew scholastic philosophy and theology, but the profound aversion felt by those of the Reformed faith (even if Calvin's own views were more subtle) towards all scholasticism is a feature of European culture. There can also be found in Huguenot political literature after St Bartholomew echoes of Lutheran resistance theories. Hotman, in his *Franco-Gallia*, a work conceived and written in the 1560s and published in 1573, embedded much of his argument and many of his allusions in the setting of a mythical and imaginary history of Gaul. But this is not the problem. Arguments were drawn from anywhere without distinction and adapted to the immediate, if unprecedented, situation, with the result that all these arguments were entirely transformed, becoming the property and indeed the invention of their authors. It was no longer the origins and the sources of inspiration that mattered, but the actual situation and the reality that had to be faced. Consequently, this political thought became for the first time in European history, a compact and coherent 'ideology'.[11]

The immediate context was obviously the massacre—or massacres—of St Bartholomew in 1572. The larger context was France and the French, in whose eyes the Calvinists constituted an intractable and rebellious minority. Hence, the pressing necessity of finding a foundation of universal validity for the political theories which crystallized in the years following St Bartholomew until 1584, when Henry of Navarre became, as a result of the Salic law, the legitimate successor to the throne. Hence, too, the wish to demonstrate that the problems the Huguenots came up against were not uniquely religious. These problems were, it was argued, by virtue of their universal aspects and their political and constitutional implications the concern of all Frenchmen—Catholics, *Politiques*, as well as Calvinists.

This was already the thesis advanced in the *Réveille-matin* of Eusèbe Philadelphe, probably Nicolas Barnaud, though the work has also been attributed to Beza. Published in 1574, the *Réveille-matin* asked that 'all our Catholics, our patriots, our good neighbours and all the rest of the French, who are treated worse than beasts, should wake up this time so as to perceive their misery and take counsel together how to remedy their misfortunes'.[12] What had evidently become the burning problem was the question of the limits to be set on the authority of a king who had become through the Massacre a conspirator against some of his people, a tyrant, and even a usurper, since he had usurped the attributes that belong to God alone. This

---

[11] D. R. Kelley, *The Beginning of Ideology* (see Further Reading) 307-14.

[12] *Le Réveille-matin des François* (Edinburgh, 1573), 81-2.

distinction is very important, since by it the usurper ceased to be a public personage against whom revolt was forbidden.

From now on the limits of royal authority were analysed in the context of the ties between king and people—people, not subjects. As early as 1573 there appeared the first important and innovatory works on the subject, of which the most celebrated is the *France gauloise* of François Hotman, or in its Latin version, the *Franco-Gallia*. In 1574 there came *Du droit des magistrats sur leurs sujets* of Theodore Beza and, finally, in 1579 the *Vindiciae contra Tyrannos* of Philippe Duplessis-Mornay. These are the three great monarchomach classics, but the harvest of pamphlets which claimed to be political treatises was extremely rich. Innocent Gentillet's best-known work was his 'Anti-Machiavel' but the *Discours sur les moyens de bien gouverner* of 1576 deserves mention. There are also the pamphlets of Pierre Fabre and Nicolas Barnaud, while a very small selection from the mass of impassioned and fiery pamphlets may be cited:—the *Déclaration des causes qui ont meu ceux de la Religion à reprendre les armes* (1575), the *Protestation des Églises Réformées de France* (n.d.), the *Discours merveilleux de la vie, actions et deportemens de Catherine de Médicis* (1575), the *Response à la question à savoir s'il est loisible de résister par armes* (1575), the *Tocsin contre les massacreurs* (1577), all printed in Simon Goulart's collection, *Mémoires de l'Estat de France*.

The monarchomachs, as their name makes plain, did not like kings. For Hotman, the history of France was the story of a gradual and continuous usurpation, the seizure of power by the kings over the people, for in earlier times the kings 'were no less under the authority and power of the people than the people were under theirs'.[13] The French monarchy was in essence a monarchy tempered by the power of the Estates, who elected, supervised, and even deposed kings. For Hotman and the pamphleteers who followed him, the assemblies played the same role in the last analysis as the ephors did for Calvin. Hotman's monarchy was a feudal monarchy, with sovereignty belonging to the people, or, rather, to the Estates who represented them. Curiously, Hotman, a lawyer, saw the *parlements* as one of the greatest dangers, along with kings of course, to the people's liberties. These precedents drawn from French history endowed Hotman's writings with a special flavour and authority; moreover he was perhaps, under his own and other names, the most active and prolific pamphleteer in the era of the Wars of Religion. One of his great innovations was the exploitation of the history of France in the service of politics and propaganda on so large a scale.

The monarchy of Beza, as it appeared in the *Droit des Magistrats*, was also a limited one. Although hereditary, it was so only by virtue of the Estates' consent. The Estates-General, which represented the people, had

---

[13] *Franco-Gallia* (1573), ed. R. E. Giesey and J. H. M. Salmon (Cambridge, 1972), 155.

full competence to act in the people's name, and it was in the Estates-General that the subordinate magistrates could express their opinions. The government of the state was based on a contract that bound king and people to each other. It was understood that kings were created for the people and not people for the kings. However, the people as such did not have the right to revolt. Again, a private person did not have the right to resist a tyrant, and so 'he had either to depart elsewhere, or having appealed to God, submit to the yoke'.[14] Only the subordinate magistrates could act in the name of the people and even appeal to foreign powers for help against a tyrant.

Pierre Mesnard summed up the *Droit des Magistrats* in the following way. 'Thus, in this state which has as its foundation a contract between the people and the sovereign, the paradoxical conclusion is reached that: (1) the regime is formally monarchical; (2) its basis is democratic; (3) its government is aristocratic. There nevertheless still remains the permanent possibility of a religious insurrection in the name of the sacred and overriding rights of truth.'[15] One addition is needed to this summary, that such an insurrection would be made not only in the name of religious truth, but also in the name of natural rights, a point rightly brought out by modern research.[16]

The *Vindiciae contra Tyrannos*[17] is not only the last, but also the most complete of the monarchomach treatises. It set out to answer four of the most difficult and burning questions of the day. These were: (1) whether subjects were obliged to obey a prince who commanded them to transgress the law of God; (2) whether they could resist him and in what way; (3) whether they could resist a prince who violated the laws of the state; (4) whether in these two last cases neighbouring princes had the right or duty to intervene.

The first two questions were easy to answer. Since God is superior to the king, God must be obeyed first. The right to resist comes from below and belongs to communities, not to individuals. France was composed essentially of a federation of communities, in which each community and each magistrate could exercise the right of self-defence. The king in Duplessis-Mornay's eyes was a king with the duty to protect the interests of his people. He was also controlled by the institutions that emanated from popular sovereignty, though, unlike Hotman, Duplessis-Mornay assigned this role to the *parlements*.

In order to answer the last two questions Duplessis-Mornay developed a double theory of contract, in which natural rights played a role of prime

---

[14] *Du Droit des Magistrats*, ed. R. M. Kingdon (Geneva, 1971), 2.

[15] Mesnard, 326.

[16] Skinner, ii. 318–38.

[17] *A Defence of Liberty against Tyrants*, ed. H. J. Laski (London, 1924), which reprints the English editions of 1648 and 1689.

importance. The contract was concluded between God, the king, and the inferior magistrates—that is, the people—for the good of the community, in this case the state. By the contract between God and the king, the king undertook to govern in the name of God, that is, with justice. It was the duty of the magistrates to ensure that the king fulfilled his duties under his contract with God. Thus it was the duty of the magistrates to resist the king should he fail in his duties.

Democracy and the sovereignty of the people are the two main conclusions of the monarchomachic theories, if they are interpreted in isolation from their historical context. But when put back into the realities of their time, their message is very different. For one thing, it should not be forgotten that, even for the monarchomachs, royal authority was conferred by God, and was therefore of divine origin. But this authority was to be exercised for the benefit of the people, and from this arose all the checks and systems of control. The people was sovereign only in the sense that power should be exercised for the good of the people, that is, for the good of the community. The people, not knowing what its proper interests were, could not act on its own and had to obey orders. The people's natural representatives, the magistrates, could alone act on behalf of the people. Seen in the context of the realities of the Wars of Religion, this is a coherent and brand-new political system which links the feudal past with a democracy that was to be born some centuries later.

Meanwhile, as early as the beginning of the 1580s, even before Henri of Navarre became heir presumptive to the throne, the fashion for monarchomachy suffered a·distinct decline. True, some scattered pamphlets can still be found which faintly echo monarchomach theories. There is, for instance, the *Miroir des Français*, published in 1582 by Nicolas de Montand, probably a pseudonym for Nicolas Barnaud. Moreover, Hotman and Duplessis-Mornay continued to be the two most prolific pamphleteers of these years. Duplessis-Mornay even inserted into his new pamphlets whole passages lifted from his older writings, published in the 1560s and 1570s. Now, however, he was preaching a new policy based on different political theories. From now on he put his stress upon a strong and authoritarian king, the best and indeed the only guarantor of national unity, a true king, who looked at the Huguenots 'with the eye of a father' and who preached toleration.[18] Hotman for his part, radically recast his *Franco-Gallia*, notably the passages on the election of kings by the Estates. Beza, alone of the monarchomach triumvirate, remained uncompromising—but then he was in Geneva.

This new policy and these new ideas resulted from a rapprochement between the Huguenots and the *Malcontents*, led by Henri de

[18] *Exhortation à la paix aux François Catholiques* (Poitiers, 1574), in *Mémoires de l'Estat de France* iii. 490.

Montmorenci-Damville, governor of Languedoc, and then with the other *Politiques*, a process which accompanied and even somewhat preceded the monarchomach explosion. There can probably be glimpsed in the feudal-federal state of the *Vindiciae* the outlines of the Languedoc of Damville.[19]

A second phase in the rapprochement with the moderate Catholics crystallized round the political moves of François, duc d'Alençon, the king's younger brother, who represented the reversionary interest. Inevitably, this ideological and political rapprochement put a new valuation upon the role of the king in the state, even of a king such as Henri III, who was practically discredited in the eyes of most Frenchmen. The third major change of direction came, of course, towards the middle of the 1580s, after the death of the duc d'Anjou, formerly Alençon, with the possibility of seeing a Huguenot, Henri de Bourbon, king of Navarre, on the throne. This time there was a rallying not only to the divine right of kings, traces of which can be detected even among the monarchomachs, but also to absolutist ideas.

These changes can also be measured by the frequency of the great propaganda themes utilized not only by Hotman and Duplessis-Mornay, but also by the innumerable anonymous pamphleteers of the time. Naturally, there was much less talk of natural rights, whereas the great theme of toleration, so extensively treated at the beginning of the 1560s but then abandoned in favour of natural rights, re-emerged along with the theme of concord, and, above all, of peace. This can be observed not only in the writings which can properly be called *politiques*, but also among soldiers, such as La Noue. The fatherland was seen to be in danger and all Frenchmen with it. The destiny of France was at stake, and only a national effort could save France from the Spanish, the Guises, or the Italians. Only thus could peace be restored to France. But there could be no peace without toleration, and there could be no toleration without a strong king capable of ensuring and giving a guarantee of its enforcement. Religion was essentially an individual problem which had to be separated from political consider-ations. Concord and toleration needed to be the future aims and inspiration of all 'true' Frenchmen, for these offered the only way by which France could be saved. It was becoming clear that the unity of France could not in future rest on religious foundations, but needed a political and national consensus. However, political and national unity was synonymous with a king, and even with absolutism.

In the last phases of the Wars of Religion Huguenot political thought gave particular emphasis to these problems. The most interesting and original expression of this trend is to be found in the writings of Michel Hurault, the Protestant grandson of the chancellor, Michel de l'Hôpital. Hurault was an absolutist by reason of his pessimism, perhaps even Calvinist pessimism. He saw man as fundamentally corrupt. On the one hand, man

[19] Cf. J. Estèbe, *Protestants du Midi, 1559–1598* (Toulouse, 1980), 179–80.

aspired to liberty, but on the other, he was incapable of using it to achieve happiness. Consequently, what he necessarily brought about was a popular state, which threatened ruin for the whole community. Contemporary France was already in such a state of disintegration. The only way of escape was a return to the monarchical form of government, alone capable of ensuring the *Concordia ordinum*. This was not the best solution, but the only one possible. The prince, from the moment he reigned, was absolute, his sovereignty knew no bounds and he shared it with no-one. There had never been anyone more absolute than the king of France in his kingdom. Never, as a result of this absolutism, had there existed a state that more perfectly represented among men 'the sovereign principality of God'. As a result, the king of France ranked first among the princes of the world. Nevertheless, the strength of the state went hand in hand with a certain degree of social injustice. Hurault analysed at length the social composition of the French monarchy; the nobility formed the mainstay of the state, while the people was 'the most trampled upon and the least esteemed; the people gave the greatest benefit to others but itself enjoyed the least honour and liberty'. Hurault, as a good Calvinist, showed a profound distrust for the clergy, whom he failed to integrate very successfully into his *concordia ordinum*.[20]

The period of the Edict of Nantes

The experience of the Religious Wars, the reconquest of France by Henri IV, and, above all, the Edict of Nantes transformed the French Protestants into good royalists, unconditionally during the peaceful years of Henri IV's reign, but with some reservations in the early years of the Regency and Louis XIII. The Edict of Nantes was the breach in royal absolutism which reassured the Protestants. They no longer feared the king, but the clergy. Many Huguenot leaders retained their influence during the peaceful years of Henri IV's reign. Sully was the most ardent defender on the king's council of the new absolutism, which contrasted with the Renaissance conception of authoritarian but mild kingship. Duplessis-Mornay retained his position as governor of Saumur, and his position was practically that of 'Pope of the Huguenots', as he was indeed called. The Huguenot party with the consistories following the great political leaders, rallied to absolutism. Nothing apparently changed following the king's assassination in 1610. Marie de Médicis reassured the Protestants when she confirmed the Edict of Nantes, and the Protestants, including political leaders, nobles and pastors, reassured the queen-mother of their fidelity and pledged again their unswerving support for royalist principles. The synod of Vitré in 1617 gave official support to the doctrine of the divine right of

---

[20] Cf. M. Yardeni, 'La pensée politique et sociale de Michel Hurault', *Revue d'histoire économique et sociale*, 46 (1968), 381–402; M. Hurault *Excellent et libre discours sur l'estat présent de la France* (n.p. 1588) 394.

kings. Nothing could have been more reassuring than the Calvinist political thought of these years, even though later on the pastor, David Blondel, deplored the failure of the Huguenots to explain clearly to French Catholic opinion the reasons for the position they had taken up in the past. He wrote that 'it is certain that in so far as we are guiltless towards France, we are to that extent guilty of negligence towards ourselves'.[21] Even the stiff-necked old captain, Agrippa d'Aubigné, was reassuring when he remarked that 'only princes who are incapable by reason of age or idiocy have found it impossible to maintain two contrary sects within their kingdoms'.[22]

It was clear, however, that only a strong king would be able to do this in France. And from now on, this strong king was the key figure around whom all French Calvinist political thought was concentrated. It was maintained that the state, its structures, and its functioning ought to concern Protestants only in so far as their religion was affected. Internal peace depended in effect, on 'our not meddling in affairs of state in our assemblies, unless something arises which directly affects our security'. On the other hand, however, it was necessary 'that the first complaint about contraventions of the Edict presented by our Deputés-Généraux should be dealt with by the Commissioners appointed to render in this respect especially good and fast justice'.[23] This can be held to be a contract, but highly sweetened and almost anodyne.

Louis XIII's harsh enforcement in Béarn of the 'Catholic' clauses of the Edict of Nantes with their effects upon taxation and property led to the 'crusades of the Midi' between 1620 and 1629. The most celebrated episode in the final phase of the Religious Wars was the siege of La Rochelle, while the great military leader of the Huguenots was the duc de Rohan. It would have been easy to advance the argument of self-defence, but the political leaders were divided and political thought did not pursue this line. No new ideology emerged in the wake of this last War of Religion. There were a few radical pamphlets which touched on the problem of legitimate defence. Thus it was said that 'the rights enjoyed by the natural subjects of the Prince are not favours nor concessions granted by his personal will. There is a reciprocal obligation between the Prince and his subjects, which does not, however, infringe upon the sovereign power of the Prince.' The great absurdity was that men such as the pastor Daniel Chamier, who actively supported the revolt of Montauban, La Milletière, Jean-Paul de Lescun in Béarn, or indeed the pastor Pierre Bérault, declared, with weapons in their hands, that the rights of kings were inviolable. They declared that if they had taken up arms, this was only because they had been constrained to do so.

[21] *Modeste déclaration de la sincérité et vérité des Eglises Réformées de France* (Sedan, 1619), 378.
[22] *Libre discours sur l'estat présent des Eglises Réformées en France* (n.p., 1619), 168, 314.
[23] J. Brachet de la Milletière, *Discours des vrayes raisons pour lesquelles ceux de la Religion en France peuvent et doivent en bonne conscience résister par armes à la persécution ouverte que leur font les ennemis de leur religion et de l'estat* (n.p., 1622), 31.

When attacked, armed struggle is merely legitimate defence. As far as other matters went, hereditary monarchy was the best political system. And as soon as the king was established on the throne, it was for God and not for the people to see that he fulfilled his duties. As for the people, all that remained for them was to pray to God to relieve their sufferings and to cause persecution to cease.[24]

But while there was a painful lack of new political ideas, new tactical arguments emerged in the 1620s directed against the state, rather than the king. To be more precise, attention was drawn, at first quite boldly and then, under Louis XIV, much more humbly, to all that could happen should the Protestants be persecuted. Thus the churches of Languedoc declared that 'this state would be badly advised to engage in a persecution which can only lead to fatal results'.[25] Yet there nevertheless persisted the danger of revolt. In 1622 La Milletière gave the warning that 'the people, fearful and full of apprehension of ill-treatment by the Prince, are taking the bit between the teeth, throwing off the duty owed to the king, resorting to rebellion, and breaking free from all obedience and service'.[26] In the time of Louis XIV, the threats became essentially economic. Writers described in apocalyptic terms the effects on France should its Protestant inhabitants be forced to leave their country, with resultant depopulation, economic decline and wretchedness. Briefly, this was what had happened to Spain after the expulsion of the Jews and the Moors, and real and imaginary analogies with Spain were frequently invoked.[27] However, there can be no doubt that this was a form of propaganda which did not impinge upon the unswerving fidelity of the French Protestants, nor upon their unconditional rallying to absolutism. Indeed, it was argued that by saving the Protestants and French Protestantism, the king and the monarchy would also be saved.

For the overwhelming majority of the French people in the seventeenth century absolutism constituted real progress by contrast with the disorders arising from local feudal loyalties, the anarchy of the Wars of Religion, and popular revolts. The absolute monarchy also became a supreme good for the French Protestants. In the first place, this was because they were Protestants, and only the king could protect them from the hatred of the clergy and their over-zealous Catholic countrymen. This was the reason why they remained faithful to the king, which was acknowledged rather candidly by an anonymous *Factum* of about 1661, which stated that 'the Protestants were well aware that their only means of survival lay in the

---

[24] Cf. H. Kretzer, 'Remarques' (see Further Reading); Brachet de La Milletière was a lawyer, who abjured in 1645 after being excommunicated by the National Synod of Charenton.
[25] *Apologie des Eglises Réformées du Languedoc* (n.p., n.d.), 40.   [26] La Milletière, 16.
[27] M. Yardeni, 'Naissance et vie d'un mythe: La Révocation de l'Édit de Nantes et le déclin économique de la France', in *Les Mythes en France, Troisième colloque de Haïfa*, ed. A. Grabois (Paris, forthcoming).

goodwill of their Prince'.[28] Secondly, the French Protestants were also monarchists and absolutists because they were, first of all, Frenchmen and Gallicans. Royal absolutism was for them the strongest rampart against the Romanist threat of which they were always conscious. Absolutism spelt social order and security, a fact always recalled and instilled into the 'trouble-makers of the Midi' by the great theologians from north of the Loire, who were much closer to the court, the great nobles, and the culture of the élite than their brethren in the south. Absolutism was also the catchword employed for consumption abroad by French theologians in order to underline the perfect respectability of French Protestantism.[29] And it was absolutism which was taught in the two great Protestant academies, that of Saumur and that of Sedan.[30]

Yet it would seem that this adherence to absolutism until 1685 was not as monolithic as it is customarily presented. Certainly there was a deification of Louis XIV which bordered on blasphemy.[31] But before the personal rule of the Sun King opinions were much more variegated than is supposed. In order to grasp this diversity within uniformity, it is necessary to go back to the period of the English Revolution, a real crisis of credibility for French Protestants, since, as Amyraut said, 'Some even bring it up against us that that what is now happening in England well reveals the spirit of our Religion'.[32] This is what lay behind the feverish activity of the Calvinist 'establishment' and Protestant intellectuals who published a series of important treatises. The pastor Samual Bochart of Caen maintained that French Protestants were always much closer to English episcopalianism than to presbyterianism, writing that 'Those of our Religion who went to England, after having learned your language, made no difficulty about attending your services, nor about receiving communion from the hands of ministers belonging to an episcopal church or from bishops themselves, if necessary.'[33] And Moïse Amyraut published a sharp warning—aimed at the Independents—to those who wished to abolish synods. Some went so far as to recognize the mistakes of the past, in order to reaffirm that 'it is never permissible for subjects to band together against their Prince, even if he should degenerate into a tyrant and persecute them for their religion'.[34]

It was at this time that Moïse Amyraut published his *Apologie*, responding under the pressure of events to an old desire of David Blondel.

[28] *Factum* (n.p., n.d.), BN Ld[176], 190, 100.

[29] Cf. E. Labrousse, 'Les doctrines politiques des Huguenots, 1600–1685', *Etudes théologiques et religieuses*, 47 (1972), 425.

[30] H. Kretzer, *Calvinismus und französische Monarchie* (see Further Reading) (Berlin, 1975).

[31] D. Ligou, *Le Protestantisme en France de 1598 à 1715* (Paris, 1968), 124.

[32] *Apologie pour ceux de la Religion sur le sujet d'aversion que plusieurs pensent avoir contre leurs personnes et leur créance* (Saumur, 1647), 61.

[33] *Lettre de Monsieur Bochart à Monsieur Morley, chapelain du Roy d'Angleterre* (Paris, 1650), 9.

[34] P. Codure, *Traicté de l'obéissance des chrétiens envers leurs magistrats et princes souverains* (Paris, 1645), 43.

The *Apologie* puts up a distinctly curious defence, if it is analysed in detail. To begin with, Amyraut vigorously defended the rights of his co-religionists to fairer treatment, in so far as they were Frenchmen. He wrote: 'We are, as everyone knows, inhabitants of this country, just like the others . . . If love of our native land extends even to the shores, rivers and fields of the place we inhabit, the affection it inspires ought to apply still more directly to the people themselves, since it is they who, strictly speaking, constitute the nation and the state much more than dumb and inanimate things . . . The greatness and strength of empires consist principally in the multitude of inhabitants.' This was a familiar theme during the Wars of Religion, used as a reminder that liberalism was still alive beneath the cinders. Amyraut listed with pride the contributions made by the Huguenots to the greatness of France, and as good Frenchmen the Huguenots were naturally monarchists. England was separated from France not merely by the sea, but—and more importantly—by language and disposition. Hence if a monarchy which was 'absolute and unlimited' suited the French character, it was 'just and reasonable that in England monarchy should be limited by the ancient laws of the state, and that the Parliament does well to seek to bring the king back to those limitations, if he has really gone too far in encroaching on the rights and liberties of his people'.[35]

These are significant passages, particularly if Amyraut's *Discours sur la Souveraineté des Rois*, published in Paris in 1650 is brought in as a comparison. That work, published during the Fronde, offers an embarrassing wealth of quotations to illustrate the blind rallying of the French Protestants to the themes of absolutism, themes thereafter repeated *ad nauseam*. French Protestants came to identify themselves with the state and the state with the king, a Sun King very close to God. A Huguenot pastor intoned that 'A monarch in his Kingdom is the true image of that great God who presides over the world. Like God, he has no superior nor equal. He alone is greater than all. He concentrates in his person all the majesty of the state'.[36]

However, towards the end of the 1670s, the pace of persecution began to accelerate. Legislation became increasingly restrictive, there was the resort to the *dragonnades*, and finally, on 22 October 1685 there came the Revocation of the Edict of Nantes. All that remained for French Protestants, after nearly a century of rallying to absolutist theses, was to try to remind the king once more of their impeccable loyalty during the Fronde, to convince him of their attachment to the monarchy and to his person, and to direct his attention to the scheming manoeuvres of the clergy with the consequent dangers that might result for France. Finally, they could pray to God, feign conversion, or emigrate.

---

[35] *Apologie*, 52–4, 90.
[36] Du Bosc, *Sermons* (Rotterdam, n.d.), iv. 109.

After the Revocation

With the Revocation, and the few preceding years can be included, there began a new 'great period' in French Calvinist political thought. The contribution made by the refugees to what Erich Haase called 'the new forms of analytic thought' is well known.[37] The literature of the *Refuge* has even been considered to be an indispensable link in the chain leading to the Enlightenment, and it is enough to recall in this context the name of Pierre Bayle.

One stimulus which led to this new phase was provided by the analysis of the legal aspects of the Revocation of the Edict of Nantes. After the failure of the sentimental and quasi-mystical arguments of fidelity, still utilized by the pastor Claude, rationalism regained the upper hand, and, with it, there came a scarcely disguised return to monarchomach theories. The Edict of Nantes was for Protestant polemicists no longer a privilege conceded by the king. One pamphlet explained that it was 'a treaty given the form of a law', and that it was 'only necessary to read the preamble to this Edict to be convinced that it is in effect a treaty that Henri IV made with our fathers'.[38] According to Jacques Abbadie, the king undertook by this contract to maintain the liberty and privileges of his subjects.[39] Moreover, it was known since the monarchomachs that if the contract was denounced by one of the parties to it, the other was automatically freed from it. Claude considered that Louis XIV, by annulling this treaty, had annulled one of the fundamental and sacrosanct laws of the kingdom. J. Coulan rejected the argument that there were no more Protestants in France and that as a consequence the Edict of Nantes had become pointless. He maintained that if only a single Protestant remained, that Protestant constituted a corporate body in himself, and the Edict had been granted to a corporate body. The monarchy itself was made up of corporate bodies, 'which shared sovereignty with the Monarch and which are even above him.'[40] As later for Montesquieu, feudalism and liberties are already joined in the eyes of some of the thinkers of the *Refuge*.

The problems which preoccupied the great figures of the *Refuge* stemmed from unprecedented situations which resulted from the mass emigration of the Huguenots. If the contract made with France and denounced by the king was no longer binding on the Huguenots, had they ceased therefore to be Frenchmen? Could they transfer their allegiance and their 'nationality'

[37] E. Haase, (see Further Reading).

[38] F. Gaultier de Saint-Blancard, *Histoire apologétique, ou défense des libertés des Eglises Réformées de France* (Mainz, 1688), i. 49.

[39] *Défense de la Nation britannique, ou les droits de Dieu, de la nature et de la société clairement établie au sujet de la Révolution d'Angleterre* (The Hague, 1693), 120. Abbadie (1654–1720), born in Béarn, was a minister in Berlin from 1680 to 1688, and subsequently in London. He was the author of a celebrated *Traité de la vérité de la Religion chrétienne* (2 vols., Rotterdam, 1684).

[40] *Défense des réfugiés contre un livre intitulé Avis important aux réfugiés* (Deventer, 1691), 120.

to their new defenders and patrons? Was being French something that lay outside the authority of the king and did not depend upon him?[41] And where was the individual to find the frontier between liberty of conscience and toleration? Such questions passionately exercised the intellectuals of the *Refuge*, who discussed them with asperity. These problems, more than once mixed up with dusty theological points, but which by their 'heterodox' perspectives already opened wide the gates of modernity,[42] were discussed until 1697, and even 1714. Indeed they were discussed as long as there was hope of a possible return of the émigrés, a hope that faded with the passing of the years.

These debates, in which almost all the intellectuals of the *Refuge* took part, pastors, journalists and teachers, were to some extent eclipsed by the great jousting match between Pierre Bayle and Pierre Jurieu. The two were old friends who became irreconcilable enemies; the one represented absolutism combined with tolerance, while the other combined sovereignty of the people in the political sphere with the strictest orthodoxy in the religious sphere.[43]

The work which best sums up the political thought of Pierre Bayle is the *Avis aux Réfugiés* published in 1690, a bitter attack on those of his co-religionists who had recently welcomed with enthusiasm the Glorious Revolution in England, and had extolled it on both theological and political grounds. In his indictment of these opinions Bayle justified the profound antipathy that the French Catholics felt towards the Protestants by the latter's spirit of revolt and satire. In his view, absolutism, even the absolutism of Louis XIV, was the best form of government, for it alone saved men from anarchy.

The unshakeable absolutism of Bayle is woven on the same loom as that of Michel Hurault or of Élie Merlat, his own contemporary, whose book on absolutism he succeeded in publishing shortly before the Revocation.[44] This absolutism was typical of French Protestantism. As a result of original sin, men, apart from the elect touched by grace, were corrupt and incapable of living in society without constraint. In view of this fallen state of man, absolutism was therefore the best of regimes. As a result, outward and professed religion was not linked with morality, for the only true religion was that of the elect. Even atheists, as the history of antiquity demonstrated, could form perfectly viable societies. This view also opens a gap for toleration, not only in terms of political, but also of moral considerations. True religion was inward. It had nothing to do with external forms of worship. The purpose of persecution was to 'externalize' religion, and that

[41] M. Yardeni, 'Problèmes de fidélités' (see Further Reading), 297–314.

[42] Cf. S. N. Eisenstadt, *Change and Modernity* (New York, 1973).

[43] E. Labrousse, 'Introduction historique' to P. Bayle, *Œuvres diverses*, v. i (Hildesheim and New York, 1982). See also ead., 'Political Ideas' (see Further Reading).

[44] *Traité du pouvoir absolu des souverains* (Cologne, 1685).

is why it was doomed to fail, for it merely created hypocrites. And, Bayle argued, politically speaking hypocrites were also the worst sort of subjects.[45] In his view, it was wiser and safer to tolerate minorities and to transform them into loyal and faithful subjects.

Bayle's strictly political and strictly religious ideas were shared by only a tiny minority in the *Refuge*, such as his friends, the brothers Basnage. But his politico-religious ideas on toleration had a much wider audience, above all because of the heterodoxy which increasingly characterized the *Refuge*, probably as an inevitable consequence of the freedom to think and to publish.

Bayle's great antagonist, Jurieu, equated toleration with impiety and therefore saw toleration as the worst enemy of states and societies.[46] He dreamed of ultimate victory for Protestantism over the Catholic church and the return of the refugees to France. This could occur either by grace touching the king, or by the propagation of the true religion, or indeed by the liberation of France by the Orangist armies.[47] Jurieu not only revived the faith and courage of the Protestants still in France by his *Lettres pastorales*,[48] but also furnished them with political and theological arguments to counter the campaign of indoctrination undertaken by the Catholic church in France.

Jurieu's political theories were the product of two influences. On the one hand, there was his belief in wild interpretations taken from the Book of Revelations, which gave him his vision of victory for Protestantism in the very near future. On the other hand, there were his links with the Orangists and their leader, the future king of England, William III, whom he saw as God's elect and the future restorer of Protestantism in France. This may well explain the highly contradictory attitudes sometimes taken up by Jurieu in the great theological and political controversies of his time, which laid him open to attack by Bayle, as well as by Bossuet and Nicole.

A preliminary sketch of Jurieu's theory of popular sovereignty can be found in his *Traité de la puissance de l'Église* of 1677, in which he analysed the problem of the authority of synods, that is whether it came from below or above. Jurieu maintained that this authority did not proceed directly from God, but from Christ, who transferred it not merely to Peter and the Apostles, but also to the whole body of the people, and it was the people who delegated this authority to its ministers. As far as Jurieu at this date was

---

[45] P. Bayle, *Ce que c'est que la France toute catholique sous le règne de Louis le Grand* (St Omer, 1686). See also the excellent new edition by E. Labrousse (Paris, 1973).

[46] A more tolerant account of Jurieu is given by F. R. Knetsch, 'Pierre Jurieu: Theologian and Politician of the Dispersion', *Acta Historiae Neerlandica*, 5 (1971), 213–42.

[47] *L'Accomplissement des prophéties: ou la délivrance prochaine de l'Église* (Rotterdam, 1686), ii. 188–92. See also G. H. Dodge, *Political Theory* (see Further Reading), 36.

[48] *Lettres pastorales adressées aux fidèles de France qui gémissent sous la captivité de Babylone* (Rotterdam, 1686–9). Nos. 16–18 contain the best exposition of Jurieu's political ideas.

concerned, this power, most certainly, was delegated to control the pope and in no way reflected upon the absolute authority of the king. But the political implications of this thesis were clear. As soon as the king of France ceased to play his role as defender of his people, meaning the Protestants of France, and indeed persecuted them, his absolutism became open to question. For the king was absolute only in order to protect his people, in conformity with divine laws and human laws, that is, with the fundamental laws of the kingdom.

In this context, Jurieu's thought evolves in two directions, embracing the theory of contract and the right of resistance. He argued that because of the need to subject themselves to civil government, the people had chosen different forms of government to which they had transferred either absolute sovereignty or limited sovereignty. But once the form of government had been chosen, the people was no longer free to change it.[49] This does not imply that the absolute sovereignty of kings is unlimited. It is limited by positive laws, in this case, the fundamental laws of the monarchy of France, and by divine laws. To extirpate true religion was to rebel against God. But it was forbidden to the king to rebel against God, just as it was forbidden to the people to rebel against God. Furthermore, taken as a whole, the people, even after the delegation of their powers and authority, remained superior to the king. In all circumstances, *salus populi suprema lex esto*. Hence arose the possibility of resistance, once the well-being and survival of the people were endangered.

Because of the differences dating from the moment of the initial contract when the people chose the form of government best suited to them, Jurieu was able to justify equally well the resistance of the visionaries of Dauphiné and the invasion and seizure of power by William of Orange in England. In both cases, though under different forms, it was the sovereignty of the people which found expression, in Dauphiné directly and in England through the agency of parliament, in accordance with the spirit of the English constitution.

The right of defence, which could mean rebellion, was perhaps the problem which most seriously divided the *Refuge*. Although the Camisards found defenders in the pamphlets and even in the newspapers of the *Refuge*, it was a different matter when some of their leaders on escaping to England provoked the 'affair of the prophets'.[50] This caused a scandal that raised

[49] Jurieu paradoxically came close on this point to the position of Élie Merlat, whom he attacked in the *Lettres pastorales*. Merlat indeed underlined the inviolability of power already established, but he explained precisely: 'We do not mean in any way to insinuate, when we speak of the absolute power of sovereigns, that the peoples are obliged either to submit themselves voluntarily to such a power when they are not already subject to it or to believe that all sovereigns may always exercise this power. On the contrary, we say frankly that all who live under a freer and milder authority do very well to stay there as long as the laws of justice and the condition of the subject permit them so to do'. This also makes plain the sensitive points of difference between France and England, *Traité*, 52 (pp. 59, 160).

[50] Cf. H. Schwarz: *The French Prophets: the History of a Millenarian Group in Eighteenth-Century England* (Berkeley, 1980).

POLITICAL THOUGHT 1534-1715

against them the entire refugee 'Establishment', which stigmatized them as dangerous visionaries.[51]

The attitude of the refugee 'Establishment' is easy to understand. With the slow fading of their hopes of returning to France, the émigrés wished to become respectable citizens. They suffered in England not only from the alarm caused by the prophets, but from the appalling dilemma of choosing between the Whigs and the Tories. The refugee 'Establishment' opted for absolute neutrality. The émigrés, frozen in a refugee mentality, were incapable of discerning the ideological differences between the two parties. However, those, who like Armand Dubourdieu, pastor of the highly aristocratic church of the Savoy, considered themselves English, no longer hesitated. In 1707 Dubourdieu published a powerful sermon, which he had preached the year before, directed against Louis XIV and France, in which he clearly drew the dividing line between the first and the second generation of refugees. He struck out against the older Huguenot tradition, saying 'There are among us those who subscribe to the thesis of the power of kings; such extreme ideas have undermined our churches. Thanks to God, I did not study my theology concerning the power of kings in the works of Amyraut and Merlat, nor in the *Avis aux Réfugiés*. I have been nurtured since my childhood on the principles of liberty in a free country. I am French by birth, but in this respect I have an English heart.'[52] It could be said that these few lines symbolize the end of French Calvinist thought in the *Refuge*, since in future intellectuals of French Huguenot origin were to think more and more as Englishmen, Prussians, or Dutchmen. Only a few aged survivors, such as Jacques Basnage and Henri Basnage de Beauval, were to continue faithful to their image of France and its government.[53]

French Calvinist political thought was a literature of combat, a literature concerned with the right to exist, even in the fifty years of false illusions between 1630 and 1680. From this there stemmed its pragmatism and its capacity for rapid adaptation to novel situations. These theorists were by necessity opportunists, but they knew how to select from the rich arsenal of the Bible, from Calvin and his precursors, and from history and natural law the arguments that in specific historical situations best served not the cause of religion, but the cause of the believers. This was political thought put at the service of men, for it was born, formed and transformed according to events. From this too there stemmed its creativeness, which although often consisting in merely a rearrangement of old and well-known arguments, yet in the end always contained something new. From this point of view, French Calvinist political thought was always in the lead, and moreover became itself an arsenal. The English Puritan Revolution drew heavily

[51] P. Joutard, *La Légende des Camisards* (Paris, 1977), 66.

[52] A. Dubourdieu, *L'Orgueil de Nebucadnetzar. Abbattu de la main de Dieu: Avec quelques applications particulières aux affaires du temps* (London, 1707), preface.

[53] J. Basnage, *Instructions pastorales aux Réformés de France sur l'obéissance due au souverain* (Rotterdam, 1720).

upon the literature of the Wars of Religion, and the Enlightenment drew upon the literature of the *Refuge*.[54] This political thought was typically French, but never provincial, and constitutes an integral part of western intellectual traditions. It was not created by giants of philosophy and theology with universal renown, even though an Amyraut and a Bayle contributed to its elaboration, but was a political thought constructed by relatively mediocre minds. Nevertheless, the contribution made by Huguenot political thought is to be ascribed to the fact that it almost always broke out of its initial bounds, probably because of the complete fusion of theory and practice, realized under the impact of events themselves.

[54] J. H. M. Salmon, *The French Religious Wars in English Political Thought* (Oxford, 1959); E. S. De Beer, 'The Huguenots and the Enlightenment', *BHSL*, xxi (1965–70), 170–95.

Further Reading

Allen, J. W., *A History of Political Thought in the Sixteenth Century* (London, 1960).

Bohatec, J., *Calvins Lehre von Staat und Kirche* (Breslau, 1937, repr. Aalen, 1968).

Caprariis, V. de, *Propaganda e pensiero politico in Francia durante le guerre di religione (1559–1572)* (Naples, 1959).

Dodge, G. H., *The Political Theory of the Huguenots of the Dispersion. With special reference to the thought and influence of Pierre Jurieu* (New York, 1922, repr. 1972).

Galland, A., 'Les pasteurs français Amyraut, Bochart, Merlat, etc. et la royauté de droit divin', *BSHPF* 77 (1928), 14 ff., 105 ff., 225 ff.

Giesey, R. E., 'When and Why Hotman wrote the *Francogallia*, *BHR* 28 (1967), 581–611.

—— 'The Monarchomach Triumvirs: Hotman, Beza and Mornay', *BHR* 32 (1970), 41–56.

—— and Salmon, J. H. M. (eds.), introduction to *François Hotman, Francogallia* (Cambridge, 1972).

Haase, E., *Einführung in die Literatur des Refuge, des Beitrags der französischen Protestanten zur Entwicklung analytischer Denksformen am Ende des 17. Jahrhunderts* (Berlin, 1959).

Kelley, D. R., *François Hotman: A Revolutionary's Ordeal* (Princeton, 1973).

—— *The Beginning of Ideology* (Cambridge, 1981).

Kingdon, R. M., 'The First Expression of Theodore Beza's Political Ideas', *Archiv für Reformationsgeschichte*, 7 (1955), 88–100.

Knetsch, F. R. J., *Pierre Jurieu* (Kempen, 1967) (For a synopsis in English, see n. 46).

Kretzer, H., *Calvinismus und französische Monarchie im 17. Jahrhundert. Die politische Lehre der Akademien Sedan und Saumur, mit besonderer Berücksichtigung von Pierre Du Moulin, Moyse Amyraut und Pierre Jurieu* (Berlin, 1975).

—— 'Remarques sur le droit de résistance des calvinistes français au début du XVIIe siècle', *BSHPF* 113 (1977), 54–75.

—— 'Calvinismus und französische Monarchie im 17. Jahrhundert. Zur politischen Lehre der Hugenotten im siècle classique', *Pietismus und Neuzeit, ein Jahrbuch zur Geschichte des neuere Protestantismus*, 6 (1980), 115–32.

Labrousse, E., *Pierre Bayle* (2 vols. The Hague, 1963–9).

—— 'La doctrine politique des Huguenots: 1630–1685'; *Études théologiques et religieuses*, 47 (1972), 421–9.

—— 'Eléments rationalistes de la controverse huguenote à la veille de la Révocation', *Recherches sur le XVIIe siècle* (1977), 91–101.

—— 'The Political Ideas of the Huguenot Diaspora' (Bayle and Jurieu), in R. M. Golden (ed.), *Church, State and Society Under the Bourbon Kings of France* (Lawrence, Kan., 1982), 222–83.

Linder, R. D., *The Political ideas of Pierre Viret* (Geneva, 1964).

Mesnard, P., *L'essor de la philosophie politique au XVIe siècle* (Paris, 1936).

Patry, R., *Philippe du Plessis-Mornay: un huguenot homme d'État* (Paris, 1933).

Rimbaud, L., *Pierre Du Moulin, 1568–1658* (Paris, 1966).

Skinner, Q., *The Foundations of Modern Political Thought*, ii. *The Age of Reformation* (Cambridge, 1978).

Yardeni, M., *La conscience nationale en France pendant les Guerres de Religion (1559–1598)* (Paris and Louvain, 1971).

—— 'Problèmes de fidélité chez les protestants français à l'époque de la Révocation', in Y. Durand (ed.), *Hommage à Roland Mousnier. Clientèles et fidélités en Europe à l'époque moderne* (Paris, 1981), 285–308.

XII

The Revocation of the Edict of Nantes: End or Renewal of French Protestantism?

PHILIPPE JOUTARD

I T may seem paradoxical or even shocking to give a title of this kind to an essay devoted to the consequences for French Calvinism of the revocation of the Edict of Nantes. Is it not generally held that the Revocation was an appalling catastrophe for the Protestants of France from which they never recovered? Nevertheless, it is not difficult to find historians who consider that the Protestant churches of France were moribund on the eve of the Edict of Fontainebleau (the act of revocation) and that persecution, far from destroying them, saved them. The earliest of these historians was Voltaire, who suggested this in *Le Siècle de Louis XIV*:

The glory surrounding Louis XIV for fifty years, his power, his firm and vigorous government banished from the Protestant party all idea of resistance. The magnificent entertainments of an elegant court also contributed to cast ridicule on the puritanical Huguenots. As good taste progressively came to be perfected, the psalms of Marot and of Beza could not but inspire unconscious feelings of distaste. Those psalms which had charmed the court of Francis II, were only suited to the common people under Louis XIV.[1]

In a quite different context, this was also the view of the Methodist minister, Mathieu Lelièvre, and also of Emile Léonard, who both underlined the weaknesses of the pastorate, of which the abjurations of the ministers provided the most obvious expression.[2]

Leaving aside its most visible effects—the destruction of temples, the flight of pastors, and the end of Reformed services in France—how effective in practice was the Edict of Fontainebleau? This is a valid question but an answer requires a detailed examination of the different solutions adopted by the *Prétendus Réformés* in the face of royal policy and also an appreciation of their respective efficacy.

The behaviour of the French Protestants can be subsumed under four possibilities. The first is conversion, which, whether sincere or not,

---

[1] Voltaire, *Le siècle de Louis XIV*, ch. 36, (Pléiade édition, Paris, 1957), 1048–9.
[2] M. Lelièvre, *De la Révocation à la Révolution*, I. *1685–1715* (Paris, 1911); E. G. Léonard, *Histoire générale du protestantisme* (Paris, 1961), ii. 346.

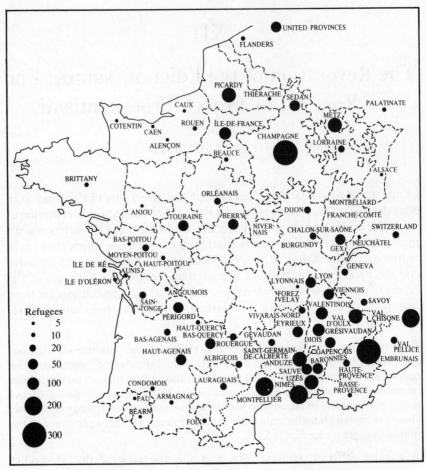

Map 4. Geographical Origin of Refugees after the Revocation
Map by M. Magdelaine and J. Bertrand, showing the origins of the 4,300 Huguenot refugees who passed through Frankfurt am Main between the end of Apr. 1686 and Nov. 1687. (Copyright Editions Armand Colin, Paris, and Verlag C. H. Beck, Munich)

obliterated, so far as the new Catholic was concerned, all traces of his old religion. His descendants all figured in the parish registers, and soon forgot their Huguenot origins. These families were definitively lost to the French Reformed community. Another form of loss, but inspired by the opposite attitude, was exile, undertaken at the risk of life, for even before the Revocation the royal authorities had forbidden emigration, except in the case of pastors and of a few privileged persons. Many of the émigrés hoped indeed to return when times improved, but were dead before that day came and meanwhile had become subjects of another prince.

Two possibilities were open for those Protestants who stayed in France and did not resign themselves to abandoning their religion: either to play a double game or to offer open resistance, whether peaceful or violent. If he played the double game, the 'new convert' (*nouveau converti*) performed only the obligatory gestures, marriage or the baptism of his children. He did not attend mass, go to confession, or communicate unless administrative pressure was strong and troops were in the neighbourhood. He continued to read the family Bible or his pocket Psalter secretly at night. When death drew near he tried to avoid having to choose between receiving extreme unction and refusing the presence of a priest. Such a refusal would entail very serious consequences for him and his heirs. He would be regarded as a relapsed heretic and thus would incur the gravest of sanctions. If he died, he would be refused burial, his body would be dragged on a hurdle and thrown on to a rubbish-dump. If he survived, he would be sentenced to the galleys, or in the case of a woman, to prison. In any event, his property would be confiscated.

Those Protestants who did not accept compromise and who were either unable or unwilling to flee abroad had no alternative but to take refuge in places remote from habitation, 'in the wilderness' (*au Désert*), to employ the biblical expression they liked to use. There they met together in clandestine gatherings. As they were often armed, they did not hesitate to fight back if they were surprised by royal troops, and the peaceful assembly would then become violent. There was no sharp division between one attitude and the other. The *nouveaux convertis* who observed more or less their obligations as Catholics might well be found at a meeting in the *Désert*, especially in a period of relative détente, or at the moment of their death they might publicly affirm their Protestant faith by refusing the ministrations of a priest. Conversely, the 'obstinate' or 'stubborn', as they were described, often faithfully attended 'popish' services for months on end.

This last observation makes apparent the difficulties encountered in any statistical estimate of these various attitudes. While it is possible to pick out the unambiguous forms of behaviour, such as emigration, the organizing of assemblies, or later on the resort to arms, it is much more difficult to distinguish between the sincere converts, the adepts of the double game and the occasionally obstinate, who formed the majority; and, this is not to mention the changes that occurred with the passage of time. This would entail following up in every parish all the families from 1685 to 1787, the date of the edict of toleration which restored civil status to the Protestants. Such work has been done only at the level of family genealogies and not for whole communities, except in terms of rough general estimates. The conclusions presented here will of necessity be largely hypothetical, showing tendencies rather than certainties.

A Deceptive Unanimity

If there is any one subject for which it is easy to produce a numerical estimate it is the campaign for abjuration. This was undertaken with the aid of the royal dragoons and the names of the *nouveaux convertis* are listed in the church registers. The success was spectacular. A correspondent of the Great Condé, Père du Rosel, wrote to him on 8 November 1685, on the basis of reports received at the court, that 'the Huguenots can sometimes show such diligence in hastening to convert that a soldier may have to change his lodging several times a day. The story is told of a soldier who, having changed his lodging eight times in the course of the day, found himself in the evening in the house of a Protestant, who instantly declared his wish for conversion. The soldier begged him to wait till morning so that he could at least have a bed for the night.' It was enough in Rouen for three or four companies of dragoons to form up on a public square for the mere sight of them to determine 'more than three hundred Huguenots to go off and abjure forthwith.'[3]

Matters could proceed even better in the areas where the Protestants were thickest on the ground, as in the Cévennes or in Lower Languedoc. There the rumour of the dragonnades in Poitou or in Béarn inspired such terror that there was no need to proceed to the billeting of troops to procure the abjuration of Protestant communities. As soon as the troops drew near a town the Protestants rushed to the curé. Marshal de Noailles, in charge of the operation, complained about the problem of billeting, writing, 'I do not know what to do with the troops, since the places I had in mind generally all convert and so quickly that the men can only sleep one night in the places where I send them'.[4]

It is worth examining the case-histories of two Protestant communities which were soon to be bastions of Huguenot resistance. Marsillargues in the plain near Nîmes was over 80 per cent Protestant with 1,100 Protestants to 260 Catholics. Before October 1685 those who weakened could be counted on the fingers of one hand. But as soon as the soldiers' arrival was announced at Nîmes, thirty-two persons abjured on the first of October; on the next day thirty-nine, and on the following day 140. On the fourth of October the curé rested, but on the fifth 500 persons crowded round the register to declare themselves Catholics. On the sixth of October there were another 131 and on the seventh there were forty-four. Since the beginning of the month more than four-fifths of the Protestants of Marsillargues had converted, over 70 per cent of them in the course of three days. Altogether, by the end of the year 1,043 inhabitants of Marsillargues figured on the list of abjurations.[5]

---

[3] F. Gonin and F. Delteil, 'La Révocation vue par les informateurs du Grand Condé, *BSHPF* (1972), 127 ff.   [4] Cited by C. Bost (see Further Reading), i. 40.
[5] J. M. Daumas, 'Les protestants de Marsillargues en Languedoc des origines à 1953' (unpublished thesis, University of Provence, 1983), 192–3.

The other example is Mialet, in the heart of the Cévennes and faithful to the Reformed religion from its beginnings. In 1559 pastors held secret meetings with a view to establishing Reformed churches in the region. The famous Camisard leader, Roland, was born in one of these hamlets, Le Mas Soubeyran, which today houses the *Musée du Desert*. The entire village was deported during the Camisard war since it was considered to be solidly on the side of the rebels. There were then nearly 1,100 Protestants. In the twenty years preceding the Revocation the curé had succeeded in persuading only sixty-eight persons to abjure, and of these twenty were outsiders. The troops were to prove more effective, but in a way which was both more gradual and slower than at Marsillargues. The harvest of conversions began on the twelfth of October. At the end of the month more than a third had already gone to Catholic services, the men showing more eagerness than the women in the proportion of three to one. By the end of the year three-quarters of the Protestants of Mialet had become *nouveaux convertis*, the rest coming over in 1686. But there were still some thirty persons figuring on the register of abjurations in 1687. This chronology suggests that there were difficulties which had not been encountered at Marsillargues. It is true that Mialet was in the mountains, but nevertheless the authorities seem to have achieved their aim, since theoretically all the inhabitants were from then on Catholics.[6]

And what of the pastors? Particular attention needs to be paid to their case, since the number of apostasies among them served as arguments for Mathieu Lelièvre and for Emile Léonard to demonstrate the debility of French Protestantism. The former puts the figure of the pastors who abjured as high as a third. It is true that the ministers alone had a choice. They could either go into exile but leave behind children over the age of seven or they could abjure and receive a pension which could revert to their widows and even to their children, quite apart from their opportunities of acquiring offices. Samuel Mours went over the whole question province by province,[7] and noted that the number of pastors still functioning on the eve of the Revocation was very much higher than that used by Lelièvre to establish his percentage. The picture is therefore less sombre. A hundred and forty pastors definitely abjured out of a total of 873, which represents little more than 16 per cent of the corps of pastors, but with surprising differences between synodal provinces. Four per cent abjured in the Île-de-France and in Burgundy, 27 per cent in the Cévennes and 41 per cent in Béarn. In general, the pastors were more faithful in the northern provinces where Protestants were very much in the minority, 8 per cent abjuring in contrast to 18 per cent in the southern provinces. In the North being a

[6] B. Atger, 'Les abjurations à Mialet', *Le lien des chercheurs cévenols* (1982).
[7] S. Mours, 'Les pasteurs à la révocation de l'édit de Nantes', *BSHPF* (1968), 67–105, 292–316, 521–4.

Protestant was more than ever before a case of personal choice, but south of the Loire it was a matter of social conformity in the various areas where Protestantism was a majority religion, as in the Cévennes, so that the pastorate was an occupation like any other. In the case of Béarn, other factors should perhaps be invoked, such as the harshness of the repression or the memory of an official religion which had varied with that of the monarchy. However the great majority of pastors preferred exile. The United Provinces received 43 per cent of those from the whole of France, followed by Switzerland, which received 27 per cent drawn largely from the eastern provinces of Dauphiné and Burgundy, but also Languedoc. England attracted 23 per cent, principally from the western maritime provinces. Finally only 7 per cent went to Germany, which lagged well behind, since conditions were doubtless more difficult and it had less prestige than the other three countries. This distribution is not surprising, since it reflects both the inclinations of French Protestantism and the geographical situation.

Even if the 'conversion' of the pastors was not so outstanding a success for the authorities as a first scrutiny would suggest, the overall balance-sheet of abjurations appeared very satisfactory: at least this was the burden of the jubilant reports reaching the court. The business was in a fair way to being settled.

There were indeed some recalcitrants, all the more incomprehensible since they belonged to the upper ranks of society. Thus an agent of the Great Condé reported that in Rouen merchants were still standing out obstinately more than a month after the Revocation. He wrote, 'there are still some forty-five Huguenot families in Rouen who do not wish to surrender and who look on without showing any impatience as their wealth is devoured by the dragoons billeted on them. I was asked yesterday by one of our Presidents of the *Parlement* to visit a merchant who has four cuirassiers billeted on him to see if I could not win him over, but he refused to enter into discussion with me, and when I prayed him to tell me what were the things he was doubtful of in our religion, he said that he doubted all, but that God had granted him the grace not to doubt anything in his own religion. He himself takes his dragoons to the butchers and eating-houses and they choose what they want while he eats and drinks with them, often telling them that his property and his life belong to the king, but that his conscience belongs to God.' But this could raise business problems, 'since because it is the richest who do not wish to convert, when bills of exchange arrive as they often do from merchants in other provinces, there are those who reply that they only have money to pay the troopers'. In December 1685 there were still twenty-five families holding out and 'since it was known that the women were preventing the conversion of their husbands, they were carried off and placed in convents . . . The women to begin with were fairly peaceable there, but now for the most part they are behaving like furies and causing great distress to the communities which harbour them, so that it will be necessary either to lock them up or to send them home.' At the beginning of January, the authorities, weary of the struggle, imprisoned ten of those who still continued obstinate.[8] The authorities in Paris had similar trouble with some upper-class Huguenots, such as Count Dolon, who was still not converted in 1687, or a *conseiller* in the *Parlement* of Paris, Muisson, who had his wife and six children carried off.

Public opinion, without exception, paid no attention to these incidents of resistance, regarding them as the final death-throes of heresy and the Edict of Fontainebleau continued to be applauded. There was even less disquiet over the relatively few signatures in the registers of abjuration, as if all Protestants were illiterate. One of the first to abjure at Marsillargues declared 'I cannot write my name' and he was a surgeon! It was also of little importance that some days after abjuring three persons in Rouen 'have not wished to receive the sacraments when dying and have declared that they will die in their first religion which they abjured only under compulsion'.[9] But one phenomenon could not be ignored for long, and this was the massive departure from France of a section of the Protestants. The correspondence of the Great Condé teems with allusions to this subject. The Prince had in his hands, in particular, a memoir from the *subdélégué* of the Pays de Gex, with the information that 5,207 persons had indeed abjured, that only 240 'remained fixed in their obstinacy', but that 2,426 had 'departed to foreign countries'.[10] This emigration was the first set-back to royal policy.

The Huguenot Diaspora: a phenomenon of European history

The Protestant emigration is, of all the consequences of the Revocation, the fact which most forcibly struck contemporaries and, later, historians. This emphasis is entirely justified: emigration was the earliest and most massive form of protest. Two-thirds of those sent to the galleys for their faith had been caught while trying to leave the country, and the initial episode of the Camisard war, the killing of the abbé du Chaila, originated in the arrest of a convoy of emigrants. The diaspora transformed a French event into a European phenomenon. This was because, first of all, the refugees were the visible sign of the consequences of a deliberate policy, and secondly, because their economic and cultural influence in several countries was not negligible, even if it has been sometimes exaggerated. The diaspora inaugurated the long series of migrations for 'ideological' reasons which have multiplied in the twentieth century. Finally, it should be added that

---

[8] Gonin and Delteil, 125, 155, 162, 365.
[9] Ibid., 144–5.
[10] Ibid., 159.

the historian has the good fortune (if this expression is permissible in the context of such a tragic event) to have at his disposal abundant documentation, covering the whole process, from departure to settlement, with all the intermediary stages, which is rare for this type of phenomenon and obviously even more so for this period. The documentation is so abundant that despite a number of scholarly studies of the nineteenth and twentieth centuries, it has scarcely begun to be exploited systematically. Even in this field therefore I can offer only provisional conclusions which may well be later revised in the light of important work in progress, undertaken in anticipation of the tercentenary of the Revocation.

The first uncertainty is how many Protestants left France? Estimates vary as between fifty thousand and one million, a twenty fold difference. Further, this quarrel over figures is not a matter of indifference, since the eulogists of Louis XIV and, in their turn, certain nineteenth-century Catholic historians minimized the haemorrhage, whereas Protestant polemicists and all those who deplored the Revocation tended to over estimate the figures. We are now beginning to form a more accurate view of the size of the emigration, even though many uncertainties remain. The higher figure cannot be accepted even approximately, since it would mean that the entire French Protestant population left the kingdom, an absurd supposition. But such an error does not arise only from polemical exaggeration, but stems from a permanent tendency on the part of historians (and further back on the part of contemporary opinion) to over estimate the number of French Protestants, and to do this from the sixteenth to the twentieth century. Nor should we criticize the underestimates for bad faith. They certainly served polemical purposes, but they also stemmed from the sources used. These were French sources which minimized the phenomenon for two reasons. The local authorities had no interest in revealing their relative failure and therefore transmitted to Versailles the lowest figures. Secondly, successful emigration depended upon secrecy, which by definition leaves no written trace. As a result of comparing French documents with German documents, we now know that many refugees installed in East Prussia were still not recorded as 'absent' from the communities from which they came.

Pastor Mours, who for years dedicated himself to minute research into a wide variety of sources, proposed the figure of 200,000 departures, which is not far from the truth, since whenever his figures have been verified locally, their reliability has been recognized.[11] If the figures need to be revised it would, in my opinion, be a matter of slightly increasing them. Recent studies of emigration all show some under estimation of the numbers involved, as compared with the figures first advanced. Furthermore one

---

[11] Table in S. Mours, *Les galériens protestants* (Paris, 1970), 58.

category often escapes inclusion in the written records; that is, all those who died on a journey which was always long and arduous.

This overall estimate needs to be followed up by a regional survey, since provinces did not furnish the same number of refugees; the contrasts in percentages are more remarkable than the predictable differences in gross totals. Thus the six synodal provinces of northern France, which scarcely represented 20 per cent of Huguenot strength, contributed more than 40 per cent of the refugee total! The Île-de-France, which lost more than half of its complement with 35,000 Huguenots going into exile, ranks first both in terms of percentage and in absolute numbers, but the five other northern provinces all saw more than 40 per cent of the faithful depart abroad. South of the Loire the only comparable region is Dauphiné, which lost 30,000 or 38 per cent of its Protestants. In contrast, Béarn, the Cévennes, and the Vivarais showed a low rate of emigration with less than 10 per cent departing. Similarly, the maritime provinces of Poitou and Saintonge, though in a favourable geographical position, did not exceed 20 per cent and 25 per cent respectively. The Southern provinces taken together lost only a fifth of their faithful.

Equally strong contrasts emerge from closer analysis made at the level of the colloquy or even of the consistory. If we take a single example from recent research on the fugitives from Gévaudan (the modern department of Lozère, corresponding to the Upper Cévennes) the parish of Saint-Martin-de-Campselade had 456 declared Protestants, none of whom left. Some miles away Saint-Frézal-de-Ventalon of a comparable size had 539 Protestants, of whom 109 fled.[12]

Why were there these differences? The facilities for flight and the proximity of the frontiers have been invoked as factors. These explain the high figures for Dauphiné or for the Île-de-France, which comprised Champagne and Picardy. But how is it possible to account for the divergence between the maritime zones with Brittany and Anjou losing 50 per cent of their Protestants but Poitou only 20 per cent? And how can the Vivarais so close to Dauphiné be explained? Is it necessary to invoke the different social structures of the consistories? Craftsmen and merchants, whose activities were linked to the urban world, showed a preference for emigration, as well as a group which was small numerically but important qualitatively, that is, the lesser nobility, who were to form the military cadres of William of Orange and of the Elector of Brandenburg. In contrast, the peasants, who could not take their land with them, departed less willingly. In so far as Protestantism in northern France was markedly more urban, this would account for the greater extent of emigration. Indeed the statistics we possess for the refugees strengthen this argument. Let us again take the

---

[12] I. Maurin, 'Les fugitifs huguenots du diocèse de Mende' (unpublished thesis, École des Chartes, 1984), 69–70.

example of the Cévennes, the more significant because agriculture, even though mixed with handicrafts, was of primary importance there. The agricultural sector accounts for only 8 per cent of the fugitives, whereas 52 per cent of them were craftsmen. Lower down, in the plain at Marsillargues, the peasant element was rather more numerous forming 12 per cent of the fugitives, with the craftsmen also rising to 56 per cent. In the south-west, in the Agenais, Périgord, and the Condomois, the rural element was even worse represented with only 4 per cent, while artisans comprised 40 per cent of the total emigration, reaching 60 per cent if merchants are included. On the other side of France the social composition was the same. Merchants and artisans accounted for 62 per cent of the emigrants from Vitry-le-François, 84 per cent from Sedan and 89 per cent from Metz.[13] Nevertheless I am bound to wonder whether the share of the rural population has not been under estimated. The peasants who passed through Frankfurt were not few and far between, especially if they came from the old Vaudois regions, the Luberon, and the valley of Freissinières, and on several occasions we find peasants at work with new techniques and products in Germany, in Switzerland, and even in England. May there not have been a tendency to take less note of the occupation of workers on the land, the predominant group in the societies of that time? To put the question in another way, may not those fugitives whose occupation is not mentioned have been those whose livelihood came from the land?

It would be absurd to deny these geographical and social factors, even if they need qualification, but I shall add two others. The first should complete the explanations already given for the imbalance between the North and the South. Elisabeth Labrousse has rightly emphasized the differences of attitude between the Protestants of the North and those of the Midi. The former were well aware that they were a minority and that they were no longer living in the days of the Wars of Religion. They could not imagine any sort of collective resistance, the more so because they were law-abiding. The only solution for them, apart from playing the double game, was exile. But the Huguenots of the Midi still felt themselves strong and believed, more or less consciously, that they could engage in a trial of strength, which they were shortly to do. Emigration for them was only one solution among others. Finally, we should not overlook the creation of a network for emigration, existing in one community but not in another, which probably explains local differences. This is too tenuous a phenomenon to appear directly in the documents, but one suspects its existence from the maps or from the mention of convoys coming from particular places.

Protestant emigration did not begin with the Revocation, but dates from

[13] D. MacKee, 'Les protestants de Sedan et la révocation de l'édit de Nantes: opposition, fuites et résistances', *BSHPF* (1981), 239.

the start of the personal reign of Louis XIV, from the moment when the first measures were taken against the Protestants. Indeed, the first edict prohibiting emigration was issued in 1669. Thus we find couples from Metz getting married in the French Reformed parishes of the Palatinate during this period.[14] Down to 1680, however, only individuals were involved, but as the threats grew, the tide of emigration swelled. Proof of this lies in the two royal declarations of 1682 and in the warning given by Louvois in March 1685 to the intendants to be vigilant. On 20 August 1685 the king granted half the property of fugitives to those who informed on them. At Sedan, for example, the professors and students of the academy, which was suppressed in 1681, escaped abroad with scarcely an exception before the Revocation. But the great wave naturally came between the end of 1685 and 1688. After that the tide slackened. The most determined had left and the War of the League of Augsburg did not make emigration easy. But a recrudescence occurred between 1698 and 1700 after the ending of the war and disappointment with the Peace of Ryswick. The Allies had not intervened firmly enough and the lot of the Huguenots was not going to improve. Further, in some provinces, such as Languedoc, repression was intensified and a new generation took the path of exile. After the Camisard war there was fresh emigration, but often officially desired and authorized. The movement never completely ceased, and continued throughout the reign of Louis XIV and beyond.

We have little information on the preparations for and the conditions of departure. There is a sense of hurried flight in the first wave of emigration. The registers of the notaries, usually so informative, are silent. Few fugitives went to see the notary before they left, though there were some exceptions, such as the Cévenol who on the day of his departure recovered some money owed to him.[15] Matters must have been settled by word of mouth. Property continued to be bequeathed to children who had already gone abroad, just as if nothing had happened. This silence speaks volumes for the atmosphere in these communities. But allusions appear from 1690, and become more and more frequent. By then it was no longer worth the bother of covering up for a fugitive.

But in compensation we know more about the journey itself, thanks to numerous written accounts, and we shall know still more in future. A large number of refugees aiming for northern Europe passed through Frankfurt and asked the Huguenot parish there for help. The secretaries were not content merely to record the name of the beneficiary and the sum given, but asked him where he came from, who was with him, what route he had followed, where he wanted to go, and what his occupation was. Some gave

[14] R. Mazauric, 'Étude sur les conséquences de la révocation de l'édit de Nantes en pays messin, un siècle de résonnances dans le village de Courcelles-Chaussy', *BSHPF* (1974), 257–8.

[15] Maurin, op. cit., 100.

detailed accounts of their journeys. This is a very rich source of information which Michelle Magdelaine is systematically exploiting with the aid of a computer program. The initial results are highly promising.[16] The first generation of refugees is clearly revealed through this source.

Surveillance was strict and informers swarmed in the strategic spots, encouraged by the rewards offered. The would-be emigrant needed therefore to be constantly on his guard. If a man was taken he was sent to the galleys and a woman went to prison. Roundabout routes had consequently to be sought, whose details were transmitted orally, or even in writing. Fugitives would travel by night, disguise themselves as pedlars or even as rosary-sellers and pilgrims. In Paris in December 1685 the watch surprised three men, one of whom was carrying a large hollow cross containing a sword. Emigration meant a brutal change in the lives of the fugitives. In a matter of hours they passed from an ordered existence to a wandering one, as an eye-witness, the pastor Élie Benoît, reported:

Women of quality, even aged sixty or seventy, who had never, so to speak, put their feet on the ground except to walk about in their homes or to stroll in an avenue, now walked eighty to a hundred leagues to the villages their guides had marked out. Girls of fifteen and sixteen, rich and poor, risked the same exhausting journeys, pushing wheelbarrows, carrying manure, baskets, or bundles. They stained their faces with dyes to brown their complexions . . . Several girls and women could be seen pretending to be ill, dumb, or mad. Some could be seen disguised as men, and some who were too delicate and small in build to pass as grown men wore the livery of lackeys, and followed on foot through the mud a guide on horseback who gave himself airs.[17]

When they drew near the frontier, it was best to engage a guide, and a good one. Some guides did not hesitate to hand over their customers to the authorities. In this way they got paid twice. Most guides were honest, but expensive, very expensive, charging according to the risks they ran in case of discovery, which until 1687 meant the galleys, but since this was not enough of a deterrent, after that the gallows.

The sea was scarcely safer. When the port authorities inspected the ships about to sail, they did not hesitate to burn sulphur so as to asphyxiate any stowaways. The ships were not always up to the open sea, and the amateur sailors might set off without enough provisions. Besides, there were captains who threw their passengers overboard after robbing them and Barbary pirates who captured ships.

[16] This is a Franco-German co-operative project financed by the Volkswagen Foundation. The first results were presented at the round table organized by the Institut d'Histoire moderne et contemporaine and published under the title 'Enquête sur le Refuge protestant à Francfort-sur-Main, à la fin du XVIIe siècle, à partir des registres de la communauté réformée française', Le Refuge huguenot en Allemagne, (IHMC-CNRS, Paris, 1981) 11–26.
[17] Gonin and Delteil, 169; C. Weiss (see Further Reading), i. 102.

The best course was to enlist as a soldier and then to slip over the frontier. This method made it even possible to indulge in the luxury of settling affairs with a notary before departure by making a will, a procedure which did not need parental approval and therefore relieved parents of future consequences. But naturally only young men could do this. The authorities grew concerned and the king was informed that 'the officers who raise recruits for their garrisons receive in the guise of soldiers or servants the richest Reformed in Paris and from various other places in the kingdom, and when these come to frontier towns and are out of danger of arrest, they easily cross to England, Holland, or Brandenburg'.[18]

It is not surprising given this sort of journey that fewer women emigrated. Women resisted in a different way. At the points of departure in the Cévennes Isabelle Maurin counted only a quarter of the refugees as women. The average age of the men, usually unmarried, was twenty-six. At Frankfurt the proportion was lower, one woman to more than five men. But what is most striking in the first statistics drawn up by Michélle Magdelaine, based on 1,360 persons who passed through the town between April and May 1686, is the large number of single persons, 783 men (nearly 60 per cent) accompanied by 55 children, and 101 women accompanied by 29 children. There were only 104 couples accompanied by 184 children. In contrast, the women at Sedan, while still in the minority, were comparatively more numerous, comprising a little more than a third of the total. But the frontier was close, which explains the greater number of families.[19]

Gradually there emerges an 'identikit portrait' of the fugitive. He was a young man, alone, about twenty-five, coming from Normandy, Picardy, Champagne, or Dauphiné, an artisan or a merchant. If he came from Dauphiné, he went first to Berne or Zürich, passing through Lyon, where care had to be taken for the town was closely watched, Geneva and Lausanne. He had little chance of being able to remain in Switzerland, for in spite of their goodwill the authorities could no longer accommodate the flood of refugees. He went further on to Frankfurt, going by Schaffhausen. There awaited him at Frankfurt the emissaries of the German princes, notably those of the great Elector and the Landgrave of Hesse-Cassel anxious to attract him to their states. According to his choice, he settled in the valley of the Weser or further afield in Prussia. If he came from Picardy he was more likely to turn his steps to 'the great ark of the refugees', as Pierre Bayle felicitously christened the United Provinces. The Protestants of northern France were accustomed to contacts with Holland; a century earlier they had supplied the first refuge, the Refuge wallon, with its population. There were still twenty-six churches where the services were

[18] Maurin, 101.
[19] MacKee, 23; Maurin, 79; Magdelaine, *Refuge huguenot*, 11.

held in French. Would our refugee find room there? Nothing could be less certain, since there was a very big influx and each European convulsion brought a new contingent of immigrants. In 1688 there came the refugees from the Palatinate, invaded by the troops of Louis XIV; in 1697 French Protestants disappointed by the Peace of Ryswick, and in 1703 the Protestants from the principality of Orange annexed by Louis XIV. Refugees periodically moved on from Holland, (a crossroads comparable to Switzerland) to Scandinavia, the German principalities and even further again. In 1687 ninety-seven families embarked for the Cape of Good Hope, where they founded a Huguenot church, which comprised at the end of the century a congregation of 3,000. The British Isles offered another outlet. In 1693, 600 families left Rotterdam for Ireland, where they would find Protestants who had come directly from the maritime provinces of western France.

This is the picture. The United Provinces incontestably ranked first among the four principal reception areas, with more than 70,000 refugees, coming not only from the north but from all over France. There were more than 2,000 in Amsterdam in March 1684, rising to around 15,000 at the end of the century, and, it seems, about the same number in The Hague and Rotterdam. Thirty-six new churches were founded to welcome the faithful. These churches enjoyed considerable prestige in the *Refuge* by virtue of the number and especially the quality of the pastors, while the intellectual brilliance of the wider Huguenot community can be seen in the universities, which benefited from the closure of the Reformed academies in France, and in the Republic of Letters in Amsterdam adorned by Pierre Bayle.[20] But, in contrast, more caution has to be shown over the Huguenot economic contribution. A census of 1684 brings out the multiplicity of crafts among the first refugees, of which some were unknown in Holland before the arrival of the Huguenots. These included the makers of *caudebecs*, rainproof felt hats made in Caudebec in Normandy, the designers of flowered silks, embroiderers in gold and silver, the manufacturers of *serges de Nîmes*, fan-makers and ivory craftsmen. But this list comes from a propaganda paper designed to demonstrate to the authorities the profits that would accrue from their hospitality. There were some resounding failures, such as that of the former director of the royal manufactures in Clermont in Languedoc, who received a credit of 50,000 guilders to make textiles, silks in particular, which the Dutch were not producing themselves, and who failed miserably, as did his compatriot, Philippe Perronneau, who was to have manufactured taffeta goods.[21]

I shall put Germany second, not so much because of the number of refugees—from 30,000 to 40,000, a figure that sets it between the two other countries, the British Isles and Switzerland—but because of the influence

[20] See pp. 331–3.
[21] Cf. H. H. Bolhuis, 'La Hollande et les deux refuges', *BSHPF*, (1969), 415.

exerted on its history by them. Germany was still at the end of the century suffering from the effects of the Thirty Years War, with deserted villages, the destruction of property and a demographic vacuum. This was particularly true of Brandenburg and Pomerania, and hence the interest of the Great Elector in skilled labour and his unremitting efforts to attract it into his lands. As a Calvinist prince ruling over a Lutheran population, this was also for him a means of strengthening his religion. Several pastors became court preachers, while Huguenot nobles took over military functions. He welcomed in all 15,000 refugees, of whom 6,000 were in Berlin, forming a fifth of the population. Other princes followed the Great Elector's example. The Landgrave of Hesse-Cassel received 3,800 refugees and created for them a whole series of settlements, Carlsdorf and Karlshafen, together with the new town of Cassel. The Margrave of Bayreuth, although a Lutheran, also installed Huguenots in a new quarter of Erlangen, which had a thousand French in 1698, the majority being artisans, making carpets, stockings, gloves, and hats. Württemburg for its part welcomed 3,000 refugees. Despite some setbacks, as at Karlshafen, the princes calculated correctly and the economic benefit was incontestable. The Huguenots improved the technology of the areas, introducing for example the stocking-frame, and widening a whole range of luxury goods, such as silks, ribbons, lace, tapestries, artificial flowers, and wigs. But they also played a role in increasing and improving the output of articles already in production, such as oil, candles, and soap, and in the agricultural sector introduced the growing of choice vegetables and tobacco. Finally, it can be said that the Huguenots laid the foundations of the first phase of industrialization in Prussia by their diffusion of modern methods of manufacture and their transmission of technical knowledge, then so dependent on personal contact.[22] In the same way, they enabled these states to be integrated more easily into the Republic of Letters, whose heart lay further to the west. Nor should we forget the determining influence exercised by the Huguenots upon the creation of the Academy of Berlin. One unexpected result has been emphasized by Rudolf von Thadden: in the Elector of Brandenburg's most easterly possessions, clearly divided between German and Polish influences, the Huguenots were a powerful influence for Germanization, in particular reinforcing the penetration of German, for they preferred to learn the language of their sovereign.[23]

Even if the number of Huguenots going to the British Isles was greater than the number going to Germany, which is an open question, their influence on English history was much less and their integration into the society which welcomed them much faster. The French émigrés played a distinct role, directly or indirectly, only at one moment. This was at the

[22] Cf. S. Jersch-Wenzel, 'La Place des réfugiés dans le développement économique allemande', *Le Refuge huguenot*, 41.
[23] 'L'acceuil des réfugiés et leur intégration dans les communautés allemandes, ibid., 27–31.

Glorious Revolution, of course no minor event. The indirect effect of the
arrival of the Huguenots was that the appearance of these victims of
Louis XIV and the accounts which they circulated aggravated anti-Popish
feeling. Anti-Papists had an enjoyable time pointing out what would
happen if a Catholic dynasty was to perpetuate itself in England. The direct
effect of the emigration was to place Huguenots in the household of William
of Orange and to make them particularly prominent in military affairs. The
Marquis de Ruvigny had been *Député général*, representing the Huguenot
churches with the Crown; he and Marshal Schomberg were among the very
few Protestants who had obtained leave to emigrate. Under their auspices,
refugees who had come from all over Europe formed three regiments of
infantry and one of cavalry, which fought in Scotland and in Ireland,
notably at the battle of the Boyne. Here Schomberg, aged eighty, originally
in charge of the Irish expedition, was killed, rallying his troops in a charge
against a French regiment with the cry, 'Voilà nos persécuteurs'.

Of the four principal countries which welcomed the Huguenots the most
uncertain immigration figures come from England. Charles Weiss found
that earlier figures of 50,000 to 70,000 were too low, and proposed 80,000,
although the census returns he quoted elsewhere do not justify the
correction.[24] The records of the Threadneedle Street church, the more
important of the Huguenot churches in London, covering the period from
August 1681 to January 1687, show 3,419 persons in receipt of aid, either
settled or passing through, for London, like Frankfurt for Germany, was a
staging-post for dispersion throughout the British isles. The rate was
comparable (though slower) with that for Frankfurt, which received 2,500
refugees between April 1686 and April 1687. The foundation of twenty-six
new churches can serve as another indicator. This was not a negligible
number, but is ten less than that of churches founded in Holland, which
logically presupposes a markedly smaller number of refugees and makes
much more credible the first estimate of a maximum of 50,000 refugees.

It should not be forgotten that some of the immigrants re-embarked for
the American colonies, for Massachusetts in particular but also for the New
York region. Refugees from La Rochelle founded New Rochelle and the
name of Étienne de Lancey can still be seen today commemorated on one of
the oldest houses in New York, near Wall Street, which became a tavern
and the meeting-place later of Washington and his friends. South Carolina
became the region most liked by the Huguenots and was known as the 'home
of the Huguenots'.[25]

[24] Weiss, 272. This observation in no way detracts from the admiration felt for this fine synthesis,
which has not yet been superseded.

[25] I. Scouloudi, 'L'aide apportée aux réfugiés français par l'église de Threadneedle Street, l'église de
Londres, 1681–1687', *BSHPF* (1969), 441. The most recent estimate puts the number of Huguenots in
America in 1700 as about 1500 and certainly not more than 2,000: Jon Butler, *The Huguenots in America*
(Harvard, 1982), 49.

The same uncertainty applies to the economic impact of the emigration. Charles Weiss presented an impressive picture—almost too impressive, for he conveyed the view that the economic expansion of England in the eighteenth century was largely due to the Huguenots. It is true that the statistics of those helped in London show two-thirds of the total as artisans and skilled craftsmen, with the textile and ready-made clothing trades predominating. These Huguenots must have brought a plus value to the country, but exactly how great? In the absence of a precise quantitative analysis of the kind which Stephi Jersch-Wenzel has made for Prussia, but which is difficult for England in the present absence of data, the question can only be raised.

Geneva and the Swiss cantons, more than any other countries, had to bear the first impact of the emigration. A contemporary bears witness to the size of the phenomenon, writing in August 1687:

An amazing number of poor French refugees pass through Geneva, entering by the new gate and leaving by the lake. Most come from Dauphiné. There are up to 350 a day; a count made on 16, 17 and 18 August showed 800 . . . It is said that in the five weeks ending on 1 September more than 8,000 will have arrived; with the result that although there are departures every day by the lake, there are always ordinarily nearly 3,000 in Geneva.[26]

Is this an exaggeration? Scarcely, for the *Bourse Française* (the relief fund) was becoming exhausted. The Genevan authorities grew alarmed at the great crowds gathering in the city squares, especially as the French resident became threatening. They resigned themselves several times to expelling the refugees when pressure mounted and granted citizenship sparingly. Until 1700 naturalization had been given to only 754, but a great number more remained. In 1693 a census returned 3,300. The others went further on; to begin with to the Pays de Vaud, French-speaking and near France, which received about 4,000. Others went to German-speaking Switzerland, particularly to Berne and Zürich, where they formed distinct communities. Others at Basle, Schaffhausen, and St Gallen rapidly merged into the population. The estimate given by Weiss of around 20,000 refugees seems reasonable. The number was not higher because of the constant effort of the authorities to evacuate the 'surplus French' towards the German lands, which were much more anxious to welcome this skilled labour.

The attitude of governments towards the refugees differed greatly from one country to another, but the German princes were the most favourably disposed. From the beginning of Louis XIV's personal rule and the first phase of persecution, the Elector of Brandenburg, Frederick William, had understood the opportunity offered to him for the development of his lands by the French Protestants. He tried to attract them by using the services of

[26] Weiss, ii. 187.

his envoy at the French court; and there followed the foundation of the Huguenot church in Berlin in 1672. It is not therefore surprising to find him publishing the celebrated Edict of Potsdam eleven days after the Revocation. This proclaimed that the Elector's agents would await the refugees coming through the United Provinces at Hamburg and those coming from France at Frankfurt, and would look after them until they reached the destination of their choice. The immigrants were to be excused customs-duties on the belongings they brought with them and were also to be exempted from taxes. They could take over ruined, empty or abandoned houses; and the Great Elector would compensate the owners if necessary. Furthermore, the immigrants would be immediately granted the rights of citizenship in the towns. Frederick William promised land to the peasants, subsidies to the entrepreneurs, offices and honours to the nobles. He would pay the French-speaking pastors, and accepted the continuance of the consistorial structure. The French community would have its own lawcourts and disputes with Germans would be settled in mixed tribunals. Finally, each province would have a commissioner appointed to protect the French refugees.

The Edict was circulated throughout France. A correspondent of the Great Condé, for example, wrote to him on 17 January 1696 that 'There has been much talk at Chalon about a circular letter from my lord of Brandenburg which came by the post to a converted Huguenot who out of curiosity sent it to another convert and then to the *lieutenant criminel*'.[27] The same policy was pursued by the Landgrave of Hesse-Cassel, who published his first declaration in April 1685 and renewed it in December 1685. This last text was accompanied by a real propaganda leaflet: 'The country is agreeable and very beautiful, the air is good and healthy and the people are easy-going and by nature kind to foreigners . . . Money is worth 10 to 12 per cent more than in France . . . taxes and dues are much less there than in France or elsewhere.'[28]

The authorities in Switzerland were much more reserved. We have already seen the attitude of Geneva subjected to French pressure, but the city-fathers of Berne, although well-disposed to begin with, grew much more reserved with the greater density of the refugees. From 1689 they ordered all those without resources to leave the canton, with the exception of the old and infirm. In face of the reactions of other Protestant powers and offers of help, the measure was not enforced. But ten years later the magistrates called upon the towns under their authority to give permanent residence 'to those of the Reformed Religion who can be useful to the community, such as schoolmasters, artisans, and those whose circumstances oblige them to remain'. The others were to leave for Germany. For example,

[27] Gonin and Delteil, 380.
[28] Text published by Weiss, ii. 415–16.

in the little town of Moudon, eleven families only remained out of the forty who had appeared on the census of 1698.[29]

The United Provinces were in an intermediate position. Numerous privileges were to begin with granted in Holland to the Huguenots, such as exemption from taxes accorded in 1681 for twelve years. But the continuance and growth of the exodus posed more and more difficult problems for the authorities, faced by the poverty of the majority of the refugees, including those of higher social status. A spy in the service of the French ambassador to the United Provinces reported in May 1686 that many officers 'to go the woods to look for snails, which they cook for lack of bread'.[30] The authorities therefore tried to send on the later arrivals to Germany or overseas.

There was also another difference between the German principalities and the other countries of the *Refuge*. In the first case, as we have seen, the princes favoured the autonomy of the Huguenot communities, but elsewhere there was a preference for integration, even at the price of being more restrictive.

In contrast to the diversity of government attitudes, popular behaviour showed a certain similarity. But if public opinion at first responded to the misfortunes of the Huguenots and to confessional solidarity, there was a progressive falling-off. A contemporary reported that: 'The magistrates of Berne have made a ruling, which is not exactly an explicit order, but a very pressing exhortation to all the bailiwicks in their territory, to require all the peasants not only to contribute alms for the upkeep of the refugees, but also to take them in, feed them, and give them all the help they can.'[31] The soldiers of the canton were detailed to accompany the French in order to open up the doors of the houses assigned to them. In Germany, jealousy was aroused by the exemption from taxes and by the various privileges enjoyed by the Huguenots. Businessmen were nervous of competition, all the more dangerous given the Huguenots' proven initiative and enterprise, while artisans feared unemployment. Cultural antagonism went with economic tension. The Lutheran population of Brandenburg found the stark simplicity of Calvinist services difficult to take. Even inside Calvinism, there were temperamental differences; the Swiss Reformed did not appreciate the expansive and voluble men of the Midi. In St Gallen the French preachers were advised to 'abstain from making unnecessary gestures in the pulpit'. It therefore becomes easier to understand the hesitations of some governments torn between religious solidarity, financial constraints, and the state of public opinion.

---

[29] Cf. Weiss, ii. 193–4 and H. Meylan, 'Aspects du Refuge huguenot en Suisse romande', *BSHPF* (1969), 535.

[30] J. Solé, 'La diplomatie de Louis XIV', *BSHPF* (1969), 632.

[31] Weiss, ii. 192.

The problem of assimilation did not arise for the first generation of refugees. To begin with this was because many Huguenots hoped to return to France either as a result of peace or because of the hope that the king would rescind the Revocation. The welcoming governments did not seek linguistic uniformity, even when they did not, on the contrary, actively favour the retention of French. Thus in Nuremberg the Lutherans forbade the Huguenots (Calvinists) to learn German, since they did not wish them to 'contaminate' their Lutheran subjects![32] Others saw the opportunity for improving the culture of their own élites, in so far as French was the language for international exchanges. The occupation of language-teacher, of interpreter, or better still of translator was regarded by many refugees as a stepping-stone to a desired position. Some countries were thus able to have their literary productions known more quickly abroad. The most famous example is the Languedoc refugee, Pierre Coste, the secretary and translator of Locke in Holland. The contribution of the Huguenot *Refuge* to the European Enlightenment was therefore not negligible.

From the double game to violent resistance

In France itself the illusion did not last long; in spite of some marked local successes, the Revocation was, in general, a failure. An informant of the Great Condé wrote to him on 18 December 1685: 'I learned when I was at Rouen from two curés that they considered *nouveaux convertis* more Huguenot after their conversion than before. They talk more freely against certain things . . . than they did before, and show no signs of devoutness in our churches.' Another letter of New Year, 1686, is even more significant; 'all the reports from the provinces say that there are many highly questionable converts, of whom some cannot bring themselves to perform the rites of our religion, while others observe them in a peculiar way.'[33]

After this general survey, let us take a single case, Vébron, a parish in the heart of the Cévennes. The curé, in obedience to the demand of the *subdélégué*, made an enquiry into the religion of his parishioners, just a little over a year after their mass abjuration in January, 1687. A third of them got bad marks and were described as 'fugitives, obstinate, . . . argumentative, and blasphemous'. There were 134 families among the remaining two-thirds, of whom sixty-six did 'quite well', fifty did 'well', and only eighteen did 'very well', though these last included three Catholics.[34] Apart from outward conduct, what about the inner conscience? The work of Michel Vovelle on testamentary formulae has shown how a corner of the veil can be lifted. Before 1685 there was a very simple Protestant formula, according to

[32] Information kindly supplied by Michelle Magdelaine.
[33] Gonin and Delteil, 163, 354.
[34] Cf. R. Poujol, *Histoire d'un village cévenol, Vébron* (Edisud-Club cévenol, Aix-en-Provence, 1982), 131.

which the testator committed his soul to divine mercy, confident in the merits of the passion of Christ, but naturally excluding the Virgin and the saints. Burial was provided for in the cemetery 'in the place where those of our Religion lie'.[35] After the Revocation, at Vébron, the Virgin was not always invoked and for the funeral a formula was used which owed little to Catholicism: 'I order the burial of my body in the form observed by those of the Christian religion'. After 1688 this formula became more irreverent— 'in the form observed by true Christians'. And since this formula might stir up reactions a prudent notary substituted at the end of November 1690: 'in the cemetery of Vébron, at the discretion of his heirs'.

Saint-Jean-du-Gard was probably more under surveillance. The *nouveaux convertis* made some concessions without fully submitting. In their wills they declared that they did indeed belong to the Catholic and Roman church, but the Virgin was never mentioned, and only half recommended themselves to the saints. From 1690 the formula 'Catholic, Apostolic, and Roman', disappears, even if the wish is still affirmed for burial in a Catholic cemetery, a wish which vanishes in 1709 after the Camisard War. The authorities seem to have been more effective at Lourmarin in Luberon, in Provence, where the invocation to the Virgin and the celestial court was normal, and to it were added all the Provençal Catholic practices of *cantats*, novenas and masses at the end of the year. The success was nevertheless ephemeral. All were docile until 1703, but from then onwards, the Catholic formulary was abandoned. The Virgin and saints went into an eclipse in one case out of every two; novenas and *cantats* were replaced by much vaguer expressions and the heir was asked to do what was appropriate.[36] The variation and evolution of the formulae show that something was at stake all the more precious for the *nouveaux convertis* since they were thereby proclaiming their first rejection of the religion and culture imposed upon them.

But there were plenty of other stakes to be played for, some apparently modest but all disputed, such as the Corpus Christi processions when many *nouveaux convertis* 'forgot' to decorate their houses. Fast days too, were another point of dispute, and it is hard to conceive the importance given to this question. The *nouveaux convertis* made it a point of honour to eat meat and the dragoons 'inspected the pots to see if meat had been cooked in them.'[37] Any pretexts served to avoid going to mass. At Saint Pierreville in the Vivarais the bell had not been heard; it was explained that it was being recast and made 'two quintals heavier' at the expense of the community. In

---

[35] M. Vovelle, 'Jalons pour une histoire du silence, les testaments réformés dans le sud-est de la France du XVIIième au XVIIIième siècle', *Cinq siècles de protestantisme à Marseille et en Provence* (Fédération historique de Provence, Marseille, 1978), 42–59.

[36] Vovelle, 51.

[37] Extract from 'Memoires de J. Gaubert', in *Journaux camisards*, ed. Ph. Joutard (Paris, 1965), 110–11.

Burgundy, illness was the excuse and everywhere people arrived late. The situation was graver at Sedan, where the *nouveaux convertis* went across the nearby frontier 'se marier à la huguenote'. At Anduze, the gateway to the Cévennes, there was a massive refusal on the part of the population in 1686 to go to confession before Lent, while at Uzès a nobleman turned his back on the elevation of the Host.[38] In several cases the clearest result of royal policy was the rise of indifference. The *nouveaux convertis* abandoned the faith of their childhood without really adhering to their new religion.

It has been said that death is a privileged moment of defiance. The curé of Sedan acknowledged that he was powerless, since 'as the dying are always surrounded by their relatives of the Religion, these turn them away from the last sacraments by prayers and threats and do not inform us, so that we only learn of the calamity after death has occured.'[39] The graph of funerals in the church at Marsillargues in Languedoc in the last years of Louis XIV's reign dipped down proportionately to the rise in the number of clandestine burials in private ground. In this little war of attrition the strength of the communities of *nouveaux convertis* lay in their grip on strategically important functions, such as those of doctors, midwives, notaries, schoolmasters. Wherever they were in a majority the Revocation paradoxically restored to them the municipal power which they had progressively lost during the last years under the Edict of Nantes, since with everyone now a Catholic they could again occupy all the administrative posts. The curés complained bitterly; typical was the priest of Vébron who wrote that: 'The sieur de Salgas, le sieur Aurès, and the sieur Boudon are the cocks of the walk of this community, to whom all the rest cling and on whom good and bad fortune depend. They are great politicians and set things in train as they please . . . The wives of Aurès, Boudon, and Lapize are cocks among the women and it is they who perform their religious duties the worst.'[40]

At one time the authorities counted on the new generation. This was the view of Madam de Maintenon and also of Bâville, Intendant of Languedoc, who wrote in 1698 that 'children who have not seen temples nor ministers will be more disposed to the good impressions which we shall make on them.'[41] Four years later the Camisards gave him an unexpected answer, clearly explained by a general in the Cévennes who, writing to the secretary of state for war, accurately defined the double game:

All the children who were in their cradles at the time of the general conversions, even those who were 4, 5, 6, 7, 8, 10, are now more Huguenot than their fathers and mothers ever were, and a great number of those who have mobilized against us

[38] All these examples are collected in S. Mours and D. Robert (see Further Reading), 18–21.
[39] MacKee, 249–50.
[40] Poujol, 132.
[41] Ibid.

never remember having seen a minister in their lives ... This is because their fathers and mothers have taken care to bring them up in these beliefs, while the majority go daily to mass and make the external observances of the good Catholic.'[42]

This lucid analysis is confirmed by witnesses of the Reformed faith, such as the Camisard prophet, Marion, who explained at the beginning of his autobiography: 'The secret teaching that I received daily from my father and mother brought my aversion for idolatry and the errors of popery to such a pitch that having reached the years of discretion, I practised no religion but that of the assemblies which met in the *déserts* and secret places.'[43] Traces of these practices can still be found in family papers, whether copies of children's catechisms, or better still short statements of belief made by the father himself, such as this one discovered in a family Bible with the explanation: 'in order that my children will be able to remember that the religion which we profess ... is altogether pure and holy, I am going to make a very faithful abridged version of what we profess ... and afterwards I shall make them see that what the Church believes is not at all in conformity with the word of God.'[44] There have also been handed down until our own day the old Bibles with the first page torn out to deceive the dragoons, the psalters, the clandestine books smuggled in from the *Refuge*, such as *Une véritable liturgie pour les chrétiens privés de pasteurs*, and numerous copies of prayers, sermons, and letters coming from Holland or Geneva.

Some did not even accept these necessary compromises. They did not abjure but took to the woods, as did the old woman of seventy-four, born at Lasalle in the Cévennes, who stayed away from her home for more than seven years, 'living in neither town nor village and hardly ever entering a house'. Very soon groups began to be formed, and ten days after the Revocation on a share-cropping farm near Anduze people could be heard chanting Ps. 69 with its lamentations but hopeful ending: 'God will save Zion, and will build the cities of Judah'. In a neighbouring parish on the following Sunday more than a hundred of the faithful organized what amounted to a service with psalms and preaching. At Vauvert near Nîmes, some days before Christmas 1685, in the cellars of a château, a candidate for the ministry, Fulcran Rey, entreated his hearers 'not to go to mass to bow the knee before the images of Baal'.[45] At the end of January 1686 more than five hundred of the 'obstinate' gathered on a mountainside close to Saint-Jean-du-Gard. On the eve of Easter in the same year in the neighbouring parish of Mialet, according to a witness from outside, there were about

---

[42] Ibid., 133.
[43] *Mémoires sur la guerre des Camisards* (Presses du Languedoc, Montpellier, 1983), 44.
[44] S. Ribard, *Notes d'histoires cévenoles* (Cazilhac, 1899), 58.
[45] Bost, i. 89.

4,000 present at an assembly. Elsewhere clandestine meetings were less remarked upon, but nevertheless they took place, in Normandy, in Lower Poitou outside Pouzauges and Montcoutant, and even in Brittany, at Vitré, for example, in March 1686, as reported by one of the Great Condé's correspondents.[46]

The first assemblies took place almost spontaneously, without a general plan and sparked off by local initiative. But from the beginning of 1686 the most obstinate had much bigger projects, wishing to restore a proper Church by replacing pastors who had emigrated or apostasized. Preachers, simple laymen, now not only led the services by readings and then by composing sermons, but presided over the Lord's Supper and baptized children, according to the tradition of universal priesthood. Charles Bost, in his highly detailed history of the Cévennes region and of Lower Languedoc, found for the period 1686–1700 more than sixty such preachers, almost all of modest background, most often textile-workers, carders or weavers. They had rudimentary schooling, the best educated among them being one-time precentors or school-masters, which was the case of one of the two leaders, Vivent. The other leader, Brousson, stands out by his social origins and education; he was a former lawyer.

At the beginning and under the influence of Vivent, the participants in these assemblies did not hesitate to carry arms to defend themselves in case of attack by the soldiers. The preachers were also in touch with the Allied powers during the War of the League of Augsburg. Several projects for landings in co-ordination with Protestant 'maquis' units were drawn up, and two in September 1689 and March 1690 were set in motion, but unsuccessfully. After the death of Vivent, Brousson became converted to the idea of non-violent and purely spiritual resistance, and he favoured unarmed assemblies.

The social composition of those who attended, seen through the judicial records, mirrors that of the preachers. Nine-tenths were of humble origin with a predominance of rural artisans, who comprised about half of those prosecuted, and among these a third were textile workers. The frequent presence of women should not cause surprise, since we have already noted the role they played in the Protestant resistance on several occasions.

This social composition explains in part the failure to understand the movement shown by influential circles in the *Refuge*. Further, moderates, such as the minister, Basnage, placed their hopes on alleviating the fate of their brothers in France by persuasion and by a redoubling of obedience. They were highly embarrassed by the developments and sanctioned family services or exile only. By contrast, zealots, such as Jurieu, rejoiced in the resistance. Here can be found re-emerging two tendencies which had already divided the French Reformed community before the Revocation. A

[46] Gonin and Delteil, 291.

final reason for distrust on the part of some was the absence of pastors and of regular church structures. This accounts for the efforts made by the preachers to go to Amsterdam or to Geneva in order to get themselves recognized as pastors, and also for the fidelity with which the assemblies kept to the traditional order of service of the Reformed churches of France, with the sole addition of the act for 'reconciliation with God', that is, counter-abjuration and the return to the Reform. In this part of the service, the repentant member of the faithful heard reminders of the theological contradictions between the two confessions and was called upon to renounce all equivocal behaviour and the double game, since going to mass was prohibited even if under duress.

It would be wrong to suppose that the holding of the assemblies was confined to the synodal provinces of the Cévennes and Lower Languedoc, simply because they were especially large and have been the subject of Bost's excellent study. More or less everywhere laymen took the initiative in reuniting the faithful. Assemblies were held in Normandy and in Poitou from 1686, in Picardy from 1688, and in Saintonge from 1689. Périgord was original in having a woman as preacher. 'Montjoie', as she was called, had never abjured and she had 'roamed the woods, going from house to house', organizing services for two years until her arrest in April 1688. A dozen assemblies were surprised between 1687 and 1689 in Upper Languedoc and rather more in Dauphiné.[47] But this last province, together with the adjacent province of the Vivarais, was characterized by another and still more original expression of Protestant resistance, prophesying.

On 3 February 1688, in a little village of Dauphiné, Saou, south-east of Valence, a young shepherdess of fifteen, Isabeau Vincent, who was illiterate, began to sing psalms and to preach in her sleep, and continued to do so in the following days. She attacked 'Popery', called for repentance, and announced that deliverance was at hand. She rapidly attracted a following; her sayings were piously collected, and some printed.[48] She continued to prophesy until 8 June, when she was arrested. But it was too late: contact with her had led to other young men and women in their turn becoming 'inspired' and roaming all over Dauphiné. In January 1689 a young farmer, Gabriel Astier, introduced the movement into the Vivarais, on the other bank of the Rhône. The prophesying assemblies multiplied; more or less everywhere young people were suddenly seized by shivering fits and convulsive trembling; some fell flat on their backs; others wept, crying out, 'Mend your ways, repent, the time of deliverance is at hand'. The movement seemed for a time to have been checked following the brutal massacre of an assembly, but it continued hidden within hamlets and

---

[47] Mours et Robert, 59.

[48] Such as the one found, copied out, in the papers of an Ardèche family, by Pastor Manen: cf. H. Manen and Ph. Joutard, (see Further Reading), 64–78.

families. Brousson in 1697 spoke with much respect of the prophetesses he had encountered.

To understand this movement it is necessary to remember the psychological climate in which the Reformed of the Midi found themselves after the Revocation. They felt despair at being deprived of their religion, which was also their culture, together with shame at having surrendered too quickly. They therefore took refuge in an imaginary world and meditated upon prophetic texts in the Bible with the greater ease because they had long been familiar with the Book in a literal interpretation. The French Protestants had for long felt themselves to be the new Israel, subjected to the same ordeals, but also bearers of the same hope. Before the recent ordeals, the Christianity of these Reformed of the Midi was already messianic, much more in sympathy with the religion of a Lutheran pastor of the sixteenth century than with a Calvinist Genevan pastor of the seventeenth century. It is enough to read the prayers copied out or the sermons of the preachers to feel the wind of prophecy already present. Besides, at the end of 1685 in the whole of the Midi from Béarn to Dauphiné, the Reformed had believed that they heard the beating of drums and the singing of psalms in the air. On top of this they learned of Jurieu's reflections on *L'Accomplissement des prophéties*, in which, taking up again the analysis made by his grandfather, Pierre du Moulin, on Rev. 11, he announced that the 'Beast' would be vanquished in 1689 and true religion re-established. The League of Augsburg, the invasion of William III, and the overthrow of James II seemed to inaugurate the realization of these prophecies and gave credibility to Jurieu's predictions. As for the manifestations of hysteria, they should not cause surprise. They were the result of traumatism. These Protestants, no longer able to express themselves through speech, which was forbidden, used the only language remaining to them, convulsions and tremors, authentic body-language. It should also be remembered that behind their confusing baffling form, the discourses of their preachers preserved a certain coherence, continuing an earlier tradition by recalling the grand themes of Calvinism—sinful man saved by the grace of God alone—and by having a constant concern with controversy.

For the preachers and prophets or more modestly, the 'stubborn and obstinate', royal power had only one answer, straightforward repression, which took the form of fines, billeting of troops, removal of children for unreliable converts; deportation, prison, and the galleys for fugitives, those who had relapsed, and participants at assemblies; execution for guides, preachers, and prophets. Up to 1700 a thousand were sent to the galleys and there were seventy executions, which included five women. Whole families were wiped out, such as that of Jean Roques, a preacher from Lasalle in the Cévennes. He was hanged and one of his brothers was sent to the galleys; his mother, his wife, his children, and one of his sisters hid in the woods; his uncle and cousin died in the Tour de Constance at Aigues-Mortes; his aunt and three female cousins died when being transported to the West Indies.[49]

In 1700 the authorities could feel that they had rid themselves of the 'evil'. This was an illusion. The worst was yet to come. Prophesyings, which had travelled across the Ardèche in the autumn of 1700, reappeared in full daylight in the heart of the Cévennes and Lower Languedoc in the void left by the persecution of the preachers. The movement quickly became violent, invoking God's vengeance. The abbé du Chaila, the inspector of Catholic missions, upon whom the *nouveaux convertis* had for years concentrated their hate, was the first victim. He had ordered some fugitives, who had been intercepted, to be locked up in his house at Pont-de-Montvert at the foot of Mont Lozère. But the 'Spirit' commanded a woolcomber, Abraham Mazel, from Saint-Jean-du-Gard to free the prisoners and in the course of the foray Du Chaila was murdered. This was the first act in the War of the Camisards.

The revolt had modest beginnings. Between July and October 1702 some groups, acting independently of each other, launched attacks in Lower Languedoc and in the Cévennes. But gradually they became organized, clustering around Roland Laporte, a wool carder, Castanet, a gamekeeper from L'Aigoual, Jouany, a brickmaker, and Jean Cavalier, an apprentice baker. Cavalier had the greatest military talent and defeated in succession the garrison of Alais on 24 December 1702 and de Broglie, commander of the army in Languedoc on 12 January 1703. Versailles now became nervous. De Broglie was replaced by Marshal de Montrevel and reinforcements were sent. European newspapers also began to show interest in these events.

The change in command brought no improvement. The rebels held the Cévennes mountains and the Languedoc countryside for fifteen months. Curés had to seek refuge in the towns, which army officers were reluctant to leave. Catholics, infuriated by the ineffectiveness of the royal troops, formed their own bands and the atrocities of one side were countered by those of the other. To crown everything Cavalier defeated one of the best royal regiments between Nîmes and Alais in March 1704.

French and foreign observers could not understand what was happening. Popular revolts had never before lasted so long. They sought for an explanation by looking for noble leadership, but found only peasants and artisans leading one of the first guerrilla campaigns of the modern type. The name *Camisard* is in itself suggestive, since it derives etymologically from *camisade*, a surprise attack by night, or *camisa*, the ordinary, everyday shirt worn by the combatants. The mountains certainly favoured the rebels, but they were equally successful in the plains of Lower Languedoc. The complicity of the local population was more important since the hard core of the rebels was thus supplied with food, hiding-places, intelligence, and

[49] Case cited by Bost, i. 204.

reinforcements. A harvester one day became a guerrilla the next. Reprisals by the army only cemented solidarity. Prophesyings were also at the heart of the revolt; they established the hierarchy and inspired all the decisions from ambushes to executions or pardons. Prophesyings above all had the merit of erasing from peasants and artisans their natural feelings of inferiority when faced by professional soldiers. It was not they who were fighting but God who was fighting through them.

The Camisards were defeated not so much in the field as by diplomacy. Following his last disaster, Montrevel was replaced by Marshal Villars, but before Montrevel left he succeeded in taking Cavalier by surprise. Further and highly important, one of his lieutenants discovered Cavalier's magazines, which enabled Villars to profit from a certain wavering on the part of the one-time baker's boy and to engage in negotiations. He had no difficulty by playing the card of his social superiority in getting Cavalier to accept unconditional surrender which was accepted very reluctantly by the other leaders in May 1704. This division was shortly followed by the death of the second leader, Roland Laporte, and general lassitude. Small groups of Camisards negotiated separate cease-fires, and by October 1704 calm had returned. Paradoxically, the Allies, who up to then had been very circumspect, now took cognizance of the Camisard movement with a view to promoting an internal insurrection, but it was too late and all their attempts to relaunch the revolt from 1705 to 1710 failed.

Was this another defeat for the French Calvinists? This is not certain. All Europe had seen that they still existed and had taken a passionate interest, whether friendly or hostile. This had included the most controversial aspect of the revolt, prophesyings, which were given an unexpected new lease of life in London. The French prophets, transporting their 'inspirations' there, gave rise to violent controversy and even mobs in the streets in 1706 and 1707. They played a part in early Methodist conversion scenes and found descendants among the Shakers. But there were more important consequences of the revolt. In future, even when the royal authorities employed coercion, care was taken not to go too far for fear of reviving the war. Persecution would never again reach the intensity of the period before the revolt.[50]

The Power of a Memory

At the end of this all too brief account, is it possible to answer the initial question? A first quantitative approach could lead to a pessimistic answer. When French Calvinism reappeared in full daylight at the beginning of the nineteenth century, its numbers had been more than halved in a France where the population had increased by a third. Whereas it represented little

[50] For a more detailed study of this question, see Ph. Joutard, *Les Camisards* (see Further Reading).

more than 4 per cent of the population before 1685, now it did not constitute more than 1.5 per cent. But once again this overall reckoning conceals great disparities, and in the first place between north and south. The divergence between them had widened again. The Reformed of the north had lost two-thirds of their numbers and constituted no more than 13 per cent of the Huguenot total, but the south had lost only a half. At the level of the provincial synods, the differences were still greater. The Protestants of the Cévennes in 1800 were almost as numerous as their ancestors in the eighteenth century, but the Bretons and Angevins were no more than a tenth of their former strength.[51] In the latter case the haemorrhage of emigration and the disheartenment of those who remained, too few to resist the pressure of the majority, and in the former case, little emigration together with a high density of population, explain the divergent development of these regions. For Protestantism to survive either larger numbers were required, if only to neutralize the authorities, or small numbers had to be compensated by high social standing. The Protestant merchant families of Marseilles, linked by an endogamy which was the only visible sign of their adherence to a proscribed religion, illustrate the latter case. They regularly performed their Catholic rites, but were all to be found in the first consistory of Marseilles under Napoleon.

Having said this, I am by no means sure that the statistics are a true reflection of reality. Between the 4 per cent of 1685 and the 1.5 per cent of 1800 there was a difference of degree and not of kind. The French Calvinists were a small minority from the time of the regime of the Edict of Nantes, and grew steadily weaker throughout the seventeenth century. It was even more serious that they were a minority with a sense of shame, seeking to compensate for its eccentricity in religion by a high degree of political conformity, breaking with its past and preferring not to recall the Wars of Religion or even Saint Bartholomew.[52] I am inclined to believe, following Voltaire, Émile Léonard, and Pierre Chaunu,[53] that but for the Revocation the Protestant minority would have been slowly and progressively absorbed into the Catholic majority, with the exception of some groups who would have become the equivalent of sects. The minority which survived the reign of Louis XIV was smaller than it had been at the time of the Edict of Nantes, but it had been tempered by war. It had endowed itself with arms to maintain itself as a minority, and had acquired a folk-memory. Henceforth there should be no more yielding, for this would be a breach of faith with

[51] A study based on figures given in S. Mours, *Les galériens protestants*, 58. G. Frèches has attempted a more precise approach at the level of the parishes of Western Languedoc in 'Contre-Réforme et dragonnades (1640–1789): Pour une orientation statistique de l'histoire du protestantisme français', *BSHPF* (1973), 362–83.

[52] See p. 298 and Élisabeth Labrousse, 'Passé et conjoncture politique: les raisons d'une discrétion', in P. Joutard (ed.), *La Saint-Barthélémy ou les résonnances d'un massacre* (Paris, 1976).

[53] P. Chaunu, 'Les crises au XVIIième siècle de l'Europe réformée', *RH* (1965), 23–60.

family traditions and the 'founding father'.[54] A mixed marriage became a betrayal.

On 25 August 1715 in a hamlet of the Lower Cévennes, Les Montèzes, a young man aged twenty gathered together about a dozen friends to reconstitute a Reformed Church in conformity with that of 1680. This was doubly symbolic. Some weeks later the old king died. Was not this the sign of the failure of a policy? But this young man, Antoine Court, who disapproved of prophesyings and the violent resistance of the Camisards, spent the second half of his life in compiling their history while he was a refugee in Lausanne.[55] He stands in contrast to his predecessors of the seventeenth century, who recognized no link with preceding generations. Between their attitude and his there had occurred the transition from a minority no longer able to survive as such to a minority whose triumphant resistance was fortified by an awareness of its own history.

[54] Resistance became essentially a family tradition, as research in private archives has shown. A family in the Cévenol hamlet of La Pervenche can be taken as an example. The family papers there contain prayers composed at the time of the Revocation, a manuscript copy of a sermon given by Brousson in 1692, and the letter from one of the family condemned to the galleys, arrested while trying to escape in 1701. Another member of the family had been compromised in the Camisard rising and in the mid-eighteenth century descendants of the same family were actively engaged in organizing clandestine Reformed gatherings. See Manen and Joutard, and P. Joutard, 'Les déserts (1685–1800)' in *Histoire des protestants en France* (Toulouse, 1977), 195 ff.

[55] Antoine Court, *Histoire des troubles des Cévennes ou de la guerre des Camisards sous de règne le Louis le Grand* (3 vols., Villefranche, 1760); P. Joutard, *La Légende des Camisards* (see Further Reading), ch. 5.

Further Reading

The *Bulletin de la Société de l'Histoire du Protestantisme Français* (*BSHPF*) is an indispensable source, particularly since its indexes of places, persons, and subjects are a model of their kind. References to the most interesting recent articles can be found in the notes.

See also:

Bost, C., *Les Prédicants protestants des Cévennes et du Bas-Languedoc* (2 vols., Paris, 1912, repr. Geneva, 1985).

Joutard, P., *Les Camisards* (Paris, 1976).

—— *La Légende des Camisards, une sensibilité au passé* (Paris, 1977).

Magdelaine, M., and Thadden, R. von (eds.), *Le Refuge huguenot, 1685–1985* (Paris, 1985), *Die Hugenotten, 1685–1985* (Munich, 1985).

Manen, H. and Joutard, P., *Une foi enracinée, La Pervenche* (Valence, 1972).

Mours, S. and Robert, D., *Le Protestantisme en France du XVIII^{ieme} siècle à nos jours* (Paris, 1972).

Weiss, C., *Histoire des réfugiés protestants de France depuis la révocation de l'édit de Nantes jusqu'à nos jours* (2 vols., Paris, 1853).

XIII

Variations on a theme by Max Weber

HERBERT LÜTHY[1]

I. *Reformation and Counter-Reformation*

MAX Weber held no high opinion of statistics, and even less so of their use for purposes for which they had not been intentionally collected. No census had ever been carried out to detect the motives of men's actions or to measure the spiritual aspirations which inform their minds and lives as influenced by the world's great religious and cultural traditions. Weber's theses on the sociology of religion and particularly on the intricate connection between Protestant—or, in a later and narrower definition, Calvinist—ethics and the economic dynamism of modernity, which he chose to call capitalism, were inspired by that other form of knowledge which is intuition, and which enables the inquirer to abstract ideal types or models from the complex evidence. Censuses and other surveys might collect figures on the proportions of different religious groups in various occupations, social classes, and status categories, and the inquirer might then infer certain affinities between creed and calling; yet he would find only what intuition had led him to expect. A strict proof can never be anticipated because in a complex and changing society it is impossible to isolate this single link from so many other factors.

The then Grand Duchy of Baden, where Max Weber was teaching first at the traditionally Catholic university of Freiburg and then at the former Palatine university of Heidelberg with its dramatic Calvinist past, seemed to be an appropriate test case, since the old and the new faiths co-existed there in roughly balanced proportions, the Catholics forming 60 per cent of the population. A doctoral thesis which Weber had had compiled by one of his students, Martin Offenbacher, on 'The Economic Condition of Catholics and Protestants in the Grand Duchy of Baden' could draw on plentiful statistical material, precisely because the coexistence of these diverse populations in a recently created state had been a major internal

---

[1] This contribution is a condensed version of three essays comprising part one of my book, *Le Passé présent* (Monaco, 1965). The first of those essays was originally published over twenty years ago in the *Cahiers Vilfredo Pareto* (Geneva, 1963), while the other two included passages from the two volumes of my *La Banque Protestante en France* (Paris, 1959, 1961). Different text-book translations in German, Italian, and English have been considered in this abridgement.

problem during its life of less than a century. This thesis, not surprisingly, confirmed most of Weber's hypotheses and, incidentally, also many popular assumptions and grievances about the unequal distribution of wealth and honours among the different groups.

At the very outset of his famous essay on 'The Protestant Ethic and the Spirit of capitalism', produced three years later, Weber pointed to this otherwise inconspicuous doctoral thesis as the best such analysis then available. In substance it came down to the conclusion that the bulk of Baden's Catholic population was rural or of immediately rural descent, overrepresented in both agricultural labour and in landed property, while the Protestants predominated in the towns and in urban occupations, as skilled workers and executives in business, in the liberal professions, and in the higher ranks of the administration and of the army. Almost tautologically, fewer Catholics than Protestants went beyond the village school, and if they did, they followed traditional classical studies rather than modern or professional training, which was more attractive to Protestants. It was plausibly calculated that the per capita income of the average Protestant was about 60 per cent higher than that of the Catholic, while that of the small and prosperous Jewish community was over six times as high as the Catholics'. Weber did not dwell on this last point, though it was always in his mind; others of course did. He was also aware of the circular fallacies of statistical correlations when the choice of criteria largely determines the conclusions: any comparison between the average monetary incomes in agricultural and industrial societies, irrespective of religion, would have given the same results.

Moreover, statistics could not yield distinctions between causal and functional connections: did a creed cause its adherents to be more enterprising in the economic sphere, or did it attract those who were more thrifty? Weber supposed that it worked both ways and only over many generations, since by 1900 church membership was seldom a deliberate personal choice. Hence the source of unequal accomplishment as far as the Christian creeds are concerned must be found in their different collective pasts, and it seemed natural enough to draw a straight line back to the Reformation as being the original parting of the ways. Certainly the time-lag between the cause in the original split and the effects reported in 1900 is disquieting. Much water had flowed down the Rhine since the time when, on both sides of this strategic waterway between the Swiss and the Flemish cities, and in the no man's land which had once been the ephemeral empire of Burgundy, princes, town councils, and even peasant communities had striven to embrace or reject the Reformation of their own free will. Two centuries of upheavals and wars had finally resulted in the fragmentation of south-western Germany into petty secular and ecclesiastical principalities of a single denomination, tiny city-states, and bizarre hybrids. Drastic simplification came only with the wars of the French Revolution and the Napoleonic era, the French annexation of the left bank of the Rhine, and the collapse of the old Holy Roman Empire, when the outlying Austrian bastions, the remnants of the Palatinate on the right bank, and all the rest of the jigsaw-puzzle were assembled in a new and makeshift state under the dynasty of the Reformed margraves of Baden. This territorial conglomeration was non-confessional, but still turbulent and incoherent. Members of different creeds met in the towns, but hardly ever in the villages; intermarriage was almost unheard-of; and even the non-confessional primary school was still a matter of bitter conflict in Weber's lifetime. The coexistence of separate traditions, linked in origin with different families, regions, and sectors of economic life, formed a largely self-reproducing structure, as Weber clearly grasped; but its very durability encouraged him to see the Reformation as the direct origin of social stratifications in his own day.

Whatever its merits Offenbacher's little study hardly mattered, since it only confirmed a much more general belief. Similar studies of other countries in which different religious groups lived side by side would certainly have yielded the same results. Switzerland in many respects was then, and was seen as, a larger prototype of Baden. There the Protestants had a narrow numerical majority but a clear political, economic, and intellectual hegemony; and there too were the only three French-speaking Protestant republics, including the prodigious republic of Geneva, proud, wealthy, and thriving, still the city of Calvin, though Catholic newcomers now outnumbered the native Protestants. Yet it must be added that in Switzerland too the boundaries between urbanized and rural cantons, or, in modern terms, between developed and underdeveloped areas, had been broadly the same before the Reformation, and had only become blurred thanks to freedom of migration and movement in the unified liberal state.

In France the disproportionate role of the tiny Protestant minority in business, political, and intellectual life was even more startling, but so too was the time-lag. French Protestantism, a mere shadow of what it had been in the age of the Reformation, was almost entirely bourgeois, not because it had been so initially but because, outside the *Désert* of the Cévennes, it had survived only in small and closed urban groups or in the diaspora. Similarly, though with an uneasy attitude towards shorthand versions of history, Weber might have pointed to the very diverse achievements of Protestants and Catholics in Ireland, then undivided, or for that matter in England or Canada. But if we turn aside from the split in the western church, what are we to make of age-old divisions in otherwise fairly homogeneous nations, such as that between northern Italy and the *Mezzogiorno*, or between Catalonia and Old Castile? Instead of speaking of traditional (equated with Catholic) elements and progressive (equated with Protestant) elements, should we not substitute simply the rural population and the urban, in order to make the pieces fall into place?

But we need not depend on such limited comparisons when we look at the wide disparity in economic achievement—still more evident in Weber's time of triumphant imperialism—between countries under Protestant leadership on the one hand and Catholic leadership on the other. The textbook paradigm would be the two halves of historical Flanders, torn asunder by Protestant revolt and Spanish reconquest. The one became for two centuries bustling Holland, the other depressed Belgium. Or, more striking, the two halves of Europe, north and south, before the First World War, or Anglo-Saxon and Latin America, the very prototypes of what were later termed developed and backward economies.

Prima facie evidence such as this may always be suspect, but it exists and invites an explanation; and Weber's interpretation in terms of ideal types, with its admittedly ambiguous link between Protestantism and capitalism (or modernity), has survived the storms of scholarly criticism. One after the other his critics, after having refuted Weber's thesis in detail, have admitted wholesale defeat, being unable to offer any comprehensive and satisfactory alternative. They accepted that there must have been in the Protestant doctrine a powerful leaven of economic and social development, that is, in Weber's terms, of capitalist development. *Quod erat demonstrandum.*

This is a fine example of a problem so posed as to allow of no solution other than that implicitly suggested by the way in which it has been formulated, and it is curious that no one in the discussion of this subject has succeeded in breaking the vicious circle. An awkward chronological gap between the period of the Reformation and that of its alleged economic effects has indeed troubled a number of scholars, yet none of them seems to have drawn conclusions from the enormous *non sequitur* in Weber's linking of causes and effects. Capitalism, the modern world, and rational thought did not begin in Wittenberg or even in Geneva.

The Reformers' attack on the spiritual authority of Rome and the Roman clergy occurred when Europe was being stirred by a dizzily accelerated advance in all spheres of secular knowledge: in technology, in scientific thought, in the emancipation of the individual, in economic expansion, and in the conquest of new horizons. In none of these can any new start, decisive progress, or even any marked interest be attributed to the Reformation. While in the seventeenth century the Roman Inquisition persecuted heretics, the Protestant authorities persecuted witches. All the intellectual or economic changes cited by or in support of Weber's thesis relate to later centuries, separated from the Reformation by too many generations, events, and changes of outlook for it to be possible to establish a clear and intelligible link with the Reformation. Moreover all had their roots in the high and late middle ages. Worse still, it is precisely in the sphere of capitalist enterprise and organization that the period of the Reformation and the Catholic counter-offensive marked the beginning of a long period of regression. Europe did not attain for another two centuries thereafter the level of development and economic organization, the vigour of individual initiative, and the flourishing of great capitalist magnates which it had known in the fifteenth and early sixteenth centuries, epitomized by the names of the Medici and the Fugger, within a still undivided Catholic Christendom. On all these planes stagnation or retreat set in about the time of Charles V's defeat and Calvin's death. Are we to blame this on the 'wars of religion', which merely prolonged and exacerbated the conflict between France and the Habsburg empire, a conflict begun in the wars for hegemony over Italy when Luther was still a child, and fully unleashed before he could have even conceived his ninety-five theses? This prolonged conflict occurred in a power-setting little affected by the religious quarrel but which largely determined adhesions or submissions to one or other of the confessional camps. After all the Reformation is wholly blameless for the sack of Rome. In this sphere it is futile to try to separate spiritual from political or even military factors. The religious demarcations were eventually imposed by force just as was the case in the Europe of 1945 with the secular creeds of our own time: *cuius regio eius religio*. Once the storm had passed, however, these demarcations became lines of division, more or less clearly defined but perfectly perceptible, between regions whose subsequent development was to diverge. On one side there was recovery, slow or rapid, often from very low previous levels. On the other there was long-term stagnation or decadence, following levels that had been very high. If on the one hand the Reformation is made answerable for a later development which was only a resumption or a continuation of a process begun much earlier, then on the other hand logic requires that the Counter-Reformation should shoulder the responsibility for its arrest or decline.

I speak of 'the Counter-Reformation' and not of 'Catholicism', for it was the Counter-Reformation which was the new fact. Was it not within the undivided Catholic world and under the Church's protection that there had taken place that brilliant rise of free cities and mercantile republics which had marked the renaissance of Europe in the high middle ages? When the proud republic of Venice, though remaining Catholic, resisted so fiercely the institutions and spirit of the Counter-Reformation, was it not defending the heritage of the medieval city against the encroachments of a church that had become 'Spanish' and was striving to re-clericalize the whole western world and to subject it to Roman police, the Inquisition, and censorship?

If we are to be content with simplifications there are excellent reasons for maintaining that under the influence of the Reformation the spirit of the medieval urban republics was allowed to survive, though only just, while wherever the Counter-Reformation triumphed it crushed, stifled, and destroyed that spirit by the terror of a relentless authoritarian reaction against everything that struggled to escape from its cumbersome control. The successive waves of refugees, Italian, Flemish, Huguenot, and the Spanish and Portuguese Jews driven out by the Inquisition, who brought to Holland, England, Switzerland, and other northern countries the knowledge, techniques, trades, and skills of the Mediterranean and Burgundian worlds, were not an exclusively religious phenomenon. There were many cases of emigration in which religious dissent was only a subsidiary factor, only one of the consequences of the intolerable burden, both spiritual and material, imposed on Tridentine Europe by this new alliance of clerical and princely despotisms.

This deliberately heightened contrast needs of course to be modified by allowing for local variations and by drawing more delicate distinctions, though the Counter-Reformation was much more unified in purpose and direction than the disparate movement we know as the Reformation. Nevertheless, a reading of European history as a whole strongly suggests that the Counter-Reformation, wherever it conquered in wholesale reaction against the spirit of heresy or independence, for long blocked the development of material and intellectual civilization; that it was, as a reconquering crusade of a monarchical and bureaucratic church, profoundly influenced by the heritage of the late Roman Empire; and that in its hierarchical structure, its means of exercising sacerdotal authority, and its baneful alliance with the most oppressive and wasteful dynastic courts it was a reactionary movement in the strict sense of that term. Rome's belated answer to the Reformers, given in the Tridentine Council, was indeed a defiant reassertion of all they had attacked as paganism: not less but more lavish pomp, cults and rites, more hagiography, more worship of the Virgin and the saints, more miracles, more thaumaturgical pictures and images, more processions, more monastic orders, more devotion to the prince who agreed to act as the secular arm of the Holy Office, less preaching of the Scriptures and stricter prohibition of their translation into the vernacular, together with a more efficient thought-control machinery and better clerical discipline: these were the external signs of Tridentine Reform in its baroque exaltation of the Visible Church.

Consider the veritable *translatio imperii* of the sciences from Italy to England in the seventeenth century, from Galileo to Newton, or the bemused silence of Catholic Germany, despite its much richer traditions, in the slow rebirth of German literature and philosophy in the eighteenth century. Or compare that part of Europe affected by the Englightenment with that very different part which had been enlivened by the Renaissance. But consider too the special and disconcerting role of the one European country which belies the general argument, France. Its kings kept the Gallican church, almost as nationalized as the Anglican, in the Roman

Catholic fold, but never received the Tridentine decrees, the Inquisition, the Roman censorship, and tilted the European balance of power in favour of the Protestant camp during the decisive conflicts of the post-Reformation century. France alone had experienced what can rightly be called wars of religion: not warfare between princes in varying alliances and affiliations, and not a Dutch war of independence, but a genuinely civil war between French Protestants and French Catholics for national power. The Protestants lost, but victory did not go to the Counter-Reformation: in a devious way it went first to the monarchy, supported by the Gallican *tiers parti*, and finally to the specifically French brand of spitefully anticlerical *Lumières*.

Let us set one overall view against another. All the foundations of the modern world—capital, wealth, the highest level of development in the arts and technology, navigation, discoveries, and overseas commerce, together with intellect and power—were, in the age of the Reformation, almost entirely in the hands of that part of Europe which was, and would remain, Catholic. Italy was the prestigious centre of the material and spiritual culture of the West. Spain and Portugal monopolized overseas conquests and the trade of both the Indies, the largest field of enterprise and the greatest source of wealth of the nascent modern world. Burgundian Flanders was the industrial, commercial, and artistic centre of northern Europe. It was in these countries that there was to be found in combination the intellectual, material, and technical conditions for what we know as the rise of capitalist economy, not in the peripheral and semi-barbarous polders and islands along the northern and north-eastern edge of Europe which were to be won for the Reformation. Yet, barely a century and a half later, all this was slackening or dying. This subject has admittedly gone out of fashion. And yet, unlike the economic historians whose curves bend only gently and belatedly, the historians of civilization have always realized what a brutal break the militant state of the Counter-Reformation made in the countries where it triumphed, how wastefully it ruled, and how deadly was the shadow it cast, a shadow from which this half of the continent began to emerge only two centuries later through the action of enlightened and anti-clerical despotism and the liberating secularization which everywhere followed the invading armies of revolutionary France. By the thoroughly repressive reaction of the endangered Roman church against not merely the Reformation but also all the dangers of free inquiry and civil autonomy which it had revealed, a ferment which had been active throughout Europe was stilled in one part of the west, and with it that vital minimum of freedom without which a society can produce neither intellectual nor industrial pioneers, neither scientific research nor economic growth.

Here we have a historical perspective which should not be reduced to a question of a possible relation between an individual's adherence to a particular religious doctrine and his effectiveness in the economic sphere. Nevertheless, even if the discussion were narrowed down to this aspect, it should have been possible to ask whether the various Reformations have not been largely beneficial by default. The simple reason is that none of their authorities, whether of northern kings or of city-states, was able to establish a traditional supremacy and an all-powerful state machine. In the narrow intolerance they exhibited in the seventeenth century they were fortunately inefficient. Was not the vast tumult known as the Reformation the minor obstacle to, rather than the cause of, the emancipation and take-off of innovating capitalism? Did not the victory of Protestantism in the northern provinces of the Low Countries, sheltered behind defences of dikes, swamps, and rivers, simply permit the preservation and development of the great industrial and commercial inheritance which was stifled in the southern part of Flanders which had remained under Spanish and clerical domination? The prosperity and prestige of Amsterdam merely captured and continued the prosperity and prestige which had been Antwerp's before it fell to the Spanish fury. Self-government and liberalism in every meaning of the term, and especially that kind of liberalism without which no entrepôt trade can thrive, counted for much in this, as Calvinism did not. In Amsterdam, cosmopolitan, sceptical, and so slow to rally to the Dutch and Protestant cause, Calvinist fervour found few adherents except among expatriates and the mob. And here is another warning against simple conclusions: the destiny of Belgium, both cockpit and pawn in Europe's politics, strangled and cut off from the sea by agreements between the powers, is not to be explained by its Catholicism alone, for, once it gained independence, Belgium, secularized and liberal but still Roman Catholic, became the first fully industrialized country on the continent.

In considering the genesis of that complex unity, the modern western world, it is certainly justifiable to isolate and study separately one particular line of development, that of capitalist industrial society. It is also justifiable to take as a working hypothesis a conventional though not self-evident starting-point in the age of the Reformation—provided that we study this age as a whole, in its own setting and with all its implications and interactions, and not merely as an exhibition of moral theology. The age of the Reformation, a time of revolutionary effervescence if ever there was one, includes that tremendous reaction, that anathema against institutional and intellectual innovation known as the Tridentine Reform; and since the clergy formed an order of feudal society this had its social and political consequences. Unless we consider the age as a whole we blind ourselves to the very nature of the antagonistic forces and to the significance of their problems, their controversies and their arguments. The historian or the sociologist is no more entitled than the theologian to seize hold of a commercial or banking ledger, even one provided with an exordium invoking the blessing of God, and cry, 'Behold how Calvin created capitalism!'

It would perhaps be unfair to reproach the social historians for being ill informed in theology, though it is rather serious that they seem to have had only hearsay knowledge of the Calvinist teaching and dogma they were discussing and to have been completely ignorant of scholastic exegeses of canon law before and after the Counter-Reformation. It is equally serious that they did not realize the extent to which both Protestant and Catholic divines were troubled by the age-old problem of predestination, the theological expression of the mystery of man's fate and man's freedom, first raised by St Paul and exhaustively formulated by St Augustine, who was followed by Luther and Calvin, together with the Jansenists. Ignorance of this led these historians to plunge headlong into crude attempts to psychoanalyse the Calvinist concept of predestination as a path to success. Less excusable is the carelessness or tendentiousness with which these scholars collected at random and misinterpreted miscellaneous facts, some significant and others irrelevant, some with and others lacking a religious connotation. It is true that they believed that they knew the definitive answers, and sought not so much proofs as striking examples. It is also true that modern social and economic history was only just emerging from its infancy. Many of the most brilliant propositions advanced in this debate have been nullified because their authors possessed only the faintest notions of the actual working of canon law on economic matters and of the basic mechanisms of banking, exchange, and accounting before the codifications of the nineteenth century. They seem to have believed quite simply, for example, that the normal activity of a banker in the seventeenth and eighteenth centuries consisted in lending money to spendthrifts and the needy. Accordingly it all seemed to them absolutely clear: Calvin authorized the charging of interest on loans, and so paved the way for capitalism.

We shall return to the question of banking and to the role played in its very inconspicuous post-Reformation development by the authorization to charge interest—a role which is a pure and simple invention of incompetent writers. But it may be observed here that banking follows trade, and that while during the seventeenth century Dutch, English, and Huguenot bankers more and more took the place of the Italians and South Germans, this was not at all due to new banking techniques (which were indeed rather more primitive than they had been in the fourteenth century), but to the fact that the centres of commerce were irreversibly shifting towards north-western Europe. As for the Huguenots, it was not their Calvinist creed but their position as descendants of a defeated and outlawed party, their membership of a community of refugees dispersed all over Europe and overseas, and yet retaining close family and business links with France, that 'predestined' them to carrying on international banking, the essence of which was international correspondence with trusted and trustworthy partners. They formed a cosmopolitan minority whose success in the eighteenth century appeared scandalous, just as, a century later, did that of the Jews after their emancipation. As with the Jews scandal monstrously exaggerated their actual and limited success. But this digression has taken us a long way, spiritually as well as chronologically, from the age of the Reformation down to that of Necker with his eirenical discussion of 'the importance of religious opinions', and his generation of Genevans brought up on Voltaire and Rousseau.

Was then the Reformation the ideology of rising capitalism and capitalists? Let us ask the first schoolboy we meet for the names of the leading representatives of commercial, financial, and industrial capitalism in the age of the Reformation. He will without hesitation name the Medici and the Fugger. The Medici, who had been princely bankers to the Roman Curia, liquidated their bank and laid their hands on the Papacy itself: it was the son of Lorenzo the Magnificent, Pope Leo X, who excommunicated Luther. Jacob Fugger, successor to the Medici as banker to the Curia, financed the election of Charles V as Emperor and was the staunchest pillar of the Empire and the Papacy in their alliance against the Reformation. He carried on simultaneously, at the head of a giant conglomerate concern, the exploitation of silver and copper mines throughout central Europe and of papal bulls of indulgence. He put up for auction, or filled with his own nephews and associates, the most important bishoprics of Germany, Hungary, and Poland; as an expert financier he managed the collection and transfer of all kinds of church revenues; and eventually he converted into cash the treasure of grace accumulated by the saints and martyrs of the Church by way of an inflated issue of drafts on the afterlife, until the crash came at Wittenberg. Never before or since have bankers so well deserved their names being given to a whole epoch.

Let us continue to question our schoolboy, for it is good to recall the most obvious and familiar facts. Everybody knows that this reckless sale of indulgences was the precise issue that provoked Luther's protest, at first humbly submitted through the hierarchical channels, and then taken into the public domain. Luther's revolt against Rome was emphatically a revolt against the cynically displayed corruption of the Church and at the same time a revolt against the great capitalist 'monopolies' of his time that had found their strongest support and their richest pastures in the financial empire of the Holy See. In so far as the Reformation concerned itself at all with the order prevailing in this world, it was also, and very explicitly, a revolt against Mammon—or, in modern terms, an outburst of deep 'anti-capitalist' indignation which had been hatching for a long time at all levels of society. At the Diet of Worms, to which Luther was summoned to answer for his seditious acts, his case was placed on the agenda at the same time as the discussion of imperial legislation against monopolies and big business, against cornering and usury, aimed first and foremost at Augsburg and the House of Fugger. These legislative proposals, long and noisily demanded, of course came to nothing. To Luther, in his wrathful pamphlet, *On Trade and Usury*, this only showed how true were the words of Isaiah: 'Thy princes have become companions of thieves.' Reread the fiery writings and speeches of the Reformer and of his early allies such as Hutten against the big capitalist companies, the money-changers who set up their tables in the Temple, against the usurers who 'devour widows' houses': here we find brought to life again for the first time in western Christendom the spirit and accent of the Old Testament Prophets, for whom the divine commandment of justice was not a promise for the afterlife but a law of God to be obeyed on this earth, here and now.

This re-emergence in the Christian consciousness of the Reformation of the Old Testament's prophetic tradition, which had lain buried for more than a millennium in the Roman Church under the Gentile patristic tradition of the late Roman Empire, was an event of immeasurable importance in the history of European thought, affecting all spheres of life, private and public, and even the deepest structures of language. We know that for the Huguenots and the English Puritans the Old Testament was more enthralling and a more powerful sources of inspiration than the New (except for the terrors of the Apocalypse). To Agrippa d'Aubigné and Oliver Cromwell Israel's battles and the wrath of the Prophets were closer than the Gospel of charity and mercy. We see the strange Hebrew names they gave to their children; we hear them, in their letters, sermons, and pamphlets, becoming intoxicated with the exultations of the Psalms and the fulminations of the Prophets. We observe how they transpose, quite naturally, the most dramatic figures and events in the history of Israel into their own time; how they hurl the curses of the Prophets at the heads of their adversaries; how, in calling down upon them the wrath of God, they make Rome the new Babylon, the Pope the priest of Baal or a new Nebuchadnezzar, the Queen of the St Bartholomew's Eve massacre a second Jezebel, King Charles I a second Rehoboam; how, when persecuted or banished, they weep with the Jews of the Captivity on the banks of the Euphrates; and how, like Cromwell after Marston Moor, they celebrate victory in singing one of David's psalms of triumph. The entire pristine spirit of the Reformation is summed up in the challenging outburst by the Prophet Amos: 'I hate, I despise your feasts, and I will take no delight in your solemn assemblies . . . Take thou away from me the noise of thy songs; for I will not hear the melody of thy viols. But let judgement roll down as waters, and righteousness as a mighty stream.' These were no mere literary flourishes. The social teaching of Zwingli and Calvin, and the revolutionary zeal of the Huguenots, the Sea Beggars, and the Puritans were all driven forward by the gale force of the Old Testament. It was in the books of Israel that they found their models, in those ordinary men and shepherds reasoning and arguing face to face with God, in the judges, prophets and popular leaders who rose against tyrannical rulers and corrupt priests, and for whom piety was not the sole duty of God's children, for they had also to bring about the reign of justice and the sanctification of this world. It is unnecessary to produce subtle interpretations of Calvinist predestination or to psychoanalyse Protestant solitude, as has been done so readily following Max Weber, in order to understand how it was that Calvinists and Puritans saw themselves as the Chosen People. That feeling sprang spontaneously from their clearly asserted identification with the People of God of the ancient books who had risen up against paganism and idols.

Calvin, the only systematic thinker among the Reformers, and a man of the Reformation's second generation, hardened in combat, was the contemporary, enemy, and intellectual brother of Ignatius Loyola and the Council of Trent. He was the spiritual and political leader of the Protestant minorities in revolt against established authority all over Europe, from Hungary and Poland to Scotland. He was the revolutionary among the Reformers, and it is in him that the imperious prophetic passion of the Old Testament, the pitiless insistence that deeds must conform to words, everyday life to doctrine, and politics to faith is most strongly expressed. He forged a type of man, proud and stern, aware that he was answerable for his way of life only to God and his own conscience—a man who was free and responsible for himself. He was the lawgiver of those Calvinist communities, fiercely resistant to any human authority in all matters of conscience, for whom the separation of the self-governing Christian community from the worldly body politic was a self-evident claim wherever political authority was not identical with the community itself, as it was in the Geneva of Calvin's time and in the Puritan settlements in New England. From Geneva, that Zion of the new People of God, there issued a spiritual revolution which changed the minds of those who followed its teaching. What made the Calvinists, hard-working and useful subjects though they were, so intolerable in the eyes of French absolutism, itself lacking in docility before the authority of Rome, was not so much their religion but rather their fierce insistence on synodal self-government and what the Intendants commonly spoke of as their 'incorrigible republican spirit'.

II. *Puritanism and 'Industrial Society'*

The affinity between the Reformation and the modern or 'capitalist' spirit acquires precision and meaning when we turn from the Lutheran princes who chose to confiscate the powers, the riches and, it must be said in justice, most of the duties of the Roman Church to the Reformers of Zürich and

Geneva, those self-governing city republics whose councils and citizens established reformed churches under their own authority. Zwingli and Calvin did not win over monarchs, though Calvin may have hoped to convince the French king: they were called to their ministry by the city magistrates to operate the tremendous transformation of their whole religious polity and administration. They were called to serve their urban communities not only as preachers but also as citizens, as legislators and statesmen, being consulted on every public issue, from the everyday problems of food supply, manufactures, poor-relief, and education to the weighty questions of war and peace. In their social teaching and in their public discipline it was the legislator no less than the theologian who spoke, and much of their effort was dedicated to reconciling the desperate needs of their encircled towns and exposed bridgeheads with the teaching of the Gospels. We shall not resume here the debate on the doctrine of predestination and the related concept of the calling. Nevertheless, when all the over-bold or over-subtle hypotheses have been discarded, there remains an irreducible element which recurs throughout the moral teaching of Calvin and his disciples: a basic conception of godly Christian life which applied to religious, ethical, social, private, and public conduct, conceived as inseparable. As Calvin put it: 'Let those who hear the gospel prove themselves to be Christian by holiness of life.' This sanctification of life, of which the sanctification of work is a chief pillar, has long shaped the spirit and character of the 'Calvinistic' city and has left an imprint on most Protestant societies, though Catholic mercantilists have tended to exaggerate the industriousness of their Protestant rivals. What Henri Hauser has called the Reformation's 'secularization of holiness' is the exact counterpart of this insistence on saintly life as the duty of every believer.

This remained an ideal, though vigorous efforts were made to enforce it with great severity; but it reflected a new conception of society. The unity of medieval hierarchical society, with the king, nobility, and clergy at its summit, maintained by the labour of common men, had simultaneously torn apart the unity of man. His faculties and aspirations were separated and distributed between different orders of society: for those of the first order the office of prayer, for those of the second that of warfare and command, and for the remainder the burden of toiling for their masters. In attributing to each individual the vocation of being a whole man, directly responsible to God and capable of hearing his voice, of praying to him, and of obeying him, with no mediator, the Reformation unsettled a social hierarchy even more than a hierarchy of values. We should have a poor understanding of the Reformers' sermons on the dignity of labour and their censures of indolence if we were to forget the precise targets they were aimed at: the lavish ostentation of cults and outward devotions, the magnificent palaces and courts of prevaricating prelates and ecclesiastical princes, and the formidable dead weight of a teeming monasticism now very far removed from its role in the early Middle Ages as the vanguard of western civilization, not only in the spiritual and intellectual spheres but also in the material activities of forest-clearing, drainage, cultivation, and technical innovation.

Ora et labora had been the complementary commands of the original monastic rule and even, in simplified form, for the lay brothers: *laborare est orare*. Only a life divided between prayer and work could be saintly. Prayer and work together formed the discipline which alone could safeguard man's heart against the temptations of pleasure and sin, whereas idleness was the open gateway to perdition. The association of prayer with work in one and the same service to God was not an innovation of the Reformers, any more than was their hostility to worldly pleasure and slackness: these are timeless topics. What was new was the insistence on the sanctification of secular life, not on ritual conformity but on an inner striving for purity and asceticism, not on the monastic communities but on the requirements for the civil community as a whole. The inexorable forbidding of all frivolity gave the Genevan republic of Calvin and Beza—and, to a lesser degree, other small city republics of the Reformed creed—the frequently ridiculed semblance of austere monasticism. This sanctification of work as an ascetic discipline embraced the everyday economic activities of the common man. Had not all the great monastic orders of the Middle Ages, before the coming of the mendicants who instituted begging as a Christian way of life, aimed at economic self-sufficiency as the very precondition of spiritual life? And had they not succeeded beyond all expectations, and so succumbed to slackness? Work then was not the wages of sin nor the punishment imposed after the Fall, but the divinely ordained human lot on this earth. It was required as a matter of public discipline and self-discipline, not as a path to salvation for which man can do nothing: God had foreordained plenty or want for the body just as he had foreordained salvation or damnation for the soul. Industriousness, like all the humble bourgeois virtues of the Christian city, was nothing more than an outward sign of the Christian life (and here we may watch the relentless dialectic of Calvin's teaching, stressing the Christian duty of activity and endeavour while simultaneously stressing man's utter impotence, as if to refute the fiendish logical equation of the dogma of predestination with fatalism).

This conception of Christian life in its integrity established a new scale of values for a new society. The separation between the superior order of those who prayed and the inferior order of those who worked, the common flock of mostly illiterate laymen, which was the institutional foundation of the Catholic Church, was thereby abolished, and with it the archetype of medieval Christendom. There was to be no hierarchy of mediators between man and God: every man was to face God individually responsible for his whole soul and his whole life, a life of prayer and work for the glorification of the Father, and also for his own and his family's needs. We should not forget that the Reformers, whether defrocked like Luther or seculars like Calvin, led family lives, and that their Christian city was an association of families where obstinate celibacy was suspect and where the citizen's first duty was to care for his dependants.

But what was the place of charity in this ordered city of prayer and work? Faced with this question most historians of Calvinism, Tawney among them, have turned away, or have talked of the hardness of those times, of deviation from or corruption of the original truth. Yet the Reformers themselves, in their writings, their regulations, and their provisions for the poor, in Zürich as in Geneva, spoke perfectly clearly. Charity, the good work *par excellence*, performed more or less wholeheartedly for centuries as a habitual exercise of Christian duty, the giving of alms to the beggars at the church door and in the street, a ritual gesture like making the sign of the cross, had no place in the reformed city. This was a busy city of craftsmen and merchants. Solidarity, mutual aid, social provision, and help to victims had their place there, conspicuously so in Calvin's city crowded with refugees; but impersonal habitual charity had not, nor had habitual pauperism. The disabled were to be looked after, but the able-bodied poor man who lived on alms insulted the divinely instituted order. He who works will earn his bread, and he who works not, neither shall he eat: that, summarized starkly, was the fundamental rule of the new social contract.

It is hard to exaggerate what this implied for the formation of societies. It is here that the commandment to be active in the world and the censuring of all forms of idleness and the *vita passiva* found their most rigorous meaning. While the Reformation, by immediatizing man's relation to God, may have contained the seeds of individualism, freedom of inquiry, and hence freedom of conscience, we must admit that the conception of society held by the post-Lutheran Reformers entailed a terrifying strict social conformity. This was not just a question of city administration: public authorities have rarely been charitable to the vagrant poor, even if it can be argued that in Protestant countries the new morality authorized them to exercise their harshness more methodically than before. It was the entire attitude of the Christian community towards pauperism and begging, the great social problem down to the nineteenth century, the attitude of the heart and mind that was hardened against *misericordia*. In Catholic piety the poor, and especially those who had freely chosen to live as beggars, had haloes of holiness as images of Christ on earth, as the favoured sons of the Father and the embodiments of evangelical poverty; whereas the rich man would find it hard to enter the Kingdom of Heaven. Begging had its place in this vision of the world, honoured in the elaborate iconography of the Church and worshipped in the sublime figure of St Francis, the *Poverello*. He who gave to the poor gave to God, and he who gave to the Church of the poor gave twofold. Here too the Reformation meant a radical re-evaluation, wounding as if deliberately all that seemed to constitute the very essence of Christian sensibility. For the Calvinist begging was not meritorious but shameful, and almsgiving, or 'inconsiderate charity', was not a good work but a sin, because by encouraging indolence it fed and perpetuated this intolerable social disorder instead of stamping it out. The only good work to be done was to work and to give work, simultaneously eliminating both the seeker and the giver of alms. Equally for Zwingli it was not the poor man nor the charitable man but the working man who 'in this world is closest to the love of God', and finally it was the worker alone who had the right to be received into the citizenship of the new Christian city. In Our Father's house there had been many mansions: henceforth it had only one, and that was a workshop.

It is the hard, merciless side of this attitude which initially strikes the eye. And indeed in generation after generation, among Calvinists and Puritans, the spirit of fraternity and human solidarity has rebelled against an orthodox social conformity that leaned too easily towards the side of the well-to-do. But none of these rebellions ever affected the central pillar of Calvinist social teaching, the ethical pre-eminence of work, which was exalted as much by the more oligarchical tendencies as by the most radical and egalitarian. The repudiation of charity was above all a repudiation of the immemorial seigneurial-clerical disdain for work and for men working for their daily bread. In a society moulded by the moral imperative of self-reliance and individual responsibility it was legitimate to fight against social inequality, monopoly, profiteering, and exploitation of the workers, but it was no longer possible to return to the age-old complacency towards mass misery as a passively accepted feature of society and begging as an established way of life. To refuse charity, and indeed mercy, and to denounce pauperism as a scandal meant an acceptance of its challenge, to make and enforce an unremitting effort to overcome it, treating it as a problem of religious and social regeneration. For Calvin this began with the institution of a general Christian education, an education of mind, character, and will, not merely of psalmody. A Christian body politic so instituted would be able to assist its aged, sick, and orphans, and would know no beggars. This was the vision. It was an austere vision, and it would be spurious to interpret it as a hymn to industrial society. The social history of Protestant communities and states with their poor laws and workhouses falls sadly short of this vision, but the model had been set forth.

It is one of the original features of Calvinism that it gave the capitalist a legitimate place in the Christian city as a prominent agent in the work of glorifying God, not through pious endowments and legacies, nor through renouncing his possessions, but through the actual exercise of his economic function. This was now, however, the parasitical function of the absentee landlord or of the rentier who lived on his unearned income from the debt-ridden treasury of spendthrift rulers so typical of the bourgeois leisure class of what was to become the *ancien régime*. The capitalist honoured in Calvinist society was the faithful and busy householder of the Gospels 'who went out early in the morning to hire labourers into his vineyard', the entrepreneur who made his capital work by setting men to work, the merchant who opened up markets for industry, and his merit could almost be measured by the number of hands for which he found employment.

Among the questions raised in the debate on the relation between 'the Protestant ethic' and 'the spirit of capitalism', those which have been formulated with the greatest theoretical pomp and circumstance are often those involving the most ambiguous general concepts or even insidious semantic traps. At the bottom of most of these confusions is the unwarranted equation, already implicit in Weber's essay, of Catholicism with medieval society and thought and of Protestantism with modern, as if the latter had not grown in the womb of the first, and as if the two had never lived side by side in controversy and competition. The very terms of Weber's comparative study are those forged in the war of words between Catholic and Protestant controversialists, given new vigour after the traumatic Vatican Council and the 'anti-capitalist' encyclical, *Rerum novarum* of 1891, not those of the real economic life and thought of Calvin's time. How should social historians draw other than word-splitting comparisons between the social teaching of Catholic and Protestant churches when their theologians had, throughout the centuries, simultaneously or successively adopted the most contradictory attitudes to such fundamental issues as private property, serfdom, taxpaying, price, value and contract? This is what gave such exceptional importance to the problem of the legitimacy of stipulating interest on loans, an apparently clear-cut, yes-or-no issue on which theology had to pronounce unequivocally. But here too there was a semantic trap: there had been only one word for usury and interest, and this had been enough for an agricultural society in which money or grain was lent to the needy peasant when his harvest had failed. It was no longer enough for the commercial town, and there the Schoolmen entered with their elaborate distinctions. A stipulated gain on a loan involving a risk or a loss of immediate income was not usurious. But this was a special law which did not alter the general law. Late medieval jurisdiction contained many particular laws and jurisdictions; and merchant guilds and merchant towns were allowed to develop under their laws merchant like so many enclosed sectors or ghettos, apparently separate from the wider society which they were to revolutionize.

It is a misfortune that for half a century the eminent scholars who took part in this large debate on 'Protestantism and capitalism' were almost all ignorant of the original teaching of the Reformers, and even more so of the highly sophisticated doctrines of the Schoolmen. Just as Raymond de Roover broke new ground in his basic studies on the development of banking and exchange instruments under canon law, beginning with his *Évolution de la lettre de change* (1953), so a Genevan theologian who is also an economist, André Biéler, did pioneer work in his *La Pensée économique et sociale de Calvin* (1959). Biéler carefully produced from the immense corpus of Calvin's writings, direct evidence of the Reformer's attitude on social and economic issues, confronting the reader with the original texts and, equally importantly, with the theological context of these pronouncements. What is generally referred to as Calvin's social teaching is nowhere set out as a body of coherent doctrines. It has to be reconstructed, with all the risks of such an undertaking, from statements scattered among his sermons and commentaries, the substance of which was the exegesis of the Scriptures, not instruction in economics. No doubt Calvin had an eye on the problems of the beleaguered city and of its citizens who had called him to the ministry, and on those of the scattered reformed communities throughout Europe, whence so many refugees flocked to Geneva as to convert it into a cosmopolitan republic. But, however receptive Calvin may have been to the social needs of his place and time, neither the corpus of theological doctrine, nor the sermons, nor the catechism lent themselves readily to economic analysis. Although Calvin was very keenly aware of the distinction between letter and spirit, symbol and significance, and of the dangers of literalism, his thought always adhered closely to the immutable sacred texts he was interpreting, which imposed upon him their archaic vocabulary and their timeless vision, and which contained no exposition of economic rules. If we consider this exclusive commitment of the minister to the Holy Scriptures we shall hardly be surprised to find a Calvin differing far less from the doctors of the Church than has been supposed, and differing above all in owing allegiance only to the Bible, not to Aristotle and the Aristotelian learning of the Dominicans. And it was from Aristotelian economics that the whole involved argument about usury was derived.

Just as on many other points which were not of primary interest to him, Calvin took up a position on lending at interest only because he could not avoid doing so. It was a standing issue, and controversialists of the old and the new faiths seized on it. Geneva, an old city of fairs which were now declining, had, like its rival Lyon, enjoyed one of those special regimes always tolerated by the Catholic Church in favour of markets and merchants. Two centuries before Calvin the lord-bishop of Geneva had granted the city in plain words unlimited freedom to practise 'usury', and municipal laws regulated the rate of interest. The question, long settled in practice, was now raised again as an issue of dogma in order to discredit the city of heretics: should not doctrinal theology steadfastly maintain the solemn general condemnation of what ecclesiastical jurisdiction had so explicitly authorized? Calvin entered this discussion unwillingly, knowing very well that whatever he might say his words would be twisted. But when obliged to speak he did so with the sharp mind of a trained lawyer, and with incomparable frankness and freshness, cutting through the frightening tangle of confusion, exegesis, casuistry, and evasion in which scholastic doctrine had wrapped up this irritating problem.

We should listen to Calvin's lucid and straightforward arguments rather than to his conclusions, which on most points coincided with traditional morality. The Gospels said: 'Give ye one to another, hoping for naught in return.' But, rejoined Calvin, 'This saying has been misunderstood when it has been applied to usury only . . . What Christ requires of his people is unrequited liberality, that they set themselves to help the poor, from whom no recompense can be expected . . . Thus Christ's words amount to a commandment to provide for the poor rather than the rich. We do not yet see that all usury is forbidden.' That is to say, what is referred to in the famous *mutuum date* text is neither lending at interest nor even lending at all, but a free gift without any idea of recovering it. The Christian is invited to give without hope of recompense if his gift is to be pleasing to God. This is the rule of charity. But no one can ignore the fact that the merchant or peasant who brings his crops to market does not come to give them away, but to sell them at a price. This is the rule of equitable exchange of goods, a rule of reciprocity and, as such, of equity. It is necessary to choose: either let no rule but that of charity apply in public life, in which case the market must be closed; or let there be a market, but in that case do not claim that it is governed by the law of the free gift. The rule of *mutuum date nihil sperantes* does not relate to economic transactions.

Do not Deuteronomy and the Prophets forbid all usury between brothers in Israel, while allowing it in dealings with outsiders? Here Calvin resorts boldly to historical and philological criticism of the sacred texts. This, he says, is a law of expediency, designed for the internal and external relations of a particular community which cannot be transferred from one epoch and people to others. 'It is notorious', he says, 'that usury was forbidden in the Old Testament, but we must at the same time admit that this was part of Jewish internal administrative practice. From this it follows that usury is not to be condemned today, except when it runs counter to equity and fraternal bonds.'

Is it not the case that the rich man who exploits the poor man by lending to him at usury violates the laws of both the Old Testament and the New, and the morality of both pagans and Christians? On this point, the only one which excited popular feelings, Calvin identified himself with the traditional condemnation with all the intransigent severity he knew how to show. But what of the man who lends to another who is not in need, to one

even richer than himself? It would be absurd to invoke the law of charity for
a transaction in which no need is involved. 'If someone rich and well-to-do,
wishing to buy a good farm, borrows part of the sum he needs from his
neighbour, why should not the lender derive some profit by way of income
until the loan has been repaid? Many such cases arise daily in which, so far
as equity is concerned, usury is no worse than a purchase.'

Finally there comes on the scene the great war-horse of the Aristotelian
Doctors of the Church. Interest, they said, is against nature, because
'money does not breed money'. Calvin did away with this sophism calmly
and cogently:

Of course I accept what even a child can see, which is that if you shut money up in a
box it will be sterile . . . I receive rent from leasing a house, but does the money
increase for this reason? Is not money employed more profitably in commerce than
in any possessions you care to mention? . . . When you buy a field does not your
money breed money? How do merchants increase their wealth? . . . No one borrows
from us on condition that the money shall lie idle without being put to profitable
use. This is why the fruit of the loan is not usury but income . . . Hence it is
necessary to conclude that, although prima facie such subtleties trouble us, if we
examine them more closely they vanish of themselves, for there is no substance in
them.

The rule of equity was stern. There is no need to dwell upon the tight and
remarkably effective regulation of interest rates in the Geneva of Calvin and
Beza, the maximum rate being 5 per cent, nor upon the moral imperatives
which were not just sound and fury, and which covered the prohibition of
interest on loans to the needy, the primacy of work over capital, the
banishment from the city of anyone practising usury. The basic hostility to
man's taking advantage of the need of others remained intact. If the
Christian citizen who went to the market were bargaining as a merchant
rather than living up to the principles of the Sermon on the Mount, reason
had to admit this, but conscience required the strict enforcement of the law
of equity, or mutual benefit and consideration for the common weal. 'In the
sixth place', wrote Calvin, 'we should not only have regard to the private
interest of the man with whom we are dealing, but we should also consider
what is expedient for the public.' The regulations which followed from this
rule of equity were administrative laws, particular to a given time and place,
not divine laws. The intellectual greatness and humility of Calvin the
theologian lay in putting theology out of court: the minister did not pretend
to be an economic expert.

This break with an immemorial tradition of impotent and preachifying
lamentation over money and merchants was an event in intellectual history
well before it worked economic change. There is nothing to suggest that
these analyses, made widely public only after Calvin's death, had any

immediate effect on economic life, either good or bad, except in the direction of greater strictness. It is probable that the practice of lending at low rates of interest helped several Italian and French refugees to rebuild their industries and trades in Geneva. It is probable that the same practice in England favoured the development and widespread use of new instruments of credit and techniques of accounting and discounting, and also stimulated economic thought. What is beyond doubt is that in the post-Reformation centuries credit was cheap and plentiful in the Protestant nations where a money market could operate legally, to the immeasurable benefit of the public as well as of the Exchequer. In Catholic countries under canon law, including France, where the money market was clandestine or deviously concealed, credit was exorbitantly expensive and inaccessible to the public at large, while the treasuries had to raise their permanent loans at usurious rates which fostered a swollen rentier class.

Credit and interest are the rational applications of the measure of time to value calculated in terms of money; and if it is true that time belongs to God—another war-horse of the Schoolmen—just as all things belong to God, it does not follow that the market and the clock-tower must be suppressed, or the eye averted from them as from a den of thieves. It was to prove no more helpful to ban mathematics from economic life than to ban it from cosmology or astronautics in the name of sacred symbolism. Calvin did not unleash usury on the world: he made usury a crime and allowed credit and interest to assume a legitimate and well-defined function in economic society; and he permitted money to be invested, and encouraged its investment in work. He did away with an inherited ideology of a static economy of manors and hamlets, stereotyped in pious images. The usurer, usually Jewish, who sucked the blood of widows and orphans belonged to the same haunted world of submissive prostration as the hallowed beggar, and it was this world and its imagery that Calvin banned from his reformed city. It was in the minds of men that a new era began.

But what of the famous Protestant bankers whose legend fills the close of the *ancien régime* in France and the beginning of the new era, and was then supplanted by that of the Jews? To this obvious question there is a simple answer. The profession of banker as it was exercised down to the end of the *ancien régime* has long been one of the most misunderstood, even by economic and social historians, partly because they imagined technical mysteries and secret combinations which never existed. For all practical purposes continental western Europe continued to be ruled by canon law until the issue of the Revolutionary and Napoleonic codes, and no banker doing business in or with a Catholic country could think of invoking Calvin's authorization of interest before a *Tribunal de commerce*. Moreover, Protestant bankers did not generally lend money at interest, and when they happened to do so indirectly, they did it in exactly the same way as their

Catholic colleagues, as for example in maritime loans. They could not revel in the rich pastures of royal tax-farmers and financiers but had, more austerely, to offer their services to the merchant community. Their profession was in no way that of money-lenders but that of 'remitters from place to place', inside and outside the country. For individual merchants, manufacturers, and other private clients they solved the essential problems of how to settle a debt, how to effect a payment, or how to recover a claim in distant parts. These were indeed intricate technical problems in pre-industrial times, and their solutions had a price. This was in perfect agreement with canon law and in no way secret, as lists of charges were currently published, setting out the cost of transfer between currencies, *le cours de change*, misleadingly translated as 'rate of exchange'. The problem was to have correspondents in distant places who would accept the papers and advance the money during the time needed for a return transaction, direct or triangular. Credit was of course implicit in the bargain, but accounted for as an indeterminate risk, never as fixed interest. The difference between a Catholic and a Protestant banker was, to repeat a truism, that the latter tended to have the requisite correspondents, preferably of the same creed and sometimes perhaps the more reliable for that reason. If this last proposition be true it might be alleged that the hard school of Calvinism played some part, though in reality Calvin had nothing to do with banking: his *Institutions* and systematic teaching, together with his ruthless forging of characters and minds, left a mark on generations of men in all walks of life who had never read, or even desired to read, a single line of his writings.

Further Reading

Weber, M., *The Protestant Ethic and the Spirit of Capitalism*, tr. Talcott Parsons; introduction by Anthony Giddens (London, 1926).

Besnard, P., *Protestantisme et Capitalisme: la Controverse Post-weberienne* (Paris, 1970), with an introduction, selected passages from various authors and a full bibliography.

Biéler, A., *La Pensée économique et sociale de Calvin* (Geneva, 1959).

George, C. and K., 'Protestantism and Capitalism in Pre-Revolutionary England', *Church History* 27 (1958).

Robertson, H. M., *Aspects of the Rise of Economic Individualism: a Criticism of Max Weber and his School* (London, 1933).

Tawney, R. H., *Religion and the Rise of Capitalism* (London, 1926).

Trevor-Roper, H. R., 'Religion, the Reformation and Social Change' in *Religion, the Reformation and Social Change* (London, 1967).

Index